WPF Recipes in C# 2008

A Problem-Solution Approach

Sam Noble, Sam Bourton, and
Allen Jones

Apress®

WPF Recipes in C# 2008: A Problem-Solution Approach

Copyright © 2008 by Sam Noble, Sam Bourton, and Allen Jones

ISBN-13 (paperback): 978-1-4302-1084-9

ISBN-13 (electronic): 978-1-4302-1083-2

Printed and bound in the United States of America (POD)

Trademarked names may appear in this book. Rather than use a trademark symbol with every occurrence of a trademarked name, we use the names only in an editorial fashion and to the benefit of the trademark owner, with no intention of infringement of the trademark.

Lead Editor: Ewan Buckingham
Technical Reviewers: Todd Meister
Editorial Board: Clay Andres, Steve Anglin, Ewan Buckingham, Tony Campbell, Gary Cornell,
    Jonathan Gennick, Matthew Moodie, Joseph Ottinger, Jeffrey Pepper, Frank Pohlmann,
    Ben Renow-Clarke, Dominic Shakeshaft, Matt Wade, Tom Welsh
Senior Project Manager: Sofia Marchant
Copy Editor: Kim Wimpsett
Associate Production Director: Kari Brooks-Copony
Senior Production Editor: Laura Cheu
Compositor: Susan Glinert Stevens and Octal Publishing, Inc.
Proofreader: April Eddy and Kim Burton
Indexer: Broccoli Information Management
Cover Designer: Kurt Krames
Manufacturing Director: Tom Debolski

Distributed to the book trade worldwide by Springer-Verlag New York, Inc., 233 Spring Street, 6th Floor, New York, NY 10013. Phone 1-800-SPRINGER, fax 201-348-4505, e-mail orders-ny@springer-sbm.com, or visit http://www.springeronline.com.

For information on translations, please contact Apress directly at 2855 Telegraph Avenue, Suite 600, Berkeley, CA 94705. Phone 510-549-5930, fax 510-549-5939, e-mail info@apress.com, or visit http://www.apress.com.

Apress and friends of ED books may be purchased in bulk for academic, corporate, or promotional use. eBook versions and licenses are also available for most titles. For more information, reference our Special Bulk Sales–eBook Licensing web page at http://www.apress.com/info/bulksales.

The source code for this book is available to readers at http://www.apress.com.

In memory of Patrick Lee.
—Sam Noble

For Helen B, thanks for being so patient and understanding.
What a year we have to look forward to!
—Sam Bourton

For my wonderful wife, Lena, and my
two amazing little girls, Anya and Alexia.
—Allen Jones

Contents at a Glance

About the Authors xv
About the Technical Reviewer xvii
Acknowledgments xix

CHAPTER 1   **Building and Debugging WPF Applications** 1
CHAPTER 2   **Working with Windows, Forms, and Layout Management** 57
CHAPTER 3   **Using Standard Controls** 99
CHAPTER 4   **Creating User and Custom Controls** 165
CHAPTER 5   **Data Binding** 229
CHAPTER 6   **Working with Styles, Templates, Skins, and Themes** 325
CHAPTER 7   **Working with Text, Documents, and Printing** 371
CHAPTER 8   **Multithreading** 453
CHAPTER 9   **Working with 2D Graphics** 511
CHAPTER 10   **Working with 3D Graphics** 563
CHAPTER 11   **Creating Animation** 595
CHAPTER 12   **Dealing with Multimedia and User Input** 653
CHAPTER 13   **Migrating and Windows Forms Interoperability** 685

INDEX 701

Contents

About the Authors xv

About the Technical Reviewer xvii

Acknowledgments xix

CHAPTER 1   Building and Debugging WPF Applications 1

    1-1. Create a Standard WPF Application 1

    1-2. Handle an Unhandled Exception 4

    1-3. Create and Use a Dependency Property 7

    1-4. Create a Read-Only Dependency Property 13

    1-5. Override a Dependency Property's Metadata 15

    1-6. Add a PropertyChangedValueCallback to Any
        Dependency Property 19

    1-7. Add Validation to a Dependency Property 20

    1-8. Create and Use an Attached Property 24

    1-9. Create a Dependency Property with Property Value Inheritance . . . 28

    1-10. Merge Two Resource Dictionaries 32

    1-11. Define Application-wide Resources 34

    1-12. Reference a ResourceDictionary in a Different Assembly 36

    1-13. Share Properties Throughout an Application 37

    1-14. Create a Single-Instance Application 42

    1-15. Manage Multiple Windows in an Application 46

    1-16. Debug Data Bindings Using an IValueConverter 51

    1-17. Debug Bindings Using Attached Properties 54

**CHAPTER 2   Working with Windows, Forms, and
Layout Management** 57

    2-1. Automatically Size the Main Application Window
        to Accommodate Its Content 58

    2-2. Arrange UI Elements in a Horizontal or Vertical Stack 59

    2-3. Arrange UI Elements into Automatically Wrapping
        Rows or Columns 61

    2-4. Dock UI Elements to the Edges of a Form 63

2-5. Arrange UI Elements in a Grid 65

2-6. Position UI Elements Using Exact Coordinates.................. 67

2-7. Display Content in a Multitabbed User Interface 69

2-8. Display Content in a Scrollable User Interface 70

2-9. Display Content in Resizable Split Panel...................... 73

2-10. Display Content in an Expander............................. 75

2-11. Place a Group Box Around a Set of UI Elements 77

2-12. Display a Message Box...................................... 78

2-13. Display a Pop-up Window 81

2-14. Display a Border 85

2-15. Display a Menu 87

2-16. Display a Toolbar... 90

2-17. Display a Status Bar 93

2-18. Control the Size of UI Elements in a Form 94

2-19. Define the Tab Order of UI Elements in a Form 97

CHAPTER 3   **Using Standard Controls** 99

3-1. Display Control Content Surrounded
by Braces.. 100

3-2. Display Simple Text.. 101

3-3. Display a Static Image 103

3-4. Get Simple Text Input from a User.......................... 104

3-5. Get Rich Text Input from a User............................ 111

3-6. Load or Save the Content of a RichTextBox 115

3-7. Display a Password Entry Box 119

3-8. Spell Check a TextBox or RichTextBox Control in Real Time 120

3-9. Handle a Button Click 122

3-10. Generate Click Events Repeatedly While a Button Is Clicked.... 124

3-11. Set a Default Button 126

3-12. Provide Quick Keyboard Access to Text Boxes 128

3-13. Provide Quick Keyboard Access to Buttons 129

3-14. Get User Input from a Slider................................ 131

3-15. Display a Context Menu 134

3-16. Display a Tool Tip on a Control 137

3-17. Display a Tool Tip on a Disabled Control 139

3-18. Control the Display Duration and Position of a Tool Tip 140

3-19. View and Select Items from a Set of Radio Buttons 142

3-20. View and Select Items from a Set of Check Boxes 145

3-21. View and Select Items Using a Tree 149

3-22. View and Select Items Using a List........................ 153

3-23. Dynamically Add Items to a List 156

3-24. View and Select Items Using a Combo Box 159

3-25. Display a Control Rotated................................. 162

CHAPTER 4   Creating User and Custom Controls...................... 165

4-1. Create a User Control 166

4-2. Set the Content Property of a User Control.................... 168

4-3. Add Properties to a User Control 171

4-4. Add Events to a User Control 176

4-5. Support Application Commands in a User Control.............. 181

4-6. Add Custom Commands to a User Control 185

4-7. Set Design Mode Behavior in a User Control 191

4-8. Create a Lookless Custom Control 193

4-9. Specify the Parts Required by a Custom Control 198

4-10. Support UI Automation in a Custom Control................. 202

4-11. Create a Custom-Drawn Element 207

4-12. Create a Numeric TextBox Control 212

4-13. Create a Scrollable Canvas Control........................ 217

4-14. Create a Zoomable Canvas Control........................ 221

4-15. Create a Drag Canvas Control 225

CHAPTER 5   Data Binding.. 229

5-1. Bind to a Property of a UI Element........................... 230

5-2. Create a Two-Way Binding................................. 231

5-3. Bind a Property of an Element to Itself 234

5-4. Bind to CLR Objects....................................... 235

5-5. Bind to an Existing Object Instance......................... 242

5-6. Bind to XML Data... 244

5-7. Bind to a Method 247

5-8. Bind to a Command.. 250

5-9. Bind to the Values of an Enumeration........................ 260

5-10. Specify a Default Value for a Binding 262

5-11. Use Data Templates to Display Bound Data.................. 264

5-12. Use Value Converters to Convert Bound Data 268

5-13. Use Data Triggers to Change the Appearance of Bound Data ... 274

5-14. Select a DataTemplate Based on Properties of the Data Object . 278

5-15. Specify Validation Rules for a Binding 283

5-16. Bind to IDataErrorInfo 288

5-17. Bind to a Collection with the Master-Detail Pattern 295

5-18. Sort Data in a Collection.................................. 302

5-19. Apply Custom Sorting Logic to a Collection................. 304

5-20. Filter Data in a Collection............................... 307

5-21. Group Data in a Collection................................ 311

5-22. Apply Custom Grouping to a Collection..................... 313

5-23. Bind to Application Settings.............................. 317

5-24. Bind to Application Resource Strings...................... 321

■CHAPTER 6   **Working with Styles, Templates, Skins, and Themes** ... 325

6-1. Create a Named Style...................................... 325

6-2. Create a Typed Style...................................... 327

6-3. Override Style Properties................................. 330

6-4. Inherit from a Common Base Style.......................... 331

6-5. Change a Control's Appearance on Mouse Over................ 333

6-6. Apply Multiple Triggers to the Same Element............... 335

6-7. Evaluate Multiple Properties for the Same Trigger......... 336

6-8. Programmatically Extract an Element's Style............... 338

6-9. Set a Style Programmatically.............................. 341

6-10. Ignore an Implicit Style................................. 343

6-11. Change the Appearance of Alternate Items in a List....... 345

6-12. Change the Appearance of a List Item When It's Selected...... 347

6-13. Create a Control Template................................ 349

6-14. Put a Control Template into a Style...................... 351

6-15. Create a Control Template That Can Be Customized
       by Properties... 353

6-16. Specify Named Parts of a Control Template................ 354

6-17. Find ControlTemplate-Generated Elements.................. 356

6-18. Create a Custom ToolTip Style............................ 358

6-19. Dynamically Change the Skin of an Application............. 361

6-20. Create Styles That Adapt to the Current OS Theme.......... 365

■CHAPTER 7   **Working with Text, Documents, and Printing**.......... 371

7-1. Programmatically Insert Text into a RichTextBox............ 372

7-2. Apply Syntax Highlighting in a Text Control............... 375

7-3. Print a WPF Visual....................................... 379

7-4. Print a Collection of WPF Visuals......................... 382

7-5. Configure Printing Options Using a PrintTicket............ 386

7-6. Print a Simple Document 393

7-7. Asynchronously Print a Multipage FixedDocument 398

7-8. Programmatically Create and Save a Simple FixedDocument 404

7-9. Use Figures and Floaters in a FlowDocument 408

7-10. Programmatically Create and Save a FlowDocument.......... 410

7-11. Asynchronously Save a FixedDocument to an XPS File 415

7-12. Display a Document 420

7-13. Annotate a Document with Sticky Notes 425

7-14. Use Highlighting in a Document 431

7-15. Load and Save User-Defined Annotations 437

7-16. Print a Document's Annotations 447

CHAPTER 8   **Multithreading**... 453

8-1. Execute a Method Asynchronously Using the
Dispatcher Queue... 454

8-2. Load the Data for a Window Asynchronously After It
Has Rendered 457

8-3. Load the Items in a ListBox Asynchronously 460

8-4. Check Whether You Are Running on the UI Thread............ 464

8-5. Ensure That You Are Running on the UI Thread............... 467

8-6. Execute a Method Asynchronously Using a Background
Worker Thread 469

8-7. Track the Progress of a Background Worker Thread 473

8-8. Support the Cancellation of a Background Worker Thread....... 476

8-9. Create a Background Worker Thread in XAML................. 480

8-10. Update the UI Asynchronously on a Timer 483

8-11. Show a Continuous Animation During an
Asynchronous Process..................................... 486

8-12. Show a ProgressBar While Processing on a
Background Thread 489

8-13. Show a Cancellable ProgressBar While Processing
on a Background Thread 493

8-14. Show a Continuous Progress Bar While Processing
on a Background Thread 496

8-15. Implement Application.DoEvents in WPF 499

8-16. Create a Separate Thread for Each Window in a
Multiwindow Application 503

CHAPTER 9 Working with 2D Graphics 511

9-1. Draw a Line 512

9-2. Draw a Sequence of Connected Lines 513

9-3. Format Lines 515

9-4. Draw a Curved Line 518

9-5. Draw Simple Shapes 521

9-6. Draw Complex Shapes 523

9-7. Create Reusable Shapes 525

9-8. Display a Tool Tip on a Shape 528

9-9. Display Graphics Elements in a Tool Tip 530

9-10. Use System Colors in Your Graphics 531

9-11. Draw or Fill a Shape Using a Solid Color 533

9-12. Fill a Shape with a Linear or Radial Color Gradient 536

9-13. Fill a Shape with an Image 539

9-14. Fill a Shape with a Pattern or Texture 542

9-15. Fill a Shape with a View of Active UI Elements 546

9-16. Apply Blur Effects on UI Elements 548

9-17. Apply a Glow Effect to Your UI Elements 552

9-18. Apply a Drop Shadow Effect to Your UI Elements 554

9-19. Scale, Skew, Rotate, or Position Graphics Elements 558

CHAPTER 10 Working with 3D Graphics 563

10-1. Use 3D in Your Application 564

10-2. Use a 3D Camera 566

10-3. Draw a 3D Model 570

10-4. Light a Scene 573

10-5. Specify a Material for a Model 578

10-6. Apply Textures to a Model 583

10-7. Interact with 3D Objects 586

10-8. Use a 2D Control in a 3D Scene 590

CHAPTER 11 Creating Animation 595

11-1. Animate the Property of a Control 596

11-2. Animate a Property of a Control Set with a Data Binding 600

11-3. Remove Animations 604

11-4. Overlap Animations 609

11-5. Animate Several Properties in Parallel 611

11-6. Create a Keyframe-Based Animation 614

11-7. Control the Progress of an Animation 617

11-8. Animate the Shape of a Path 620

11-9. Loop and Reverse an Animation 623

11-10. Limit the Frame Rate of a Storyboard. 626

11-11. Limit the Frame Rate for All Animations in an Application 629

11-12. Animate an Object Along a Path 632

11-13. Play Back Audio or Video with a MediaTimeline 635

11-14. Synchronize Timeline Animations with a MediaTimeline 637

11-15. Receive Notification When an Animation Completes 641

11-16. Animate the Color of a Brush with Indirect Property Targeting . 644

11-17. Control Animations Through Triggers 646

11-18. Animate Text 651

CHAPTER 12   Dealing with Multimedia and User Input. 653

12-1. Play System Sounds 653

12-2. Use Triggers to Play Audio When a User Interacts
with a Control 656

12-3. Play a Media File 658

12-4. Respond When the User Clicks a UI Element with the Mouse . . . 663

12-5. Respond When the User Clicks a UI Element in a
Container with the Mouse 666

12-6. Respond When the User Rotates the Mouse Wheel 669

12-7. Drag Items from a List and Drop Them on a Canvas 672

12-8. Handle Keyboard Events. 676

12-9. Query Keyboard State 679

12-10. Suppress Keyboard and Mouse Events 682

CHAPTER 13   Migrating and Windows Forms Interoperability 685

13-1. Use WPF Windows in a Windows Forms Application 686

13-2. Use WPF Controls in Windows Forms 689

13-3. Use Windows Forms in a WPF Application 693

13-4. Use Windows Forms Controls in a WPF Window 696

INDEX 701

About the Authors

SAM NOBLE is a software developer who has been using .NET for several years in the land of academia, creating 3D graphics pipelines, artificial neural networks, image-processing tools, and a theoretical 4D spacetime computer compiler and emulator, amongst other things. Sam is currently a developer for SmithBayes where he has been using .NET 3.0+ industrially since the early CTP releases, fully embracing WPF and all it has to offer to create sophisticated strategic visualization tools.

SAM BOURTON is a technologist with ten years of commercial experience as a software designer and developer, across a wide variety of industries including e-commerce, telecoms, and Formula 1 motor racing. He has been using the .NET Framework since the very first beta and has been using WPF since the early CTPs. He has a passion for design patterns, application architecture, and best-practice object-oriented design and methodologies.

ALLEN JONES has 20 years of experience covering a wide range of IT disciplines in a variety of sectors; however, his true passion has always been software development. Allen is currently the the Chief Architect at SmithBayes, a UK-based firm that develops an agile decision platform which provides strategic decision support to senior executives in large corporations.

About the Technical Reviewer

 **TODD MEISTER** has been developing and using Microsoft technologies for more than ten years. He has been a technical editor on more than 50 books on topics ranging from SQL Server to the .NET Framework. Besides technical editing books, he is an assistant director for computing services at Ball State University in Muncie, Indiana. He lives in central Indiana with his wife, Kimberly, and their four children. Contact Todd at tmeister@sycamoresolutions.com.

Acknowledgments

I would like to give thanks to everyone at Apress who made this book possible, in particular Sofia Marchant for her patience and guidance, Todd Meister for his technical edits, Kim Wimpsett for correcting all of my dodgy prose, Laura Cheu for the final reviews, and everyone else who I didn't have the fortune of talking to. To my coauthors and colleagues at SmithBayes, my family for all the love and support, and my friends for all the distractions and good times. Most importantly of all, to my wonderful girlfriend, Jayne, for all the love, support, encouragement, and understanding.

Sam Noble

I would like to thank everyone at Apress for working so hard to make this book a reality. And I would like to say a special thank you to my lovely Helen B. for being so patient and understanding, even whilst this book gradually and remorselessly sucked up all our free time together. I love you always. Finally, thanks must go to Little Kev and Rose "Miss Geek" Cobb, for love, adventures, and tech support.

Sam Bourton

Thanks again to all the crew at Apress for helping us get this book published: Dominic, Ewan, Sofia, Kim, Todd, Laura, and Tina. Thanks also to the two Sams for joining me in this endeavor and making this book possible.

Allen Jones

CHAPTER 1

Building and Debugging WPF Applications

WPF provides a great deal of powerful functionality that you can leverage to simplify and speed up the development and debugging processes of your applications. This includes functionality that would have required a great deal of effort in WinForms. From sharing resources across your application to creating custom properties that you can use in animations and bindings to narrowing down the debugging process of data bindings, there's something for everyone.

This chapter focuses on the basics of building a rich WPF application and some methods that you can use to help ease the debugging of data bindings. The recipes in this chapter describe how to:

- Create a standard WPF application (recipe 1-1)

- Handle an unhandled exception (recipe 1-2)

- Create and use dependency properties (recipes 1-3, 1-4, 1-5, 1-6, 1-7, 1-8, and 1-9)

- Handle resources in an application (recipes 1-10, 1-11, and 1-12)

- Share properties throughout an application (recipe 1-13)

- Create a single-instance application (recipe 1-14)

- Manage multiple windows in an application (recipe 1-15)

- Debug data bindings (recipes 1-16 and 1-17)

1-1. Create a Standard WPF Application

Problem

You need to create a new, rich WPF desktop application.

Solution

Create a new project with a single App.xaml file, containing the main entry point for your application.

How It Works

In its simplest form, an application is defined by creating a System.Windows.Application object. When creating a new Windows Application project in Visual Studio, you are given the default definition of the Application object. The Application object provides useful functionality such as the following:

- A last chance to handle an unhandled exception

- Handling application-wide resources and properties

- Providing access to the windows contained in the application

The application definition needs a special MSBuild property to indicate that it contains the application's definition. This can be set using the Properties window of Microsoft Visual Studio, specifically, by setting the value of Build Action to ApplicationDefinition. If you attempt to compile a Windows Application project that doesn't have a file marked with a build action of ApplicationDefinition, you will receive an error stating that no main entry point was found in the application. One of the side effects of the ApplicationDefinition build action adds a definition of a Main method to your application's code-behind. This is the entry point for your application.

■**Note** The Application class uses the Singleton pattern to ensure that only one instance of the Application object is created per AppDomain, because the Application object is shared throughout an AppDomain. For more information on the Singleton pattern, please refer to http://en.wikipedia.org/wiki/Singleton_pattern.

The Code

The following example details the default application structure for a simple Microsoft Windows application. The example comprises the following: the App.xaml file defines the markup for a System.Windows.Application object, with a build action of ApplicationDefinition; the App.xaml.cs, which contains the Application object's code-behind; the Window1.xaml file, which contains the markup for the application's main window; and Window1.xaml.cs, which contains the window's code-behind.

This is the code for App.xaml:

```
<Application x:Class="Recipe_01_01.App"
    xmlns="http://schemas.microsoft.com/winfx/2006/xaml/presentation"
    xmlns:x="http://schemas.microsoft.com/winfx/2006/xaml"
    StartupUri="Window1.xaml">
    <Application.Resources>

    </Application.Resources>
</Application>
```

This is the code for App.xaml.cs:

```
using System.Windows;

namespace Recipe_01_01
{
    /// <summary>
    /// Interaction logic for App.xaml
    /// </summary>
    public partial class App : Application
    {
        public App()
        {
            InitializeComponent();
        }
    }
}
```

This is the code for Window1.xaml:

```
<Window
  x:Class="Recipe_01_01.Window1"
  xmlns="http://schemas.microsoft.com/winfx/2006/xaml/presentation"
  xmlns:x="http://schemas.microsoft.com/winfx/2006/xaml"
  Title="Window1"
  Height="300"
  Width="300">
  <Grid>

  </Grid>
</Window>
```

This is the code for Window1.xaml.cs:

```
using System.Windows;

namespace Recipe_01_01
{
    /// <summary>
    /// Interaction logic for Window1.xaml
    /// </summary>
    public partial class Window1 : Window
    {
        public Window1()
        {
            InitializeComponent();
        }
    }
}
```

1-2. Handle an Unhandled Exception

Problem

You need to handle any unexpected exceptions, allowing you to present the user with an informative dialog box and or log useful debug data.

Solution

Add an event handler to the `System.Windows.Application.DispatcherUnhandledException` event of your application. This will be invoked when an exception has not been handled in code; it allows you to handle the event, allowing the application to continue processing.

How It Works

The default exception handling in WPF will catch any unhandled exceptions that are thrown in the application's main UI thread and display a message to the user. Once the user handles the dialog box, the application shuts down. It is possible, though, to override this default behavior, which allows you to decide what action should be taken. This could be writing to some log file or handling the exception and allowing the application to continue.

To allow an application to provide its own unhandled exception behavior, you need to add a `System.Windows.Threading.DispatcherUnhandledExceptionEventHandler` to the `DispatcherUnhandledException` event on the current application. The handler is passed a `System.Windows.Threading.DispatcherUnhandledExceptionEventArgs` object, which contains a reference to the exception that was unhandled and a flag to indicate whether the exception has been handled. If the exception is marked as being handled, the default WPF exception handling will not kick in. Instead, the operation that was running is halted, but the application will continue running, unless otherwise instructed.

Exceptions raised on threads other than the main UI thread will not be rethrown on the UI thread by default; thus, `DispatcherUnhandledException` does not get raised. If this behavior is required, it will need to be implemented by handling the exception on the owning thread, dispatching it to the UI thread and then rethrowing the exception from the UI thread.

■ **Note** When using the `DispatcherUnhandledException` event to catch unhandled exceptions, you may still find your IDE breaking on an exception and informing you that it is unhandled. This is to be expected if you have your IDE configured to break on unhandled exceptions. Continue the program's execution, and you will see the exception being handled by your custom code.

The Code

The following code demonstrates how to handle the `Application.DispatcherUnhandledException` event. The following markup defines the content of the `App.xaml` file, or whatever name you have given to the file in your project with a build action of `ApplicationDefinition`.

```xml
<Application
  x:Class="Recipe_01_02.App"
  xmlns="http://schemas.microsoft.com/winfx/2006/xaml/presentation"
  xmlns:x="http://schemas.microsoft.com/winfx/2006/xaml"
  StartupUri="Window1.xaml"
  DispatcherUnhandledException="App_DispatcherUnhandledException"
/>
```

The following code block defines the code for the code-behind of the previous markup and contains the declaration for App_DispatcherUnhandledException:

```csharp
using System;
using System.Windows;
using System.Windows.Threading;

namespace Recipe_01_02
{
    /// <summary>
    /// Interaction logic for App.xaml
    /// </summary>
    public partial class App : Application
    {
        private void App_DispatcherUnhandledException (object sender,
                                        DispatcherUnhandledExceptionEventArgs e)
        {
            string msg =
                string.Format("An unhandled exception has occurred.{0}{0}{1}",
                            Environment.NewLine,
                            e.Exception);

            MessageBox.Show(msg, "Recipe_01_02");

            //Handling this event will result in the application
            //remaining alive. This is useful if you are able to
            //recover from the exception.
            e.Handled = true;
        }
    }
}
```

The next code block gives the markup used to define the application's main window. The window contains three System.Windows.Controls.Button controls, which demonstrate the behavior of the default WPF exception handling and how it can be overridden.

```xml
<Window
  x:Class="Recipe_01_02.Window1"
  xmlns="http://schemas.microsoft.com/winfx/2006/xaml/presentation"
  xmlns:x="http://schemas.microsoft.com/winfx/2006/xaml"
  Title="Window1"
```

```xml
      Height="135"
      Width="300">
      <StackPanel>
        <Button
          x:Name="btnThrowHandledException"
          Click="btnThrowHandledException_Click"
          Content="Throw Handled Exception"
          Margin="10,10,10,5"
        />

        <Button
          x:Name="btnThrowUnhandledException"
          Click="btnThrowUnhandledException_Click"
          Content="Throw Unhandled Exception"
          Margin="10,5,10,5"
        />

        <Button
          x:Name="btnThrowUnhandledExceptionFromThread"
          Click="btnThrowUnhandledExceptionFromThread_Click"
          Content="Throw Unhandled Exception From a New Thread"
          Margin="10,5,10,10"
        />
      </StackPanel>
    </Window>
```

The final code block defines the code-behind for the window defined earlier. It contains the three Button.Click event handlers that execute the examples. The first button throws a new System.NotImplementedException, which is caught using a try...catch block and doesn't progress any further. The second button throws a new NotImplementedException that is not handled in code and invokes DispatcherUnhandledException, which is handled by App. The third button throws a new NotImplementedException from a System.ComponentModel.BackgroundWorker, illustrating that the exception does not invoke DispatcherUnhandledException.

```csharp
using System;
using System.Windows;
using System.ComponentModel;

namespace Recipe_01_02
{
    /// <summary>
    /// Interaction logic for Window1.xaml
    /// </summary>
    public partial class Window1 : Window
    {
        public Window1()
        {
```

```csharp
        InitializeComponent();
    }

    private void btnThrowHandledException_Click(object sender,
                                                RoutedEventArgs e)
    {
        try
        {
            throw new NotImplementedException();
        }
        catch (NotImplementedException ex)
        {
            MessageBox.Show(ex.Message);
        }
    }

    private void btnThrowUnhandledException_Click(object sender,
                                                  RoutedEventArgs e)
    {
        throw new NotImplementedException();
    }

    private void btnThrowUnhandledExceptionFromThread_Click(object sender,
                                                            RoutedEventArgs e)
    {
        BackgroundWorker backgroundWorker = new BackgroundWorker();

        backgroundWorker.DoWork += delegate
            {
                throw new NotImplementedException();
            };

        backgroundWorker.RunWorkerAsync();
    }
    }
}
```

1-3. Create and Use a Dependency Property

Problem

You need to add a property to a System.Windows.DependencyObject that provides support for any or all of the following:

- Data bindings

- Animation

- Setting with a dynamic resource reference

- Automatically inheriting a property value from a super-class

- Setting in a style

- Using property value inheritance (see recipe 1-9)

- Notification through a callback when the value changes

This could be for a new UI control you are creating or simply a type that descends from `DependencyObject`.

Solution

Use a `System.Windows.DependencyProperty` as the backing store for the required property on your class.

How It Works

A dependency property is implemented using a standard Common Language Runtime (CLR) property, but instead of using a private field to back the property, a `DependencyProperty` is used. A `DependencyProperty` is instantiated using the static method `DependencyProperty.Register(string name, System.Type propertyType, Type ownerType)`, which returns a `DependencyProperty` instance that is stored using a static, read-only field. There are also two overrides that allow you to specify metadata and a callback for validation.

The first argument passed to the `DependencyProperty.Register` method specifies the name of the dependency property being registered. This name must be unique within registrations that occur in the owner type's namespace (see recipe 1-5 for how to use the same name for a dependency property on several objects inside a common namespace). The next two arguments simply give the type of property being registered and the class against which the dependency property is being defined, respectively. It is important to note that the owning type derives from `DependencyObject`; otherwise, an exception will be raised when the dependency property is initialized.

The first override for the `Register` method allows a `System.Windows.PropertyMetadata` object, or one of the several derived types, to be specified for the property. Property metadata is used to define characteristics of a dependency property, allowing for greater richness than simply using reflection or common CLR characteristics. The use of property metadata can be broken down into three areas:

- Specifying a default value for the property

- Providing callback implementations for property changes and value coercion

- Reporting framework-level characteristics used in layout, inheritance, and so on

Caution Because values for dependency properties can be set in several places, a set of rules define the precedence of these values and any default value specified in property metadata. These rules are beyond the scope of this recipe; for more information, you can look at the subject of dependency property value precedence at http://msdn.microsoft.com/en-us/library/ms743230.aspx.

In addition to specifying a default value, property-changed callbacks, and coercion callbacks, the System.Windows.FrameworkPropertyMetadata object allows you to specify various options given by the System.Windows.FrameworkPropertyMetadataOptions enumeration. You can use as many of these options as required, combining them as flags. Table 1-1 details the values defined in the FrameworkPropertyMetadataOptions enumeration.

Table 1-1. *Values for the FrameworkPropertyMetadataOptions Class*

Property	Description
None	The property will adopt the default behavior of the WPF property system.
AffectsMeasure	Changes to the dependency property's value affect the owning control's measure.
AffectsArrange	Changes to the dependency property's value affect the owning control's arrangement.
AffectsParentMeasure	Changes to the dependency property's value affect the parent of the owning control's measure.
AffectsParentArrange	Changes to the dependency property's value affect the parent of the owning control's arrangement.
AffectsRender	Changes to the dependency property's value affect the owning control's render or layout composition.
Inherits	The value of the dependency property is inherited by any child elements of the owning type.
OverridesInheritenceBehaviour	The value of the dependency property spans disconnected trees in the context of property value inheritance.
NotDataBindable	Binding operations cannot be performed on this dependency property.
BindsTwoWayByDefault	When used in data bindings, the System.Windows.BindingMode is TwoWay by default.
Journal	The value of the dependency property saved or restored through any journaling processes or URI navigations.
SubPropertiesDoNotAffectRender	Properties of the value of the dependency property do not affect the owning type's rendering in any way.

■**Caution** When implementing a dependency property, it is important to use the correct naming convention. The identifier used for the dependency property must be the same as the identifier used to name the CLR property it is registered against, appended with `Property`. For example, if you were defining a property to store the velocity of an object, the CLR property would be named `Velocity`, and the dependency property field would be named `VelocityProperty`. If a dependency property isn't implemented in this fashion, you may experience strange behavior with property system–style applications and some visual designers not correctly reporting the property's value.

Value coercion plays an important role in dependency properties and comes into play when the value of a dependency property is set. By supplying a `CoerceValueCallback` argument, it is possible to alter the value to which the property is being set. An example of value coercion is when setting the value of the `System.Windows.Window.RenderTransform` property. It is not valid to set the `RenderTransform` property of a window to anything other than an identity matrix. If any other value is used, an exception is thrown. It should be noted that any coercion callback methods are invoked before any `System.Windows.ValidateValueCallback` methods.

The Code

The following example demonstrates the definition of a custom `DependencyProperty` on a simple `System.Windows.Controls.UserControl` (`MyControl`, defined in `MyControl.xaml`). The `UserControl` contains two text blocks: one of which is set by the control's code-behind; the other is bound to a dependency property defined in the control's code-behind.

```
<UserControl
  x:Class="Recipe_01_03.MyControl"
  xmlns="http://schemas.microsoft.com/winfx/2006/xaml/presentation"
  xmlns:x="http://schemas.microsoft.com/winfx/2006/xaml">
  <Grid>
    <Grid.RowDefinitions>
      <RowDefinition Height="20" />
      <RowDefinition Height="*" />
    </Grid.RowDefinitions>

    <TextBlock x:Name="txblFontWeight" Text="FontWeight set to: Normal."  />

    <Viewbox Grid.Row="1">
      <TextBlock
        Text="{Binding Path=TextContent}"
        FontWeight="{Binding Path=TextFontWeight}" />
    </Viewbox>
  </Grid>
</UserControl>
```

The following code block details the code-behind for the previous markup (MyControl.xaml.cs):

```
using System.Windows;
using System.Windows.Controls;

namespace Recipe_01_03
{
    public partial class MyControl : UserControl
    {
        public MyControl()
        {
            InitializeComponent();
            DataContext = this;
        }

        public FontWeight TextFontWeight
        {
            get { return (FontWeight)GetValue(TextFontWeightProperty); }
            set { SetValue(TextFontWeightProperty, value); }
        }

        public static readonly DependencyProperty TextFontWeightProperty =
            DependencyProperty.Register(
                "TextFontWeight",
                typeof(FontWeight),
                typeof(MyControl),
                new FrameworkPropertyMetadata(FontWeights.Normal,
                            FrameworkPropertyMetadataOptions.AffectsArrange
                            & FrameworkPropertyMetadataOptions.AffectsMeasure
                            & FrameworkPropertyMetadataOptions.AffectsRender,
                            TextFontWeight_PropertyChanged,
                            TextFontWeight_CoerceValue));

        public string TextContent
        {
            get { return (string)GetValue(TextContentProperty); }
            set { SetValue(TextContentProperty, value); }
        }

        public static readonly DependencyProperty TextContentProperty =
            DependencyProperty.Register(
                "TextContent",
                typeof(string),
                typeof(MyControl),
```

```
            new FrameworkPropertyMetadata(
                "Default Value",
                FrameworkPropertyMetadataOptions.AffectsArrange
                & FrameworkPropertyMetadataOptions.AffectsMeasure
                & FrameworkPropertyMetadataOptions.AffectsRender));


    private static object TextFontWeight_CoerceValue(DependencyObject d,
            object value)
    {
        FontWeight fontWeight = (FontWeight)value;


        if (fontWeight == FontWeights.Bold
            || fontWeight == FontWeights.Normal)
        {
            return fontWeight;
        }

        return FontWeights.Normal;
    }

    private static void TextFontWeight_PropertyChanged(DependencyObject d,
                            DependencyPropertyChangedEventArgs e)
    {
        MyControl myControl = d as MyControl;

        if (myControl != null)
        {
            FontWeight fontWeight = (FontWeight)e.NewValue;
            string fontWeightName;

            if (fontWeight == FontWeights.Bold)
                fontWeightName = "Bold";
            else
                fontWeightName = "Normal";

            myControl.txblFontWeight.Text =
                    string.Format("Font weight set to: {0}.", fontWeightName);
        }
    }
}
```

1-4. Create a Read-Only Dependency Property

Problem

You need to add a read-only dependency property to an object that inherits from System.Windows.
DependencyObject.

Solution

When registering a dependency property, use System.Windows.DependencyProperty.
RegisterReadOnly instead of DependencyProperty.Register to obtain a reference to a System.
Windows.DependencyPropertyKey. This is stored in a private field and used to look up the value
of the property.

How It Works

The RegisterReadOnly method of DependencyProperty is similar to the Register method in
terms of their parameters, although they differ in their return values. Where Register
returns a reference to a DependencyProperty object, RegisterReadOnly returns a reference
to a DependencyPropertyKey object. The DependencyPropertyKey exposes two members: a
DependencyProperty property containing a reference to the DependencyProperty created against the
key and an OverrideMetadata method allowing you to alter the metadata used to describe the
property's characteristics.

    The DependencyProperty property on DependencyPropertyKey can directly be used in calls
to the SetValue and ClearValue methods. The GetValue method, though, has no such signature.
To make a call to GetValue, simply pass in the value of DependencyPropertyKey.DependencyProperty.

    When defining the access modifiers for the various members, it is important to remember
that if the field that stores the DependencyPropertyKey is public, then other objects will be able
to set the value of the property, defeating the object of making the property read-only. The
DependencyProperty property of the DependencyPropertyKey can be exposed, though, and it is
recommended that you do so as a public static readonly DependencyProperty property. This
ensures that certain property system operations can still take place whilst the property remains
read-only to external types. Any attempt to create a two-way binding against a read-only property
will result in a runtime exception.

The Code

The following code demonstrates a simple XAML file that defines a System.Windows.Window.
The window contains a System.Windows.Controls.Viewbox, which is used to display a System.
Windows.Controls.TextBlock. The value of the TextBlock's Text property is bound to a custom
dependency property defined in the window's code-behind file.

```xaml
<Window
  x:Name="winThis"
  x:Class="Recipe_01_04.Window1"
  xmlns="http://schemas.microsoft.com/winfx/2006/xaml/presentation"
  xmlns:x="http://schemas.microsoft.com/winfx/2006/xaml"
  Title="Recipe_01_04"
  Height="300"
  Width="300">
    <Grid>
      <Viewbox>
        <TextBlock
          Text="{Binding ElementName=winThis, Path=Counter}"
        />
      </Viewbox>
    </Grid>
</Window>
```

The following code demonstrates a simple application that contains a single System.Windows.Window. The window defines a single read-only CLR property that is backed by a System.Windows.DependencyProperty, referenced using a System.Windows.DependencyPropertyKey. A System.Windows.Threading.DispatcherTimer is used to increment the value of the Counter property every second.

```csharp
using System;
using System.Windows;
using System.Windows.Threading;

namespace Recipe_01_04
{
    /// <summary>
    /// Interaction logic for Window1.xaml
    /// </summary>
    public partial class Window1 : Window
    {
        /// <summary>
        /// Contructor for the demo's main window. Here a simple dispatcher
        /// timer is created simply for the purpose of demonstrating how
        /// a read-only dependency property can be set.
        /// </summary>
        public Window1()
        {
            InitializeComponent();

            DispatcherTimer timer =
                new DispatcherTimer(TimeSpan.FromSeconds(1),
                                    DispatcherPriority.Normal,
                                    delegate
                                    {
```

```
                                   //Increment the value stored in Counter
                                   int newValue = Counter == int.MaxValue
                                                      ? 0
                                                      : Counter + 1;
                                   //Uses the SetValue that accepts a
                                   //System.Windows.DependencyPropertyKey
                                   SetValue(counterKey, newValue);
                               },
                               Dispatcher);
        }


        /// <summary>
        /// The standard CLR property wrapper. Note the wrapper is
        /// read-only too, so as to maintain consistency.
        /// </summary>
        public int Counter
        {
            get { return (int)GetValue(counterKey.DependencyProperty); }
        }


        /// <summary>
        /// The <see cref="System.Windows.DependencyPropertyKey"/> field which
        /// provides access to the <see cref="System.Windows.DependencyProperty"/>
        /// which backs the above CLR property.
        /// </summary>
        private static readonly DependencyPropertyKey counterKey =
            DependencyProperty.RegisterReadOnly("Counter",
                                                typeof(int),
                                                typeof(Window1),
                                                new PropertyMetadata(0));
    }
}
```

1-5. Override a Dependency Property's Metadata

Problem

You need to override the metadata for a System.Windows.DependencyProperty defined in a class higher up in the type's inheritance tree.

Solution

Use the OverrideMetadata method of the dependency property for which you want to override the metadata.

■ **Note** It is also possible to override metadata for attached properties, which are, after all, dependency properties. Overridden metadata for an attached property is used only when the attached property is set on an instance of the class performing the overriding.

How It Works

The `OverrideMetadata` method on a `DependencyProperty` allows you to specify new property metadata for a type that has inherited the `DependencyProperty` in question. This is particularly useful if you want to alter any characteristics of the property's metadata. This can be the property's default value, `System.Windows.PropertyMetadata.PropertyChangedCallback` or `System.Windows.PropertyMetadata.CoerceValueCallback`.

There are some things to be aware of when overriding a dependency property's metadata that may make it more favorable to implement your own custom dependency property (see recipe 1-3). It is important to note that a new `ValidateValueCallback` cannot be specified because this is defined outside the scope of the property's metadata. It is also not possible to override the property's value type.

Another caveat is that when overriding property metadata, the overriding metadata's object type must match that of the metadata being overridden. For example, if you are overriding the property metadata on a `System.Windows.FrameworkElement.DataContextProperty`, where the original metadata is defined using a `System.Windows.FrameworkPropertyMetadata` object, overriding metadata must also be a `FrameworkPropertyMetadata` object.

Each characteristic that can be overridden behaves slightly differently in the way it handles existing values, either replacing the existing data with the new data or merging the new data with any existing values. Table 1-2 covers the three characteristics and describes the way in which it acts if any other data is present.

Table 1-2. *Merge/Replacement Behavior for Overidden Metadata*

Characteristic	Description
`DefaultValue`	A new default value will replace the default value of the dependency property for the new owner's type. If no new default value is supplied in the overridden metadata, the default value in the closest ancestor will be used.
`PropertyChangedCallback`	A new `PropertyChangedCallback` implementation will be merged with any existing ones. `PropertyChangedCallback` implementations are executed starting with the most derived type. If no `PropertyChangedCallback` is supplied in the overridden metadata, the `PropertyChangedCallback` in the closest ancestor will be used.
`CoerceValueCallback`	A new `CoerceValueCallback` implementation will replace any existing implementation. If a `CoerceValueCallback` implementation is provided, it will be the only callback to be invoked. If the `CoerceValueCallback` is not overridden, the implementation in the closest ancestor will be used.

The Code

The following example demonstrates a simple System.Windows.Window that contains a System.
Windows.Controls.TextBox and a System.Windows.Controls.Button. In the window's code-behind,
the metadata for the window's DataContextProperty is overridden. The overriding data specifies a new default value and registers a property-changed callback. The first code block defines
the window's markup file, and the second defines the window's code-behind.

```
<Window
  x:Class="Recipe_01_05.Window1"
  xmlns="http://schemas.microsoft.com/winfx/2006/xaml/presentation"
  xmlns:x="http://schemas.microsoft.com/winfx/2006/xaml"
  Title="Window1"
  Height="102"
  Width="200">
  <StackPanel>
    <TextBox
      x:Name="tbxUserText"
      Text="Enter some text..."
      Margin="10,10,10,5"
    />
    <Button
      Click="Button_Click"
      Content="Update DataContext"
      Margin="10,5,10,10"
    />
  </StackPanel>
</Window>
```

The following code block defines the code-behind file for the window:

```
using System.Windows;
using System;

namespace Recipe_01_05
{
    /// <summary>
    /// Interaction logic for Window1.xaml
    /// </summary>
    public partial class Window1 : Window
    {
        public Window1()
        {
            InitializeComponent();

            // Override the metadata for the DataContextProperty
            // of the window, altering the default value and
            // registering a property-changed callback.
```

```
            DataContextProperty.OverrideMetadata(
                typeof(Window1),
                new FrameworkPropertyMetadata(
                    100d,
                    new PropertyChangedCallback(DataContext_PropertyChanged)));

        }

        private static void DataContext_PropertyChanged(DependencyObject d,
                                DependencyPropertyChangedEventArgs e)
        {
            string msg =
                string.Format(
                    "DataContext changed.{0}{0}Old Value: {1}{0}New Value: {2}",
                    Environment.NewLine,
                    e.OldValue.ToString(),
                    e.NewValue.ToString());

            MessageBox.Show(msg, "Recipe_01_05");
        }

        private void Button_Click(object sender, RoutedEventArgs e)
        {
            DataContext = tbxUserText.Text;
        }
    }
}
```

Figure 1-1 shows the dialog box the user will see after clicking the button.

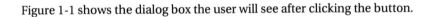

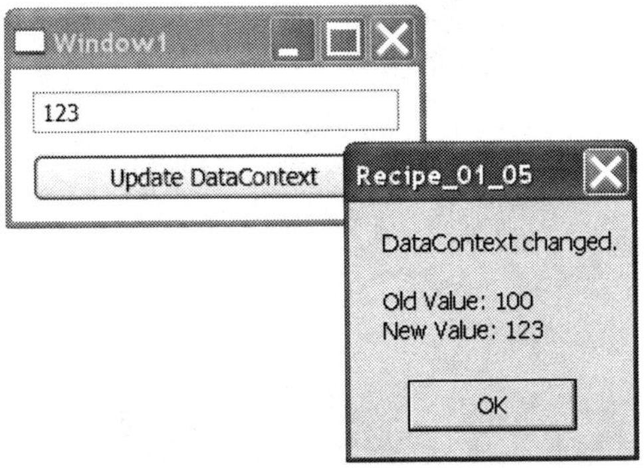

Figure 1-1. *The dialog box shown to the user after clicking the button*

1-6. Add a PropertyChangedValueCallback to Any Dependency Property

Problem

You need to add a `PropertyChangedValueCallback` to a dependency property but are not able to override the property's metadata or access the source property.

Solution

Use the static method `System.ComponentModel.DependencyPropertyDescriptor.FromProperty` to obtain a reference to a `System.ComponentModel.DependencyPropertyDescriptor`. Using the descriptor, you are able to add new `PropertyChangedValueCallback` handlers through the descriptor's `AddValueChanged` method.

How It Works

In obtaining a reference to a `DependencyPropertyDescriptor`, you have a collection of methods and properties that allow you to work with the underlying dependency property, even accessing the property directly. Some of the members of this type are aimed at designers, so they can be ignored.

The method you are interested in is `AddValueChanged`, which accepts two parameters. The first is a reference to the object that owns the dependency property in question. The second parameter is a `System.Windows.EventHandler`, pointing to the method to be called when the dependency property's value changes. There is also a conjugate method named `RemoveValueChanged`, which, as the name suggests, allows you to remove a value-changed event handler. It is best practice to remove any event handlers that are added to objects to ensure that they are properly cleaned up once they are done with.

The Code

```
using System;
using System.ComponentModel;
using System.Windows;
using System.Windows.Controls;

namespace Recipe_01_06
{
    /// <summary>
    /// Interaction logic for Window1.xaml
    /// </summary>
    public partial class Window1 : Window
    {
        public Window1()
        {
            InitializeComponent();
        }
```

```
        private void Window1_Loaded(object sender, RoutedEventArgs e)
        {
            DependencyPropertyDescriptor descriptor =
                DependencyPropertyDescriptor.FromProperty(TextBox.TextProperty,
                                                    typeof(TextBox));

            descriptor.AddValueChanged(tbxEditMe, tbxEditMe_TextChanged);

        }

        private void tbxEditMe_TextChanged(object sender, EventArgs e)
        {
            //Do something
        }
    }
}
```

1-7. Add Validation to a Dependency Property

Problem

You need to validate a dependency property, ensuring the value being set is in the context of your application's business rules.

Solution

Add a ValidationValueCallback handler when specifying the metadata of a dependency property.

How It Works

When setting the value of a dependency property, there are several opportunities to inspect the value and, based on its validity, take some action. The first chance you get to handle the new value coming in is through the CoerceValueCallback, which allows you to shape the input data, if required (see recipe 1-3). The second chance is through a ValidationValueCallback. Simply supply a method to be used for validation when defining a dependency property's metadata object.

The validation method returns a bool indicating the validity of the new value. This allows you to determine whether the value meets your requirements of any business rules, returning true if the conditions are met and otherwise false. If the validation phase passes successfully, any supplied PropertyChangedCallback methods are invoked, notifying any listeners that the value of the property has changed.

Validation callbacks are used when the dependency property's value is set in several different scenarios. This covers the default value of the property, default value overrides through overridden property metadata, or setting the property through System.Windows. DependencyObject.SetValue, either explicitly through code or implicitly through data binding.

The validation callback takes only a value to validate as an object and does not take a reference to the owning System.Windows.DependencyObject. As such, validation callbacks are intended to provide generic validation to the property in question. Because the type of the object is not known, it is assumed that validation callback methods are aware of the type they are validating. This makes them useful for validating numerical ranges, executing regular expression matches, and so on. They are not useful if the validity of the value in question is in any way influenced by other property values.

Should the validation callback handler return false, a `System.ArgumentException` exception will be raised and handled within the property system. The result of a validation callback returning false is that the value being validated will not be set, and the dependency property will not change and hence not invoke any `PropertyChangedCallbacks`.

Note Because the validation callback parameter is not part of the property's metadata, the validation methods cannot be overridden.

The Code

The following code demonstrates a simple application with a single window. The window contains a text block into which the user can enter a number. The `Text` property of the `System.Windows.Controls.TextBox` control is bound to a `System.Windows.DependencyProperty`, `UserValue`, defined in the window's code-behind. The value of the `UserValue` dependency property is also bound to a text block in the window, reflecting the actual value of the property. The color of the text in the text box is set to green when the given value is valid; otherwise, it is set to red.

Note When the value input into the text box goes from being invalid to valid, through the deletion of the characters entered to invalidate it, the text box's text color will remain red. This is a result of the dependency property holding the last valid value it was set with. In this scenario, when the text goes from invalid to valid, the value will be equal to that held by the dependency property; therefore, the property's value doesn't actually change. For example, try entering the number 1000 and then delete the last 0.

```
<Window
  x:Class="Recipe_01_07.Window1"
  xmlns="http://schemas.microsoft.com/winfx/2006/xaml/presentation"
  xmlns:x="http://schemas.microsoft.com/winfx/2006/xaml"
  Title-"Window1"
  Height="300"
  Width="300">
  <Grid>
    <StackPanel>
      <TextBlock
        Text="Please enter a value between 1 and 100, inclusive."
        Margin="5" />
```

```xml
    <TextBox
      x:Name="uv"
      Text="{Binding Path=UserValue, UpdateSourceTrigger=PropertyChanged}"
      Margin="5"
      PreviewKeyDown="TextBox_PreviewKeyDown" />
    <StackPanel Orientation="Horizontal">
      <TextBlock
        Margin="5"
        Text="UserValue1 Value:" />
      <TextBlock
        x:Name="userValueValue"
        Margin="5"
        Text="{Binding Path=UserValue}" />
    </StackPanel>
  </StackPanel>
  </Grid>
</Window>
```

The following code provides the listing for the window's code-behind file. The single dependency property is bound to the window's TextBox.Text property. A validation callback is supplied, as is a property-changed callback. The property-changed callback will be invoked only if the validation callback returns true. As text is entered into the text box, the text box's foreground color is set to red, indicating it is invalid. When the property-changed handler is invoked, it sets the color to green, indicating the entered value is valid.

```csharp
using System.Windows;
using System.Windows.Controls;
using System.Windows.Media;

namespace Recipe_01_07
{
    public partial class Window1 : Window
    {
        public Window1()
        {
            InitializeComponent();
            //Set the window's DataContext to itself to simplify
            //the binding paths for the UserValue property.
            DataContext = this;
        }

        //The CLR wrapper for the DependencyProperty
        public int UserValue
        {
            get { return (int)GetValue(UserValueProperty); }
            set { SetValue(UserValueProperty, value); }
        }
```

```csharp
//The dependency property backing store.
public static readonly DependencyProperty UserValueProperty =
    DependencyProperty.Register("UserValue",
                                typeof(int),
                                typeof(Window1),
                                new PropertyMetadata(
                                        1,
                                        UserValue_PropertyChangedCallback),
                                ValidateIntRange_ValidationCallbackHandler);

//Validation callback for the above UserValue dependency property.
private static bool ValidateIntRange_ValidationCallbackHandler(object value)
{
    //Try to parse the value to an int.
    int intValue;

    if (int.TryParse(value.ToString(), out intValue))
    {
        //The value is an integer so test its value.
        if (intValue >= 1 && intValue <= 100)
        {
            return true;
        }
    }

    return false;
}

//Property-changed callback for the above UserValue dependency property.
private static void UserValue_PropertyChangedCallback(DependencyObject d,
                                    DependencyPropertyChangedEventArgs e)
{
    Window1 window1 = d as Window1;

    if (window1 != null)
    {
        window1.uv.Foreground = Brushes.SeaGreen;
    }
}

//Handler for the PreviewKeyDown event on the TextBox
private void TextBox_PreviewKeyDown(object sender, RoutedEventArgs e)
{
    TextBox textBox = sender as TextBox;
```

```
                if (textBox != null)
                {
                    textBox.Foreground = Brushes.Firebrick;
                }
            }
        }
}
```

1-8. Create and Use an Attached Property

Problem

You need to add a dependency property to a class but are not able to access the class in a way that would allow you to add the property, or you want to use a property that can be set on any child objects of the type.

Solution

Create an attached property by registering a `System.Windows.DependencyProperty` using the static `DependencyProperty.RegisterAttached` method.

How It Works

You can think of an attached property as a special type of dependency property that doesn't get exposed using a CLR property wrapper. You will more than likely have come across a few examples of attached properties in your XAML travels. Examples of everyday attached properties are `System.Windows.Controls.Canvas.Top`, `System.Windows.Controls.DockPanel.Dock`, and `System.Windows.Controls.Grid.Row`.

As attached properties are registered in a similar way to dependency properties, you are still able to provide metadata for handling property changes, and so on. In addition to metadata, it is possible to enable property value inheritance on attached properties (see recipe 1-9).

Attached properties are not set like dependency properties using a CLR wrapper property; they are instead accessed through a method for getting and setting their value. These methods have specific signatures and naming conventions so that they can be matched up to the correct attached property. The signatures for the property's getter and setter methods can be found in the following code listing.

The Code

The following code defines a simple `System.Windows.Window` that contains a few controls. In the window's code-behind, an attached property is defined with `SystemWindows.UIElement` as the target type. The window's markup defines four controls, three of which have the value of `Window1.Rotation` set in XAML. The button's value for this property is not set and will therefore return the default value for the property, 0 in this case.

```xml
<Window
  x:Class="Recipe_01_08.Window1"
  xmlns="http://schemas.microsoft.com/winfx/2006/xaml/presentation"
  xmlns:x="http://schemas.microsoft.com/winfx/2006/xaml"
  xmlns:local="clr-namespace:Recipe_01_08"
  Title="Recipe_01_08"
  Height="350"
  Width="350">
  <UniformGrid>
    <Button
      Content="Click me!"
      Click="UIElement_Click"
      Margin="10"
    />

    <Border
      MouseLeftButtonDown="UIElement_Click"
      BorderThickness="1"
      BorderBrush="Black"
      Background="Transparent"
      Margin="10"
      local:Window1.Rotation="3.14"
    />

    <ListView
      PreviewMouseLeftButtonDown="UIElement_Click"
      Margin="10"
      local:Window1.Rotation="1.57">
      <ListViewItem Content="Item 1" />
      <ListViewItem Content="Item 1" />
      <ListViewItem Content="Item 1" />
      <ListViewItem Content="Item 1" />
    </ListView>

    <local:UserControl1
      Margin="10"
      local:Window1.Rotation="1.0"
    />
  </UniformGrid>
</Window>

using System.Windows;
using System.Windows.Controls;
```

```csharp
namespace Recipe_01_08
{
    /// <summary>
    /// Interaction logic for Window1.xaml
    /// </summary>
    public partial class Window1 : Window
    {
        public Window1()
        {
            InitializeComponent();
        }

        private void UIElement_Click(object sender, RoutedEventArgs e)
        {
            UIElement uiElement = (UIElement)sender;

            MessageBox.Show("Rotation = " + GetRotation(uiElement), "Recipe_01_08");
        }

        public static readonly DependencyProperty RotationProperty =
            DependencyProperty.RegisterAttached("Rotation",
                                            typeof(double),
                                            typeof(Window1),
                                            new FrameworkPropertyMetadata(
                    0d, FrameworkPropertyMetadataOptions.AffectsRender));

        public static void SetRotation(UIElement element, double value)
        {
            element.SetValue(RotationProperty, value);
        }

        public static double GetRotation(UIElement element)
        {
            return (double)element.GetValue(RotationProperty);
        }
    }
}
```

The following markup and code-behind define a simple System.Windows.Controls.
UserControl that demonstrates the use of the custom attached property in code:

```xml
<UserControl
  x:Class="Recipe_01_08.UserControl1"
  xmlns="http://schemas.microsoft.com/winfx/2006/xaml/presentation"
  xmlns:x="http://schemas.microsoft.com/winfx/2006/xaml"
  MouseLeftButtonDown="UserControl_MouseLeftButtonDown"
  Background="Transparent">
  <Viewbox>
    <TextBlock Text="I'm a UserControl" />
  </Viewbox>
</UserControl>
```

```csharp
using System.Windows;
using System.Windows.Controls;

namespace Recipe_01_08
{
    /// <summary>
    /// Interaction logic for UserControl1.xaml
    /// </summary>
    public partial class UserControl1 : UserControl
    {
        public UserControl1()
        {
            InitializeComponent();
        }

        private void UserControl_MouseLeftButtonDown(object sender,
                                                     RoutedEventArgs e)
        {
            UserControl1 uiElement = (UserControl1)sender;

            MessageBox.Show("Rotation = " + Window1.GetRotation(uiElement),
                    "Recipe_01_08");
        }
    }
}
```

Figure 1-2 shows the result of clicking the button. A value for the Window1.Rotation property is not explicitly set on the button; therefore, it is displaying the default value.

Figure 1-2. *The result of clicking the button*

1-9. Create a Dependency Property with Property Value Inheritance

Problem

You need to create a dependency property on a dependency object where the value is pushed down the visual tree.

Solution

When registering the dependency property, use a `FrameworkPropertyMetadata` object and include `FrameworkPropertyMetadataOptions.Inherits` when specifying the framework-level options.

How It Works

Property value inheritance can be extremely useful under the right circumstances. It applies only to objects that reside in a visual tree and have one or more child objects. Property value inheritance is used to push the value of a property down onto each child object that also contains the same property.

One of the most common examples of property value inheritance can be found in the `DataContext` dependency property defined in `System.Windows.FrameworkElement`. The behavior can be observed when the data context of a parent control is set. For example, if you have a grid that contains several text elements, the value set on the data context on the grid will be pushed down to each of the text elements. This is useful for reducing the code required when the value of a property is applicable to its children.

The Code

The following code details the content of the markup for the application's main window. The window contains four System.Windows.Controls.TextBlock controls to display the values of four properties. Two of the properties belong to a control that is the child of another control.

The PropertyThatInherits property uses property value inheritance. Any value assigned to that property will be pushed down to any child controls. The PropertyThatDoesNotInherit property is used to show that a property that does not use the FrameworkPropertyMetadataOptions.Inherits does not employ property value inheritance.

```
<Window
  x:Class="Recipe_01_09.Window1"
  xmlns="http://schemas.microsoft.com/winfx/2006/xaml/presentation"
  xmlns:local="clr-namespace:Recipe_01_09"
  xmlns:x="http://schemas.microsoft.com/winfx/2006/xaml"
  Title="Window1"
  Height="175"
  Width="320"
  Loaded="Window1_Loaded">
  <StackPanel>

    <Border
      BorderThickness="1"
      BorderBrush="Black"
      Margin="10,10,10,5">
      <StackPanel>
        <StackPanel Orientation="Horizontal" Margin="10,10,10,5">
          <TextBlock Text="Parent.PropertyThatInherits: " />
          <TextBlock Text="{Binding Path=[0].PropertyThatInherits}" />
        </StackPanel>
        <StackPanel Orientation="Horizontal" Margin="10,5,10,5">
          <TextBlock Text="Child.PropertyThatInherits: " />
          <TextBlock Text="{Binding Path=[1].PropertyThatInherits}" />
        </StackPanel>
      </StackPanel>
    </Border>

    <Border
      BorderThickness="1"
      BorderBrush="Black"
      Margin="10,5,10,10">
```

```xml
    <StackPanel>
      <StackPanel Orientation="Horizontal" Margin="10,5,10,10">
        <TextBlock Text="Parent.PropertyThatDoesNotInherit: " />
        <TextBlock Text="{Binding Path=[0].PropertyThatDoesNotInherit}" />
      </StackPanel>
      <StackPanel Orientation="Horizontal" Margin="10,5,10,10">
        <TextBlock Text="Child.PropertyThatDoesNotInherit: " />
        <TextBlock Text="{Binding Path=[1].PropertyThatDoesNotInherit}" />
      </StackPanel>
    </StackPanel>
  </Border>
</StackPanel>
</Window>
```

The following code defines the content of the code-behind for the window defined in the previous markup:

```csharp
using System.Windows;

namespace Recipe_01_09
{
    /// <summary>
    /// Interaction logic for Window1.xaml
    /// </summary>
    public partial class Window1 : Window
    {
        public Window1()
        {
            InitializeComponent();
        }

        private void Window1_Loaded(object sender, RoutedEventArgs e)
        {
            Parent parent = new Parent();
            parent.PropertyThatInherits = "Still Inherits.";
            parent.PropertyThatDoesNotInherit = "Still not inheriting.";

            Child child = new Child();
            parent.Children.Add(child);

            DataContext = new object[]{parent, child};
        }
    }
}
```

The next code block details the Parent class in which the two dependency properties are defined:

```
using System.Windows;
using System.Windows.Controls;

namespace Recipe_01_09
{
    public class Parent : StackPanel
    {
        public string PropertyThatInherits
        {
            get { return (string)GetValue(PropertyThatInheritsProperty); }
            set { SetValue(PropertyThatInheritsProperty, value); }
        }

        public static readonly DependencyProperty PropertyThatInheritsProperty
            = DependencyProperty.RegisterAttached("PropertyThatInherits",
                                                typeof(string),
                                                typeof(UIElement),
                        new FrameworkPropertyMetadata("Inherits.",
                                FrameworkPropertyMetadataOptions.Inherits));

        public string PropertyThatDoesNotInherit
        {
            get { return (string)GetValue(PropertyThatDoesNotInheritProperty); }
            set { SetValue(PropertyThatDoesNotInheritProperty, value); }
        }

        public static readonly DependencyProperty PropertyThatDoesNotInheritProperty
            = DependencyProperty.RegisterAttached("PropertyThatDoesNotInherit",
                                                typeof(string),
                                                typeof(UIElement),
                        new FrameworkPropertyMetadata("Does not inherit."));
    }
}
```

The final code block details the Child class. This class inherits from Parent and contains no new members. Its sole purpose is to illustrate property value inheritance.

```
namespace Recipe_01_09
{
    public class Child : Parent
    {
    }
}
```

Figure 1-3 shows the values of the parent and child's dependency properties.

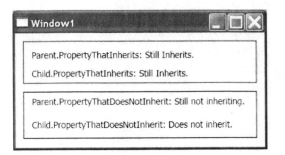

Figure 1-3. *Values of the parent and child's dependency properties*

1-10. Merge Two Resource Dictionaries

Problem

You need to reference objects contained in some System.Windows.ResourceDictionary that is not part of your System.Windows.Controls.Control.

Solution

Use the ResourceDictionary.MergedDictionaries property to merge a ResourceDictionary into any other ResourceDictionary.

How It Works

The ResourceDictionary.MergedDictionaries property gets a System.Collections.ObjectModel. Collection<ResourceDictionary>, containing any ResourceDictionary objects that are to be merged into the original ResourceDictionary. Each ResourceDictionary that is added to the collection of resource dictionaries does not contain any elements but instead references a ResourceDictionary by setting the Source property with a System.Uri. The URI can point to a ResourceDictionary in the same assembly or in an entirely different assembly (see recipe 1-12); the only stipulation is that the destination of the URI must be a XAML file with ResourceDictionary as its root element.

Each time a ResourceDictionary is added to the collection, it becomes the first ResourceDictionary to be searched when a resource is referenced. The search will stop as soon as it finds the required key. One would assume that this would mean a ResourceDictionary cannot be merged into another ResourceDictionary if they have any common keys. In reality, duplicate keys are valid because each merged ResourceDictionary is held in its own scope, just under the scope of the parent ResourceDictionary.

The fact that merged resource dictionaries are held outside the scope of the parent ResourceDictionary means that if a key exists in both the parent and a merged resource dictionary, the value that is returned will always be the object that maps to the key found in the parent.

The Code

The following example demonstrates the merging of an external ResourceDictionary into a local ResourceDictionary, defined within a window's local resources. The System.Windows. Window defines a System.Windows.Media.SolidColorBrush resource in its local resources that is used as the color for the System.Windows.Controls.Button background property. A second SolidColorBrush is defined in a resource dictionary that lies outside the window's XAML file. This second brush is used to provide the background color for the window (see Figure 1-4).

```xaml
<Window
  x:Class="Recipe_01_10.Window1"
  xmlns="http://schemas.microsoft.com/winfx/2006/xaml/presentation"
  xmlns:x="http://schemas.microsoft.com/winfx/2006/xaml"
  Title="Recipe_01_10"
  Height="300"
  Width="300"
  Background="{DynamicResource WindowBackgroundBrush}">
  <Window.Resources>
    <ResourceDictionary>
      <ResourceDictionary.MergedDictionaries>
        <ResourceDictionary Source="ExternalResourceDictionary.xaml" />
      </ResourceDictionary.MergedDictionaries>

      <SolidColorBrush x:Key="ButtonBackground" Color="Yellow" />
    </ResourceDictionary>
  </Window.Resources>

  <Button
    Background="{DynamicResource ButtonBackground}"
    Height="20"
    Width="20"
  />
</Window>
```

The following code gives the content of the external resource dictionary that is merged into the previous window's local resources:

```xaml
<ResourceDictionary
  xmlns="http://schemas.microsoft.com/winfx/2006/xaml/presentation"
  xmlns:x="http://schemas.microsoft.com/winfx/2006/xaml">

  <SolidColorBrush x:Key="WindowBackgroundBrush" Color="HotPink" />

</ResourceDictionary>
```

Figure 1-4. *Using resources from both local and external resource dictionaries*

1-11. Define Application-wide Resources

Problem

You have several resources that you want to make available throughout your application.

Solution

Merge all the required System.Windows.ResourceDictionary objects into the application's ResourceDictionary.

How It Works

ResourceDictionary objects are by default available to all objects that are within the scope of the application. This means that some System.Windows.Controls.Control that is placed within a System.Windows.Window will be able to reference objects contained within any of the ResourceDictionary objects referenced at the application level. This ensures the maintainability of your styles because you will need to update the objects only in a single place.

It is important to know that each time a ResourceDictionary is referenced by a System.Windows.Controls.Control, a local copy of that ResourceDictionary is made for each instance of the control. This means that if you have several large ResourceDictionary objects that are referenced by a control that is instantiated several times, you may notice a performance hit.

▪Note System.Windows.Controls.ToolTip styles need to be referenced once per control. If several controls all use a ToolTip style referenced at the application level, you will observe strange behavior in your tool tips.

The Code

The following example demonstrates the content of an application's App.xaml. Two System.Windows.Media.SolidColorBrush resources are defined that are referenced in other parts of the application.

```
<Application
  x:Class="Recipe_01_11.App"
  xmlns="http://schemas.microsoft.com/winfx/2006/xaml/presentation"
  xmlns:x="http://schemas.microsoft.com/winfx/2006/xaml"
  StartupUri="Window1.xaml">
  <Application.Resources>
    <SolidColorBrush x:Key="FontBrush" Color="#FF222222" />
    <SolidColorBrush x:Key="BackgroundBrush" Color="#FFDDDDDD" />
  </Application.Resources>
</Application>
```

The following example demonstrates the content of the application's Window1.xaml file. The two resources that were defined in the application's resources are used by controls in the System.Windows.Window. The first resource is used to set the background property of the outer System.Windows.Controls.Grid, and the second resource is used to set the foreground property of a System.Windows.Controls.TextBlock (see Figure 1-5).

```
<Window
  x:Class="Recipe_01_11.Window1"
  xmlns="http://schemas.microsoft.com/winfx/2006/xaml/presentation"
  xmlns:x="http://schemas.microsoft.com/winfx/2006/xaml"
  Title="Recipe_01_11"
  Height="300"
  Width="300">
  <Grid Background="{StaticResource BackgroundBrush}">
    <Viewbox>
      <TextBlock
        Text="Some Text"
        Foreground="{StaticResource FontBrush}"
        Margin="5"
      />
    </Viewbox>
  </Grid>
</Window>
```

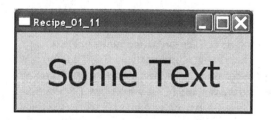

Figure 1-5. *Using an application-level resource to set properties on controls*

1-12. Reference a ResourceDictionary in a Different Assembly

Problem

You need to reference a System.Windows.ResourceDictionary that is held in a different assembly than the current one.

Solution

You add the required ResourceDictionary using the same approach as merging a ResourceDictionary within the same assembly (see recipe 1-10) but use a Pack URI to specify the value for the resource dictionary's Source property.

How It Works

The only difference between referencing a local ResourceDictionary and a ResourceDictionary contained in some other assembly, referenced by the project, is that the Source for the external ResourceDictionary is specified using a Pack URI.

Amongst other things, the Pack URI approach allows you to reference components in assemblies referenced by your project. A Pack URI uses the pack prefix to indicate the pack scheme is being used. The scheme has two components that define an authority and a path, taking the form of pack://authority/path. Of the two supported authorities, we are interested in application:///, which is used when the target resources are files known at compile time. Because the authority is an embedded URI, the / character must be replaced with a comma (,) character.

Note As well as / characters, other reserved characters such as ? and & must be escaped. For a full definition of the restrictions, see the open packaging conventions on naming restrictions at http://www.ecma-international.org/news/TC45_current_work/Office%20Open%20XML%20Part%201%20-%20Fundamentals.pdf, section 9.1.1 in particular.

The path component of the URI consists of the name of the external assembly being referenced, which is ;component: to indicate that the assembly being referenced in the URI is referenced by the current assembly. The remainder of the path component is then used to define the path to the target resource, relative to the project folder of the assembly being referenced. For example, to reference a resource file called ResourceFile.xaml located in a folder named Resources within the assembly MyExternalAssembly, the URI would take the form of pack://application:,,,/MyExternalAssembly;component:Resources/ResourceFile.xaml.

Note The Pack URI also supports two optional parameters in the path component that can be used when referencing an assembly different from the owning one. These parameters can be used to indicate a specific version of the assembly to be used or a public key that was used to sign the assembly. The full format for the path component is `pack://application,,,/AssemblyName[;Version][;PublicKey];component/Path`.

At least one of these parameters is required when different versions of the same assembly are referenced by the assembly. For example, to specify that version 1.2.3.4 of the assembly `MyExternalAssembly` should be used when accessing the `ResourceFile.xaml` resource, the following URI would be used: `pack://application:,,,/MyExternalAssembly;1.2.3.4;component:Resources/ResourceFile.xaml`.

The Code

The following example demonstrates the merging of an external `ResourceDictionary` object into a local resource dictionary. The external dictionary is defined in the `Recipe_01_10` project; thus, that project must be referenced by this project. The `App.xaml` and `Window1.xaml.cs` files are unchanged and have been omitted.

```
<Window
  x:Class="Recipe_01_12.Window1"
  xmlns="http://schemas.microsoft.com/winfx/2006/xaml/presentation"
  xmlns:x="http://schemas.microsoft.com/winfx/2006/xaml"
  Title="Window1"
  Height="200"
  Width="200"
  Background="{DynamicResource WindowBackgroundBrush}">
  <Window.Resources>
    <ResourceDictionary>
      <ResourceDictionary.MergedDictionaries>
        <ResourceDictionary Source=➥
"pack://application:,,,/Recipe_01_10;component/ExternalResourceDictionary.xaml" />
      </ResourceDictionary.MergedDictionaries>
    </ResourceDictionary>
  </Window.Resources>
</Window>
```

1-13. Share Properties Throughout an Application

Problem

You need to share a set of properties throughout the scope of your application, such as user preferences, and so on.

Solution

Use the `Properties` property on your `System.Windows.Application` object.

How It Works

The `Application` type provides a thread-safe method for sharing properties throughout your application, accessible by any thread within the current `AppDomain`. The `Properties` property returns a `System.Collections.IDictionary` in which objects can be stored using some predefined key.

The Code

The following example demonstrates a very trivial use of the `Application.Properties` property. Because the application's definition is unchanged, it has been omitted (see Figure 1-6). The next code block details markup for the main window in the application.

```xml
<Window
  x:Class="Recipe_01_13.Window1"
  xmlns="http://schemas.microsoft.com/winfx/2006/xaml/presentation"
  xmlns:x="http://schemas.microsoft.com/winfx/2006/xaml"
  Title="Window1"
  Height="102"
  Width="300">
  <StackPanel>
    <TextBox
      x:Name="tbxUserText"
      Text="Enter some text..."
      Margin="10,10,10,5"
    />
    <Button
      Click="Button_Click"
      Content="Open a New Window..."
      Margin="10,5,10,10"
    />
  </StackPanel>
</Window>
```

The following code block details a simple helper class that wraps interaction with the `Application.Properties` property:

```csharp
using System.Windows;

namespace Recipe_01_13
{
    /// <remark>
    /// This helper is intended to provide the base for a helper,
    /// which simplifies use of the Application.Properties property.
    /// The obvious next step in extending the class is to add
```

```
/// argument validation.
/// </remark>
public static class ApplicationPropertiesHelper
{
    /// <summary>
    /// Tries to retrieve a property from the Application's Properties
    /// collection. If the object with the specified key cannot be found,
    /// the default value for the supplied type is returned.
    /// </summary>
    /// <typeparam name="T">The type of object to retrieve.</typeparam>
    /// <param name="key">The key with which the object was stored.</param>
    /// <returns>If the specified key exists, then the associated
    /// value is returned, otherwise the default value for the
    /// specified type.</returns>
    public static T GetProperty<T>(object key)
    {
        if (Application.Current.Properties.Contains(key)
            && Application.Current.Properties[key] is T)
        {
            return (T)Application.Current.Properties[key];
        }

        return default(T);
    }

    /// <summary>
    /// Retrieves the property associated with the given key.
    /// </summary>
    /// <param name="key">The key with which the object was stored.</param>
    /// <returns>If the specified key exists, the associated
    /// value is returned, otherwise the return value is null.</returns>
    public static object GetProperty(object key)
    {
        if (Application.Current.Properties.Contains(key))
        {
            return Application.Current.Properties[key];
        }

        return null;
    }

    /// <summary>
    /// Adds a value to the Application's properties collection,
    /// indexed by the supplied key.
    /// </summary>
    /// <param name="key">
    /// The key against which the value should be stored.</param>
```

```
        /// <param name="value">The value to be stored.</param>
        public static void SetProperty(object key, object value)
        {
            Application.Current.Properties[key] = value;
        }
    }
}
```

The following code block details the code for the previous window's code-behind. When the button in the window is clicked, the ApplicationPropertiesHelper object is used to set a value in the Application.Properties property. A second window is then opened.

```
using System.Windows;

namespace Recipe_01_13
{
    /// <summary>
    /// Interaction logic for Window1.xaml
    /// </summary>
    public partial class Window1 : Window
    {
        public Window1()
        {
            InitializeComponent();
        }

        private void Button_Click(object sender, RoutedEventArgs e)
        {
            ApplicationPropertiesHelper.SetProperty("PropertyKey",
                                                    tbxUserText.Text);

            Window2 window2 = new Window2();

            window2.ShowDialog();
        }
    }
}
```

The final two code blocks define the markup and code-behind for a second window. This second window looks up a known key in the application's shared properties collection and displays the value in a System.Windows.Controls.TextBlock.

```
<Window
  x:Class="Recipe_01_13.Window2"
  xmlns="http://schemas.microsoft.com/winfx/2006/xaml/presentation"
  xmlns:x="http://schemas.microsoft.com/winfx/2006/xaml"
  Title="Window2"
  Height="300"
  Width="300"
```

```
    Loaded="Window_Loaded">
    <Viewbox Margin="10">
      <TextBlock x:Name="tbxUserText" />
    </Viewbox>
</Window>

using System.Windows;

namespace Recipe_01_13
{
    /// <summary>
    /// Interaction logic for Window2.xaml
    /// </summary>
    public partial class Window2 : Window
    {
        public Window2()
        {
            InitializeComponent();
        }

        private void Window_Loaded(object sender, RoutedEventArgs e)
        {
            string value =
                ApplicationPropertiesHelper.GetProperty<string>("PropertyKey");

            if (string.IsNullOrEmpty(value))
            {
                value = "Nothing to display!";
            }

            tbxUserText.Text = value;
        }
    }
}
```

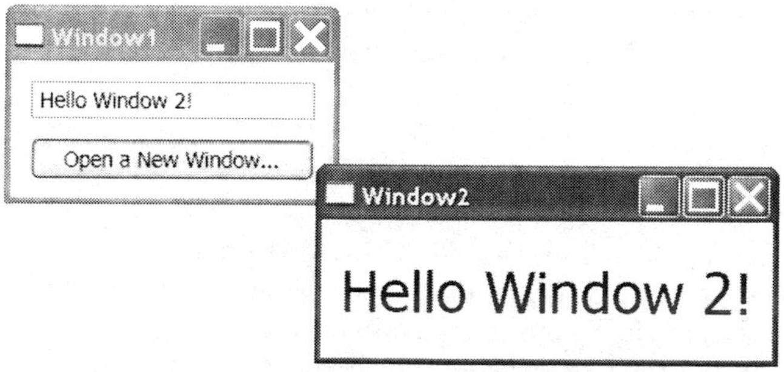

Figure 1-6. *The second window, shown in the foreground, opened from clicking the button in the first window, shown in the background*

1-14. Create a Single-Instance Application

Problem

You need to ensure that only one instance of your application is running at any one time. Each time a new instance of the application is started, you need to receive any startup arguments.

Solution

Create a class that derives from `Microsoft.VisualBasic.ApplicationServices.WindowsFormsApplicationBase`, and use it to wrap your WPF `System.Windows.Application`. The wrapper is initialized by supplying your own implementation of `Main`.

How It Works

The `WindowsFormsApplicationBase` class provides all the necessary functionality to ensure only a single instance of your application is running, whilst providing notification of any command-line arguments passed to new instances of your application. It also allows you to do this without getting your hands dirty with `System.Thread.Mutex` objects, and so on. This is ideally suited to some form of MDI object viewer, for example, a tabbed XPS reader where any new documents that are opened are added to an existing instance in a new tab.

To use this functionality, you need to change the basic structure of your project and create the class that will wrap your application's `Application` object. This will allow you to control what happens when a new instance of your application is started. The first step is to create a class that inherits from `WindowsFormsApplicationBase`. In the constructor of your wrapper, you will need to set the `IsSingleInstance` to true, indicating you want only one instance of the application to be permitted.

The next step is to override the `OnStartup` method. This method is invoked when the application first runs and is used to start up your WPF application. One more method will require overriding, but only if you need to be notified of attempts to create a new instance of your application. This is the aptly named `OnStartupNextInstance` method. The `Microsoft.VisualBasic.ApplicationServices.StartupNextInstanceEventArgs` passed to the method can be used to retrieve any arguments used when the creation of a new instance of the application is attempted.

Now that you have your wrapper, you need a place to create it when the application runs. The best place for this is in the application's `Main` method, which in WPF applications you no longer need to explicitly define. To define your own implementation of `Main`, add a new public class to your project in a file named `App.cs`. The class should contain a single method with the following signature:

```
public static void Main(string[] args)
```

It will be this method that is responsible for creating a new instance of your wrapper and calling its `Run` method, passing the application's startup arguments. The `Run` method carries out a lot of work behind the scenes so that it can intercept any new attempts at starting the application. The final modification required for the project is to modify the build action of your application's `App.xaml` file. All you need to do here is change the build action in the Properties window from ApplicationDefinition to Page. Failure to do so will result in a compile-time error because the compiler will detect that your application has two entry points.

The Code

The following code demonstrates a simple single-instance application. The main window of the application contains controls that allow a new instance of the application to be started, with some user-defined arguments, entered into a System.Windows.Controls.TextBox. If a new instance of the application is started and another instance already exists, the System.Windows. MessageBox is shown, displaying the arguments that were passed to the already running instance. Because the code contained in the default App.xaml and App.xaml.cs files does not require changing, its code is not listed here.

The first code block details the implementation of the SingleInstanceManager, responsible for initializing the inner WPF application when Run is called and handling new arguments that are passed to an already running instance.

```
using System;
using System.Windows;
using Microsoft.VisualBasic.ApplicationServices;

namespace Recipe_01_14
{
    public class SingleInstanceManager : WindowsFormsApplicationBase
    {
        public SingleInstanceManager()
        {
            this.IsSingleInstance = true;
        }

        protected override bool OnStartup(
            Microsoft.VisualBasic.ApplicationServices.StartupEventArgs eventArgs)
        {
            base.OnStartup(eventArgs);

            App app = new App();
            app.Run();

            return false;
        }

        protected override void OnStartupNextInstance(
            StartupNextInstanceEventArgs eventArgs)
        {
            base.OnStartupNextInstance(eventArgs);

            string args = Environment.NewLine;
```

```
        foreach(string arg in eventArgs.CommandLine)
        {
            args += Environment.NewLine + arg;
        }

        string msg = string.Format("New instance started with {0} args.{1}",
                                eventArgs.CommandLine.Count,
                                args);
        MessageBox.Show(msg);
    }
  }
}
```

The next code block details the content of the App.cs file where the application's main entry point is defined:

```
using System;

namespace Recipe_01_14
{
    public class MyApp
    {
        [STAThread]
        public static void Main(string[] args)
        {
            //Create our new single-instance manager
            SingleInstanceManager manager = new SingleInstanceManager();
            manager.Run(args);
        }
    }
}
```

The next code block details the content of the application's main window markup:

```
<Window
  x:Class="Recipe_01_14.Window1"
  xmlns="http://schemas.microsoft.com/winfx/2006/xaml/presentation"
  xmlns:x="http://schemas.microsoft.com/winfx/2006/xaml"
  Title="Window1" Height="300" Width="300">
  <Grid>
    <Grid.RowDefinitions>
      <RowDefinition Height="30" />
      <RowDefinition Height="30" />
    </Grid.RowDefinitions>
```

```
    <TextBox x:Name="tbxArgs" />

    <Button
      Content="Start New Process"
      Click="btnCreateNewInstance_Click"
      Grid.Row="1"
    />
  </Grid>
</Window>
```

The final code block details the content of the code-behind for the application's main window:

```
using System;
using System.Diagnostics;
using System.Windows;

namespace Recipe_01_14
{
    /// <summary>
    /// Interaction logic for Window1.xaml
    /// </summary>
    public partial class Window1 : Window
    {
        public Window1()
        {
            InitializeComponent();
        }

        private void btnCreateNewInstance_Click(object sender, RoutedEventArgs e)
        {
            Process proc = new Process();

            proc.StartInfo.FileName =
                string.Format("{0}{1}",
                            Environment.CurrentDirectory,
                            "\\Recipe_01_14.exe");

            proc.StartInfo.Arguments = tbxArgs.Text;

            proc.Start();
        }
    }
}
```

1-15. Manage Multiple Windows in an Application

Problem

You need to manage several different windows within your application, performing such tasks as preventing a window from closing, displaying a list of thumbnails of the windows, showing or hiding a window, and bringing a window into view or closing the window.

Solution

Use the System.Windows.Application.Current.Windows collection to get a System.Windows.WindowCollection, containing all the applications that are contained within your project.

How It Works

The Windows property of an Application object maintains a list of all the windows within the current System.AppDomain. Any window that is created on the UI thread is automatically added to the collection and removed when the window's Closing event has been handled but before the Closed event is raised (see Figure 1-7).

The Code

```
<Window
  x:Class="Recipe_01_15.Window1"
  xmlns="http://schemas.microsoft.com/winfx/2006/xaml/presentation"
  xmlns:system="clr-namespace:System.Windows;assembly=PresentationFramework"
  xmlns:x="http://schemas.microsoft.com/winfx/2006/xaml"
  Title="Main Window"
  Height="310"
  Width="280"
  Loaded="Window1_Loaded"
  Closing="Window1_Closing">
  <Window.Resources>
    <DataTemplate DataType="{x:Type Window}" x:Key="WindowTemplate">
      <StackPanel>
        <Rectangle Height="50" Width="50">
          <Rectangle.Fill>
            <VisualBrush Visual="{Binding}" />
          </Rectangle.Fill>
        </Rectangle>

        <TextBlock Text="{Binding Path=Title}" />
      </StackPanel>
    </DataTemplate>
  </Window.Resources>
```

```xml
<Grid>
  <Grid.RowDefinitions>
    <RowDefinition Height="100" />
    <RowDefinition Height="*" />
  </Grid.RowDefinitions>

  <ListBox x:Name="lbxWindows" ItemTemplate="{StaticResource WindowTemplate}">
    <ListBox.ItemsPanel>
      <ItemsPanelTemplate>
        <WrapPanel />
      </ItemsPanelTemplate>
    </ListBox.ItemsPanel>
  </ListBox>

  <StackPanel Grid.Row="1">
    <CheckBox
      x:Name="cbxIsVisibleInTaskBar"
      Content="IsVisibleInTaskbar"
      IsChecked="{Binding ElementName=lbxWindows,
                          Path=SelectedItem.ShowInTaskbar}"
      Margin="10"
    />

    <CheckBox
      x:Name="cbxIsVisible"
      Content="IsVisible"
      IsChecked="{Binding ElementName=lbxWindows,
                          Path=SelectedItem.IsVisible,
                          Mode=OneWay}"
      Checked="CheckBox_Checked_Changed"
      Unchecked="CheckBox_Checked_Changed"
      Margin="10"
    />

    <CheckBox
      x:Name="cbxCanClose"
      Content="CanClose"
      IsChecked="True"
      Margin="10"
    />

    <Button Content="Bring To Front" Click="btnBringToFront_Click" Margin="10" />
    <Button Content="Close" Click="btnClose_Click" Margin="10" />
  </StackPanel>
</Grid>
</Window>
```

The following code block contains the code-behind for the previous markup file. The code handles several control events and sets up some windows.

```csharp
using System;
using System.Collections.Generic;
using System.ComponentModel;
using System.Windows;
using System.Windows.Controls;
using System.Windows.Documents;
using System.Windows.Media;

namespace Recipe_01_15
{
    /// <summary>
    /// Interaction logic for Window1.xaml
    /// </summary>
    public partial class Window1 : Window
    {
        public Window1()
        {
            InitializeComponent();
        }

        /// <summary>
        /// When the main window is loaded, we want to spawn some
        /// windows to play with.
        /// </summary>
        /// <param name="sender"></param>
        /// <param name="e"></param>
        private void Window1_Loaded(object sender, RoutedEventArgs e)
        {
            Brush[] backgrounds = new Brush[5]{ Brushes.Red,
                                               Brushes.Blue,
                                               Brushes.Green,
                                               Brushes.Yellow,
                                               Brushes.HotPink};
            //Create 5 windows.
            for (int i = 1; i <= 5; i++)
            {
                Window window = new Window();

                SetupWindow(window, "Window " + i, backgrounds[i - 1]);
                //Show the window.
                window.Show();
            }

            RebuildWindowList();
        }
```

```csharp
/// <summary>
/// When the main window closes, we want to close all the child windows.
/// </summary>
/// <param name="sender"></param>
/// <param name="e"></param>
private void Window1_Closing(object sender, CancelEventArgs e)
{
    Application.Current.Shutdown();
}


private void SetupWindow(Window window, string title, Brush background)
{
    // We want to know when a window is closing so we can prevent
    // it from being closed if required.
    window.Closing += new CancelEventHandler(Window_Closing);

    // We want to know when a window has been closed so we can
    // rebuild our list of open windows.
    window.Closed += new EventHandler(Window_Closed);

    // Give the window a title so we can track it.
    window.Title = title;
    window.Width = 100d;
    window.Height = 100d;

    // Create a text block displaying the window's title inside
    // a view box for the window's content.
    Viewbox viewBox = new Viewbox();
    TextBlock textBlock = new TextBlock();

    //Set the window's background to make it easier to identify.
    window.Background = background;
    viewBox.Child = textBlock;
    textBlock.Text = window.Title;
    window.Content = viewBox;
}


/// <summary>
/// This method iterates all the windows for this application
/// and adds them to the list box lbxWindows.
/// </summary>
private void RebuildWindowList()
{
    List<Window> windows = new List<Window>();
```

```csharp
        foreach (Window window in Application.Current.Windows)
        {
            if (window == this)
                continue;

            windows.Add(window);
        }

        lbxWindows.ItemsSource = windows;
    }

    private void Window_Closed(object sender, EventArgs e)
    {
        RebuildWindowList();
    }

    private void Window_Closing(object sender, CancelEventArgs e)
    {
        Window w = sender as Window;

        if (w == null)
            return;

        e.Cancel = !cbxCanClose.IsChecked == true;
    }

    private void CheckBox_Checked_Changed(object sender, RoutedEventArgs e)
    {
        //Get the selected window.
        Window window = lbxWindows.SelectedItem as Window;

        if (window == null)
            return;

        if (cbxIsVisible.IsChecked == true)
            window.Show();
        else
            window.Hide();
    }

    private void btnBringToFront_Click(object sender, RoutedEventArgs e)
    {
        Window window = lbxWindows.SelectedItem as Window;

        if (window != null)
            window.Activate();
    }
```

```
        private void btnClose_Click(object sender, RoutedEventArgs e)
        {
            Window window = lbxWindows.SelectedItem as Window;

            if (window != null)
                window.Close();
        }
    }
}
```

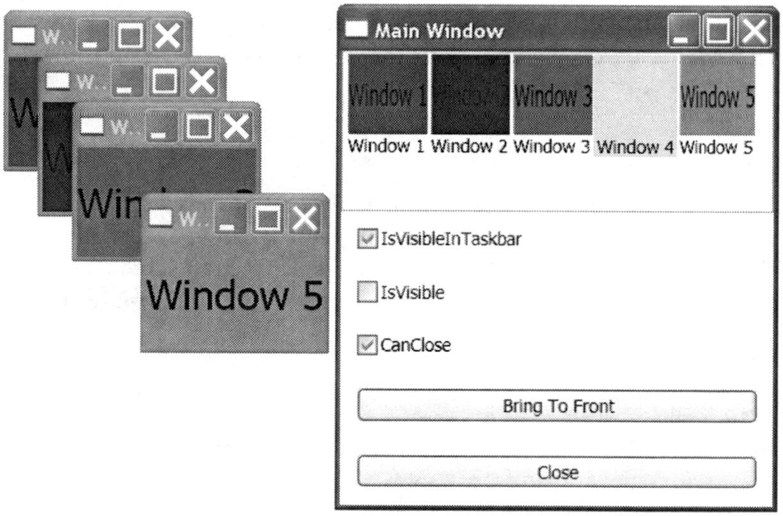

Figure 1-7. *Interacting with the windows in an application*

1-16. Debug Data Bindings Using an IValueConverter

Problem

You need to debug a binding that is not working as expected and want to make sure the correct values are going in.

Solution

Create a converter class that implements System.Windows.Data.IValueConverter (see Chapter 5) and returns the value it receives for conversion, setting a breakpoint or tracepoint within the converter.

How It Works

Debugging a data binding can sometimes be quite tricky and consume a lot of time. Because data bindings are generally defined in XAML, you don't have anywhere you can set a breakpoint to make sure things are working as you intended. In some cases, you will be able to place a breakpoint on a property of the object that is being bound, but that option isn't always available, such as when binding to a property of some other control in your application. This is where a converter comes in.

When using a simple converter that returns the argument being passed in, unchanged, you immediately have some code that you can place a breakpoint on or write some debugging information to the Output window or some log. This can tell you whether the value coming in is the wrong type, in a form that means it is not valid for the binding, or is coming in with a strange value. You'll also soon realize whether the binding is not being used, because the converter will never be hit.

The Code

The following example demonstrates a System.Windows.Window that contains a System.Windows.Controls.Grid. Inside the Grid are a System.Windows.Controls.CheckBox and a System.Windows.Controls.Expander. The IsExpanded property of the Expander is bound to the IsChecked property of the CheckBox. This is a very simple binding, but it gives an example where you are able to place a breakpoint in code.

```
<Window
  x:Class="Recipe_01_16.Window1"
  xmlns="http://schemas.microsoft.com/winfx/2006/xaml/presentation"
  xmlns:x="http://schemas.microsoft.com/winfx/2006/xaml"
  xmlns:local="clr-namespace:Recipe_01_16"
  Title="Recipe_01_13"
  Width="200"
  Height="200">
  <Window.Resources>
    <local:DummyConverter x:Key="DummyConverter" />
  </Window.Resources>
  <Grid>
    <Grid.RowDefinitions>
      <RowDefinition Height="0.5*" />
      <RowDefinition Height="0.5*"/>
    </Grid.RowDefinitions>

    <CheckBox
      x:Name="chkShouldItBeOpen"
      IsChecked="False"
      Content="Open Sesame!"
      Margin="10"
    />
```

```
      <Expander
        IsExpanded="{Binding
                        ElementName=chkShouldItBeOpen,
                        Path=IsChecked,
                        Converter={StaticResource DummyConverter}}"
        Grid.Row="1"
        Background="Black"
        Foreground="White"
        Margin="10"
        VerticalAlignment="Center"
        HorizontalAlignment="Center"
        Header="I'm an Expander!">
        <TextBlock Text="Sesame Open!" Foreground="White"/>
      </Expander>
    </Grid>
</Window>
```

The following code defines the code-behind for the previous XAML:

```
using System.Windows;

namespace Recipe_01_16
{
    /// <summary>
    /// Interaction logic for Window1.xaml
    /// </summary>
    public partial class Window1 : Window
    {
        public Window1()
        {
            InitializeComponent();
        }
    }
}
```

The following code defines a dummy converter class that returns the value passed to it:

```
using System;
using System.Globalization;
using System.Windows.Data;

namespace Recipe_01_16
{
    public class DummyConverter : IValueConverter
    {
        #region IValueConverter Members
```

```
        public object Convert(object value,
                              Type targetType,
                              object parameter,
                              CultureInfo culture)
        {
            return value;
        }

        public object ConvertBack(object value,
                                  Type targetType,
                                  object parameter,
                                  CultureInfo culture)
        {
            return value;
        }

        #endregion
    }
}
```

1-17. Debug Bindings Using Attached Properties

Problem

You need to debug a binding that is not working as expected and want to make sure the correct values are going in. Using a converter is either undesired or not feasible.

Solution

Use the System.Diagnostics.PresentationTraceSources.TraceLevel attached property defined in the WindowsBase assembly, setting the level of detail required. If the data binding is defined in code, use the static method PresentationTraceLevel.SetTraceLevel.

█Caution Using the PresentationTraceSources.TraceLevel attached property can affect the performance of a WPF application and should be removed as soon as it is no longer required.

How It Works

The PresentationTraceSources.TraceLevel attached property allows you to specify the level of information written to the Output window for data bindings, on a per-binding basis. The higher the System.Diagnostics.PresentationTraceLevel value that is used, the more information that will be generated. The PresentationTraceSources.TraceLevel can be used on the following object types:

- System.Windows.Data.BindingBase

- System.Windows.Data.BindingExpressionBase

- System.Windows.Data.ObjectDataProvider

- System.Windows.Data.XmlDataProvider

It is important to remember to remove any trace-level attached properties from your code once you are finished debugging a binding; otherwise, your Output window will continue to be filled with binding information. Table 1-3 details the values of the PresentationTraceSource.TraceLevel enumeration.

Table 1-3. *Values for the* PresentationTraceSources.TraceLevel

Property	Description
None	Generates no additional information.
Low	Generates some information about binding failures. This generally details the target and source properties involved and any exception that is thrown. No information is generated for bindings that work properly.
Medium	Generates a medium amount of information about binding failures and a small amount of information for valid bindings. When a binding fails, information is generated for the source and target properties, some of the transformations that are applied to the value, any exceptions that occur, the final value of the binding, and some of the steps taken during the whole process. For valid bindings, information logging is light.
High	Generates the most amount of binding state information for binding failures and valid bindings. When a binding fails, a great deal of information about the binding process is logged, covering all the previous data in a more verbose manner.

The Code

The following markup demonstrates how to use the PresentationTraceSource.TraceLevel property in two different bindings. One of the bindings is valid and binds the value of the text block to the width of the parent grid; the other is invalid and attempts to bind the width of the parent grid to the height of the text block. Set the values of the PresentatonTraceSource.TraceLevel attached properties to see how they behave.

```
<Window
  x:Class="Recipe_01_17.Window1"
  xmlns="http://schemas.microsoft.com/winfx/2006/xaml/presentation"
  xmlns:x="http://schemas.microsoft.com/winfx/2006/xaml"
  xmlns:diagnostics="clr-namespace:System.Diagnostics;assembly=WindowsBase"
  Title="Recipe_01_17"
  Height="300"
  Width="300">
```

```xml
<Grid x:Name="gdLayoutRoot">
  <Viewbox>
    <TextBlock x:Name="tbkTextBlock">
      <TextBlock.Text>
        <Binding
          ElementName="gdLayoutRoot"
          Path="ActualWidth"
          diagnostics:PresentationTraceSources.TraceLevel="High"
        />
      </TextBlock.Text>
      <TextBlock.Height>
        <Binding
          ElementName="gdLayoutRoot"
          Path="Name"
          diagnostics:PresentationTraceSources.TraceLevel="High" />
      </TextBlock.Height>
    </TextBlock>
  </Viewbox>
</Grid>
</Window>
```

CHAPTER 2

■ ■ ■

Working with Windows, Forms, and Layout Management

Amajor challenge in the development of good Windows user interfaces is creating a window and control layout that is not only functional but also attractive and easy to use. Another challenge is ensuring your interface can adapt correctly (preferably elegantly) to different localizations, window sizes, and screen resolutions.

The layout system provided by WPF is a significant change from that provided by Windows Forms and is closer in style to how web developers control layout using HTML and CSS. Generally, you should avoid positioning content directly using fixed coordinates and instead rely on the capabilities of various layout panels to size and arrange the content depending on the space the panel has available at runtime.

This chapter focuses on how to use the windows and frames that provide the basic building blocks of your application's user interface and how to use panels to manage the layout of controls contained in your application's UI. The recipes in this chapter describe how to:

- Create an autosized main window (recipe 2-1)

- Manage the size and layout of controls in your application using standard layout panels (recipes 2-2, 2-3, 2-4, 2-5, and 2-6)

- Display content in a tabbed user interface (recipe 2-7)

- Display content in a scrollable user interface (recipe 2-8)

- Display content in a resizable split panel (recipe 2-9)

- Display content in an expander (recipe 2-10)

- Place a group box around a group of UI elements (recipe 2-11)

- Display a message box or a pop-up window (recipes 2-12 and 2-13)

- Display a border around a group of UI elements (recipe 2-14)

- Display a menu, toolbar, or status bar (recipes 2-15, 2-16, and 2-17)

- Control the size, spacing, and tab order of UI elements in a form (recipes 2-18 and 2-19)

■**Note** Recipes 2-2, 2-3, 2-4, 2-5, and 2-6 describe how to use specific layout panels. Even for relatively simple user interfaces, you will rarely use a single layout panel. Instead, you will need to combine the capabilities of different panels to achieve the layout you require. This involves placing panels within panels to achieve the UI structure you need. To do this effectively, it is essential that you understand the purpose and capabilities of each panel.

2-1. Automatically Size the Main Application Window to Accommodate Its Content

Problem

You need to have the main application window determine its size automatically based on its content instead of specifying a fixed size.

Solution

Remove the Height and Width properties from the System.Windows.Window element in XAML, and set its SizeToContent property to the value WidthAndHeight.

How It Works

Usually, you will fix the initial size of your main application Window object and allow WPF to scale and position the window's content based on the window's size. Occasionally, you will want the main window to autoscale to accommodate its content.

Removing the Height and Width properties of the Window element and setting its SizeToContent property to the value WidthAndHeight causes WPF to determine the Window object's dimensions based on its content. When the SizeToContent property is set to the value WidthAndHeight, any values you assign to the Height and Width properties are ignored.

You can also autosize a Window object in only one dimension by setting the SizeToContent property to the value Height or Width. In this case, you fix the size of the other dimension using the appropriate Height or Width property.

The Code

The following XAML demonstrates how to define a Window element that has a height and width based on the dimensions of its content:

```
<Window x:Class="Recipe_02_01.Window1"
    xmlns="http://schemas.microsoft.com/winfx/2006/xaml/presentation"
    xmlns:x="http://schemas.microsoft.com/winfx/2006/xaml"
    Title="WPF Recipes 2_01" SizeToContent="WidthAndHeight">
    <StackPanel Height="23" Orientation="Horizontal">
        <Button Content="Button 1" Margin="2" />
```

```
        <Button Content="Button 2" Margin="2" />
        <Button Content="Button 3" Margin="2" />
        <Button Content="Button 4" Margin="2" />
        <Button Content="Button 5" Margin="2" />
    </StackPanel>
</Window>
```

2-2. Arrange UI Elements in a Horizontal or Vertical Stack

Problem

You need to arrange a group of UI elements in a horizontal or vertical stack.

Solution

Place the UI elements in a System.Windows.Controls.StackPanel. Use the Orientation property of the StackPanel to control the flow of the stacking (vertical or horizontal).

How It Works

The StackPanel arranges the elements it contains in a horizontal or vertical stack. The order of the elements is determined by the order in which they are declared in the XAML (that is, the order in which they occur in the Children collection of the StackPanel). By default, the StackPanel will arrange the elements vertically (one under another). You can control the direction of the stack using the Orientation property. To stack the elements horizontally (next to each other), set the Orientation property to the value Horizontal.

Note If the StackPanel is smaller than the space required to display its content, the content is visually cropped. However, you can still interact with visual elements that are cropped by using keyboard shortcuts or by tabbing to the control and pressing Enter. For information on how to create a scrollable user interface, see recipe 2-8.

The default height and width of elements in a StackPanel depends on the type of element and the orientation of the StackPanel. When the Orientation property of the StackPanel has the value Vertical, text is left justified, but buttons are stretched to the width of the StackPanel. You can override this default behavior by directly configuring the width of the element (see recipe 2-18) or by setting the HorizontalAlignment property of the contained element to the value Left, Center, or Right. These values force the element to take a width based on its content and position it in the left, center, or right of the StackPanel.

Similarly, when the Orientation property of the StackPanel has the value Horizontal, the text is top justified, but the height of buttons is stretched to fill the height of the StackPanel.

You can override this behavior by directly configuring the height of the element (see recipe 2-18) or by setting the VerticalAlignment property of the contained element to the value Top, Center, or Bottom. These values force the element to take a height based on its content and position it in the top, center, or bottom of the StackPanel.

The Code

The following XAML demonstrates how to use three StackPanel panels. An outer StackPanel allows you to stack two inner StackPanel panels vertically. The first inner StackPanel has a horizontal orientation and contains a set of System.Windows.Controls.Button controls. The Button controls show the effects of the various VerticalAlignment property values on the positioning of the controls. This panel also shows the cropping behavior of the StackPanel on the elements it contains (see Figure 2-1). You can see that Button 4 is partially cropped and that Button 5 is not visible at all. However, you can still tab to and interact with Button 5.

The second inner StackPanel has a vertical orientation and also contains a set of Button controls. These buttons show the effects of the various HorizontalAlignment property values on the positioning of a control in the StackPanel.

```
<Window x:Class="Recipe_02_02.Window1"
    xmlns="http://schemas.microsoft.com/winfx/2006/xaml/presentation"
    xmlns:x="http://schemas.microsoft.com/winfx/2006/xaml"
    Title="WPF Recipes 2_02" Height="240" Width="250">
    <StackPanel Width="200">
        <StackPanel Height="50" Margin ="5" Orientation="Horizontal">
            <Button Content="Button _1" Margin="2" />
            <Button Content="Button _2" Margin="2"
                    VerticalAlignment="Top"/>
            <Button Content="Button _3" Margin="2"
                    VerticalAlignment="Center"/>
            <Button Content="Button _4" Margin="2"
                    VerticalAlignment="Bottom"/>
            <Button Content="Button _5" Margin="2" />
        </StackPanel>
        <Separator />
        <StackPanel Margin="5" Orientation="Vertical">
            <Button Content="Button _A" Margin="2" />
            <Button Content="Button _B" HorizontalAlignment="Left"
                    Margin="2" />
            <Button Content="Button _C" HorizontalAlignment="Center"
                    Margin="2" />
            <Button Content="Button _D" HorizontalAlignment="Right"
                    Margin="2" />
            <Button Content="Button _E" Margin="2" />
        </StackPanel>
    </StackPanel>
</Window>
```

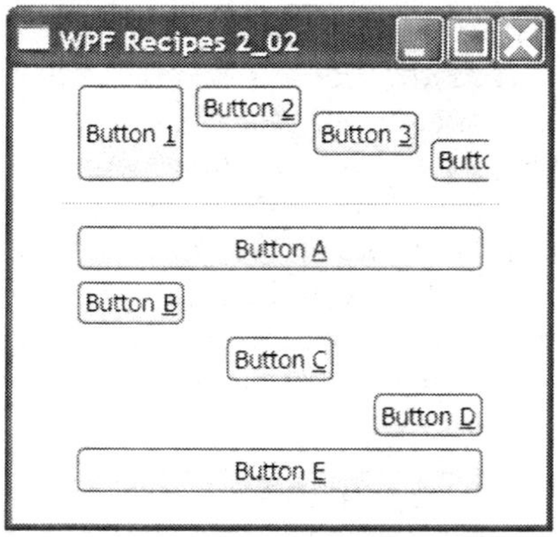

Figure 2-1. *Using a* StackPanel *to control the layout of UI elements*

2-3. Arrange UI Elements into Automatically Wrapping Rows or Columns

Problem

You need to arrange a group of UI elements in horizontal or vertical rows that wrap as the elements fill the available space.

Solution

Place the UI elements in a System.Windows.Controls.WrapPanel. Use the Orientation property of the WrapPanel to control whether the controls are displayed in rows or columns.

How It Works

The WrapPanel arranges the elements it contains in rows or columns. The order of the elements is determined by the order in which they are declared in the XAML (that is, the order in which they occur in the Children collection of the WrapPanel). By default, the WrapPanel will arrange the elements in a row (left to right), automatically moving elements onto another row if the WrapPanel does not have enough space to display the entire element.

You can force the WrapPanel to arrange the contained elements in columns by setting the Orientation property to Vertical. If the WrapPanel does not have enough space to display an entire element, it automatically moves the element to the next column.

The WrapPanel also provides the FlowDirection property, which allows you to control the direction in which elements flow and wrap. By default, the WrapPanel arranges the elements it contains from left to right. To arrange the elements in the WrapPanel from right to left, set the FlowDirection property to the value RightToLeft. Regardless of the value of the FlowDirection property, elements in a WrapPanel with its Orientation property set to Vertical are always arranged from top to bottom.

The Code

The following XAML demonstrates how to use two WrapPanel panels. The first WrapPanel has a horizontal orientation and contains a set of System.Windows.Controls.Button controls. You can see (in Figure 2-2) how the WrapPanel wraps the buttons it cannot fit on the first row onto a second row.

The second WrapPanel has a vertical orientation and also contains a set of Button controls. This WrapPanel also has its FlowDirection property set to RightToLeft, causing the columns to start on the right and work toward the left. Note that, as mentioned, the buttons are still laid out from the top to the bottom irrespective of the change to the FlowDirection property.

```
<Window x:Class="Recipe_02_03.Window1"
    xmlns="http://schemas.microsoft.com/winfx/2006/xaml/presentation"
    xmlns:x="http://schemas.microsoft.com/winfx/2006/xaml"
    Title="WPF Recipes 2_03" Height="240" Width="240">
    <StackPanel>
        <WrapPanel Height="50" Margin ="5">
            <Button Content="Button _1" Margin="2" />
            <Button Content="Button _2" Margin="2" />
            <Button Content="Button _3" Margin="2" />
            <Button Content="Button _4" Margin="2" />
            <Button Content="Button _5" Margin="2" />
        </WrapPanel>
        <Separator />
        <WrapPanel Margin="5" MaxHeight="150" Orientation="Vertical"
                FlowDirection="RightToLeft">
            <Button Content="Button _A" Margin="2" />
            <Button Content="Button _B" Margin="2" />
            <Button Content="Button _C" Margin="2" />
            <Button Content="Button _D" Margin="2" />
            <Button Content="Button _E" Margin="2" />
            <Button Content="Button _F" Margin="2" />
            <Button Content="Button _G" Margin="2" />
            <Button Content="Button _H" Margin="2" />
        </WrapPanel>
    </StackPanel>
</Window>
```

Figure 2-2. *Using a* WrapPanel *to control the layout of UI elements*

2-4. Dock UI Elements to the Edges of a Form

Problem

You need to dock UI elements to specific edges of a form.

Solution

Place the UI elements in a System.Windows.Controls.DockPanel. Use the DockPanel.Dock attached property on each element in the DockPanel to position the element on a particular edge.

How It Works

The DockPanel allows you to arrange UI elements (including other panels) along its edges. This is very useful in achieving the basic window layout common to many Windows applications with menus and toolbars along the top of the window and control panels along the sides.

When you apply the DockPanel.Dock attached property to the elements in a DockPanel, the DockPanel places the UI element along the specified edge: Left, Right, Top, or Bottom. The DockPanel assigns the elements' positions in the same order they are declared in the XAML (that is, in the order in which they occur in the Children collection of the DockPanel).

As each element is placed on an edge, it takes up all the space available along that edge. This means you must consider the layout you want when ordering the contained elements. Also, if there are multiple elements on a given edge, the DockPanel stacks them in order.

By default, the last element added to the DockPanel fills all the remaining space in the panel regardless of its DockPanel.Dock property value. You can stop this behavior by setting the LastChildFill property of the DockPanel to False. The DockPanel places any elements without a DockPanel.Dock property value along the left edge.

Figure 2-3 provides examples of the different layouts you can achieve by declaring elements in different orders. The third example also shows how the DockPanel stacks elements when specified on a common edge.

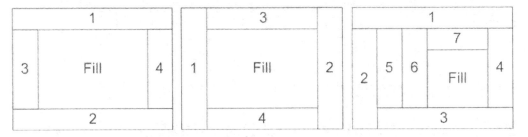

Figure 2-3. *Layout examples using a* DockPanel

The Code

The following XAML demonstrates how to use a DockPanel to dock a System.Windows.Controls. StackPanel containing a set of System.Windows.Controls.Button controls along its top edge and another along its left edge. The final Button added to the DockPanel stretches to fill all the remaining space in the panel (see Figure 2-4).

```
<Window x:Class="Recipe_02_04.Window1"
    xmlns="http://schemas.microsoft.com/winfx/2006/xaml/presentation"
    xmlns:x="http://schemas.microsoft.com/winfx/2006/xaml"
    Title="WPF Recipes 2_04" Height="200" Width="300">
    <DockPanel >
        <StackPanel DockPanel.Dock="Top" Orientation="Horizontal">
            <Button Content="Button 1" Margin="2" />
            <Button Content="Button 2" Margin="2" />
            <Button Content="Button 3" Margin="2" />
            <Button Content="Button 4" Margin="2" />
            <Button Content="Button 5" Margin="2" />
        </StackPanel>
        <StackPanel DockPanel.Dock="Left">
            <Button Content="Button A" Margin="2" />
            <Button Content="Button B" Margin="2" />
            <Button Content="Button C" Margin="2" />
            <Button Content="Button D" Margin="2" />
            <Button Content="Button E" Margin="2" />
        </StackPanel>
        <Button Content="Fill Button" />
    </DockPanel>
</Window>
```

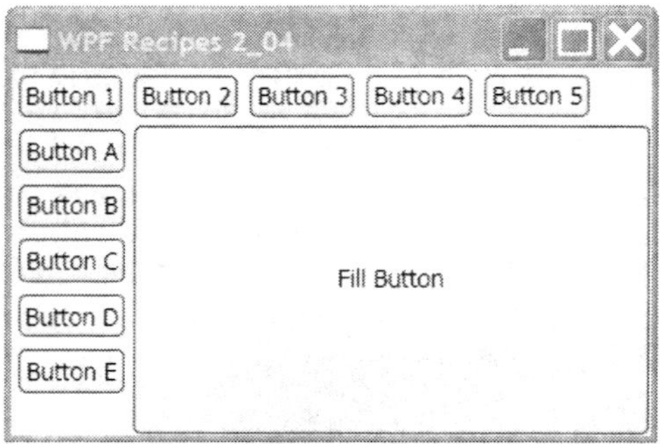

Figure 2-4. *Arranging UI elements in a DockPanel*

2-5. Arrange UI Elements in a Grid

Problem

You need to arrange a group of UI elements in a two-dimensional grid layout.

Solution

Place the UI elements in a System.Windows.Controls.Grid. Define the number of rows and columns in the Grid. For each UI element in the Grid, define its row and column coordinates using the Grid.Row and Grid.Column attached properties.

How It Works

To define the number of rows in a Grid panel, you must include a Grid.RowDefinitions element inside the Grid. Within the Grid.RowDefinitions element, you declare one RowDefintion element for each row you need. You must do the same thing for columns, but you use elements named Grid.ColumnDefinitions and ColumnDefinition.

Tip Although you will rarely want it in live production code, it is often useful during development to be able to see where the row and column boundaries are within your Grid panel. Setting the ShowGridLines property of the Grid panel to True will turn visible grid lines on.

Using the Height property of the RowDefinition element and the Width property of the ColumnDefinition, you have fine-grained control over the layout of a Grid. Both the Height and Width properties can take absolute values if you require fixed sizes. You must define the size of the column or row as a number and an optional unit identifier. By default, the unit is assumed to be px (pixels) but can also be in (inches), cm (centimeters), or pt (points).

If you do not want fixed sizes, you can assign the value Auto to the Height or Width property, in which case the Grid allocates only the amount of space required by the elements contained in the row or column.

If you do not specify absolute or auto values, the Grid will divide its horizontal space equally between all columns and its vertical space equally between all rows. You can override this default behavior and change the proportions of available space assigned to each row or column using an asterisk (*) preceded by the relative weighting the Grid should give the row or column. For example, a RowDefinition element with the Height property of 3* will get three times as much space allocated to it as a RowDefinition element with a Height property of *. Most often, you will use a mix of auto and proportional sizing.

Once you have defined the structure of your Grid, you specify where in the Grid each element should go using the Grid.Row and Grid.Column attached properties. Both the Grid.Row and Grid.Column properties are zero-based and default to zero if you do not define them for an element contained within the Grid.

If you want elements in the Grid that span multiple rows or columns, you can assign them Grid.RowSpan and Grid.ColumnSpan attached properties that specify the number of rows or columns that the element should span.

The Code

The following XAML demonstrates how to use a three-by-three Grid to lay out a set of System.Windows.Controls.Button controls. The Grid uses a mix of fixed, auto, and proportional row and column sizing, and the Grid lines are turned on so that you can see (in Figure 2-5) the resulting Grid structure. The top left Button controls span multiple rows or columns, and the leftmost Button is rotated (see recipe 3-25 for details on how to do this).

```xml
<Window x:Class="Recipe_02_05.Window1"
    xmlns="http://schemas.microsoft.com/winfx/2006/xaml/presentation"
    xmlns:x="http://schemas.microsoft.com/winfx/2006/xaml"
    Title="WPF Recipes 2_05" Height="200" Width="250">
    <Grid ShowGridLines="True">
        <Grid.RowDefinitions>
            <RowDefinition MinHeight="50" />
            <RowDefinition Height="2*" />
            <RowDefinition Height="*" />
        </Grid.RowDefinitions>
        <Grid.ColumnDefinitions>
            <ColumnDefinition Width="50" />
            <ColumnDefinition Width="2*" />
            <ColumnDefinition Width="3*" />
        </Grid.ColumnDefinitions>
        <Button Content="Button spanning 3 rows" Grid.RowSpan="3">
            <Button.LayoutTransform>
                <RotateTransform Angle="90" />
            </Button.LayoutTransform>
        </Button>
        <Button Content="Button spanning 2 columns" Grid.Column="1"
                Grid.Row="0" Grid.ColumnSpan="2" />
```

```
        <Button Content="Button" Grid.Column="2" Grid.Row="2"/>
    </Grid>
</Window>
```

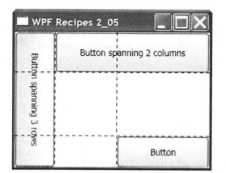

Figure 2-5. *Arranging UI elements in a Grid*

2-6. Position UI Elements Using Exact Coordinates

Problem

You need complete control over the positioning of the UI elements in a form.

Solution

Place the UI elements in a System.Windows.Controls.Canvas panel. Use the Canvas.Top, Canvas.Bottom, Canvas.Left, and Canvas.Right attached properties to define the position of each element.

How It Works

The Canvas panel allows you to place UI elements using exact coordinates. Unlike other layout panels, the Canvas does not provide special layout logic to position and size the elements it contains based on the space it has available. Instead, the Canvas simply places each element at its specified location and gives it the exact dimensions it requires. This does not facilitate maintainable user interfaces that are easy to localize, but in certain circumstances (such as drawing and graphical design applications) it may be necessary.

By default, the Canvas positions the elements it contains in its top-left corner. To position an element elsewhere in the Canvas, you can define the Canvas.Top, Canvas.Bottom, Canvas.Left, and Canvas.Right attached properties on the element. Each property takes a number and an optional unit identifier. By default, the unit is assumed to be px (pixels) but can also be in (inches), cm (centimeters), or pt (points). The value can even be negative, which allows the Canvas to draw elements outside its own visual boundaries.

If you define both Canvas.Top and Canvas.Bottom on an element, the Canvas ignores the Canvas.Bottom value. Similarly, if you define both Canvas.Left and Canvas.Right on an element, the Canvas ignores the Canvas.Right value.

Because you have complete control over element position when using a Canvas, it is easy to get elements that overlap. The Canvas draws the elements in the same order they are declared in the XAML (that is, the order in which they occur in the Children collection of the Canvas). So, elements declared later are visible on top of elements declared earlier. You can override this default stacking order (referred to as the *z-order*) by defining the Canvas.ZIndex attached property on the element. The default Canvas.ZIndex is zero, so by assigning a higher integer value to the Canvas.ZIndex property on an element, the Canvas will draw that element over the top of elements with a lower value.

The Code

The following XAML demonstrates how to use a Canvas to lay out a set of System.Windows. Controls.Button controls. In Figure 2-6, the shaded area shows the boundary of the Canvas. You can see how using negative position values for Button 1 and Button 5 place them wholly or partially outside the boundary of the Canvas. Despite Button 4 being declared after Button 2, the higher Canvas.ZIndex assigned on Button 2 forces the Canvas to draw Button 2 over the top of Button 4.

```
<Window x:Class="Recipe_02_06.Window1"
    xmlns="http://schemas.microsoft.com/winfx/2006/xaml/presentation"
    xmlns:x="http://schemas.microsoft.com/winfx/2006/xaml"
    Title="WPF Recipes 2_06" Height="300" Width="300">
    <Canvas Background="LightGray" Margin="1cm">
        <Button Content="Button _1" Canvas.Top="-1cm" Canvas.Left="1cm" />
        <Button Content="Button _2" Canvas.Bottom="1cm" Canvas.Left="1cm"
            Canvas.ZIndex="1"/>
        <Button Content="Button _3" Canvas.Top="1cm" Canvas.Right="1cm" />
        <Button Content="Button _4" Canvas.Bottom="1.2cm" Canvas.Left="1.5cm" />
        <Button Content="Button _5" Canvas.Bottom="1cm" Canvas.Right="-1cm" />
    </Canvas>
</Window>
```

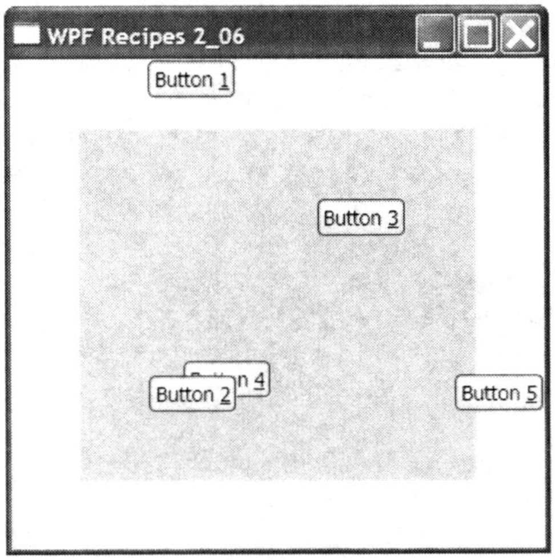

Figure 2-6. *Arranging UI elements using a Canvas*

2-7. Display Content in a Multitabbed User Interface

Problem

You need to display a set of tabbed pages, with each page containing separate content.

Solution

Use a System.Windows.Controls.TabControl object, and declare one TabItem element inside it for each content page you need. Declare the content for each page inside the appropriate TabItem element.

How It Works

The TabControl is a container for TabItem elements. The TabControl displays one selectable tab for each TabItem it contains, and each tab provides the user with access to a different page of content—which you declare within the TabItem element. The content of the TabItem must be a single element, but this can be a panel, allowing you to declare rich structured content within the panel.

You can assign a simple name for display in each tab using the Heading attribute of the TabItem element. You can also include rich structured content (including images) as part of the tab heading by declaring the TabItem.Header element within the TabItem. Again, this content must be a single item but can be a panel.

The first tab declared is the default selected tab, but you can change this by setting the IsSelected property of a TabItem to True. The default display position of the tabs is along the top of the TabControl, but you can also control this by setting the TabStripPlacement property of the TabControl to one of these values: Left, Right, Top, or Bottom.

The Code

The following XAML demonstrates a TabControl containing three TabItem objects. As you can see in Figure 2-7, the tabs are on the left side of the TabControl because the TabStripPlacement property of the TabControl has the value Left. Each TabItem contains a set of System.Windows.Controls.Button objects in a System.Windows.Controls.StackPanel. The headers of the first two tabs are simple text, but the third contains an image. The second TabItem is selected by default because its IsSelected property is set to the value True.

```
<Window x:Class="Recipe_02_07.Window1"
    xmlns="http://schemas.microsoft.com/winfx/2006/xaml/presentation"
    xmlns:x="http://schemas.microsoft.com/winfx/2006/xaml"
    Title="WPF Recipes 2_07" Height="150" Width="250">
    <TabControl TabStripPlacement="Left">
        <TabItem Header="Tab 1">
```

```
            <StackPanel HorizontalAlignment="Center">
                <Button Content="Button _1" Margin="5" />
                <Button Content="Button _2" Margin="5" />
                <Button Content="Button _3" Margin="5" />
            </StackPanel>
        </TabItem>
        <TabItem Header="Tab 2" IsSelected="True">
            <StackPanel HorizontalAlignment="Center">
                <Button Content="Button _A" Margin="5" />
                <Button Content="Button _B" Margin="5" />
                <Button Content="Button _C" Margin="5" />
            </StackPanel>
        </TabItem>
        <TabItem >
            <TabItem.Header>
                <Image Source="ApressLogo.gif" ToolTip="Apress" Width="50"/>
            </TabItem.Header>
            <StackPanel HorizontalAlignment="Center">
                <Button Content="Button _X" Margin="5" />
                <Button Content="Button _Y" Margin="5" />
                <Button Content="Button _Z" Margin="5" />
            </StackPanel>
        </TabItem>
    </TabControl>
</Window>
```

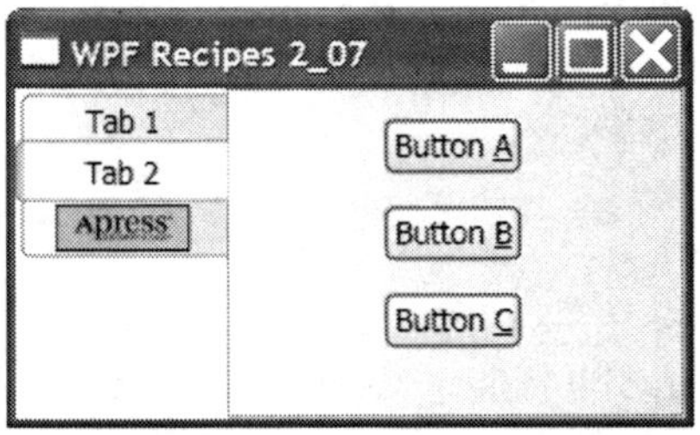

Figure 2-7. *Arranging UI elements using a TabControl*

2-8. Display Content in a Scrollable User Interface

Problem

You need to support scrolling in a panel so that the user has access to content that occupies more screen space than the panel currently has available.

Solution

Place the content that needs to scroll in a System.Windows.Controls.ScrollViewer container.

How It Works

None of the basic panels (discussed in recipes 2-2 through 2-6) contains inherent support for scrolling to support content that is bigger than the current size of the panel. But scrollable content is an essential part of almost every Windows application. WPF delegates the responsibility for scrolling to a separate control—the ScrollViewer. To support scrolling, declare a ScrollViewer element, and place the scrollable content—typically a layout panel—inside the ScrollViewer element.

You can control the visibility of the horizontal and vertical scrollbars using the HorizontalScrollBarVisibility and VerticalScrollBarVisibility properties of the ScrollViewer element. You can set these properties to the values listed in Table 2-1.

Table 2-1. *Property Values for Controlling Scrollbar Visibility*

Value	Description
Disabled	Scrolling is disabled in the horizontal or vertical direction regardless of the size of the content contained in the ScrollViewer. The virtual height or width of the ScrollViewer is fixed to its visible size and the content.
Auto	A scrollbar is always visible, but it is enabled only when required to provide access to content outside the visible bounds of the ScrollViewer.
Hidden	Scrollbars are never visible, but the virtual dimensions of the ScrollViewer are not constrained to its physical dimensions. You must use the arrow keys or tab between controls to scroll around the content.
Visible	The scrollbar is always visible regardless of the content in the ScrollViewer. However, it is visibly disabled if no scrolling is possible.

The Code

The following XAML demonstrates how to use a ScrollViewer to support scrolling content that does not fit in the current window dimensions. The example (shown in Figure 2-8) contains two tabs, each containing a panel inside a ScrollViewer element. Both have content (a set of Button objects inside a StackPanel) that is too large for the default panel size.

The first tab has the HorizontalScrollBarVisibility and VerticalScrollBarVisibility properties of the ScrollViewer element set to Visible so that you can use the scrollbars to move around the scrollable surface. The second tab has the HorizontalScrollBarVisibility and VerticalScrollBarVisibility properties set to Hidden, meaning you need to use the arrow keys or tab between buttons to move the scrollable surface.

```
<Window x:Class="Recipe_02_08.Window1"
    xmlns="http://schemas.microsoft.com/winfx/2006/xaml/presentation"
    xmlns:x="http://schemas.microsoft.com/winfx/2006/xaml"
    Title="WPF Recipes 2_08" Height="200" Width="250">
    <TabControl>
```

```xml
        <TabItem Header="Visible ScrollBars">
            <ScrollViewer HorizontalScrollBarVisibility="Visible"
                          VerticalScrollBarVisibility="Visible" >
                <StackPanel>
                    <StackPanel Orientation="Horizontal">
                        <Button Content="Button 1" Margin="2" />
                        <Button Content="Button 2" Margin="2" />
                        <Button Content="Button 3" Margin="2" />
                        <Button Content="Button 4" Margin="2" />
                        <Button Content="Button 5" Margin="2" />
                    </StackPanel>
                    <StackPanel HorizontalAlignment="Left">
                        <Button Content="Button A" Margin="2" />
                        <Button Content="Button B" Margin="2" />
                        <Button Content="Button C" Margin="2" />
                        <Button Content="Button D" Margin="2" />
                        <Button Content="Button E" Margin="2" />
                    </StackPanel>
                </StackPanel>
            </ScrollViewer>
        </TabItem>
        <TabItem Header="Hidden ScrollBars">
            <ScrollViewer HorizontalScrollBarVisibility="Hidden"
                          VerticalScrollBarVisibility="Hidden">
                <StackPanel>
                    <StackPanel Orientation="Horizontal">
                        <Button Content="Button 1" Margin="2" />
                        <Button Content="Button 2" Margin="2" />
                        <Button Content="Button 3" Margin="2" />
                        <Button Content="Button 4" Margin="2" />
                        <Button Content="Button 5" Margin="2" />
                    </StackPanel>
                    <StackPanel HorizontalAlignment="Left">
                        <Button Content="Button A" Margin="2" />
                        <Button Content="Button B" Margin="2" />
                        <Button Content="Button C" Margin="2" />
                        <Button Content="Button D" Margin="2" />
                        <Button Content="Button E" Margin="2" />
                    </StackPanel>
                </StackPanel>
            </ScrollViewer>
        </TabItem>
    </TabControl>
</Window>
```

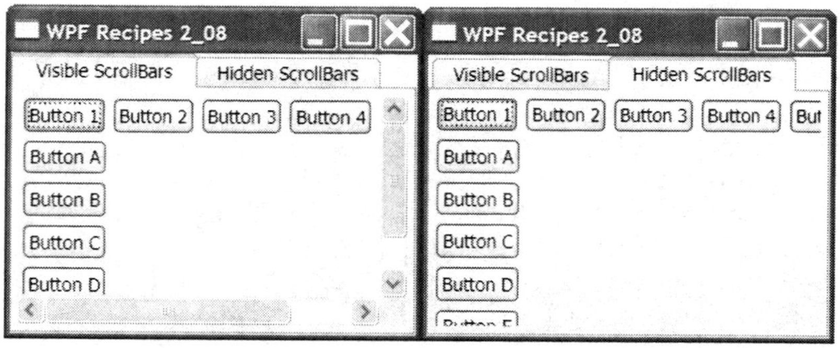

Figure 2-8. *Making content scrollable (with and without scrollbars) using a* ScrollViewer

2-9. Display Content in Resizable Split Panel

Problem

You need to display a set of UI elements in a panel divided by a movable splitter bar.

Solution

Place the UI elements in a System.Windows.Controls.Grid. Declare a System.Windows.Controls.GridSplitter in the Grid row or column where you want the movable splitter bar to appear.

How It Works

The GridSplitter control allows you to turn a Grid panel into a resizable splitter panel. You insert the GridSplitter control at the row or column in the Grid where you want the splitter bar to appear. Use the Grid.Row or Grid.Column attached properties to position the GridSplitter (described in recipe 2-5).

You should set the height or width of the row or column that will contain the GridSplitter and stretch the GridSplitter to fill the available space by setting its HorizontalAlignment property to the value Stretch. If you need the splitter to go across multiple rows or columns, use the Grid.RowSpan or Grid.ColumnSpan attached properties (also described in recipe 2-5).

The Code

The following XAML demonstrates how to create a three-sectioned UI using two GridSplitter controls. The first GridSplitter creates two resizable vertical sections, and the second GridSplitter divides the right vertical section into two horizontal sections. Figure 2-9 shows the result and also shows the default double-headed arrow used for the mouse pointer when you move the mouse over the splitter bar.

```
<Window x:Class="Recipe_02_09.Window1"
    xmlns="http://schemas.microsoft.com/winfx/2006/xaml/presentation"
    xmlns:x="http://schemas.microsoft.com/winfx/2006/xaml"
    Title="WPF Recipes 2_09" Height="200" Width="300">
```

```xml
<Grid>
    <Grid.ColumnDefinitions>
        <ColumnDefinition Width="1*" />
        <ColumnDefinition Width="5" />
        <ColumnDefinition Width="3*" />
    </Grid.ColumnDefinitions>
    <TextBlock HorizontalAlignment="Center" Text="Left Panel"
            VerticalAlignment="Center">
        <TextBlock.LayoutTransform>
            <RotateTransform Angle="90" />
        </TextBlock.LayoutTransform>
    </TextBlock>
    <GridSplitter Grid.Column="1" HorizontalAlignment="Stretch" />
    <Grid Grid.Column="3">
        <Grid.RowDefinitions>
            <RowDefinition />
            <RowDefinition Height="5"/>
            <RowDefinition />
        </Grid.RowDefinitions>
        <TextBlock Grid.Row="0" HorizontalAlignment="Center"
                Text="Top Panel" VerticalAlignment="Center" />
        <GridSplitter Grid.Row="1" HorizontalAlignment="Stretch" />
        <TextBlock Grid.Row="2" HorizontalAlignment="Center"
                Text="Bottom Panel" VerticalAlignment="Center" />
    </Grid>
</Grid>
</Window>
```

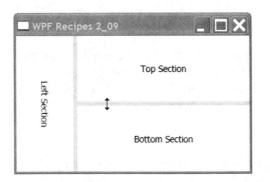

Figure 2-9. *Creating a resizable splitter panel using a GridSplitter*

2-10. Display Content in an Expander

Problem

You need to allow the user to expand and collapse sections of the user interface that contain groups of UI elements or content.

Solution

Place the UI elements or content that needs to be expanded and collapsed into a System.Windows. Controls.Expander control.

How It Works

The Expander control allows you to wrap a set of UI elements (usually a content panel) so that they can be expanded and collapsed by the user. You can specify a simple text title for the collapsible section using the Header property of the Expander control. Alternatively, you can specify richer header content by defining the Expander.Header element within the Expander element. Within the Expander.Header element, you define the content that represents your header.

You control whether the Expander is expanded or collapsed using the IsExpanded property, which takes the value True or False. To configure the direction in which the Expander content expands, set the ExpandDirection of the Expander to one of these values: Up, Down, Left, or Right.

The Code

The following XAML (shown running in Figure 2-10) demonstrates how to use two Expander objects embedded in a System.Windows.Controls.StackPanel. The first Expander expands horizontally and uses an image in its header. The second Expander contains a set of System.Windows. Controls.Button objects and expands downward. Using a System.Windows.Controls.ScrollViewer (discussed in recipe 2-8) around the outer StackPanel provides scrollbar support when the expansion of the Expander objects results in the displayed content being larger than the window area available.

```
<Window x:Class="Recipe_02_10.Window1"
    xmlns="http://schemas.microsoft.com/winfx/2006/xaml/presentation"
    xmlns:x="http://schemas.microsoft.com/winfx/2006/xaml"
    Title="WPF Recipes 2_10" Height="200" Width="300">
    <ScrollViewer HorizontalScrollBarVisibility="Auto"
        VerticalScrollBarVisibility="Auto" >
        <StackPanel HorizontalAlignment="Left">
            <Expander ExpandDirection="Right" IsExpanded="True">
                <Expander.Header>
                    <Image Source="Apress.gif" />
                </Expander.Header>
```

```xml
        <TextBlock TextWrapping="Wrap" MaxWidth="200">
            Lorem ipsum dolor sit amet, consectetur adipisicing elit, sed do
            eiusmod tempor incididunt ut labore et dolore magna aliqua. Ut
            enim ad minim veniam, quis nostrud exercitation ullamco laboris
            nisi ut aliquip ex ea commodo consequat. Duis aute irure dolor
            in reprehenderit in voluptate velit esse cillum dolore eu fugiat
        </TextBlock>
    </Expander>
    <Expander Header="Buttons">
        <StackPanel>
            <StackPanel Orientation="Horizontal">
                <Button Content="Button 1" Margin="2" />
                <Button Content="Button 2" Margin="2" />
                <Button Content="Button 3" Margin="2" />
                <Button Content="Button 4" Margin="2" />
                <Button Content="Button 5" Margin="2" />
            </StackPanel>
            <StackPanel HorizontalAlignment="Left">
                <Button Content="Button A" Margin="2" />
                <Button Content="Button B" Margin="2" />
                <Button Content="Button C" Margin="2" />
                <Button Content="Button D" Margin="2" />
                <Button Content="Button E" Margin="2" />
            </StackPanel>
        </StackPanel>
    </Expander>
    </StackPanel>
    </ScrollViewer>
</Window>
```

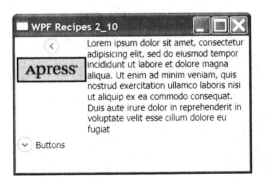

Figure 2-10. *Displaying content in an Expander*

2-11. Place a Group Box Around a Set of UI Elements

Problem

You need to surround a group of related UI elements with a group box.

Solution

Place the UI elements that need to be grouped in a System.Windows.Controls.GroupBox control.

How It Works

The GroupBox control allows you to easily place a group of controls in a visual container that has a heading and a border. You can specify a simple text title for the GroupBox using the Header property of the GroupBox control. Alternatively, you can specify richer header content by defining the GroupBox.Header element as a child of the GroupBox element. Within the GroupBox.Header element, you define the content that represents your header.

The Code

The following XAML demonstrates how to use two GroupBox controls to group radio buttons. The GroupBox controls are positioned in a System.Windows.Controls.Grid. One GroupBox uses a simple text header, and the other uses an image (see Figure 2-11).

```xml
<Window x:Class="Recipe_02_11.Window1"
    xmlns="http://schemas.microsoft.com/winfx/2006/xaml/presentation"
    xmlns:x="http://schemas.microsoft.com/winfx/2006/xaml"
    Title="WPF Recipes 2_11" Height="200" Width="400">
    <Grid>
        <Grid.ColumnDefinitions>
            <ColumnDefinition />
            <ColumnDefinition />
        </Grid.ColumnDefinitions>
        <GroupBox Grid.Column="0" Header="Simple Text" Margin="5">
            <StackPanel>
                <RadioButton Content="Radio 1" IsChecked="True" Margin="5" />
                <RadioButton Content="Radio 2" Margin="5" />
                <RadioButton Content="Radio 3" Margin="5" />
                <RadioButton Content="Radio 4" Margin="5" />
                <RadioButton Content="Radio 5" Margin="5" />
            </StackPanel>
        </GroupBox>
        <GroupBox Grid.Column="1" Margin="5">
            <GroupBox.Header>
                <Image Source="Apress.gif" />
            </GroupBox.Header>
```

```
        <StackPanel>
            <RadioButton Content="Radio A" IsChecked="True" Margin="5" />
            <RadioButton Content="Radio B" Margin="5" />
            <RadioButton Content="Radio C" Margin="5" />
            <RadioButton Content="Radio D" Margin="5" />
            <RadioButton Content="Radio E" Margin="5" />
        </StackPanel>
    </GroupBox>
  </Grid>
</Window>
```

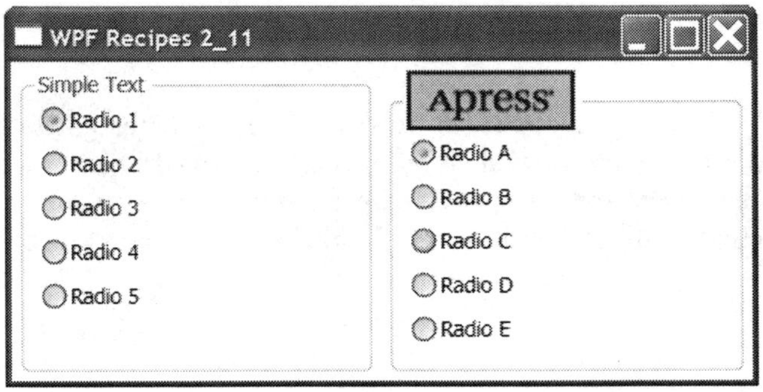

Figure 2-11. *Displaying UI elements in a GroupBox*

2-12. Display a Message Box

Problem

You need to display a message box.

Solution

Call an overload of the Show method from the System.Windows.MessageBox class, and pass arguments specifying the content you want displayed in the MessageBox. For example, you can define the header, body text, icons, and buttons to show to the user.

How It Works

The MessageBox class provides a wrapper around the standard Windows message box. To display a MessageBox, call one of the static overloads of the MessageBox.Show method, of which there are 12. Each overload takes a different set of arguments that give you varying levels of control over the behavior and content of the MessageBox.

The MessageBox.Show method returns a value from the System.Windows.MessageBoxResult enumeration that identifies the button the user clicked to close the MessageBox. The possible values are None, OK, Cancel, Yes, and No.

Table 2-2 summarizes the parameters taken by the 12 overloads of the MessageBox.Show method.

Table 2-2. *Summary of the MessageBox.Show Parameters*

Parameter	Description
Window	A System.Windows.Window object identifying the owner of the MessageBox.
Body Text	A System.String containing the text to display in the body of the MessageBox.
Caption	A System.String containing the text to display in the title bar of the MessageBox.
Button	A value from the System.Windows.MessageBoxButton enumeration that specifies the buttons you want shown in the MessageBox. The possible values are OK, OKCancel, YesNoCancel, and YesNo.
Icon	A value from the System.Windows.MessageBoxImage enumeration that specifies the icon you want shown in the MessageBox. The possible values are None, Hand, Question, Exclamation, Asterisk, Stop, Error, Warning, and Information.
Default Result	The default result of the message box expressed as a value of the System.Windows.MessageBoxResult enumeration. The possible values are None, OK, Cancel, Yes, and No.
Options	A value from the System.Windows.MessageBoxOptions enumeration that allows you to enable specific options relating to the MessageBox. The possible values are None, ServiceNotification, DefaultDesktopOnly, RightAlign, and RtlReading.

The Code

The following XAML defines a set of System.Windows.Controls.Button controls that, when clicked, display a MessageBox. Each Button uses a different overload of the MessageBox.Show method to control the MessageBox displayed.

```
<Window x:Class="Recipe_02_12.Window1"
    xmlns="http://schemas.microsoft.com/winfx/2006/xaml/presentation"
    xmlns:x="http://schemas.microsoft.com/winfx/2006/xaml"
    Title="WPF Recipes 2_12" Height="170" Width="300">
    <StackPanel>
        <Button Click="btnMessageOnly_Click" Content="Message Only"
                Margin="5" Name="btnMessageOnly" />
        <Button Click="btnMessageHeader_Click" Content="Message and Header"
                Margin="5" Name="btnMessageHeader" />
        <Button Click="btnMessageHeaderButton_Click"
                Content="Message, Header, and Button"
                Margin="5" Name="btnMessageHeaderButton" />
        <Button Click="btnMessageHeaderButtonImage_Click"
                Content="Message, Header, Button, and Image"
                Margin="5" Name="btnMessageHeaderButtonImage" />
    </StackPanel>
</Window>
```

The following is the code-behind to support the previous XAML. Figure 2-12 shows what the MessageBox displayed by the btnMessageHeaderButtonImage_Click event handler (fourth button) looks like (running on Windows XP).

```
namespace Recipe_02_12
{
    /// <summary>
    /// Interaction logic for Window1.xaml
    /// </summary>
    public partial class Window1 : Window
    {
        public Window1()
        {
            InitializeComponent();
        }

        private void btnMessageOnly_Click(object sender, RoutedEventArgs e)
        {
            MessageBox.Show("A simple MessageBox.");
        }

        private void btnMessageHeader_Click(object sender, RoutedEventArgs e)
        {
            MessageBox.Show("A MessageBox with a title.",
                "WPF Recipes Chapter 2");
        }

        private void btnMessageHeaderButton_Click(object sender,
            RoutedEventArgs e)
        {
            MessageBox.Show("A MessageBox with a title and buttons.",
                "WPF Recipes Chapter 2",
                MessageBoxButton.YesNoCancel);
        }

        private void btnMessageHeaderButtonImage_Click(object sender,
            RoutedEventArgs e)
        {
            MessageBox.Show("A MessageBox with a title, buttons, and an icon.",
                "WPF Recipes Chapter 2",
                MessageBoxButton.YesNoCancel,
                MessageBoxImage.Warning);
        }
    }
}
```

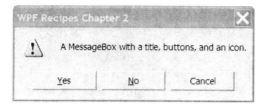

Figure 2-12. *A* MessageBox *with a title, body, buttons, and an icon*

2-13. Display a Pop-up Window

Problem

You need to show a pop-up window containing rich interactive content to the user.

Solution

Declare the content in a System.Windows.Controls.Primitives.Popup control. When you want to display the pop-up window, set the Popup.IsOpen property to the value True. To close the pop-up, set the Popup.IsOpen property to False.

How It Works

The System.Windows.Controls.ToolTip control (discussed in recipe 3-16) allows you to show rich content in a pop-up window, but it does not allow the contained UI elements to receive the input focus; as such, there is no way for the user to interact with the controls on the ToolTip. If you want the user to interact with the controls on the pop-up window, you should use a Popup control.

A Popup control contains a single element. Usually this is a layout panel allowing you to create rich structured content within the Popup, as described in recipes 2-2 through 2-6. To display the Popup, set its IsOpen property to the value True.

You control the basic placement of the Popup using its PlacementTarget and Placement properties. By default, the placement target is the main application window but can be over-ridden using the Popup.PlacementTarget property.

The Popup.Placement property takes a value from the System.Windows.Controls.Primitives. PlacementMode enumeration, which determines where WPF places the Popup when it is displayed. The PlacementMode enumeration contains 12 values, offering a wide choice of how you place your Popup. Many of the PlacementMode options are relative to the element referenced in the PlacementTarget property of the Popup. Table 2-3 summarizes some of the more commonly used PlacementMode values.

The Popup.HorizontalOffset and Popup.VerticalOffset properties allow you to specify System.Double values to fine-tune the position of the Popup depending on the value of the Popup.Placement property. By default, the offset values are assumed to be in px (pixels) but can also be in (inches), cm (centimeters), or pt (points).

Table 2-3. *Property Values for the Placement of Popup Controls*

Value	Description
Bottom	The top of the Popup is aligned with the bottom of the placement target, and the left edge of the Popup is aligned with the left edge of the placement target.
Center	The Popup is centered over the placement target.
Left	The right of the Popup is aligned with the left of the placement target, and the upper edge of the Popup is aligned with the upper edge of the placement target.
Mouse	The top of the Popup is aligned with the bottom of the mouse's bounding box, and the left edge of the Popup is aligned with the left edge of the mouse's bounding box.
Relative	The upper-left corner of the Popup is placed relative to the upper-left corner of the placement target.
Right	The left of the Popup is aligned with the right of the placement target, and the upper edge of the ToolTip is aligned with the upper edge of the placement target.

Tip WPF provides fine-grained control over the placement of Popup controls using the PlacementTarget, PlacementRectangle, HorizontalOffset, and VerticalOffset properties. For a thorough description of Popup placement logic, see the MSDN article at http://msdn2.microsoft.com/en-us/library/ bb613596.aspx.

You can also control the animation effect WPF uses when displaying the Popup by setting the PopupAnimation property. The default animation is None, meaning the Popup simply appears at the specified position. Other options are Fade, Slide, and Scroll. However, to use any of these animations, you must set the AllowTransparency property of the Popup to the value True.

The StaysOpen property of the Popup control determines how the Popup is closed. If StaysOpen is True (the default), the Popup will remain open until its IsOpen property is set to False. If StaysOpen is False, the Popup will close as soon as the user clicks something other than the Popup.

The Code

The following XAML defines a Popup that is displayed when the user clicks one of four buttons on the main window. Each of the four buttons uses a different form of animation to open the Popup. The Popup contains a System.Windows.Controls.DockPanel to provide structure for its content and is placed 1 centimeter to the right of the main window. The Popup contains a button that calls an event handler in the code-behind that sets IsOpen to False and closes the Popup (see Figure 2-13).

```
<Window x:Class="Recipe_02_13.Window1"
    xmlns="http://schemas.microsoft.com/winfx/2006/xaml/presentation"
    xmlns:x="http://schemas.microsoft.com/winfx/2006/xaml"
    Title="WPF Recipes 2_13" Height="150" Width="200">
```

```xml
<StackPanel>
    <Popup AllowsTransparency="True" Height="100"
            HorizontalOffset="1cm" Name="popRecipe2_13"
            Placement="Right" StaysOpen="True" Width="200" >
        <Border BorderBrush="Black" BorderThickness="2">
            <DockPanel Background="White" LastChildFill="True">
                <TextBlock Background="AliceBlue" DockPanel.Dock="Top"
                            FontSize="16" HorizontalAlignment="Stretch"
                            Margin="5" Text="A WPF Popup" />
                    <Button Click="btnClosePopup_Click" Content="Close"
                            DockPanel.Dock="Bottom" Margin="5"
                            HorizontalAlignment="Right" MaxHeight="23"/>
                    <Image DockPanel.Dock="Top" Margin="5"
                            Source="Apress.gif" />
            </DockPanel>
        </Border>
    </Popup>
    <StackPanel>
        <StackPanel.Resources>
            <Style TargetType="{x:Type Button}">
                <Setter Property="Margin" Value="2" />
                <EventSetter Event="Click" Handler="btnShowPopup_Click" />
            </Style>
        </StackPanel.Resources>
        <Button Content="Show Popup" Name="btnShowPopup" />
        <Button Content="Fade Popup" Name="btnFadePopup" />
        <Button Content="Scroll Popup" Name="btnScrollPopup" />
        <Button Content="Slide Popup" Name="btnSlidePopup" />
    </StackPanel>
</StackPanel>
</Window>
```

The following code-behind shows the button event handlers used to open and close the Popup in the previous example:

```csharp
namespace Recipe_02_13
{
    /// <summary>
    /// Interaction logic for Window1.xaml
    /// </summary>
    public partial class Window1 : Window
    {
        public Window1()
        {
            InitializeComponent();
        }
```

```
private void btnClosePopup_Click(object sender, RoutedEventArgs e)
{
    popRecipe2_13.IsOpen = false;
}

private void btnShowPopup_Click(object sender, RoutedEventArgs e)
{
    // Determine the correct animation based on the button clicked.
    if (sender == btnFadePopup)
    {
        popRecipe2_13.PopupAnimation = PopupAnimation.Fade;
    }
    else if (sender == btnScrollPopup)
    {
        popRecipe2_13.PopupAnimation = PopupAnimation.Scroll;
    }
    else if (sender == btnSlidePopup)
    {
        popRecipe2_13.PopupAnimation = PopupAnimation.Slide;
    }
    else
    {
        popRecipe2_13.PopupAnimation = PopupAnimation.None;
    }

    // Close the pop-up if it is open.
    popRecipe2_13.IsOpen = false;

    // Display the pop-up.
    popRecipe2_13.IsOpen = true;
}
}
}
```

Figure 2-13. *A WPF Popup placed 1 centimeter to the right of its placement target*

2-14. Display a Border

Problem

You need to display a border around a group of UI elements.

Solution

Place the content you want surrounded by a border in a System.Windows.Controls.Border control. Define the appearance of the Border control using its Background, BorderBrush, BorderThickness, and CornerRadius properties.

How It Works

Many UI elements (those derived from System.Windows.Controls.Control) already provide the ability to display a configurable border. When you want to place a border around other elements, you can use the Border control. The Border control can contain only a single UI element, so if you need to surround a group of elements, you must place them in a layout panel (as described in recipes 2-2 through 2-6). Table 2-4 describes the properties you will use most frequently to configure the appearance of the Border control.

Table 2-4. *Properties of the Border Control*

Value	Description
Background	The System.Windows.Media.Brush object used to paint the area covered by the Border control. Content within the Border control is drawn on top of the background.
BorderBrush	The Brush object used to paint the outer border of the Border control.
BorderThickness	The thickness of the border expressed as a number and an optional unit identifier. By default, the unit is assumed to be px (pixels) but can also be in (inches), cm (centimeters), or pt (points). You can specify a single value that is applied to all sides, or you can specify a different value for each side using a comma-separated list—the order is left, top, right, and then bottom.
CornerRadius	The degree, expressed as a System.Double, to which the corners of the border are rounded. You can specify a single value that is applied to all corners, or you can specify a different value for each corner using a comma-separated list—the order is top left, top right, bottom right, and then bottom left.

■ **Note** You can use many different brush types to configure the Background and BorderBrush properties of the Border control. See Chapter 9 for details on how to use brushes.

The Code

The following XAML defines a System.Windows.Controls.UniformGrid that contains four
Border controls with different configurations in each of its cells. You can see the output in
Figure 2-14.

```xml
<Window x:Class="Recipe_02_14.Window1"
    xmlns="http://schemas.microsoft.com/winfx/2006/xaml/presentation"
    xmlns:x="http://schemas.microsoft.com/winfx/2006/xaml"
    Title="WPF Recipes 2_14" Height="300" Width="300">
    <UniformGrid>
        <UniformGrid.Resources>
            <Style TargetType="{x:Type TextBlock}">
                <Setter Property="FontSize" Value="14" />
                <Setter Property="HorizontalAlignment" Value="Center" />
                <Setter Property="VerticalAlignment" Value="Center" />
            </Style>
        </UniformGrid.Resources>
        <Border CornerRadius="90" Background="LightBlue" BorderThickness="2px"
                Margin="10">
            <TextBlock Text="A circular border" />
        </Border>
        <Border CornerRadius="15" BorderBrush="Black"
                BorderThickness="2px, 5px, 2px, 5px" Margin="10">
            <TextBlock Text="A rounded border" />
        </Border>
        <Border CornerRadius="0, 5, 30, 90" Background="LightGray"
                BorderBrush="LightGray" BorderThickness="2px, 5px, 2px, 5px"
                Margin="10">
            <TextBlock Text="A wonky border" />
        </Border>
        <Border BorderBrush="Black" BorderThickness="4px, 4px, 0px, 0px"
                Margin="10">
            <TextBlock Text="A half border" />
        </Border>
    </UniformGrid>
</Window>
```

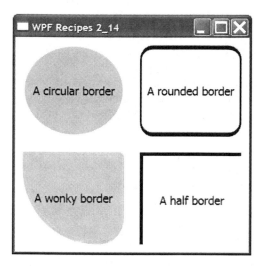

Figure 2-14. *A variety of Border controls arranged in a UniformGrid*

2-15. Display a Menu

Problem

You need to display a menu from which the user can select a particular action they want to perform.

Solution

Use the System.Windows.Controls.Menu control to represent the menu. Inside the Menu, use a hierarchy of System.Windows.Controls.MenuItem controls to define the menu structure you need. Define Click event handlers or Command bindings to associate actions with each MenuItem.

How It Works

The WPF Menu class provides the functionality of a traditional Windows menu but is not limited in its use only as a menu at the top of a form or window. You can place Menu objects anywhere you like and even have multiple menus in a single window. To achieve the normal Windows menu behavior, you would usually position the Menu at the top of a System.Windows.Controls. DockPanel, which is discussed in recipe 2-4. To identify which Menu gets the focus when a user presses Alt or F10, you set the IsMainMenu property of the Menu to True.

To define the actions listed in the Menu, you create a hierarchy of MenuItem objects. By declaring MenuItem elements within the body of another MenuItem element, you create a submenu that opens when the user clicks the parent MenuItem.

The Header property of the MenuItem specifies the text that appears for that item in the Menu structure. MenuItem supports basic formatting of the Header, including things such as the font family, size, style, and weight. You can also define access keys by prefixing the appropriate character in the Header with an underscore (_).

To place horizontal separator lines between groups of menu actions, declare System. Windows.Controls.Separator controls between the relevant MenuItem elements.

To define the functionality of the MenuItem elements, you can either define Click event handlers on each MenuItem or define Command bindings.

Note Chapter 4 contains detailed examples of how to use commands and command bindings.

The Code

The following XAML declares a Menu that contains MenuItem objects configured to allow the editing of a System.Windows.Controls.TextBox. The Menu is positioned as a traditional Windows menu using a DockPanel (see Figure 2-15).

```xml
<Window x:Class="Recipe_02_15.Window1"
    xmlns="http://schemas.microsoft.com/winfx/2006/xaml/presentation"
    xmlns:x="http://schemas.microsoft.com/winfx/2006/xaml"
    Title="WPF Recipes 2_15" Height="200" Width="300">
    <DockPanel LastChildFill="True">
        <Menu DockPanel.Dock="Top">
            <MenuItem Header="_Edit">
                <MenuItem Header="Cu_t"
                        Command="ApplicationCommands.Cut" />
                <MenuItem Header="_Copy"
                        Command="ApplicationCommands.Copy" />
                <MenuItem Header="_Paste"
                        Command="ApplicationCommands.Paste"/>
                <Separator/>
                <MenuItem Click="SelectAll_Click" Header="_Select All" />
                <MenuItem Click="Clear_Click" Header="_Clear" />
            </MenuItem>
            <MenuItem Header="_Format">
                <MenuItem Click="TextStyle_Click" Header="_Normal"
                        Name="miNormal" />
                <MenuItem Click="TextStyle_Click" FontWeight="Bold"
                        Header="_Bold" Name="miBold" />
                <MenuItem Click="TextStyle_Click" FontStyle="Italic"
                        Header="_Italic" Name="miItalic" />
            </MenuItem>
        </Menu>
```

```
    <TextBox Name="txtTextBox" TextWrapping="Wrap">
        Lorem ipsum dolor sit amet, consectetur adipisicing elit, sed do
        eiusmod tempor incididunt ut labore et dolore magna aliqua. Ut
        enim ad minim veniam, quis nostrud exercitation ullamco laboris
        nisi ut aliquip ex ea commodo consequat. Duis aute irure dolor
        in reprehenderit in voluptate velit esse cillum dolore eu fugiat
    </TextBox>
  </DockPanel>
</Window>
```

The following code-behind contains the shared Click event handler to handle format changes and individual Click event handlers for the Clear and Select All menu items:

```
namespace Recipe_02_15
{
    /// <summary>
    /// Interaction logic for Window1.xaml
    /// </summary>
    public partial class Window1 : Window
    {
        public Window1()
        {
            InitializeComponent();
        }

        // Handles Clear Button Click.
        private void Clear_Click(object sender, RoutedEventArgs e)
        {
            txtTextBox.Clear();
        }

        // Handles the Select All Button Click.
        private void SelectAll_Click(object sender, RoutedEventArgs e)
        {
            txtTextBox.SelectAll();
        }

        // Handles all the Button Click events that format the TextBox.
        private void TextStyle_Click(object sender, RoutedEventArgs e)
        {
            if (sender == miNormal)
            {
                txtTextBox.FontWeight = FontWeights.Normal;
                txtTextBox.FontStyle = FontStyles.Normal;
            }
```

```
            else if (sender == miBold)
            {
                txtTextBox.FontWeight = FontWeights.Bold;
            }
            else if (sender == miItalic)
            {
                txtTextBox.FontStyle = FontStyles.Italic;
            }
        }
    }
}
```

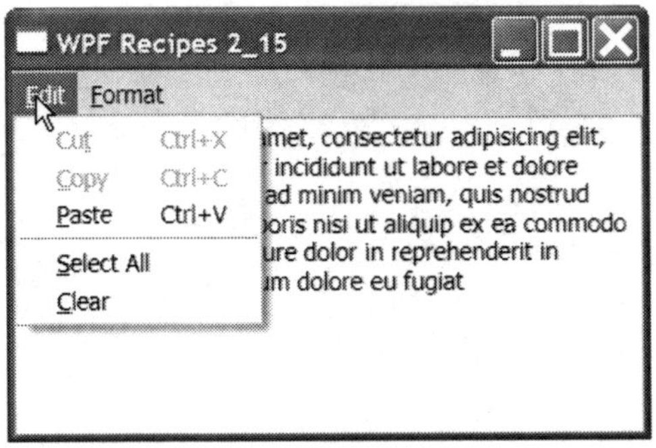

Figure 2-15. *Using a Menu to support editing of a TextBox*

2-16. Display a Toolbar

Problem

You need to display a Windows-style toolbar at the top of a form so that the user has visibility of, and quick access to, application functionality.

Solution

Place the UI elements you want the user to access in a System.Windows.Controls.ToolBar container. If you need multiple toolbars, place them in a System.Windows.Controls.ToolBarTray container to allow greater control over their position and organization.

How It Works

The ToolBar control allows you to quickly create Windows-style toolbars with little effort. All you need to do is define a ToolBar element and declare the controls you want to display on the toolbar within the ToolBar element body. You are not limited in placing the ToolBar at the top of the form or window, but you would typically put it in a System.Windows.Controls.DockPanel (discussed in recipe 2-4) and dock it to the top edge of the panel.

The ToolBar control handles most of the functionality you would want to emulate a traditional Windows-style toolbar, including overriding the styles of many common control types to make them look appropriate for display within a toolbar. For example, System.Windows.Controls. Button controls look more like menu items, and System.Windows.Controls.RadioButton controls behave like toggle buttons.

The Toolbar control also handles the overflow of items if the window is too small to display everything defined in the ToolBar. The toolbar provides a drop-down menu that gives temporary access to the items that do not fit in the main window.

If you have multiple ToolBar objects, wrap them in a ToolBarTray container. A ToolBarTray provides special functionality for managing ToolBar controls over simply placing them in a standard layout panel. By default, the ToolBarTray displays each menu in a single line in the order you define them. But you can provide a zero-based integer index for each ToolBar object using the ToolBar.Rank property to define the row on which you want the ToolBarTray to display each ToolBar.

The Code

The following XAML uses two ToolBar objects organized in a ToolBarTray container to provide access to the controls necessary for a user to edit and format the text in a System.Windows. Controls.RichTextBox. You can see the sample running in Figure 2-16, which shows the ToolBar overflow area open to reveal the buttons that are not able to fit within the available window space.

■**Note** The example uses binding and built-in command types. Chapter 4 contains more information about data binding and Chapter 5 contains more information about commands.

```xml
<Window x:Class="Recipe_02_16.Window1"
    xmlns="http://schemas.microsoft.com/winfx/2006/xaml/presentation"
    xmlns:x="http://schemas.microsoft.com/winfx/2006/xaml"
    Title="WPF Recipes 2_16" Height="200" Width="300">
    <DockPanel FocusManager.FocusedElement="{Binding ElementName=rtbTextBox}"
            LastChildFill="True">
        <ToolBarTray DockPanel.Dock="Top">
            <ToolBar Band="0">
                <Button Command="ApplicationCommands.Cut" Content="Cut" />
                <Button Command="ApplicationCommands.Copy" Content="Copy" />
                <Button Command="ApplicationCommands.Paste" Content="Paste" />
            </ToolBar>
            <ToolBar Band="1">
                <TextBlock Text="Font Size" VerticalAlignment="Center" />
                <ComboBox Name="cbxFontSize">
                    <ComboBoxItem Content="12" IsSelected="True" Margin="2" />
                    <ComboBoxItem Content="14" Margin="2" />
                    <ComboBoxItem Content="16" Margin="2" />
```

```
                        </ComboBox>
                        <Separator Margin="5"/>
                        <RadioButton Command="EditingCommands.AlignLeft" Content="Left"
                                     IsChecked="True"/>
                        <RadioButton Command="EditingCommands.AlignCenter"
                                     Content="Center" />
                        <RadioButton Command="EditingCommands.AlignRight"
                                     Content="Right" />
                        <Separator Margin="5"/>
                        <Button Command="EditingCommands.ToggleBold"
                                Content="Bold" />
                        <Button Command="EditingCommands.ToggleItalic"
                                Content="Italic" />
                        <Button Command="EditingCommands.ToggleUnderline"
                                Content="Underline" />
                    </ToolBar>
                </ToolBarTray>
                <RichTextBox Name="rtbTextBox">
                    <FlowDocument>
                        <Paragraph FontSize="{Binding ElementName=cbxFontSize,
                            Path=SelectedItem.Content}">
                            Lorem ipsum dolor sit amet, consectetuer adipiscing elit,
                            sed diam nonummy nibh euismod tincidunt ut laoreet dolore
                            magna aliquam erat volutpat.
                        </Paragraph>
                    </FlowDocument>
                </RichTextBox>
            </DockPanel>
        </Window>
```

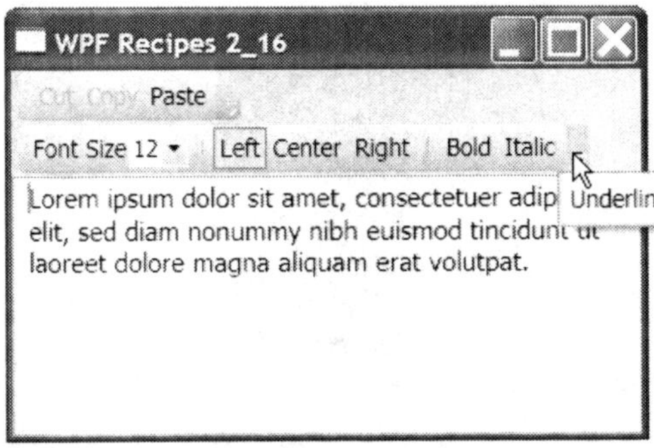

Figure 2-16. *Using ToolBar objects to support editing of a RichTextBox*

2-17. Display a Status Bar

Problem

You need to display a Windows-style status bar at the bottom of a form.

Solution

Place the UI elements you want to display in a System.Windows.Controls.Primitives.StatusBar container.

How It Works

To implement a Windows-style status bar, declare a StatusBar element, and place the UI elements you want to appear on the status bar within the StatusBar element. You are not limited to placing the StatusBar at the bottom of the form or window, but you would typically put it in a DockPanel (discussed in recipe 2-4) and dock it to the bottom edge of the panel.

The StatusBar, unlike the System.Windows.Controls.ToolBar container (described in recipe 2-16), is intended predominantly to display data and is not for user interaction. As such, the StatusBar container is far less capable of styling other controls to fit them into the traditional StatusBar look and feel.

The Code

The following XAML demonstrates how to use a StatusBar control to present a set of UI elements to the user. The example uses a DockPanel to position the StatusBar across the bottom of the window. In the example, the controls in the StatusBar allow the user to manipulate the size and position of the text in a System.Windows.Controls.RichTextBox (see Figure 2-17).

Note The example uses binding and built-in command types. Chapter 4 contains more information about data binding and Chapter 5 contains more information about commands.

```
<Window x:Class="Recipe_02_17.Window1"
    xmlns="http://schemas.microsoft.com/winfx/2006/xaml/presentation"
    xmlns:x="http://schemas.microsoft.com/winfx/2006/xaml"
    Title="WPF Recipes 2_17" Height="150" Width="300">
    <DockPanel LastChildFill="True">
        <StatusBar DockPanel.Dock="Bottom">
            <TextBlock  Text="Font size: " />
                <ComboBox Name="cbxFontSize" >
                    <ComboBoxItem Content="12" IsSelected="True" Margin="2" />
                    <ComboBoxItem Content="14" Margin="2" />
                    <ComboBoxItem Content="16" Margin="2" />
                </ComboBox>
```

```
                    <Separator Margin="5"/>
                    <RadioButton Command="EditingCommands.AlignLeft"
                                 CommandTarget="{Binding ElementName=rtbTextBox}"
                                 Content="Left" IsChecked="True"/>
                    <RadioButton Command="EditingCommands.AlignCenter"
                                 CommandTarget="{Binding ElementName=rtbTextBox}"
                                 Content="Center" />
                    <RadioButton Command="EditingCommands.AlignRight"
                                 CommandTarget="{Binding ElementName=rtbTextBox}"
                                 Content="Right" />
            </StatusBar>
            <RichTextBox Name="rtbTextBox">
                <FlowDocument>
                    <Paragraph FontSize="{Binding ElementName=cbxFontSize,
                        Path=SelectedItem.Content}">
                        Lorem ipsum dolor sit amet, consectetuer adipiscing elit,
                        sed diam nonummy nibh euismod tincidunt ut laoreet dolore
                        magna aliquam erat volutpat.
                    </Paragraph>
                </FlowDocument>
            </RichTextBox>
        </DockPanel>
</Window>
```

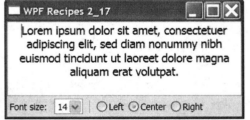

Figure 2-17. *Using a StatusBar to display UI elements*

2-18. Control the Size of UI Elements in a Form

Problem

You need fine-grained control over the size of UI elements on a form but the flexibility to create dynamically user interfaces.

Solution

When required, use the Height and Width properties inherited from System.Windows. FrameworkElement to explicitly set the dimensions of a UI element. However, to give the UI element's container more flexibility in laying out its content and better support dynamic resizing, use the MinHeight, MinWidth, MaxHeight, and MaxWidth properties (also inherited from FrameworkElement) to define the minimum and maximum dimensions for the UI element. Use the Margin property to define the amount of space between elements.

How It Works

The layout of UI elements is determined by the type and configuration of the panel in which they are placed. But the panel's layout logic is driven by the demands (often expressed using attached properties) of the elements it contains. Some panels allow UI elements to specify the order in which they appear, the panel edge or cell on which they are placed, or even the exact coordinates where the element should be positioned (see recipes 2-2 through 2-6 for examples of using various types of panels).

The size of each UI element is a major factor in the ability of a panel to lay out the elements it contains. You can use the Height and Width properties of a UI element to explicitly set its dimensions. You express the Height and Width as a number and an optional unit identifier. By default, the unit is assumed to be px (pixels) but can also be in (inches), cm (centimeters), or pt (points). However, setting explicit dimensions for individual controls does not facilitate the creation of flexible resizable interfaces because it often constrains the options available to the control's containing panel.

Table 2-5 describes a set of UI element properties (less explicit than Height and Width) that give you control over the dimensions of UI elements while still retaining a high level of flexibility to allow for resizable user interfaces. All of these properties with the exception of HorizontalAlignment and VerticalAlignment take numbers with optional unit identifiers like the Height and Width properties just discussed.

Table 2-5. *Properties for Controlling the Size of a UI Element*

Value	Description
HorizontalAlignment	Defines how a panel positions a UI element when the panel has extra horizontal space beyond the current width of the UI element. You can specify one of Left, Center, Right, or Stretch. If you specify Stretch, the container will stretch the UI element to fill all available horizontal space.
VerticalAlignment	Defines how a panel positions a UI element when the panel has extra vertical space beyond the current height of the UI element. You can specify one of Top, Center, Bottom, or Stretch. If you specify Stretch, the container will stretch the UI element to fill all available vertical space.
Margin	Defines the amount of space to leave empty around a UI element. You can specify a single value that is applied to all sides or specify a different value for each side using a comma-separated list—the order is left, top, right, and then bottom.
MinWidth, MinHeight	Sets the minimum width or height of a UI element. The container will never scale the UI element smaller than this, although it may crop the UI element depending on the container.
MaxWidth, MaxHeight	Sets the maximum width or height of a UI element. The container will never scale the UI element larger than this, even if the HorizontalAlignment or VerticalAlignment properties of the UI element are set to Stretch.

The Code

The following XAML demonstrates how to apply the properties discussed in this recipe to control the dimensions of a set of System.Windows.Controls.Button controls. Figure 2-18 shows the sample when run in an expanded and a compressed state. The figure comes with some indication as to how the different buttons respond when housed in a compressed System.Windows.Controls.StackPanel (see recipe 2-2).

```xml
<Window x:Class="Recipe_02_18.Window1"
    xmlns="http://schemas.microsoft.com/winfx/2006/xaml/presentation"
    xmlns:x="http://schemas.microsoft.com/winfx/2006/xaml"
    Title="WPF Recipes 2_18" Height="300" Width="400">
    <StackPanel Margin="5" Orientation="Vertical">
        <Button Content="Button _A" Margin="2" />
        <Button Content="Button _B" HorizontalAlignment="Left" />
        <Button Content="Button _C" HorizontalAlignment="Center" />
        <Button Content="Button _D" HorizontalAlignment="Right" />
        <Button Content="Button _E" Height="40" Margin="2" />
        <Button Content="Button _F" Width="80" Margin="2" />
        <Button Content="Button _G" MinHeight="30" Margin="2" />
        <Button Content="Button _H" MinWidth="120" Margin="10,5,5,10" />
        <Button Content="Button _I" MaxWidth="200" Margin="2" />
    </StackPanel>
</Window>
```

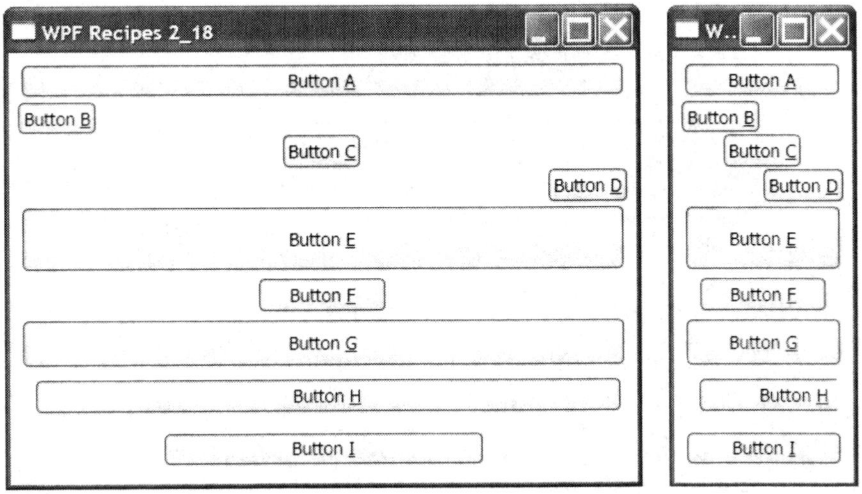

Figure 2-18. *Using flexible sizing for UI elements*

2-19. Define the Tab Order of UI Elements in a Form

Problem

You need to define the order in which a user tabs through a set of controls.

Solution

Specify the tab order using a zero-based index, and assign the index value to the TabIndex property (inherited from System.Window.Controls.Control) of each control.

How It Works

The Control class defines the TabIndex property as the means by which WPF determines the order in which controls receive focus when a user presses the Tab key. When the user presses Tab, WPF will give focus to the next control that has a TabIndex equal to or higher than the TabIndex of the control with the current focus.

The Code

The following XAML shows how to use the TabIndex property to control the tab order through a set of System.Windows.Controls.Button controls:

```
<Window x:Class="Recipe_02_19.Window1"
    xmlns="http://schemas.microsoft.com/winfx/2006/xaml/presentation"
    xmlns:x="http://schemas.microsoft.com/winfx/2006/xaml"
    Title="WPF Recipe 2_19" Height="200" Width="300">
    <StackPanel>
        <Button Content="Button _A (1st tab)" TabIndex="0" Margin="2" />
        <Button Content="Button _B (4th tab)" TabIndex="3" Margin="2" />
        <Button Content="Button _C (2nd tab)" TabIndex="1" Margin="2" />
        <Button Content="Button _D (5th tab)" TabIndex="4" Margin="2" />
        <Button Content="Button _E (3rd tab)" TabIndex="1" Margin="2" />
        <Button Content="Button _F (6th tab)" TabIndex="5" Margin="2" />
    </StackPanel>
</Window>
```

CHAPTER 3

■■■

Using Standard Controls

WPF makes it relatively easy for the average software developer to create rich and exciting user interfaces that integrate print-quality text, 2D and 3D graphics, animation, and multimedia content. However, for the foreseeable future, most business applications will still require a user interface constructed predominantly from the everyday Windows-style controls that users have become familiar with over the past 15 years.

Note For those readers coming from a Windows Forms background, it will help to be able to know which WPF control is equivalent to each of the familiar Windows Forms controls. The .NET Framework documentation summarizes the equivalent controls at http://msdn2.microsoft.com/en-us/library/ms750559.aspx.

WPF provides a rich set of highly functional controls in the System.Windows.Controls namespace that meet the everyday needs of the business application developer. The recipes in this chapter focus on how to use these standard controls and describe how to do the following:

- Display text (recipes 3-1 and 3-2)

- Display static images (recipe 3-3)

- Handle text input by a user (recipes 3-4, 3-5, and 3-6)

- Validate and spell check text input by a user (recipes 3-7 and 3-8)

- Handle and generate button clicks and set a default button for a form (recipes 3-9, 3-10, and 3-11)

- Provide quick keyboard access to text buttons and boxes (recipes 3-12 and 3-13)

- Get user input from a slider (recipe 3-14)

- Display a context menu on a control (recipe 3-15)

- Display and control the display properties of tool tips (recipes 3-16, 3-17, and 3-18)

- Display and allow the user to select items from a set of radio buttons (recipe 3-19)

- Display and allow the user to select items from a set of check boxes (recipe 3-20)

- Display and allow the user to select items from a hierarchical tree (recipe 3-21)

- Display and allow the user to select items from a list (recipe 3-22)

- Change the content of a list dynamically (recipe 3-23)

- Display and allow the user to select items from a combo box (recipe 3-24)

- Display any control rotated from its default orientation (recipe 3-25)

Note This chapter focuses on how to use the standard capabilities of the WPF controls found in the `System.Windows.Controls` namespace. All of these controls are highly customizable in terms of behavior and appearance; these advanced features will be discussed in Chapter 5 and Chapter 6.

3-1. Display Control Content Surrounded by Braces

Problem

You need to display text surrounded by braces (curly brackets) as the content of a control, as in {surrounded by braces}. Curly braces are used to denote markup extensions in XAML and are not normally valid in control content.

Solution

Place the content within the XAML element (where braces are permitted), or if you must use a content attribute, prefix the text with a pair of braces ({}).

How It Works

In XAML, braces identify the use of markup extension syntax within XAML control attributes. WPF will attempt to process any such string with a markup extension handler. On the occasions you need to surround the text within a control's content with braces, you must signal to WPF that the content is not markup extension syntax. You do this by prefixing the text with a pair of braces.

The Code

The following XAML demonstrates a `Button`, `RadioButton`, `TextBox`, and `TextBlock` (all from the `System.Windows.Controls` namespace) that display content surrounded by braces (see Figure 3-1):

```xml
<Window x:Class="Recipe_03_01.Window1"
    xmlns="http://schemas.microsoft.com/winfx/2006/xaml/presentation"
    xmlns:x="http://schemas.microsoft.com/winfx/2006/xaml"
    Title="WPF Recipes 3_01" Height="200" Width="250">
    <StackPanel>
        <Button Content="{}{A Button}" Margin="10"
            Name="button1" Width="75" />
        <RadioButton Content="{}{A RadioButton}"
            HorizontalAlignment="Center" Margin="10" />
        <TextBox Text="{}{A TextBox}" HorizontalAlignment="Center"
            Margin="10" />
        <TextBlock HorizontalAlignment="Center" Margin="10"
            Text="{}{A TextBlock}" />
    </StackPanel>
</Window>
```

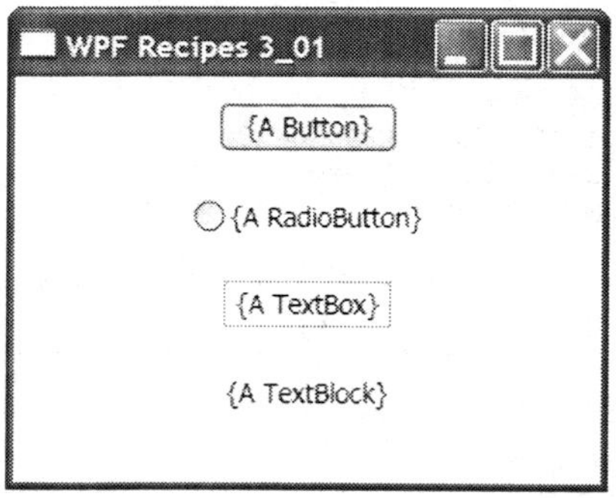

Figure 3-1. *Control content surrounded by braces*

3-2. Display Simple Text

Problem

You need to display small amounts of simple text.

Solution

Use the System.Windows.Controls.TextBlock control.

How It Works

The TextBlock control provides a lightweight and easy-to-use way to include small amounts (typically up to one paragraph) of flow content in your UI. The properties of the TextBlock provide extensive control over the formatting of the contained text. Table 3-1 lists some of the more commonly used properties of the TextBlock control.

Table 3-1. *Commonly Used Properties of the TextBlock Control*

Property	Description
FontFamily	The name of the font family to apply to the text, for example, Tahoma or Arial. You can specify multiple font names separated by commas. The first font is the primary font, and the others are fallback fonts used only if the preceding fonts are not available.
FontSize	The size of the text expressed as a number and an optional unit identifier. By default, the unit is assumed to be px (pixels) but can also be in (inches), cm (centimeters), or pt (points).
FontStyle	The style to apply to the text; available styles include Italic, Normal, and Oblique (generally, oblique fonts are optically skewed but lack the individual letter forms and cursive accoutrements of true italics). See the System.Windows.FontStyles class for more information.
FontWeight	The weight to apply to the text; some of the available weights are Thin, Light, Normal, Medium, Bold, Heavy, and UltraBlack. See the System.Windows.FontWeight class for more information.
TextAlignment	The alignment of the text within the TextBlock control. Possible values are Left, Right, Center, and Justify.
TextDecoration	One or more comma-separated decoration styles to apply to the text. Possible values are Overline, Strikethrough, Baseline, and Underline. See the System.Windows.TextDecorations class for more information.
TextWrapping	The wrapping behavior of text within the TextBlock control. Possible values are WrapWithOverflow, NoWrap, and Wrap.

The Code

The following XAML demonstrates how to create the formatted TextBlock control shown in Figure 3-2:

```
<Window x:Class="Recipe_03_02.Window1"
    xmlns="http://schemas.microsoft.com/winfx/2006/xaml/presentation"
    xmlns:x="http://schemas.microsoft.com/winfx/2006/xaml"
    Title="WPF Recipes 3_02" Height="100" Width="300">
    <Grid>
        <TextBlock FontFamily="Tahoma, Arial"
                   FontSize="20"
                   FontStyle="Italic"
                   FontWeight="Light"
                   HorizontalAlignment="Center"
                   TextAlignment="Right"
                   TextDecorations="Underline, Strikethrough"
                   TextWrapping="Wrap"
                   VerticalAlignment="Center">
            The quick brown fox jumped over the lazy brown dog.
        </TextBlock>
    </Grid>
</Window>
```

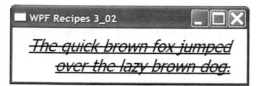

Figure 3-2. *A formatted TextBlock control*

3-3. Display a Static Image

Problem

You need to display a simple static (nonanimated) image on a form.

Solution

Use the `Sytem.Windows.Controls.Image` control, and specify the path to the image you want to
display in the `Image.Source` property.

How It Works

The `Image` control provides an easy way to display static images and supports the following
image types:

- `.bmp`
- `.gif`
- `.ico`
- `.jpg`
- `.png`
- `.wdp`
- `.tiff`

To control the size of the image, you can use the `Width` or `Height` property of the `Image` control.
You specify the size of the image as a number with an optional unit identifier. By default, the
unit is assumed to be `px` (pixels) but can also be `in` (inches), `cm` (centimeters), or `pt` (points).

You should only ever set one, and not both, of `Width` or `Heigth`. WPF will determine the
appropriate size for the unspecified property in order to keep the aspect ratio of the image
unchanged. If you specify both properties, the image will likely appear stretched or squashed.

As a standard control, the `Image` class inherits many useful features from its parent classes,
making it straightforward to control things such as the position, opacity, and tool tip associated
with your image.

The Code

The following XAML demonstrates how to size and place images on a form using the Image
control. It also demonstrates how easy it is to associate a tool tip (discussed in recipe 3-16) and
an opacity setting with an image (see Figure 3-3).

```xaml
<Window x:Class="Recipe_03_03.Window1"
    xmlns="http://schemas.microsoft.com/winfx/2006/xaml/presentation"
    xmlns:x="http://schemas.microsoft.com/winfx/2006/xaml"
    Title="WPF Recipes 3_03" Height="300" Width="400">
    <StackPanel Orientation="Horizontal">
        <Image Margin="10" ToolTip="Bottom Image" Width="100"
                Source="ApressLogo.gif" />
        <Image Margin="-30" Opacity=".7" Source="ApressLogo.gif"
                ToolTip="Middle Image" Width="150" />
        <Image Source="ApressLogo.gif" ToolTip="Top Image"
                VerticalAlignment="Top" Width="150" />
    </StackPanel>
</Window>
```

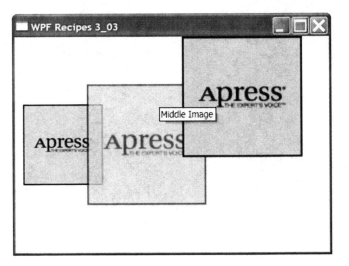

Figure 3-3. *Displaying images using the Image control*

3-4. Get Simple Text Input from a User

Problem

You need a simple way to allow a user to enter text.

Solution

Use the System.Windows.Controls.TextBox control.

How It Works

The easiest control to use for getting text input from a user is the TextBox control. The TextBox control supports only simple text formatting , so if you need more complex formatting, you should use the System.Windows.Controls.RichTextBox control (discussed in recipe 3-5).

Despite its limitations, the TextBox is a highly functional control that supports features such as multiline text entry, word wrap, scrolling, text selection, text alignment, cut/copy/paste, and drag and drop. Table 3-2 summarizes some of the more commonly used members of the TextBox control.

Table 3-2. *Commonly Used Members of the TextBox Control*

Member	Summary
Properties	
AcceptsReturn	Controls whether the TextBox allows multiline text entry by controlling what happens when the user presses the Enter key. If set to False, the TextBox ignores the Enter key, resulting in a TextBox that takes only a single line of input.
AcceptsTab	Controls whether the user can insert Tab characters in the TextBox content or whether pressing Tab takes the user out of the TextBox and moves to the next control marked as a tab stop.
CaretIndex	Gets or sets the current insertion position index of the TextBox.
IsReadOnly	Controls whether the TextBox is read-only or whether the user can also edit the content of the TextBox. Even if IsReadOnly is set to True, you can still programmatically change the content of the TextBox.
LineCount	Gets the total number of lines in the TextBox.
MaxLength	Controls the maximum number of characters that the user can type into the TextBox. The default value of 0 (zero) means there is no limit.
SelectedText	Gets or sets the currently selected TextBox content.
Text	Gets or sets the content of the TextBox. Alternatively, place the desired text within the body of the XAML TextBox element.
TextAlignment	Controls the alignment of text in the TextBox. Possible values are Left, Right, Center, and Justify.
TextWrapping	Controls the word wrapping behavior of text in the TextBox. Possible values are WrapWithOverflow, NoWrap, and Wrap.
Methods	
AppendText	Appends text to the existing content of the TextBox.
Clear	Clears all the contents of the TextBox.
Copy	Copies the currently selected TextBox content to the clipboard.
Cut	Cuts the currently selected TextBox content and places it in the clipboard.
Paste	Pastes the current content of the clipboard over the currently selected TextBox content or inserts it at the cursor position if nothing is selected.
Select	Selects a specified range of text in the TextBox control.

Table 3-2. *Commonly Used Members of the TextBox Control (Continued)*

Member	Summary
SelectAll	Selects the entire content of the TextBox control.
Undo	Undoes the most recent undoable action on the TextBox control.
Event	
TextChanged	The event fired when the text in a TextBox changes.

Note The TextBox is not a lightweight control, containing anywhere from 10 to 30 individual visual elements depending on its configuration. This can become a performance problem if you try to display a large number of TextBox controls. If you only need to display and not edit text, you should use a System.Windows. Controls.TextBlock control (see recipe 3-2).

The Code

The following XAML demonstrates how to use a TextBox control that supports multiline input with word wrap and vertical scrolling. The buttons provide simple demonstrations of how to apply some of the functionality listed in Table 3-2.

```xml
<Window x:Class="Recipe_03_04.Window1"
    xmlns="http://schemas.microsoft.com/winfx/2006/xaml/presentation"
    xmlns:x="http://schemas.microsoft.com/winfx/2006/xaml"
    Title="WPF Recipes 3_04" Height="300" Width="300">
    <StackPanel>
        <TextBox AcceptsReturn="True" Height="100" IsReadOnly="True"
                Name="textBox1" TextAlignment="Left" TextWrapping="Wrap"
                VerticalScrollBarVisibility="Auto">
            Default starting text.
        </TextBox>
        <WrapPanel Margin="10">
            <Button Margin="5" Name="textButton" Width="75"
                    Click="TextButton_Click">Set Text</Button>
            <Button Margin="5" Name="selectAllButton" Width="75"
                    Click="SelectAllButton_Click">Select All</Button>
            <Button Margin="5" Name="clearButton" Width="75"
                    Click="ClearButton_Click">Clear</Button>
            <Button Margin="5" Name="prependButton" Width="75"
                    Click="PrependButton_Click">Prepend</Button>
            <Button Margin="5" Name="insertButton" Width="75"
                    Click="InsertButton_Click">Insert</Button>
```

```xml
                <Button Margin="5" Name="appendButton" Width="75"
                        Click="AppendButton_Click">Append</Button>
                <Button Margin="5" Name="cutButton" Width="75"
                        Click="CutButton_Click">Cut</Button>
                <Button Margin="5" Name="pasteButton" Width="75"
                        Click="PasteButton_Click">Paste</Button>
                <Button Margin="5" Name="undoButton" Width="75"
                        Click="UndoButton_Click">Undo</Button>
            </WrapPanel>
            <Grid>
                <Grid.ColumnDefinitions>
                    <ColumnDefinition/>
                    <ColumnDefinition/>
                </Grid.ColumnDefinitions>
                <RadioButton Checked="EditableChecked" Grid.Column="0"
                             HorizontalAlignment="Center" IsChecked="True"
                             Margin="5" Name="editableRadioButton" >
                    Editable</RadioButton>
                <RadioButton Checked="EditableChecked" Grid.Column="1"
                             HorizontalAlignment="Center" Margin="5"
                             Name="readonlyRadioButton">
                    Read Only</RadioButton>
            </Grid>
            <Grid>
                <Grid.ColumnDefinitions>
                    <ColumnDefinition/>
                    <ColumnDefinition/>
                    <ColumnDefinition/>
                </Grid.ColumnDefinitions>
                <RadioButton Checked="AlignmentChecked" Grid.Column="0"
                             HorizontalAlignment="Center" IsChecked="True"
                             Margin="5" Name="leftAlignRadioButton">
                    Left</RadioButton>
                <RadioButton Checked="AlignmentChecked" Grid.Column="1"
                             HorizontalAlignment="Center" Margin="5"
                             Name="centerAlignRadioButton">
                    Center</RadioButton>
                <RadioButton Checked="AlignmentChecked" Grid.Column="2"
                             HorizontalAlignment="Center" Margin="5"
                             Name="rightAlignRadioButton">
                    Right</RadioButton>
            </Grid>
        </StackPanel>
</Window>
```

The following code-behind handles the events fired by the buttons and radio buttons:

```
using System.Windows;
using System.Windows.Controls;

namespace Recipe_03_04
{
    /// <summary>
    /// Interaction logic for Window1.xaml
    /// </summary>
    public partial class Window1 : Window
    {
        public Window1()
        {
            InitializeComponent();
        }

        // Handles the checking of the Text Alignment RadioButtons.
        private void AlignmentChecked(object sender, RoutedEventArgs e)
        {
            RadioButton button = e.OriginalSource as RadioButton;

            if (e.OriginalSource == leftAlignRadioButton)
            {
                textBox1.TextAlignment = TextAlignment.Left;
            }
            else if (e.OriginalSource == centerAlignRadioButton)
            {
                textBox1.TextAlignment = TextAlignment.Center;
            }
            else if (e.OriginalSource == rightAlignRadioButton)
            {
                textBox1.TextAlignment = TextAlignment.Right;
            }

            textBox1.Focus();
        }

        // Handles the click of the Append button. Adds text to the end
        // of the TextBox content.
        private void AppendButton_Click(object sender, RoutedEventArgs e)
        {
            textBox1.AppendText(" *** appended text ***");
        }
```

```csharp
// Handles the click of the Clear button. Clears all content from
// the TextBox.
private void ClearButton_Click(object sender, RoutedEventArgs e)
{
    textBox1.Clear();
}


// Handles the click of the Cut button. Cuts the currently
// selected text and places it in the clipboard.
private void CutButton_Click(object sender, RoutedEventArgs e)
{
    if (textBox1.SelectionLength == 0)
    {
        MessageBox.Show("Select text to cut first.", Title);
    }
    else
    {
        MessageBox.Show("Cut: " + textBox1.SelectedText, Title);

        textBox1.Cut();
    }
}


// Handles the checking of the Editable / ReadOnly RadioButtons.
private void EditableChecked(object sender, RoutedEventArgs e)
{
    RadioButton button = e.OriginalSource as RadioButton;

    if (e.OriginalSource == editableRadioButton)
    {
        textBox1.IsReadOnly = false;
    }
    else if (e.OriginalSource == readonlyRadioButton)
    {
        textBox1.IsReadOnly = true;
    }

    textBox1.Focus();
}

// Handles the click of the Insert button. Inserts text into
// the TextBox at the current cursor location.
```

```csharp
        private void InsertButton_Click(object sender, RoutedEventArgs e)
        {
            textBox1.Text = textBox1.Text.Insert(
                textBox1.CaretIndex, " *** inserted text *** ");
        }

        // Handles the click of the Paste button. Pastes the current
        // content of the clipboard into the TextBox at the current
        // cursor location.
        private void PasteButton_Click(object sender, RoutedEventArgs e)
        {
            textBox1.Paste();
        }

        // Handles the click of the Prepend button. Adds text to the start
        // of the TextBox content.
        private void PrependButton_Click(object sender, RoutedEventArgs e)
        {
            textBox1.Text =
                textBox1.Text.Insert(0, "*** Prepended text *** ");
        }

        // Handles the click of the Select All button. Selects all the
        // content in the TextBox.
        private void SelectAllButton_Click(object sender, RoutedEventArgs e)
        {
            textBox1.SelectAll();

            // Set the focus on the TextBox to make the selection visible.
            textBox1.Focus();
        }

        // Handles the click of the Set Text Button. Sets the content
        // of the TextBox to a default value.
        private void TextButton_Click(object sender, RoutedEventArgs e)
        {
            textBox1.Text = "Replace default text with initial text value";
        }

        // Handles the click of the Undo Button. Undoes the last undoable
        // event.
        private void UndoButton_Click(object sender, RoutedEventArgs e)
        {
            textBox1.Undo();
        }
    }
}
```

3-5. Get Rich Text Input from a User

Problem

You need to allow the user to edit large amounts of text and give them fine-grained control over the formatting of text they enter.

Solution

Use the `System.Windows.Controls.RichTextBox` control.

How It Works

The `RichTextBox` is a sophisticated and highly functional control designed to allow you to display and edit `System.Windows.Documents.FlowDocument` objects. The combination of the `RichTextBox` and `FlowDocument` objects provides the user with access to advanced document-editing capabilities that you do not get in a `System.Windows.Controls.TextBox` control. These features include mixed text formatting, hyphenation, tables, lists, paragraphs, and embedded images.

To populate the content of a `RichTextBox` statically, you include a `FlowDocument` element as the content of the `RichTextBox` XAML declaration. Within the `FlowDocument` element, you can define richly formatted content using elements of the flow document content model. Key structural elements of this content model include `Figure`, `Hyperlink`, `List`, `ListItem`, `Paragraph`, `Section`, and `Table`.

To populate the `RichTextBox` in code, you must work with a `FlowDocument` object directly. You can either create a new `FlowDocument` object or obtain one currently in a `RichTextBox` through the `RichTextBox.Document` property.

You manipulate the content of the `FlowDocument` by selecting portions of its content using a `System.Windows.Documents.TextSelection` object. The `TextSelection` object contains two properties, `Start` and `End`, which identify the beginning and end positions of the `FlowDocument` content you want to manipulate. Once you have a suitable `TextSelection` object, you can manipulate its content using the `TextSelection` members.

■Note Chapter 7 contains more recipes using the `RichTextBox` control and `FlowDocument` object. For detailed information about flow content, see the .NET Framework documentation at `http://msdn2.microsoft.com/en-us/library/ms753113.aspx`.

To simplify the manipulation of `FlowDocument` objects, the `RichTextBox` supports standard commands defined by the `ApplicationCommands` and `EditingCommands` classes from the `System.Windows.Input` namespace. The `RichTextBox` also supports standard key combinations to execute basic text-formatting operations such as applying bold, italic, and underline formats to text as well as cutting, copying, and pasting selected content. Table 3-3 summarizes some of the more commonly used members of the `RichTextBox` control.

Table 3-3. *Commonly Used Members of the RichTextBox Control*

Member	Summary
Properties	
AcceptsTab	Controls whether the user can insert Tab characters in the RichTextBox content or whether pressing Tab takes the user out of the RichTextBox and moves to the next control marked as a tab stop.
CaretPostion	Gets or sets the current insertion position index of the RichTextBox.
Document	Gets or sets the FlowDocument object that represents the RichTextBox content.
HorizontalScrollBarVisibility	Determines whether the RichTextBox displays a horizontal scrollbar.
IsReadOnly	Controls whether the RichTextBox is read-only or whether the user can also edit the content of the TextBox. Even if IsReadOnly is set to True, you can still programmatically change the content of the RichTextBox.
Selection	Gets a System.Windows.Documents.TextSelection object representing the current selection in the RichTextBox.
VerticalScrollBarVisibility	Determines whether the RichTextBox displays a vertical scrollbar.
Methods	
AppendText	Appends text to the existing content of the RichTextBox.
Copy	Copies the currently selected RichTextBox content to the clipboard.
Cut	Cuts the currently selected RichTextBox content and places it in the clipboard.
Paste	Pastes the current content of the clipboard over the currently selected RichTextBox content or inserts it at the cursor position if nothing is selected.
SelectAll	Selects the entire content of the RichTextBox control.
Undo	Undoes the most recent undoable action on the RichTextBox control.
Event	
TextChanged	The event fired when the text in a RichTextBox changes.

The Code

The following code provides a simple example of a RichTextBox used to edit a FlowDocument. The XAML defines a static FlowDocument that contains a variety of structural and formatting elements. The user interface provides a set of buttons to manipulate the RichTextBox content. The buttons rely on the application and editing command support provided by the RichTextBox control and use a style (discussed further in Chapter 6) to make the RichTextBox the target of the button's command.

```xml
<Window x:Class="Recipe_03_05.Window1"
    xmlns="http://schemas.microsoft.com/winfx/2006/xaml/presentation"
    xmlns:x="http://schemas.microsoft.com/winfx/2006/xaml"
    Title="WPF Recipes 3_05" Height="350" Width="500">
    <DockPanel>
        <StackPanel DockPanel.Dock="Top" Orientation="Horizontal">
            <StackPanel.Resources>
                <Style TargetType="{x:Type Button}">
                    <Setter Property="CommandTarget"
                            Value="{Binding ElementName=rtbTextBox1}" />
                </Style>
            </StackPanel.Resources>
            <Button Content="Clear" Name="btnClear" Click="btnClear_Click" />
            <Separator Margin="5"/>
            <Button Content="Cu_t" Command="ApplicationCommands.Cut" />
            <Button Content="_Copy" Command="ApplicationCommands.Copy" />
            <Button Content="_Paste" Command="ApplicationCommands.Paste" />
            <Separator Margin="5"/>
            <Button Content="_Undo" Command="ApplicationCommands.Undo" />
            <Button Content="_Redo" Command="ApplicationCommands.Redo" />
            <Separator Margin="5"/>
            <Button Content="_Bold" Command="EditingCommands.ToggleBold" />
            <Button Content="_Italic" Command="EditingCommands.ToggleItalic" />
            <Button Content="Underline"
                    Command="EditingCommands.ToggleUnderline" />
            <Separator Margin="5"/>
            <Button Content="_Right" Command="EditingCommands.AlignRight" />
            <Button Content="C_enter" Command="EditingCommands.AlignCenter" />
            <Button Content="_Left" Command="EditingCommands.AlignLeft" />
        </StackPanel>
        <RichTextBox DockPanel.Dock="Bottom" Name="rtbTextBox1"
                     HorizontalScrollBarVisibility="Visible"
                     VerticalScrollBarVisibility="Visible">
            <FlowDocument>
                <Paragraph FontSize="12">
                    Lorem ipsum dolor sit amet, consectetuer adipiscing elit,
                    sed diam nonummy nibh euismod tincidunt ut laoreet dolore
                    magna aliquam erat volutpat.
                </Paragraph>
                <Paragraph FontSize="15">
                    Ut wisi enim ad minim veniam, quis nostrud exerci tation
                    ullamcorper suscipit lobortis nisl ut aliquip ex ea
                    commodo consequat. Duis autem vel eum iriure.
                </Paragraph>

                <Paragraph FontSize="18">A List</Paragraph>
```

```
                    <List>
                        <ListItem>
                            <Paragraph>
                                <Bold>Bold List Item</Bold>
                            </Paragraph>
                        </ListItem>
                        <ListItem>
                            <Paragraph>
                                <Italic>Italic List Item</Italic>
                            </Paragraph>
                        </ListItem>
                        <ListItem>
                            <Paragraph>
                                <Underline>Underlined List Item</Underline>
                            </Paragraph>
                        </ListItem>
                    </List>
                </FlowDocument>
            </RichTextBox>
        </DockPanel>
</Window>
```

The following code-behind contains the event handler that handles the Clear button provided on the user interface defined earlier:

```
using System.Windows;

namespace Recipe_03_05
{
    /// <summary>
    /// Interaction logic for Window1.xaml
    /// </summary>
    public partial class Window1 : Window
    {
        public Window1()
        {
            InitializeComponent();
        }

        // Handles Clear Button click event.
        private void btnClear_Click(object sender, RoutedEventArgs e)
        {
            // Select all the text in the FlowDocument and cut it.
            rtbTextBox1.SelectAll();
            rtbTextBox1.Cut();
        }
    }
}
```

Figure 3-4 shows what the RichTextBox looks like when the example is first run.

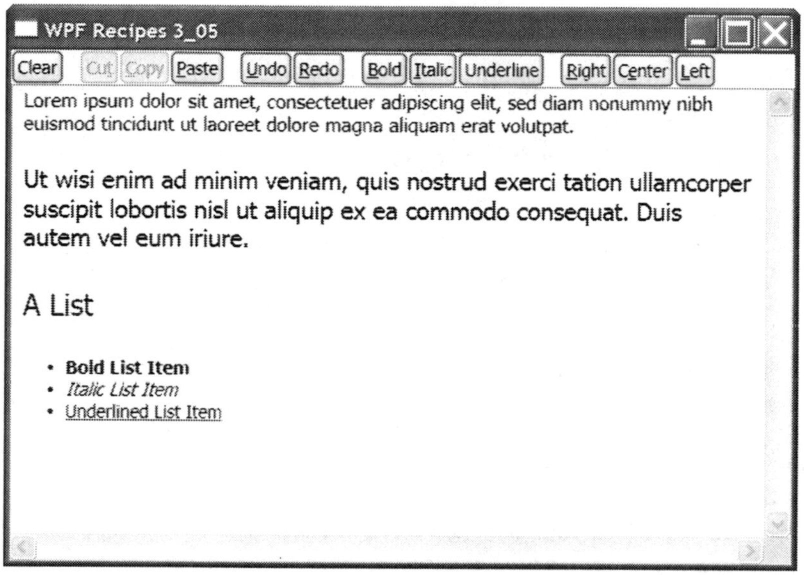

Figure 3-4. *Using a RichTextBox to edit a FlowDocument*

3-6. Load or Save the Content of a RichTextBox

Problem

You need to load the content of a System.Windows.Controls.RichTextBox from a file or save the current content to a file.

Solution

Load the content of the System.Windows.Documents.FlowDocument object contained in the RichTextBox.Document from a file using the XamlReader class. Save the content of the FlowDocument object using the XamlWriter class. Both the XamlReader and XamlWriter classes are members of the System.Windows.Markup namespace.

How It Works

The XamlReader and XamlWriter classes make it easy to serialize XAML to and from disk. Because you can represent a FlowDocument (the content model used within a RichTextBox) as XAML, the XamlReader and XamlWriter classes provide an excellent way to store and retrieve the content of a RichTextBox.

To load a FlowDocument stored in a XAML file into a RichTextBox, pass a System.IO. FileStream object representing the file to the static XamlReader.Load method. You must cast the returned System.Object to a FlowDocument and handle any formatting or casting errors that occur in the process. Once you have the FlowDocument, assign it to the Document property of the RichTextBox.

To write the FlowDocument content of a RichTextBox to a file, pass the FlowDocument from the RichTextBox.Document property and a FileStream object representing the destination file to the XamlWriter.Save method.

The Code

The following XAML displays a RichTextBox containing some default text along with the buttons necessary to create a new empty FlowDocument, open a FlowDocument, and save a FlowDocument:

```xml
<Window x:Class="Recipe_03_06.Window1"
    xmlns="http://schemas.microsoft.com/winfx/2006/xaml/presentation"
    xmlns:x="http://schemas.microsoft.com/winfx/2006/xaml"
    Title="WPF Recipes 3_06" Height="300" Width="300">
    <DockPanel>
        <StackPanel DockPanel.Dock="Top" Orientation="Horizontal">
            <Button Content="_New" Name="btnNew" Click="btnNew_Click" />
            <Button Content="_Open" Name="btnOpen" Click="btnOpen_Click" />
            <Button Content="_Save" Name="btnSave" Click="btnSave_Click" />
        </StackPanel>
        <RichTextBox DockPanel.Dock="Bottom" Name="rtbTextBox1"
                    HorizontalScrollBarVisibility="Visible"
                    VerticalScrollBarVisibility="Visible">
            <FlowDocument>
                <Paragraph>
                    Lorem ipsum dolor sit amet, consectetuer adipiscing elit,
                    sed diam nonummy nibh euismod tincidunt ut laoreet dolore
                    magna aliquam erat volutpat.
                </Paragraph>
                <Paragraph>
                    Ut wisi enim ad minim veniam, quis nostrud exerci tation
                    ullamcorper suscipit lobortis nisl ut aliquip ex ea
                    commodo consequat. Duis autem vel eum iriure.
                </Paragraph>
            </FlowDocument>
        </RichTextBox>
    </DockPanel>
</Window>
```

The following code-behind shows the event handlers for the New, Open, and Save buttons. The btnOpen_Click event handler uses the Microsoft.Win32.OpenFileDialog to provide a standard Windows dialog box to allow the user to select the file to open. Similarly, the btnSave_Click event handler uses the Microsoft.Win32.SaveFileDialog.

```csharp
using Microsoft.Win32;
using System;
using System.IO;
using System.Windows;
using System.Windows.Documents;
using System.Windows.Markup;
```

```
namespace Recipe_03_06
{
    /// <summary>
    /// Interaction logic for Window1.xaml
    /// </summary>
    public partial class Window1 : Window
    {
        private String currentFileName = String.Empty;

        public Window1()
        {
            InitializeComponent();
        }

        // Handles the Open Button Click event
        private void btnOpen_Click(object sender, RoutedEventArgs e)
        {
            // Use a standard OpenFileDialog to allow the user to
            // select the file to open.
            OpenFileDialog dialog = new OpenFileDialog();
            dialog.FileName = currentFileName;
            dialog.Filter = "XAML Files (*.xaml)|*.xaml";

            // Display the OpenFileDialog and read if the user
            // provides a file name.
            if (dialog.ShowDialog() == true)
            {
                // Remember the new file name.
                currentFileName = dialog.FileName;

                {
                    using (FileStream stream = File.Open(currentFileName,
                        FileMode.Open))
                    {
                        // TODO: Need logic to handle incorrect file format errors.
                        FlowDocument doc = XamlReader.Load(stream) as FlowDocument;

                        if (doc == null)
                        {
                            MessageBox.Show("Could not load document.", Title);
                        }
                        else
                        {
                            rtbTextBox1.Document = doc;
                        }
                    }
                }
```

```csharp
            }
        }

        // Handles the New Button Click event
        private void btnNew_Click(object sender, RoutedEventArgs e)
        {
            // Create a totally new FlowDocument for the RichTextBox.
            rtbTextBox1.Document = new FlowDocument();

            currentFileName = String.Empty;
        }

        // Handles the Save Button Click event
        private void btnSave_Click(object sender, RoutedEventArgs e)
        {
            // Use a standard SaveFileDialog to allow the user to
            // select the file to save.
            SaveFileDialog dialog = new SaveFileDialog();
            dialog.FileName = currentFileName;
            dialog.Filter = "XAML Files (*.xaml)|*.xaml";

            // Display the SaveFileDialog and save if the user
            // provides a file name.
            if (dialog.ShowDialog() == true)
            {
                // Remember the new file name.
                currentFileName = dialog.FileName;

                using (FileStream stream = File.Open(currentFileName,
                    FileMode.Create))
                {
                    XamlWriter.Save(rtbTextBox1.Document, stream);
                }
            }
        }
    }
}
```

3-7. Display a Password Entry Box

Problem

You need to allow the user to enter secret information (such as a password) and mask the characters entered so they cannot be read from the screen.

Solution

Use a System.Windows.Controls.PasswordBox control to get the user input.

How It Works

The PasswordBox control works like a simplified System.Windows.Controls.TextBox control. But for each character the user types, the PasswordBox control displays a placeholder symbol instead of the character entered. You can define the placeholder character by setting the PasswordChar property of the PasswordBox control; an asterisk (*) is the default.

In an extra effort to improve the security of the data entered by the user, the PasswordBox control stores its content internally in a System.Security.SecureString. This stores the string encrypted in memory, ensuring that if the memory is paged or written to disk as part of a memory dump, then the password remains secure. However, you can get the password from the PasswordBox via the Password property as a System.String, meaning you have to be very careful with the data if you want to maintain the same level of protection throughout your code.

The Code

The following example demonstrates how to use a PasswordBox to allow the user to enter a password, which it then displays when the user clicks the OK button (which is not very secure but demonstrates how to use the Password property). The example uses an exclamation mark as the password character.

```
<Window x:Class="Recipe_03_07.Window1"
    xmlns="http://schemas.microsoft.com/winfx/2006/xaml/presentation"
    xmlns:x="http://schemas.microsoft.com/winfx/2006/xaml"
    Title="WPF Recipes 3_07" Height="100" Width="300">
    <StackPanel Orientation="Horizontal">
        <TextBlock Margin="5" VerticalAlignment="Center">
            Enter Password:
        </TextBlock>
        <PasswordBox Name="passwordBox" PasswordChar="!"
                    VerticalAlignment="Center" Width="150" />
        <Button Content="OK" IsDefault="True" Margin="5" Name="button1"
                VerticalAlignment="Center" Click="button1_Click" />
    </StackPanel>
</Window>
```

The following code-behind handles the button click event:

```
using System.Windows;

namespace Recipe_03_07
{
    /// <summary>
    /// Interaction logic for Window1.xaml
    /// </summary>
    public partial class Window1 : Window
    {
        public Window1()
        {
            InitializeComponent();
        }

        // Handles the Button Click event
        private void button1_Click(object sender, RoutedEventArgs e)
        {
            MessageBox.Show("Password entered: " + passwordBox.Password,
                Title);
        }
    }
}
```

Figure 3-5 shows how the PasswordBox masks the user input with a selectable substitute character.

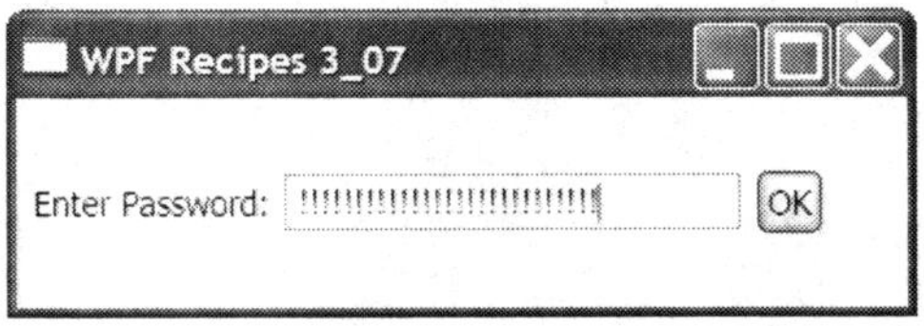

Figure 3-5. *Using the PasswordBox to mask user input*

3-8. Spell Check a TextBox or RichTextBox Control in Real Time

Problem

You need to do a spell check as the user enters text into a System.Windows.Controls.TextBox or System.Windows.Controls.RichTextBox control.

Solution

Enable spell checking on the TextBox or RichTextBox control by setting the attached property SpellCheck.IsEnabled to True.

How It Works

The System.Windows.Controls.SpellCheck class provides real-time spell-checking functionality for text-editing controls. When enabled on a TextBox or RichTextBox control, as the user types text into the control, any unrecognized words are underlined in red. If the user right-clicks a high-lighted word, they get a context menu, and they can select to replace the word from a set of suggested alternatives. The user can also choose to ignore the highlighted word, which will clear the highlighting of that word while the text entry control exists.

The SpellCheck control provides multilingual support. A TextBox control will use the language defined by the xml:lang attribute. For RichTextBox, the SpellCheck control determines which dictionary to use based on the current keyboard input language.

As of this writing, the SpellCheck control supports only US English (xml:lang="en-US"), UK English (xml:lang="en-GB"), French (xml:lang="fr-FR"), and German (xml:lang="de-DE"). You must have the appropriate language pack installed to enable multilingual dictionary support. Unfortunately, there is currently no way to create new dictionaries or to customize the content of the dictionaries provided.

The Code

The following XAML declares a TextBox with spell checking enabled:

```
<Window x:Class="Recipe_03_08.Window1"
    xmlns="http://schemas.microsoft.com/winfx/2006/xaml/presentation"
    xmlns:x="http://schemas.microsoft.com/winfx/2006/xaml"
    Title="WPF Recipes 3_08" Height="100" Width="300">
    <StackPanel>
        <TextBlock FontSize="14" FontWeight="Bold"
                    Text="A spell-checking TextBox:"/>
        <TextBox AcceptsReturn="True" AcceptsTab="True" FontSize="14"
                Margin="5" SpellCheck.IsEnabled="True" TextWrapping="Wrap">
            The qick red focks jumped over the lasy brown dog.
        </TextBox>
    </StackPanel>
</Window>
```

Figure 3-6 shows the spell-check-enabled TextBox from the previous example. It also shows the context menu displayed to allow the user to select suggested alternatives to the word identified as being misspelled.

Figure 3-6. *Spell-check-enabled TextBox*

3-9. Handle a Button Click

Problem

You need to display a button and take an action when the user clicks it.

Solution

Use the System.Windows.Controls.Button control, and handle its Click event in the code-behind.

How It Works

When the user clicks a Button control, WPF raises the Button control's Click event, which in turn invokes the method that is configured to handle the event. In XAML, the easiest way to register a method to handle a Click event is to specify the name of the handler method as the value of the Click attribute of the Button element.

Depending on what you are doing and the number of buttons you need to accommodate, you can create individual Click handler methods for each Button, or you can create a single method that determines which Button generated the Click event and takes the appropriate action.

To use the second approach, you can use the OriginalSource property of the System. Windows.RoutedEventArgs object that is passed to the Click event handler to determine which Button raised the event. The OriginalSource property contains a System.Object reference to the control that raised the event. You can compare the Object reference to see whether it is the same as a particular Button, or you can cast the Object reference to a Button and inspect its properties to determine which action to take.

■**Note** Chapter 12 contains recipes that provide more detail on the various mouse and keyboard input events and how to handle them appropriately.

The Code

The following example presents three Button controls. When the user clicks a Button, the example displays a System.Windows.MessageBox containing the name of the Button selected. This example casts the Object in the RoutedEventArgs.OriginalSource property to a Button to access the Name of the Button. Recipe 3-4 contains an example that directly compares a known Button control with the Object in the OriginalSource property.

```xml
<Window x:Class="Recipe_03_09.Window1"
    xmlns="http://schemas.microsoft.com/winfx/2006/xaml/presentation"
    xmlns:x="http://schemas.microsoft.com/winfx/2006/xaml"
    Title="WPF Recipes 3_09" Height="200" Width="200">
    <StackPanel>
        <Button Click="SharedButtonClickHandler" Height="23" Margin="10"
                Name="button1" Width="75">Button One</Button>
        <Button Click="SharedButtonClickHandler" Height="23" Margin="10"
                Name="button2" Width="75">Button Two</Button>
        <Button Click="SharedButtonClickHandler" Height="23" Margin="10"
                Name="button3" Width="75">Button Three</Button>
    </StackPanel>
</Window>
```

Here is the code-behind containing the shared Click event handler:

```csharp
using System.Windows;
using System.Windows.Controls;

namespace Recipe_03_09
{
    /// <summary>
    /// Interaction logic for Window1.xaml
    /// </summary>
    public partial class Window1 : Window
    {
        public Window1()
        {
            InitializeComponent();
        }
```

```
        private void SharedButtonClickHandler(object sender,
            RoutedEventArgs e)
        {
            Button source = e.OriginalSource as Button;

            if (source != null)
            {
                MessageBox.Show("You pressed " + source.Name, Title);
            }
        }
    }
}
```

3-10. Generate Click Events Repeatedly While a Button Is Clicked

Problem

You need to repeatedly generate click events for as long as a user "holds down" a button.

Solution

Use the System.Windows.Controls.Primitives.RepeatButton control.

How It Works

A standard System.Windows.Controls.Button control raises click events when the user clicks, releases, or hovers over the button (controlled by the Button.ClickMode property). The RepeatButton control provides an easy way to repeatedly raise Click events for the entire duration during which the user "holds down" a button.

Two properties control the timing of the Click events raised by the RepeatButton. The Delay property defines (in milliseconds) the delay from when the user first activates the RepeatButton to when it raises the first Click event. The default Delay value is the same as that of the keyboard delay obtained via the System.Windows.SystemParameters.KeyboardDelay property. The Interval property defines (in milliseconds) the time between subsequent Click events (as long as the user is still holding down the RepeatButton). The default Interval value is the same as that of the keyboard speed obtained via the System.Windows.SystemParameters.KeyboardSpeed property.

The Code

The following example uses two RepeatButton controls to move a slider. The first RepeatButton must be clicked and held to move the slider to the left. The second RepeatButton moves the slider to the right while the mouse hovers over the button.

```
<Window x:Class="Recipe_03_10.Window1"
    xmlns="http://schemas.microsoft.com/winfx/2006/xaml/presentation"
    xmlns:x="http://schemas.microsoft.com/winfx/2006/xaml"
    Title="WPF Recipes 3_10" Height="100" Width="200">
    <StackPanel>
        <Slider Name="slider" Maximum="100" Minimum="0" Value="50" />
        <StackPanel Orientation="Horizontal">
            <RepeatButton Click="SliderLeft_Click" Content="Click Me"
                        Height="23" Margin="10" Width="70"
                        ToolTip="Click to move slider left" />
            <RepeatButton Click="SliderRight_Click" ClickMode="Hover"
                        Content="Touch Me" Height="23" Margin="10"
                        ToolTip="Hover to move slider right" Width="70" />
        </StackPanel>
    </StackPanel>
</Window>
```

The following code-behind shows how to handle the Click events raised by the RepeatButton controls:

```
using System.Windows;

namespace Recipe_03_10
{
    /// <summary>
    /// Interaction logic for Window1.xaml
    /// </summary>
    public partial class Window1 : Window
    {
        public Window1()
        {
            InitializeComponent();
        }

        // Handles the SliderLeft Click event.
        private void SliderLeft_Click(object sender, RoutedEventArgs e)
        {
            // Reduce the value of the slider by one for each click.
            slider.Value -= 1;
        }

        // Handles the SliderRight Click event.
        private void SliderRight_Click(object sender, RoutedEventArgs e)
        {
            // Increase the value of the slider by one for each click.
            slider.Value += 1;
        }
    }
}
```

3-11. Set a Default Button

Problem

You need to identify one default button from a group of buttons that is "clicked" when the user presses Enter.

Solution

Set the IsDefault property of the System.Windows.Controls.Button control to True.

How It Works

It is standard behavior in a data entry form that the currently selected button is "clicked" when the user presses the Enter key. But when the user is active in a nonbutton control such as a text entry control or a list, users expect forms to have a default button that is "clicked" when they press Enter. Usually, this will be the OK, Next, Send, or Submit button.

By default, the currently selected Button (as you tab through them, for example) has a colored border identifying that it is the Button that will be clicked if you press Enter. By setting the IsDefault property of a Button control to True, you identify that Button as the default. Whenever the user is focused on a nonbutton control, the default Button will have a colored border to indicate that it will be "clicked" if the user presses Enter.

If you configure two default Button controls, when the user presses Enter, focus jumps to the first default Button in the tab order (making it active), but it is not clicked automatically.

The Code

The following example contains a System.Windows.Controls.TextBox and three Button controls. The button3 Button is configured as the default. As the default, btnThree is selected when the application first loads and is "clicked" when you press Enter while editing the TextBox.

```
<Window x:Class="Recipe_03_11.Window1"
    xmlns="http://schemas.microsoft.com/winfx/2006/xaml/presentation"
    xmlns:x="http://schemas.microsoft.com/winfx/2006/xaml"
    Title="WPF Recipes 3_11" Height="100" Width="300">
    <DockPanel>
        <TextBox DockPanel.Dock="Top" Margin="5">
            Button three is the default button.
        </TextBox>
        <StackPanel HorizontalAlignment="Center" DockPanel.Dock="Bottom"
                Orientation="Horizontal">
            <Button Click="SharedButtonClickHandler" Content="Button One"
                Margin="5" Name="btnOne" Width="75" />
            <Button Click="SharedButtonClickHandler" Content="Button Two"
                Margin="5" Name="btnTwo" Width="75" />
```

```
        <Button Click="SharedButtonClickHandler" Content="Button Three"
                IsDefault="True" Margin="5" Name="btnThree" />
    </StackPanel>
  </DockPanel>
</Window>
```

Here is the code-behind containing the shared Click event handler:

```
using System.Windows;
using System.Windows.Controls;

namespace Recipe_03_11
{
    /// <summary>
    /// Interaction logic for Window1.xaml
    /// </summary>
    public partial class Window1 : Window
    {
        public Window1()
        {
            InitializeComponent();
        }

        // Handles the click event for all buttons.
        private void SharedButtonClickHandler(object sender,
            RoutedEventArgs e)
        {
            Button source = e.OriginalSource as Button;

            if (source != null)
            {
                MessageBox.Show("You pressed " + source.Name, Title);
            }
        }
    }
}
```

Figure 3-7 shows how a default button is identified when the user is focused on a text entry control.

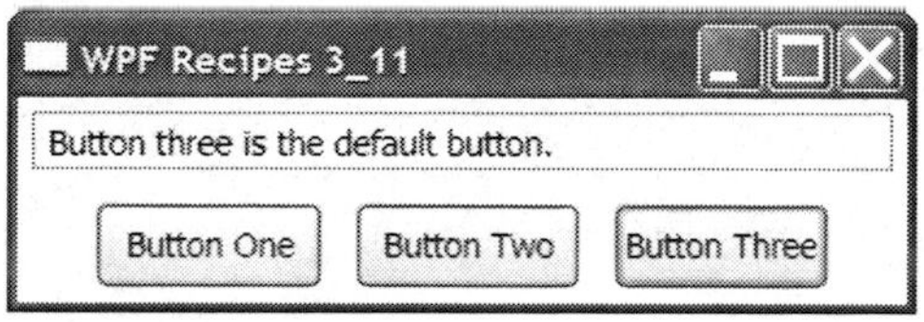

Figure 3-7. *Setting a default Button*

3-12. Provide Quick Keyboard Access to Text Boxes

Problem

You need to provide a keyboard shortcut so that users can jump to specific System.Windows. Controls.TextBox controls.

Solution

Create a label for the TextBox using the System.Windows.Controls.Label control. Define access keys within the content of the Label control by preceding the desired access character with an underscore (_). Then use the Target property of the Label control to identify the TextBox that is the intended target when the user presses the access key.

How It Works

The TextBox is one of the most common controls users want to access quickly from the keyboard (another being buttons, which are discussed in recipe 3-13). However, the TextBox itself has no constant text in which you can embed an access key. Using a Label control, you can specify an access key in the content of the Label and then identify a TextBox target for the access key.

To define an access key in a Label, precede the letter you want to be the access key with an underscore (_). By default, the first underscore identifies the access key, so if you need to use underscores in the Label prior to the desired access key, use double underscores (__) so that WPF doesn't treat it as an access key and instead displays a normal underscore.

When a user presses the access key for the Label (while pressing Alt), instead of jumping to the Label, the user's focus is redirected to the targeted TextBox.

The Code

The following XAML displays a window containing three Label and TextBox control pairs. Each Label defines a numeric quick access key (1, 2, or 3) that, when pressed in conjunction with the Alt key, takes you to the TextBox associated with the Label. In Windows Vista, the default configuration displays only the underscore when you press the Alt key.

```
<Window x:Class="Recipe_03_12.Window1"
    xmlns="http://schemas.microsoft.com/winfx/2006/xaml/presentation"
    xmlns:x="http://schemas.microsoft.com/winfx/2006/xaml"
    Title="WPF Recipes 3_12" Height="200" Width="250">
    <StackPanel>
        <StackPanel Margin="10" Orientation="Horizontal">
            <Label Target="{Binding ElementName=textBox1}">Label _1</Label>
            <TextBox Name="textBox1" Width="150"></TextBox>
        </StackPanel>
```

```
        <StackPanel Margin="10" Orientation="Horizontal">
            <Label Target="{Binding ElementName=textBox2}">Label _2</Label>
            <TextBox Name="textBox2" Width="150"></TextBox>
        </StackPanel>
        <StackPanel Margin="10" Orientation="Horizontal">
            <Label Target="{Binding ElementName=textBox3}">Label _3</Label>
            <TextBox Name="textBox3" Width="150"></TextBox>
        </StackPanel>
    </StackPanel>
</Window>
```

3-13. Provide Quick Keyboard Access to Buttons

Problem

You need to provide a keyboard shortcut so that users can quickly "click" a System.Windows.
Controls.Button control without using the mouse.

Solution

In the Content property of the Button, precede the letter you want to be the access key with an
underscore (_).

How It Works

The first underscore character in the Content property of a Button control identifies the access
key for that Button. If the user presses one of the available access keys while holding the Alt key,
WPF raises the Click event on the Button as if the user had clicked the Button with the mouse.

Because the first underscore identifies the access key, if you need to use underscores in the
content prior to the desired access key, use double underscores (__) so that WPF doesn't treat
it as an access key and instead displays a normal underscore.

▓ **Note** Even though the access key underscore is not displayed onscreen as a normal part of the Button
content, it is still there. You must take this into consideration if you need to work with the Button content
programmatically.

The Code

The following XAML demonstrates how to use underscores to define access keys for the three
Button controls:

```xml
<Window x:Class="Recipe_03_13.Window1"
    xmlns="http://schemas.microsoft.com/winfx/2006/xaml/presentation"
    xmlns:x="http://schemas.microsoft.com/winfx/2006/xaml"
    Title="WPF Recipes 3_13" Height="100" Width="300">
    <StackPanel HorizontalAlignment="Center" Orientation="Horizontal">
        <Button Click="SharedButtonClickHandler" Height="23" Margin="5"
                Name="button1" Width="75">Button _One</Button>
        <Button Click="SharedButtonClickHandler" Height="23" Margin="5"
                Name="button2" Width="75">Button _Two</Button>
        <Button Click="SharedButtonClickHandler" Height="23" Margin="5"
                Name="button3" Width="75">Button T_hree</Button>
    </StackPanel>
</Window>
```

The following code-behind provides the Click event handler for the preceding XAML:

```csharp
using System;
using System.Windows;
using System.Windows.Controls;

namespace Recipe_03_13
{
    /// <summary>
    /// Interaction logic for Window1.xaml
    /// </summary>
    public partial class Window1 : Window
    {
        public Window1()
        {
            InitializeComponent();
        }

        private void SharedButtonClickHandler(object sender, RoutedEventArgs e)
        {
            Button source = e.OriginalSource as Button;

            if (source != null)
            {
                string message = String.Format("{0} was pressed.", source.Content);
                MessageBox.Show(message, Title);
            }
        }
    }
}
```

3-14. Get User Input from a Slider

Problem

You need to allow the user to provide input to your application using a slider.

Solution

Use the System.Windows.Controls.Slider control. You can obtain the current value of the Slider from its Value property or handle the ValueChanged event to respond dynamically as the Slider value changes.

How It Works

A Slider control allows a user to choose one value from a range of values by moving a thumb along a track. You set the values for the extremes of the track using the Minimum and Maximum properties of the Slider control and get or set the current position of the thumb using the Value property.

Other properties of the Slider control allow you to control the frequency and location of tick marks that divide the length of the track and how the thumb moves along the track in response to user interaction. Table 3-4 summarizes some of the most commonly used properties of the Slider control.

Table 3-4. *Commonly Used Properties of the Slider Control*

Property	Description
IsSnapToTickEnabled	Determines whether the Slider automatically moves the thumb to the closest tick mark.
LargeChange	The size of the change in the Value property when the Slider control receives an IncreaseLarge or DecreaseLarge command. By default, this occurs when the user clicks the central track of the slider to either side of the thumb.
Maximum	The maximum value the Slider.Value can contain when the user moves the thumb all the way to the right.
Minimum	The minimum value the Slider.Value can contain when the user moves the thumb all the way to the left.
SmallChange	The size of the change in the Value property when the Slider control receives an IncreaseSmall or DecreaseSmall command. By default, this occurs when the user presses the left or right arrow keys when the thumb of the Slider is selected.
TickFrequency	The interval between ticks along the Slider track. The TickPlacement property must have a value other than None for the tick marks to be visible.
TickPlacement	The location of the tick marks relative to the Slider track. Possible values are None, TopLeft, BottomRight, or Both. Also, changes the style of the thumb to point more precisely at the ticks if the value is TopLeft or BottomRight.

Table 3-4. *Commonly Used Properties of the Slider Control (Continued)*

Property	Description
Ticks	A set of specific tick marks to show along the length of the Slider expressed as a comma-separated list of values. Values outside the range defined by the Minimum and Maximum properties are ignored. The TickPlacement property must have a value other than None for the tick marks to be visible.
Value	The current value of the Slider, which defines the position of the thumb along the Slider control's track. Setting Value less than the Minimum property defaults to the value of Minimum, and setting Value greater than the Maximum property defaults to the value of Maximum.

The Code

The following XAML displays two Slider controls. The top Slider allows the user to move the thumb freely between the Minimum and Maximum values but specifies a LargerChange value of 10 for when the user clicks the track. The bottom Slider uses a TickFrequency value of 25 and forces the thumb to align to a tick using the IsSnapToTickEnabled property. This results in a slider that always moves in increments of 25.

```
<Window x:Class="Recipe_03_14.Window1"
    xmlns="http://schemas.microsoft.com/winfx/2006/xaml/presentation"
    xmlns:x="http://schemas.microsoft.com/winfx/2006/xaml"
    Title="WPF Recipes 3_14" Height="200" Width="300">
    <StackPanel>
        <TextBlock Margin="5" Text="0" FontSize="20"
                HorizontalAlignment="Center" Name="txtSliderValue" />
        <Slider LargeChange="10" Margin="5" Maximum="1000" Minimum="0"
                Name="slider1" TickPlacement="TopLeft"
                Ticks="100, 200, 400, 800" Value="0"
                ValueChanged="slider_ValueChanged" />
        <Button Name="btnGetSliderValue1" Width="100"
                Click="GetSliderValue_Click">Get Slider 1 Value</Button>
        <Slider IsSnapToTickEnabled="True" Margin="5" Maximum="1000"
                Minimum="0" Name="slider2" TickFrequency="25"
                TickPlacement="BottomRight" Value="1000"
                ValueChanged="slider_ValueChanged" />
        <Button Name="btnGetSliderValue2" Width="100"
                Click="GetSliderValue_Click">Get Slider 2 Value</Button>
    </StackPanel>
</Window>
```

The following code-behind demonstrates how to obtain the current Value of a Slider in response to a button click and also shows how to handle the ValueChanged event to respond dynamically to the movement of the Slider thumb:

```csharp
using System.Windows;
using System.Windows.Controls;

namespace Recipe_03_14
{
    /// <summary>
    /// Interaction logic for Window1.xaml
    /// </summary>
    public partial class Window1 : Window
    {
        public Window1()
        {
            InitializeComponent();
        }

        // Handles all GetSliderValue Button Clicks
        private void GetSliderValue_Click(object sender, RoutedEventArgs e)
        {
            Button button = e.OriginalSource as Button;
            string message = "Unknown slider.";

            if (button == btnGetSliderValue1)
            {
                message = "Slider1 value = " + slider1.Value;
            }
            else if (button == btnGetSliderValue2)
            {
                message = "Slider2 value = " + slider2.Value;
            }

            MessageBox.Show(message, Title);
        }

        // Handles all Slider ValueChangedEvents.
        private void slider_ValueChanged(object sender,
            RoutedPropertyChangedEventArgs<double> e)
        {
            Slider slider = e.OriginalSource as Slider;

            if (slider != null)
            {
                txtSliderValue.Text = slider.Value.ToString();
            }
        }
    }
}
```

Figure 3-8 shows the sample code where the number at the top of the window shows the Value property of the top slider.

Figure 3-8. *Getting user input from a* Slider

3-15. Display a Context Menu

Problem

You need to show a context menu when a user right-clicks a control.

Solution

Set the ContextMenu property of the control, and configure the context menu using a hierarchy of System.Windows.Controls.MenuItem objects to define each menu option.

How It Works

You attach a context menu to an element by setting that element's ContextMenu property. With the ContextMenu property defined, right-clicking the control will bring up the context menu.

You define the structure and content of the context menu by creating a hierarchy of MenuItem objects. The Header property of the MenuItem defines the name displayed for the menu option. MenuItem supports the basic formatting of the Header, including things such as the font family, size, style, and weight. You can also define access keys by prefixing the appropriate character in the Header with an underscore (_).

To define the functionality of the ContextMenu items, you can either define Click event handlers on each MenuItem or define Command bindings. If the control the ContextMenu is attached to is aware of the bound Command, then you do not need to implement special logic because WPF passes the Command to the parent control when the user clicks the MenuItem.

▪**Note** Chapter 4 contains more examples of using commands and command bindings.

The ContextMenu also supports properties that make it easy to create rich visual effects such as HasDropShadow to turn on a shadow behind the ContextMenu and Opacity to control the opacity of the ContextMenu.

The Code

The following XAML demonstrates how to define a ContextMenu for a TextBox that lets the user clear, select, cut, copy, and paste content from the TextBox. A submenu allows the user to change the format of the TextBox content. The example uses a shared Click event handler to handle format changes, individual Click event handlers for the Clear and Select All menu items, and standard Command bindings for the Cut, Copy, and Paste commands, which the TextBox knows how to handle.

```xml
<Window x:Class="Recipe_03_15.Window1"
    xmlns="http://schemas.microsoft.com/winfx/2006/xaml/presentation"
    xmlns:x="http://schemas.microsoft.com/winfx/2006/xaml"
    Title="WPF Recipes 3_15" Height="100" Width="300">
    <Grid>
        <TextBox FontSize="16"  Height="23" Name="txtTextBox" >
            <TextBox.ContextMenu>
                <ContextMenu HasDropShadow="True" Opacity=".8">
                    <MenuItem Command="Cut" Header="Cu_t" />
                    <MenuItem Command="Copy" Header="_Copy" />
                    <MenuItem Command="Paste" Header="_Paste" />
                    <Separator/>
                    <MenuItem Click="SelectAll_Click" Header="_Select All" />
                    <MenuItem Click="Clear_Click" Header="_Clear" />
                    <Separator/>
                    <MenuItem Header="Format">
                        <MenuItem Click="TextStyle_Click" Header="_Normal"
                            Name="miNormal"></MenuItem>
                        <MenuItem Click="TextStyle_Click" FontWeight="Bold"
                            Header="_Bold" Name="miBold"></MenuItem>
                        <MenuItem Click="TextStyle_Click" FontStyle="Italic"
                            Header="_Italic" Name="miItalic"></MenuItem>
                    </MenuItem>
                </ContextMenu>
            </TextBox.ContextMenu>
            A TextBox control with ContextMenu.</TextBox>
    </Grid>
</Window>
```

The following code-behind contains the shared Click event handler to handle format changes and individual Click event handlers for the Clear and Select All context menu items:

```csharp
using System.Windows;

namespace Recipe_03_15
{
    /// <summary>
    /// Interaction logic for Window1.xaml
    /// </summary>
    public partial class Window1 : Window
    {
        public Window1()
        {
            InitializeComponent();
        }

        // Handles Clear Button Click.
        private void Clear_Click(object sender, RoutedEventArgs e)
        {
            txtTextBox.Clear();
        }

        // Handles the Select All Button Click.
        private void SelectAll_Click(object sender, RoutedEventArgs e)
        {
            txtTextBox.SelectAll();
        }

        // Handles all the Button Click events that format the TextBox.
        private void TextStyle_Click(object sender, RoutedEventArgs e)
        {
            if (sender == miNormal)
            {
                txtTextBox.FontWeight = FontWeights.Normal;
                txtTextBox.FontStyle = FontStyles.Normal;
            }
            else if (sender == miBold)
            {
                txtTextBox.FontWeight = FontWeights.Bold;
            }
            else if (sender == miItalic)
            {
                txtTextBox.FontStyle = FontStyles.Italic;
            }
        }
    }
}
```

Figure 3-9 shows the two levels of `ContextMenu` open over the `TextBox` as defined in this recipe's sample code.

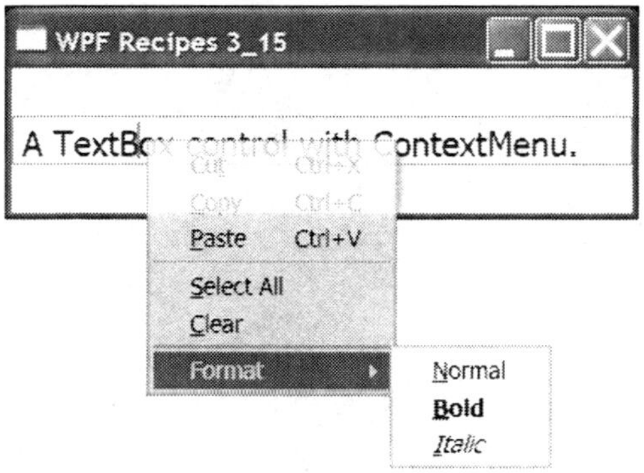

Figure 3-9. *A ContextMenu on a TextBox*

3-16. Display a Tool Tip on a Control

Problem

You need to display a tool tip when a user hovers over a UI control with the mouse pointer.

Solution

Assign a `System.Windows.Controls.ToolTip` control to the `ToolTip` property of the control on which you want to display the tool tip.

How It Works

The `System.Windows.FrameworkElement` class implements the `ToolTip` property, providing a simple mechanism through which to display a tool tip on any `FrameworkElement`-derived control.

The `ToolTip` property is of type `System.Object`, so you can assign it any object, and the property will attempt to render the object as a tool tip for display. This provides a great deal of flexibility in how you define tool tip content. For simple textual tool tips, you can specify the text to display as the value of the control's `ToolTip` attribute. When creating richer, more complex tool tips, you should use property element syntax to specify structured `ToolTip` content.

■ **Caution** The content of a `ToolTip` can contain interactive controls such as buttons, but they never get focus; you can't click or otherwise interact with them.

The Code

The following XAML demonstrates both how to use the ToolTip attribute to specify the tool tip of a Button and how to use a ToolTip object defined using property element syntax to create a tool tip that contains larger and more structured content comprising a label and a list of values:

```xml
<Window x:Class="Recipe_03_16.Window1"
    xmlns="http://schemas.microsoft.com/winfx/2006/xaml/presentation"
    xmlns:x="http://schemas.microsoft.com/winfx/2006/xaml"
    Title="WPF Recipes 3_16" Height="150" Width="300">
    <StackPanel Name="stackPanel1">
        <Button Height="23" Margin="10" Name="button1"
                ToolTip="A simple textual ToolTip" Width="175">
            Button with Simple ToolTip
        </Button>
        <Button Content="Button with a Richer ToolTip" Height="23"
                Margin="10" Name="button2" Width="175">
            <Button.ToolTip>
                <StackPanel Name="stackPanel2" Width="200">
                    <Label Name="label1" HorizontalAlignment="Left">
                        List of Things:
                    </Label>
                    <ListBox Name="listBox1" Margin="10" >
                        <ListBoxItem>Thing 1</ListBoxItem>
                        <ListBoxItem>Thing 2</ListBoxItem>
                        <ListBoxItem>Thing 3</ListBoxItem>
                    </ListBox>
                </StackPanel>
            </Button.ToolTip>
        </Button>
    </StackPanel>
</Window>
```

Figure 3-10 shows the previous example with the ToolTip visible for the lower Button.

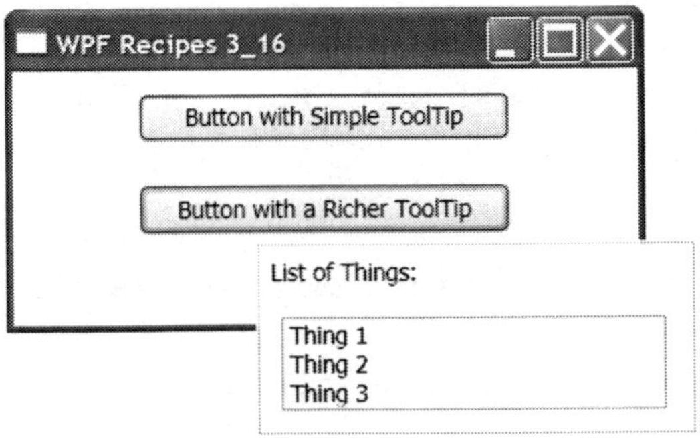

Figure 3-10. *Displaying a ToolTip on a Button*

3-17. Display a Tool Tip on a Disabled Control

Problem

You need to display a tool tip on a control even when the control is disabled.

Solution

On the control you want to associate the tool tip with, set the ShowOnDisabled attached property of the System.Windows.Controls.ToolTipService class to True.

How It Works

Usually, disabled controls (those with IsEnabled set to False) do not display tool tips when the user hovers over them with the mouse pointer. The ToolTipService class provides a set of global services that you can use to control the behavior of ToolTip objects. The ToolTipService property that enables the display of tool tips on disabled controls is named ShowOnDisabled. By assigning True to this attached property on a control, you override the default ToolTip behavior and force WPF to display the ToolTip even though the control is disabled.

The Code

The following XAML demonstrates how to use the ToolTipService.ShowOnDisabled attached property to enable the display of a ToolTip for a disabled Button control. The code contains two Button controls: the first shows the default behavior of a ToolTip on a disabled control, and the second shows the effect of setting the ToolTipService.ShowOnDisabled property to True.

```xaml
<Window x:Class="Recipe_03_17.Window1"
    xmlns="http://schemas.microsoft.com/winfx/2006/xaml/presentation"
    xmlns:x="http://schemas.microsoft.com/winfx/2006/xaml"
    Title="WPF Recipes 3_17" Height="150" Width="300">
    <StackPanel>
        <Button Content="Disabled Button without ToolTipService"
            Height="23" IsEnabled="False" Margin="10" Name="button1"
            Width="200">
            <Button.ToolTip>
                ToolTip on a disabled control
            </Button.ToolTip>
        </Button>
        <Button Content="Disabled Button with ToolTipService"
            Height="23" IsEnabled="False" Margin="10" Name="button2"
                ToolTipService.ShowOnDisabled="True" Width="200">
            <Button.ToolTip>
                ToolTip on a disabled control
            </Button.ToolTip>
        </Button>
    </StackPanel>
</Window>
```

3-18. Control the Display Duration and Position of a Tool Tip

Problem

You need to control how long your application displays a System.Windows.Controls.ToolTip or where the ToolTip is located relative to the associated control.

Solution

Apply the attached properties of the System.Windows.Controls.ToolTipService class to the control with which the ToolTip is associated. The ToolTipService.ShowDuration property controls the display duration of the ToolTip. The ToolTipService.Placement property along with the ToolTipService.HorizontalOffset and ToolTipService.VerticalOffset properties control the position of the ToolTip.

How It Works

The ToolTipService class provides a set of attached properties that you can use to control the behavior of ToolTip objects. The ToolTipService.ShowDuration property takes a System.Int32 value that specifies the number of milliseconds for which to display the ToolTip. The default value is 5000.

The ToolTipService.Placement property takes a value from the System.Windows. Controls.Primitives.PlacementMode enumeration, which determines where WPF places the ToolTip when it is displayed. The PlacementMode enumeration contains 12 values, offering a wide choice of how you place your ToolTip. Many of the PlacementMode options are relative to the placement target of the ToolTip. By default, the placement target is the control on which the ToolTip is defined but can be overridden using the ToolTipService.PlacementTarget property. Table 3-5 summarizes some of the more commonly used PlacementMode values.

Table 3-5. *Property Values for the Placement of ToolTip Controls*

Value	Description
Bottom	The top of the ToolTip is aligned with the bottom of the placement target, and the left edge of the ToolTip is aligned with the left edge of the placement target.
Center	The ToolTip is centered over the placement target.
Left	The right of the ToolTip is aligned with the left of the placement target, and the upper edge of the ToolTip is aligned with the upper edge of the placement target.
Mouse	The top of the ToolTip is aligned with the bottom of the mouse's bounding box, and the left edge of the ToolTip is aligned with the left edge of the mouse's bounding box.
Relative	The upper-left corner of the ToolTip is placed relative to the upper-left corner of the placement target.
Right	The left of the ToolTip is aligned with the right of the placement target, and the upper edge of the ToolTip is aligned with the upper edge of the placement target.

The ToolTipService.HorizontalOffset and ToolTipService.VerticalOffset properties allow you to specify System.Double values to fine-tune the position of the ToolTip depending on the value of the ToolTipService.Placement property. By default, the offset values are assumed to be in px (pixels) but can also be in (inches), cm (centimeters), or pt (points).

Tip WPF provides fine-grained control over the placement of ToolTip controls using the PlacementTarget, PlacementRectangle, HorizontalOffset, and VerticalOffset properties provided by the ToolTipService. For a thorough description of ToolTip placement logic, see the MSDN article at http://msdn2.microsoft.com/en-us/library/bb613596.aspx.

The Code

The following XAML declares three buttons, each with ToolTip controls using different properties of the ToolTipService class to control position and display duration:

```
<Window x:Class="Recipe_03_18.Window1"
    xmlns="http://schemas.microsoft.com/winfx/2006/xaml/presentation"
    xmlns:x="http://schemas.microsoft.com/winfx/2006/xaml"
    Title="WPF Recipes 3_18" Height="200" Width="300">
    <StackPanel>
        <Button Height="40" Margin="5" ToolTipService.Placement="Mouse"
                ToolTipService.ShowDuration="1000">
            <Button.ToolTip>
                <ToolTip>
                    ToolTip displayed for 1 second...
                </ToolTip>
            </Button.ToolTip>
            Button with ToolTip under Mouse
        </Button>
        <Button Height="40" Margin="5" ToolTipService.Placement="Center">
            <Button.ToolTip>
                <ToolTip>
                    ToolTip displayed for 5 seconds...
                </ToolTip>
            </Button.ToolTip>
            Button with Centered ToolTip
        </Button>
        <Button Height="40" Margin="5" ToolTipService.HorizontalOffset="5cm"
                ToolTipService.Placement="Relative"
                ToolTipService.ShowDuration="10000"
                ToolTipService.VerticalOffset="50px">
            <Button.ToolTip>
                <ToolTip >
                    ToolTip displayed for 10 seconds...
                </ToolTip>
```

```
            </Button.ToolTip>
            Button with offset ToolTip
        </Button>
    </StackPanel>
</Window>
```

3-19. View and Select Items from a Set of Radio Buttons

Problem

You need to display a set of radio buttons and allow the user to select an item.

Solution

Create a set of System.Windows.Controls.RadioButton controls. To know which particular RadioButton is selected, either test its IsSelected property when the user exits the form containing the RadioButton or handle the RadioButton.Checked event.

How It Works

All RadioButton controls in a single parent container form a single group by default. To create multiple independent groups in a single parent container or to create groups that span multiple containers, set the GroupName property on each RadioButton to define its group membership.

Typically, you consider the state of a set of radio controls when the user submits a form via the click of a button. Unfortunately, there is no straightforward way to identify which RadioButton in a group is checked. Instead, as part of the form-processing logic, you must individually check the IsSelected property of each RadioButton. When you have large numbers or a dynamic set of RadioButton controls, it is easiest to loop through all the controls in a container and filter out those that are not RadioButton controls and those that do not belong to the correct group.

Alternatively, if you need to take an action as the user clicks the RadioButton, assign an event handler to its Checked event.

The Code

The following example demonstrated how to create two groups of RadioButton controls. Using the GroupName property, the example creates two groups within a single System.Windows. Controls.StackPanel (on the left) and also creates a group (Group1) that spans the left and right StackPanel containers.

```
<Window x:Class="Recipe_03_19.Window1"
    xmlns="http://schemas.microsoft.com/winfx/2006/xaml/presentation"
    xmlns:x="http://schemas.microsoft.com/winfx/2006/xaml"
    Title="WPF Recipes 3_19" SizeToContent="Height" Width="300">
```

```xml
<Grid Name="grid">
    <Grid.RowDefinitions>
        <RowDefinition Height="Auto"/>
        <RowDefinition Height="*"/>
    </Grid.RowDefinitions>
    <Grid.ColumnDefinitions>
        <ColumnDefinition/>
        <ColumnDefinition/>
    </Grid.ColumnDefinitions>
    <Border Grid.Column="0" BorderBrush="Gray" BorderThickness="1" />
    <Border Grid.Column="1" BorderBrush="Gray" BorderThickness="1" />
    <StackPanel Grid.Column="0" HorizontalAlignment="Center" Margin="5"
                Name="spLeftContainer">
        <TextBlock FontSize="16" Text="Radio Group 1" />
        <RadioButton Content="Radio Button 1A" GroupName="Group1"
                    IsChecked="True" Margin="5" Name="rbnOneA" />
        <RadioButton Content="Radio Button 1B" GroupName="Group1"
                    Margin="5" Name="rbnOneB" />
        <RadioButton Content="Radio Button 1C" GroupName="Group1"
                    Margin="5" Name="rbnOneC" />
        <Separator/>
        <TextBlock FontSize="16" Text="Radio Group 2" />
        <RadioButton Checked="RadioButton_Checked" GroupName="Group2"
                    Content="Radio Button 2A" IsChecked="True"
                    Margin="5" Name="rbnTwoA" />
        <RadioButton Checked="RadioButton_Checked" GroupName="Group2"
                    Content="Radio Button 2B" Margin="5" Name="rbnTwoB"/>
        <RadioButton Checked="RadioButton_Checked" GroupName="Group2"
                    Content="Radio Button 2C" Margin="5" Name="rbnTwoC"/>
    </StackPanel>
    <StackPanel Grid.Column="1" HorizontalAlignment="Center" Margin="5"
                Name="spRightContainer">
        <TextBlock FontSize="16" Text="Radio Group 1" />
        <RadioButton Content="Radio Button 1D" GroupName="Group1"
                    Margin="5" Name="rbnOneD" />
        <RadioButton Content="Radio Button 1E" GroupName="Group1"
                    Margin="5" Name="rbnOneE" />
    </StackPanel>
    <Button Content="Show Group1 Selection" Grid.ColumnSpan="2"
            Grid.Row="1" HorizontalAlignment="Center"
            Margin="10" MaxHeight="25" Click="Button_Click" />
</Grid>
</Window>
```

The following code-behind demonstrates how to handle the RadioButton.Checked event and also how to loop through the children of a container to determine which RadioButton from a particular group is checked:

```csharp
using System;
using System.Linq;
using System.Windows;
using System.Windows.Controls;

namespace Recipe_03_19
{
    /// <summary>
    /// Interaction logic for Window1.xaml
    /// </summary>
    public partial class Window1 : Window
    {
        public Window1()
        {
            InitializeComponent();
        }

        // Handles the Submit Button Click event.
        private void Button_Click(object sender, RoutedEventArgs e)
        {
            RadioButton radioButton = null;

            // Try the first (left) container to see if one of
            // the radio buttons in Group1 is checked.
            radioButton = GetCheckedRadioButton(
                spLeftContainer.Children, "Group1");

            // If no RadioButton in the first container is checked, try
            // the second (right) container.
            if (radioButton == null)
            {
                radioButton = GetCheckedRadioButton(
                    spRightContainer.Children, "Group1");
            }

            // We must have at least one RadioButton checked to display.
            MessageBox.Show(radioButton.Content + " checked.", Title);
        }

        // A method that loops through a UIElementCollection and identifies
        // a checked RadioButton with a specified group name.
        private RadioButton GetCheckedRadioButton(
            UIElementCollection children, String groupName)
        {
```

```
            return children.OfType<RadioButton>().
                FirstOrDefault( rb => rb.IsChecked == true
                    && rb.GroupName == groupName);
        }

        // Handles the RadioButton Checked event for all buttons in Group2.
        private void RadioButton_Checked(object sender, RoutedEventArgs e)
        {
            // Don't handle events until the Window is fully initialized.
            if (!this.IsInitialized) return;

            RadioButton radioButton = e.OriginalSource as RadioButton;

            if (radioButton != null)
            {
                MessageBox.Show(radioButton.Content + " checked.", Title);
            }
        }
    }
}
```

Figure 3-11 shows the two groups of RadioButton controls created in the previous example.

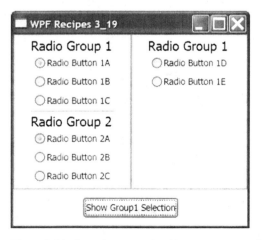

Figure 3-11. *Creating sets of RadioButton controls*

3-20. View and Select Items from a Set of Check Boxes

Problem

You need to display a set of check boxes and allow the user to select items.

Solution

Create a set of System.Windows.Controls.CheckBox controls. To know which particular CheckBox is selected, test the IsChecked property of each CheckBox when the user exits the form containing the set of CheckBox controls. To respond as soon as the user clicks a CheckBox to change its state, handle the Checked, Unchecked, and Indeterminate events of the CheckBox control.

How It Works

To determine the state of a CheckBox, test the value of its IsChecked property. The IsChecked property is of type bool?, meaning it can be True, False, or Null. A value of True means the CheckBox is checked, False means it is unchecked, and Null means it is in an indeterminate state. By default, the user cannot switch a CheckBox into an indeterminate state, but by setting CheckBox.IsThreeState to True, the user can click the CheckBox to toggle through the three states.

To respond as soon as the user clicks a CheckBox, you could handle the CheckBox.Click event and determine what state the CheckBox is in, but it is easier to handle the Checked, Unchecked, and Indeterminate events that the CheckBox raises as it is entering the appropriate state (that is, as the CheckBox gets unchecked, it raises the Unchecked event).

The Code

The following example demonstrates two approaches to determining the state of a set of CheckBox controls. The XAML defines a simple window containing four CheckBox controls (two enabled with tristate support). Each time the user changes the state of a CheckBox, the example shows a message box describing the change. The user can also click a button, which will populate a list with the names of the CheckBox controls that are currently checked.

```xaml
<Window x:Class="Recipe_03_20.Window1"
    xmlns="http://schemas.microsoft.com/winfx/2006/xaml/presentation"
    xmlns:x="http://schemas.microsoft.com/winfx/2006/xaml"
    Title="WPF Recipes 3_20" Height="250" Width="300">
    <StackPanel Name="panel">
        <CheckBox Checked="CheckBox_Checked" Content="First CheckBox"
                IsChecked="True" Margin="2" Name="checkbox1"
                Unchecked="CheckBox_Unchecked"/>
        <CheckBox Checked="CheckBox_Checked" Content="Second CheckBox"
                IsChecked="False" Margin="2" Name="checkbox2"
                Unchecked="CheckBox_Unchecked"/>
        <CheckBox Checked="CheckBox_Checked"
                Content="Third CheckBox (Tri-State Enabled)"
                Indeterminate="CheckBox_Indeterminate"  IsChecked="True"
                IsThreeState="True" Margin="2" Name="checkbox3"
                Unchecked="CheckBox_Unchecked"/>
        <CheckBox Checked="CheckBox_Checked"
                Content="Fourth CheckBox (Tri-State Enabled)"
                Indeterminate="CheckBox_Indeterminate" IsChecked="False"
                IsThreeState="True" Margin="2" Name="checkbox4"
                Unchecked="CheckBox_Unchecked"/>
```

```
        <Button Content="Get Selected" Margin="5" MaxWidth="100"
                Click="Button_Click" />
        <TextBlock FontWeight="Bold" Text="Selected CheckBoxes:" />
        <ListBox Margin="5" MinHeight="2cm" Name="listbox" />
    </StackPanel>
</Window>
```

The following code-behind provides the logic for processing the Button.Cick event to populate the list with the names of the checked CheckBox controls and the event handlers for displaying message boxes as the state of a CheckBox changes:

```
using System.Linq;
using System.Windows;
using System.Windows.Controls;

namespace Recipe_03_20
{
    /// <summary>
    /// Interaction logic for Window1.xaml
    /// </summary>
    public partial class Window1 : Window
    {
        public Window1()
        {
            InitializeComponent();
        }

        // Handles Button Click event to populate the ListBox with
        // the names of the currently checked CheckBox controls.
        private void Button_Click(object sender, RoutedEventArgs e)
        {
            // Clear the content of the ListBox.
            listbox.Items.Clear();

            // Process each CheckBox control in the main StackPanel.
            foreach (CheckBox checkbox in panel.Children.OfType<CheckBox>()
                .Where( cb => cb.IsChecked == true))
            {
                listbox.Items.Add(checkbox.Name);
            }
        }

        // Handles all the CheckBox Checked events to display a message
        // when a CheckBox changes to a checked state.
        private void CheckBox_Checked(object sender, RoutedEventArgs e)
        {
            // Don't handle these events during initialization.
            if (!IsInitialized) return;
```

```csharp
            CheckBox checkbox = e.OriginalSource as CheckBox;

            if (checkbox != null)
            {
                MessageBox.Show(checkbox.Name + " is checked.", Title);
            }
        }

        // Handles all the CheckBox Indeterminate events to display a message
        // when a CheckBox changes to an indeterminate state.
        private void CheckBox_Indeterminate(object sender, RoutedEventArgs e)
        {
            // Don't handle these events during initialization.
            if (!IsInitialized) return;

            CheckBox checkbox = e.OriginalSource as CheckBox;

            if (checkbox != null)
            {
                MessageBox.Show(checkbox.Name + " is indeterminate.", Title);
            }
        }

        // Handles all the CheckBox Unchecked events to display a message
        // when a CheckBox changes to an unchecked state.
        private void CheckBox_Unchecked(object sender, RoutedEventArgs e)
        {
            // Don't handle these events during initialization.
            if (!IsInitialized) return;

            CheckBox checkbox = e.OriginalSource as CheckBox;

            if (checkbox != null)
            {
                MessageBox.Show(checkbox.Name + " is unchecked.", Title);
            }
        }
    }
}
```

Figure 3-12 shows the previous example after the user has toggled the fourth CheckBox into an indeterminate state and has clicked the Get Selected Button.

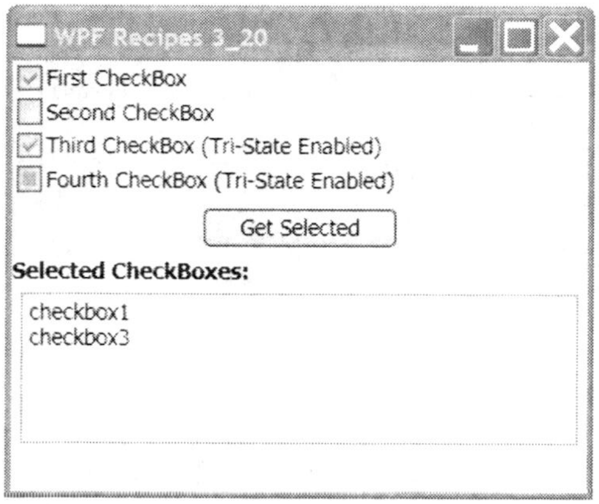

Figure 3-12. *Creating sets of CheckBox controls*

3-21. View and Select Items Using a Tree

Problem

You need to present a hierarchical set of data as a tree with collapsible branches and allow a user to select an item from the tree.

Solution

Use the System.Windows.Controls.TreeView control to present an expandable tree of items. Use the SelectedItem property of the TreeView control to determine the currently selected item. To respond to the selection of items in the ListBox dynamically, handle the TreeView. SelectionChanged event or the Selected event raised by the System.Windows.Controls. TreeViewItem objects that wrap each element contained in the TreeView controls.

How It Works

The easiest way to define the content of a static TreeView is to include the content elements directly within the XAML TreeView element. You can include controls directly within the TreeView element XAML or, for greater control over the formatting of the contained items, wrap them in a TreeViewItem element.

Note A more flexible way to define the content of a TreeView is to data bind it to a collection. Chapter 5 describes how to use data binding.

To determine the current TreeView selection, you can get the SelectedItem property of the TreeView at an appropriate time (that is, when the user submits or closes the form containing the TreeView), or you can handle selection dynamically by handling events raised by the TreeView and the individual TreeViewItem objects.

On a change in selection, the TreeView raises a SelectedItemChanged. The individual TreeViewItem objects raise a Selected event that contains details that allow you to identify that the TreeViewItem has changed. When a TreeViewItem raises the Selected event, the hierarchy of parent TreeViewItem objects that contain the item each raise a Selected event in turn.

The Code

The following example demonstrates how to use a TreeView control to display hierarchical information. As the user selects an item, the example shows a MessageBox for each TreeViewItem. Selected event raised. The user can also click the Button to see a message box identifying the header of the currently selected TreeViewItem. The example uses a Style with an EventSetter element to assign a common Selected event handler to all instances of TreeViewItem.

```xaml
<Window x:Class="Recipe_03_21.Window1"
    xmlns="http://schemas.microsoft.com/winfx/2006/xaml/presentation"
    xmlns:x="http://schemas.microsoft.com/winfx/2006/xaml"
    Title="WPF Recipes 3_21" Height="200" Width="300">
    <DockPanel LastChildFill="True">
        <DockPanel.Resources>
            <Style TargetType="{x:Type TreeViewItem}">
                <EventSetter Event="Selected"
                            Handler="TreeViewItem_Selected" />
            </Style>
        </DockPanel.Resources>
        <Button Click="Button_Click" DockPanel.Dock="Bottom"
                Content="Show Selected" MaxHeight="23" MaxWidth="100" />
        <TreeView FontSize="16" Name="tvTree">
            <TreeViewItem Header="Birds" IsExpanded="True">
                <TreeViewItem Header="Flighted">
                    <TreeViewItem Header="Falcon" />
                    <TreeViewItem Header="Starling" />
                </TreeViewItem>
                <TreeViewItem Header="Flightless" IsExpanded="True">
                    <TreeViewItem Header="Emu" />
                    <TreeViewItem Header="Kiwi" />
                </TreeViewItem>
            </TreeViewItem>
            <TreeViewItem Header="Reptiles">
                <TreeViewItem Header="Lizards">
                    <TreeViewItem Header="Blue Tonge" />
                    <TreeViewItem Header="Frilled" />
                    <TreeViewItem Header="Iguana" />
                </TreeViewItem>
```

```xml
                    <TreeViewItem Header="Snakes">
                        <TreeViewItem Header="Anaconda" />
                        <TreeViewItem Header="Cobra" />
                        <TreeViewItem Header="Rattlesnake" />
                    </TreeViewItem>
                </TreeViewItem>
            </TreeView>
        </DockPanel>
</Window>
```

The following code contains the event-handling logic for the TreeView example:

```csharp
using System;
using System.Windows;
using System.Windows.Controls;

namespace Recipe_03_21
{
    /// <summary>
    /// Interaction logic for Window1.xaml
    /// </summary>
    public partial class Window1 : Window
    {
        public Window1()
        {
            InitializeComponent();
        }

        // Handles the Selected event for all TreeViewItems.
        private void TreeViewItem_Selected(object sender,
            RoutedEventArgs e)
        {
            String message = String.Empty;

            // As the Selected event is fired by successive
            // parent TreeViewItem controls of the actually
            // selected TreeViewItem, the sender will change,
            // but the e.OriginalSource will continue to
            // refer to the TreeViewItem that was actually
            // clicked.
            TreeViewItem item = sender as TreeViewItem;

            if (item == e.OriginalSource)
            {
                // Event raised by clicked item.
                message =
                    String.Format("Item selected: {0} ({1} child items)",
                    item.Header, item.Items.Count);
            }
```

```
            else
            {
                // Event raised by a parent of clicked item.
                message =
                    String.Format("Parent of selected: {0} ({1} child items)",
                    item.Header, item.Items.Count);
            }

            MessageBox.Show(message, Title);
        }

        // Handles the Button Click event.
        private void Button_Click(object sender, RoutedEventArgs e)
        {
            TreeViewItem item = tvTree.SelectedItem as TreeViewItem;

            if (item != null)
            {
                MessageBox.Show("Item selected: " + item.Header, Title);
            }
            else
            {
                MessageBox.Show("No item selected", Title);
            }
        }
    }
}
```

Figure 3-13 shows the example in its initial state with the Birds and Flightless items expanded by default.

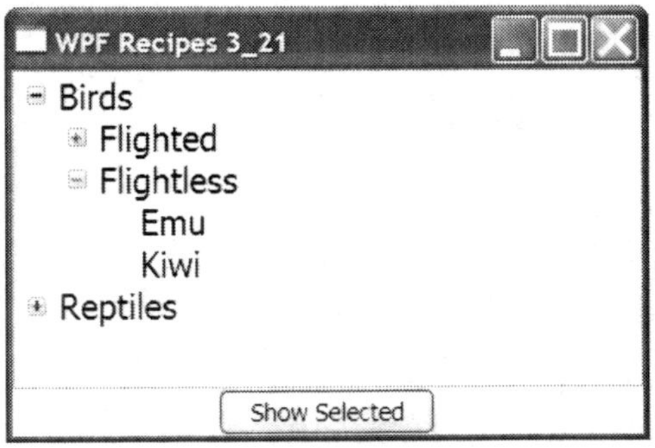

Figure 3-13. *Hierarchical data shown in a TreeView control*

3-22. View and Select Items Using a List

Problem

You need to present a scrollable list of items and allow the user to select an item from the list.

Solution

Use the System.Windows.Controls.ListBox control to present a list of items. Use the SelectedItem property of the ListBox control to determine the currently selected item (use SelectedItems for multiselect lists). To respond to the selection of items in the ListBox dynamically, handle the ListBox.SelectionChanged event or the Selected event raised by the System.Windows.Controls. ListBoxItem objects that wrap each element contained in the ListBox controls.

How It Works

The ListBox control makes it incredibly easy to present a set of things to the user as a list. In fact, you can put anything that derives from System.Object into a ListBox. Any list item derived from System.Windows.UIElement will render according to its OnRender implementation, whereas other items will be rendered using ToString.

The easiest way to define the content of a static list is to include the content elements directly within the XAML ListBox element. You can include controls directly within the ListBox element XAML or, for greater control over the formatting of the contained items, wrap them in a ListBoxItem element.

To determine the current ListBox selection, you can process the SelectedItem or SelectedItems properties of the ListBox at an appropriate time (that is, when the user submits or closes the form containing the ListBox), or you can handle selection dynamically by handling events raised by the ListBox and the individual ListBoxItem objects. On a change in selection, the ListBox raises a SelectionChanged event that passes details of all the items currently selected along with those that were just unselected. The individual ListBoxItem objects also raise a Selected event that contains details that allow you to identify the ListBoxItem that has changed.

■ **Note** Recipe 3-23 describes how to add and remove items from a ListBox programmatically. Also, the flexibility of the ListBox control means that it is a useful base from which to create rich custom controls that look and behave differently than the generic ListBox (see Chapter 4 and Chapter 6 for more details).

The Code

The following XAML defines in single-select ListBox containing a variety of other controls, including a nested ListBox. Some items are contained directly within the ListBox, while others are wrapped in ListBoxItem elements.

```xml
<Window x:Class="Recipe_03_22.Window1"
    xmlns="http://schemas.microsoft.com/winfx/2006/xaml/presentation"
    xmlns:x="http://schemas.microsoft.com/winfx/2006/xaml"
    Title="WPF Recipes 3_22" Height="300" Width="300">
    <StackPanel>
        <ListBox SelectionChanged="OuterListBox_SelectionChanged"
                 Name="outerListBox">
            <ListBoxItem Content="List Box Item 1" FontFamily="Tahoma"
                         FontSize="14" HorizontalContentAlignment="Left" />
            <ListBoxItem Content="List Box Item 2" FontFamily="Algerian"
                         FontSize="16" HorizontalContentAlignment="Center" />
            <ListBoxItem Content="List Box Item 3" FontSize="20"
                         FontFamily="FreeStyle Script"
                         HorizontalContentAlignment="Right" />
            <Button Content="Button directly in a list" Margin="5" />
            <ListBoxItem HorizontalContentAlignment="Center" Margin="5">
                <Button Content="Button wrapped in ListBoxItem" />
            </ListBoxItem>
            <ListBox Height="50" Margin="5">
                <ListBoxItem Content="Inner List Item 1"
                             Selected="InnerListBoxItem_Selected" />
                <ListBoxItem Content="Inner List Item 2"
                             Selected="InnerListBoxItem_Selected" />
                <ListBoxItem Content="Inner List Item 3"
                             Selected="InnerListBoxItem_Selected" />
                <ListBoxItem Content="Inner List Item 4"
                             Selected="InnerListBoxItem_Selected" />
            </ListBox>
            <StackPanel Margin="5" Orientation="Horizontal">
                <Label Content="Enter some text:" />
                <TextBox MinWidth="150" />
            </StackPanel>
        </ListBox>
        <TextBlock Text="No item currently selected." Margin="10"
                   HorizontalAlignment="Center" Name="txtSelectedItem" />
    </StackPanel>
</Window>
```

The following code-behind contains the logic used to handle the event raised by the outer ListBox and the items contained in the inner ListBox. When the user selects an item in the outer ListBox, the code handles the ListBox.SelectionChanged event and displays the ToString output of the selected item at the bottom of the form. When the user selects an item in the inner ListBox, the code handles the ListBoxItem.Selected event and displays the Content property of the selected item in a MessageBox.

```csharp
using System.Windows;
using System.Windows.Controls;

namespace Recipe_03_22
{
    /// <summary>
    /// Interaction logic for Window1.xaml
    /// </summary>
    public partial class Window1 : Window
    {
        public Window1()
        {
            InitializeComponent();
        }

        // Handles ListBoxItem Selected events for the ListBoxItems in the
        // inner ListBox.
        private void InnerListBoxItem_Selected(object sender,
            RoutedEventArgs e)
        {
            ListBoxItem item = e.OriginalSource as ListBoxItem;

            if (item != null)
            {
                MessageBox.Show(item.Content + " was selected.", Title);
            }
        }

        // Handles ListBox SelectionChanged events for the outer ListBox.
        private void OuterListBox_SelectionChanged(object sender,
            SelectionChangedEventArgs e)
        {
            object item = outerListBox.SelectedItem;

            if (item == null)
            {
                txtSelectedItem.Text = "No item currently selected.";
            }
            else
            {
                txtSelectedItem.Text = item.ToString();
            }
        }
    }
}
```

Figure 3-14 shows the ListBox from the example. The first button is the currently selected item.

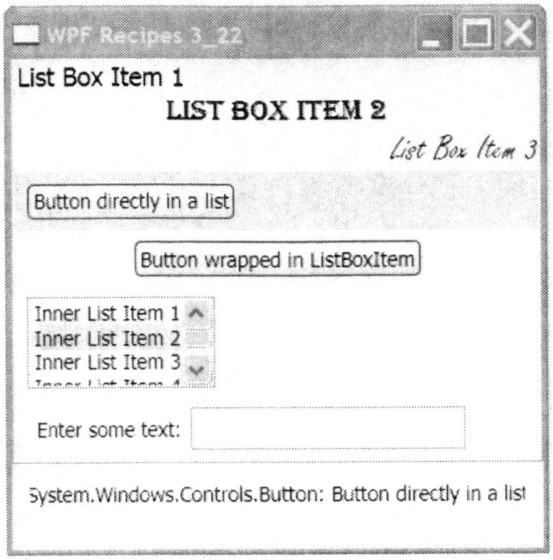

Figure 3-14. *A* ListBox *containing a rich set of controls as list elements*

3-23. Dynamically Add Items to a List

Problem

You need to add items to, and remove items from, a System.Windows.Controls.ListBox control at runtime.

Solution

To add an item, create a new System.Windows.Controls.ListBoxItem object, configure it, and add it to the ListBox using the ListBox.Items.Add method. To remove an item, use the ListBox.Items.Remove method.

How It Works

The content of a ListBox is contained in a System.Windows.Controls.ItemCollection collection, which is accessed via the ListBox.Items property. By modifying the content of the ItemCollection, you control the visible content of the ListBox.

You can add any object to the ItemCollection. Any list item derived from System.Windows.UIElement will render according to its OnRender implementation, whereas other items will be rendered using ToString. Wrapping the object in a ListBoxItem gives you greater control over the format and layout of the item when it is displayed in the ListBox.

Note Recipe 3-22 describes the basic structure of a ListBox and ListBoxItem in more detail.

The Code

The following XAML defines a simple ListBox control in Extended selection mode containing some statically defined items. The example contains System.Windows.Controls.TextBox and System.Windows.Controls.Button controls that allow the user to add and remove items from the list.

```
<Window x:Class="Recipe_03_23.Window1"
    xmlns="http://schemas.microsoft.com/winfx/2006/xaml/presentation"
    xmlns:x="http://schemas.microsoft.com/winfx/2006/xaml"
    Title="WPF Recipes 3_23" Height="300" Width="300">
    <StackPanel>
        <ListBox FontSize="16" Height="150" Margin="5" Name="listBox1"
                SelectionMode="Extended">
            <ListBoxItem>List Item 1</ListBoxItem>
            <ListBoxItem>List Item 2</ListBoxItem>
            <ListBoxItem>List Item 3</ListBoxItem>
        </ListBox>
        <StackPanel HorizontalAlignment="Center" Orientation="Horizontal">
            <Label Content="_New item text:" VerticalAlignment="Center"
                    Target="{Binding ElementName=textBox}"  />
            <TextBox Margin="5" Name="textBox" MinWidth="120" />
        </StackPanel>
        <StackPanel HorizontalAlignment="Center" Orientation="Horizontal">
            <Button Click="btnAddListItem_Click" Content="Add Item"
                    IsDefault="True" Margin="5" Name="btnAddListItem" />
            <Button Click="btnDeleteListItem_Click" Content="Delete Items"
                    Margin="5" Name="btnDeleteListItem" />
            <Button Click="btnSelectAll_Click" Content="Select All"
                    Margin="5" Name="btnSelectAll" />
        </StackPanel>
    </StackPanel>
</Window>
```

The following code-behind handles the Button click events that add and remove items from the list. When the user clicks the Add Item Button, the event handler gets the content of the TextBox, wraps it in a ListBoxItem, formats it, and adds it to the ListBox. When the user clicks the Delete Items Button, the event handler loops through the set of currently selected items and removes them from the ListBox.

```
using System.Windows;
using System.Windows.Controls;
using System.Windows.Media;

namespace Recipe_03_23
{
    /// <summary>
    /// Interaction logic for Window1.xaml
    /// </summary>
```

```csharp
public partial class Window1 : Window
{
    public Window1()
    {
        InitializeComponent();
    }

    // Handles the Add Item Button Click event.
    private void btnAddListItem_Click(object sender,
        RoutedEventArgs e)
    {
        // Ensure there is text to add.
        if (textBox.Text.Length == 0)
        {
            MessageBox.Show("Enter text to add to the list.", Title);
        }
        else
        {
            // Wrap the text in a ListBoxItem and configure.
            ListBoxItem item = new ListBoxItem();
            item.Content = textBox.Text;
            item.IsSelected = true;
            item.HorizontalAlignment = HorizontalAlignment.Center;
            item.FontWeight = FontWeights.Bold;
            item.FontFamily = new FontFamily("Tahoma");

            // Add the ListBoxItem to the ListBox
            listBox1.Items.Add(item);

            // Clear the content of the textBox and give it focus.
            textBox.Clear();
            textBox.Focus();
        }
    }

    // Handles the Delete Item Button Click event.
    private void btnDeleteListItem_Click(object sender,
        RoutedEventArgs e)
    {
        // Ensure there is at least one item selected.
        if (listBox1.SelectedItems.Count == 0)
        {
            MessageBox.Show("Select list items to delete.", Title);
        }
```

```
        else
        {
            // Iterate through the selected items and remove each one.
            // Cannot use foreach because we are changing the underlying
            // data.
            while (listBox1.SelectedItems.Count > 0)
            {
                listBox1.Items.Remove(listBox1.SelectedItems[0]);
            }
        }
    }

    // Handles the Select All Button Click event.
    private void btnSelectAll_Click(object sender, RoutedEventArgs e)
    {
        listBox1.SelectAll();
    }
  }
}
```

3-24. View and Select Items Using a Combo Box

Problem

You need to present a list of items as an expandable combo box and allow the user to select an item from the list.

Solution

Use the System.Windows.Controls.ComboBox control to present the expandable list of items. Use the SelectedItem property of the ComboBox control to identify the currently selected item. To respond to the selection of items in the ComboBox dynamically, handle the ComboBox.SelectionChanged event or the Selected event raised by the System.Windows.Controls.ComboBoxItem objects that wrap each element contained in the ComboBox control.

How It Works

The ComboBox control inherits from the System.Windows.Controls.ItemsControl the same as the System.Windows.Controls.ListBox, and they are similar in their use (recipes 3-22 and 3-23 demonstrate how to use the ListBox control). The key difference between the ListBox and the ComboBox is the way they are rendered, which results in the ComboBox allowing the user to select only one item at a time. The other key difference is that by setting the ComboBox.IsEditable property to True, you allow the user to type a value into the ComboBox instead of being able to choose only one of the values in the drop-down list.

As with a ListBox, you can put anything that derives from System.Object into a ComboBox. Any list item derived from System.Windows.UIElement will render according to its OnRender implementation, whereas other items will be rendered using ToString.

To define static content for a ComboBox, include the content elements directly within the XAML ComboBox element. You can include controls directly within the ComboBox element XAML or, for greater control over the formatting of the contained items, wrap them in a ComboBoxItem element.

To determine the current ComboBox selection, you can query the SelectedItem property of the ComboBox at an appropriate time (that is, when the user submits or closes the form containing the ComboBox). If the SelectedItem property is Null and IsEditable is True, you can determine whether the user has typed a value into the ComboBox via the ComboBox.Text property.

To handle ComboBox selection more dynamically, you can handle the events raised by the ComboBox and the individual ComboBoxItem objects. On a change in selection, the ComboBox raises a SelectionChanged event that passes details of the item currently selected. Alternatively, when newly selected, a ComboBoxItem raises a Selected event, which contains details that allow you to identify the individual ComboBoxItem that raised the event.

The Code

The following XAML defines a ComboBox containing five ComboBoxItem items and sets the third item to be selected using the IsSelected property. The Get Selected button causes the example to determine which ComboBoxItem is currently selected. As the user changes their selection, the example handles both ComboBoxItem.Selected and ComboBox.SelectionChanged events, displaying messages about which item is now selected.

```xaml
<Window x:Class="Recipe_03_24.Window1"
    xmlns="http://schemas.microsoft.com/winfx/2006/xaml/presentation"
    xmlns:x="http://schemas.microsoft.com/winfx/2006/xaml"
    Title="WPF Recipes 3_24" Height="100" Width="300">
    <StackPanel>
        <ComboBox Name="comboBox" IsEditable="True" Margin="5"
                SelectionChanged="ComboBox_SelectionChanged">
            <ComboBoxItem Content="ComboBox Item 1"
                        Selected="ComboBoxItem_Selected" />
            <ComboBoxItem Content="ComboBox Item 2"
                        Selected="ComboBoxItem_Selected" />
            <ComboBoxItem Content="ComboBox Item 3"
                        Selected="ComboBoxItem_Selected" IsSelected="True"/>
            <ComboBoxItem Content="ComboBox Item 4"
                        Selected="ComboBoxItem_Selected" />
            <ComboBoxItem Content="ComboBox Item 5"
                        Selected="ComboBoxItem_Selected" />
        </ComboBox>
        <Button Content="Get Selected" Margin="5" Width="100"
                Click="Button_Click" />
    </StackPanel>
</Window>
```

The following code-behind contains the event handlers used by the preceding XAML:

```
using System;
using System.Windows;
using System.Windows.Controls;

namespace Recipe_03_24
{
    /// <summary>
    /// Interaction logic for Window1.xaml
    /// </summary>
    public partial class Window1 : Window
    {
        public Window1()
        {
            InitializeComponent();
        }

        // Gets the currently selected ComboBoxItem when the user
        // clicks the Button. If the SelectedItem of the ComboBox
        // is null, the code checks to see if the user has entered
        // text into the ComboBox instead.
        private void Button_Click(object sender, RoutedEventArgs e)
        {
            ComboBoxItem item = comboBox.SelectedItem as ComboBoxItem;

            if (item != null)
            {
                MessageBox.Show("Current item: " + item.Content, Title);
            }
            else if (!String.IsNullOrEmpty(comboBox.Text))
            {
                MessageBox.Show("Text entered: " + comboBox.Text, Title);
            }
        }

        // Handles ComboBox SelectionChanged events.
        private void ComboBox_SelectionChanged(object sender,
            SelectionChangedEventArgs e)
        {
            // Do not handle events until Window is fully initialized.
            if (!IsInitialized) return;

            ComboBoxItem item = comboBox.SelectedItem as ComboBoxItem;
```

```
                if (item != null)
                {
                    MessageBox.Show("Selected item: " + item.Content, Title);
                }
            }

            // Handles ComboBoxItem Selected events.
            private void ComboBoxItem_Selected(object sender,
                RoutedEventArgs e)
            {
                // Do not handle events until Window is fully initialized.
                if (!IsInitialized) return;

                ComboBoxItem item = e.OriginalSource as ComboBoxItem;

                if (item != null)
                {
                    MessageBox.Show(item.Content + " was selected.", Title);
                }
            }
        }
    }
}
```

3-25. Display a Control Rotated

Problem

You need to display a control rotated from its normal horizontal or vertical axis.

Solution

Apply a LayoutTransform or a RenderTransform to the control.

How It Works

WPF makes many things trivial that are incredibly complex to do in Windows Forms programming. One of those things is the ability to rotate controls to any orientation yet still have them appear and function as normal. Admittedly, it is not every day you need to display a rotated control, but when you do, you will appreciate how easy it is in WPF. Most frequently, the ability to rotate controls becomes important when you start to customize the appearance of standard controls using templates (as discussed in Chapter 6) or when you create custom controls (as discussed in Chapter 4).

Both the LayoutTransform and RenderTransform have a RotateTransform property, in which you specify the angle in degrees you want your control rotated by. Positive values rotate the control clockwise, and negative values rotate the control counterclockwise. The rotation occurs around the point specified by the CenterX and CenterY properties. These properties refer to the coordinate space of the control that is being transformed, with (0,0) being the upper-left corner. Alternatively, you can use the RenderTransformOrigin property on the control you are rotating; this allows you to specify a point a relative distance from the origin using values between 0 and 1 that WPF automatically converts to specific values.

The difference between the LayoutTransform and RenderTransform is the order in which WPF executes the transformation. WPF executes the LayoutTransform as part of the layout processing, so the rotated position of the control affects the layout of controls around it. The RenderTransform, on the other hand, is executed after layout is determined, which means the rotated control does not affect the positioning of other controls and can therefore end up appearing partially over or under other controls.

The Code

The following XAML demonstrates a variety of rotated controls. The bottom left shows the difference in behavior of a LayoutTransform compared to a RenderTransform (shown in the bottom-right corner). See Figure 3-15.

```
<Window x:Class="Recipe_03_25.Window1"
    xmlns="http://schemas.microsoft.com/winfx/2006/xaml/presentation"
    xmlns:x="http://schemas.microsoft.com/winfx/2006/xaml"
    Title="WPF Recipes 3_25" Height="350" Width="400">
    <Grid ShowGridLines="True">
        <Grid.RowDefinitions>
            <RowDefinition MinHeight="140" />
            <RowDefinition MinHeight="170" />
        </Grid.RowDefinitions>
        <Grid.ColumnDefinitions>
            <ColumnDefinition />
            <ColumnDefinition />
        </Grid.ColumnDefinitions>
        <TextBox Grid.Row="0" Grid.Column="0" Height="23"
                HorizontalAlignment="Center" Text="An upside down TextBox."
                Width="140">
            <TextBox.LayoutTransform>
                <RotateTransform Angle="180"/>
            </TextBox.LayoutTransform>
        </TextBox>
        <Button Content="A rotated Button" Grid.Row="0" Grid.Column="1"
                Height="23" Width="100">
            <Button.LayoutTransform>
                <RotateTransform Angle="-120"/>
            </Button.LayoutTransform>
        </Button>
        <StackPanel Grid.Row="1" Grid.Column="0" >
            <TextBlock HorizontalAlignment="Center" Margin="5">
                Layout Tranform
            </TextBlock>
            <Button Margin="5" Width="100">Top Button</Button>
```

```
        <Button Content="Middle Button" Margin="5" Width="100">
            <Button.LayoutTransform>
                <RotateTransform Angle="30" />
            </Button.LayoutTransform>
        </Button>
        <Button Margin="5" Width="100">Bottom Button</Button>
    </StackPanel>
    <StackPanel Grid.Row="1" Grid.Column="1" >
        <TextBlock HorizontalAlignment="Center" Margin="5">
            Render Tranform
        </TextBlock>
        <Button Margin="5" Width="100">Top Button</Button>
        <Button Content="Middle Button" Margin="5"
                RenderTransformOrigin="0.5, 0.5" Width="100">
            <Button.RenderTransform>
                <RotateTransform Angle="30" />
            </Button.RenderTransform>
        </Button>
        <Button Margin="5" Width="100">Bottom Button</Button>
    </StackPanel>
</Grid>
</Window>
```

Figure 3-15 shows a variety of rotated controls.

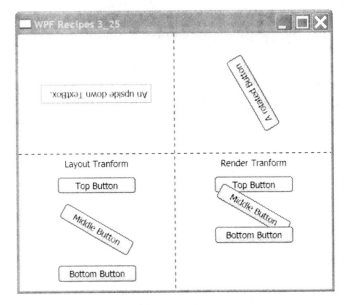

Figure 3-15. *A set of rotated controls*

CHAPTER 4

Creating User and Custom Controls

WPF provides developers with unparalleled options in customizing and modifying the visual appearance of controls.

In the first instance, you can simply assign custom values to the appearance properties of the built-in WPF controls. For example, you could set the Background property of a System.Windows.Controls.Button control to silver and the FontWeight property to bold.

If you wanted to reuse this Button control in different places within your application, you could define an application-wide System.Windows.Style to set these property values and then apply this Style to all Button objects automatically (see Chapter 6).

Alternatively, suppose you wanted every Button to display an image surrounded by a border. The content model in WPF makes this easy. Simply declare a System.Windows.Controls.Border and a System.Windows.Controls.Image in the inline XAML for your button. If you wanted to reuse this type of button across your application, you could define a System.Windows.Controls.ControlTemplate with an application-wide Style (see Chapter 6).

These mechanisms for changing the appearance offer a great deal of power and flexibility to change individual controls and elements. However, when you want to create reusable groups of controls and functionality, you need to create a user or custom control. User controls are ideal for situations where you need to encapsulate a group of visual elements and behaviors into one component that can be reused in different parts of your application.

However, because user controls encapsulate much of their visual appearance, you cannot change their style and control template in different contexts. This is where custom controls come in. They separate their interaction logic from their visual implementation, allowing other developers to reuse them within different applications and to customize their appearance themselves.

Finally, you can also create custom-drawn controls and render them to the screen using custom drawing logic.

This chapter focuses on how to create user and custom controls and custom-drawn elements, and it demonstrates some examples of all these types of controls. The recipes in this chapter describe how to:

- Create a user control (recipe 4-1)

- Incorporate it into the content model in WPF (recipe 4-2)

- Add properties, events, and commands to user controls (recipes 4-3, 4-4, 4-5, and 4-6)

- Set design-mode behavior in a user control (recipe 4-7)

- Create a lookless custom control (recipes 4-9 and 4-10)

- Support UI automation in a custom control (recipe 4-11)

- Create a custom-drawn element (recipe 4-12)

- Create a numeric text box control (recipe 4-13)

- Create scrollable, zoomable, and draggable canvas controls (recipes 4-13, 4-14, and 4-15)

4-1. Create a User Control

Problem

You need to create a user control to reuse part of the UI in different contexts within your application, without duplicating appearance or behavior logic.

Solution

Create a class that derives from System.Windows.Controls.UserControl or System.Windows.Controls.ContentControl, and place the visual elements you need in your reusable component in the XAML for the user control. Put custom logic in the code-behind for the UserControl to control custom behavior and functionality.

■**Tip** A control that derives from UserControl is useful for creating a reusable component within an application but is less useful if it can be shared by other applications, software teams, or even companies. This is because a control that derives from UserControl cannot have its appearance customized by applying custom styles and templates in the consumer. If this is needed, then you need to use a custom control, which is a control that derives from System.Windows.UIElement.FrameworkElement or System.Windows.Controls.Control.

How It Works

User controls provide a simple development model that is similar to creating WPF elements in standard windows. They are ideal for composing reusable UI controls out of existing components or elements, provided you do not need to allow them to be extensively customized by consumers of your control. If you do want to provide full control over the visual appearance of your control, or allow it to be a container for other controls, then a custom control is more suitable. Custom controls are covered later in this chapter.

To create a user control, right-click your project in Visual Studio, click Add, and then click the User Control option in the submenu. This creates a new XAML file and a corresponding code-behind file. The root element of the new XAML file is a System.Windows.Controls.UserControl class. Inside this XAML file, you can create the UI elements that compose your control.

The Code

The following example demonstrates how to create a FileInputControl, a custom reusable
user control to encapsulate the functionality of browsing to a file and displaying the file name.
This user control is then used in a window, as shown in Figure 4-1.

The XAML for the FileInputControl is as follows:

```xml
<UserControl x:Class="Recipe_04_01.FileInputControl"
    xmlns="http://schemas.microsoft.com/winfx/2006/xaml/presentation"
    xmlns:x="http://schemas.microsoft.com/winfx/2006/xaml">
    <DockPanel>

        <Button
                DockPanel.Dock="Right"
                Margin="2,0,0,0"
                Click="BrowseButton_Click">
            Browse...
        </Button>

        <TextBox x:Name="txtBox"
                IsReadOnly="True" />

    </DockPanel>
</UserControl>
```

The code-behind for the control is as follows:

```csharp
using System.Windows.Controls;
using Microsoft.Win32;

namespace Recipe_04_01
{
    public partial class FileInputControl : UserControl
    {
        public FileInputControl()
        {
            InitializeComponent();
        }

        private void BrowseButton_Click(
            object sender,
            System.Windows.RoutedEventArgs e)
        {
            OpenFileDialog dlg = new OpenFileDialog();
            if(dlg.ShowDialog() == true)
            {
                this.FileName = dlg.FileName;
            }
        }
```

```
        public string FileName
        {
            get
            {
                return txtBox.Text;
            }
            set
            {
                txtBox.Text = value;
            }
        }
    }
}
```

The XAML for the window that consumes this user control is as follows:

```
<Window x:Class="Recipe_04_01.Window1"
    xmlns="http://schemas.microsoft.com/winfx/2006/xaml/presentation"
    xmlns:x="http://schemas.microsoft.com/winfx/2006/xaml"
    xmlns:Recipe_04_01="clr-namespace:Recipe_04_01;assembly="
    Title="WPF Recipes 4_01" Height="72" Width="300">
    <Grid>
        <Recipe_04_01:FileInputControl Margin="8" />
    </Grid>
</Window>
```

Figure 4-1. *Creating and using a* FileInput *user control*

4-2. Set the Content Property of a User Control

Problem

You need to specify the Content property of your System.Windows.Controls.UserControl so that when the consumer defines an instance of your UserControl, the consumer can set the value of this property as the inline content.

Solution

Use the System.Windows.Markup.ContentPropertyAttribute attribute to decorate your user control's class declaration, and specify the name of the property you want to designate as the Content property.

How It Works

Because `UserControl` ultimately inherits from `System.Windows.Controls.ContentControl`, the `Content` property is the default property to receive the value of any inline XAML declarations. For example, a consumer of a `FileInputControl` (see the following code) might declare the instance of the control with the following XAML:

```
<local:FileInputControl>c:\readme.txt</local:FileInputControl>
```

Without the `ContentProperty` attribute on the user control, this XAML declaration would replace the control elements inside the `FileInputControl` and simply display a string. The `ContentProperty` attribute tells the user control to instead use another property to set whenever a value is passed as inline content.

■ **Caution** An explicit setting of the `Content` property would still replace the visual elements inside the control, for example, `<local:FileInputControl Content="c:\readme.txt" />`. If this is a real possibility and you need to prevent this case as well, then you should create a custom control rather than a user control and specify the visual elements of the control in a control template. In this case, you could use a template binding to bind `TextBox.Text` to the `Content` property.

The Code

The following example demonstrates how to set the `Content` property of a `UserControl`. It defines a `UserControl` called `FileInputControl` that can be used to browse to a file using the `Microsoft.Win32.OpenFileDialog` and to display the file name in a `System.Windows.Controls.TextBox`. In the code-behind, the `FileInputControl` class is decorated with the `ContentProperty` attribute and passed the name of the `FileName` property in the parameter of its constructor. The user control is then used in a window called `Window1`. In the XAML for this window, an initial file name is set by specifying the text as the inline content.

The XAML for the `FileInputControl` is as follows:

```xml
<UserControl x:Class="Recipe_04_02.FileInputControl"
    xmlns="http://schemas.microsoft.com/winfx/2006/xaml/presentation"
    xmlns:x="http://schemas.microsoft.com/winfx/2006/xaml">
    <DockPanel>

        <Button
                DockPanel.Dock="Right"
                Margin="2,0,0,0"
                Click="BrowseButton_Click">
            Browse...
        </Button>
```

```
            <TextBox x:Name="txtBox"
                     IsReadOnly="True" />

    </DockPanel>

</UserControl>
```

The code-behind for the FileInputControl is as follows:

```csharp
using System.Windows.Controls;
using System.Windows.Markup;
using Microsoft.Win32;

namespace Recipe_04_02
{
    /// <summary>
    /// ContentProperty attribute
    /// </summary>
    [ContentProperty("FileName")]
    public partial class FileInputControl : UserControl
    {
        public FileInputControl()
        {
            InitializeComponent();
        }

        private void BrowseButton_Click(
            object sender,
            System.Windows.RoutedEventArgs e)
        {
            OpenFileDialog dlg = new OpenFileDialog();
            if(dlg.ShowDialog() == true)
            {
                this.FileName = dlg.FileName;
            }
        }

        public string FileName
        {
            get
            {
                return txtBox.Text;
            }
            set
            {
                txtBox.Text = value;
            }
        }
    }
}
```

The following XAML shows how to use the `FileInputControl` in a window and declares a file name in the inline content of the declaration, which then automatically sets the value of the `FileName` property:

```
<Window x:Class="Recipe_04_02.Window1"
    xmlns="http://schemas.microsoft.com/winfx/2006/xaml/presentation"
    xmlns:x="http://schemas.microsoft.com/winfx/2006/xaml"
    xmlns:Recipe_04_02="clr-namespace:Recipe_04_02;assembly="
    Title="WPF Recipes 4_02" Height="72" Width="300">
    <Grid>
        <Recipe_04_02:FileInputControl
            Margin="8">
            c:\readme.txt
        </Recipe_04_02:FileInputControl>
    </Grid>
</Window>
```

4-3. Add Properties to a User Control

Problem

You need to allow internal aspects of the behavior and appearance of your `System.Windows.Controls.UserControl` to be changed by the control consumer and to be accessible to WPF features such as data binding, styles, and animations.

Solution

Create a standard .NET property in the code-behind of your user control, and use it in the internal configuration of the control to determine aspects of behavior or appearance. Create a static `System.Windows.DependencyProperty` field, with the word *Property* added to the end of your property name, and use it to back the standard .NET property. Register the dependency property in the static constructor of the user control.

How It Works

By using a `DependencyProperty` to hold the value of behavioral or appearance properties of your user control, you can use the full range of WPF features such as data binding, styling, and animations to interact with these values.

The Code

The following example demonstrates how to use `DependencyProperties` to interact with a custom `PageNumberControl` that displays a descriptive page number string, for example, "Page 2 of 8."

The user control exposes `Count` and `Total` dependency properties in the code-behind, which are then used in the control's XAML to construct the display string.

```csharp
using System.Windows;
using System.Windows.Controls;

namespace Recipe_04_03
{
    /// <summary>
    /// Show the page number text in the format:
    ///     <!-- Page <Current> of <Total>
    /// </summary>
    public partial class PageNumberControl : UserControl
    {
        public PageNumberControl()
        {
            InitializeComponent();
        }

        public int Current
        {
            get
            {
                return (int) GetValue(CurrentProperty);
            }
            set
            {
                if(value <= Total
                   && value >= 0)
                {
                    SetValue(CurrentProperty, value);
                }
            }
        }

        public static readonly DependencyProperty CurrentProperty =
            DependencyProperty.Register("Current",
                                    typeof(int),
                                    typeof(PageNumberControl),
                                    new PropertyMetadata(0));

        public int Total
        {
            get
            {
                return (int) GetValue(TotalProperty);
            }
```

```
        set
        {
            if(value >= Current
               && value >= 0)
            {
                SetValue(TotalProperty, value);
            }
        }
    }

    public static readonly DependencyProperty TotalProperty =
        DependencyProperty.Register("Total",
                                    typeof(int),
                                    typeof(PageNumberControl),
                                    new PropertyMetadata(0));
}
}
```

The XAML for the PageNumberControl is as follows:

```xml
<UserControl
    x:Class="Recipe_04_03.PageNumberControl"
    xmlns="http://schemas.microsoft.com/winfx/2006/xaml/presentation"
    xmlns:x="http://schemas.microsoft.com/winfx/2006/xaml"
    x:Name="rootControl"
    Height="100" Width="200">
    <StackPanel
        Orientation="Horizontal"
        HorizontalAlignment="Center"
        VerticalAlignment="Center"
        Margin="10">

        <!-- Show the page number text in the format: -->
        <!-- Page <Current> of <Total> -->
        <TextBlock Text="Page "/>
        <TextBlock
            Text="{Binding
            ElementName=rootControl,
            Path=Current}"
            />
        <TextBlock Text=" of "/>
        <TextBlock
            Text="{Binding
            ElementName=rootControl,
            Path=Total}"
            />
    </StackPanel>
</UserControl>
```

The following XAML shows how to use the PageNumberControl in a window and contains buttons that, when clicked, change the Current and Total properties and automatically update the display. Figure 4-2 shows the resulting window.

```xml
<Window x:Class="Recipe_04_03.Window1"
    xmlns="http://schemas.microsoft.com/winfx/2006/xaml/presentation"
    xmlns:x="http://schemas.microsoft.com/winfx/2006/xaml"
    xmlns:Recipe_04_03="clr-namespace:Recipe_04_03;assembly="
    Title="WPF Recipes 4_03" Height="120" Width="260">
    <Grid>

        <Grid.RowDefinitions>
            <RowDefinition Height="0.25*" />
            <RowDefinition Height="0.75*" />
        </Grid.RowDefinitions>

        <Recipe_04_03:PageNumberControl
            x:Name="pageNumberControl"
            HorizontalAlignment="Center"
            VerticalAlignment="Center"
            Margin="4"
            Current="2"
            Total="5"
            />

        <GroupBox Header="Test"
                Margin="4"
                Grid.Row="1"
                HorizontalAlignment="Stretch"
                VerticalAlignment="Stretch">
            <StackPanel
                Orientation="Horizontal">
                <Button Click="DecreaseCurrent_Click"
                    Margin="4">
                    Current--
                </Button>
                <Button Click="IncreaseCurrent_Click"
                    Margin="4">
                    Current++
                </Button>
                <Button Click="DecreaseTotal_Click"
                    Margin="4">
                    Total--
                </Button>
                <Button Click="IncreaseTotal_Click"
                    Margin="4">
                    Total++
                </Button>
```

```
            </StackPanel>
        </GroupBox>

    </Grid>
</Window>
```

The code in the window's code-behind handles the click events of the buttons and simply increments or decrements the PageNumberControl's dependency properties:

```
using System.Windows;

namespace Recipe_04_03
{
    public partial class Window1 : Window
    {
        public Window1()
        {
            InitializeComponent();
        }

        private void DecreaseCurrent_Click(object sender,
                                        RoutedEventArgs e)
        {
            pageNumberControl.Current--;
        }

        private void IncreaseCurrent_Click(object sender,
                                        RoutedEventArgs e)
        {
            pageNumberControl.Current++;
        }

        private void DecreaseTotal_Click(object sender,
                                        RoutedEventArgs e)
        {
            pageNumberControl.Total--;
        }

        private void IncreaseTotal_Click(object sender,
                                        RoutedEventArgs e)
        {
            pageNumberControl.Total++;
        }
    }
}
```

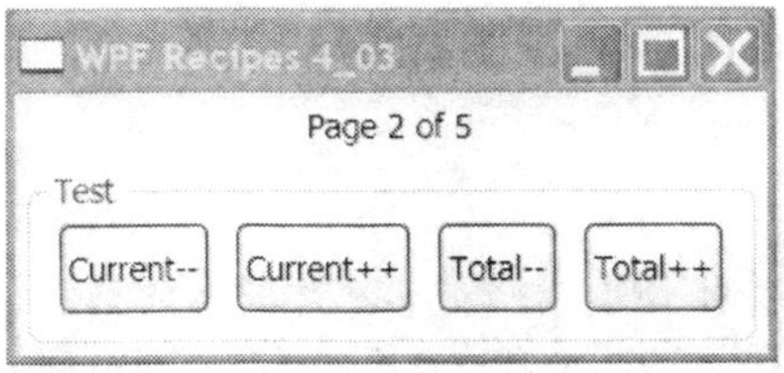

Figure 4-2. *Using* DependencyProperties *in a* PageNumberControl *to allow the current and total page numbers to be manipulated*

4-4. Add Events to a User Control

Problem

You need to notify the control consumer when something happens in your System.Windows.Controls.UserControl and allow it to use this event with WPF features such as triggers, animations, and event bubbling and tunneling.

Solution

Create a static property of type System.Windows.RoutedEvent in the code-behind of your user control, with the word *Event* added to the end of the name of the event you want to raise, and register it with the EventManager:

```
public static RoutedEvent SearchChangedEvent =
          EventManager.RegisterRoutedEvent(
                                        "SearchChanged",
                                        RoutingStrategy.Bubble,
                                        typeof(SearchChangedEventHandler),
                                        typeof(SearchControl));
```

Then use the RaiseEvent method of the base System.Windows.UIElement class to notify the consumer of the user control:

```
SearchChangedEventArgs args = new SearchChangedEventArgs(txtSearch.Text);
args.RoutedEvent = SearchChangedEvent;
RaiseEvent(args);
```

How It Works

By using a RoutedEvent to wrap an ordinary .NET event, you can expose this event to the consumer of your user control and allow it to use the full range of WPF features such as triggers, animations, and event bubbling and tunneling.

The Code

The following example demonstrates how to use a RoutedEvent to notify the control consumer when the search text is changed within a custom search user control. The SearchControl defined next contains a System.Windows.Controls.TextBox for entering a new search string, as well as a System.Windows.Controls.Button to raise a SearchChanged event. The SearchChanged event is also raised when the Enter key is pressed within the search TextBox. An instance of this SearchControl is defined in a window, and an event handler is added to the SearchChanged events, which displays the new search text in a System.Windows.MessageBox.

The XAML for the SearchControl user control is as follows:

```xml
<UserControl x:Class="Recipe_04_04.SearchControl"
    xmlns="http://schemas.microsoft.com/winfx/2006/xaml/presentation"
    xmlns:x="http://schemas.microsoft.com/winfx/2006/xaml"
    Height="Auto" Width="Auto">

    <UserControl.Resources>
        <ResourceDictionary>
            <ResourceDictionary.MergedDictionaries>
                <ResourceDictionary Source="SearchImage.xaml"/>
            </ResourceDictionary.MergedDictionaries>
        </ResourceDictionary>
    </UserControl.Resources>

    <Grid>

        <Grid.ColumnDefinitions>
            <ColumnDefinition Width="*"/>
            <ColumnDefinition Width="48"/>
        </Grid.ColumnDefinitions>

        <Grid.RowDefinitions>
            <RowDefinition />
            <RowDefinition />
        </Grid.RowDefinitions>

        <TextBlock>
            Enter your search text:
        </TextBlock>

        <TextBox
            x:Name="txtSearch"
            KeyDown="txtSearch_KeyDown"
            Grid.Row="1"/>

        <Button Grid.Column="1"
                Grid.RowSpan="2"
                Margin="4,0,0,0"
                Click="SearchButton_Click">
            <Image Source="{StaticResource SearchImage}"/>
        </Button>

    </Grid>
</UserControl>
```

The code-behind declares the SearchChanged RoutedEvent:

```csharp
using System.Windows;
using System.Windows.Controls;
using System.Windows.Input;

namespace Recipe_04_04
{
    /// <summary>
    /// A reusable Search UserControl that raises a
    /// RoutedEvent when a new search is requested.
    /// </summary>
    public partial class SearchControl : UserControl
    {
        public SearchControl()
        {
            InitializeComponent();
        }

        public static RoutedEvent SearchChangedEvent =
            EventManager.RegisterRoutedEvent(
                "SearchChanged",
                RoutingStrategy.Bubble,
                typeof(SearchChangedEventHandler),
                typeof(SearchControl));

        /// <summary>
        /// The SearchChanged event that can be handled
        /// by the consuming control.
        /// </summary>
        public event SearchChangedEventHandler SearchChanged
        {
            add
            {
                AddHandler(SearchChangedEvent, value);
            }
            remove
            {
                RemoveHandler(SearchChangedEvent, value);
            }
        }

        private void SearchButton_Click(
            object sender,
            RoutedEventArgs e)
        {
            // Raise the SearchChanged RoutedEvent when
            // the Search button is clicked
```

```
            OnSearchChanged();
        }

        private void txtSearch_KeyDown(
            object sender,
            KeyEventArgs e)
        {
            if(e.Key == Key.Enter)
            {
                // Raise the SearchChanged RoutedEvent when
                // the Enter key is pressed in the Search TextBox
                OnSearchChanged();
            }
        }

        private void OnSearchChanged()
        {
            SearchChangedEventArgs args =
                new SearchChangedEventArgs(txtSearch.Text);
            args.RoutedEvent = SearchChangedEvent;
            RaiseEvent(args);
        }
    }

    public delegate void SearchChangedEventHandler(
        object sender,
        SearchChangedEventArgs e);

    public class SearchChangedEventArgs
        : RoutedEventArgs
    {
        private readonly string searchText;

        public SearchChangedEventArgs(
            string searchText)
        {
            this.searchText = searchText;
        }

        public string SearchText
        {
            get
            {
                return searchText;
            }
        }
    }
}
```

The following XAML shows how to use the SearchControl in a window and adds an event handler to the SearchChanged event. Figure 4-3 shows the resulting window.

```
<Window x:Class="Recipe_04_04.Window1"
    xmlns="http://schemas.microsoft.com/winfx/2006/xaml/presentation"
    xmlns:x="http://schemas.microsoft.com/winfx/2006/xaml"
    xmlns:Recipe_04_04="clr-namespace:Recipe_04_04;assembly="
    Title="WPF Recipes 4_04" Height="86" Width="240">

    <Grid>
        <Recipe_04_04:SearchControl
            Margin="8"
            SearchChanged="SearchControl_SearchChanged"/>
    </Grid>
</Window>
```

The code in the code-behind for the window handles the SearchControl's SearchChanged RoutedEvent and shows the new search text in a message box:

```
using System.Windows;
using Recipe_04_04;

namespace Recipe_04_04
{
    /// <summary>
    /// This window creates an instance of SearchControl
    /// and handles the SearchChanged event, showing the
    /// new search text in a message box
    /// </summary>
    public partial class Window1 : Window
    {
        public Window1()
        {
            InitializeComponent();
        }

        private void SearchControl_SearchChanged(
            object sender,
            SearchChangedEventArgs e)
        {
            MessageBox.Show("New Search: " + e.SearchText);
        }
    }
}
```

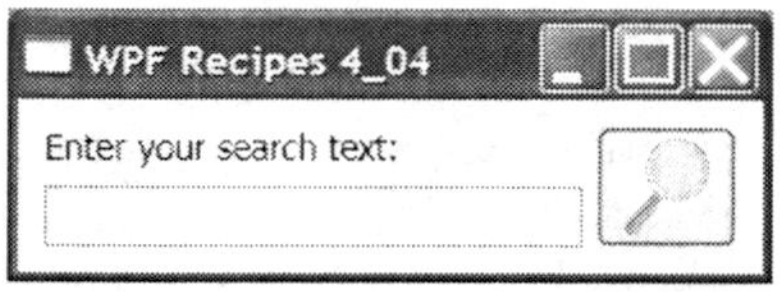

Figure 4-3. *Using a* RoutedEvent *in a reusable search user control*

4-5. Support Application Commands in a User Control

Problem

You need to support common application commands in your System.Windows.Controls. UserControl, such as Undo, Redo, Open, Copy, Paste, and so on, so that your control can respond to a command without needing any external code.

Solution

Use the System.Windows.Input.CommandManager to register an instance of the System.Windows. Input.CommandBinding class for each member of System.Windows.Input.ApplicationCommands you need to support in your user control. The CommandBinding specifies the type of command you want to receive notification of, specifies an event handler to determine when the command can be executed, and specifies another event handler to be called when the command is executed. These event handlers are called the CanExecute and Executed event handlers.

How It Works

There are many predefined commands in WPF to support common scenarios, grouped as static properties on five different classes, mostly in the System.Windows.Input namespace, as shown in Table 4-1.

Table 4-1. *Predefined Common Commands*

Value	Description
ApplicationCommands	Common commands for an application, for example, Copy, Paste, Undo, Redo, Find, Open, SaveAs, Print, and so on
ComponentCommands	Common commands for user interface components, for example, MoveLeft, MoveToEnd, ScrollPageDown, and so on
MediaCommands	Common commands used for multimedia, for example, Play, Pause, NextTrack, IncreaseVolume, ToggleMicrophoneOnOff, and so on
NavigationCommands	A set of commands used for page navigation, for example, BrowseBack, GoToPage, NextPage, Refresh, Zoom, and so on
EditingCommands	A set of commands for editing documents, for example, AlignCenter, IncreaseFontSize, EnterParagraphBreak, ToggleBold, and so on

Each command has a System.Windows.Input.InputGestureCollection that specifies the possible mouse or keyboard combinations that trigger the command. These are defined by the command itself, which is why you are able to register to receive these automatically by registering a CommandBinding for a particular command.

A CommandBinding for a particular command registers the CanExecute and Executed handlers so that the execution and the validation of the execution of the command are routed to these event handlers.

The Code

The following example creates a UserControl called FileInputControl that can be used to browse to a file using Microsoft.Win32.OpenFileDialog and display the file name in a System.Windows. Controls.TextBox.

It registers a CommandBinding for two application commands, Open and Find. When the user control has focus and the keyboard shortcuts for the Open and Find command (Ctrl+O and Ctrl+F, respectively) are used, the Executed event handler for the respective command is invoked.

The Executed event handler for the Find command launches the OpenFileDialog, as if the user has clicked the Browse button. This command can always be executed, so the CanExecute event handler simply sets the CanExecute property of System.Windows.Input.CanExecuteRoutedEventArgs to True.

The Executed event handler for the Open command launches the file that is currently displayed in the TextBox. Therefore, the CanExecute event handler for this command sets the CanExecuteRoutedEventArgs to True only if there is a valid FileName.

The XAML for the FileInputControl is as follows:

```xml
<UserControl x:Class="Recipe_04_05.FileInputControl"
    xmlns="http://schemas.microsoft.com/winfx/2006/xaml/presentation"
    xmlns:x="http://schemas.microsoft.com/winfx/2006/xaml">
    <DockPanel>

        <Button
                DockPanel.Dock="Right"
                Margin="2,0,0,0"
                Click="BrowseButton_Click">
            Browse...
        </Button>

        <TextBox x:Name="txtBox" />

    </DockPanel>
</UserControl>
```

The code-behind for the FileInputControl is as follows:

```csharp
using System.Diagnostics;
using System.IO;
using System.Windows.Controls;
using System.Windows.Input;
```

```csharp
using Microsoft.Win32;

namespace Recipe_04_05
{
    public partial class FileInputControl : UserControl
    {
        public FileInputControl()
        {
            InitializeComponent();

            // Register command bindings

            // ApplicationCommands.Find
            CommandManager.RegisterClassCommandBinding(
                typeof(FileInputControl),
                new CommandBinding(
                    ApplicationCommands.Find,
                    FindCommand_Executed,
                    FindCommand_CanExecute));

            // ApplicationCommands.Open
            CommandManager.RegisterClassCommandBinding(
                typeof(FileInputControl),
                new CommandBinding(
                    ApplicationCommands.Open,
                    OpenCommand_Executed,
                    OpenCommand_CanExecute));
        }

        #region Find Command

        private void FindCommand_CanExecute(
            object sender,
            CanExecuteRoutedEventArgs e)
        {
            e.CanExecute = true;
        }

        private void FindCommand_Executed(
            object sender,
            ExecutedRoutedEventArgs e)
        {
            DoFindFile();
        }

        #endregion
```

```csharp
#region Open Command

private void OpenCommand_CanExecute(
    object sender,
    CanExecuteRoutedEventArgs e)
{
    e.CanExecute =
        !string.IsNullOrEmpty(this.FileName)
        && File.Exists(this.FileName);
}

private void OpenCommand_Executed(
    object sender,
    ExecutedRoutedEventArgs e)
{
    Process.Start(this.FileName);
}

#endregion

private void BrowseButton_Click(
    object sender,
    System.Windows.RoutedEventArgs e)
{
    DoFindFile();
}

private void DoFindFile()
{
    OpenFileDialog dlg = new OpenFileDialog();
    if(dlg.ShowDialog() == true)
    {
        this.FileName = dlg.FileName;
    }
}

public string FileName
{
    get
    {
        return txtBox.Text;
    }
```

```
        set
        {
            txtBox.Text = value;
        }
    }
  }
}
```

The following XAML shows how to use the FileInputControl in a window.

If the TextBox has the focus, then pressing the keyboard shortcut Ctrl+F will automatically open the OpenFileDialog. If a file is selected and a valid file name appears in the TextBox, then the shortcut Ctrl+O will launch it.

```
<Window x:Class="Recipe_04_05.Window1"
    xmlns="http://schemas.microsoft.com/winfx/2006/xaml/presentation"
    xmlns:x="http://schemas.microsoft.com/winfx/2006/xaml"
    xmlns:Recipe_04_05="clr-namespace:Recipe_04_05;assembly="
    Title="WPF Recipes 4_05" Height="72" Width="300">
    <Grid>
        <Recipe_04_05:FileInputControl
            Margin="8"/>
    </Grid>
</Window>
```

4-6. Add Custom Commands to a User Control

Problem

You need to add custom commands to your System.Windows.Controls.UserControl to enable consumers of your control to bind to and execute units of functionality and custom behavior.

Solution

Create a static System.Windows.Input.RoutedCommand property in the code-behind of your user control. In the static constructor, initialize a class-level instance of this RoutedCommand and give it a name, the type of your user control, and any input gestures you want to associate with it. A System.Windows.Input.InputGesture associates keyboard and mouse inputs with your commands so that when a certain key combination is pressed, for example, Ctrl+W, the System.Windows. Input.CommandManager will execute your command.

Create an instance of the System.Windows.Input.CommandBinding class for your RoutedCommand, and specify an event handler to determine when the command can be executed and another event handler to be called when the command is executed.

Consumers of your control can now define visual elements that data bind directly to your static command property.

How It Works

Three types of command classes in WPF support data binding, and they can all be found in the System.Windows.Input namespace (see Table 4-2).

Table 4-2. *Three Types of WPF Commands*

Value	Description
ICommand	The basic command interface in WPF. This exposes two methods, Execute and CanExecute, and a CanExecuteChanged event.
RoutedCommand	Implements ICommand and adds support for event tunneling and bubbling and input gestures.
RoutedUICommand	Derives from RoutedCommand and adds a localizable Text property.

Creating a RoutedCommand or RoutedUICommand allows you to expose custom command functionality and automatically plug in to the event tunneling and bubbling mechanisms in WPF that route a consumer of your command to your custom event handlers.

The Code

The following example creates a user control called PageNumberControl that displays a descriptive page number string, for example, "Page 2 of 8."

The code-behind for the user control exposes a public RoutedCommand property called IncreaseTotal, which increases the total number of pages when executed. The static constructor initializes a CommandBinding that binds this command to the CanExecute and Executed event handlers.

The control is then consumed in a window, which demonstrates how to bind a System.Windows.Controls.Button to the custom command in XAML.

The XAML for the PageNumberControl is as follows:

```
<UserControl
    x:Class="Recipe_04_06.PageNumberControl"
    xmlns="http://schemas.microsoft.com/winfx/2006/xaml/presentation"
    xmlns:x="http://schemas.microsoft.com/winfx/2006/xaml"
    x:Name="rootControl"
    Height="100" Width="200">
    <StackPanel
        Orientation="Horizontal"
        HorizontalAlignment="Center"
        VerticalAlignment="Center"
        Margin="10">

        <!-- Show the page number text in the format: -->
        <!-- Page <Current> of <Total> -->
        <TextBlock Text="Page "/>
        <TextBlock
```

```
                Text="{Binding
                ElementName=rootControl,
                Path=Current}"
                />
        <TextBlock Text=" of "/>
        <TextBlock
            Text="{Binding
            ElementName=rootControl,
            Path=Total}"
            />
    </StackPanel>
</UserControl>
```

The code-behind for the PageNumberControl is as follows:

```
using System.Windows;
using System.Windows.Controls;
using System.Windows.Input;

namespace Recipe_04_06
{
    /// <summary>
    /// Show the page number text in the format:
    ///     <!-- Page <Current> of <Total>
    /// </summary>
    public partial class PageNumberControl : UserControl
    {
        private static RoutedCommand increaseTotalCommand;

        public static RoutedCommand IncreaseTotal
        {
            get
            {
                return increaseTotalCommand;
            }
        }

        static PageNumberControl()
        {
            // Create an input gesture so that the command
            // is executed when the Add (+) key is pressed
            InputGestureCollection myInputs =
                new InputGestureCollection();
            myInputs.Add(
                new KeyGesture(
                    Key.Add,
                    ModifierKeys.Control));
```

```csharp
        // Create a RoutedCommand
        increaseTotalCommand =
            new RoutedCommand(
                "IncreaseTotal",
                typeof(PageNumberControl),
                myInputs);

        // Create a CommandBinding, specifying the
        // Execute and CanExecute handlers
        CommandBinding binding =
            new CommandBinding();

        binding.Command = increaseTotalCommand;
        binding.Executed +=
            new ExecutedRoutedEventHandler(binding_Executed);
        binding.CanExecute +=
            new CanExecuteRoutedEventHandler(binding_CanExecute);

        // Register the CommandBinding
        CommandManager.RegisterClassCommandBinding(
            typeof(PageNumberControl), binding);
    }

    public PageNumberControl()
    {
        InitializeComponent();
    }

    static void binding_CanExecute(
        object sender,
        CanExecuteRoutedEventArgs e)
    {
        // The command can execute as long as the
        // Total is less than the maximum integer value
        PageNumberControl control = (PageNumberControl) sender;
        e.CanExecute = control.Total < int.MaxValue;
    }

    private static void binding_Executed(
        object sender,
        ExecutedRoutedEventArgs e)
    {
        // Increment the value of Total when
        // the command is executed
        PageNumberControl control = (PageNumberControl) sender;
        control.Total++;
    }
```

```csharp
public int Current
{
    get
    {
        return (int) GetValue(CurrentProperty);
    }
    set
    {
        if(value <= Total
           && value >= 0)
        {
            SetValue(CurrentProperty, value);
        }
    }
}

public static readonly DependencyProperty CurrentProperty =
    DependencyProperty.Register("Current",
                                typeof(int),
                                typeof(PageNumberControl));

public int Total
{
    get
    {
        return (int) GetValue(TotalProperty);
    }
    set
    {
        if(value >= Current
           && value >= 0)
        {
            SetValue(TotalProperty, value);
        }
    }
}

public static readonly DependencyProperty TotalProperty =
    DependencyProperty.Register("Total",
                                typeof(int),
                                typeof(PageNumberControl));
    }
}
```

The following XAML shows how to use the PageNumberControl in a window, with a Button control that data binds to the IncreaseTotal command:

```xml
<Window x:Class="Recipe_04_06.Window1"
    xmlns="http://schemas.microsoft.com/winfx/2006/xaml/presentation"
    xmlns:x="http://schemas.microsoft.com/winfx/2006/xaml"
    xmlns:Recipe_04_06="clr-namespace:Recipe_04_06;assembly="
    Title="WPF Recipes 4_06" Height="120" Width="260">
    <Grid>

        <Grid.RowDefinitions>
            <RowDefinition Height="0.25*" />
            <RowDefinition Height="0.75*" />
        </Grid.RowDefinitions>

        <Recipe_04_06:PageNumberControl
            x:Name="pageNumberControl"
            HorizontalAlignment="Center"
            VerticalAlignment="Center"
            Margin="4"
            Current="2"
            Total="5"
            />

        <GroupBox Header="Test"
                Margin="4"
                Grid.Row="1"
                HorizontalAlignment="Stretch"
                VerticalAlignment="Stretch">
            <StackPanel
                Orientation="Horizontal">

                <Button
                    Command="Recipe_04_06:PageNumberControl.IncreaseTotal"
                    CommandTarget=
                        "{Binding ElementName=pageNumberControl}"
                    Margin="4">
                    Total++
                </Button>
            </StackPanel>
        </GroupBox>

    </Grid>
</Window>
```

Figure 4-4 shows the resulting window.

Figure 4-4. *Data binding to a custom RoutedCommand in a user control*

4-7. Set Design Mode Behavior in a User Control

Problem

You need to determine whether your System.Windows.Controls.UserControl is running in design mode (for example, being displayed in the Visual Studio or Expression Blend designer) and set specific behavior.

Solution

Use the System.ComponentModel.DesignerProperties.GetIsInDesignMode method in the constructor for your user control.

How It Works

The static System.ComponentModel.DesignerProperties exposes an IsInDesignMode attached property that returns true if the control is currently running in design mode.

Tip Setting specific behavior for your user control when it is in design mode can be useful for priming your user control with the kind of data or property values that would normally be set only at runtime. This enables your control to display itself realistically for designers, even when there is no actual data or property values available for it during design.

The Code

The following example demonstrates a simple user control called MyUserControl that contains a button with some text as Content. The constructor for the control calls the GetIsInDesignMode method and changes the button's Text property depending on whether it is currently being displayed in design mode.

The XAML for the control is as follows:

```
<UserControl x:Class="Recipe_04_07.MyUserControl"
    xmlns="http://schemas.microsoft.com/winfx/2006/xaml/presentation"
    xmlns:x="http://schemas.microsoft.com/winfx/2006/xaml">
    <Grid>
        <Button x:Name="btnMode">
            Set Design Mode Behavior
        </Button>
    </Grid>
</UserControl>
```

The code-behind for the control calls the GetIsInDesignMode:

```
using System.Windows.Controls;

namespace Recipe_04_07
{
    public partial class MyUserControl : UserControl
    {
        public MyUserControl()
        {
            InitializeComponent();

            // Call the GetIsInDesignMode method
            if(System.ComponentModel.DesignerProperties.GetIsInDesignMode(this))
            {
                btnMode.Content = "In Design Mode";
            }
            else
            {
                btnMode.Content = "Runtime";
            }
        }
    }
}
```

Figure 4-5 shows the control when displayed by the Visual Studio designer.

Figure 4-5. *Displaying the user control in design mode*

Figure 4-6 shows the control when displayed at runtime.

Figure 4-6. *Displaying the user control in a window at runtime*

4-8. Create a Lookless Custom Control

Problem

You need to create a custom control that encapsulates functionality and behavior logic but that can have its visual appearance changed by consumers. For example, you need consumers to be able to change the style, template, or visual theme of your control for a particular context, application, or operating system theme.

Solution

Create a lookless custom control class that contains interaction and behavior logic but little or no assumptions about its visual implementation. Then declare the default visual elements for it in a control template within a default style.

■Tip When creating the code for a custom control, you need to ensure it is lookless and assumes as little as possible about the actual implementation of the visual elements in the control template, because it could well be different across different consumers. This means ensuring that the UI is decoupled from the interaction logic by using commands and bindings, avoiding event handlers, and referencing elements in the ControlTemplate whenever possible.

How It Works

The first step in creating a lookless custom control is choosing which control to inherit from. You should derive from the most basic option available to you, because it provides the minimum required functionality and gives the control consumer the maximum freedom. On the other hand, it also makes sense to leverage as much built-in support as possible by deriving from an existing WPF control if it possesses similar behavior and functionality to your custom control. For example, if your control will be clickable, then it might make sense to inherit from the Button class. If your control is not only clickable but also has the notion of being in a selected or unselected state, then it might make sense to inherit from ToggleButton.

Some of the main base classes you can choose from are listed in Table 4-3.

Table 4-3. *Main Base Classes for Creating a Custom Control*

Name	Description
FrameworkElement	This is usually the most basic element from which you will derive. Use this when you need to draw your own element by overriding the OnRender method and explicitly defining the component visuals. FrameworkElement classes tend not to interact with the user; for example, the WPF Image and Border controls are FrameworkElement classes.
Control	Control is the base class used by most of the existing WPF controls. It allows you to define its appearance by using control templates, and it adds properties for setting the background and foreground, font, padding, tab index, and alignment of content. It also supports double-clicking through the MouseDoubleClick and PreviewMouseDoubleClick events.
ContentControl	This inherits from Control and adds a Content property that provides the ability to contain a single piece of content, which could be a string or another visual element. For example, a button ultimately derives from ContentControl, which is why it has the ability to contain any arbitrary visual element such as an image. Use this as your base class if you need your control to contain other objects defined by the control consumer.
Panel	This has a property called Children that contains a collection of System.Windows.UIElements, and it provides the layout logic for positioning these children within it.
Decorator	This wraps another control to decorate it with a particular visual effect or feature. For example, the Border is a Decorator control that draws a line around an element.

After choosing an appropriate base class for your custom control, you can create the class and put the logic for the interaction, functionality, and behavior of your control in the custom control class.

However, don't define your visual elements in a XAML file for the class, like you would with a user control. Instead, put the default definition of visual elements in a System.Windows. ControlTemplate, and declare this ControlTemplate in a default System.Windows.Style.

The next step is to specify that you will be providing this new style; otherwise, your control will continue to use the default template of its base class. You specify this by calling the OverrideMetadata method of DefaultStyleKeyProperty in the static constructor for your class.

Next, you need to place your style in the Generic.xaml resource dictionary in the Themes subfolder of your project. This ensures it is recognized as the default style for your control. You can also create other resource dictionaries in this subfolder, which enables you to target specific operating systems and give your custom controls a different visual appearance for each one.

■**Tip** When a custom control library contains several controls, it is often better the keep their styles separate instead of putting them all in the same Generic.xaml resource dictionary. You can use resource dictionary merging to keep each style in a separate resource dictionary file and then merge them into the main Generic.xaml one.

The custom style and template for your control must use the System.Type.TargetType attribute to attach it to the custom control automatically.

Tip In Visual Studio, when you add a new WPF custom control to an existing project, it does a number of the previous steps for you. It automatically creates a code file with the correct call to DefaultStyleKeyproperty. OverrideMetadata. It creates the Themes subfolder and Generic.xaml resource dictionary if they don't already exist, and it defines a placeholder Style and ControlTemplate in there.

When creating your custom control class and default control template, you have to remember to make as few assumptions as possible about the actual implementation of the visual elements. This is in order to make the custom control as flexible as possible and to give control consumers as much freedom as possible when creating new styles and control templates.

You can enable this separation between the interaction logic and the visual implementation of your control in a number of ways.

First, when binding a property of a visual element in the default ControlTemplate to a dependency property of the control, use the System.Windows.Data.RelativeSource property instead of naming the element and referencing it via the ElementName property.

Second, instead of declaring event handlers in the XAML for the template, for example, for the Click event of a Button, either add the event handler programmatically in the control constructor or bind to commands. If you choose to use event handlers and bind them programmatically, override the OnApplyTemplate method and locate the controls dynamically.

Furthermore, give names only to those elements that without which the control would not be able to function as intended. By convention, give these intrinsic elements the name PART_ElementName so that they can be identified as part of the public interface for your control. For example, it is intrinsic to a ProgressBar that it has a visual element representing the total value at completion and a visual element indicating the relative value of the current progress. The default ControlTemplate for the System.Windows.Controls.ProgressBar therefore defines two named elements, PART_Track and PART_Indicator. These happen to be Border controls in the default template, but there is no reason why a control consumer could not provide a custom template that uses different controls to display these functional parts.

Tip If your control requires named elements, as well as using the previously mentioned naming convention, apply the System.Windows.TemplatePart attribute to your control class, which documents and signals this requirement to users of your control and to design tools such as Expression Blend.

The following code example demonstrates how to separate the interaction logic and the visual implementation using these methods.

The Code

The following example demonstrates how to create a lookless custom control to encapsulate the functionality of browsing to a file and displaying the file name. Figure 4-7 shows the control in use.

The FileInputControl class derives from Control and uses the TemplatePart attribute to signal that it expects a Button control called PART_Browse. It overrides the OnApplyTemplate method and calls GetTemplateChild to find the button defined by its actual template. If this exists, it adds an event handler to the button's Click event.

The code for the control is as follows:

```
using System.Windows;
using System.Windows.Controls;
using System.Windows.Markup;
using Microsoft.Win32;

namespace Recipe_04_08
{
    [TemplatePart(Name = "PART_Browse", Type = typeof(Button))]
    [ContentProperty("FileName")]
    public class FileInputControl : Control
    {
        static FileInputControl()
        {
            DefaultStyleKeyProperty.OverrideMetadata(
                typeof(FileInputControl),
                new FrameworkPropertyMetadata(
                    typeof(FileInputControl)));
        }

        public override void OnApplyTemplate()
        {
            base.OnApplyTemplate();

            Button browseButton = base.GetTemplateChild("PART_Browse") as Button;

            if(browseButton != null)
                browseButton.Click += new RoutedEventHandler(browseButton_Click);
        }

        void browseButton_Click(object sender, RoutedEventArgs e)
        {
            OpenFileDialog dlg = new OpenFileDialog();
            if(dlg.ShowDialog() == true)
            {
                this.FileName = dlg.FileName;
            }
        }
```

```
    public string FileName
    {
        get
        {
            return (string) GetValue(FileNameProperty);
        }
        set
        {
            SetValue(FileNameProperty, value);
        }
    }

    public static readonly DependencyProperty FileNameProperty =
        DependencyProperty.Register (
                    "FileName",
                    typeof(string),
                    typeof(FileInputControl));
    }
}
```

The default style and control template for FileInputControl is in a ResourceDictionary in the Themes subfolder and is merged into the Generic ResourceDictionary. The XAML for this style is as follows:

```
<ResourceDictionary
    xmlns="http://schemas.microsoft.com/winfx/2006/xaml/presentation"
    xmlns:x="http://schemas.microsoft.com/winfx/2006/xaml"
    xmlns:Recipe_04_08="clr-namespace:Recipe_04_08;assembly=">

    <Style TargetType="{x:Type Recipe_04_08:FileInputControl}">
        <Setter Property="Template">
            <Setter.Value>
                <ControlTemplate
                    TargetType="{x:Type Recipe_04_08:FileInputControl}">
                    <Border Background="{TemplateBinding Background}"
                            BorderBrush="{TemplateBinding BorderBrush}"
                            BorderThickness="{TemplateBinding BorderThickness}">
                        <DockPanel>

                            <Button
                                x:Name="PART_Browse"
                                DockPanel.Dock="Right"
                                Margin="2,0,0,0">
                                Browse...
                            </Button>
```

```
                            <TextBox
                                IsReadOnly="True"
                                Text="{Binding
                                    Path=FileName,
                                    RelativeSource=
                                        {RelativeSource TemplatedParent}}"
                                />

                        </DockPanel>
                    </Border>
                </ControlTemplate>
            </Setter.Value>
        </Setter>
    </Style>

</ResourceDictionary>
```

The XAML for the window that consumes this custom control is as follows:

```
<Window x:Class="Recipe_04_08.Window1"
    xmlns="http://schemas.microsoft.com/winfx/2006/xaml/presentation"
    xmlns:x="http://schemas.microsoft.com/winfx/2006/xaml"
    xmlns:Recipe_04_08="clr-namespace:Recipe_04_08;assembly="
    Title="WPF Recipes 4_08" Height="72" Width="300">
    <Grid>
        <Recipe_04_08:FileInputControl
            Margin="8"
            />
    </Grid>
</Window>
```

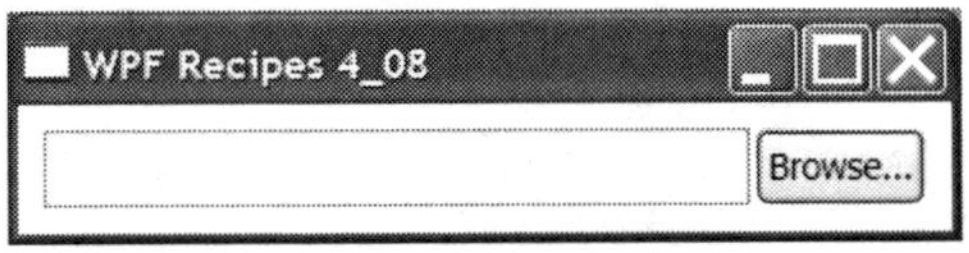

Figure 4-7. *Creating and using a* FileInput *custom control*

4-9. Specify the Parts Required by a Custom Control

Problem

You need to specify that consumers of your custom control should define certain elements within the control template in order for the control to function correctly.

Solution

In the default control template for your custom control, name any elements that are required by your control to function correctly, according to the naming convention PART_ElementName.

You should then document each part's existence by marking your class with System.Windows.TemplatePartAttribute, specifying the name and System.Type as parameters.

In the code for your custom control, add any event handlers to these elements dynamically by overriding the OnApplyTemplate method and locating the actual implementation of the element by calling GetTemplateChild.

How It Works

By documenting any parts required by your custom control using TemplatePartAttribute, you signal this requirement to consumers of your control and to design tools such as Expression Blend.

Furthermore, by attaching any necessary event handlers to the control parts programmatically, you ensure that they do not have to be specified in every template defined for your control by a consumer.

Tip When locating these parts in the code for your custom control, it is recommended that you handle any omissions gracefully. If a template does not define a specific element, it should not cause an exception in your code. This not only allows consumers of your control to support just the functionality they require, but it also prevents issues when your control is used within design tools such as Expression Blend.

The Code

The following example demonstrates how to create a lookless custom control to encapsulate the functionality of browsing to a file and displaying the file name. Figure 4-8 shows the control in use.

The FileInputControl class derives from Control and uses the TemplatePart attribute to signal that it expects a Button control called PART_Browse. It overrides the OnApplyTemplate method and calls GetTemplateChild to find the button defined by its actual template. If this exists, it adds an event handler to the button's Click event.

The code for the control is as follows:

```
using System.Windows;
using System.Windows.Controls;
using Microsoft.Win32;

namespace Recipe_04_09
{
    /// <summary>
    /// The TemplatePart attribute specifies that the control
    /// expects the Control Template to contain a Button called
    /// PART_Browse
    /// </summary>
    [TemplatePart(Name = "PART_Browse", Type = typeof(Button))]
```

```csharp
public class FileInputControl : Control
{
    static FileInputControl()
    {
        DefaultStyleKeyProperty.OverrideMetadata(
            typeof(FileInputControl),
            new FrameworkPropertyMetadata(
                typeof(FileInputControl)));
    }

    public override void OnApplyTemplate()
    {
        base.OnApplyTemplate();

        // Use the GetTemplateChild method to locate
        // the button called PART_Browse
        Button browseButton = base.GetTemplateChild("PART_Browse") as Button;

        // Do not cause or throw an exception
        // if it wasn't supplied by the Template
        if(browseButton != null)
            browseButton.Click += new RoutedEventHandler(browseButton_Click);
    }

    void browseButton_Click(object sender, RoutedEventArgs e)
    {
        OpenFileDialog dlg = new OpenFileDialog();
        if(dlg.ShowDialog() == true)
        {
            this.FileName = dlg.FileName;
        }
    }

    public string FileName
    {
        get
        {
            return (string) GetValue(FileNameProperty);
        }
        set
        {
            SetValue(FileNameProperty, value);
        }
    }

    public static readonly DependencyProperty FileNameProperty =
        DependencyProperty.Register(
```

```
                "FileName",
                typeof(string),
                typeof(FileInputControl));
    }
}
```

The default style and control template for FileInputControl is in a ResourceDictionary in the Themes subfolder and is merged into the generic ResourceDictionary. The XAML for this style is as follows:

```xml
<ResourceDictionary
    xmlns="http://schemas.microsoft.com/winfx/2006/xaml/presentation"
    xmlns:x="http://schemas.microsoft.com/winfx/2006/xaml"
    xmlns:Recipe_04_09="clr-namespace:Recipe_04_09;assembly=">

    <Style TargetType="{x:Type Recipe_04_09:FileInputControl}">
        <Setter Property="Template">
            <Setter.Value>
                <ControlTemplate
                    TargetType="{x:Type Recipe_04_09:FileInputControl}">
                    <Border Background="{TemplateBinding Background}"
                            BorderBrush="{TemplateBinding BorderBrush}"
                            BorderThickness="{TemplateBinding BorderThickness}">
                        <DockPanel>

                            <Button
                                x:Name="PART_Browse"
                                DockPanel.Dock="Right"
                                Margin="2,0,0,0">
                                Browse...
                            </Button>

                            <TextBox
                                IsReadOnly="True"
                                Text="{Binding
                                    Path=FileName,
                                    RelativeSource=
                                        {RelativeSource TemplatedParent}}"
                                />

                        </DockPanel>
                    </Border>
                </ControlTemplate>
            </Setter.Value>
        </Setter>
    </Style>

</ResourceDictionary>
```

The XAML for the window that consumes this custom control is as follows:

```
<Window x:Class="Recipe_04_09.Window1"
    xmlns="http://schemas.microsoft.com/winfx/2006/xaml/presentation"
    xmlns:x="http://schemas.microsoft.com/winfx/2006/xaml"
    xmlns:Recipe_04_09="clr-namespace:Recipe_04_09;assembly="
    Title="WPF Recipes 4_09" Height="72" Width="300">
    <Grid>
        <Recipe_04_09:FileInputControl
            Margin="8"
            />
    </Grid>
</Window>
```

Figure 4-8. *Creating and using a FileInput custom control*

4-10. Support UI Automation in a Custom Control

Problem

You need to support UI automation in your custom control to allow test scripts to interact with the UI.

Solution

Create a companion class called ControlNameAutomationPeer for your custom control that derives from System.Windows.Automation.Peers.FrameworkElementAutomationPeer.

Override the OnCreateAutomationPeer method in your custom control, and return an instance of your companion class.

How It Works

The FrameworkElementAutomationPeer companion class describes your control to the automation system. Whenever an event occurs that should be communicated to the automation system, you can retrieve the companion class and call the Invoke method of System.Windows.Automation.Provider.IInvokeProvider.

The Code

The following example demonstrates how to create a lookless custom control to encapsulate the functionality of browsing to a file and displaying the file name.

The code for the control also defines a class called FileInputControlAutomationPeer that provides UI automation support and returns an instance of this class in the OnCreateAutomationPeer method.

The code for the control is as follows:

```
using System;
using System.Windows;
using System.Windows.Automation.Peers;
using System.Windows.Automation.Provider;
using System.Windows.Controls;
using System.Windows.Markup;
using Microsoft.Win32;

namespace Recipe_04_10
{
    [TemplatePart(Name = "PART_Browse", Type = typeof(Button))]
    [ContentProperty("FileName")]
    public class FileInputControl : Control
    {
        static FileInputControl()
        {
            DefaultStyleKeyProperty.OverrideMetadata(
                typeof(FileInputControl),
                new FrameworkPropertyMetadata(
                    typeof(FileInputControl)));
        }

        public override void OnApplyTemplate()
        {
            base.OnApplyTemplate();

            Button browseButton = base.GetTemplateChild("PART_Browse") as Button;

            if(browseButton != null)
                browseButton.Click += new RoutedEventHandler(browseButton_Click);
        }

        void browseButton_Click(object sender, RoutedEventArgs e)
        {
            OpenFileDialog dlg = new OpenFileDialog();
            if(dlg.ShowDialog() == true)
            {
                this.FileName = dlg.FileName;
            }
        }
```

```csharp
public string FileName
{
    get
    {
        return (string) GetValue(FileNameProperty);
    }
    set
    {
        SetValue(FileNameProperty, value);
    }
}

public static readonly DependencyProperty FileNameProperty =
    DependencyProperty.Register(
            "FileName",
            typeof(string),
            typeof(FileInputControl));

/// <summary>
/// Identifies SimpleButton.Click routed event.
/// </summary>
public static readonly RoutedEvent ClickEvent
        = EventManager.RegisterRoutedEvent(
                "Click",
                RoutingStrategy.Bubble,
                typeof(EventHandler),
                typeof(FileInputControl));

/// <summary>
/// Occurs when a Simple button is clicked.
/// </summary>
public event RoutedEventHandler Click
{
    add
    {
        AddHandler(ClickEvent, value);
    }
    remove
    {
        RemoveHandler(ClickEvent, value);
    }
}

/// <summary>
/// Overriding of this method provides an UI Automation support
/// </summary>
/// <returns></returns>
```

```csharp
        protected override AutomationPeer OnCreateAutomationPeer()
        {
            return new FileInputControlAutomationPeer(this);
        }
    }

    /// <summary>
    /// Class that provides UI Automation support
    /// </summary>
    public class FileInputControlAutomationPeer
        : FrameworkElementAutomationPeer,
          IInvokeProvider
    {
        public FileInputControlAutomationPeer(FileInputControl control)
            : base(control)
        {
        }

        protected override string GetClassNameCore()
        {
            return "FileInputControl";
        }

        protected override string GetLocalizedControlTypeCore()
        {
            return "FileInputControl";
        }

        protected override AutomationControlType GetAutomationControlTypeCore()
        {
            return AutomationControlType.Button;
        }

        public override object GetPattern(PatternInterface patternInterface)
        {
            if(patternInterface == PatternInterface.Invoke)
            {
                return this;
            }

            return base.GetPattern(patternInterface);
        }

        private FileInputControl MyOwner
        {
```

```
                get
                {
                    return (FileInputControl) base.Owner;
                }
            }

            #region IInvokeProvider Members

            public void Invoke()
            {
                RoutedEventArgs newEventArgs
                        = new RoutedEventArgs(FileInputControl.ClickEvent);
                MyOwner.RaiseEvent(newEventArgs);
            }
            #endregion
        }
    }
```

The control is then used in the following window. It contains a button that, when clicked, invokes the Click event of the FileInputControl via the automation peer.

The code-behind for this window is as follows:

```
using System.Windows;
using System.Windows.Automation.Peers;
using System.Windows.Automation.Provider;
using Recipe_04_10;

namespace Recipe_04_10
{
    public partial class Window1 : Window
    {
        public Window1()
        {
            InitializeComponent();

            ctlFileInput.Click +=
                new RoutedEventHandler(ctlFileInput_Click);
        }

        private void Button_Click(object sender, RoutedEventArgs e)
        {
            // Get the AutomationPeer for this control
            FileInputControlAutomationPeer peer =
                new FileInputControlAutomationPeer(ctlFileInput);

            IInvokeProvider invokeProvider =
                peer.GetPattern(PatternInterface.Invoke)
                as IInvokeProvider;
```

```csharp
            // Call the Invoke method
            invokeProvider.Invoke();
        }

        private void ctlFileInput_Click(
            object sender,
            RoutedEventArgs e)
        {
            MessageBox.Show("Invoked via the Automation Peer");
        }
    }
}
```

4-11. Create a Custom-Drawn Element

Problem

You need to be able to draw a custom element.

Solution

Create a class that derives from System.Windows.FrameworkElement, and override the OnRender method of the base class System.Windows.UIElement. Add code to render the custom element to the System.Windows.Media.DrawingContext.

How It Works

The OnRender method of UIElement is provided with a DrawingContext. This context provides methods for drawing text and geometries.

When the parent of the UIElement detects that the size has changed, OnRender is called automatically. It can also be invoked when any data or properties change by calling the InvalidateVisual method of UIElement.

The Code

The following example demonstrates how to render a custom pie chart control using the OnRender method.

The PieChartControl contains a Slices property that tells the control the slices it needs to draw. In the OnRender method, it draws each slice to the DrawingContext object.

The code for the PieChartControl is as follows:

```csharp
using System;
using System.Collections.Generic;
using System.Windows;
using System.Windows.Media;
```

```
namespace Recipe_04_11
{
    public class PieChartControl : FrameworkElement
    {
        #region Slices

        public List<double> Slices
        {
            get
            {
                return (List<double>) GetValue(SlicesProperty);
            }
            set
            {
                SetValue(SlicesProperty, value);
            }
        }

        // Using a DependencyProperty as the backing store for slices.
        // This enables animation, styling, binding, etc...
        public static readonly DependencyProperty SlicesProperty =
            DependencyProperty.Register("Slices",
                                        typeof(List<double>),
                                        typeof(PieChartControl),
                                        new FrameworkPropertyMetadata(
                                            null,
                                            FrameworkPropertyMetadataOptions.
                                            AffectsRender,
                                            new PropertyChangedCallback(
                                                OnPropertyChanged)));
        #endregion

        /// <summary>
        /// Override the OnRender and draw the slices
        /// for the pie chart
        /// </summary>
        /// <param name="drawingContext"></param>
        protected override void OnRender(DrawingContext drawingContext)
        {
            List<double> segments = this.Slices;

            if(segments != null)
            {
                Size radius = new Size(
                    this.RenderSize.Width * 0.5,
                    this.RenderSize.Height * 0.5);
```

```csharp
            Point startPoint = new Point(radius.Width, 0);

            foreach(double slice in segments)
            {
                startPoint = DrawSlice(
                    drawingContext,
                    slice,
                    startPoint,
                    radius);
            }
        }
}

private Point DrawSlice(

                                DrawingContext drawingContext,
                                double slice,
                                Point startPoint,
                                Size radius)
{
    // double theta = (slice.Percentage / 100) * 360;
    double theta = (slice / 100) * 360;

    // nb. This caters for the condition where we have one slice
    theta = (theta == 360) ? 359.99 : theta;

    //Note - we need to translate the point first.
    // Could be rolled into a single affine transformation.
    Point endPoint =
        RotatePoint(
            new Point(
                startPoint.X - radius.Width,
                startPoint.Y - radius.Height),
            theta);

    endPoint = new Point(
        endPoint.X + radius.Width,
        endPoint.Y + radius.Height);

    bool isLargeArc = (theta > 180);

    PathGeometry geometry = new PathGeometry();
    PathFigure figure = new PathFigure();

    geometry.Figures.Add(figure);

    figure.IsClosed = true;
    figure.StartPoint = startPoint;
```

```
            figure.Segments.Add(
                        new ArcSegment(endPoint, radius, 0, isLargeArc,
                                                SweepDirection.Clockwise, false));
            figure.Segments.Add(new LineSegment(startPoint, false));
            figure.Segments.Add(new LineSegment(endPoint, false));
            figure.Segments.Add(
                        new LineSegment(
                                new Point(
                                        radius.Width, radius.Height), false));

            SolidColorBrush brush = new SolidColorBrush(GetRandomColor());
            drawingContext.DrawGeometry(brush, new Pen(brush, 1), geometry);

            startPoint = endPoint;
            return startPoint;
        }

        private const double _pi_by180 = Math.PI / 180;

        private Point RotatePoint(Point a, double phi)
        {
            double theta = phi * _pi_by180;
            double x = Math.Cos(theta) * a.X + -Math.Sin(theta) * a.Y;
            double y = Math.Sin(theta) * a.X + Math.Cos(theta) * a.Y;
            return new Point(x, y);
        }

        protected static void OnPropertyChanged(
                                        DependencyObject o,
                                        DependencyPropertyChangedEventArgs args)
        {
            PieChartControl pcc = o as PieChartControl;
            if(null != pcc)
                pcc.InvalidateVisual();
        }

        private static Random seed = new Random();

        private Color GetRandomColor()
        {
            Color newColor = new Color();

            newColor.A = (byte) 255;
            newColor.R = (byte) seed.Next(0, 256);
            newColor.G = (byte) seed.Next(0, 256);
            newColor.B = (byte) seed.Next(0, 256);
```

```
        return newColor;
      }
   }
}
```

The following XAML defines a window displaying three `PieChartControl` controls.

```
<Window x:Class="Recipe_04_11.Window1"
    xmlns="http://schemas.microsoft.com/winfx/2006/xaml/presentation"
    xmlns:x="http://schemas.microsoft.com/winfx/2006/xaml"
    xmlns:Recipe_04_11="clr-namespace:Recipe_04_11;assembly="
    Title="WPF Recipes 4_11" Height="120" Width="180">
    <Grid>

        <StackPanel
            Orientation="Horizontal"
            Margin="4">

            <Recipe_04_11:PieChartControl
            x:Name="pieChart1"
            Width="36"
            Height="36"
            Margin="8"
            />
            <Recipe_04_11:PieChartControl
            x:Name="pieChart2"
            Width="36"
            Height="36"
            Margin="8"
            />
            <Recipe_04_11:PieChartControl
            x:Name="pieChart3"
            Width="36"
            Height="36"
            Margin="8"
            />
        </StackPanel>

    </Grid>
</Window>
```

In the constructor for the window, the pie charts are given their slices:

```
using System.Collections.Generic;
using System.Windows;

namespace Recipe_04_11
{
    public partial class Window1 : Window
```

```
{
    public Window1()
    {
        InitializeComponent();

        // Set up the slices
        pieChart1.Slices = new List <double>();
        pieChart1.Slices.Add(30);
        pieChart1.Slices.Add(60);
        pieChart1.Slices.Add(160);

        pieChart2.Slices = new List <double>();
        pieChart2.Slices.Add(30);
        pieChart2.Slices.Add(90);

        pieChart3.Slices = new List <double>();
        pieChart3.Slices.Add(90);
        pieChart3.Slices.Add(180);
    }
}
}
```

Figure 4-9 shows the resulting window.

Figure 4-9. *Creating a custom-drawn* PieChartControl

4-12. Create a Numeric TextBox Control

Problem

You need a System.Windows.Controls.TextBox control that accepts only numeric values as the input.

Solution

Create a control that inherits from TextBox, add a System.Windows.DependencyProperty to the code-behind called Number, and specify a type of double.

Override the OnPreviewTextInput method of the TextBox control, and if the text that is being input cannot be parsed to a double, set the Handled property of the System.Windows. Input.TextCompositionEventArgs to True.

Add code to ensure that when the Number property is changed, the Text property is also changed, and vice versa.

Tip If you need the TextBox to contain only integer values, then simply change the type of Number property to int, and use int.TryParse instead of double.TryParse to check whether a new text input should be allowed.

How It Works

By inheriting from a TextBox control, you get a custom control with all the behavior and appearance properties of a TextBox, but you also get the ability to override and modify certain aspects or features for the specific needs of a situation.

In this case, you override the OnPreviewTextInput method to intercept the inputting of text into the base TextBox and allow text to be input only if it can be parsed to a double. This is possible because the TextCompositionEventArgs class has a Handled property, and the text is input only if this property is not set to False.

By using DependencyProperty to store the numeric value of the Text, you can use the full range of WPF features such as data binding, styles, and animations to interact with the control.

The Code

The following code-behind shows a class called NumericTextboxControl that inherits from the TextBox class and adds a Number property of type double, backed by a DependencyProperty. There is code in the OnPreviewTextInput method to allow only text that can be converted to a double as input. Then, there is code in the OnNumberChanged and OnTextChanged methods to ensure that the values in the Text and Number properties are synchronized.

```
using System;
using System.Windows;
using System.Windows.Controls;
using System.Windows.Input;

namespace Recipe_04_12
{
    public partial class NumericTextboxControl : TextBox
    {
        // Flag is True if the Text property is changed
        private bool isTextChanged = false;

        // Flag is True if the Number property is changed
        private bool isNumberChanged = false;
```

```csharp
public NumericTextboxControl()
{
    InitializeComponent();
}

/// <summary>
/// Public property to store the numeric
/// value of the control's Text property
/// </summary>
public double Number
{
    get
    {
        return (double) GetValue(NumberProperty);
    }
    set
    {
        SetValue(NumberProperty, value);
    }
}

public static readonly DependencyProperty NumberProperty =
    DependencyProperty.Register("Number",
                        typeof(double),
                        typeof(NumericTextboxControl),
                        new PropertyMetadata(
                            new PropertyChangedCallback(
                                    OnNumberChanged)));

private static void OnNumberChanged(
                                DependencyObject sender,
                                DependencyPropertyChangedEventArgs e)
{
    NumericTextboxControl control = (NumericTextboxControl) sender;

    if(!control.isTextChanged)
    {
        // Number property has been changed from the outside,
        // via a binding or control, so set the Text property
        control.isNumberChanged = true;
        control.Text = control.Number.ToString();
        control.isNumberChanged = false;
    }
}
```

```csharp
protected override void OnTextChanged(TextChangedEventArgs e)
{
    if(!isNumberChanged)
    {
        // Text property has been changed from
        // text input, so set the Number property
        // nb. It will default to 0 if the text
        // is empty or "-"
        isTextChanged = true;
        double number;
        double.TryParse(this.Text, out number);
        this.Number = number;
        isTextChanged = false;
    }

    base.OnTextChanged(e);
}

protected override void OnPreviewTextInput(TextCompositionEventArgs e)
{
    // Get the preview of the new text
    string newTextPreview =
        this.Text.Insert(
            this.SelectionStart,
            e.Text);

    // Try to parse it to a double
    double number;
    if(!double.TryParse(newTextPreview, out number)
        && newTextPreview != "-")
    {
        // Mark the event as being handled if
        // the new text can't be parsed to a double
        e.Handled = true;
    }

    base.OnPreviewTextInput(e);
}
}
}
```

The following XAML shows how to use a NumericTextBoxControl in a window. There is also a button to demonstrate changing the value of the Number property and updating the text, as well as a System.Windows.Controls.TextBlock control that demonstrates binding to the Number property.

```xml
<Window x:Class="Recipe_04_12.Window1"
    xmlns="http://schemas.microsoft.com/winfx/2006/xaml/presentation"
    xmlns:x="http://schemas.microsoft.com/winfx/2006/xaml"
    xmlns:Recipe_04_12="clr-namespace:Recipe_04_12;assembly="
    Title="WPF Recipes 4_12" Height="120" Width="300">
    <Grid>
        <Grid.ColumnDefinitions>
            <ColumnDefinition Width="0.5*"/>
            <ColumnDefinition Width="0.5*"/>
        </Grid.ColumnDefinitions>

        <Grid.RowDefinitions>
            <RowDefinition />
            <RowDefinition />
        </Grid.RowDefinitions>

        <TextBlock
            Grid.Column="0"
            VerticalAlignment="Center"
            HorizontalAlignment="Center">
                Only accepts numbers:
         </TextBlock>

        <Recipe_04_12:NumericTextboxControl
            x:Name="numTextBox"
            Width="80"
            Height="20"
            Grid.Column="1"
            VerticalAlignment="Center"
            HorizontalAlignment="Center"
            />

        <Button Click="Button_Click"
                Grid.Row="1"
                Grid.Column="0"
                VerticalAlignment="Center"
                Width="120"
                Height="24" >
            Increment the number
        </Button>

        <StackPanel
            Orientation="Horizontal"
            VerticalAlignment="Center"
            Grid.Row="1"
            Grid.Column="1">
            <TextBlock>The number is:</TextBlock>
```

```
          <TextBlock
            Margin="4,0,0,0"
            Text="{Binding
            ElementName=numTextBox,
            Path=Number,
            UpdateSourceTrigger=PropertyChanged}"
              />
        </StackPanel>

      </Grid>
</Window>
```

4-13. Create a Scrollable Canvas Control

Problem

You need to provide scroll functionality in a System.Windows.Controls.Canvas control.

Solution

Create a class that derives from System.Windows.Controls.Canvas, and override the MeasureOverride method. In this method, iterate through the FrameworkElements in the Children collection, call the Measure method of each child, and determine the highest value for the Top and Left properties. Then return these as the dimensions the canvas should occupy based on the layout of its children.

This new Canvas control can be wrapped in a System.Windows.Controls.ScrollViewer, and if the Canvas contains child elements that require scrolling in order to be brought into view, the ScrollViewer now provides the correct scroll amount.

Caution The default value for the VerticalScrollBarVisibility property of a ScrollViewer is System.Windows.Controls.ScrollBarVisibility.Visible, but the default value for the HorizontalScrollBarVisibility property is Hidden. So if this property is not explicitly changed to Visible, the ScrollViewer will not show the horizontal scrollbar regardless of whether there are any child elements out of view and to the right.

How It Works

By default, a Canvas has no height or width. This causes issues if you want to use a Canvas in a ScrollViewer because the ScrollViewer doesn't ever see the Canvas spill out of its viewport. When overriding the Canvas's MeasureOverride method, you can determine a bounding rectangle for all the child items in the Canvas and return this as the Canvas's size. Then if the Canvas contains child elements that require scrolling to be brought into view, the ScrollViewer provides the correct scroll amount.

The Code

The following example demonstrates how to create a ScrollableCanvasControl, a custom reusable canvas control that can be wrapped in a ScrollViewer and display horizontal and vertical scrollbars to scroll the child items into view. This user control is then used in a window, which is shown in Figure 4-10.

The code for the ScrollableCanvasControl is as follows:

```
using System;
using System.Windows;
using System.Windows.Controls;

namespace Recipe_04_13
{
    public class ScrollableCanvasControl : Canvas
    {
        static ScrollableCanvasControl()
        {
            DefaultStyleKeyProperty.OverrideMetadata(
                typeof(ScrollableCanvasControl),
                new FrameworkPropertyMetadata(
                    typeof(ScrollableCanvasControl)));
        }

        protected override Size MeasureOverride(
            Size constraint)
        {
            double bottomMost = 0d;
            double rightMost = 0d;

            // Loop through the child FrameworkElements,
            // and track the highest Top and Left value
            // amongst them.
            foreach(object obj in Children)
            {
                FrameworkElement child = obj as FrameworkElement;

                if(child != null)
                {
                    child.Measure(constraint);
```

```
            bottomMost = Math.Max(
                bottomMost,
                GetTop(child) +
                child.DesiredSize.Height);
            rightMost = Math.Max(
                rightMost,
                GetLeft(child) +
                child.DesiredSize.Width);
        }
    }

    if(double.IsNaN(bottomMost)
       || double.IsInfinity(bottomMost))
    {
        bottomMost = 0d;
    }

    if(double.IsNaN(rightMost)
       || double.IsInfinity(rightMost))
    {
        rightMost = 0d;
    }

    // Return the new size
    return new Size(rightMost, bottomMost);
    }
  }
}
```

The following XAML defines a window with two ScrollView controls side by side. The one on the left contains a normal Canvas, which in turn contains two System.Windows.Controls. Button controls. One of the buttons is positioned in the view; one is positioned below the bottom of the window. Because this is a normal Canvas, the second button is not displayed and cannot be scrolled into view. The Canvas on the right is a ScrollableCanvasControl containing identical buttons. However, this time, the vertical scrollbar is displayed, and the bottom button can be scrolled into view. Figure 4-10 shows the results.

```
<Window x:Class="Recipe_04_13.Window1"
    xmlns="http://schemas.microsoft.com/winfx/2006/xaml/presentation"
    xmlns:x="http://schemas.microsoft.com/winfx/2006/xaml"
    xmlns:Recipe_04_13="clr-namespace:Recipe_04_13;assembly="
    Title="WPF Recipes 4_13" Height="200" Width="400" >
```

```xml
<Window.Resources>
    <Style TargetType="Button">
        <Setter Property="Width" Value="Auto" />
        <Setter Property="Height" Value="24" />
    </Style>
</Window.Resources>

<Grid>

    <Grid.ColumnDefinitions>
        <ColumnDefinition Width="0.5*"/>
        <ColumnDefinition Width="0.5*"/>
    </Grid.ColumnDefinitions>

    <ScrollViewer Grid.Column="0">
        <Canvas>
            <Button
                Canvas.Top="80"
                Canvas.Left="80">
                In View
            </Button>
            <Button
                Canvas.Top="300"
                Canvas.Left="80">
                Out of view
            </Button>
        </Canvas>
    </ScrollViewer>

    <ScrollViewer Grid.Column="1">
        <Recipe_04_13:ScrollableCanvasControl>
            <Button
                Canvas.Top="80"
                Canvas.Left="80">
                In View
            </Button>
            <Button
                Canvas.Top="300"
                Canvas.Left="80">
                Out of View
            </Button>
        </Recipe_04_13:ScrollableCanvasControl>
    </ScrollViewer>

</Grid>
</Window>
```

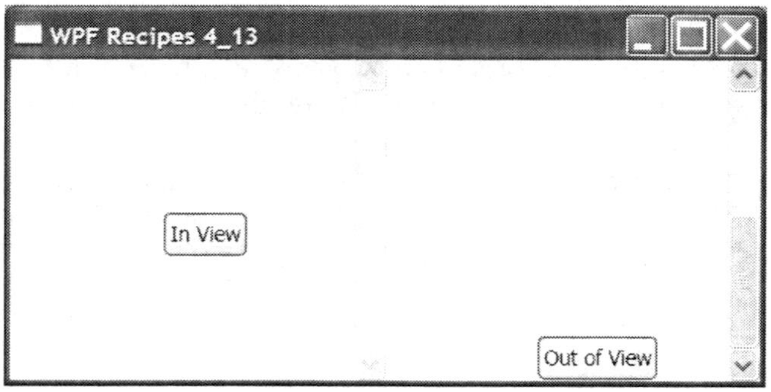

Figure 4-10. *Creating a scrollable Canvas control*

4-14. Create a Zoomable Canvas Control

Problem

You need to provide zoom functionality in a System.Windows.Controls.Canvas control.

Solution

Create a class that derives from System.Windows.Controls.Canvas, and override the MeasureOverride method. In this method, iterate through the FrameworkElements in the Children collection, call the Measure method of each child, and determine the highest value for the Top and Left properties. Then return these as the dimensions the canvas should occupy based on the layout of its children.

This new Canvas control can be wrapped in a System.Windows.Controls.ScrollViewer, and if the Canvas contains child elements that require scrolling in order to be brought into view, the ScrollViewer now provides the correct scroll amount.

Set the System.Windows.Media.Transform.LayoutTransform property of the Canvas to a System.Windows.Media.ScaleTransform, and bind the ScaleX and ScaleY properties of the ScaleTransform to the Value property of a System.Windows.Controls.Slider control.

How It Works

In overriding the Canvas's MeasureOverride method, you can determine a bounding rectangle for all the child items in the Canvas and return this as the Canvas's size. Then if the Canvas contains child elements that require scrolling to be brought into view, the ScrollViewer provides the correct scroll amount.

By setting the LayoutTransform property of the Canvas to a ScaleTransform, you can automatically transform the scale of the Canvas control by a factor provided by the value of a Slider control.

The Code

The following example demonstrates how to create a ZoomableCanvasControl, which is a custom reusable Canvas control that can be wrapped in a ScrollViewer, and it sets the LayoutTransform property of the Canvas to a ScaleTransform.

This user control is then used in a window that contains a Slider control, and it binds the ScaleX and ScaleY properties of the ScaleTransform to the value of the Slider control.

Figure 4-11 shows the resulting window. As the Slider moves left and right, the contents of the Canvas zoom in and out.

The code for the ZoomableCanvasControl is as follows:

```
using System;
using System.Windows;
using System.Windows.Controls;

namespace Recipe_04_14
{
    public class ZoomableCanvasControl : Canvas
    {
        static ZoomableCanvasControl()
        {
            DefaultStyleKeyProperty.OverrideMetadata(
                typeof(ZoomableCanvasControl),
                new FrameworkPropertyMetadata(
                    typeof(ZoomableCanvasControl)));
        }

        protected override Size MeasureOverride(
            Size constraint)
        {
            double bottomMost = 0d;
            double rightMost = 0d;

            // Loop through the child FrameworkElements,
            // and track the highest Top and Left value
            // amongst them.
            foreach(object obj in Children)
            {
                FrameworkElement child = obj as FrameworkElement;

                if(child != null)
                {
                    child.Measure(constraint);

                    bottomMost = Math.Max(
                        bottomMost,
                        GetTop(child) +
                        child.DesiredSize.Height);
```

```
                rightMost = Math.Max(
                    rightMost,
                    GetLeft(child) +
                    child.DesiredSize.Width);
            }
        }

        if(double.IsNaN(bottomMost)
           || double.IsInfinity(bottomMost))
        {
            bottomMost = 0d;
        }

        if(double.IsNaN(rightMost)
           || double.IsInfinity(rightMost))
        {
            rightMost = 0d;
        }

        // Return the new size
        return new Size(rightMost, bottomMost);
    }
  }
}
```

The following XAML defines a window with a ZoomableCanvasControl inside a ScrollViewer control. There is a Slider control docked to the bottom of the window, whose Value property is bound to the ScaleX and ScaleY properties of a ScaleTransform within the ZoomableCanvasControl.

```xml
<Window x:Class="Recipe_04_14.Window1"
    xmlns="http://schemas.microsoft.com/winfx/2006/xaml/presentation"
    xmlns:x="http://schemas.microsoft.com/winfx/2006/xaml"
    xmlns:Recipe_04_14="clr-namespace:Recipe_04_14;assembly="
  Title="WPF Recipes 4_14" Height="300" Width="300" >

    <Window.Resources>
        <Style TargetType="Button">
            <Setter Property="Width" Value="Auto" />
            <Setter Property="Height" Value="24" />
        </Style>
    </Window.Resources>

    <DockPanel>
```

```xml
            <Slider
                DockPanel.Dock="Bottom"
                x:Name="zoomSlider"
                Minimum="0.1"
                Maximum="5"
                Value="1"
                />

            <ScrollViewer
                VerticalScrollBarVisibility="Auto"
                HorizontalScrollBarVisibility="Auto">

                <Recipe_04_14:ZoomableCanvasControl x:Name="zoomControl">
                    <Canvas.LayoutTransform>
                        <ScaleTransform
                            ScaleX="{Binding Path=Value, ElementName=zoomSlider}"
                            ScaleY="{Binding Path=Value, ElementName=zoomSlider}"
                            />
                    </Canvas.LayoutTransform>
                    <Rectangle
                        Canvas.Top="0"
                        Canvas.Left="0"
                        StrokeThickness="2"
                        Stroke="Red"
                        Width="50"
                        Height="50"
                        />
                    <Rectangle
                        Canvas.Top="50"
                        Canvas.Left="50"
                        StrokeThickness="2"
                        Stroke="Blue"
                        Width="150"
                        Height="150"
                        />
                    <Rectangle
                        Canvas.Top="200"
                        Canvas.Left="200"
                        StrokeThickness="2"
                        Stroke="Green"
                        Width="200"
                        Height="200"
                        />
                </Recipe_04_14:ZoomableCanvasControl>
            </ScrollViewer>

        </DockPanel>
    </Window>
```

Figure 4-11 shows the resulting window.

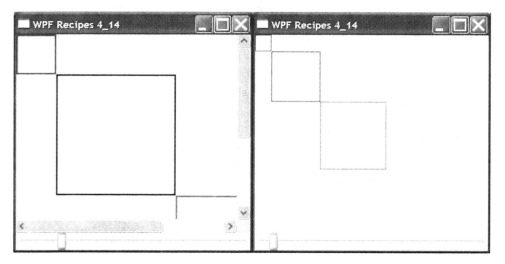

Figure 4-11. *Creating a zoomable Canvas control*

4-15. Create a Drag Canvas Control

Problem

You need to be able to drag elements inside your System.Windows.Controls.Canvas control.

Solution

Create a class that derives from System.Windows.Controls.Canvas, and override the OnPreviewMouseLeftButtonDown, OnPreviewMouseLeftButtonUp, and OnPreviewMouseMove methods. Add logic to these methods to determine when the left mouse button is pressed down on an element within the Canvas and where the element should be moved to if the mouse is moved before the button is released.

How It Works

In the Canvas control's OnPreviewMouseLeftButtonDown method, store the current mouse position and the current position of the selected UI element on the Canvas. In the OnPreviewMouseMove method, get the new position of the mouse, and use it to calculate the desired position of the UI element. Call the Canvas.SetLeft and Canvas.SetTop methods to set this position.

The Code

The following example demonstrates how to create a DragCanvasControl, a custom reusable Canvas control that overrides the OnPreviewMouseLeftButtonDown, OnPreviewMouseLeftButtonUp, and OnPreviewMouseMove methods to automatically drag elements inside the Canvas when the left mouse button is pressed down and the mouse is moved.

Figure 4-12 shows the resulting window. The shape elements in the canvas can be dragged around the Canvas by clicking them.

The code for the DragCanvasControl is as follows:

```
using System.Windows;
using System.Windows.Controls;
using System.Windows.Input;

namespace Recipe_04_15
{
    public class DragCanvasControl : Canvas
    {
        private Point startPoint;
        private Point selectedElementOrigins;
        private bool isDragging;
        private UIElement selectedElement;

        static DragCanvasControl()
        {
            DefaultStyleKeyProperty.OverrideMetadata(
                typeof(DragCanvasControl),
                new FrameworkPropertyMetadata(
                    typeof(DragCanvasControl)));
        }

        protected override void OnPreviewMouseLeftButtonDown(MouseButtonEventArgs e)
        {
            base.OnPreviewMouseLeftButtonDown(e);

            if(e.Source != this)
            {
                if(!isDragging)
                {
                    startPoint = e.GetPosition(this);
                    selectedElement = e.Source as UIElement;
                    this.CaptureMouse();

                    isDragging = true;

                    selectedElementOrigins =
                        new Point(
                            Canvas.GetLeft(selectedElement),
                            Canvas.GetTop(selectedElement));
                }
                e.Handled = true;
            }
        }
```

```
        protected override void OnPreviewMouseLeftButtonUp(MouseButtonEventArgs e)
        {
            base.OnPreviewMouseLeftButtonUp(e);

            if(this.IsMouseCaptured)
            {
                isDragging = false;
                this.ReleaseMouseCapture();

                e.Handled = true;
            }
        }

        protected override void OnPreviewMouseMove(MouseEventArgs e)
        {
            base.OnPreviewMouseMove(e);

            if(this.IsMouseCaptured)
            {
                if(isDragging)
                {
                    Point currentPosition = e.GetPosition(this);

                    double elementLeft = (currentPosition.X - startPoint.X) +
                                            selectedElementOrigins.X;
                    double elementTop = (currentPosition.Y - startPoint.Y) +
                                            selectedElementOrigins.Y;

                    Canvas.SetLeft(selectedElement, elementLeft);
                    Canvas.SetTop(selectedElement, elementTop);
                }
            }
        }
    }
}
```

The following XAML defines a window with a DragCanvasControl containing three shape elements:

```
<Window x:Class="Recipe_04_15.Window1"
    xmlns="http://schemas.microsoft.com/winfx/2006/xaml/presentation"
    xmlns:x="http://schemas.microsoft.com/winfx/2006/xaml"
    xmlns:Recipe_04_15="clr-namespace:Recipe_04_15;assembly="
    Title="WPF Recipes 4_15" Height="200" Width="300">
```

```xml
<Recipe_04_15:DragCanvasControl>

    <Rectangle
        Canvas.Top="8"
        Canvas.Left="8"
        Width="32"
        Height="32"
        Fill="Blue"
        />

    <Ellipse
        Canvas.Top="36"
        Canvas.Left="48"
        Width="40"
        Height="24"
        Fill="Yellow" />

    <Ellipse
        Canvas.Top="60"
        Canvas.Left="96"
        Width="32"
        Height="32"
        Fill="Red" />

</Recipe_04_15:DragCanvasControl>

</Window>
```

Figure 4-12 shows the resulting window.

Figure 4-12. *Creating a draggable Canvas control*

CHAPTER 5

Data Binding

WPF has an extremely rich data binding model. It revolves around the notion that you can take almost any object as your binding source and bind it to almost any target UI element. The binding source can be another UI element, a property of the same element, an XML file, a custom business object, a database, or an in-memory collection. The binding target can be a WPF property, an individual UI element, or a WPF user control or window. But the essential idea is that once a binding is established, the data in the source is automatically and dynamically propagated to the binding target, and vice versa.

How the data object is displayed visually is controlled primarily by data templates, data converters, and data triggers. These take an object as the binding source and translate it for display into a visual structure of UI elements. It is through this mechanism that you can, for example, take a collection of custom business objects, representing products in a product catalog, and display them in a rich and visually compelling manner. Any object can be converted via the data binding system into the UI elements you specify in templates and converters and can adapt and change its display based on your triggers and data template selectors.

Once you become familiar with the data binding system in WPF, you will find it an immensely productive, simple, and effective approach to rich GUI development. The amount of custom application logic you find yourself writing in the code-behind files will dwindle to nonexistence. Before long, you will be enthusiastically and whole-heartedly embracing the wonders of true object-orientated GUI development and wondering how you ever managed without it! This chapter aims to get you up to speed as quickly as possible.

The recipes in this chapter describe how to:

- Bind to a property of a UI element (recipe 5-1)

- Create a two-way binding (recipe 5-2)

- Bind a property of a UI element to itself (recipe 5-3)

- Bind to CLR objects, existing object instances, and XML data (recipes 5-4, 5-5, and 5-6)

- Bind to a method, a command, and the values in an enumeration (recipes 5-7, 5-8, and 5-9)

- Specify a default value for a binding (recipe 5-10)

- Use data templates, value converters, and data triggers to display bound data (recipes 5-11, 5-12, 5-13, and 5-14)

- Validate bound data (recipes 5-15 and 5-16)

- Bind to collections and sort, group, and filter their data (recipes 5-17 - 5-22)

- Bind to application settings and resource strings (recipes 5-23 and 5-24)

5-1. Bind to a Property of a UI Element

Problem

You need to bind a property of a UI element to a property of another UI element. For example, you need to bind the Text property of a System.Windows.Controls.TextBlock control to the Value property of a System.Windows.Controls.Slider control so that the text is automatically and dynamically updated when the slider is changed.

Solution

Use the System.Windows.Data.Binding markup extension, and specify the ElementName and Path attributes.

How It Works

The Binding class creates a relationship between two properties: a binding source and a binding target. In this case, the target is the property of the element with the value you want to set. The source is the property of the element you want to get the value from. The target property must be a System.Windows.DependencyProperty, is designed to support data binding.

In the XAML for the property you want to set, declare a Binding statement inside curly braces. Set the ElementName attribute to the name of the element to use as the binding source object. Set the Path attribute to the property on the source where the data should come from.

The Code

The following example demonstrates a window containing a Slider control and a TextBlock control. The XAML statement for the Text property of the TextBlock specifies a Binding statement. This statement binds it to the Value property of the slider so that when the slider's value changes, the Text property automatically changes to reflect it.

The XAML for the window is as follows:

```
<Window
    x:Class="Recipe_05_01.Window1"
    xmlns="http://schemas.microsoft.com/winfx/2006/xaml/presentation"
    xmlns:x="http://schemas.microsoft.com/winfx/2006/xaml"
    Title="WPF Recipes 5_01" Height="100" Width="260">
    <StackPanel>
        <Slider Name="slider"
                Margin="4" Interval="1"
                TickFrequency="1"
```

```
                IsSnapToTickEnabled="True"
                Minimum="0" Maximum="100"/>
        <StackPanel Orientation="Horizontal" >
            <TextBlock Width="Auto" HorizontalAlignment="Left" Margin="4"
                        Text="The value property of the slider is:" />
            <TextBlock Width="40" HorizontalAlignment="Center" Margin="4"
                        Text="{Binding
                                ElementName=slider,
                                Path=Value}" />
        </StackPanel>
    </StackPanel>
</Window>
```

Figure 5-1 shows the resulting window.

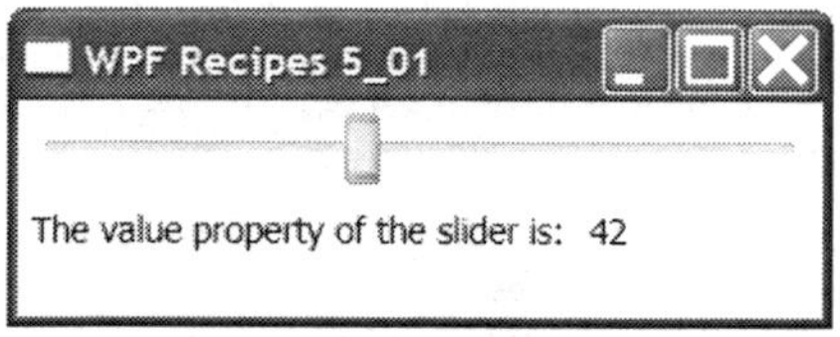

Figure 5-1. *Binding to a property of another element*

5-2. Create a Two-Way Binding

Problem

You need to create a two-way binding so that when the value of either property changes, the other one automatically updates to reflect it.

Solution

Use the System.Windows.Data.Binding markup extension, and set the Mode attribute to System.Windows.Data.BindingMode.TwoWay. Use the UpdateSourceTrigger attribute to specify when the binding source should be updated.

How It Works

The data in a binding can flow from the source property to the target property, can flow from the target property to the source property, or can flow in both directions. For example, suppose the Text property of a System.Windows.Controls.TextBox control is bound to the Value property of a System.Windows.Controls.Slider control. In this case, the Text property of the TextBox control is the target of the binding, and the Value property of the Slider control is the binding source. The direction of data flow between the target and the source can be configured in a number of different ways. It could be configured such that when the Value of the Slider control changes, the Text property of the TextBox is updated. This is called a *one-way binding*. Alternatively, you could configure the binding so that when the Text property of the TextBox changes, the Slider control's Value is automatically updated to reflect it. This is called a *one-way binding to the source*. A *two-way binding* means that a change to either the source property or the target property automatically updates the other. This type of binding is useful for editable forms or other fully interactive UI scenarios.

It is the Mode property of a Binding object that configures its data flow. This stores an instance of the System.Windows.Data.BindingMode enumeration and can be configured with the values listed in Table 5-1.

Table 5-1. *BindingMode Values for Configuring the Data Flow in a Binding*

Value	Description
Default	The Binding uses the default Mode value of the binding target, which varies for each dependency property. In general, user-editable control properties, such as those of text boxes and check boxes, default to two-way bindings, whereas most other properties default to one-way bindings.
OneTime	The target property is updated when the control is first loaded or when the data context changes. This type of binding is appropriate if the data is static and won't change once it has been set.
OneWay	The target property is updated whenever the source property changes. This is appropriate if the target control is read-only, such as a System.Windows.Controls. Label or System.Windows.Controls.TextBlock. If the target property does change, the source property will not be updated.
OneWayToSource	This is the opposite of OneWay. The source property is updated when the target property changes.
TwoWay	Changes to either the target property or the source automatically update the other.

Bindings that are TwoWay or OneWayToSource listen for changes in the target property and update the source. It is the UpdateSourceTrigger property of the binding that determines when this update occurs. For example, suppose you created a TwoWay binding between the Text property of a TextBox control and the Value property of a Slider control. You could configure the binding so that the slider is updated either as soon as you type text into the TextBox or when the TextBox loses its focus. Alternatively, you could specify that the TextBox is updated only when you explicitly call the UpdateSource property of the System.Windows.Data.BindingExpression class. These options are configured by the Binding's UpdateSourceTrigger property, which stores an instance of the System.Windows.Data.UpdateSourceTrigger enumeration. Table 5-2 lists the possible values of this enumeration.

Therefore, to create a two-way binding that updates the source as soon as the target property changes, you need to specify TwoWay as the value of the Binding's Mode attribute and PropertyChanged for the UpdateSourceTrigger attribute.

Table 5-2. *UpdateSourceTrigger Values for Configuring When the Binding Source Is Updated*

Value	Description
Default	The Binding uses the default UpdateSourceTrigger of the binding target property. For most dependency properties, this is PropertyChanged, but for the TextBox.Text property, it is LostFocus.
Explicit	Updates the binding source only when you call the System.Windows.Data.BindingExpression.UpdateSource method.
LostFocus	Updates the binding source whenever the binding target element loses focus.
PropertyChanged	Updates the binding source immediately whenever the binding target property changes.

Note To detect source changes in OneWay and TwoWay bindings, if the source property is not a System.Windows.DependencyProperty, it must implement System.ComponentModel. INotifyPropertyChanged to notify the target that its value has changed.

The Code

The following example demonstrates a window containing a System.Windows.Controls.Slider control and a System.Windows.Controls.TextBlock control. The XAML statement for the Text property of the TextBlock specifies a Binding statement that binds it to the Value property of the Slider control. In the binding statement, the Mode attribute is set to TwoWay, and the UpdateSourceTrigger attribute is set to PropertyChanged. This ensures that when a number from 1 to 100 is typed into the TextBox, the Slider control immediately updates its value to reflect it.

The XAML for the window is as follows:

```
<Window x:Class="Recipe_05_02.Window1"
    xmlns="http://schemas.microsoft.com/winfx/2006/xaml/presentation"
    xmlns:x="http://schemas.microsoft.com/winfx/2006/xaml"
    Title="WPF Recipes 5_02" Height="100" Width="260">
    <StackPanel>
        <Slider Name="slider"
                Margin="4" Interval="1"
                TickFrequency="1"
                IsSnapToTickEnabled="True"
                Minimum="0" Maximum="100"/>
        <StackPanel Orientation="Horizontal" >
            <TextBlock Width="Auto" HorizontalAlignment="Left"
                    VerticalAlignment="Center" Margin="4"
                    Text="Gets and sets the value of the slider:" />
```

```
            <TextBox Width="40" HorizontalAlignment="Center" Margin="4"
                Text="{Binding
                        ElementName=slider,
                        Path=Value,
                        Mode=TwoWay,
                        UpdateSourceTrigger=PropertyChanged}" />
        </StackPanel>
    </StackPanel>
</Window>
```

Figure 5-2 shows the resulting window.

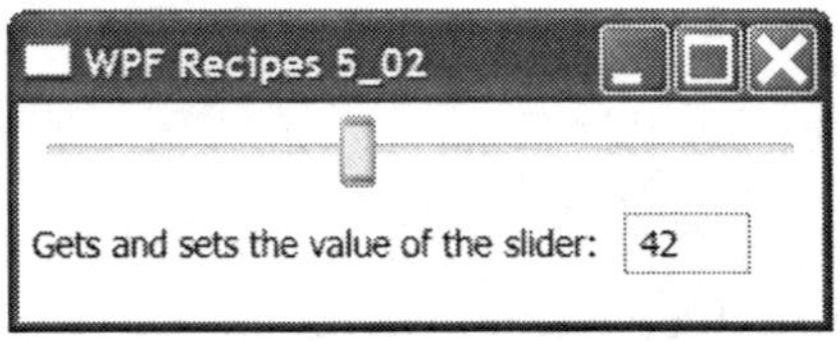

Figure 5-2. *Creating a two-way binding*

5-3. Bind a Property of an Element to Itself

Problem

You need to bind one property of an element to another property of the same element.

Solution

Use the RelativeSource property of the System.Windows.Data.Binding markup extension, and specify a System.Windows.Data.RelativeSource of Self.

How It Works

The RelativeSource property of a Binding designates the binding source by specifying its relationship to the binding target. If the value of this property is set to RelativeSource.Self, then the source element is the same as the target element.

The Code

The following example demonstrates a window containing a System.Windows.Controls.Slider control. The XAML statement for the ToolTip property of the Slider control specifies a Binding statement that binds it to the Value property of itself.

The XAML for the window is as follows:

```
<Window x:Class="Recipe_05_03.Window1"
    xmlns="http://schemas.microsoft.com/winfx/2006/xaml/presentation"
    xmlns:x="http://schemas.microsoft.com/winfx/2006/xaml"
```

```
        Title="WPF Recipes 5_03" Height="100" Width="240">
    <Grid>
        <Slider Name="slider"
                Margin="4" Interval="1"
                TickFrequency="1"
                IsSnapToTickEnabled="True"
                Minimum="0" Maximum="100"
                ToolTip="{Binding
                        RelativeSource=
                            {RelativeSource Self},
                            Path=Value}"/>
    </Grid>
</Window>
```

Figure 5-3 shows the resulting window.

Figure 5-3. *Binding a property of an element to itself*

5-4. Bind to CLR Objects

Problem

You need to bind the properties of UI elements to a CLR object, such as a custom business object.

Solution

To use a CLR object as a binding source, implement a property change notification mechanism such as the System.ComponentModel.INotifyPropertyChanged interface.

How It Works

If you are binding to a CLR object using a System.Windows.Data.BindingMode of either OneWay or TwoWay, you must implement a property change notification mechanism if you want your UI to update dynamically when the source CLR properties change. Such a mechanism is necessary to inform the System.Windows.Data.Binding that it should update the binding target with the new value in the binding source.

The recommended notification mechanism is for the CLR class to implement the INotifyPropertyChanged interface. This interface has just one member, an event called PropertyChanged. When you raise this event, you pass in an instance of the System.

ComponentModel.PropertyChangedEventArgs class. This contains a property called PropertyName, which informs the binding mechanism that the property of the binding source with the specified name has changed its value.

There are alternative notification systems to INotifyPropertyChanged. You can provide change notifications by supporting the PropertyChanged pattern for each property that you want change notifications for. To implement this system, you define a *PropertyName*Changed event for each property, where *PropertyName* is the name of the property. You need to raise this event every time the property changes. This was the preferred method to bind to CLR objects in version 1.0 of the .NET Framework and is still supported.

Another option is to back your CLR properties with a corresponding System.Windows.DependencyProperty. These provide built-in support for data binding.

The recommended pattern for implementing INotifyPropertyChanged in a CLR class is as follows. Create a method called OnPropertyChanged that takes the name of the property that has changed as a parameter. In this method, raise the PropertyChanged event, passing in a new instance of the PropertyChangedEventArgs class as the event arguments. Initialize the event arguments with the name of the property passed in to the method. It is common practice to implement this pattern in a base CLR class that all your custom business objects derive from. Then, in the setter part of each property in your class, simply call OnPropertyChanged whenever it is assigned a new value.

The Code

The following example demonstrates a window that data binds to an instance of the Person class in its constructor. It uses three System.Windows.Controls.TextBox controls and a System.Windows.Controls.ComboBox control to display the name, age, and occupation data for a person. These UI elements have two-way data bindings to the corresponding CLR properties of the Person class.

Additionally, there is a System.Windows.Controls.TextBlock control that has a one-way binding to the read-only Description property. The value of this CLR property changes whenever the values of the other properties change. To notify the TextBlock that the description has changed, the Person class implements the INotifyPropertyChanged interface.

In the setters for the properties in the Person class, the OnPropertyChanged method is called twice. It's called first to notify any bound targets that the value of this property has changed. It's called a second time to notify them that the Description property has also changed. The OnPropertyChanged method raises the PropertyChanged event, passing in the property name.

Figure 5-4 shows the resulting window. If the value in any of the TextBox controls or the ComboBox control is changed, then when it loses focus, the description of the person will automatically and dynamically update.

In the code-behind for the window, there is code in the constructor to create and configure an instance of the Person class and assign it to the DataContext of the window.

The XAML for the window is as follows:

```
<Window
    x:Class="Recipe_05_04.Window1"
    xmlns="http://schemas.microsoft.com/winfx/2006/xaml/presentation"
    xmlns:x="http://schemas.microsoft.com/winfx/2006/xaml"
    Title="WPF Recipes 5_04" Height="180" Width="260">
    <Grid>
```

```xml
<Grid.ColumnDefinitions>
    <ColumnDefinition Width="74"/>
    <ColumnDefinition Width="*"/>
</Grid.ColumnDefinitions>

<Grid.RowDefinitions>
    <RowDefinition Height="26"/>
    <RowDefinition Height="26"/>
    <RowDefinition Height="26"/>
    <RowDefinition Height="26"/>
    <RowDefinition Height="10"/>
    <RowDefinition Height="26"/>
</Grid.RowDefinitions>

<TextBlock
    Margin="4"
    Text="First Name"
    VerticalAlignment="Center"/>
<TextBox
    Text="{Binding Path=FirstName, Mode=TwoWay}"
    Margin="4" Grid.Column="1"/>

<TextBlock
    Margin="4"
    Text="Last Name"
    Grid.Row="1"
    VerticalAlignment="Center"/>
<TextBox
    Margin="4"
    Text="{Binding Path=LastName, Mode=TwoWay}"
    Grid.Column="1" Grid.Row="1"/>

<TextBlock
    Margin="4"
    Text="Age"
    Grid.Row="2"
    VerticalAlignment="Center"/>
<TextBox
    Margin="4"
    Text="{Binding Path=Age, Mode=TwoWay}"
    Grid.Column="1"
    Grid.Row="2"/>

<TextBlock
    Margin="4"
    Text="Occupation"
    Grid.Row="3"
    VerticalAlignment="Center"/>
```

```xml
<ComboBox
    x:Name="cboOccupation"
    IsEditable="False"
    Grid.Column="1"
    Grid.Row="3"
    HorizontalAlignment="Left"
    Text="{Binding Path=Occupation, Mode=TwoWay}"
    Margin="4" Width="140">
  <ComboBoxItem>Student</ComboBoxItem>
  <ComboBoxItem>Skilled</ComboBoxItem>
  <ComboBoxItem>Professional</ComboBoxItem>
</ComboBox>

<TextBlock
    Margin="4"
    Text="Description"
    FontWeight="Bold"
    FontStyle="Italic"
    Grid.Row="5"
    VerticalAlignment="Center"/>
<TextBlock
    Margin="4"
    Text="{Binding Path=Description, UpdateSourceTrigger=PropertyChanged}"
    VerticalAlignment="Center"
    FontStyle="Italic"
    Grid.Column="1"
    Grid.Row="5"/>

    </Grid>
</Window>
```

The code-behind for the window is as follows:

```csharp
using System.Windows;

using System.Windows;

namespace Recipe_05_04
{
    public partial class Window1 : Window
    {
        public Window1()
        {
            InitializeComponent();

            // Set the DataContext to a Person object
            this.DataContext =
                new Person()
```

```
                        {
                            FirstName = "Elin",
                            LastName = "Binkles",
                            Age = 26,
                            Occupation = "Professional"
                        };
                }
        }
}
```

The code for the Person class is as follows:

```
using System.ComponentModel;

namespace Recipe_05_04
{
    public class Person : INotifyPropertyChanged
    {
        private string firstName;
        private string lastName;
        private int age;
        private string occupation;

        // Each property calls the OnPropertyChanged method
        // when its value changed, and each property that
        // affects the Person's Description also calls the
        // OnPropertyChanged method for the Description property.

        public string FirstName
        {
            get
            {
                return firstName;
            }
            set
            {
                if(firstName != value)
                {
                    firstName = value;
                    OnPropertyChanged("FirstName");
                    OnPropertyChanged("Description");
                }
            }
        }
```

```csharp
public string LastName
{
    get
    {
        return lastName;
    }
    set
    {
        if(this.lastName != value)
        {
            this.lastName = value;
            OnPropertyChanged("LastName");
            OnPropertyChanged("Description");
        }
    }
}

public int Age
{
    get
    {
        return age;
    }
    set
    {
        if(this.age != value)
        {
            this.age = value;
            OnPropertyChanged("Age");
            OnPropertyChanged("Description");
        }
    }
}

public string Occupation
{
    get { return occupation; }
    set
    {
        if (this.occupation != value)
        {
            this.occupation = value;
            OnPropertyChanged("Occupation");
            OnPropertyChanged("Description");
        }
    }
}
```

```csharp
// The Description property is read-only
// and is composed of the values of the
// other properties.
public string Description
{
    get
    {
        return string.Format("{0} {1}, {2} ({3})",
                            firstName, lastName, age, occupation);
    }
}

#region INotifyPropertyChanged Members

/// Implement INotifyPropertyChanged to notify the binding
/// targets when the values of properties change.
public event PropertyChangedEventHandler PropertyChanged;

private void OnPropertyChanged(
    string propertyName)
{
    if(this.PropertyChanged != null)
    {
        // Raise the PropertyChanged event
        this.PropertyChanged(
            this,
            new PropertyChangedEventArgs(
                propertyName));
    }
}

#endregion
    }
}
```

Figure 5-4 shows the resulting window.

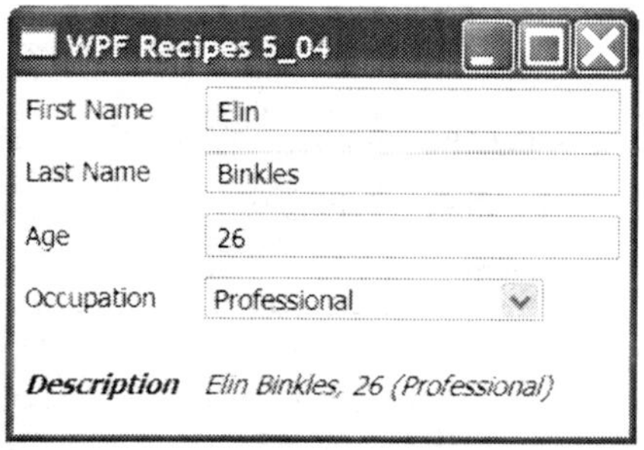

Figure 5-4. *Binding to CLR objects*

5-5. Bind to an Existing Object Instance

Problem

You need to bind a number of UI elements to an object that can be created and populated only at runtime, for example, a custom business object containing live data or a System.Data.DataSet object that's created in response to a database query.

Solution

Create System.Windows.Data.Binding statements in the XAML for your elements to bind the properties of your UI elements to the properties of your data source. Use the Path property of the Binding class to specify the name of the property of the data source to bind to, but do not specify a value for its Source property.

At runtime, assign an existing object instance to the DataContext property of a System.Windows.FrameworkElement. This FrameworkElement must be a UI element that is a parent element of all the child elements that need to bind to it.

■Tip This is also the recommended method of data binding when you need to bind more than one property to a particular source. Because the DataContext of a parent element is inherited by all its child elements, as explained in the "How It Works" section, you don't need to specify the source multiple times. However, when you need to bind only one property to a source, it can be simpler and more convenient to define a data source as a static resource and reference it in the Source property of the binding. This can be easier to debug, because you can see all the information about the binding in one place, instead of having to search for the nearest DataContext to understand what is happening.

How It Works

In this chapter, you have so far seen three different ways of specifying the data source of a Binding: using its ElementName, RelativeSource, and Source properties. Table 5-3 lists these different options.

Table 5-3. *Ways of Specifying the Data Source for a Binding*

Property	Description
Source	Use this to reference an instance of an object created as a resource.
RelativeSource	Use this to specify a UI element that is relative to the binding target.
ElementName	Use this to specify another UI element on your application.

However, if none of these properties has been set, the binding system will traverse up the tree of elements, looking for the nearest one with a value for its DataContext property. This allows a DataContext to be established for one root element and then inherited automatically by all its child elements.

Setting the DataContext of a FrameworkElement programmatically at runtime automatically updates any inherited bindings on its child elements. This makes it an ideal candidate to use when binding multiple elements to multiple properties of the same source object. It also makes it ideal when you want to bind your controls to a different instance of the same class at runtime.

The Code

The following example demonstrates a window containing three System.Windows.Controls. TextBox objects that display the name and age data for a person. The Person class is defined in the code-behind for the window and represents a simple custom business object.

In the XAML for the window, the Text property of each TextBox is set to a Binding. Each Binding specifies a property of the Person class as its Path but doesn't specify anything for its Source.

In the code-behind for the window, there is code in the constructor to create and configure an instance of the Person class and assign it to the DataContext of the window.

The XAML for the window is as follows:

```
<Window x:Class="Recipe_05_05.Window1"
    xmlns="http://schemas.microsoft.com/winfx/2006/xaml/presentation"
    xmlns:x="http://schemas.microsoft.com/winfx/2006/xaml"
    Title="WPF Recipes 5_05" Height="120" Width="300">
    <Grid>
        <Grid.ColumnDefinitions>
            <ColumnDefinition Width="60"/>
            <ColumnDefinition Width="*"/>
        </Grid.ColumnDefinitions>

        <Grid.RowDefinitions>a
            <RowDefinition Height="26"/>
            <RowDefinition Height="26"/>
            <RowDefinition Height="26"/>
        </Grid.RowDefinitions>

        <TextBlock Margin="4" Text="First Name" VerticalAlignment="Center"/>
        <TextBox Margin="4" Text="{Binding Path=FirstName}"
                Grid.Column="1"/>

        <TextBlock
                Margin="4" Text="Last Name"
                Grid.Row="1" VerticalAlignment="Center"/>
        <TextBox Margin="4" Text="{Binding Path=LastName}"
                Grid.Column="1"
                Grid.Row="1"/>
```

```
            <TextBlock Margin="4" Text="Age" Grid.Row="2" VerticalAlignment="Center"/>
            <TextBox Margin="4" Text="{Binding Path=Age}"
                     Grid.Column="1"
                     Grid.Row="2"/>
        </Grid>
</Window>
```

The code-behind for the window is as follows:

```
using System.Windows;
using Recipe_05_05;

namespace Recipe_05_05
{
    public partial class Window1 : Window
    {
        public Window1()
        {
            InitializeComponent();

            // Set the DataContext to a Person object
            this.DataContext = new Person()
                                    {
                                        FirstName = "Nelly",
                                        LastName = "Blinks",
                                        Age = 26
                                    };
        }
    }
}
```

Figure 5-5 shows the resulting window.

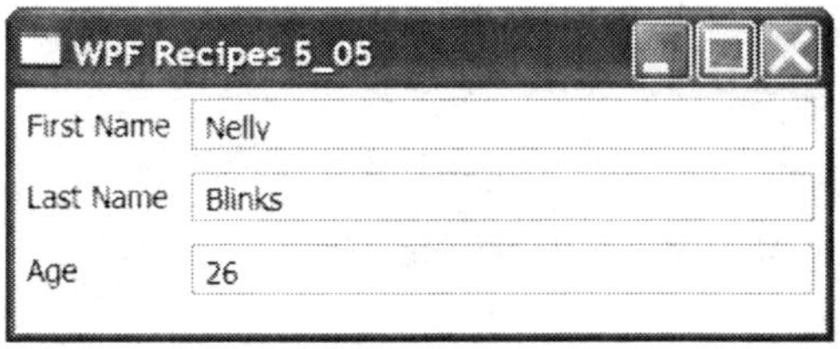

Figure 5-5. *Binding a number of controls to an existing object instance*

5-6. Bind to XML Data

Problem

You need to display XML data in a WPF control.

Solution

Create a `System.Windows.Data.XmlDataProvider` in the `System.Windows.ResourceDictionary` for your window, and either embed the XML data inline as a *data island* or set the `Source` property to reference an embedded XML file and then use this `XmlDataProvider` as the `Source` of a binding.

How It Works

The `XmlDataProvider` class provides a simple way to create a bindable data source from XML data. It can be declared in a `Resources` section and then referenced via a key. Its data can be declared either inline via the `XmlDataProvider`'s `Content` property; or, if the XML resides in a separate file, you can use the `Source` property to reference it via an appropriate `Uri`.

The `XmlDataProvider` can be referenced in a binding as a static resource, and the `XPath` property of the binding can be used to set an XPath query to populate it with the required subset of data. XPath, short for XML Path Language, is a W3C Recommendation published at `http://www.w3.org/TR/xpath`.

Tip When embedding XML data directly into the `Content` property of an `XmlDataProvider`, it must be given an empty `xmlns` attribute, or your XPath queries will not work as expected. Instead, they will be qualified by the `System.Windows` namespace, and your output window will show that a `System.Windows.Data.Error` exception has occurred.

The Code

The following example demonstrates a window that creates an `XmlDataProvider` as a static resource and sets its content to embedded XML data containing a list of countries. The `XmlDataProvider` is given a key and is then referenced in the `ItemsSource` property of a `System.Windows.Controls.ListBox`.

The `XPath` property of the `ListBox` specifies that the relevant data is the `Name` attribute of each `Country` in `Countries`.

```
<Window x:Class="Recipe_05_06.Window1"
    xmlns="http://schemas.microsoft.com/winfx/2006/xaml/presentation"
    xmlns:x="http://schemas.microsoft.com/winfx/2006/xaml"
    Title="WPF Recipes 5_06" Height="240" Width="200">
    <Window.Resources>

        <!-- Use the Source attribute to specify an embedded XML Data File-->
        <!--<XmlDataProvider x:Key="CountriesXML"
                            Source="Countries.xml"
                            XPath="Countries"/>-->

        <!-- Or embed the data directly -->
        <XmlDataProvider x:Key="CountriesXML">
            <x:XData>
```

```
            <Countries xmlns="" >
                <Country Name="Great Britan" Continent="Europe" />
                <Country Name="USA" Continent="NorthAmerica" />
                <Country Name="Canada" Continent="NorthAmerica" />
                <Country Name="France" Continent="Europe" />
                <Country Name="Germany" Continent="Europe" />
                <Country Name="Italy" Continent="Europe" />
                <Country Name="Spain" Continent="Europe" />
                <Country Name="Brazil" Continent="SouthAmerica" />
                <Country Name="Argentina" Continent="SouthAmerica" />
                <Country Name="China" Continent="Asia" />
                <Country Name="India" Continent="Asia" />
                <Country Name="Japan" Continent="Asia" />
                <Country Name="South Africa" Continent="Africa" />
                <Country Name="Tunisia" Continent="Africa" />
                <Country Name="Egypt" Continent="Africa" />
            </Countries>
        </x:XData>
    </XmlDataProvider>
</Window.Resources>
<Grid>
    <ListBox
        ItemsSource="{Binding Source={StaticResource CountriesXML},
        XPath=/Countries/Country/@Name}"
    />
</Grid>
</Window>
```

Figure 5-6 shows the resulting window.

Figure 5-6. *Binding to XML data in a control*

5-7. Bind to a Method

Problem

You need to bind a property of a UI element to the value returned by a method.

Solution

Use the System.Windows.Data.ObjectDataProvider class to make a method of a class available as a binding source, and bind to its results.

How It Works

The ObjectDataProvider can be created as a resource in your window or control and acts as a wrapper to expose a method as a binding source. Use its ObjectType and MethodName properties to specify the names of the class and the method to bind to. Then simply reference the ObjectDataProvider in a binding statement, and the target property will receive the return value of the method.

If the method expects any parameters, they must be declared in the ObjectDataProvider's MethodParameters collection. To specify the values of the parameters to pass to the method, you can create separate bindings that pull in the values from other UI elements. To do this, create binding statements that reference the ObjectDataProvider as the binding source. Then set the Path attribute to the relevant item in the MethodParameters collection. Set the BindsDirectlyToSource property of the ObjectDataProvider to True. This signals to the ObjectDataProvider that the binding Path statement should be evaluated relative to itself, not to the data item it wraps.

The Code

The following example demonstrates a window containing an ObjectDataProvider that creates a binding source for a method called Convert on the DistanceConverter class. The purpose of this method is to convert miles into kilometers, and vice versa. It takes two parameters: a double specifying the amount and a DistanceType enumeration that represents the unit that the amount is in. These parameters are declared in the ObjectDataProvider's MethodParameters collection.

The window displays a System.Windows.Controls.TextBlock control that binds to the result of the method. There is also a System.Windows.Controls.TextBox control and a System.Windows.Controls.ComboBox control. These bind to the first and second parameters of the method, respectively.

The XAML for the window is as follows:

```
<Window
    x:Class="Recipe_05_07.Window1"
    xmlns="http://schemas.microsoft.com/winfx/2006/xaml/presentation"
    xmlns:x="http://schemas.microsoft.com/winfx/2006/xaml"
    xmlns:system="clr-namespace:System;assembly=mscorlib"
    xmlns:Recipe_05_07="clr-namespace:Recipe_05_07"
```

```xml
            Title="WPF Recipes 5_07" Width="240" Height="150" >
            <Window.Resources>

                <Recipe_05_07:DoubleToString x:Key="doubleToString" />

                <!-- The ObjectDataProvider exposes the method as a binding source -->
                <ObjectDataProvider
                    x:Key="convertDistance"
                    ObjectType="{x:Type Recipe_05_07:DistanceConverter }"
                    MethodName="Convert" >

                    <!-- Declare the parameters the method expects-->
                    <ObjectDataProvider.MethodParameters>
                        <system:Double>0</system:Double>
                        <Recipe_05_07:DistanceType>Miles</Recipe_05_07:DistanceType>
                    </ObjectDataProvider.MethodParameters>
                </ObjectDataProvider>

            </Window.Resources>

            <Grid Margin="10">

                <Grid.ColumnDefinitions>
                    <ColumnDefinition Width="0.5*"/>
                    <ColumnDefinition Width="0.5*"/>
                </Grid.ColumnDefinitions>

                <Grid.RowDefinitions>
                    <RowDefinition Height="31" />
                    <RowDefinition Height="31" />
                    <RowDefinition Height="31" />
                </Grid.RowDefinitions>

                <TextBlock Margin="5" Grid.ColumnSpan="2"
                            VerticalAlignment="Center"
                            Text="Enter a distance to convert:"/>

                <!-- This TextBox binds to the 1st paramter of the method -->
                <TextBox
                    Grid.Row="1" Grid.Column="0" Margin="5"
                    Text ="{Binding
                            Source={StaticResource convertDistance},
                            Path=MethodParameters[0],
                            BindsDirectlyToSource=true,
                            UpdateSourceTrigger=PropertyChanged,
                            Converter={StaticResource doubleToString}}"/>
```

```xml
<!-- This TextBox binds to the 1st paramter of the method -->
<ComboBox
    Grid.Row="1" Grid.Column="1" Margin="5" Width="80"
    HorizontalAlignment="Left"
    SelectedValue="{Binding
                    Source={StaticResource convertDistance},
                    Path=MethodParameters[1],
                    BindsDirectlyToSource=true}" >
    <Recipe_05_07:DistanceType>Miles</Recipe_05_07:DistanceType>
    <Recipe_05_07:DistanceType>Kilometres</Recipe_05_07:DistanceType>
</ComboBox>

<TextBlock Grid.Row="2" HorizontalAlignment="Right" Margin="5"
        Text="Result:"/>

<!-- The TextBlock that binds to the results of the method.-->
<TextBlock
    Grid.Row="2" Grid.Column="1" Margin="5"
    Text="{Binding
            Source={StaticResource convertDistance}}"/>

    </Grid>
</Window>
```

The code for the DistanceConverter class is as follows:

```csharp
using System;

namespace Recipe_05_07
{
    public enum DistanceType
    {
        Miles,
        Kilometres
    }

    public class DistanceConverter
    {
        /// <summary>
        /// Convert miles to kilometres and vice versa.
        /// </summary>
        /// <param name="amount">The amount to convert.</param>
        /// <param name="distancetype">The units the amount is in.</param>
        /// <returns>A string containing the converted amount.</returns>
        public string Convert(
            double amount,
            DistanceType distancetype)
```

```
        {
            if(distancetype == DistanceType.Miles)
                return (amount * 1.609344).ToString("0.##") + " km";

            if(distancetype == DistanceType.Kilometres)
                return (amount * 0.621371192).ToString("0.##") + " m";

            throw new ArgumentOutOfRangeException("distanceType");
        }
    }
}
```

Figure 5-7 shows the resulting window.

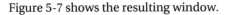

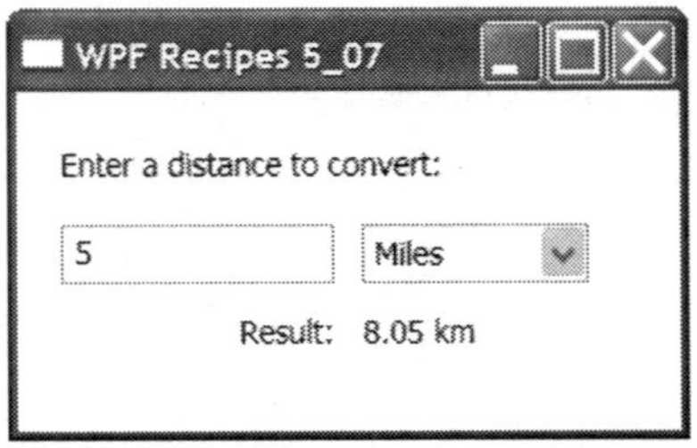

Figure 5-7. *Binding to a method and its parameters*

5-8. Bind to a Command

Problem

You need to bind a System.Windows.Controls.Button control directly to a System.Windows.Input.ICommand. This enables you to execute custom logic when the Button is clicked, without having to handle its Click event and call a method. You can also bind the IsEnabled property of the Button to the ICommand object's CanExecute method.

Solution

Create a class that implements ICommand, and expose an instance of it as a property on another class or business object. Bind this property to a Button control's Command property.

How It Works

The Button control derives from the System.Windows.Controls.Primitives.ButtonBase class. This implements the System.Windows.Input.ICommandSource interface and exposes an ICommand property called Command. The ICommand interface encapsulates a unit of functionality. When its Execute method is called, this functionality is executed. The CanExecute method determines whether the ICommand can be executed in its current state. It returns True if the ICommand can be executed and returns False if not.

To execute custom application logic when a Button is clicked, you would typically attach an event handler to its Click event. However, you can also encapsulate this custom logic in a command and bind it directly to the Button control's Command property. This approach has several advantages. First, the IsEnabled property of the Button will automatically be bound to the CanExecute method of the ICommand. This means that when the CanExecuteChanged event is fired, the Button will call the command's CanExecute method and refresh its own IsEnabled property dynamically. Second, the application functionality that should be executed when the Button is clicked does not have to reside in the code-behind for the window. This enables greater separation of presentation and business logic, which is always desirable in object-oriented programming in general, and even more so in WPF development, because it makes it easier for UI designers to work alongside developers without getting in each other's way.

To bind the Command property of a Button to an instance of an ICommand, simply set the Path attribute to the name of the ICommand property, just as you would any other property. You can also optionally specify parameters using the CommandParameter attribute. This in turn can be bound to the properties of other elements and is passed to the Execute and CanExecute methods of the command.

The Code

The following example demonstrates a window containing three System.Windows.Controls.TextBox controls. These are bound to the FirstName, LastName, and Age properties of a custom Person object. The Person class also exposes an instance of the AddPersonCommand and SetOccupationCommand as read-only properties. There are two Button controls on the window that have their Command attribute bound to these command properties. Custom logic in the CanExecute methods of the commands specifies when the Buttons should be enabled or disabled. If the ICommand can be executed and the Button should therefore be enabled, the code in the CanExecute method returns True. If it returns False, the Button will be disabled. The Set Occupation Button control also binds its CommandParameter to the Text property of a System.Windows.Controls.ComboBox control. This demonstrates how to pass parameters to an instance of an ICommand.

The XAML for the window is as follows:

```xml
<Window x:Class="Recipe_05_08.Window1"
    xmlns="http://schemas.microsoft.com/winfx/2006/xaml/presentation"
    xmlns:x="http://schemas.microsoft.com/winfx/2006/xaml"
    Title="WPF Recipes 5_08" Height="224" Width="300">
    <Grid>
        <Grid.ColumnDefinitions>
            <ColumnDefinition Width="60"/>
            <ColumnDefinition Width="*"/>
        </Grid.ColumnDefinitions>

        <Grid.RowDefinitions>
            <RowDefinition Height="26"/>
            <RowDefinition Height="26"/>
            <RowDefinition Height="26"/>
            <RowDefinition Height="40"/>
```

```xml
        <RowDefinition Height="34"/>
        <RowDefinition Height="26"/>
    </Grid.RowDefinitions>

    <TextBlock
        Margin="4"
        Text="First Name"
        VerticalAlignment="Center"/>
    <TextBox
        Text="{Binding Path=FirstName}"
        Margin="4" Grid.Column="1"/>

    <TextBlock
        Margin="4"
        Text="Last Name"
        Grid.Row="1"
        VerticalAlignment="Center"/>
    <TextBox
        Margin="4"
        Text="{Binding Path=LastName}"
        Grid.Column="1" Grid.Row="1"/>

    <TextBlock
        Margin="4"
        Text="Age"
        Grid.Row="2"
        VerticalAlignment="Center"/>
    <TextBox
        Margin="4"
        Text="{Binding Path=Age}"
        Grid.Column="1"
        Grid.Row="2"/>

    <!-- Bind the Button to the Add Command -->
    <Button
        Command="{Binding Path=Add}"
        Content="Add"
        Margin="4"
        Grid.Row="3"
        Grid.Column="2"/>

    <StackPanel
        Orientation="Horizontal"
        Grid.Column="2"
        Grid.Row="4">
```

```xml
<ComboBox
    x:Name="cboOccupation"
    IsEditable="False"
    Margin="4" Width="100">
    <ComboBoxItem>Student</ComboBoxItem>
    <ComboBoxItem>Skilled</ComboBoxItem>
    <ComboBoxItem>Professional</ComboBoxItem>
</ComboBox>

<Button
    Command="{Binding Path=SetOccupation}"
    CommandParameter="{Binding ElementName=cboOccupation, Path=Text}"
    Content="Set Occupation"
    Margin="4"
  />

</StackPanel>

<TextBlock
    Margin="4"
    Text="Status"
    Grid.Row="5"
    VerticalAlignment="Center"/>
<TextBlock
    Margin="4"
    Text="{Binding Path=Status, UpdateSourceTrigger=PropertyChanged}"
    VerticalAlignment="Center"
    FontStyle="Italic"
    Grid.Column="1"
    Grid.Row="5"/>

    </Grid>
</Window>
```

The code-behind for the window sets its DataContext property to a new Person object. The code for this is as follows:

```csharp
using System.Windows;
using Recipe_05_08;

namespace Recipe_05_08
{
    public partial class Window1 : Window
    {
        public Window1()
        {
            InitializeComponent();
```

```
                    // Set the DataContext to a Person object
                    this.DataContext =
                        new Person()
                            {
                                FirstName = "Ellin",
                                LastName = "Blinks",
                            };
            }
        }
}
```

The code for the Person class, which also contains the command classes, is as follows:

```
using System;
using System.ComponentModel;
using System.Windows.Input;

namespace Recipe_05_08
{
    public class Person : INotifyPropertyChanged
    {
        private string firstName;
        private int age;
        private string lastName;
        private string status;
        private string occupation;

        private AddPersonCommand addPersonCommand;
        private SetOccupationCommand setOccupationCommand;

        public string FirstName
        {
            get
            {
                return firstName;
            }
            set
            {
                if(firstName != value)
                {
                    firstName = value;
                    OnPropertyChanged("FirstName");
                }
            }
        }
```

```csharp
public string LastName
{
    get
    {
        return lastName;
    }
    set
    {
        if(this.lastName != value)
        {
            this.lastName = value;
            OnPropertyChanged("LastName");
        }
    }
}

public int Age
{
    get
    {
        return age;
    }
    set
    {
        if(this.age != value)
        {
            this.age = value;
            OnPropertyChanged("Age");
        }
    }
}

public string Status
{
    get
    {
        return status;
    }
    set
    {
        if(this.status != value)
        {
            this.status = value;
            OnPropertyChanged("Status");
        }
    }
}
```

```csharp
public string Occupation
{
    get
    {
        return occupation;
    }
    set
    {
        if(this.occupation != value)
        {
            this.occupation = value;
            OnPropertyChanged("Occupation");
        }
    }
}

/// Gets an AddPersonCommand for data binding
public AddPersonCommand Add
{
    get
    {
        if(addPersonCommand == null)
            addPersonCommand = new AddPersonCommand(this);

        return addPersonCommand;
    }
}

/// Gets a SetOccupationCommand for data binding
public SetOccupationCommand SetOccupation
{
    get
    {
        if(setOccupationCommand == null)
            setOccupationCommand = new SetOccupationCommand(this);

        return setOccupationCommand;
    }
}

#region INotifyPropertyChanged Members

/// Implement INotifyPropertyChanged to notify the binding
/// targets when the values of properties change.
public event PropertyChangedEventHandler PropertyChanged;
```

```
    private void OnPropertyChanged(string propertyName)
    {
        if(this.PropertyChanged != null)
        {
            this.PropertyChanged(
                this, new PropertyChangedEventArgs(propertyName));
        }
    }

    #endregion
}

public class AddPersonCommand : ICommand
{
    private Person person;

    public AddPersonCommand(Person person)
    {
        this.person = person;

        this.person.PropertyChanged +=
            new PropertyChangedEventHandler(person_PropertyChanged);
    }

    // Handle the PropertyChanged event of the person to raise the
    // CanExecuteChanged event
    private void person_PropertyChanged(
        object sender, PropertyChangedEventArgs e)
    {
        if(CanExecuteChanged != null)
        {
            CanExecuteChanged(this, EventArgs.Empty);
        }
    }

    #region ICommand Members

    /// The command can execute if there are valid values
    /// for the person's FirstName, LastName, and Age properties
    /// and if it hasn't already been executed and had its
    /// Status property set.
    public bool CanExecute(object parameter)
    {
        if(!string.IsNullOrEmpty(person.FirstName))
            if(!string.IsNullOrEmpty(person.LastName))
                if(person.Age > 0)
                    if(string.IsNullOrEmpty(person.Status))
                        return true;
```

```
            return false;
        }

        public event EventHandler CanExecuteChanged;

        /// When the command is executed, update the
        /// status property of the person.
        public void Execute(object parameter)
        {
            person.Status =
                string.Format("Added {0} {1}",
                                person.FirstName, person.LastName);
        }

        #endregion
}

public class SetOccupationCommand : ICommand
{
    private Person person;

    public SetOccupationCommand(Person person)
    {
        this.person = person;

        this.person.PropertyChanged +=
            new PropertyChangedEventHandler(person_PropertyChanged);
    }

    // Handle the PropertyChanged event of the person to raise the
    // CanExecuteChanged event
    private void person_PropertyChanged(
        object sender, PropertyChangedEventArgs e)
    {
        if(CanExecuteChanged != null)
        {
            CanExecuteChanged(this, EventArgs.Empty);
        }
    }

    #region ICommand Members

    /// The command can execute if the person has been added,
    /// which means its Status will be set, and if the occupation
```

```
/// parameter is not null
public bool CanExecute(object parameter)
{
    if(!string.IsNullOrEmpty(parameter as string))
        if(!string.IsNullOrEmpty(person.Status))
            return true;

    return false;
}

public event EventHandler CanExecuteChanged;

/// When the command is executed, set the Occupation
/// property of the person, and update the Status.
public void Execute(object parameter)
{
    // Get the occupation string from the command parameter
    person.Occupation = parameter.ToString();

    person.Status =
        string.Format("Added {0} {1}, {2}",
                        person.FirstName, person.LastName, person.Occupation);
}
#endregion
    }
}
```

Figure 5-8 shows the resulting window.

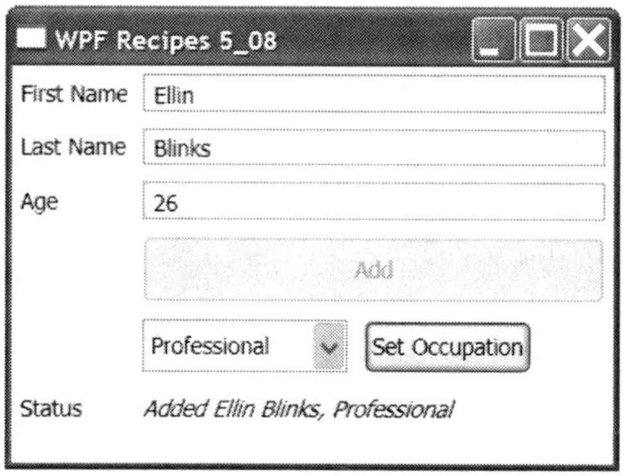

Figure 5-8. *Binding to a command*

5-9. Bind to the Values of an Enumeration

Problem

You need to bind a System.Windows.Controls.ItemsControl to all the possible values of an enumeration.

Solution

Use the System.Windows.Data.ObjectDataProvider class to make the values of a System.Enum available as a binding source. Bind the ObjectDataProvider to the ItemsSource property of an ItemsControl.

How It Works

You can create the ObjectDataProvider as a resource in your window or control and can expose the values of an Enum as a binding source. In your XAML, declare an ObjectDataProvider, and set the MethodName and ObjectType attributes to the GetValues method of the System.Enum class. Add the type of the Enum you want to convert to the MethodParameters collection of the ObjectDataProvider. Then simply bind the ItemsSource property of an ItemsControl, such as a System.Windows.Controls.ComboBox or System.Windows.Controls.ListBox control, to this ObjectDataProvider.

The Code

The following example demonstrates a window containing an ObjectDataProvider that creates a binding source for an enumeration called DaysOfTheWeek. Unsurprisingly, this enumerates the days of the week, from Monday to Sunday. The window contains a ComboBox that binds to the ObjectDataProvider and displays the values of this Enum.

The XAML for the window is as follows:

```
<Window
    x:Class="Recipe_05_09.Window1"
    xmlns="http://schemas.microsoft.com/winfx/2006/xaml/presentation"
    xmlns:x="http://schemas.microsoft.com/winfx/2006/xaml"
    xmlns:System="clr-namespace:System;assembly=mscorlib"
    xmlns:Recipe_05_09="clr-namespace:Recipe_05_09"
    Title="WPF Recipes 5_09" Height="100" Width="180">

    <Window.Resources>

        <!-- The ObjectDataProvider exposes the enum as a binding source -->
        <ObjectDataProvider
            x:Key="daysData"
            MethodName="GetValues"
            ObjectType="{x:Type System:Enum}" >
```

```
                    <!-- Pass the DaysOfTheWeek type to the -->
                    <!-- GetValues property of System.Enum. -->
                    <ObjectDataProvider.MethodParameters>
                        <x:Type TypeName="Recipe_05_09:DaysOfTheWeek"/>
                    </ObjectDataProvider.MethodParameters>
                </ObjectDataProvider>

        </Window.Resources>

        <StackPanel>
            <TextBlock
                Margin="5"
                Text="Select the day of the week:"/>

            <!-- Binds to the ObjectDataProvider -->
            <ComboBox
                Margin="5"
                ItemsSource="{Binding
                             Source={StaticResource daysData}}" />
        </StackPanel>
</Window>
```

The DaysOfTheWeek enumeration is declared in the code-behind for the window, which is as follows:

```
using System.Windows;

namespace Recipe_05_09
{
    /// <summary>
    /// The Days of the Week enumeration
    /// </summary>
    public enum DaysOfTheWeek
    {
        Monday,
        Tuesday,
        Wednesday,
        Thursday,
        Friday,
        Saturday,
        Sunday
    }
```

```
public partial class Window1 : Window
{
    public Window1()
    {
        InitializeComponent();
    }
}
}
```

Figure 5-9 shows the resulting window.

Figure 5-9. *Binding to the values of an enumeration*

5-10. Specify a Default Value for a Binding

Problem

You need to specify a default value for a data binding as a fallback in case the source property of the binding cannot always be resolved.

Solution

Use the FallbackValue property of System.Windows.Data.BindingBase.

How It Works

The FallbackValue property specifies the value to use when the binding is unable to return a value. A binding may be unable to return a value for any of the following reasons:

- The path to the binding cannot be resolved successfully.

- The value converter, if there is one, cannot convert the resulting value.

- The resulting value is not valid for the binding target property.

In any of these cases, the target property is set to the value of the FallbackValue, if one is available.

Tip Specifying a default value for a binding can be very useful when working with design tools such as Microsoft Expression Blend. If the data source for a binding is assigned only at runtime, then the target property will not display anything in design mode. This means designers don't see a realistic view of the UI they are designing.

The Code

The following example demonstrates a window containing three System.Windows.Controls. TextBox objects that display the name and age of a person. The window is never actually assigned a data source, so when the application is run, the TextBox objects are empty by default. However, in the binding statement for each TextBox, the FallbackValue is specified. This ensures that when the application is run, the TextBox objects display default values.

The XAML for the window is as follows:

```
<Window x:Class="Recipe_05_10.Window1"
    xmlns="http://schemas.microsoft.com/winfx/2006/xaml/presentation"
    xmlns:x="http://schemas.microsoft.com/winfx/2006/xaml"
     Title="WPF Recipes 5_10" Height="120" Width="300">
    <Grid>
        <Grid.ColumnDefinitions>
            <ColumnDefinition Width="60"/>
            <ColumnDefinition Width="*"/>
        </Grid.ColumnDefinitions>

        <Grid.RowDefinitions>
            <RowDefinition Height="28"/>
            <RowDefinition Height="28"/>
            <RowDefinition Height="28"/>
        </Grid.RowDefinitions>

        <TextBlock Margin="4" Text="First Name" VerticalAlignment="Center"/>
        <TextBox Margin="4"
                    Text="{Binding
                            Path=FirstName,
                            FallbackValue=First name goes here}"
                    FontStyle="Italic" Grid.Column="1"/>

        <TextBlock Margin="4" Text="Last Name"
                    Grid.Row="1" VerticalAlignment="Center"/>
```

```
            <TextBox Margin="4"
                        Text="{Binding
                                 Path=LastName,
                                 FallbackValue=Second name goes here}"
                        FontStyle="Italic"
                        Grid.Column="1" Grid.Row="1"/>

            <TextBlock Margin="4" Text="Age"
                        Grid.Row="2" VerticalAlignment="Center"/>
            <TextBox Margin="4"
                        Text="{Binding
                                 Path=Age,
                                 FallbackValue=Age goes here}"
                        FontStyle="Italic"
                        Grid.Column="1" Grid.Row="2"/>

    </Grid>
</Window>
```

Figure 5-10 shows the resulting window.

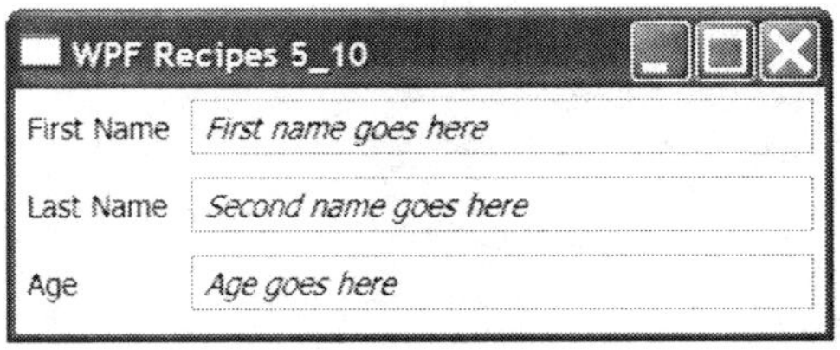

Figure 5-10. *Specifying default values for a binding*

5-11. Use Data Templates to Display Bound Data

Problem

You need to specify a set of UI elements to use to visualize your bound data objects.

Solution

Create a System.Windows.DataTemplate to define the presentation of your data objects. This specifies the visual structure of UI elements to use to display your data.

How It Works

When you bind to a data object, the binding target displays a string representation of the object by default. Internally, this is because without any specific instructions the binding mechanism calls the ToString method of the binding source when binding to it. Creating a DataTemplate enables you to specify a different visual structure of UI elements when displaying your data object. When the binding mechanism is asked to display a data object, it will use the UI elements specified in the DataTemplate to render it.

The Code

The following example demonstrates a window that contains a System.Windows.Controls. ListBox control. The ItemsSource property of the ListBox is bound to a collection of Person objects. The Person class is defined in the Data.cs file and exposes FirstName, LastName, Age and Photo properties. It also overrides the ToString method to return the full name of the person it represents. Without a DataTemplate, the ListBox control would just display this list of names. Figure 5-11 shows what this would look like.

Figure 5-11. *Binding to a list of data objects, without specifying a* DataTemplate

However, the ItemTemplate property of the ListBox is set to a static resource called personTemplate. This is a DataTemplate resource defined in the window's System.Windows. ResourceDictionary. The DataTemplate creates a System.Windows.Controls.Grid control inside a System.Windows.Controls.Border control. Inside the Grid, it defines a series of System. Windows.Controls.TextBlock controls and a System.Windows.Controls.Image control. These controls have standard binding statements that bind their properties to properties on the Person class. When the window opens and the ListBox binds to the collection of Person objects, the binding mechanism uses the set of UI elements in the DataTemplate to display each item. Figure 5-12 shows the same ListBox as in Figure 5-11 but with its ItemTemplate property set to the DataTemplate.

The XAML for the window is as follows:

```
<Window
    x:Class="Recipe_05_11.Window1"
    xmlns="http://schemas.microsoft.com/winfx/2006/xaml/presentation"
    xmlns:x="http://schemas.microsoft.com/winfx/2006/xaml"
    xmlns:Recipe_05_11="clr-namespace:Recipe_05_11"
    Title="WPF Recipes 5_11" Height="298" Width="260">

    <Window.Resources>
```

```xml
<!-- Creates the local data source for binding -->
<Recipe_05_11:People x:Key="people"/>

<!-- Styles used by the UI elements in the DataTemplate -->
<Style
    x:Key="lblStyle"
    TargetType="{x:Type TextBlock}">
    <Setter Property="FontFamily" Value="Tahoma"/>
    <Setter Property="FontSize" Value="11pt"/>
    <Setter Property="VerticalAlignment" Value="Center"/>
    <Setter Property="Margin" Value="2"/>
    <Setter Property="Foreground" Value="Red"/>
</Style>

<Style
    x:Key="dataStyle"
    TargetType="{x:Type TextBlock}"
    BasedOn="{StaticResource lblStyle}">
    <Setter Property="Margin" Value="10,2,2,2"/>
    <Setter Property="Foreground" Value="Blue"/>
    <Setter Property="FontStyle" Value="Italic"/>
</Style>

<!-- DataTemplate to use for displaying each Person item -->
<DataTemplate x:Key="personTemplate">
    <Border
        BorderThickness="1"
        BorderBrush="Gray"
        Padding="4"
        Margin="4"
        Height="Auto"
        Width="Auto">
        <Grid>
            <Grid.ColumnDefinitions>
                <ColumnDefinition Width="80"/>
                <ColumnDefinition Width="*"/>
            </Grid.ColumnDefinitions>

            <StackPanel>
                <TextBlock
                    Style="{StaticResource lblStyle}"
                    Text="First Name" />
                <TextBlock
                    Style="{StaticResource dataStyle}"
                    Text="{Binding Path=FirstName}"/>
```

```xml
                <TextBlock
                    Style="{StaticResource lblStyle}"
                    Text="Last Name" />
                <TextBlock
                    Style="{StaticResource dataStyle}"
                    Text="{Binding Path=LastName}" />

                <TextBlock
                    Style="{StaticResource lblStyle}"
                    Text="Age" />
                <TextBlock
                    Style="{StaticResource dataStyle}"
                    Text="{Binding Path=Age}" />
            </StackPanel>

            <Image
                Margin="4"
                Grid.Column="1"
                Width="96"
                Height="140"
                Source="{Binding Path=Photo}"/>
        </Grid>
      </Border>
    </DataTemplate>


</Window.Resources>

<Grid>
    <!-- The ListBox binds to the people collection, and sets the -->
    <!-- DataTemplate to use for displaying each item -->
    <ListBox
        Margin="10"
        ItemsSource="{Binding Source={StaticResource people}}"
        ItemTemplate="{StaticResource personTemplate}"/>

    <!-- Without specifying a DataTemplate, the ListBox just -->
    <!-- displays a list of names. -->
    <!--<ListBox
        Margin="10"
        ItemsSource="{Binding Source={StaticResource people}}"/>-->
</Grid>
</Window>
```

Figure 5-12 shows the resulting window.

Figure 5-12. *Binding to a list of data objects and specifying a* DataTemplate

5-12. Use Value Converters to Convert Bound Data

Problem

You need to convert the source value of a binding in order to assign it to the target value. For example, you need to bind one type of property to a completely different type of property, such as binding an integer value to a System.Windows.Controls.Control.Foreground property. Alternatively, you may need to bind two values of the same type but derive the value of the target property from a calculation based on the value of the source. For example, your data has a property of type double that you want to bind to a System.Windows.FrameworkElement.Width property.

Solution

Create a class that implements the System.Windows.Data.IValueConverter interface. Add custom logic to the Convert method to apply a conversion to the data that will be assigned to the binding. Declare this converter class as a static resource, and reference it as the Converter property of a System.Windows.Data.Binding in your XAML.

Tip WPF includes a few value converters out of the box for common data binding scenarios. For example, the System.Windows.Controls.BooleanToVisibilityConverter class, which converts a Boolean value to a System.Windows.Visibility value. This is extremely useful for specifying whether a particular UI element and its children should be displayed at runtime, based on the value of a Boolean property.

How It Works

The IValueConverter interface has two methods, Convert and ConvertBack. When you specify the Converter property of a binding, the source value is not bound directly to the target value. Instead, it is passed in as the value parameter to the Convert method of the converter. The Convert method that receives the value is then free to apply conversion logic based on its value. It returns an instance of the type expected by the binding target.

The ConvertBack method is called in a two-way binding, when the binding target propagates a value to the binding source. In one-way bindings, it can simply throw a System. NotImplementedException instance, because it should never be called.

If you need to convert the values from multiple properties into a single value to assign to a binding target, use a System.Windows.Data.IMultiValueConverter. This associates a converter with a System.Windows.Data.MultiBinding class, which attaches a collection of System.Windows. Data.Binding objects to a single binding target property. This is useful when the value of a bound property should be updated whenever the values of multiple source properties change.

■ **Tip** When naming a converter, it is good practice to use the convention <Source Type or Name>To<Target Type>Converter, for example, DoubleToWidthProperty or ProbabilityToOpacityConverter. It is also good practice to decorate the converter class with the System.Windows.Data. ValueConversionAttribute to indicate to development tools the data types involved in the conversion.

The Code

The following example demonstrates a window containing a System.Windows.Controls. ItemsControl that displays a collection of DataItem objects. This object exposes a Percent property, which contains a double value from –100 to +100. The window contains a System.Windows. DataTemplate in its Resources collection. This specifies that each DataItem should be displayed as a System.Windows.Shapes.Rectangle, which has the effect of presenting the data items in the form of a simple bar graph.

The window declares two converter classes. These are referenced in the binding statements in the XAML for the rectangle. The Height property of each rectangle is bound to the Percent property of its DataItem and is sent through an instance of the PercentToHeightConverter. In this case, both the source property, Percent, and the target property, Height, are double values. However, a conversion has to take place to translate the value of Percent, into a valid Height value. The Fill property of the rectangle is also bound to the Percent property of DataItem. However, this binding requires a value converter, because a double value cannot be converted directly to a System.Windows.Media.Brush value. The PercentToFillConverter intercepts the binding and returns one color of Brush if the Percent value is positive and another value if it is negative.

The XAML for the window is as follows:

```
<Window
    x:Class="Recipe_05_12.Window1"
    xmlns="http://schemas.microsoft.com/winfx/2006/xaml/presentation"
    xmlns:x="http://schemas.microsoft.com/winfx/2006/xaml"
```

```
    xmlns:local="clr-namespace:Using_Value_Converters"
    xmlns:Recipe_05_12="clr-namespace:Recipe_05_12"
    x:Name="thisWindow"
    Title="WPF Recipes 5_12" Height="240" Width="280">

<Window.Resources>

    <local:DataItems x:Key="dataItems"/>

    <!-- Declare two converter classes -->
    <Recipe_05_12:PercentToHeightConverter x:Key="percentToHeightConverter" />
    <Recipe_05_12:PercentToFillConverter x:Key="percentToFillConverter" />

    <!-- Bind the rectangle's height and color to the data's -->
    <!-- Percent property, but apply a conversion -->
    <!-- to it using the two converter classes. -->
    <DataTemplate x:Key="dataItemtemplate">
        <Rectangle
            Margin="4"
            Width="30"
            VerticalAlignment="Bottom"

            Height="{Binding
                    Path=Percent,
                    Converter={StaticResource
                                    percentToHeightConverter}}"
            Fill="{Binding
                    Path=Percent,
                    Converter={StaticResource
                                    percentToFillConverter}}"/>
    </DataTemplate>

</Window.Resources>

<Grid Margin="20">

    <Grid.ColumnDefinitions>
        <ColumnDefinition Width="1"/>
        <ColumnDefinition />
    </Grid.ColumnDefinitions>

    <Grid.RowDefinitions>
        <RowDefinition/>
        <RowDefinition Height="1"/>
    </Grid.RowDefinitions>
```

```xml
        <ItemsControl
            Grid.Column="1"
            Margin="4,0,0,4"
            ItemsSource="{Binding Source={StaticResource dataItems}}"
            ItemTemplate="{StaticResource dataItemtemplate}">
            <ItemsControl.ItemsPanel>
                <ItemsPanelTemplate>
                    <StackPanel Orientation="Horizontal"/>
                </ItemsPanelTemplate>
            </ItemsControl.ItemsPanel>
        </ItemsControl>

        <Line Grid.RowSpan="2"
            Stroke="Black"
            StrokeThickness="2"
            X1="0" Y1="0"
            X2="0"
            Y2="{Binding ElementName=thisWindow, Path=ActualHeight}"/>

        <Line Grid.Row="1"
            Grid.ColumnSpan="2"
            Stroke="Black"
            StrokeThickness="2"
            X1="0" Y1="0"
            X2="{Binding ElementName=thisWindow, Path=ActualWidth}"
            Y2="0"/>
    </Grid>
</Window>
```

The code for the `PercentToHeightConverter` class is as follows:

```csharp
using System;
using System.Windows.Data;
using System.Globalization;

namespace Recipe_05_12
{
    [ValueConversion(typeof (double), typeof (double))]
    public class PercentToHeightConverter : IValueConverter
    {
        // Converts a Percent value to a new height value.
        // The data binding engine calls this method when
        // it propagates a value from the binding source to the binding target.
        public Object Convert(
            Object value,
            Type targetType,
            Object parameter,
            CultureInfo culture)
```

```
        {
            double percent =
                System.Convert.ToDouble(value);

            // if the value is negative, invert it
            if(percent < 0)
                percent *= -1;

            return percent * 2;
        }

        // Converts a value. The data binding engine calls this
        // method when it propagates a value from the binding
        // target to the binding source.
        // As the binding is one-way, this is not implemented.
        public object ConvertBack(
            object value,
            Type targetType,
            object parameter,
            CultureInfo culture)
        {
            throw new NotImplementedException();
        }
    }
}
```

The code for the PercentToFillConverter is as follows:

```
using System;
using System.Windows;
using System.Windows.Data;
using System.Windows.Media;
using System.Globalization;
using System.Collections.Generic;

namespace Recipe_05_12
{
    [ValueConversion(typeof (double), typeof (Brush))]
    public class PercentToFillConverter : IValueConverter
    {
        // Declares a Brush to use for negative data items
        private static readonly Brush negativeColor =
            new LinearGradientBrush(
                new GradientStopCollection(
                    new List<GradientStop>(
                        new GradientStop[]
```

```csharp
                    {
                        new GradientStop(
                            Color.FromArgb(255, 165, 0, 0), 0),
                        new GradientStop(
                            Color.FromArgb(255, 132, 0, 0), 0)
                    }
                )),
            new Point(0.5,0),
            new Point(0.5,1));

// Declares a Brush to use for positive data items
private static readonly Brush positiveColor =
    new LinearGradientBrush(
        new GradientStopCollection(
            new List<GradientStop>(
                new GradientStop[]
                    {
                        new GradientStop(
                            Color.FromArgb(255, 0, 165, 39), 1),
                        new GradientStop(
                            Color.FromArgb(255, 0, 132, 37), 0)
                    }
                )),
        new Point(0.5, 0),
        new Point(0.5, 1));


// Converts a Percent value to a Fill value.
// Returns a Brush based on whether Percent is positive or negative.
// The data binding engine calls this method when
// it propagates a value from the binding source to the binding target.
public Object Convert(
    Object value,
    Type targetType,
    Object parameter,
    CultureInfo culture)
{
    double percent = System.Convert.ToDouble(value);

    if(percent > 0)
    {
        return  positiveColor;
    }
    else
    {
        return negativeColor;
    }
}
```

```
// Converts a value. The data binding engine calls this
// method when it propagates a value from the binding
// target to the binding source.
// As the binding is one-way, this is not implemented.
public object ConvertBack(
    object value,
    Type targetType,
    object parameter,
    CultureInfo culture)
{
    throw new NotImplementedException();
}
    }
}
```

Figure 5-13 shows the resulting window.

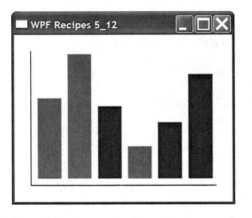

Figure 5-13. *Converting bound data*

5-13. Use Data Triggers to Change the Appearance of Bound Data

Problem

You need to change the appearance of a bound data object when its property values meet a certain condition. For example, you are binding to a list of products, and you want those items that are out of stock to be given a different visual appearance than the others.

Solution

Create a System.Windows.DataTemplate to define the visual structure of your data object, and add a System.Windows.DataTrigger to it. The DataTrigger sets appearance property values on the UI elements in the DataTemplate when the property value of the data object matches a specified condition.

How It Works

Like the System.Windows.Style and System.Windows.Controls.ControlTemplate classes, the DataTemplate class has a collection of triggers. A trigger applies property values or performs actions when the bound data meets a specified condition.

Create a DataTrigger in the Triggers collection of your DataTemplate. A DataTrigger has three components to configure. First, it has a Binding property that specifies the property of the data object it should be bound to. Set this using a standard binding statement, and assign the name of the property in the binding's Path attribute. It is this property that the trigger will be evaluating to determine whether it should be applied. Second, specify the DataTrigger's Value attribute. This stores the value that the bound property should contain in order for the trigger to be applied. For example, suppose you want to apply a different visual appearance to out-of-stock items in a product catalog. You could create a DataTrigger, set its Binding property to the IsOutOfStock property of the data object, and set its Value property to True.

The third component in a DataTrigger is its Setters property. This contains a collection of System.Windows.Setter objects, which describe the appearance property values to apply when the bound property has the specified value. Each Setter object specifies the UI element in the template to target, the property of that target it should set, and the value to set it to. For example, if you wanted to highlight the names of out-of-stock products in red, you would create a Setter with a TargetName of txtName, a Property of Foreground, and a Value of Red.

A DataTrigger can contain multiple Setter objects that change the visual appearance of the DataTemplate in different ways when the trigger's condition is met. For example, if a product is out of stock, you might want to not only highlight its name in red but also hide the Add to Shopping Basket button.

The Code

The following example demonstrates a window containing a System.Windows.Controls.ItemsControl that displays a collection of DataItem objects. The window contains a System.Windows.DataTemplate in its Resources collection, which specifies that each DataItem should be displayed as a System.Windows.Shapes.Rectangle. This has the effect of presenting the data items in the form of a simple bar graph.

The DataTemplate contains a DataTrigger. This binds to a Boolean property on the DataItem class called IsPositive. When the value of this property is True, the Setter in the DataTrigger changes the Fill color of the rectangle to red.

The XAML for the window is as follows:

```
<Window x:Class="Recipe_05_13.Window1"
    xmlns="http://schemas.microsoft.com/winfx/2006/xaml/presentation"
    xmlns:x="http://schemas.microsoft.com/winfx/2006/xaml"
    xmlns:Recipe_05_13="clr-namespace:Recipe_05_13"
    x:Name="thisWindow"
    Title="WPF Recipes 5_13" Height="240" Width="280">

    <Window.Resources>

        <Recipe_05_13:DataItems x:Key="dataItems"/>
```

```xml
<!-- Declare two converter classes -->
<Recipe_05_13:AmountToHeightConverter x:Key="amountToHeightConverter" />

<!-- Creates a DataTemplate that displays a colored bar -->
<!-- for each DataItem. Its height is calculated by a converter.-->
<DataTemplate x:Key="dataItemtemplate">
    <Rectangle
        x:Name="rectangle"
        Margin="4"
        Width="30"
        VerticalAlignment="Bottom"
        Fill="Green"
        Height="{Binding
                Path=Amount,
                Converter={StaticResource
                                    amountToHeightConverter}}"/>

    <!-- A DataTigger that binds to the IsPositive property  -->
    <!-- of a DataItem, and changes the color of the bar to -->
    <!-- red if IsPositive is False. -->
    <DataTemplate.Triggers>
        <DataTrigger
                Binding="{Binding
                    Path=IsPositive}"
                Value="False">
            <Setter
                TargetName="rectangle"
                Property="Fill"
                Value="Red"/>
        </DataTrigger>
    </DataTemplate.Triggers>
</DataTemplate>

</Window.Resources>

<Grid Margin="20">

    <Grid.ColumnDefinitions>
        <ColumnDefinition Width="1"/>
        <ColumnDefinition />
    </Grid.ColumnDefinitions>

    <Grid.RowDefinitions>
        <RowDefinition/>
        <RowDefinition Height="1"/>
    </Grid.RowDefinitions>
```

```
        <ItemsControl
            Grid.Column="1"
            Margin="4,0,0,4"
            ItemsSource="{Binding Source={StaticResource dataItems}}"
            ItemTemplate="{StaticResource dataItemtemplate}">
            <ItemsControl.ItemsPanel>
                <ItemsPanelTemplate>
                    <StackPanel Orientation="Horizontal"/>
                </ItemsPanelTemplate>
            </ItemsControl.ItemsPanel>
        </ItemsControl>

        <Line Grid.RowSpan="2"
            Stroke="Black"
            StrokeThickness="2"
            X1="0" Y1="0"
            X2="0"
            Y2="{Binding ElementName=thisWindow, Path=ActualHeight}"/>

        <Line Grid.Row="1"
            Grid.ColumnSpan="2"
            Stroke="Black"
            StrokeThickness="2"
            X1="0" Y1="0"
            X2="{Binding ElementName=thisWindow, Path=ActualWidth}"
            Y2="0"/>
    </Grid>
</Window>
```

Figure 5-14 shows the resulting window.

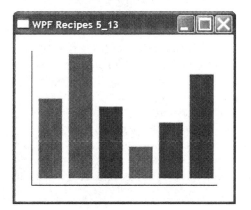

Figure 5-14. *Using triggers to change the appearance of a* DataTemplate

5-14. Select a DataTemplate Based on Properties of the Data Object

Problem

You need to select a different DataTemplate to display a data object, based on properties of the data object or custom application logic.

Solution

Create two or more System.Windows.DataTemplate instances that define the UI elements to display a data object. Create a class that inherits from System.Windows.Controls.DataTemplateSelector, and override the SelectTemplate method. Supply custom application logic to determine which DataTemplate to return for a given data object. Assign this DataTemplateSelector to the target element in your binding.

How It Works

The DataTemplateSelector class provides a way to choose a DataTemplate, based on the data object and custom application logic. This allows you to define multiple templates and dynamically choose which one to apply to any given data object.

Create a class that derives from DataTemplateSelector, and override the SelectTemplate method. This method takes a parameter called item, which is the instance of your data object for which the binding requires a template. If you are binding to a list of items, it will call this method once for each item in the list. You can define custom application logic to determine which DataTemplate to return. Use the FindResource method of System.Windows.FrameworkElememt to locate the required template resource.

Assign your DataTemplateSelector to an appropriate property of the binding target element, instead of assigning a single DataTemplate to it. For example, instead of setting the ItemTemplate property of a System.Windows.Controls.ListBox control, set its ItemTemplateSelector property.

Several other controls in the standard WPF control suite also expose a DataTemplateSelector property. For example, both the System.Windows.Controls.ContentControl and System.Windows.Controls.ContentPresenter classes expose a DataTemplateSelector via their ContentTemplateSelector properties. Assigning a DataTemplateSelector to either of these properties, or the controls that derive from them, allows you to dynamically choose different UI elements to display their content. The HeaderTemplateSelector property of both System.Windows.Controls.HeaderedItemsControl and System.Windows.Controls.HeaderedContentControl allows you to dynamically select a template to use to display a header. Furthermore, when using a System.Windows.Controls.GridView control, you can select templates for cells and column headers. The System.Windows.Controls.TabControl control also exposes DataTemplateSelector properties for selecting the template to use to display the content of its tabs and its selected tab.

Tip To make your DataTemplateSelector behave nicely in designers, such as the WPF designer for Visual Studio or Microsoft Expression Blend, return null in the SelectTemplate method at design time. This is because the DataTemplate resources referenced by the FindResource method of FrameworkElement might not be available at design time. This results in an exception being shown when you try to open your window or control in a designer. By checking for design mode and returning null, your controls will display themselves in the designer, albeit without applying your custom DataTemplate instances.

The Code

The following example demonstrates a window containing a System.Windows.Controls.ListBox control that displays a collection of TaskItem objects. The ItemTemplateSelector property of the ListBox is set to a DataTemplateSelector class called TaskItemDataTemplateSelector. In the SelectTemplate method of this class, there is custom logic to check the value of the Priority property of each TaskItem. If this value is 1, it returns a DataTemplate called highPriorityTaskTemplate. If not, it returns a DataTemplate called defaultTaskTemplate.

Both templates are defined in the window's Resources collection. Note that the DataTemplateSelector is also defined as a static resource in this collection.

The XAML for the window is as follows:

```xml
<Window
    x:Class="Recipe_05_14.Window1"
    xmlns="http://schemas.microsoft.com/winfx/2006/xaml/presentation"
    xmlns:x="http://schemas.microsoft.com/winfx/2006/xaml"
    xmlns:Recipe_05_14="clr-namespace:Recipe_05_14"
    Title="WPF Recipes 5_14" Height="360" Width="330">
    <Window.Resources>

        <!-- Create the TaskList data -->
        <Recipe_05_14:TaskList x:Key="taskList"/>

        <!-- Create the DataTemplateSelector -->
        <Recipe_05_14:TaskItemDataTemplateSelector
                        x:Key="taskItemDataTemplateSelector"/>

        <!-- Default DataTemplate for tasks -->
        <DataTemplate
            x:Key="defaultTaskTemplate">
            <Border Name="border"
                    BorderBrush="LightBlue"
                    BorderThickness="1"
                    Padding="5"
                    Margin="5">
```

```xml
            <Grid>
                <Grid.RowDefinitions>
                    <RowDefinition/>
                    <RowDefinition/>
                </Grid.RowDefinitions>
                <Grid.ColumnDefinitions>
                    <ColumnDefinition Width="80" />
                    <ColumnDefinition />
                </Grid.ColumnDefinitions>
                <TextBlock Grid.Row="0" Grid.Column="0"
                        Text="Name:"/>
                <TextBlock Grid.Row="0" Grid.Column="1"
                        Text="{Binding Path=Name}" />
                <TextBlock Grid.Row="1" Grid.Column="0"
                        Text="Description:"/>
                <TextBlock Grid.Row="1" Grid.Column="1"
                        Text="{Binding Path=Description}"/>
            </Grid>
        </Border>
    </DataTemplate>

    <!-- DataTemplate for high priority tasks -->
    <DataTemplate
        x:Key="highPriorityTaskTemplate">

        <Border
            Name="border"
            BorderBrush="Red"
            BorderThickness="2"
            Margin="5">
            <DockPanel
                Margin="4"
                HorizontalAlignment="Center">
                <TextBlock
                    FontSize="18"
                    Text="{Binding Path=Description}" />
                <Image
                    Margin="20,4,4,4"
                    Height="55" Width="39"
                    Source="Exclamation.png"/>
            </DockPanel>
        </Border>
    </DataTemplate>
```

```xml
        </Window.Resources>

        <Grid>
            <Grid.RowDefinitions>
                <RowDefinition Height="24"/>
                <RowDefinition Height="*"/>
            </Grid.RowDefinitions>

            <TextBlock
                Margin="4"
                HorizontalAlignment="Center"
                VerticalAlignment="Center"
                FontSize="14"
                Text="Task List:"/>

            <!-- Bind the ListBox to the data -->
            <!-- and assign the DataTemplateSelector -->
            <ListBox
                Margin="10"
                Grid.Row="1"
                HorizontalContentAlignment="Stretch"
                ItemsSource="{Binding
                            Source={StaticResource taskList}}"
                ItemTemplateSelector="{StaticResource
                                    taskItemDataTemplateSelector}"/>

        </Grid>
</Window>
```

The code for the DataTemplateSelector is as follows:

```csharp
using System.Windows;
using System.Windows.Controls;
using Recipe_05_14;

namespace Recipe_05_14
{
    public class TaskItemDataTemplateSelector
        : DataTemplateSelector
    {
        // Override the SelectTemplate method to
        // return the desired DataTemplate.
        //
        public override DataTemplate SelectTemplate(
            object item,
            DependencyObject container)
```

```
        {
            if (item != null &&
                item is TaskItem)
            {
                TaskItem taskitem = item as TaskItem;

                Window window = Application.Current.MainWindow;

                // To run in design mode test for design mode, and
                // return null, as it will not find the DataTemplate resources
                // in the following code.
                if (System.ComponentModel.DesignerProperties.GetIsInDesignMode(
                    window))
                    return null;

                // Check the Priority of the TaskItem to
                // determine the DataTemplate to display it.
                //
                if (taskitem.Priority == 1)
                {
                    // Use the window's FindResource method to
                    // locate the DataTemplate
                    return
                        window.FindResource(
                            "highPriorityTaskTemplate") as DataTemplate;
                }
                else
                {
                    return
                        window.FindResource(
                            "defaultTaskTemplate") as DataTemplate;
                }
            }

            return null;
        }
    }
}
```

Figure 5-15 shows the resulting window.

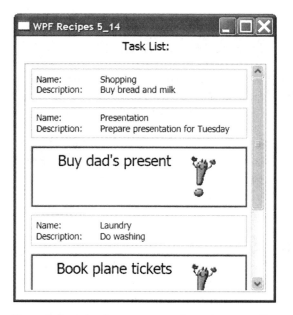

Figure 5-15. *Selecting a* DataTemplate *dynamically*

5-15. Specify Validation Rules for a Binding

Problem

You need to validate user input in a bound UI element, reject invalid data, and give feedback to the user as to why the input is invalid.

Solution

Create a class that derives from System.Windows.Controls.ValidationRule, and specify custom validation logic. Add it to the ValidationRules collection property of a System.Windows. Data.Binding. Optionally, create a custom control template to override the default Validation. ErrorTemplate, and change the appearance of a UI element when its data is invalid.

How It Works

The ValidationRules collection of a Binding provides a way to check the data passed into a binding and mark it as invalid if it fails any of the rules. The ValidationRule class has a method called Validate, which can be overridden to provide the custom validation logic. The Validate method takes the data passed into the binding as a parameter and returns an instance of the System.Windows.Controls.ValidationResult class. The IsValid property of the ValidationResult specifies whether the rule has passed or failed. Set this property to False if the data should be marked as invalid. The ValidationResult class also has an ErrorContent property, which can be used to inform the user as to why the data is invalid. In the following example, this property is used to set an error message that is then displayed in a System.Windows.FrameworkElement.ToolTip control.

In the XAML for a UI element, declare a Binding object as a nested element, instead of as an inline attribute. This allows you to add rules to the Binding's ValidationRules property.

By default, when a binding for a UI element is invalid, its control template is altered so that it is displayed with a thin red border around it. However, you can create a custom System.Windows.Style that assigns a different control template to the Validation.ErrorTemplate attached property on the target element. This allows you to give a control a more sophisticated appearance when its data is invalid. It also allows you to give feedback to the user by exposing the ErrorContent value of the ValidationResult.

The Code

The following example demonstrates a window containing a System.Windows.Controls.Slider control and a System.Windows.Controls.TextBlock control. The XAML statement for the Text property of the TextBlock specifies a Binding statement that binds it to the Value property of the Slider control. In the binding statement, the Mode attribute is set to TwoWay and the UpdateSourceTrigger attribute to PropertyChanged. This ensures that when a number from 1 to 100 is typed into the TextBox, the Slider control immediately updates its value to reflect it.

In the Binding declaration, a local ValidationRule called PercentageRule is added to the ValidationRules collection. This class checks that the value entered into the TextBox is a number between 0 and 100. If it is not, the ValidationRule returns a ValidationResult with the IsValid property set to False and an ErrorContent that states "Must be a number between 0 and 100."

The TextBox is assigned a Style called textBoxInErrorStyle, which is declared in the window's Resources collection. This Style does two things. First, it ensures that when the attached property Validation.HasError is set to True, it assigns the value of the ErrorContent to the ToolTip property of the TextBox. Second, it assigns a new control template to the Validation.ErrorTemplate property. This ensures that when the TextBox is invalid, an error icon is shown to the right of it, and if the user hovers over this icon with the mouse, the error description is displayed in its ToolTip.

The XAML for the window is as follows:

```
<Window
    x:Class="Recipe_05_15.Window1"
    xmlns="http://schemas.microsoft.com/winfx/2006/xaml/presentation"
    xmlns:x="http://schemas.microsoft.com/winfx/2006/xaml"
    xmlns:Recipe_05_15="clr-namespace:Recipe_05_15"
    Title="WPF Recipes 5_15" Height="100" Width="260">

    <Window.Resources>

        <!-- A TextBox style to replace the default ErrorTemplate. -->
        <!-- When the validation rule fails, an error icon is       -->
        <!-- shown next to the TextBox, and the error message is    -->
        <!-- displayed in the ToolTip.                              -->
```

```xml
<Style
    x:Key="textBoxInErrorStyle"
    TargetType="{x:Type TextBox}" >
    <Style.Triggers>

        <!-- A Property Trigger that sets the value of the  -->
        <!-- Tooltip to the error message, when the binding -->
        <!-- has a validation error.                        -->
        <Trigger
            Property="Validation.HasError"
            Value="true">
            <Setter
                Property="ToolTip"
                Value="{Binding
                        RelativeSource={x:Static
                                        RelativeSource.Self},
                        Path=(Validation.Errors)[0].ErrorContent}"/>
        </Trigger>
    </Style.Triggers>

    <!-- A Property Setter that sets the ErrorTemplate to   -->
    <!-- display an error icon to the right of the TextBox. -->
    <Setter
        Property="Validation.ErrorTemplate">
        <Setter.Value>
            <ControlTemplate>
                <DockPanel DockPanel.Dock="Right">
                    <AdornedElementPlaceholder/>
                    <Image
                        Source="Error.png"
                        Width="16"
                        Height="16"
                        ToolTip="{Binding
                                  Path=AdornedElement.ToolTip,
                                  RelativeSource={RelativeSource
                                     Mode=FindAncestor,
                                     AncestorType={x:Type Adorner}}}"/>
                </DockPanel>
            </ControlTemplate>
        </Setter.Value>
    </Setter>
</Style>
</Window.Resources>

<StackPanel>
```

```xml
            <!-- A Slider control that displays a value from 0 to 100 -->
            <Slider Name="slider"
                    Margin="4" Interval="1"
                    TickFrequency="1"
                    IsSnapToTickEnabled="True"
                    Minimum="0" Maximum="100"/>

            <StackPanel Orientation="Horizontal" >
                <TextBlock
                    Width="Auto" Margin="4"
                    HorizontalAlignment="Left"
                    VerticalAlignment="Center"
                    Text="Gets and sets the value of the slider:" />

                <!-- A TextBox with a two-way binding between its Text property -->
                <!-- and the Slider control's Value property. The -->
                <!-- textBoxInErrorStyle resource is assigned as its Style property. -->
                <TextBox
                    Width="40" Margin="4"
                    Style="{StaticResource textBoxInErrorStyle}"
                    HorizontalAlignment="Center" >
                  <TextBox.Text>
                        <Binding
                            ElementName="slider"
                            Path="Value"
                            Mode="TwoWay"
                            UpdateSourceTrigger="PropertyChanged" >

                            <!-- Adds a ValidationRule, specifiying -->
                            <!-- the local PercentageRule class. -->
                            <Binding.ValidationRules>
                                <Recipe_05_15:PercentageRule/>
                            </Binding.ValidationRules>
                        </Binding>
                  </TextBox.Text>
                </TextBox>
            </StackPanel>
        </StackPanel>
</Window>
```

The code for the PercentageRule class is as follows:

```csharp
using System.Globalization;
using System.Windows.Controls;
```

```csharp
namespace Recipe_05_15
{
    /// <summary>
    /// ValidationRule class to validate that a value is a
    /// number from 0 to 100.
    /// </summary>
    public class PercentageRule : ValidationRule
    {
        // Override the Validate method to add custom validation logic
        //
        public override ValidationResult Validate(
            object value,
            CultureInfo cultureInfo)
        {
            string stringValue = value as string;

            // Check whether there is a value
            if(!string.IsNullOrEmpty(stringValue))
            {
                // Check whether the value can be converted to a double
                double doubleValue;
                if(double.TryParse(stringValue, out doubleValue))
                {
                    // Check whether the double is between 0 and 100
                    if(doubleValue >= 0 && doubleValue <= 100)
                    {
                        // Return a ValidationResult with the IsValid
                        // property set to True
                        return new ValidationResult(true, null);
                    }
                }
            }

            // Return a ValidationResult with the IsValid
            // property set to False. Also specify an error message,
            // which will be displayed in the ToolTip.
            return
                new ValidationResult(
                    false, "Must be a number between 0 and 100");
        }

    }
}
```

Figure 5-16 shows the resulting window.

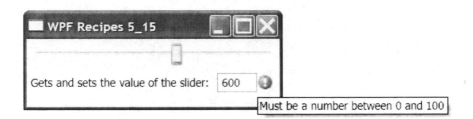

Figure 5-16. *Validating a binding*

5-16. Bind to IDataErrorInfo

Problem

You need to bind to a data object that implements the System.ComponentModel.IDataErrorInfo interface and display its error messages when the object is in an invalid state.

Solution

Create a class that implements IDataErrorInfo, and specify custom validation logic that returns error messages when a property value is invalid. Set the ValidatesOnErrors property of a System.Windows.Data.Binding to True. Optionally, create a custom control template to override the default Validation.ErrorTemplate, and change the appearance of a UI element when its data is invalid.

How It Works

The IDataErrorInfo interface is the standard construct in .NET for supporting the validation of CLR objects. It returns error messages for properties that are in an invalid state. Typically, you would implement a business rules engine or validation framework to determine whether any property values are invalid. Alternatively, you can simply embed your validation logic in your classes, as in the following example.

   To enable a binding for validation, set the ValidatesOnDataErrors property of your Binding object to True. Internally, this will add a System.Windows.Controls.DataErrorValidationRule to the Binding's ValidationRules collection. The WPF binding system will now interrogate the data source's IDataErrorInfo members for validation errors.

   By default, when a binding for a UI element is invalid, its control template is altered so that it is displayed with a thin red border around it. However, you can create a custom System.Windows.Style that assigns a different control template to the Validation.ErrorTemplate attached property on the target element.

The Code

The following example demonstrates a window that displays the name and age data of a Person object using three System.Windows.Controls.TextBox controls. The Person object is assigned to the DataContext property of the window in its constructor. The Person class implements the IDataErrorInfo and contains custom validation logic to check that its properties have valid values. In the binding statements for the controls, the ValidatesOnErrors property is set to True. A custom System.Windows.Style resource is also assigned to the TextBox. This ensures that when the data in the TextBox is invalid, an error icon is displayed to its right, and the ToolTip property displays the error message.

The XAML for the window is as follows:

```xml
<Window
    x:Class="Recipe_05_16.Window1"
    xmlns="http://schemas.microsoft.com/winfx/2006/xaml/presentation"
    xmlns:x="http://schemas.microsoft.com/winfx/2006/xaml"
    Title="WPF Recipes 5_16" Height="116" Width="260">

    <Window.Resources>

        <!-- A TextBox style to replace the default ErrorTemplate. -->
        <!-- When the validation rule fails, an error icon is        -->
        <!-- shown next to the TextBox, and the error message is     -->
        <!-- displayed in the ToolTip.                               -->
        <Style
            x:Key="textBoxInErrorStyle"
            TargetType="{x:Type TextBox}" >
            <Style.Triggers>

                <!-- A Property Trigger that sets the value of the  -->
                <!-- Tooltip to the error message, when the binding -->
                <!-- has a validation error.                        -->
                <Trigger
                    Property="Validation.HasError"
                    Value="true">
                    <Setter
                        Property="ToolTip"
                        Value="{Binding
                                    RelativeSource={x:Static
                                                    RelativeSource.Self},
                                Path=(Validation.Errors)[0].ErrorContent}"/>
                </Trigger>
            </Style.Triggers>

            <!-- A Property Setter that sets the ErrorTemplate to  -->
            <!-- display an error icon to the right of the TextBox. -->
            <Setter
                Property="Validation.ErrorTemplate">
                <Setter.Value>
                    <ControlTemplate>
                        <DockPanel DockPanel.Dock="Right">
```

```
                            <AdornedElementPlaceholder/>
                            <Image
                                Source="Error.png"
                                Width="16"
                                Height="16"
                                ToolTip="{Binding
                                            Path=AdornedElement.ToolTip,
                                            RelativeSource={RelativeSource
                                                Mode=FindAncestor,
                                                AncestorType={x:Type Adorner}}}"/>
                        </DockPanel>
                    </ControlTemplate>
                </Setter.Value>
            </Setter>
        </Style>

</Window.Resources>

<Grid>
    <Grid.ColumnDefinitions>
        <ColumnDefinition Width="74"/>
        <ColumnDefinition Width="*"/>
        <ColumnDefinition Width="14"/>
    </Grid.ColumnDefinitions>

    <Grid.RowDefinitions>
        <RowDefinition Height="26"/>
        <RowDefinition Height="26"/>
        <RowDefinition Height="26"/>
    </Grid.RowDefinitions>

    <TextBlock
        Margin="4"
        Text="First Name"
        VerticalAlignment="Center"/>
    <TextBox
        Style="{StaticResource textBoxInErrorStyle}"
        Text="{Binding Path=FirstName,
                    Mode=TwoWay,
                    UpdateSourceTrigger=PropertyChanged,
                    ValidatesOnDataErrors=True}"
        Margin="4" Grid.Column="1"/>

    <TextBlock
        Margin="4"
        Text="Last Name"
```

```
            Grid.Row="1"
            VerticalAlignment="Center"/>
        <TextBox
            Margin="4"
            Style="{StaticResource textBoxInErrorStyle}"
            Text="{Binding Path=LastName,
                        Mode=TwoWay,
                        UpdateSourceTrigger=PropertyChanged,
                        ValidatesOnDataErrors=True}"
            Grid.Column="1" Grid.Row="1"/>

        <TextBlock
            Margin="4"
            Text="Age"
            Grid.Row="2"
            VerticalAlignment="Center"/>
        <TextBox
            Style="{StaticResource textBoxInErrorStyle}"
            Margin="4"
            Text="{Binding Path=Age,
                        Mode=TwoWay,
                        UpdateSourceTrigger=PropertyChanged,
                        ValidatesOnDataErrors=True}"
            Grid.Column="1"
            Grid.Row="2"/>

    </Grid>
</Window>
```

The code-behind for the window is as follows:

```
using System.Windows;
using Recipe_05_16;

namespace Recipe_05_16
{
    public partial class Window1 : Window
    {
        public Window1()
        {
            InitializeComponent();

            // Set the DataContext to a Person object
            this.DataContext =
                new Person()
```

```
                        {
                            FirstName = "Elin",
                            LastName = "Binkles",
                            Age = 26,
                        };
            }
        }
    }
```

The code for the Person class is as follows:

```
using System.ComponentModel;

namespace Recipe_05_16
{
    public class Person
        : INotifyPropertyChanged,
          IDataErrorInfo
    {
        private string firstName;
        private string lastName;
        private int age;

        public Person()
        {
            FirstName = "spod";
        }
        public string FirstName
        {
            get
            {
                return firstName;
            }
            set
            {
                if(firstName != value)
                {
                    firstName = value;
                    OnPropertyChanged("FirstName");
                }
            }
        }

        public string LastName
        {
            get
```

```
    {
        return lastName;
    }
    set
    {
        if(this.lastName != value)
        {
            this.lastName = value;
            OnPropertyChanged("LastName");
        }
    }
}

public int Age
{
    get
    {
        return age;
    }
    set
    {
        if(this.age != value)
        {
            this.age = value;
            OnPropertyChanged("Age");
        }
    }
}


#region INotifyPropertyChanged Members

/// Implement INotifyPropertyChanged to notify the binding
/// targets when the values of properties change.
public event PropertyChangedEventHandler PropertyChanged;

private void OnPropertyChanged(
    string propertyName)
{
    if(this.PropertyChanged != null)
    {
        // Raise the PropertyChanged event
        this.PropertyChanged(
            this,
            new PropertyChangedEventArgs(
                propertyName));
    }
}
```

```csharp
#endregion

#region IDataErrorInfo Members

// Implement IDataErrorInfo to return custom
// error messages when a property value
// is invalid.

public string Error
{
    get
    {
        return string.Empty;
    }
}

public string this[string propertyName]
{
    get
    {
        // Return an empty string if there are no errors
        string message = string.Empty;

        switch(propertyName)
        {
            case "FirstName":
                if(string.IsNullOrEmpty(firstName))
                    message = "A person must have a first name.";
                break;

            case "LastName":
                if(string.IsNullOrEmpty(lastName))
                    message = "A person must have a last name.";
                break;

            case "Age":
                if(age < 1)
                    message = "A person must have an age.";
                break;

            case "Occupation":
                if(string.IsNullOrEmpty(firstName))
                    message = "A person must have an occupation.";
                break;
            default:
                break;
        }
```

```
                    return message;
                }
            }

        #endregion
    }
}
```

Figure 5-17 shows the resulting window. If you delete the values in any of the TextBox controls, the error icon is displayed, and the tool tip shows the error message.

Figure 5-17. *Binding to* IDataErrorInfo

5-17. Bind to a Collection with the Master-Detail Pattern

Problem

You need to bind to the items in a data collection and display more information about the selected item. For example, you might display a list of product names and prices on one side of the screen and a more detailed view of the selected product on the other side.

Solution

Bind a data collection to the ItemsSource property of a System.Windows.Controls.ItemsControl such as a System.Windows.Controls.ListBox, System.Windows.Controls.ListView, or System.Windows.Controls.TreeView. Implement the System.Collections.Specialized. INotifyCollectionChanged on the data collection to ensure that insertions or deletions in the collection update the UI automatically. Implement the master-detail pattern by binding a System.Windows.Controls.ContentControl to the same collection.

How It Works

To bind an ItemsControl to a collection object, set its ItemsSource property to an instance of a collection class. This is a class that implements the System.Collections.IEnumerable interface, such as System.Collections.Generic.List<T> or System.Collections.ObjectModel.Collection<T>, or the System.Collections.IList and System.Collections.ICollection interfaces. However, if you bind to any of these objects, the binding will be one-way and read-only. To set up dynamic bindings so that insertions or deletions in the collection update the UI automatically, the collection must implement the System.Collections.Specialized.INotifyCollectionChanged interface. This interface provides the mechanism for notifying the binding target of changes to the source collection, in much the same way as the System.ComponentModel.INotifyPropertyChanged interface notifies bindings of changes to properties in single objects.

INotifyCollectionChanged exposes an event called CollectionChanged that should be raised whenever the underlying collection changes. When you raise this event, you pass in an instance of the System.Collections.Specialized.NotifyCollectionChangedEventArgs class. This contains properties that specify the action that caused the event, for example, whether items were added, moved, or removed from the collection and the list of affected items. The binding mechanism listens for these events and updates the target UI element accordingly.

You do not need to implement INotifyCollectionChanged on your own collection classes. WPF provides the System.Collections.ObjectModel.ObservableCollection<T> class, which is a built-in implementation of a data collection that exposes INotifyCollectionChanged. If your collection classes are instances of the ObservableCollection<T> class or they inherit from it, you will get two-way dynamic data binding for free.

Note To fully support transferring data values from source objects to targets, each object in your collection that supports bindable properties must also implement the INotifyPropertyChanged interface. It is common practice to create a base class for all your custom business objects that implements INotifyPropertyChanged and a base collection class for collections of these objects that inherits from ObservableCollection<T>. This automatically enables all your custom objects and collection classes for data binding.

To implement the master-detail scenario of binding to a collection, you simply need to bind two or more controls to the same System.Windows.Data.CollectionView object. A CollectionView represents a wrapper around a binding source collection that allows you to navigate, sort, filter, and group the collection, without having to manipulate the underlying source collection itself. When you bind to any class that implements IEnumerable, the WPF binding engine creates a default CollectionView object automatically behind the scenes. So if you bind two or more controls to the same ObservableCollection<T> object, you are in effect binding them to the same default CollectionView class. If you want to implement custom sorting, grouping, and filtering of your collection, you will need to define a CollectionView explicitly yourself. You do this by creating a System.Windows.Data.CollectionViewSource class in your XAML. This approach is demonstrated in the next few recipes in this chapter. However, for the purpose of implementing the master-detail pattern, you can simply bind directly to an ObservableCollection<T> and accept the default CollectionView behind the scenes.

To display the master aspect of the pattern, simply bind your collection to the ItemsSource property of an ItemsControl, such as a System.Windows.Controls.ListBox, System.Windows. Controls.ListView, or System.Windows.Controls.TreeView. If you do not specify a DataTemplate for the ItemTemplate property of the ItemsControl, you can use the DisplayMemberPath property to specify the name of the property the ItemsControl should display. If you do not support a value for DisplayMemberPath, it will display the value returned by the ToString method of each data item in the collection.

To display the detail aspect of the pattern for the selected item, simply bind a singleton object to the collection, such as a ContentControl. When a singleton object is bound to a CollectionView, it automatically binds to the CurrentItem of the view.

If you are explicitly creating a CollectionView using a CollectionViewSource object, it will automatically synchronize currency and selection between the binding source and targets. However, if you are bound directly to an ObservableCollection<T> or other such IEnumerable object, then you will need to set the IsSynchronizedWithCurrentItem property of your ListBox to True for this to work. Setting the IsSynchronizedWithCurrentItem property to True ensures that the item selected always corresponds to the CurrentItem property in the ItemCollection. For example, suppose there are two ListBox controls with their ItemsSource property bound to the same ObservableCollection<T>. If you set IsSynchronizedWithCurrentItem to True on both ListBox controls, the selected item in each is the same.

The Code

The following example demonstrates a window that data binds to an instance of the PersonCollection class in its constructor. The PersonCollection class is an ObservableCollection<T> of Person objects. Each Person object exposes name, age, and occupation data, as well as a description.

In the top half of the window, a ListBox is bound to the window's DataContext. This is assigned an instance of the PersonCollection in the code-behind for the window. The ItemTemplate property of the ListBox references a DataTemplate called masterTemplate defined in the window's Resources collection. This shows the value of the Description property for each Person object in the collection. It sets the UpdateSourceTrigger attribute to System.Windows.Data. UpdateSourceTrigger.PropertyChanged. This ensures that the text in the ListBox item is updated automatically and immediately when the Description property of a Person changes. In the bottom half of the window, a ContentControl binds to the same collection. Because it is a singleton UI element and does not display a collection of items, it automatically binds to the current item in the PersonCollection class. Because the IsSynchronizedWithCurrentItem property of the ListBox is set to True, this corresponds to the selected item in the ListBox. The ContentControl uses a DataTemplate called detailTemplate to display the full details of the selected Person.

When the data displayed in the details section is changed, it automatically updates the corresponding description in the master section above it. This is made possible for two reasons. First, the System.Windows.Controls.TextBox controls in the details section specify a System. Windows.Data.Binding.BindingMode of TwoWay, which means that when new text is input, it is automatically marshaled to the binding source. Second, the Person class implements the INotifyPropertyChanged interface. This means that when a value of a property changes, the binding target is automatically notified.

At the bottom of the window, there is a System.Windows.Controls.Button control marked Add Person. When this button is clicked, it adds a new Person object to the collection. Because the PersonCollection class derives from ObservableCollection<T>, which in turn implements INotifyCollectionChanged, the master list of items automatically updates to show the new item.

The XAML for the window is as follows:

```
<Window x:Class="Recipe_05_17.Window1"
    xmlns="http://schemas.microsoft.com/winfx/2006/xaml/presentation"
    xmlns:x="http://schemas.microsoft.com/winfx/2006/xaml"
    Title="WPF Recipes 5_17" Height="370" Width="280">
    <Window.Resources>

        <DataTemplate
            x:Key="masterTemplate">
            <TextBlock
                Margin="4"
                Text="{Binding
                        Path=Description,
                        UpdateSourceTrigger=PropertyChanged}"/>
        </DataTemplate>

        <DataTemplate x:Key="detailTemplate">
            <Border
                BorderBrush="LightBlue"
                BorderThickness="1">
                <Grid Margin="10">
                    <Grid.ColumnDefinitions>
                        <ColumnDefinition Width="74"/>
                        <ColumnDefinition Width="*"/>
                    </Grid.ColumnDefinitions>

                    <Grid.RowDefinitions>
                        <RowDefinition Height="26"/>
                        <RowDefinition Height="26"/>
                        <RowDefinition Height="26"/>
                        <RowDefinition Height="26"/>
                    </Grid.RowDefinitions>

                    <TextBlock
            Margin="4"
            Text="First Name"
            VerticalAlignment="Center"/>
        <TextBox
            Text="{Binding Path=FirstName, Mode=TwoWay}"
            Margin="4" Grid.Column="1"/>

        <TextBlock
            Margin="4"
            Text="Last Name"
            Grid.Row="1"
            VerticalAlignment="Center"/>
```

```xml
<TextBox
    Margin="4"
    Text="{Binding Path=LastName, Mode=TwoWay}"
    Grid.Column="1" Grid.Row="1"/>

<TextBlock
    Margin="4"
    Text="Age"
    Grid.Row="2"
    VerticalAlignment="Center"/>
<TextBox
    Margin="4"
    Text="{Binding Path=Age, Mode=TwoWay}"
    Grid.Column="1"
    Grid.Row="2"/>

 <TextBlock
     Margin="4"
     Text="Occupation"
     Grid.Row="3"
     VerticalAlignment="Center"/>

 <ComboBox
     x:Name="cboOccupation"
     IsEditable="False"
     Grid.Column="1"
     Grid.Row="3"
     HorizontalAlignment="Left"
     Text="{Binding Path=Occupation, Mode=TwoWay}"
     Margin="4" Width="140">
      <ComboBoxItem>Student</ComboBoxItem>
      <ComboBoxItem>Engineer</ComboBoxItem>
      <ComboBoxItem>Professional</ComboBoxItem>
 </ComboBox>

</Grid>
        </Border>
    </DataTemplate>
</Window.Resources>

<StackPanel Margin="5">

    <TextBlock
        VerticalAlignment="Center"
        FontSize="14"
        Margin="4"
        Text="People"/>
```

```xml
        <!-- The ItemsControls binds to the collection. -->
        <ListBox
            ItemsSource="{Binding}"
            ItemTemplate="{StaticResource masterTemplate}"
            IsSynchronizedWithCurrentItem="True" />

        <TextBlock
            VerticalAlignment="Center"
            FontSize="14"
            Margin="4"
            Text="Details"/>

        <!-- The ContentControl binds to the CurrentItem of the collection. -->
        <ContentControl
          Content="{Binding}"
          ContentTemplate="{StaticResource detailTemplate}" />

        <!-- Add a new person to the collection. -->
        <Button
            Margin="4"
            Width="100"
            Height="34"
            HorizontalAlignment="Right"
            Click="AddButton_Click">
            Add Person
        </Button>
    </StackPanel>
</Window>
```

The code-behind for the window is as follows:

```csharp
using System.Windows;
using Recipe_05_17;

namespace Recipe_05_17
{
    public partial class Window1 : Window
    {
        // Create an instance of the PersonCollection class
        PersonCollection people =
            new PersonCollection();

        public Window1()
        {
            InitializeComponent();

            // Set the DataContext to the PersonCollection
            this.DataContext = people;
        }
```

```
        private void AddButton_Click(
            object sender, RoutedEventArgs e)
        {
            people.Add(new Person()
                        {
                            FirstName = "Nelly",
                            LastName = "Bonks",
                            Age = 26,
                            Occupation = "Professional"
                        });
        }
    }
}
```

The code for the Person class is omitted for brevity. It is identical to the Person class used in recipe 5-4, so you can see the full code in that recipe. The code for the PersonCollection class is as follows:

```
using System.Collections.ObjectModel;
using Recipe_05_17;

namespace Recipe_05_17
{
    public class PersonCollection
        : ObservableCollection<Person>
    {
        public PersonCollection()
        {
            // Load the collection with dummy data
            //
            Add(new Person(){FirstName = "Elin",
                            LastName = "Binkles",
                            Age = 26,
                            Occupation = "Professional"});

            Add(new Person(){FirstName = "Samuel",
                            LastName = "Bourts",
                            Age = 28,
                            Occupation = "Engineer"});

            Add(new Person(){FirstName = "Alan",
                            LastName = "Jonesy",
                            Age = 37,
                            Occupation = "Engineer"});
```

```
              Add(new Person(){FirstName = "Sam",
                               LastName = "Nobles",
                               Age = 25,
                               Occupation = "Engineer"});
        }
    }
}
```

Figure 5-18 shows the resulting window.

Figure 5-18. *Binding to a collection using the master-detail pattern*

5-18. Sort Data in a Collection

Problem

You need to sort a collection of items based on the value of a property.

Solution

Create a System.Windows.Data.CollectionViewSource as a static resource, and bind it to the data collection. Specify a System.ComponentModel.SortDescription using the name of the property you want to sort on.

How It Works

A CollectionViewSource is a layer on top of the binding source collection that allows you to expose a custom System.Windows.Data.CollectionView class for your data. A CollectionView represents a view of the items in a data collection and can supply custom grouping, sorting, filtering, and navigation.

To specify how the items in the collection view are sorted, create a System.ComponentModel. SortDescription object, and add it to the CollectionViewSource's SortDescriptions collection. A SortDescription defines the direction and the property name to be used as the criteria for sorting the data.

The Code

The following example creates a CollectionViewSource as a static resource that binds to a collection of countries. The CollectionViewSource has a SortDescription property that sorts the data according to each item's Name property. A System.Windows.Controls.ItemsControl binds to the CollectionViewSource and shows the sorted collection.

The XAML for the window is as follows:

```
<Window x:Class="Recipe_05_18.Window1"
    xmlns="http://schemas.microsoft.com/winfx/2006/xaml/presentation"
    xmlns:x="http://schemas.microsoft.com/winfx/2006/xaml"
    xmlns:ComponentModel="clr-namespace:System.ComponentModel;assembly=WindowsBase"
    xmlns:local="clr-namespace:Recipe_05_18"
    Title="WPF Recipes 5_18" Height="244" Width="124">
  <Window.Resources>

      <!-- Create an instance of the collection class -->
      <local:Countries x:Key="countries"/>

      <!-- Wrap it in a CollectionViewSource -->
      <CollectionViewSource
          x:Key="cvs"
          Source="{Binding
                  Source={StaticResource countries}}">

          <!-- Add a SortDescription to sort by the Name -->
          <CollectionViewSource.SortDescriptions>
              <ComponentModel:SortDescription
                            PropertyName="Name" />
          </CollectionViewSource.SortDescriptions>
      </CollectionViewSource>

  </Window.Resources>

  <Grid>
      <!-- Bind an ItemsControl to the CollectionViewSource -->
      <!-- Set its DisplayMemberPath to display the Name property -->
```

```
    <ItemsControl
        ItemsSource="{Binding
                       Source={StaticResource cvs}}"
        DisplayMemberPath="Name" />
  </Grid>

</Window>
```

The code for the data collection and data object is omitted for brevity. Figure 5-19 shows the resulting window.

Figure 5-19. *Sorting a collection*

5-19. Apply Custom Sorting Logic to a Collection

Problem

You need to sort a collection of data items based on custom sorting logic.

Solution

Create a custom class that implements the System.Collections.IComparer interface. Add the custom sorting logic to the Compare method to sort the collection of data items based on your custom sort criteria. Use the static GetDefaultView method of the System.Windows.Data. CollectionViewSource class to get the default view your collection. Set the CustomSort property of this view to an instance of your IComparer class.

How It Works

When you bind to a collection class, the WPF binding system creates a default System.Windows. Data.CollectionView behind the scenes. Internally, this wraps your collection and exposes it as a binding source. There is a static method on the CollectionViewSource class called GetDefaultView. This gets the default collection view from your collection. This will be an instance of the System. Windows.Data.ListCollectionView class if your data collection is a System.Collections.IList.

Once you have your ListCollectionView object, you can set its CustomSort property to a class that implements IComparer. This interface exposes a method that compares two objects. Add custom logic to this method to sort your data collection.

The Code

The following example demonstrates a window that creates a System.Collections.ObjectModel. ObservableCollection<T> of strings called SortableCountries as a static resource. The collection contains names of countries prefixed by a number and is displayed in a System.Windows. Controls.ItemsControl. Using the normal SortDescription property of a CollectionViewSource to sort the countries would result in all those beginning with a 1 being before the others. For example, "14 USA" would be above "4 China." In the code-behind for the window, there is an implementation of IComparer called SortCountries. When the System.Windows.Controls. Button control marked Sort is clicked, there is code in the event handler to get the default view from the collection and set an instance of this SortCountries class to the CustomSort property.

The XAML for the window is as follows:

```
<Window
    x:Class="Recipe_05_19.Window1"
    xmlns="http://schemas.microsoft.com/winfx/2006/xaml/presentation"
    xmlns:x="http://schemas.microsoft.com/winfx/2006/xaml"
    xmlns:local="clr-namespace:Recipe_05_19"
    Title="WPF Recipes 5_19" Height="300" Width="180">

    <Window.Resources>

        <!-- Create an instance of the collection class -->
        <local:SortableCountries x:Key="sortableCountries"/>

    </Window.Resources>

    <Grid Margin="16">
        <StackPanel>

            <ItemsControl
                ItemsSource="{StaticResource sortableCountries}" />

            <Button
                Click="SortButton_Click"
                Content="Sort"
                Margin="8" />

        </StackPanel>

    </Grid>

</Window>
```

In the SortCountries implementation of IComparer, there is custom logic to sort the numeric prefixes as numbers, not as strings. The full code for this comparison logic is omitted for brevity. However, you can find the code to apply the IComparer in the following code-behind for the window:

```
using System;
using System.Collections;
using System.Windows;
using System.Windows.Data;
using Recipe_05_19;

namespace Recipe_05_19
{
    public partial class Window1 : Window
    {
        public Window1()
        {
            InitializeComponent();
        }

        private void SortButton_Click(
            object sender, RoutedEventArgs args)
        {
            // Get the ObservableCollection from the window Resources
            SortableCountries sortableCountries =
                (SortableCountries)
                (this.Resources["sortableCountries"]);

            // Get the Default View from the ObservableCollection
            ListCollectionView lcv =
                (ListCollectionView)
                CollectionViewSource.GetDefaultView(sortableCountries);

            // Set the Custom Sort class
            lcv.CustomSort = new SortCountries();
        }
    }

    public class SortCountries
        : IComparer
    {
        public int Compare(object x, object y)
        {
            // Custom sorting logic goes here.
            // (Omitted for brevity).
            //
            string stringX = x.ToString();
            string stringY = y.ToString();
```

```
        int ret = 0;

        // […]

        return ret;
    }
  }
}
```

Figure 5-20 shows the difference between the two lists, before and after the custom sorting logic is applied.

Figure 5-20. *Applying custom sorting logic*

5-20. Filter Data in a Collection

Problem

You need to filter a collection of items based on a value of a property.

Solution

Create a System.Windows.Data.CollectionViewSource as a static resource, and bind it to the data collection. Set the Filter property of the CollectionViewSource to a System.Windows.Data.FilterEventHandler. In the code for this event handler, add custom logic to determine which items in the collection should be displayed.

How It Works

A CollectionViewSource wraps a binding source collection and allows you to expose a custom view of its data based on sort, filter, and group queries. When a FilterEventHandler is assigned to its Filter property, the event handler is called for each item in the collection. The event handler takes an instance of the System.Windows.Data.FilterEventArgs class as its event argument. If a data item should be included in the collection view, set the Accepted property of the FilterEventArgs to True. If it should not pass through the filter, simply set the Accepted property to False.

The Code

The following example creates a CollectionViewSource as a static resource that binds to a collection of countries. The CollectionViewSource has a Filter property that references an EventHandler called CollectionViewSource_EuropeFilter in the code-behind for the window. This event handler filters out countries in the collection that are not in Europe.

The XAML for the window is as follows:

```
<Window
    x:Class="Recipe_05_20.Window1"
    xmlns="http://schemas.microsoft.com/winfx/2006/xaml/presentation"
    xmlns:x="http://schemas.microsoft.com/winfx/2006/xaml"
    xmlns:local="clr-namespace:Recipe_05_20"
    Title="WPF Recipes 5_20" Height="124" Width="124">
    <Window.Resources>

        <!-- Create an instance of the collection class -->
        <local:Countries x:Key="countries"/>

        <!-- Wrap it in a CollectionViewSource -->
        <!-- Set the Filter property to a FilterEventHandler -->
        <CollectionViewSource
            x:Key="cvs"
            Source="{Binding
                    Source={StaticResource countries}}"
            Filter="CollectionViewSource_EuropeFilter" />

    </Window.Resources>

    <Grid>
        <!-- Bind an ItemsControl to the CollectionViewSource -->
        <!-- Set its DisplayMemberPath to display the Name property -->
        <ItemsControl
            ItemsSource="{Binding
                        Source={StaticResource cvs}}"
            DisplayMemberPath="Name"/>
    </Grid>
```

```
</Window>
```

The code-behind for the window is as follows:

```csharp
using System.Windows;
using System.Windows.Data;
using Recipe_05_20;

namespace Recipe_05_20
{
    public partial class Window1 : Window
    {
        public Window1()
        {
            InitializeComponent();
        }

        // Filter the collection of countries.
        private void CollectionViewSource_EuropeFilter(
            object sender, FilterEventArgs e)
        {
            // Get the data item
            Country country = e.Item as Country;

            // Accept it into the collection view, if its
            // Continent property equals Europe.
            e.Accepted = (country.Continent == Continent.Europe);
        }
    }
}
```

The data for the collection and its data items is as follows:

```csharp
using System.Collections.ObjectModel;

namespace Recipe_05_20
{
    public class Country
    {
        private string name;
        private Continent continent;

        public string Name
        {
            get{ return name;}
            set{name = value;}
        }
```

```csharp
        public Continent Continent
        {
            get{return continent;}
            set{continent = value;}
        }

        public Country(string name, Continent continent)
        {
            this.name = name;
            this.continent = continent;
        }
    }

public enum Continent
{
    Asia,
    Africa,
    Europe,
    NorthAmerica,
    SouthAmerica,
    Australasia
}

public class Countries : Collection<Country>
{
    public Countries()
    {
        this.Add(new Country("Great Britan", Continent.Europe));
        this.Add(new Country("USA", Continent.NorthAmerica));
        this.Add(new Country("Canada", Continent.NorthAmerica));
        this.Add(new Country("France", Continent.Europe));
        this.Add(new Country("Germany", Continent.Europe));
        this.Add(new Country("Italy", Continent.Europe));
        this.Add(new Country("Spain", Continent.Europe));
        this.Add(new Country("Brazil", Continent.SouthAmerica));
        this.Add(new Country("Argentina", Continent.SouthAmerica));
        this.Add(new Country("China", Continent.Asia));
        this.Add(new Country("India", Continent.Asia));
        this.Add(new Country("Japan", Continent.Asia));
        this.Add(new Country("South Africa", Continent.Africa));
        this.Add(new Country("Tunisia", Continent.Africa));
        this.Add(new Country("Egypt", Continent.Africa));
    }
  }
}
```

Figure 5-21 shows the resulting window.

Figure 5-21. *Filtering a collection*

5-21. Group Data in a Collection

Problem

You need to group a collection of items based on a value of a property.

Solution

Use a System.Windows.Data.CollectionViewSource to wrap a collection and group its items, and create a System.Windows.Controls.GroupStyle to control how the group headers are displayed.

How It Works

A CollectionViewSource is a layer on top of the binding source collection that allows you to expose a custom view of the collection based on sort, filter, and group queries.

Create the CollectionViewSource as a static resource in the System.Windows. ResourceDictionary for your window, and bind it to the collection you want to group. Add a System.Windows.Data.PropertyGroupDescription to the GroupDescriptions collection property of the CollectionViewSource, and specify the name of the property you want to group the items by. Use the GroupStyle property of the System.Windows.Controls. ItemsControl to specify a HeaderTemplate to use for the group headers.

The Code

The following example creates a CollectionViewSource as a static resource that binds to a collection of countries. The Country class has two properties, Name and Continent, and the CollectionViewSource uses a PropertyGroupDescription to group the countries according to the value of their Continent property. A System.Windows.Controls.ItemsControl binds to the CollectionViewSource and shows the grouped collection. It declares a GroupStyle that references a System.Windows.DataTemplate called groupingHeaderTemplate. This DataTemplate defines the display style for group headers.

The XAML for the window is as follows:

```xml
<Window x:Class="Recipe_05_21.Window1"
    xmlns="http://schemas.microsoft.com/winfx/2006/xaml/presentation"
    xmlns:x="http://schemas.microsoft.com/winfx/2006/xaml"
    xmlns:Recipe_05_21="clr-namespace:Recipe_05_21"
    Title="WPF Recipes 5_21" Height="294" Width="160">
    <Window.Resources>

        <!-- Create an instance of the collection class -->
        <Recipe_05_21:Countries x:Key="countries"/>

        <!-- Wrap it in a CollectionViewSource -->
        <CollectionViewSource
            x:Key="cvs"
            Source="{Binding
                    Source={StaticResource countries}}">

            <!-- Add a PropertyGroupDescription to group by the Continent -->
            <CollectionViewSource.GroupDescriptions>
                <PropertyGroupDescription PropertyName="Continent"/>
            </CollectionViewSource.GroupDescriptions>
        </CollectionViewSource>

        <!-- DataTemplate to display the group header -->
        <DataTemplate x:Key="groupingHeaderTemplate">
            <Border Height="28">
                <Label VerticalAlignment="Center" Content="{Binding}"
                    BorderBrush="#FF8F8D8D" BorderThickness="0,0,0,0.5"
                    Foreground="#FF666666">
                    <Label.Background>
                        <LinearGradientBrush
                            EndPoint="0.506,-0.143" StartPoint="0.502,11.643">
                            <GradientStop Color="#FF000000" Offset="0"/>
                            <GradientStop Color="#FFFFFFFF" Offset="1"/>
                        </LinearGradientBrush>
                    </Label.Background>
                </Label>
            </Border>
        </DataTemplate>

    </Window.Resources>

    <Grid>
        <!-- Bind an ItemsControl to the CollectionViewSource -->
        <!-- Set its DisplayMemberPath to display the Name property -->
```

```
    <ItemsControl
        ItemsSource="{Binding
                      Source={StaticResource cvs}}"
        DisplayMemberPath="Name">

        <!-- Create a GroupStyle that uses the DataTemplate -->
        <ItemsControl.GroupStyle>
            <GroupStyle HeaderTemplate=
                        "{StaticResource groupingHeaderTemplate}" />
        </ItemsControl.GroupStyle>
    </ItemsControl>
    </Grid>
</Window>
```

Figure 5-22 shows the resulting window.

Figure 5-22. *Grouping a collection*

5-22. Apply Custom Grouping to a Collection

Problem

You need to group a collection of items based on custom logic, not just on a value of a property.

Solution

Create a System.Windows.Data.CollectionViewSource as a static resource, and bind it to the collection. Create a class that implements the System.Windows.Data.IValueConverter interface and contains the custom grouping logic. Declare the IValueConverter implementation as a static resource. Add a PropertyGroupDescription to the GroupDescriptions collection property of the `CollectionViewSource`, and specify the `Converter` property. Use the `GroupStyle` property of the `System.Windows.Controls.ItemsControl` to specify the default `GroupStyle`.

How It Works

When the `CollectionViewSource` is bound to the collection, the `IValueConverter.Convert` method is invoked for each item in the collection. This contains custom logic in the code-behind for deciding to which group each item belongs.

The Code

The following example creates a `CollectionViewSource` as a static resource that binds to a collection of countries. It also declares an `IValueConverter` class as a static resource, which is defined in the code-behind for the window and which contains the code to divide the countries into two groups. The resulting grouped data collection is displayed in an `ItemsControl`.

■**Note** If you don't create a custom `DataTemplate` to define the display of your groups' headers, you have to specify the default `GroupStyle`. This indents the items in a group. For more sophisticated visualizations, create a `DataTemplate` to display a group header, and specify it as the `HeaderTemplate` property of your `ItemsControl`'s `GroupStyle`.

The XAML for the window is as follows:

```
<Window
    x:Class="Recipe_05_22.Window1"
    xmlns="http://schemas.microsoft.com/winfx/2006/xaml/presentation"
    xmlns:x="http://schemas.microsoft.com/winfx/2006/xaml"
    xmlns:Recipe_05_22="clr-namespace:Recipe_05_22"
    Title="WPF Recipes 5_22" Height="294" Width="160">

    <Window.Resources>

        <!-- Create an instance of the collection class -->
        <Recipe_05_22:Countries x:Key="countries"/>

        <!-- Create an instance of the GroupByContinentConverter class -->
        <Recipe_05_22:GroupByContinentConverter
            x:Key="GroupByContinentConverter"/>

        <!-- Wrap the collection in a CollectionViewSource -->
        <!-- Set the Filter property to a FilterEventHandler -->
        <CollectionViewSource
            x:Key="cvs"
            Source="{Binding
                    Source={StaticResource countries}}">
```

```xml
            <!-- Add a PropertyGroupDescription that uses -->
            <!-- the GroupByContinentConverter class to create the groups -->
            <CollectionViewSource.GroupDescriptions>
                <PropertyGroupDescription
                    Converter="{StaticResource GroupByContinentConverter}" />
            </CollectionViewSource.GroupDescriptions>
        </CollectionViewSource>

    </Window.Resources>

    <Grid>
        <!-- Bind an ItemsControl to the CollectionViewSource. -->
        <!-- Set its DisplayMemberPath to display the Name property. -->
        <!-- Set the GroupStyle to use the Default. -->
        <ItemsControl
            Margin="10"
             ItemsSource="{Binding Source={StaticResource cvs}}"
             DisplayMemberPath="Name" >

            <!-- The default GroupStyle indents the items in a group -->
            <ItemsControl.GroupStyle>
                <x:Static Member="GroupStyle.Default"/>
            </ItemsControl.GroupStyle>
        </ItemsControl>

    </Grid>
</Window>
```

The code in the IValueConverter checks the Continent property of each country and decides whether it should be in the "Americas" or the "Rest of the World" group:

```csharp
using System;
using System.Globalization;
using System.Windows.Data;
using Recipe_05_22;

namespace Recipe_05_22
{
    public class GroupByContinentConverter
        : IValueConverter
    {
        public object Convert(object value,
                              Type targetType,
                              object parameter,
                              CultureInfo culture)
        {
            Country country = (Country)value;
```

```
        // Decide which group the country belongs in
        switch (country.Continent)
        {
            case Continent.NorthAmerica:
            case Continent.SouthAmerica:
                return "Americas";

            default:
                return "Rest of the World";
        }
    }

    public object ConvertBack(object value,
                              Type targetType,
                              object parameter,
                              CultureInfo culture)
    {
        throw new NotImplementedException();
    }
    }
}
```

Figure 5-23 shows the resulting window.

Figure 5-23. *Applying custom grouping to a collection*

5-23. Bind to Application Settings

Problem

You need to bind UI elements to application settings to automatically use and update their values.

Solution

Reference your application's `Properties.Settings.Default` class as a static binding source in your binding statements.

How It Works

Visual Studio provides a handy mechanism for storing and retrieving application settings dynamically. Using the Settings page of the Project Designer, you can add custom properties and give each one a name, a type, and an initial value. Visual Studio then automatically generates a `Settings` class and creates standard .NET properties for each setting. It exposes the properties via a static `Settings` property called `Default`.

To bind your application settings to UI elements, set the `Source` property of a `System.Windows.Data.Binding` to the static `Properties.Settings.Default` class, and set the `Path` property to the name of a setting. Set the `Mode` property to `System.Windows.Data.BindingMode.TwoWay` to automatically update the application setting when it is changed by your target UI element.

To save changes to your settings, override the `OnClosing` method of your window, and call the `Properties.Savings.Default.Save` method.

The Code

The following example demonstrates a window that displays the values of the window's `Height`, `Width`, `Left`, and `Top` properties. On the project's Settings page, there are four corresponding double properties. Figure 2-24 shows these application settings.

In the XAML for the window, the window's `Height`, `Width`, `Left`, and `Top` properties are bound to the values of these application settings. The binding statements reference the `Properties.Settings.Default` class as a static binding source. This ensures that when the window opens, it gets its initial size and position from the application settings.

In the code-behind for the window, the `Settings.Default.Save` method is called in the `OnClosing` method. This ensures that when you move or resize the window, these settings are saved and restored the next time the application runs.

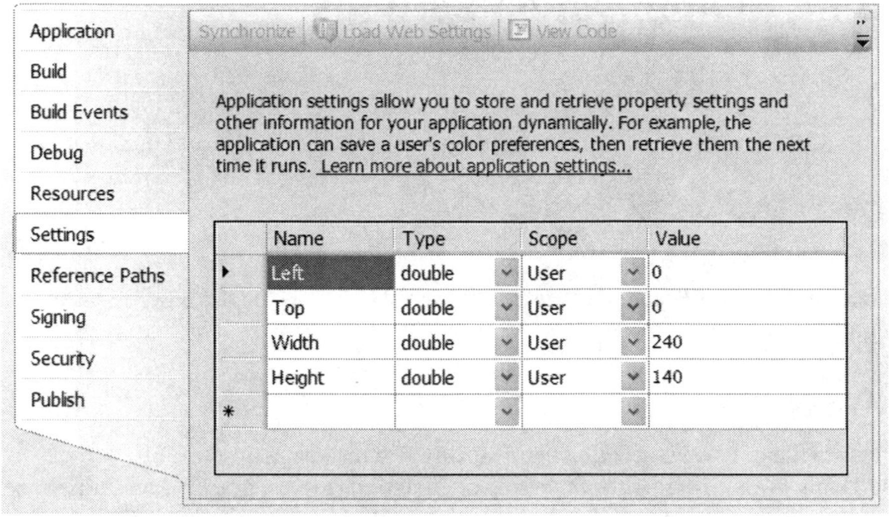

Figure 5-24. *Application settings on the Settings page of the Project Designer*

The XAML for the window is as follows:

```
<Window
    x:Class="Recipe_05_23.Window1"
    xmlns="http://schemas.microsoft.com/winfx/2006/xaml/presentation"
    xmlns:x="http://schemas.microsoft.com/winfx/2006/xaml"
    xmlns:Properties="clr-namespace:Recipe_05_23.Properties"
    x:Name="MainWindow"
    WindowStartupLocation="Manual"
    Title="WPF Recipes 5_23"
    Height="{Binding
            Source={x:Static
                Properties:Settings.Default},
            Path=Height,
            Mode=TwoWay}"
    Width="{Binding
            Source={x:Static
                Properties:Settings.Default},
            Path=Width,
            Mode=TwoWay}"
    Left="{Binding
            Source={x:Static
                Properties:Settings.Default},
            Path=Left,
            Mode=TwoWay}"
    Top="{Binding
            Source={x:Static
                Properties:Settings.Default},
```

```
        Path=Top,
        Mode=TwoWay}" >

<Grid>
    <Grid VerticalAlignment="Center" HorizontalAlignment="Center">

    <Grid.ColumnDefinitions>
        <ColumnDefinition Width="100"/>
        <ColumnDefinition Width="40"/>
    </Grid.ColumnDefinitions>

    <Grid.RowDefinitions>
        <RowDefinition Height="24"/>
        <RowDefinition Height="24"/>
        <RowDefinition Height="24"/>
        <RowDefinition Height="24"/>
    </Grid.RowDefinitions>

    <TextBlock
        Text="Window Height:"/>
    <TextBlock
        Text="{Binding
              ElementName=MainWindow,
              Path=Height,
              UpdateSourceTrigger=PropertyChanged}"
        Grid.Column="1"
        FontWeight="Bold"/>

    <TextBlock
        Text="Window Width:"
        Grid.Row="1"/>
    <TextBlock
        Text="{Binding
              ElementName=MainWindow,
              Path=Width,
              UpdateSourceTrigger=PropertyChanged}"
        Grid.Column="1"
        Grid.Row="1"
        FontWeight="Bold"/>

    <TextBlock
        Text="Window Left:" Grid.Row="2"/>
    <TextBlock
        Text="{Binding
              ElementName=MainWindow,
              Path=Left,
              UpdateSourceTrigger=PropertyChanged}"
```

```
                    Grid.Column="1"
                    Grid.Row="2"
                    FontWeight="Bold"/>

            <TextBlock
                Text="Window Top:"
                Grid.Row="3"/>
            <TextBlock
                Text="{Binding
                        ElementName=MainWindow,
                        Path=Top,
                        UpdateSourceTrigger=PropertyChanged}"
                    Grid.Column="1"
                    Grid.Row="3"
                    FontWeight="Bold"/>

        </Grid>

    </Grid>
</Window>
```

The code-behind for the window is as follows:

```
using System.Windows;
using Recipe_05_23.Properties;

namespace Recipe_05_23
{
    public partial class Window1 : Window
    {
        public Window1()
        {
            InitializeComponent();
        }

        /// <summary>
        /// Override the OnClosing method and save the current settings
        /// </summary>
        /// <param name="e"></param>
        protected override void OnClosing(
            System.ComponentModel.CancelEventArgs e)
        {
            // Save the settings
            Settings.Default.Save();

            base.OnClosing(e);
        }
    }
}
```

Figure 5-25 shows the resulting window.

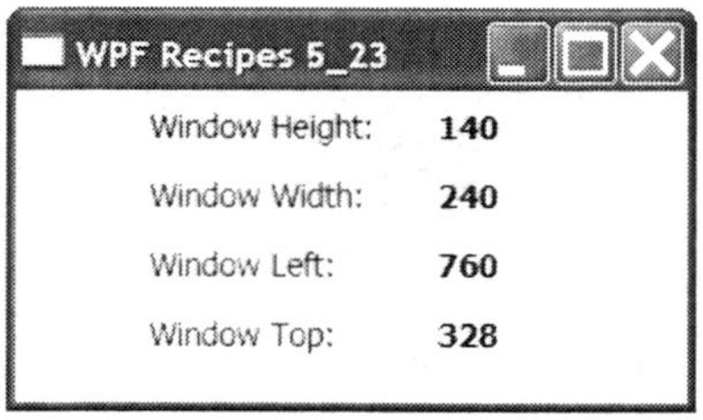

Figure 5-25. *Binding to application settings*

5-24. Bind to Application Resource Strings

Problem

You need to bind UI elements to application resource strings to automatically use their values in your controls.

Solution

Use the System.Reflection namespace to add the resource strings to the System.Windows. Application instance's System.Windows.ResourceDictionary when your application starts up. Reference the names of your resource strings in your binding statements using the ResourceKey property of the System.Windows.StaticResourceExtension class.

How It Works

You can add resource strings to your application on the Resources page of the Project Designer in Visual Studio. This automatically generates corresponding .NET properties on your application's Resources class. However, because these properties are marked as static, you cannot bind to them directly. Instead, override the OnStartup method of your Application class in the App.xaml.cs file, and use reflection to retrieve all the string properties from the Properties. Resources class. Add these properties and their values to the Application's Resources collection. This makes them available for data binding throughout your application.

To bind the resource strings to your UI elements, use the StaticResource markup extension in your binding statements, and set the value of the ResourceKey property to the name of a resource string.

■ **Note** The resource strings are added to the Application's Resources collection at runtime. This means that when you reference them in your XAML, you may see error messages warning you that the StaticResource reference was not found. However, the project will still compile and run perfectly.

The Code

The following example demonstrates a window that displays two System.Windows.Controls. TextBlock controls and binds them to two resource strings that contain a welcome message and a copyright notice. These resource strings are defined on the project's Resources page, which is shown in Figure 5-26.

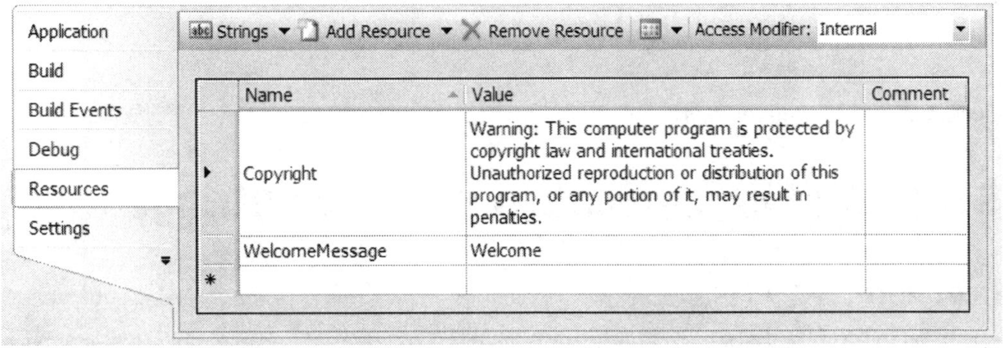

Name		Value	Comment
▶	Copyright	Warning: This computer program is protected by copyright law and international treaties. Unauthorized reproduction or distribution of this program, or any portion of it, may result in penalties.	
	WelcomeMessage	Welcome	

Application / Build / Build Events / Debug / Resources / Settings tabs shown at left. Toolbar: Strings ▼ | Add Resource ▼ | ✕ Remove Resource | ▼ Access Modifier: Internal ▼

Figure 5-26. *Application resource strings on the Resources page of the Project Designer*

In the App.xaml.cs file, the OnStartup method of the Application class is overridden, and the resource strings are added to the resource dictionary. The code-behind for this is as follows:

```csharp
using System;
using System.Reflection;
using System.Windows;

namespace Recipe_05_24
{
    public partial class App : Application
    {
        /// <summary>
        /// Override the OnStartup method to add the
        /// resource strings to the Application's ResourceDictionary
        /// </summary>
        /// <param name="e"></param>
        protected override void OnStartup(
            StartupEventArgs e)
        {
            // Use reflection to get the PropertyInfo
            // for the Properties.Resources class
            Type resourcesType = typeof(Recipe_05_24.Properties.Resources);
            PropertyInfo[] properties =
                resourcesType.GetProperties(
                    BindingFlags.Static | BindingFlags.NonPublic);
```

```
            // Add properties to XAML Application.Resources
            foreach(PropertyInfo property in properties)
            {
                // If the property is a string, add it to the
                // application's resources dictionary
                if(property.PropertyType == typeof(string))
                    Resources.Add(
                        property.Name,
                        property.GetValue(null, null));
            }

            base.OnStartup(e);
        }
    }
}
```

The XAML for the window is as follows:

```xml
<Window
    x:Class="Recipe_05_24.Window1"
    xmlns="http://schemas.microsoft.com/winfx/2006/xaml/presentation"
    xmlns:x="http://schemas.microsoft.com/winfx/2006/xaml"
    WindowStartupLocation="Manual"
    Title="WPF Recipes 5_24"
    Height="180" Width="240">

    <StackPanel Margin="10">

        <TextBlock
            Text="{StaticResource
                    ResourceKey=WelcomeMessage}"
            HorizontalAlignment="Center"
            FontSize="16" FontWeight="Bold"/>

        <TextBlock
            Text="{StaticResource
                    ResourceKey=Copyright}"
            HorizontalAlignment="Center"
            Margin="10"
            Grid.Row="1"
            TextWrapping-"Wrap"/>

    </StackPanel>
</Window>
```

Figure 5-27 shows the resulting window.

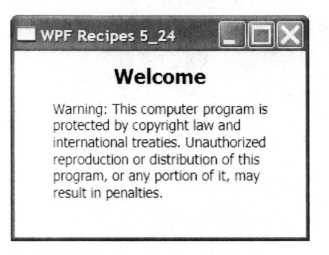

Figure 5-27. *Binding to application resource strings*

CHAPTER 6

Working with Styles, Templates, Skins, and Themes

One of the most remarkable aspects of WPF is the ability to separate and customize the visual appearance of user interface elements from the built-in behavior and functionality they provide. You can do this using styles and control templates.

The recipes in this chapter describe how to:

- Create custom visual styles for control elements (recipes 6-1 and 6-2)

- Customize, override, inherit from, and dynamically change these visual styles (recipes 6-3, 6-4, 6-5, 6-6, 6-7, and 6-8)

- Set a style programmatically and ignore an implicit style (recipes 6-9 and 6-10)

- Create styles to control the appearance of items in a collection (recipes 6-11 and 6-12)

- Create custom control templates that specify how an element should be constructed and displayed (recipes 6-13 and 6-14)

- Manipulate, manage, and dynamically change the elements in a control's visual tree (recipes 6-15, 6-16, and 6-17)

- Create custom tool tip styles for elements (recipe 6-18)

- Dynamically change the skin of an application and create styles that adapt to the current Windows operating system theme (recipes 6-19 and 6-20)

6-1. Create a Named Style

Problem

You need to display a UI control, or set of controls, with a custom look and style, instead of using the default display style.

Solution

Create a System.Windows.Style resource, and specify the Key attribute. The Style can set control properties and reference custom brush resources. Then reference this Key in the System.Windows.Style property of a control.

How It Works

A Style is a collection of property values that can be applied to one or more controls. Primarily, it does this via its Setters collection, which holds System.Windows.Setter objects. Each Setter object specifies the name of a property to act on and the value to assign to it. This allows you to create a group of values for visual appearance properties, declare this group of values in a System.Windows.ResourceDictionary, and reference it from different parts of your application.

All UI controls ultimately derive from System.Windows.FrameworkElement, and this class exposes a Style property. You can set this property to a named Style using the System.Windows.StaticResourceExtension markup extension class.

The Code

The following example declares two brush resources and a Style. The Style has a key of My Style; changes the System.Windows.FontWeight, System.Windows.Media.Brush.Background, and System.Windows.Media.Brush.BorderBrush properties of a control; and sets the width, height, and margin. There are three System.Windows.Controls.Button controls; two specify the My Style resource as the Style property, and the other receives the default for this control type.

```
<Window x:Class="Recipe_06_01.Window1"
    xmlns="http://schemas.microsoft.com/winfx/2006/xaml/presentation"
    xmlns:x="http://schemas.microsoft.com/winfx/2006/xaml"
    Title="WPF Recipes 6_01" Height="100" Width="300">

    <Window.Resources>

        <!-- Brush Resources -->
        <LinearGradientBrush x:Key="NormalBrush"
                             EndPoint="0,1"
                             StartPoint="0,0">
            <GradientStop Color="White" Offset="0.0"/>
            <GradientStop Color="LightGray" Offset="1.0"/>
        </LinearGradientBrush>

        <LinearGradientBrush x:Key="NormalBorderBrush"
                             EndPoint="0,1"
                             StartPoint="0,0">
            <GradientStop Color="Gainsboro" Offset="0.0"/>
            <GradientStop Color="DarkGray" Offset="1.0"/>
        </LinearGradientBrush>
```

```xml
    <!-- Named Style -->
    <Style x:Key="MyStyle">
        <Setter Property="Control.FontWeight" Value="Bold"/>
        <Setter Property="Control.Background"
                Value="{DynamicResource NormalBrush}"/>
        <Setter Property="Control.BorderBrush"
                Value="{DynamicResource NormalBorderBrush}"/>
        <Setter Property="Control.Width" Value="88"/>
        <Setter Property="Control.Height" Value="24"/>
        <Setter Property="Control.Margin" Value="4"/>
    </Style>

</Window.Resources>

<Grid>
    <StackPanel Orientation="Horizontal">

        <Button Style="{StaticResource MyStyle}"
                Content="Named Style"/>

        <Button Style="{StaticResource MyStyle}"
                Content="Named Style"/>

        <Button Width="88" Height="24" Margin="4"
                Content="Default Style"/>

    </StackPanel>
</Grid>

</Window>
```

Figure 6-1 shows the resulting window.

Figure 6-1. *Applying a named style to Button controls*

6-2. Create a Typed Style

Problem

You need to apply the same custom style to all instances of a control type.

Solution

Create a System.Windows.Style resource, and specify the TargetType attribute. The Style can set control properties and reference custom brush resources. It will be automatically applied to every instance of this control type, within the scope of the Style resource.

How It Works

If a Style is given a TargetType, then it will automatically be applied to any instance of this control type within the scope of the resource. (See Chapter 2 for more information on resource scopes.) The System.Windows.FrameworkElement and System.Windows.FrameworkContentElement base classes both have a Resources property, so Style resources can be added to most WPF classes. If a typed Style is added to a control's Resources collection, then any child of this type within the logical tree will have the Style applied to it.

Tip A System.Type can also be specified as the Key property of a style, which achieves the same result as specifying the TargetType. For example, `<Style TargetType="{x:Type ListView}">` is the same as `<Style Key="{x:Type ListView}">`.

The Code

The following example demonstrates a window that declares two brush resources and a Style. Instead of giving the Style a key, the TargetType of System.Windows.Controls.Button is specified. The Style sets some display properties for a Button, including the Margin, Size, and Background. The window displays two Button controls, neither of which have been explicitly given a style property, and they both automatically receive the custom typed style.

Note If a TargetType is specified, notice that the Control. prefix is not needed in the Setter properties. This is because the style knows what type of control it can be applied to and therefore what properties are available to it.

The XAML for the window is as follows:

```
<Window x:Class="Recipe_06_02.Window1"
    xmlns="http://schemas.microsoft.com/winfx/2006/xaml/presentation"
    xmlns:x="http://schemas.microsoft.com/winfx/2006/xaml"
    Title="WPF Recipes 6_02" Height="120" Width="240">

    <Window.Resources>

        <!-- Brush Resources -->
        <LinearGradientBrush x:Key="NormalBrush"
                             EndPoint="0,1"
                             StartPoint="0,0">
```

```xml
        <GradientStop Color="White" Offset="0.0"/>
        <GradientStop Color="LightGray" Offset="1.0"/>
    </LinearGradientBrush>

    <LinearGradientBrush x:Key="NormalBorderBrush"
                         EndPoint="0,1"
                         StartPoint="0,0">
        <GradientStop Color="Gainsboro" Offset="0.0"/>
        <GradientStop Color="DarkGray" Offset="1.0"/>
    </LinearGradientBrush>

    <!-- Typed Style -->
    <Style TargetType="{x:Type Button}">
        <Setter Property="Margin" Value="4"/>
        <Setter Property="Width" Value="80"/>
        <Setter Property="Height" Value="24"/>
        <Setter Property="FontWeight" Value="Bold"/>
        <Setter Property="Background"
                Value="{DynamicResource NormalBrush}"/>
        <Setter Property="BorderBrush"
                Value="{DynamicResource NormalBorderBrush}"/>
    </Style>

</Window.Resources>

<Grid Margin="20">
    <StackPanel Orientation="Horizontal">

        <Button>One</Button>
        <Button>Two</Button>

    </StackPanel>
</Grid>
</Window>
```

Figure 6-2 shows the resulting window, with the custom style automatically applied to both instances of the Button control.

Figure 6-2. Button *controls with a typed style*

6-3. Override Style Properties

Problem

You need to override the value of a property that has been set by a named or typed System.Windows.Style.

Solution

Set the property or properties in the inline XAML declaration for a specific instance.

How It Works

Styles set the initial appearance of a control, but you can override any of the values they set in the inline XAML for any element. The control will automatically use these instead of taking the values from a named or typed style.

The Code

The following example declares a Style for all System.Windows.Button controls within the window's Resources collection. There are two Button controls that will automatically receive the typed Style, but the second Button has overridden the System.Windows.FontWeight property.

```
<Window x:Class="Recipe_06_03.Window1"
    xmlns="http://schemas.microsoft.com/winfx/2006/xaml/presentation"
    xmlns:x="http://schemas.microsoft.com/winfx/2006/xaml"
    Title=" WPF Recipes 6_03" Height="120" Width="240">

    <Window.Resources>

        <!-- Typed Style -->
        <Style TargetType="{x:Type Button}">
            <Setter Property="Margin" Value="4"/>
            <Setter Property="Width" Value="80"/>
            <Setter Property="Height" Value="24"/>
            <Setter Property="FontWeight" Value="Bold"/>
        </Style>

    </Window.Resources>

    <Grid Margin="20">
        <StackPanel Orientation="Horizontal">

            <Button>One</Button>
            <Button FontWeight="Thin">Two</Button>

        </StackPanel>
    </Grid>
</Window>
```

Figure 6-3 shows the resulting window.

Figure 6-3. *Overriding style properties*

6-4. Inherit from a Common Base Style

Problem

You need to create a System.Windows.Style that defines some common display properties for all your controls and then allow different custom styles to inherit from, and extend, this base style.

Solution

When defining a Style, use the BasedOn attribute to inherit the properties of a base Style.

How It Works

You can define a named Style with a TargetType of a common base type such as System. Windows.Control and give the Style all the display properties you want to share across different types of controls. Then define typed styles for the specific controls you want to use, and set the BasedOn attribute to ensure these styles inherit the properties of the base Style. The derived styles can still override and extend the properties set on the base Style.

The Code

The following example demonstrates a window that declares a Style called BaseControlStyle with a TargetType of Control. The Style specifies the values of the FontFamily, FontSize, FontStyle, and Margin properties. There are three typed styles that specify this base Style in the BasedOn attribute. A group of controls are then displayed in a System.Windows.Controls.StackPanel. Some of the controls have a typed Style defined for them, namely, the System.Windows. CheckBox, System.Windows.Controls.TextBox, and System.Windows.Button controls. These inherit the common properties defined in the base Style. The other controls do not have a typed Style declared for them, namely, the System.Windows.Controls.TextBlock and the System.Windows.Controls.ComboBox, and so do not inherit any of the appearance properties specified in the Style. The Style targeting the Button control demonstrates how to extend a property in an inherited Style. And the inline XAML declaration for one of the Button instances demonstrates how to override a Style's property.

```xml
<Window x:Class="Recipe_06_04.Window1"
    xmlns="http://schemas.microsoft.com/winfx/2006/xaml/presentation"
    xmlns:x="http://schemas.microsoft.com/winfx/2006/xaml"
    Title="WPF Recipes 6_04" Height="220" Width="300">
    <Window.Resources>

        <!-- Base Style -->
        <Style x:Key="BaseControlStyle"
               TargetType="{x:Type Control}">
            <Setter Property="FontFamily" Value="Tahoma" />
            <Setter Property="FontSize" Value="14pt"/>
            <Setter Property="FontStyle" Value="Italic" />
            <Setter Property="Margin" Value="4" />
        </Style>

        <!-- Button Style -->
        <Style TargetType="{x:Type Button}"
               BasedOn="{StaticResource BaseControlStyle}">
            <!-- Add any overriding property values here -->
            <Setter Property="FontWeight" Value="Bold" />
        </Style>

        <!-- CheckBox Style -->
        <Style TargetType="{x:Type CheckBox}"
               BasedOn="{StaticResource BaseControlStyle}">
        </Style>

        <!-- TextBox Style -->
        <Style TargetType="{x:Type TextBox}"
               BasedOn="{StaticResource BaseControlStyle}">
        </Style>

    </Window.Resources>

    <Grid>
        <StackPanel>
            <CheckBox>CheckBox with inherited style</CheckBox>
            <TextBox>TextBox with inherited style</TextBox>
            <Button>Button with inherited style</Button>
            <Button FontWeight="Light">Button with overridden style</Button>
            <TextBlock>TextBlock with default style</TextBlock>
            <ComboBox>ComboBox with default style</ComboBox>
        </StackPanel>
    </Grid>
</Window>
```

Figure 6-4 shows the resulting window.

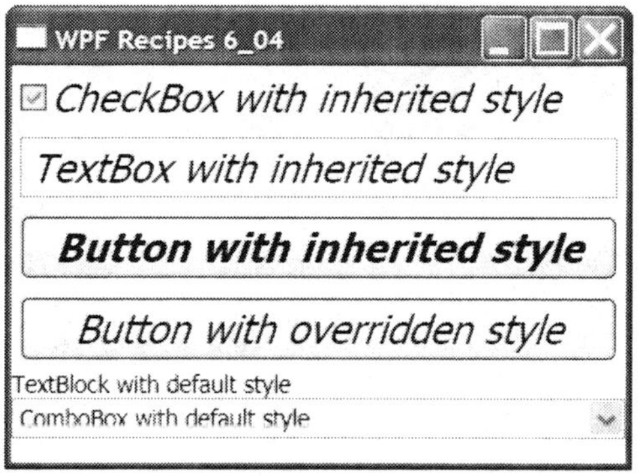

Figure 6-4. *Inheriting style properties*

6-5. Change a Control's Appearance on Mouse Over

Problem

You need to change the appearance of a control when the mouse moves over it.

Solution

Create a `System.Windows.Style` resource for the `System.Windows.Controls.Control`, and use a "property trigger" to change the properties of the `Style` when the `IsMouseOver` property is `True`.

How It Works

Every control ultimately inherits from `System.Windows.UIElement`. This exposes a dependency property called `IsMouseOverProperty`. A `System.Windows.Trigger` can be defined in the `Style` of the control, which receives notification when this property changes and can subsequently change the control's `Style`. When the mouse leaves the control, the property is set back to `False`, which notifies the trigger, and the control is automatically set back to the default state.

The Code

The following example demonstrates a window with a `Style` resource and two `System.Windows.Controls.Button` controls. The `Style` uses a `Trigger` to change the `System.Windows.FontWeight` and `BitmapEffect` properties of the `Button` controls when the mouse is over them.

The XAML for the window is as follows:

```
<Window x:Class="Recipe_06_05.Window1"
    xmlns="http://schemas.microsoft.com/winfx/2006/xaml/presentation"
    xmlns:x="http://schemas.microsoft.com/winfx/2006/xaml"
    Title="WPF Recipes 6_05" Height="120" Width="240">
```

```
<Window.Resources>

    <Style TargetType="{x:Type Button}">
        <Style.Triggers>
            <Trigger Property="IsMouseOver" Value="True">
                <Setter Property="FontWeight" Value="Bold" />
                <Setter Property="BitmapEffect">
                    <Setter.Value>
                        <OuterGlowBitmapEffect
                                GlowColor="Orange"
                                GlowSize="5"
                            />
                    </Setter.Value>
                </Setter>
            </Trigger>
        </Style.Triggers>
    </Style>

</Window.Resources>

<StackPanel Margin="8">
    <Button Height="25" Width="100" Margin="4">
        Mouse Over Me!
    </Button>
    <Button Height="25" Width="100" Margin="4">
        Mouse Over Me!
    </Button>
</StackPanel>

</Window>
```

Figure 6-5 shows the resulting window.

Figure 6-5. *Changing a control's appearance on mouse over*

6-6. Apply Multiple Triggers to the Same Element

Problem

You need to make the same change to the appearance of a control but under different scenarios. This is the same as saying "If property x is true *or* property y is true, then change the appearance to this…."

Solution

Create a System.Windows.Style resource for the control, and add multiple triggers to the style's System.Windows.Triggers collection. In the Trigger, set the values of the properties to achieve the desired appearance.

How It Works

It's possible to create multiple Trigger objects that apply to the same element at once. If they set the values of different properties, then the multiple Trigger objects do not affect each other. If they affect the same properties and they assign the same values, then it is the same as saying that the controls should have a certain visual appearance under multiple circumstances. However, if there are multiple Trigger objects affecting the same property and they assign different values, then the last one to set the value will win.

The Code

The following example specifies a Style resource for a System.Windows.Controls.TextBox control with two triggers. The triggers set the value of the Background property when either the mouse is over the control or when the control has the focus.

```
<Window x:Class="Recipe_06_06.Window1"
    xmlns="http://schemas.microsoft.com/winfx/2006/xaml/presentation"
    xmlns:x="http://schemas.microsoft.com/winfx/2006/xaml"
    Title="WPF Recipes 6_06" Height="100" Width="300">
    <Window.Resources>
        <Style TargetType="{x:Type TextBox}">
            <Style.Triggers>
                <Trigger Property="IsMouseOver"
                        Value="True">
                    <Setter Property="Background"
                            Value="Orange" />
                </Trigger>
                <Trigger Property="IsFocused"
                        Value="True" >
                    <Setter Property="Background"
                            Value="Orange" />
```

```
            </Trigger>
        </Style.Triggers>
    </Style>
</Window.Resources>

<Grid>
    <TextBox Height="20" Width="200">
        Mouse over or give me focus!
    </TextBox>
</Grid>
</Window>
```

Figure 6-6 shows the resulting window.

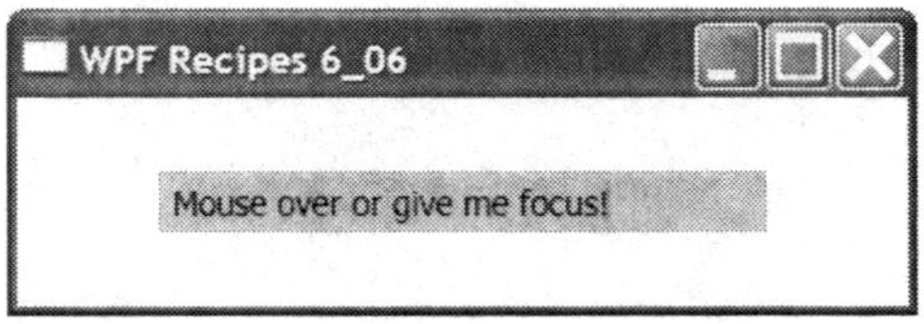

Figure 6-6. *Applying multiple triggers to the same element*

6-7. Evaluate Multiple Properties for the Same Trigger

Problem

You need to make changes to the appearance of a control when multiple conditions are true. This is the same as saying "If property x is true *and* property y is true, then change the appearance to this...."

Solution

Create a System.Windows.Style resource for the control, and add a System.Windows.MultiTrigger to the Style's Triggers collection. Then create multiple instances of the System.Windows. Condition class, and add them to the MultiTrigger's Conditions collection. In the MultiTrigger, set the values of the properties to achieve the desired appearance.

How It Works

A MultiTrigger exposes a Conditions collection that lets you define a series of property and value combinations. The MultiTrigger's Setters are applied to the control only when all the Conditions evaluate to True.

The Code

The following example specifies a Style resource for a System.Windows.Controls.TextBox control with one MultiTrigger. The MultiTrigger sets the Background property of the TextBox and specifies two conditions: when the mouse is over the control and when it has the focus.

```xml
<Window x:Class="Recipe_06_07.Window1"
    xmlns="http://schemas.microsoft.com/winfx/2006/xaml/presentation"
    xmlns:x="http://schemas.microsoft.com/winfx/2006/xaml"
    Title="WPF Recipes 6_07" Height="100" Width="300">
    <Window.Resources>
        <Style
            TargetType="{x:Type TextBox}">
            <Style.Triggers>
                <MultiTrigger>
                    <MultiTrigger.Conditions>
                        <Condition
                            Property="IsMouseOver"
                            Value="True"/>
                        <Condition
                            Property="IsFocused"
                            Value="True"/>
                    </MultiTrigger.Conditions>
                    <Setter
                        Property="Background"
                        Value="Orange" />
                </MultiTrigger>
            </Style.Triggers>
        </Style>
    </Window.Resources>

    <Grid>
        <TextBox Height="20" Width="200">
            Mouse over and give me focus!
        </TextBox>
    </Grid>

</Window>
```

Figure 6-7 shows the resulting window.

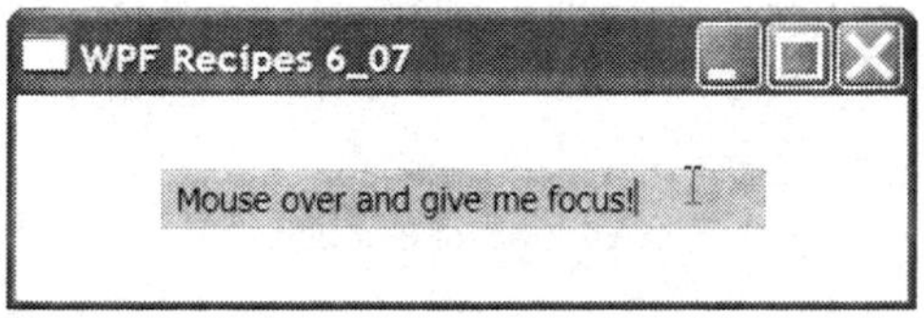

Figure 6-7. *Evaluating multiple properties for the same trigger*

6-8. Programmatically Extract an Element's Style

Problem

You need to programmatically extract a UI element's System.Windows.Style to XAML, for example, because you want to modify a default System.Windows.Controls.ControlTemplate for a standard WPF control.

Solution

Get the key for the element's Style, and use it to find the Style in the application's resources. Programmatically extract the Style by saving it to a string or System.IO.Stream.

How It Works

The FrameworkElement class has a dependency property called DefaultStyleKeyProperty. This property holds the key to the element's Style in the application's resources. You can use the System.Reflection namespace to get the value of this key for a given element and then use the Application.Current.FindResource method to find the relevant Style. Save the Style to XAML with the System.Windows.Markup.XamlWriter.Save method.

The Code

The following example defines a custom Style for a System.Windows.Controls.ProgressBar control. There is a named ProgressBar element that uses this Style and a System.Windows.Button that can be clicked to extract the Style in the code-behind.

```
<Window x:Class="Recipe_06_08.Window1"
    xmlns="http://schemas.microsoft.com/winfx/2006/xaml/presentation"
    xmlns:x="http://schemas.microsoft.com/winfx/2006/xaml"
    Title="WPF Recipes 6_08" Height="120" Width="220">
    <Window.Resources>

        <Style
            x:Key="CustomProgressBarStyle"
            TargetType="{x:Type ProgressBar}">
            <Setter Property="Template">
                <Setter.Value>
                    <ControlTemplate
                        TargetType="{x:Type ProgressBar}">
                        <Grid MinHeight="20" MinWidth="240">
                            <Border
                            Name="PART_Track"
                            Background="{DynamicResource
                              {x:Static SystemColors.InactiveCaptionBrushKey}}"
```

```xml
                                BorderBrush="{DynamicResource
                                  {x:Static SystemColors.InactiveBorderBrushKey}}"
                                BorderThickness="1"
                                    />
                                  <Border
                                Name="PART_Indicator"
                                Background="{DynamicResource
                                  {x:Static SystemColors.ActiveCaptionBrushKey}}"
                                BorderBrush="{DynamicResource
                                  {x:Static SystemColors.ActiveBorderBrushKey}}"
                                BorderThickness="1"
                                HorizontalAlignment="Left"
                                    />
                            </Grid>
                        </ControlTemplate>
                    </Setter.Value>
                </Setter>
            </Style>

    </Window.Resources>

    <StackPanel>

        <ProgressBar x:Name="MyProgressBar"
                        Value="30"
                        Width="200"
                        HorizontalAlignment="Center"
                        Margin="8"
                        Style="{DynamicResource CustomProgressBarStyle}"
                        />

        <Button Click="Button_Click"
                Width="100"
                Height="28"
                Margin="8"

                Content="Extract Style"/>

    </StackPanel>

</Window>
```

In the Click event handler for the Button, the following code extracts the Style from the ProgressBar and saves it to XAML:

```csharp
using System;
using System.Reflection;
using System.Windows;
using System.Windows.Markup;

namespace Recipe_06_08
{
    public partial class Window1 : Window
    {
        public Window1()
        {
            InitializeComponent();
        }

        private void Button_Click(object sender, RoutedEventArgs e)
        {
            Type type = typeof(FrameworkElement);

            // Get the DefaultStyleKeyProperty dependency
            // property of FrameworkElement
            FieldInfo fieldInfo = type.GetField(
                              "DefaultStyleKeyProperty",
                              BindingFlags.Static
                              | BindingFlags.NonPublic);

            DependencyProperty defaultStyleKeyProperty =
                        (DependencyProperty)fieldInfo.GetValue
                            (MyProgressBar);

            // Get the value of the property for the
            //progress bar element
            object defaultStyleKey =
                MyProgressBar.GetValue(defaultStyleKeyProperty);

            // Get the style from the application's resources
            Style style =
                (Style)Application.Current.FindResource
                    (defaultStyleKey);

            // Save the style to a string
            string styleXaml = XamlWriter.Save(style);
        }
    }
}
```

6-9. Set a Style Programmatically

Problem

You need to set which System.Windows.Style to apply to a UI element programmatically, based on custom application logic.

Solution

Use the System.Windows.FrameworkElement.FindResource method to locate and apply the required Style resource to the UI element.

How It Works

When a Style is given a name, it can be retrieved from the resources using the FindResource method. This method will search all the available resource dictionaries within the scope of the FrameworkElement on which it is called. If it is unable to find a resource with the specified key, it will throw a System.Windows.ResourceReferenceKeyNotFoundException.

The Code

The following example demonstrates a window that displays a System.Windows.Controls.Image and a System.Windows.Controls.TextBox. In the window's Resources collection, there are two sets of styles for both of these controls. There is custom logic in the window's Loaded event to programmatically set which Style should be used for the controls, based on the hour of the day.

The XAML for the window is as follows:

```
<Window x:Class="Recipe_06_09.Window1"
    xmlns="http://schemas.microsoft.com/winfx/2006/xaml/presentation"
    xmlns:x="http://schemas.microsoft.com/winfx/2006/xaml"
    Loaded="Window_Loaded"
    Title="WPF Recipes 6_09"
    Height="230" Width="140">
    <Window.Resources>
        <Style x:Key="lblDaytimeStyle">
            <Setter Property="Label.Background" Value="LightYellow" />
            <Setter Property="Label.BorderBrush" Value="Orange" />
            <Setter Property="Label.BorderThickness" Value="1" />
            <Setter Property="Label.FontSize" Value="20" />
            <Setter Property="Label.Width" Value="96" />
            <Setter Property="Label.Height" Value="36" />
            <Setter Property="Label.Margin" Value="4" />
            <Setter Property="Label.Foreground" Value="Orange" />
            <Setter Property="Label.HorizontalContentAlignment" Value="Center" />
```

```xml
        </Style>
        <Style x:Key="imgDaytimeStyle">
            <Setter Property="Image.Source" Value="authorDay.png" />
            <Setter Property="Image.Height" Value="140" />
            <Setter Property="Image.Width" Value="96" />
        </Style>
        <Style x:Key="lblNighttimeStyle">
            <Setter Property="Label.Background" Value="AliceBlue" />
            <Setter Property="Label.BorderBrush" Value="DarkBlue" />
            <Setter Property="Label.BorderThickness" Value="1" />
            <Setter Property="Label.FontSize" Value="20" />
            <Setter Property="Label.Width" Value="96" />
            <Setter Property="Label.Height" Value="36" />
            <Setter Property="Label.Margin" Value="4" />
            <Setter Property="Label.Foreground" Value="DarkBlue" />
            <Setter Property="Label.HorizontalContentAlignment" Value="Center" />
        </Style>
        <Style x:Key="imgNighttimeStyle">
            <Setter Property="Image.Source" Value="authorNight.png" />
            <Setter Property="Image.Height" Value="140" />
            <Setter Property="Image.Width" Value="96" />
        </Style>
    </Window.Resources>
    <Grid>
        <Grid.RowDefinitions>
            <RowDefinition Height="148"/>
            <RowDefinition Height="*"/>
        </Grid.RowDefinitions>

        <Image x:Name="img"/>
        <Label Grid.Row="1" x:Name="lbl" Content="Hello" />
    </Grid>
</Window>
```

The code-behind for the window is as follows:

```csharp
using System;
using System.Windows;

namespace Recipe_06_09
{
    public partial class Window1 : Window
    {
        public Window1()
        {
            InitializeComponent();
        }
```

```
private void Window_Loaded(object sender, RoutedEventArgs e)
{
    if (DateTime.Now.TimeOfDay.Hours >= 18
        || DateTime.Now.TimeOfDay.Hours < 6 )
    {
        lbl.Style = (Style)FindResource("lblNighttimeStyle");
        img.Style = (Style)FindResource("imgNighttimeStyle");
    }
    else
    {
        lbl.Style = (Style)FindResource("lblDaytimeStyle");
        img.Style = (Style)FindResource("imgDaytimeStyle");
    }
}
}
}
```

Figure 6-8 shows the resulting windows.

Figure 6-8. *Setting styles programmatically*

6-10. Ignore an Implicit Style

Problem

You need to specify that a UI element should ignore a typed System.Windows.Style.

Solution

Set the Style property of the element to the System.Windows.Markup.NullExtension markup extension.

How It Works

Each System.Windows.Control, such as System.Windows.Controls.Button, has two styles: the local Style, as specified by the Style property and the theme or default Style, which is defined by the control or in the system. When you set the Style property of a Control to null, it overrides a typed Style and forces it to use the default theme Style. To set a Style property to null, use the x:Null markup extension.

The Code

The following example demonstrates a window with two Button controls. The window's Resources collection contains a simple Style that targets Button controls and changes their Background and FontWeight properties. The Button at the top will inherit this Style automatically, but the one after it will ignore it, because its Style is set to {x:Null}.

```
<Window x:Class="Recipe_06_10.Window1"
    xmlns="http://schemas.microsoft.com/winfx/2006/xaml/presentation"
    xmlns:x="http://schemas.microsoft.com/winfx/2006/xaml"
    xmlns:Recipe_06_10="clr-namespace:Recipe_06_10;assembly="
    Title="WPF Recipes 6_10" Height="88" Width="180">

    <Window.Resources>

        <Style TargetType="{x:Type Button}">
            <Setter Property="Background" Value="LightGray"/>
            <Setter Property="FontWeight" Value="Bold"/>
        </Style>

    </Window.Resources>

    <StackPanel Margin="4">
        <Button>Implicit Style</Button>
        <Button Style="{x:Null}">Ignores Style</Button>
    </StackPanel>

</Window>
```

Figure 6-9 shows the resulting window.

Figure 6-9. *Ignoring implicit styles*

6-11. Change the Appearance of Alternate Items in a List

Problem

You need to change the System.Windows.Style of items in a System.Windows.Controls.ListBox to change the appearance of alternate rows.

Solution

Create a System.Windows.Controls.StyleSelector class, and override the SelectStyle method.

How It Works

When you set the ItemContainerStyleSelector property of a ListBox to a StyleSelector, it will evaluate each item and apply the correct Style. This allows you to specify custom logic to vary the appearance of items based on any particular value or criteria.

The Code

The following example demonstrates a window that displays a list of country names in a ListBox. In the XAML for the ListBox, its ItemContainerStyleSelector property is set to a local StyleSelector class called AlternatingRowStyleSelector. This class has a property called AlternateStyle, which is set to a Style resource that changes the Background property of a ListBoxItem.

The AlternatingRowStyleSelector class overrides the SelectStyle property and returns either the default or the alternate Style, based on a boolean flag.

The XAML for the window is as follows:

```
<Window x:Class="Recipe_06_11.Window1"
    xmlns="http://schemas.microsoft.com/winfx/2006/xaml/presentation"
    xmlns:x="http://schemas.microsoft.com/winfx/2006/xaml"
    xmlns:local="clr-namespace:Recipe_06_11;assembly="
    Title="WPF Recipes 6_11" Height="248" Width="128">

    <Window.Resources>
        <local:Countries x:Key="countries"/>

        <Style x:Key="AlternateStyle">
            <Setter Property="ListBoxItem.Background" Value="LightGray"/>
        </Style>

    </Window.Resources>

    <Grid Margin="4">
        <ListBox
            DisplayMemberPath="Name"
```

```
            ItemsSource="{Binding
                Source={StaticResource countries}}" >

            <ListBox.ItemContainerStyleSelector>
                <local:AlternatingRowStyleSelector
                    AlternateStyle="{StaticResource AlternateStyle}" />
            </ListBox.ItemContainerStyleSelector>
        </ListBox>
    </Grid>
</Window>
```

The code for the StyleSelector is as follows:

```
using System.Windows;
using System.Windows.Controls;

namespace Recipe_06_11
{
    public class AlternatingRowStyleSelector : StyleSelector
    {
        public Style DefaultStyle
        {
            get;
            set;
        }

        public Style AlternateStyle
        {
            get;
            set;
        }

        // Flag to track the alternate rows
        private bool isAlternate = false;

        public override Style SelectStyle(object item, DependencyObject container)
        {
            // Select the style, based on the value of isAlternate
            Style style = isAlternate ? AlternateStyle : DefaultStyle;

            // Invert the flag
            isAlternate = !isAlternate;

            return style;
        }
    }
}
```

Figure 6-10 shows the resulting window.

Figure 6-10. *Changing the appearance of alternate rows*

6-12. Change the Appearance of a List Item When It's Selected

Problem

You need to change the appearance of an item in a System.Windows.Controls.ListBox when it is selected.

Solution

Create a System.Windows.Style resource that targets the System.Windows.Controls.ListBoxItem type, and use a property trigger to change the appearance of an item when the IsSelected property is True.

How It Works

The ListBoxItem class exposes a DependencyProperty called IsSelectedProperty. A System.Windows.Trigger can be defined in the Style of the ListBoxItem, which receives notification when this property changes and can subsequently change the appearance properties.

The Code

The following example creates a System.Windows.Controls.ListBox and specifies a style resource for a ListBoxItem. In the style, a property trigger changes the FontWeight and FontSize properties when the IsSelected property is True.

```
<Window x:Class="Recipe_06_12.Window1"
    xmlns="http://schemas.microsoft.com/winfx/2006/xaml/presentation"
    xmlns:x="http://schemas.microsoft.com/winfx/2006/xaml"
    xmlns:Recipe_06_12="clr-namespace:Recipe_06_12;assembly="
```

```xml
      Title="WPF Recipes 6_12" Height="248" Width="128">
  <Window.Resources>

      <Recipe_06_12:Countries x:Key="countries"/>

      <Style TargetType="{x:Type ListBoxItem}">
          <Setter Property="Content"
                  Value="{Binding Path=Name}"/>
          <Setter Property="Margin"
                  Value="2"/>
          <Style.Triggers>
              <Trigger Property="IsSelected" Value="True">
                  <Setter Property="FontWeight"
                          Value="Bold" />
                  <Setter Property="FontSize"
                          Value="14" />
              </Trigger>
          </Style.Triggers>
      </Style>


  </Window.Resources>

  <Grid Margin="4">
      <ListBox
          ItemsSource="{Binding
              Source={StaticResource countries}}"
          Width="100"
          />
  </Grid>

</Window>
```

Figure 6-11 shows the appearance of the selected item in a list box.

Figure 6-11. *Modifying the appearance of the selected item*

6-13. Create a Control Template

Problem

You need to replace an element's visual tree while keeping all its functionality intact.

Solution

Create a `System.Windows.Controls.ControlTemplate`, and apply it to the `Template` property of a `System.Windows.Controls.Control`.

How It Works

The `ControlTemplate` contains the desired visual tree of elements and can be changed independently from the `Control`'s behavior and functionality. For example, you can choose to use a `System.Windows.Controls.ToggleButton` in your application if you want `ToggleButton`-like behavior. That is, if you want a `Control` that can be clicked and that can be in one of two states: checked or unchecked. However, you are free to change the appearance and visual behavior of the `ToggleButton`, including what it looks like and how it reacts when you mouse over it or press it. You do this by replacing its `ControlTemplate` with a new declaration of visual elements and by specifying `System.Windows.Triggers` to change the appearance of the elements in response to property changes.

Tip One thing to keep in mind is that once you create a `ControlTemplate` for your control, you are replacing the *entire* `ControlTemplate`. This is in contrast to `System.Windows.Styles`, where any property that doesn't get explicitly set by its `Style` will automatically inherit the value from the control's default style.

The Code

The following example demonstrates a window that displays a `ToggleButton` control. The `ToggleButton` is given a new `ControlTemplate` that displays a `System.Windows.Controls.Image` inside a `System.Windows.Controls.Border`. The `ControlTemplate` contains three `Trigger` objects. The first two change the `Border`'s `Background` and `BorderBrush` when you mouse over it, and the second one changes the image when the `ToggleButton` is in a checked state.

```
<Window x:Class="Recipe_06_13.Window1"
    xmlns="http://schemas.microsoft.com/winfx/2006/xaml/presentation"
    xmlns:x="http://schemas.microsoft.com/winfx/2006/xaml"
    Title="WPF Recipes 6_13" Height="240" Width="160">
```

```
<Grid>
    <ToggleButton Width="122" Height="170">
        <ToggleButton.Template>
            <ControlTemplate
                    TargetType="{x:Type ToggleButton}">
                <Border x:Name="border"
                            CornerRadius="4"
                            BorderThickness="3"
                            BorderBrush="DarkGray"
                            Background="LightGray">
                    <Image x:Name="img"
                            Source="authorDay.png"
                            Margin="10"
                            />
                </Border>
                <ControlTemplate.Triggers>
                    <Trigger Property="IsMouseOver" Value="True">
                        <Setter TargetName="border"
                                Property="BorderBrush"
                                Value="Black"
                                />
                    </Trigger>
                    <Trigger Property="IsMouseOver" Value="True">
                        <Setter TargetName="border"
                                Property="Background"
                                Value="DarkGray"
                                />
                    </Trigger>
                    <Trigger Property="IsChecked" Value="True">
                        <Setter TargetName="img"
                                Property="Source"
                                Value="authorNight.png"
                                />
                    </Trigger>
                </ControlTemplate.Triggers>
            </ControlTemplate>
        </ToggleButton.Template>

    </ToggleButton>
</Grid>

</Window>
```

Figure 6-12 shows the appearance of the window in the three states: mouse over, unchecked, and checked.

Figure 6-12. *Creating a control template*

6-14. Put a Control Template into a Style

Problem

You need to share a System.Windows.Controls.ControlTemplate across multiple instances of a System.Windows.Controls.Control.

Solution

Create a typed System.Windows.Style, and set the Template property to an inline ControlTemplate.

How It Works

A Style can be defined as a resource and given the TargetType attribute to apply it to all instances of the specified control type, within the scope of that resource. A System.Windows.Setter can be used to set the value of the Template property to an inline ControlTemplate.

The Code

The following example demonstrates a window that displays five System.Windows.Controls. ToggleButton controls. Three of these are in a checked state; two are unchecked. There is a typed Style in the window's Resources collection, which sets the Template property to an inline ControlTemplate. This ControlTemplate specifies that a ToggleButton should be displayed as a System.Windows.Shapes.Path in the shape of a star. There are two System.Windows.Trigger objects that change the Fill property of the Path when the mouse is over it or when the ToggleButton is checked.

The XAML for the window is as follows:

```
<Window x:Class="Recipe_06_14.Window1"
  xmlns="http://schemas.microsoft.com/winfx/2006/xaml/presentation"
  xmlns:x="http://schemas.microsoft.com/winfx/2006/xaml"
  Title="WPF Recipes 6_14" Height="120" Width="260">
```

```xml
<Window.Resources>

    <!-- Typed Style -->
    <Style TargetType="{x:Type ToggleButton}">
        <Setter Property="Width" Value="36"/>
        <Setter Property="Height" Value="30"/>
        <Setter Property="Template" >
            <Setter.Value>
                <!-- Control Template -->
                <ControlTemplate
                    TargetType="{x:Type ToggleButton}">
                    <Canvas Canvas.Left="5" Canvas.Top="20">
                        <Path x:Name="pth" Stroke="#000080" Fill="#C0C0C0"
                          StrokeThickness="3" StrokeStartLineCap="Round"
                          StrokeEndLineCap="Round" StrokeLineJoin="Round"
                          Data="M 0,0 l 10,0 l 5,-10 l 5,
                              10 l 10,0 l -7,10 l 2,10 l -10,
                              -5 l -10,5 l 2,-10 Z"
                          />
                    </Canvas>
                    <ControlTemplate.Triggers>
                        <Trigger Property="IsMouseOver" Value="True">
                            <Setter TargetName="pth"
                                Property="Fill"
                                Value="#000080"
                                />
                        </Trigger>
                        <Trigger Property="IsChecked" Value="True">
                            <Setter TargetName="pth"
                                Property="Fill"
                                Value="#FFFF00"
                                />
                        </Trigger>
                    </ControlTemplate.Triggers>
                </ControlTemplate>
            </Setter.Value>
        </Setter>
    </Style>

</Window.Resources>

<StackPanel VerticalAlignment="Center"
            HorizontalAlignment="Center"
            Margin="10" Orientation="Horizontal">
    <ToggleButton IsChecked="True"/>
    <ToggleButton IsChecked="True"/>
    <ToggleButton IsChecked="True"/>
```

```
        <ToggleButton IsChecked="False"/>
        <ToggleButton IsChecked="False"/>
    </StackPanel>

</Window>
```

Figure 6-13 shows the resulting window with the five `ToggleButton` controls.

Figure 6-13. *Putting a control template into a style*

6-15. Create a Control Template That Can Be Customized by Properties

Problem

You need to replace an element's visual tree whilst keeping all its functionality intact and also expose it to customization by the user of the control via properties.

Solution

Create a `System.Windows.Controls.ControlTemplate` resource, and specify it as the `Template` property of a control. Use the `System.Windows.TemplateBindingExtension` markup extension to specify that values of properties within the `ControlTemplate` should be bound to a property on the templated element.

How It Works

The `TemplateBinding` markup extension is a lightweight one-way data binding that maps the values of properties on the `System.Windows.Controls.Control` being templated to properties within the template itself. This allows you to customize the appearance of the controls by setting their properties in the inline XAML, which will then be adopted by the elements in the template.

The Code

The following example demonstrates a window that defines a custom `ControlTemplate` for the `System.Windows.Controls.Label` control. Within the `ControlTemplate` there is a `System.Windows.Controls.Border` control that uses the `TemplateBinding` markup extension to declare that its `Background` property should derive its value from the `Background` property of the `Label` element, which in this case is set to `LightBlue`.

The XAML for the window is as follows:

```xaml
<Window x:Class="Recipe_06_15.Window1"
    xmlns="http://schemas.microsoft.com/winfx/2006/xaml/presentation"
    xmlns:x="http://schemas.microsoft.com/winfx/2006/xaml"
    Title="WPF Recipes 6_15" Height="100" Width="180">

    <Window.Resources>
        <ControlTemplate
                x:Key="labelTemplate"
                TargetType="{x:Type Label}">
            <Border x:Name="border"
                CornerRadius="4"
                BorderThickness="3"
                BorderBrush="DarkGray"
                Background="{TemplateBinding
                Property=Background}">
                <ContentPresenter
                    HorizontalAlignment="Center"
                    VerticalAlignment="Center"/>
            </Border>
        </ControlTemplate>
    </Window.Resources>
    <Grid>
        <Label Width="100" Height="24"
            Margin="4" Content="Custom Label"
            Template="{StaticResource labelTemplate}"
            Background="LightBlue"/>
    </Grid>
</Window>
```

Figure 6-14 shows the resulting window.

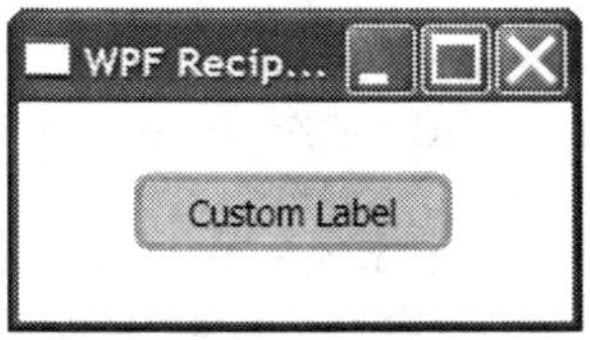

Figure 6-14. *Creating a control template that can be customized by properties*

6-16. Specify Named Parts of a Control Template

Problem

You need to restyle a WPF control without modifying or replacing expected behavior.

Solution

Identify the names of expected elements in your System.Windows.Controls.ControlTemplate by looking for the System.Windows.TemplatePartAttribute on the class declaration for the control. Apply these names to corresponding elements in your ControlTemplate to maintain expected behavior.

How It Works

System.Windows.Controls.Control elements use the TemplatePartAttribute to specify named parts of the visual element that the code expects. Look at the documentation for a given control to determine which named elements the ControlTemplate requires. The names are always of the form PART_Xxx.

Create a typed System.Windows.Style, and set the Template property to an inline System.Windows.Controls.ControlTemplate. Define elements in the ControlTemplate, and give them the expected PART_Xxx names. The expected behaviors will automatically be applied to them.

The Code

The following example demonstrates a window that defines a Style resource with a TargetType of System.Windows.Controls.ProgressBar and an inline ControlTemplate. The ControlTemplate contains two System.Windows.Shapes.Rectangle elements within a grid. The Rectangle elements are given the names PART_Track and PART_Indicator, which are the two template parts defined using the TemplatePartAttribute in the ProgressBar class. This ensures that the width of PART_Indicator automatically remains the correct size relative to the width of PART_Track, based on the Value, Minimum, and Maximum properties.

The XAML for the window is as follows:

```
<Window x:Class="Recipe_06_16.Window1"
    xmlns="http://schemas.microsoft.com/winfx/2006/xaml/presentation"
    xmlns:x="http://schemas.microsoft.com/winfx/2006/xaml"
    Title="WPF Recipes 6_16" Height="120" Width="300">

    <Window.Resources>
        <Style
            TargetType="{x:Type ProgressBar}">
            <Setter Property="Template">
                <Setter.Value>
                    <ControlTemplate
                        TargetType="{x:Type ProgressBar}">
                        <Grid MinHeight="20" MinWidth="240">
                            <Rectangle
                              Name="PART_Track"
                              Fill="Gainsboro"
                              Stroke="Gray"
                              StrokeThickness="1" />
                            <Rectangle
```

```
                                Name="PART_Indicator"
                                Fill="DarkGray"
                                Stroke="Gray"
                                StrokeThickness="1"
                                HorizontalAlignment="Left" />
                    </Grid>
                </ControlTemplate>
            </Setter.Value>
        </Setter>
    </Style>
</Window.Resources>

<StackPanel>
    <ProgressBar x:Name="progress" Value="30"
                 HorizontalAlignment="Center"
                 Margin="10"/>
    <Slider Value="{Binding ElementName=progress, Path=Value, Mode=TwoWay}"
            Minimum="0" Maximum="100"  Margin="10"/>
</StackPanel>
</Window>
```

Figure 6-15 shows the resulting window.

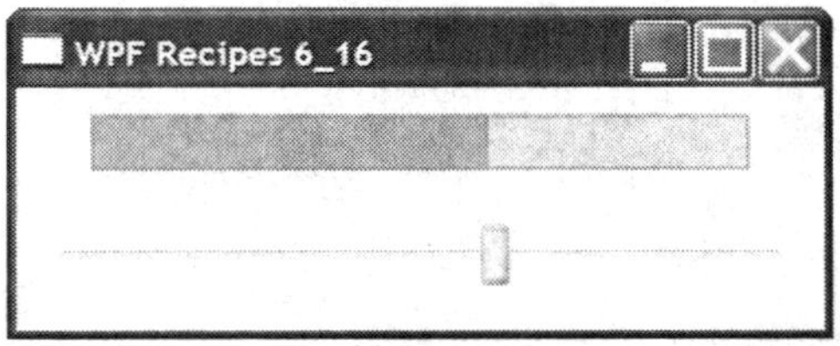

Figure 6-15. *Specifying named parts of a control template*

6-17. Find ControlTemplate-Generated Elements

Problem

You need to locate an element in the visual tree of a System.Windows.Controls.ControlTemplate and access the values of its properties.

Solution

Use the FindName method of a System.Windows.FrameworkTemplate.

How It Works

The FindName method finds the element associated with the specified name, defined within the template.

The Code

The following example demonstrates a window that defines a `ControlTemplate` resource and creates a `System.Windows.Button` element that references this template. There is a `System.Windows.Controls.Border` control within the `ControlTemplate` called border. In the code-behind for the `Click` event of the `Button`, the `Template.FindName` method is used to return the `Border` within the `Button` template and read the value of its `ActualWidth` property.

The XAML for the window is as follows:

```xml
<Window x:Class="Recipe_06_17.Window1"
    xmlns="http://schemas.microsoft.com/winfx/2006/xaml/presentation"
    xmlns:x="http://schemas.microsoft.com/winfx/2006/xaml"
   Title="WPF Recipes 6_17" Height="100" Width="160">

    <Window.Resources>
        <ControlTemplate
                    x:Key="buttonTemplate"
                    TargetType="{x:Type Button}">
            <Border x:Name="border"
                    CornerRadius="4"
                    BorderThickness="3"
                    BorderBrush="DarkGray"
                    Background="LightGray">
                <ContentPresenter
                    HorizontalAlignment="Center"
                    VerticalAlignment="Center"
                    />
            </Border>
            <ControlTemplate.Triggers>
                <Trigger
                    Property="IsMouseOver"
                    Value="True">
                    <Setter
                        TargetName="border"
                        Property="Background"
                        Value="Orange"
                        />
                </Trigger>
            </ControlTemplate.Triggers>
        </ControlTemplate>
    </Window.Resources>
    <Grid>
        <Button x:Name="button"
                Height="24"
                HorizontalAlignment="Stretch"
                Margin="4"
                Content="Custom Template"
                Template="{StaticResource buttonTemplate}"
```

```
                    Click="Button_Click">
        </Button>
    </Grid>
</Window>
```

The code-behind for the window is as follows:

```
using System.Windows;
using System.Windows.Controls;

namespace Recipe_06_17
{
    public partial class Window1 : Window
    {
        public Window1()
        {
            InitializeComponent();
        }

        private void Button_Click(object sender, RoutedEventArgs e)
        {
            // Finding the border that is generated by the
            // ControlTemplate of the Button
            //
            Border borderInTemplate = (Border)
                button.Template.FindName("border", button);

            // Do something to the ControlTemplate-generated border
            //
            MessageBox.Show(
                "The actual width of the border in the ControlTemplate: "
                + borderInTemplate.GetValue(Border.ActualWidthProperty));
        }
    }
}
```

6-18. Create a Custom ToolTip Style

Problem

You need to create a custom System.Windows.Style for the System.Windows.Controls.ToolTip
for an element.

Solution

Define a typed Style for the ToolTip class, and specify custom content and appearance
properties.

How It Works

The System.Windows.FrameworkElement class exposes a ToolTip property that allows you to set the text that should appear in the tool tip. Because the ToolTip class derives from System.Windows.Controls.ContentControl, you can create a typed Style for it and define a custom System.Windows.Controls.ControlTemplate.

■**Caution** The content of a ToolTip can contain interactive controls such as Button controls, but they never get focus, and you can't click or otherwise interact with them.

The Code

The following example displays a System.Windows.Controls.TextBox with a ToolTip and a custom ToolTip style:

```
<Window x:Class="Recipe_06_18.Window1"
    xmlns="http://schemas.microsoft.com/winfx/2006/xaml/presentation"
    xmlns:x="http://schemas.microsoft.com/winfx/2006/xaml"
    Title="WPF Recipes 6_18" Height="160" Width="300">
    <Window.Resources>

        <Style TargetType="{x:Type ToolTip}">
            <Setter Property="HasDropShadow"
                    Value="True"/>
            <Setter Property="OverridesDefaultStyle"
                    Value="True"/>
            <Setter Property="Template">
                <Setter.Value>
                    <ControlTemplate
                        TargetType="{x:Type ToolTip}">
                        <Border Name="Border"
                            BorderBrush="DarkGray"
                            BorderThickness="1"
                            Width="{TemplateBinding Width}"
                            Height="{TemplateBinding Height}"
                            CornerRadius="4">
                            <Border.Background>
                                <LinearGradientBrush
                                    StartPoint="0,0"
                                    EndPoint="0,1">
                                    <GradientStop
                                        Color="Snow"
                                        Offset="0.0"/>
```

```
                                    <GradientStop
                                            Color="Gainsboro"
                                            Offset="1.0"/>
                                    </LinearGradientBrush>
                            </Border.Background>
                            <StackPanel Orientation="Horizontal">
                                <Image Margin="4,4,0,4" Source="help.gif"/>
                                <ContentPresenter
                                  Margin="4"
                                  HorizontalAlignment="Left"
                                  VerticalAlignment="Top" />
                            </StackPanel>
                        </Border>
                    </ControlTemplate>
                </Setter.Value>
            </Setter>
        </Style>

    </Window.Resources>

    <Grid>
        <Border Margin="8"
                BorderThickness="1"
                BorderBrush="Black"
                Width="160"
                Height="60">
            <TextBlock Foreground="DarkGray"
                        VerticalAlignment="Center"
                        HorizontalAlignment="Center"
                        ToolTip="This is a custom tooltip"
                        Text="Mouse Over for tooltip"/>
        </Border>
    </Grid>

</Window>
```

Figure 6-16 shows this custom tool tip.

Figure 6-16. *A tool tip with a custom style*

6-19. Dynamically Change the Skin of an Application

Problem

You need to dynamically customize the look and feel of an entire application.

Solution

Create a System.Windows.ResourceDictionary for each custom skin, and use the System. Windows.Application.LoadComponent method to dynamically load one at runtime.

How It Works

Each System.Windows.ResourceDictionary should contain the named resources such as VisualBrush, Style, and ControlTemplate for each custom skin you want the application to be able to use. The Application.LoadComponent method can dynamically load one of the resource dictionaries at runtime and apply it to the Application.Current.Resources property. If the visual elements in your XAML use the DynamicResource markup extension, instead of StaticResource, then they can change their styles and visual appearance dynamically, pulling them from the selected ResourceDictionary.

The Code

The following example demonstrates an application that creates four resource dictionaries in separate XAML files. Figure 6-17 shows the solution tree. In each resource dictionary, there are two named styles, which are referenced as dynamic resources in the XAML for a window containing a number of different elements.

When the selected index of the SkinsComboBox System.Windows.Controls.ComboBox is changed, there is application logic in the code-behind to dynamically load the appropriate resource dictionary and use it to set the application's current resources.

Figure 6-17 shows the solution tree with the four resource dictionaries.

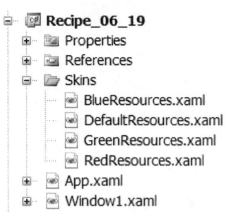

Figure 6-17. *Creating multiple resource dictionaries*

The XAML for the window is as follows:

```
<Window x:Class="Recipe_06_19.Window1"
    xmlns="http://schemas.microsoft.com/winfx/2006/xaml/presentation"
    xmlns:x="http://schemas.microsoft.com/winfx/2006/xaml"
    xmlns:s="clr-namespace:System;assembly=mscorlib"
    xmlns:Recipe_06_19="clr-namespace:Recipe_06_19;assembly="
    Title="WPF Recipes 6_19" Height="228" Width="300">

    <Window.Resources>

        <!-- Base Style -->
        <Style x:Key="baseControlStyle"
              TargetType="{x:Type Control}">
           <Setter Property="FontFamily" Value="Tahoma" />
           <Setter Property="FontSize" Value="11pt"/>
           <Setter Property="Margin" Value="4"/>
           <Setter Property="Foreground"
                  Value="{DynamicResource TextForegroundBrush}" />
           <Setter Property="Background"
                  Value="{DynamicResource BackgroundBrush}" />
        </Style>

        <!-- Button Style -->
        <Style TargetType="{x:Type Button}"
              BasedOn="{StaticResource baseControlStyle}">
        </Style>

        <!-- CheckBox Style -->
        <Style TargetType="{x:Type CheckBox}"
              BasedOn="{StaticResource baseControlStyle}">
```

```
            </Style>

            <!-- TextBox Style -->
            <Style TargetType="{x:Type TextBox}"
                    BasedOn="{StaticResource baseControlStyle}">
            </Style>

            <!-- ComboBox Style -->
            <Style TargetType="{x:Type ComboBox}"
                    BasedOn="{StaticResource baseControlStyle}">
            </Style>

            <!-- Skins -->
            <ObjectDataProvider x:Key="Skins"
                                MethodName="GetValues"
                                ObjectType="{x:Type s:Enum}">
                <ObjectDataProvider.MethodParameters>
                    <x:Type TypeName="Recipe_06_19:Skin" />
                </ObjectDataProvider.MethodParameters>
            </ObjectDataProvider>

    </Window.Resources>

    <Grid>
        <StackPanel>
            <StackPanel Orientation="Horizontal" >
                <Label Content="Choose a skin:"
                        VerticalAlignment="Center"
                        Foreground="{DynamicResource
                        TextForegroundBrush}"/>
                <ComboBox x:Name="SkinsComboBox"
                        Height="24" Width="160"
                        IsSynchronizedWithCurrentItem="True"
                        SelectionChanged="SkinsComboBox_SelectionChanged"
                        ItemsSource="{Binding Mode=OneWay,
                        Source={StaticResource Skins}}"/>
            </StackPanel>

            <CheckBox>Hello World</CheckBox>
            <TextBox>Hello World</TextBox>
            <Button>Hello World</Button>
            <Button>Hello World</Button>
            <ComboBox>Hello World</ComboBox>


        </StackPanel>
    </Grid>
</Window>
```

The code-behind for the window is as follows:

```csharp
using System;
using System.Windows;
using System.Windows.Controls;

namespace Recipe_06_19
{
    public partial class Window1 : Window
    {
        public Window1()
        {
            InitializeComponent();
        }

        private void SkinsComboBox_SelectionChanged(
                    object sender,
                    SelectionChangedEventArgs e)
        {
            ResourceDictionary resourceDictionary;
            Skin skin = (Skin)((ComboBox)sender).SelectedItem;

            switch (skin)
            {
                case Skin.Red:
                    resourceDictionary = Application.LoadComponent(
                        new Uri(@"Skins/RedResources.xaml",
                            UriKind.Relative)) as ResourceDictionary;
                    break;

                case Skin.Green:
                    resourceDictionary = Application.LoadComponent(
                        new Uri(@"Skins/GreenResources.xaml",
                            UriKind.Relative)) as ResourceDictionary;
                    break;

                case Skin.Blue:
                    resourceDictionary = Application.LoadComponent(
                        new Uri(@"Skins/BlueResources.xaml",
                            UriKind.Relative)) as ResourceDictionary;
                    break;

                default:
                    resourceDictionary = Application.LoadComponent(
                        new Uri(@"Skins/DefaultResources.xaml",
                            UriKind.Relative)) as ResourceDictionary;
                    break;
            }
```

```
            Application.Current.Resources = resourceDictionary;
        }
    }

    public enum Skin
    {
        Default,
        Red,
        Green,
        Blue
    }
}
```

Figure 6-18 shows the resulting window with a blue skin applied to the controls.

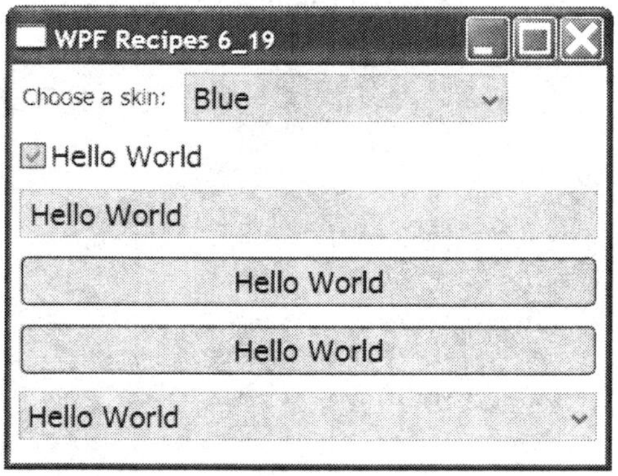

Figure 6-18. *Dynamically changing the skin of an application*

6-20. Create Styles That Adapt to the Current OS Theme

Problem

You need to create styles and templates that adapt to the current operating system (OS) theme.

Solution

Use the System.Windows.SystemColors, System.Windows.SystemFonts, and System.Windows. SystemParameters classes in System.Windows.Styles to specify the values for brushes, colors, and fonts. Define theme-specific resource dictionaries in a themes subfolder in your application.

How It Works

The values of SystemColors, SystemFonts, and SystemParameters are automatically updated when the Windows OS theme changes.

Create a themes subfolder in the root of your project, and put theme-specific resource dictionaries in the subfolder. The resource dictionary files need to be named themes\<ThemeName>.<ThemeColor>.xaml, where ThemeName and ThemeColor correspond to the following valid Microsoft themes (case is insensitive):

- The Windows Vista theme: aero.normalcolor.xaml

- The default blue Windows XP theme: luna.normalcolor.xaml

- The olive green Windows XP theme: luna.homestead.xaml

- The silver Windows XP theme: luna.metallic.xaml

- The Windows XP Media Center Edition 2005 and Windows XP Tablet PC Edition 2005 theme: Royale.NormalColor.xaml

- The Windows Classic theme: Classic.xaml

- The Zune Windows XP theme: Zune.NormalColor.xaml

You can also specify a generic dictionary that gets used if there isn't a dictionary corresponding to the current theme and color. This should be named Generic.xaml.

You must then specify the ThemeInfoAttribute in the application's AssemblyInfo.cs file. This specifies where the automatic theming mechanism should look for the theme dictionaries and the generic dictionary. Each option can be set to one of the following values:

- None (default): Don't look for a resource dictionary.

- SourceAssembly: The dictionary is the current assembly.

- ExternalAssembly: The dictionary is in a different assembly, which must be named <AssemblyName>.<ThemeName>.dll, where <AssemblyName> is the current assembly's name.

If the theme dictionaries specify styles for controls that are defined in external assemblies, for example, the WPF controls such as System.Windows.Controls.ProgressBar and System.Windows.Button, then you must use the ThemeDictionaryExtension to specify the application as the source for the theme dictionaries.

The Code

The following example creates a ProgressBar and two Button elements. It uses the SystemColors class for the Foreground property of one Button and references a custom brush for the other and a custom style for the ProgressBar.

```
<Window x:Class="Recipe_06_20.Window1"
    xmlns="http://schemas.microsoft.com/winfx/2006/xaml/presentation"
    xmlns:x="http://schemas.microsoft.com/winfx/2006/xaml"
    Title="WPF Recipes 6_20" Height="134" Width="200">
```

```
<StackPanel>
    <ProgressBar Value="30"
                 HorizontalAlignment="Center"
                 Margin="4"
                 Style="{DynamicResource CustomProgressBarStyle}"/>
    <Button Margin="4"
            Content="Custom Brush"
            Foreground="{DynamicResource ButtonText}"/>
    <Button Margin="4"
            Content="System Brush"
            Foreground="{DynamicResource
                {x:Static SystemColors.ActiveCaptionBrushKey}}"/>
</StackPanel>
</Window>
```

There is a themes subfolder in the solution tree, which contains the theme dictionaries, named according to the Windows themes convention. Each theme dictionary contains its version of the custom resources used by the ProgressBar and Button controls.

Figure 6-19 shows the solution tree with the themes subfolder and the theme dictionaries.

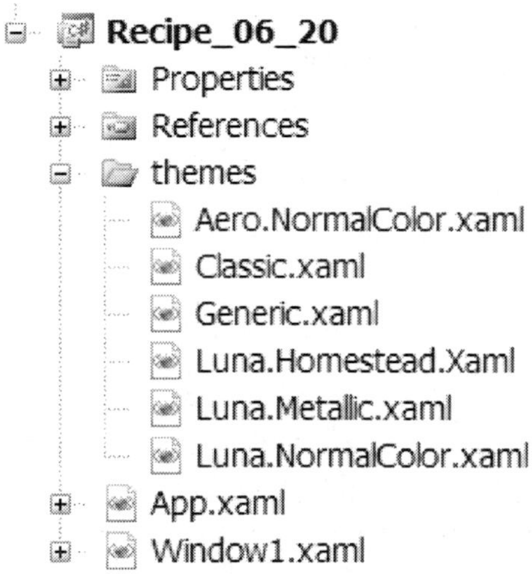

Figure 6-19. *Creating theme dictionaries in a project*

For example, the Luna.Homestead.xaml resource dictionary contains the following Brush and Style definitions:

```
<ResourceDictionary
    xmlns="http://schemas.microsoft.com/winfx/2006/xaml/presentation"
    xmlns:x="http://schemas.microsoft.com/winfx/2006/xaml">

    <SolidColorBrush x:Key="ButtonText" Color="Green"/>
```

```xml
<Style
    x:Key="CustomProgressBarStyle"
    TargetType="{x:Type ProgressBar}">
    <Setter Property="Template">
        <Setter.Value>
            <ControlTemplate
                    TargetType="{x:Type ProgressBar}">
                <Grid MinHeight="20" MinWidth="240">
                    <Border
                      Name="PART_Track"
                      Background="{DynamicResource
                        {x:Static SystemColors.InactiveCaptionBrushKey}}"
                      BorderBrush="{DynamicResource
                        {x:Static SystemColors.InactiveBorderBrushKey}}"
                      BorderThickness="1"
                        />
                    <Border
                      Name="PART_Indicator"
                      Background="{DynamicResource
                        {x:Static SystemColors.ActiveCaptionBrushKey}}"
                      BorderBrush="{DynamicResource
                        {x:Static SystemColors.ActiveBorderBrushKey}}"
                      BorderThickness="1"
                      HorizontalAlignment="Left"
                        />
                </Grid>
            </ControlTemplate>
        </Setter.Value>
    </Setter>
</Style>

</ResourceDictionary>
```

The ThemeInfoAttribute is declared in the application's AssemblyInfo.cs file, specifying the current assembly as the source of both the theme dictionaries and the generic dictionary:

```
[assembly: ThemeInfo(
    ResourceDictionaryLocation.SourceAssembly,
    ResourceDictionaryLocation.SourceAssembly
)]
```

Furthermore, in App.xaml, the ThemeDictionaryExtension is used to specify the application as the source of theme styles for externally defined elements:

```xml
<Application x:Class="Recipe_06_20.App"
    xmlns="http://schemas.microsoft.com/winfx/2006/xaml/presentation"
    xmlns:x="http://schemas.microsoft.com/winfx/2006/xaml"
```

```
StartupUri="Window1.xaml">
<Application.Resources>

    <ResourceDictionary>
        <ResourceDictionary.MergedDictionaries>
            <ResourceDictionary
                Source="{ThemeDictionary Recipe_06_20}"/>
        </ResourceDictionary.MergedDictionaries>
    </ResourceDictionary>

</Application.Resources>

</Application>
```

Figure 6-20 shows the same window, viewed in two different Windows themes.

Tip To change the OS theme in Windows XP, right-click the Windows desktop and select Properties. Then select the Appearance tab in the dialog box, and set the required theme in the Color Scheme drop-down box.

Figure 6-20. *The same progress bar and buttons under the Windows XP blue theme and the olive green theme*

CHAPTER 7

■ ■ ■

Working with Text, Documents, and Printing

Document handling and printing have been greatly overhauled in .NET 3.5. With the introduction of XPS documents, creating, editing, managing, and printing documents have all been hugely simplified. It is now possible to quickly provide print functionality for various object types and user scenarios.

The new printing and document functionality is built on the XML Paper Specification (XPS) technology. XPS defines an electronic file format, a spool file format, and a page description format on which the new XPS print path is built. The print path allows a document to remain in an XPS format from creation to the final processing of a printing device.

With the added richness of WPF controls and handling of text, programmatically manipulating the way text is displayed and used has been made easier than traditional approaches.

The recipes in this chapter describe how to:

- Programmatically interact with a rich-text control to provide text insertion and text formatting (recipes 7-1 and 7-2)

- Print visual elements (recipes 7-3 and 7-4)

- Print simple documents (recipes 7-5, 7-6, and 7-7)

- Create and serialize a fixed document (recipe 7-8)

- Use rich content inline in a flow document (recipe 7-9)

- Create and serialize a flow document (recipe 7-10)

- Asynchronously save a fixed document to an XPS document file on disk (recipe 7-11)

- Display fixed and flow documents (recipe 7-12)

- Annotate, manage, and print user annotations (recipes 7-13, 7-14, 7-15, and 7-16)

7-1. Programmatically Insert Text into a RichTextBox

Problem

You need to programmatically insert text into a System.Windows.Controls.RichTextBox, with the text being inserted at the caret's position.

Solution

Get a System.Windows.Documents.TextPointer representing the caret's current position in the RichTextBox, and then use the InsertTextIntoRun method on the TextPointer, passing in the text to insert as a System.String.

How It Works

The TextPointer object is provided to help move through text elements in a flow content, providing methods to examine, manipulate, or add text elements into the flow content with which the TextPointer is associated.

A RichTextBox control tracks the position of the caret and stores this in a TextPointer, accessible through the CaretPosition property. This allows easy access to the caret's position, enabling you to easily insert any text at the caret's position.

The TextPointer object provides an InsertTextIntoRun method, which takes a single argument, a String, containing the text to insert. The method inserts the supplied text into the current System.Windows.Document.Run that the TextPointer is in. If the TextPointer is not in the scope of a Run, a new Run is created and inserted into the flow content.

If the user has selected some text in the RichTextBox control that should be replaced by the text to be inserted, the selected text must be cleared first. This is easily achieved by modifying the RichTextBox control's Selection property. This property stores a System.Windows.Documents.TextSelection object (which derives from System.Windows.Documents.TextRange). The Text property of the TextSelection can be set to String.Empty, thus clearing the text.

After the new text is inserted, the caret is positioned at the start of the inserted text by default. To ensure that the caret is moved to the end of the newly inserted text, you'll need to obtain a reference to a TextPointer that points to the next element after the caret. Once the text has been inserted, the caret's position can be set to the recently obtained TextPointer, thus positioning the caret at the end of the inserted text. Getting the next element on from the caret is achieved using the GetPositionAtOffset method on a TextPointer.

The GetPositionAtOffset method takes two arguments and returns a TextPointer. The first is a System.Int32 indicating the offset, in symbols, from the beginning of the TextPointer. The second argument is a System.Windows.LogicalDirection and specifies the direction in which to move.

By calling the BeginChange method on the RichTextBox control before inserting the text, you can ensure that no text content or selection changed events will be raised until the EndChange method is called. This means the insertion can take place more efficiently because it will not be interrupted by code possibly listening to and acting on such events, such as syntax highlighting and so on. Another advantage is that any changes made after BeginChange and before EndChange will be combined into a single undo action.

The Code

The following example gives the XAML and code-behind used to display a window containing a RichTextBox with a System.Windows.Controls.TextBox and a System.Windows.Controls.Button. Both the RichTextBox and TextBox can be edited. The TextBox at the bottom of the window is where the insertion text is entered. Clicking the Button will take the text from the TextBox and insert it into the RichTextBox at the location of the caret.

```
<Window
  x:Class-"Recipe_07_01.Window1"
  xmlns="http://schemas.microsoft.com/winfx/2006/xaml/presentation"
  xmlns:x="http://schemas.microsoft.com/winfx/2006/xaml"
  Title="Window1" Height="600" Width="800">
  <DockPanel>
    <StackPanel DockPanel.Dock="Bottom" Orientation="Horizontal">
      <TextBox x:Name="tbxInsertionText" Width="200" Margin="5,0" />
      <Button
        DockPanel.Dock="Bottom"
        Content="Insert"
        Width="40"
        Margin="5,0"
        Click="btnInsert_Click"
      />
    </StackPanel>
    <RichTextBox x:Name="rtbTextContent" />
  </DockPanel>
</Window>
```

The following code describes the content of the previous markup's code-behind file:

```
using System.Windows;
using System.Windows.Documents;
using System.Windows.Input;

namespace Recipe_07_01
{
    /// <summary>
    /// Interaction logic for Window1.xaml
    /// </summary>
    public partial class Window1 : Window
    {
        public Window1()
        {
            InitializeComponent();
        }
```

```csharp
private void btnInsert_Click(object sender, RoutedEventArgs e)
{
    // Check to see we have some valid insertion text.
    if (string.IsNullOrEmpty(tbxInsertionText.Text))
    {
        return;
    }

    // Mark the text control as being changed. This prevents
    // any text content or selection changed events and
    // combines any steps performed before the EndChange into
    // a single undo action.
    rtbTextContent.BeginChange();

    // First clear any selected text.
    if (rtbTextContent.Selection.Text != string.Empty)
    {
        rtbTextContent.Selection.Text = string.Empty;
    }

    // Get the text element adjacent to the caret in its current
    // position.
    TextPointer tp =
        rtbTextContent.CaretPosition.GetPositionAtOffset(0,
            LogicalDirection.Forward);

    // Insert the text we have supplied
    rtbTextContent.CaretPosition.InsertTextInRun(tbxInsertionText.Text);

    // Now restore the caret's position so that it is placed
    // after the newly inserted text.
    rtbTextContent.CaretPosition = tp;

    //We have finished making our changes.
    rtbTextContent.EndChange();

    // Now set the focus back to RichTextBox so the user can
    // continue typing.
    Keyboard.Focus(rtbTextContent);
    }
  }
}
```

7-2. Apply Syntax Highlighting in a Text Control

Problem

You need to color words in a `System.Windows.Controls.RichTextBox` based on some rule set; for example, all numerical characters are given a bold font weight.

Solution

Use a `System.Windows.Documents.TextPointer` to work your way through each element in the `RichTextBox`'s document, and apply the appropriate formatting.

How It Works

When the content of the `RichTextBox` is changed, the content of the `RichTextBox` is formatted according to some simple rules.

Before the formatting is applied, any existing formatting first needs to be cleared. This is done by creating a `System.Windows.Documents.TextRange`, which spans the entire content of the `RichTextBox`, and then calling the `ClearAllProperties` method on the `TextRange`.

To apply some simple formatting in this example, each block of text in the document is examined to see whether it is one of four operators (+, -, /, *), an integer, or text. Based on this, the block of text is formatted by modifying the value of a property on the `TextRange`. This property can be any dependency property defined in the `System.Windows.Documents.TextElement` class.

The method that finds the next block of text works by looking at the category of the content adjacent to the `TextPointer`. The category is defined using the `System.Windows.Documents.TextPointerContext` enum. If this value is anything other than `TextPointerContext.Text`, the method continues to examine the next content element.

The Code

```
<Window
  x:Class="Recipe_07_02.Window1"
  xmlns="http://schemas.microsoft.com/winfx/2006/xaml/presentation"
  xmlns:x="http://schemas.microsoft.com/winfx/2006/xaml"
  Title="Window1"
  Height="600"
  Width="800">
  <Grid>
    <RichTextBox
      x:Name="rlbTexlContent"
      TextChanged="RichTextBox_TextChanged"
    />
  </Grid>
</Window>
```

The following code defines the content of the previous markup's code-behind file:

```
using System.Windows;
using System.Windows.Controls;
using System.Windows.Documents;
using System.Windows.Media;

namespace Recipe_07_02
{
    public enum TokenType
    {
        Numerical,
        Operator,
        Other
    }


    /// <summary>
    /// Interaction logic for Window1.xaml
    /// </summary>
    public partial class Window1 : Window
    {
        public Window1()
        {
            InitializeComponent();
        }

        private void RichTextBox_TextChanged(object sender, TextChangedEventArgs e)
        {
            // Get the content from the rich text box.
            TextRange textRange =
                new TextRange(rtbTextContent.Document.ContentStart,
                            rtbTextContent.Document.ContentEnd);

            // We don't want to know about any more changes while we're
            // making changes.
            rtbTextContent.TextChanged -= RichTextBox_TextChanged;

            // First clear any formatting applied to the text.
            textRange.ClearAllProperties();

            ApplyFormatting();

            // Start listening for changes again.
            rtbTextContent.TextChanged += RichTextBox_TextChanged;
        }
```

```csharp
private void ApplyFormatting()
{
    // We want to start from the beginning of the document.
    TextPointer tp = rtbTextContent.Document.ContentStart;

    //Find the next block of text.
    tp = FindNextString(tp);

    while (tp != null)
    {
        TextPointer textRangeEnd = tp.GetPositionAtOffset(1,
            LogicalDirection.Forward);

        TextRange tokenTextRange = new TextRange(tp,
            tp.GetPositionAtOffset(1, LogicalDirection.Forward));

        TokenType tokenType = ClassifyToken(tokenTextRange.Text);

        switch (tokenType)
        {
            case TokenType.Numerical:
                tokenTextRange.ApplyPropertyValue(
                    TextElement.ForegroundProperty,  Brushes.Blue);
                break;
            case TokenType.Operator:
                tokenTextRange.ApplyPropertyValue(
                    TextElement.FontWeightProperty, FontWeights.Bold);
                break;
            case TokenType.Other:
                tokenTextRange.ApplyPropertyValue(
                    TextElement.FontSizeProperty, 20d);
                break;
        }

        tp = FindNextString(textRangeEnd);
    }
}

private TokenType ClassifyToken(string text)
{
    int temp;

    if (int.TryParse(text, out temp))
    {
        return TokenType.Numerical;
    }
```

```
        switch(text)
        {
            case "+":
            case "-":
            case "/":
            case "*":
                return TokenType.Operator;
            default:
                return TokenType.Other;
        }
    }

    private TextPointer FindNextString(TextPointer tp)
    {
        //Skip over anything that isn't text
        while (tp.GetPointerContext(
            LogicalDirection.Forward) != TextPointerContext.Text)
        {
            tp = tp.GetPositionAtOffset(1, LogicalDirection.Forward);

            if (tp == null)
            {
                return tp;
            }
        }

        //Skip over any whitespace we meet
        char[] buffer = new char[1];
        tp.GetTextInRun(LogicalDirection.Forward, buffer, 0, 1);

        while (IsWhiteSpace(buffer))
        {
            tp = tp.GetPositionAtOffset(1, LogicalDirection.Forward);

            if (tp == null)
            {
                break;
            }

            tp.GetTextInRun(LogicalDirection.Forward, buffer, 0, 1);
        }

        return tp;
    }
```

```
        private bool IsWhiteSpace(char[] buffer)
        {
            return (buffer[0] == '\n'
                    || buffer[0] == '\t'
                    || buffer[0] == '\r'
                    || buffer[0] == ' ');
        }
    }
}
```

7-3. Print a WPF Visual

Problem

You need to print a visual element within your application.

The Solution

Use a System.Windows.Xps.XpsDocumentWriter to print a visual object to a System.Printing.
PrintQueue.

How It Works

The Write method of a System.Windows.Documents.XpsDocumentWriter has several overloads that allow several different object types to be written to the target against which the
XpsDocumentWriter was created. One of these overloads takes a single argument of type
System.Windows.Media.Visual. By creating the XpsDocumentWriter against a PrintQueue,
content written by the XpsDocumentWriter will be written to the PrintQueue.

You can create a PrintQueue using several different approaches. These are two examples of
creating a PrintQueue:

- Selecting a PrintQueue from a selection of printers discovered using a System.Printing.
  PrintServer object

- Presenting the user with a System.Windows.Dialogs.PrintDialog where a target printer
  is selected

The method of choice will depend on the level of user interaction required and the security
levels of the machine. Of the previous two examples for obtaining a PrintQueue, a PrintServer
object can be instantiated only in a full-trust environment, whereas the PrintDialog approach
will work in both full and partial-trust environments.

To ensure that the visual being printed appears within the bounds of the printed page, it
may be necessary to scale the visual before it is written to the PrintQueue. Without scaling the
visual, it will be printed at the size it appears on the screen. If this size is greater than that of the
paper size (taking into account the resolution of the printout), the visual will appear clipped.
The target page size can be obtained through the PrintQueue's System.Printing.PrintTicket.
(See recipe 7-5 for more information on the PrintTicket class.)

Note You will need to add references to the `System.Printing` and `ReachFramework` assemblies in your project for this example.

The Code

This example shows you how to print a `Visual` object using a `PrintQueue` obtained from a `PrintDialog`. The following XAML defines a window with a few visual objects that are to be printed. A button at the bottom of the form calls a method in the code-behind that initiates the printing process.

```
<Window
  x:Class="Recipe_07_03.Window1"
  xmlns="http://schemas.microsoft.com/winfx/2006/xaml/presentation"
  xmlns:x="http://schemas.microsoft.com/winfx/2006/xaml"
  Title="Window1">
  <Grid>
    <Grid x:Name="VisualRoot">
      <Ellipse
        Fill="Blue"
        Height="300"
        Width="300"
        HorizontalAlignment="Center"
        VerticalAlignment="Center"
      />

      <TextBlock
        FontSize="24"
        Foreground="White"
        Text="A Printed Visual"
        HorizontalAlignment="Center"
        VerticalAlignment="Center"
      />
    </Grid>

    <Button
      Click="btnPrintVisual_Click"
      Content="Print Visual..."
      Width="150"
      VerticalAlignment="Bottom"
      HorizontalAlignment="Center"
    />
  </Grid>
</Window>
```

The following code-behind contains a handler for the click event of the button defined earlier. When the button is clicked, a PrintDialog is presented to the user, from which they select the printer to which they want to print.

If the dialog box is closed via the OK button, a PrintQueue for the selected printer is obtained, and an XpsDocumentWriter is created. The visual is then written to the PrintQueue using the Write method on the XpsDocumentWriter.

```csharp
using System.Printing;
using System.Windows;
using System.Windows.Controls;
using System.Windows.Media;
using System.Windows.Xps;

namespace Recipe_07_03
{
    /// <summary>
    /// Interaction logic for Window1.xaml
    /// </summary>
    public partial class Window1 : Window
    {
        public Window1()
        {
            InitializeComponent();
        }

        private Visual GetVisual()
        {
            return new Grid();
        }

        private void btnPrintVisual_Click(object sender, RoutedEventArgs e)
        {
            //Get hold of the visual you want to print.
            Visual visual = GetVisual();

            // Create a Print dialog.
            PrintDialog printDialog = new PrintDialog();

            if (printDialog.ShowDialog() != true)
            {
                return;
            }

            // Get the default print queue
            PrintQueue pq = printDialog.PrintQueue;

            //Scale the visual
            Visual scaledVisual = ScaleVisual(visual, pq);
```

```
        // Get an XpsDocumentWriter for the default print queue
        XpsDocumentWriter xpsdw = PrintQueue.CreateXpsDocumentWriter(pq);

        xpsdw.Write(scaledVisual);
    }

    //We want to be able to scale the visual so it fits within the page.
    private Visual ScaleVisual(Visual v, PrintQueue pq)
    {
        ContainerVisual root = new ContainerVisual();
        const double inch = 96;

        // Set the margins.
        double xMargin = 1.25 * inch;
        double yMargin = 1 * inch;

        PrintTicket pt = pq.UserPrintTicket;
        double printableWidth = pt.PageMediaSize.Width.Value;
        double printableHeight = pt.PageMediaSize.Height.Value;

        double xScale = (printableWidth - xMargin * 2) / printableWidth;
        double yScale = (printableHeight - yMargin * 2) / printableHeight;

        root.Children.Add(v);
        root.Transform
            = new MatrixTransform(xScale, 0, 0, yScale, xMargin, yMargin);

        return root;
    }
  }
}
```

7-4. Print a Collection of WPF Visuals

Problem

You have a collection of System.Windows.Media.Visual objects that you want to print, with each Visual being printed on a separate page.

Solution

Write the Visuals to a System.Printing.PrintQueue using the batched write capability of a System.Windows.Xps.VisualsToXpsDocument object.

How It Works

In recipe 7-3, a single Visual is printed by obtaining a reference to an XpsDocumentWriter and calling its Write method, passing in the Visual to be printed. To print a collection of visual objects, you must use a System.Windows.Xps.VisualsToXpsDocument object (an implementation of a System.Windows.Documents.Serialization.SerializerWriterCollator) to perform a batch write of the visuals to the PrintQueue.

To obtain a VisualsToXpsDocument, you first create a System.Windows.Xps.XpsDocumentWriter against a PrintQueue, as described in recipe 7-3. Using the CreateVisualCollator method on the XpsDocumentWriter, you get an instance of a VisualsToXpsWriterDocument object.

To write the Visual objects to the PrintQueue, the Write method on the VisualsToXpsDocument is called for each Visual object you want to print, creating a new System.Windows.Documents. FixedPage for each Visual in the document. As such, only visual elements that can be written to a FixedPage can be passed to the Write method of the VisualsToXpsDocument.

Once each Visual has been written, a call to EndBatchWrite on the VisualsToXpsDocument is called, writing the document to the PrintQueue.

Note You will need to add references to the System.Printing and ReachFramework assemblies in your project for this example.

The Code

```xml
<Window
  x:Class="Recipe_07_04.Window1"
  xmlns="http://schemas.microsoft.com/winfx/2006/xaml/presentation"
  xmlns:x="http://schemas.microsoft.com/winfx/2006/xaml"
  Title="Window1">
  <Grid>
    <Grid x:Name="VisualRoot">
      <Ellipse
        Fill="Blue"
        Height="300"
        Width="300"
        HorizontalAlignment="Center"
        VerticalAlignment="Center"
      />

      <TextBlock
        FontSize="24"
        Foreground="White"
        Text="A Printed Visual"
        HorizontalAlignment="Center"
        VerticalAlignment="Center"
      />
    </Grid>
```

```xml
      <Button
        Click="btnPrintVisuals_Click"
        Content="Print Visuals..."
        Width="150"
        VerticalAlignment="Bottom"
        HorizontalAlignment="Center"
      />
    </Grid>
</Window>
```

The following code-behind defines a handler for the click event of the System.Windows.Controls.Button defined earlier. A System.Windows.Dialogs.PrintDialog is created and presented to the user. If the PrintDialog is closed by clicking the OK button, a collection of Visual objects is sent to the chosen printer using a VisualsToXpsDocument collator.

```csharp
using System.Collections.Generic;
using System.Printing;
using System.Windows;
using System.Windows.Controls;
using System.Windows.Media;
using System.Windows.Xps;

namespace Recipe_07_04
{
    /// <summary>
    /// Interaction logic for Window1.xaml
    /// </summary>
    public partial class Window1 : Window
    {
        public Window1()
        {
            InitializeComponent();
        }

        private List<Visual> GetVisuals()
        {
            return new List<Visual>(new Visual[]
                                        {
                                            VisualRoot,
                                            VisualRoot,
                                            VisualRoot
                                        });
        }

        private void btnPrintVisuals_Click(object sender, RoutedEventArgs e)
        {
            //Get hold of the visual you want to print.
            List<Visual> visuals = GetVisuals();
```

```csharp
    // Create a Print dialog.
    PrintDialog printDialog = new PrintDialog();

    if (printDialog.ShowDialog() != true)
    {
        return;
    }

    // Get the default print queue
    PrintQueue printQueue = printDialog.PrintQueue;

    // Get an XpsDocumentWriter for the default print queue
    XpsDocumentWriter xpsdw
        = PrintQueue.CreateXpsDocumentWriter(printQueue);

    VisualsToXpsDocument vtxd =
        (VisualsToXpsDocument)xpsdw.CreateVisualsCollator();

    //Indicate we want any writes to be performed in a batch operation.
    vtxd.BeginBatchWrite();

    //Write out each visual.
    visuals.ForEach(delegate(Visual visual)
    {
        //Scale the visual
        Visual scaledVisual = ScaleVisual(visual, printQueue);

        vtxd.Write(scaledVisual);
    });

    //Mark the end of the batch operation.
    vtxd.EndBatchWrite();
}

//We want to be able to scale the visual so it fits within the page.
private Visual ScaleVisual(Visual visual, PrintQueue printQueue)
{
    ContainerVisual root = new ContainerVisual();

    //An inch is 96 DIPs, use this to scale up sizes given in inches.
    double inch = 96;

    //Calculate our margins.
    double xMargin = 1.25 * inch;
    double yMargin = 1 * inch;
```

```
                    //Get the current print ticket from which the paper size can be
                    //obtained.
                    PrintTicket printTicket = printQueue.UserPrintTicket;

                    //Retrieve the dimensions of the target page.
                    double pageWidth = printTicket.PageMediaSize.Width.Value;
                    double pageHeight = printTicket.PageMediaSize.Height.Value;

                    double xScale = (pageWidth - xMargin * 2) / pageWidth;
                    double yScale = (pageHeight - yMargin * 2) / pageHeight;

                    root.Children.Add(visual);

                    root.Transform
                        = new MatrixTransform(xScale, 0, 0, yScale, xMargin, yMargin);

                    return root;
                }
            }
        }
```

7-5. Configure Printing Options Using a PrintTicket

Problem

You need to be able to check for and configure the available features of a printer such as duplexing, stapling, collation, page size, and so on.

Solution

Using the GetPrintCapabilities method of a System.Printing.PrintQueue, it is possible to detect what functionality is available on a given printer. By configuring the System.Printing. PrintTicket property on the PrintQueue, functionality can be enabled or disabled as required.

How It Works

The GetPrintCapabilities method on a PrintQueue returns a System.Printing.PrintCapabilities, defining what functionality the printer provides. The PrintCapabilities object represents a PrintCapabilities document, which is an XML document detailing a printer's capabilities and current settings.

For each feature that the printer offers, an element appears in the document; for example, if the printer supported collation, there would exist a Collation element. The PrintCapabilities object contains properties for each possible feature, for example, CollationCapability. The CollationCapability property is a collection of System.Printing.Collation, indicating the collation capabilities of the printer. If the printer does not support a feature, the value of the capability property is set to null.

To configure the printing options, the appropriate property on the PrintTicket object is set to the desired value.

Note You will need to add references to the System.Printing and ReachFramework assemblies in your project for this example.

The Code

```xml
<Window
  x:Class="Recipe_07_05.Window1"
  xmlns="http://schemas.microsoft.com/winfx/2006/xaml/presentation"
  xmlns:x="http://schemas.microsoft.com/winfx/2006/xaml"
  Title="Window1"
  Height="300"
  Width="300"
  Loaded="Window_Loaded">
  <StackPanel>
    <GroupBox
      x:Name="gbStage1"
      Header="Stage 1 - Select a Printer"
      BorderBrush="Black"
      Margin="5">
      <Button
        Content="Select Printer..."
        Margin="5"
        Click="btnSelectPrinter_Click" />
    </GroupBox>

    <GroupBox
      x:Name="gbStage2"
      Header="Stage 2 - Configure Options"
      BorderBrush="Black"
      Margin="5">
      <WrapPanel>

        <GroupBox Header="Duplexing" Margin="5,0,2.5,0">
          <StackPanel>
            <RadioButton
              x:Name="rbDuplexing1"
              GroupName="duplexing"
              Content="One Sided" />
            <RadioButton
              x:Name="rbDuplexing2"
              GroupName="duplexing"
              Content="Two Sided (Long Edge)" />
```

```xml
                <RadioButton
                  x:Name="rbDuplexing3"
                  GroupName="duplexing"
                  Content="Two Sided (Short Edge)" />
              </StackPanel>
            </GroupBox>

            <GroupBox Header="Collation" Margin="2.5,0">
              <StackPanel>
                <RadioButton
                  x:Name="rbCollation1"
                  GroupName="collation"
                  Content="Collated" />
                <RadioButton
                  x:Name="rbCollation2"
                  GroupName="collation"
                  Content="Uncollated" />
              </StackPanel>
            </GroupBox>

            <GroupBox Header="Duplexing" Margin="2.5,0,5,0">
              <StackPanel>
                <RadioButton
                  x:Name="rbOrientation1"
                  GroupName="orientation"
                  Content="Landscape" />
                <RadioButton
                  x:Name="rbOrientation2"
                  GroupName="orientation"
                  Content="Portrait" />
              </StackPanel>
            </GroupBox>
          </WrapPanel>
        </GroupBox>

        <GroupBox
          x:Name="gbStage3"
          Header="Stage 3 - Print"
          BorderBrush="Black"
          Margin="5">
          <Button
            Content="Print"
            Margin="5"
            Click="btnPrint_Click" />
        </GroupBox>

      </StackPanel>
    </Window>
```

The following code defines the content of the Window1.xaml.cs file:

```csharp
using System.Printing;
using System.Windows;
using System.Windows.Controls;
using System.Windows.Documents;
using System.Windows.Markup;
using System.Windows.Xps;

namespace Recipe_07_05
{
    /// <summary>
    /// Interaction logic for Window1.xaml
    /// </summary>
    public partial class Window1 : Window
    {
        private PrintQueue printQueue;
        private PrintTicket printTicket;

        public Window1()
        {
            InitializeComponent();
        }

        //When the Window loads, set the initial control states.
        private void Window_Loaded(object sender, RoutedEventArgs e)
        {
            gbStage1.IsEnabled = true;
            gbStage2.IsEnabled = false;
            gbStage3.IsEnabled = false;
        }

        private void btnSelectPrinter_Click(object sender, RoutedEventArgs e)
        {
            //Set the state of the options controls
            printQueue = GetPrintQueue();

            if (printQueue == null)
            {
                return;
            }

            // Get default PrintTicket from printer
            printTicket = printQueue.UserPrintTicket;

            PrintCapabilities printCapabilites = printQueue.GetPrintCapabilities();
```

```
        SetControlStates(printCapabilites, printTicket);
    }

    private void btnPrint_Click(object sender, RoutedEventArgs e)
    {
        SetPrintTicket(printTicket);

        XpsDocumentWriter documentWriter =
            PrintQueue.CreateXpsDocumentWriter(printQueue);

        documentWriter.Write(CreateMultiPageFixedDocument(), printTicket);

        MessageBox.Show("Document printed.",
                        "Recipe 07 05",
                        MessageBoxButton.OK,
                        MessageBoxImage.Information);
    }

    private PrintQueue GetPrintQueue()
    {
        // Create a Print dialog.
        PrintDialog printDialog = new PrintDialog();

        if (printDialog.ShowDialog() != true)
        {
            return null;
        }

        // Get the default print queue
        PrintQueue printQueue = printDialog.PrintQueue;

        return printQueue;
    }

    public FixedDocument CreateMultiPageFixedDocument()
    {
        FixedDocument fixedDocument = new FixedDocument();

        //Set the size of each page to be A4 (8.5" x 11").
        Size a4PageSize = new Size(8.5 * 96, 11 * 96);
        fixedDocument.DocumentPaginator.PageSize = a4PageSize;

        //Add 5 pages to the document.
        for (int i = 1; i < 6; i++)
        {
            PageContent pageContent = new PageContent();
            fixedDocument.Pages.Add(pageContent);
```

```
        FixedPage fixedPage = new FixedPage();
        //Create a TextBlock
        TextBlock textBlock = new TextBlock();
        textBlock.Margin = new Thickness(10, 10, 0, 0);
        textBlock.Text = string.Format("Page {0}", i);
        textBlock.FontSize = 24;
        //Add the TextBlock to the page.
        fixedPage.Children.Add(textBlock);
        //Add the page to the page's content.
        ((IAddChild)pageContent).AddChild(fixedPage);
    }

    return fixedDocument;
}


//Set the states of the controls defined in the markup
//for this Window.
private void SetControlStates(
    PrintCapabilities printCapabilities,
    PrintTicket printTicket)
{
    gbStage1.IsEnabled = false;
    gbStage2.IsEnabled = true;
    gbStage3.IsEnabled = true;

    //Set duplexing options.
    rbDuplexing1.IsEnabled =
        printCapabilities.DuplexingCapability.Contains(
            Duplexing.OneSided);

    rbDuplexing1.IsChecked =
        printTicket.Duplexing == Duplexing.OneSided;

    rbDuplexing2.IsEnabled =
        printCapabilities.DuplexingCapability.Contains(
            Duplexing.TwoSidedLongEdge);

    rbDuplexing2.IsChecked =
        printTicket.Duplexing == Duplexing.TwoSidedLongEdge;

    rbDuplexing3.IsEnabled =
        printCapabilities.DuplexingCapability.Contains(
            Duplexing.TwoSidedShortEdge);

    rbDuplexing3.IsChecked =
        printTicket.Duplexing == Duplexing.TwoSidedShortEdge;
```

```csharp
        //Set collation properties.
        rbCollation1.IsEnabled =
            printCapabilities.CollationCapability.Contains(
                Collation.Collated);

        rbCollation1.IsChecked =
            printTicket.Collation == Collation.Collated;

        rbCollation2.IsEnabled =
            printCapabilities.CollationCapability.Contains(
                Collation.Uncollated);

        rbCollation2.IsChecked =
            printTicket.Collation == Collation.Uncollated;

        //Set the orientation properties
        rbOrientation1.IsEnabled =
            printCapabilities.PageOrientationCapability.Contains(
                PageOrientation.Landscape);

        rbOrientation1.IsChecked =
            printTicket.PageOrientation == PageOrientation.Landscape;

        rbOrientation2.IsEnabled =
            printCapabilities.PageOrientationCapability.Contains(
                PageOrientation.Portrait);

        rbOrientation2.IsChecked =
            printTicket.PageOrientation == PageOrientation.Portrait;
    }

    private void SetPrintTicket(PrintTicket printTicket)
    {
        //Determine the Duplexing value.
        if (rbDuplexing1.IsEnabled
            && rbDuplexing2.IsChecked == true)
        {
            printTicket.Duplexing = Duplexing.OneSided;
        }
        else if (rbDuplexing2.IsEnabled
                && rbDuplexing2.IsChecked == true)
        {
            printTicket.Duplexing = Duplexing.TwoSidedLongEdge;
        }
        else if (rbDuplexing3.IsEnabled
                && rbDuplexing3.IsChecked == true)
```

```
            {
                printTicket.Duplexing = Duplexing.TwoSidedShortEdge;
            }

            //Determine the Collation setting.
            if (rbCollation1.IsEnabled
                && rbDuplexing2.IsChecked == true)
            {
                printTicket.Collation = Collation.Collated;
            }
            else if (rbCollation2.IsEnabled
                    && rbDuplexing2.IsChecked == true)
            {
                printTicket.Collation = Collation.Uncollated;
            }

            //Determine the Orientation value.
            if (rbOrientation1.IsEnabled
                && rbOrientation1.IsChecked == true)
            {
                printTicket.PageOrientation = PageOrientation.Landscape;
            }
            else if (rbOrientation2.IsEnabled
                    && rbOrientation2.IsChecked == true)
            {
                printTicket.PageOrientation = PageOrientation.Portrait;
            }
        }
    }
}
```

7-6. Print a Simple Document

Problem

You have a System.Windows.Documents.FixedDocument or System.Windows.Documents.FlowDocument containing a single page that you want to print. The document may have been created programmatically or loaded from an XPS package.

Solution

Printing a FixedDocument or FlowDocument is a relatively simple process and not too unlike that of printing a Visual (recipe 7-3). Obtain a System.Windows.Printing.PrintQueue object, and use it to create a System.Windows.Xps.XpsDocumentWriter. The XpsDocumentWriter is used to write the document using overloaded versions of the Write method, writing the document to the PrintQueue against which it was created.

■**Note** You will need to add references to the System.Printing and ReachFramework assemblies in your project for this example.

How It Works

In this recipe, a PrintQueue is obtained through displaying a System.Windows.Dialogs.PrintDialog to the user, allowing the user to choose a printer to print the document on (see recipe 7-3 for more information on obtaining a PrintQueue). From this, a PrintQueue object is obtained, and an XpsDocumentWriter is created using the CreateXpsDocumentWriter method on the PrintQueue.

The document that is to be printed can then be passed to the Write method of the XpsDocumentWriter. For FixedDocument objects, the FixedDocument itself is passed to the write method, because XPS documents are themselves fixed documents. For FlowDocument objects, though, you need to get the document's DocumentPaginator to pass in. This is achieved by casting the FlowDocument object to an IDocumentPaginatorSource and reading the DocumentPaginator property. This can then be passed to the XpsDocumentWriter.

Each page in the document will be printed onto a separate page of paper and will be sent to the printer at full size that it appears in the document. As such, you may want to scale each page to the size selected by the user in the PrintDialog. You can find the target paper size by looking at the System.Printing.PrintTicket that gets created based on the user's choices in the PrintDialog.

The Code

```xml
<Window
  x:Class="Recipe_07_06.Window1"
  xmlns="http://schemas.microsoft.com/winfx/2006/xaml/presentation"
  xmlns:x="http://schemas.microsoft.com/winfx/2006/xaml"
  Title="Window1"
  Height="100"
  Width="300">
  <StackPanel>
    <Button
      Margin="10,5"
      Content="Print FixedDocument"
      Click="btnPrintFixedDocument_Click"
    />
    <Button
      Margin="10,5"
      Content="Print FlowDocument"
      Click="btnPrintFlowDocument_Click"
    />
  </StackPanel>
</Window>
```

```csharp
using System.Printing;
using System.Windows;
using System.Windows.Controls;
using System.Windows.Documents;
using System.Windows.Markup;
using System.Windows.Media;
using System.Windows.Shapes;
using System.Windows.Xps;

namespace Recipe_07_06
{
    /// <summary>
    /// Interaction logic for Window1.xaml
    /// </summary>
    public partial class Window1 : Window
    {
        public Window1()
        {
            InitializeComponent();
        }

        public FixedDocument GetFixedDocument()
        {
            // Create a FixedDocument
            FixedDocument fixedDocument = new FixedDocument();
            //Set the size of each page to be A4.
            Size a4PageSize = new Size(8.5 * 96, 11 * 96);
            fixedDocument.DocumentPaginator.PageSize = a4PageSize;

            //Add 5 pages to the document.
            for (int i = 1; i < 6; i++)
            {
                PageContent pageContent = new PageContent();
                fixedDocument.Pages.Add(pageContent);

                FixedPage fixedPage = new FixedPage();
                //Create a TextBlock
                TextBlock textBlock = new TextBlock();
                textBlock.Margin = new Thickness(10, 10, 0, 0);
                textBlock.Text = string.Format("Page {0}", 1);
                textBlock.FontSize = 24;
                //Add the TextBlock to the page.
                fixedPage.Children.Add(textBlock);
                //Add the page to the page's content.
                ((IAddChild)pageContent).AddChild(fixedPage);
            }
```

```
        return fixedDocument;
    }

    public FlowDocument GetFlowDocument()
    {
        //Programmatically create a FlowDocument
        FlowDocument flowDocument = new FlowDocument();

        //Create a new paragraph to add to the document.
        Paragraph paragraph = new Paragraph();

        //Add some text to the paragraph.
        paragraph.Inlines.Add("This is the printed document.");

        //Add the paragraph to the document.
        flowDocument.Blocks.Add(paragraph);

        //Create a new figure and add an Ellipse to it.
        Figure figure = new Figure();
        paragraph = new Paragraph();
        Ellipse ellipse = new Ellipse();
        ellipse.Width = 50;
        ellipse.Height = 50;
        ellipse.Fill = Brushes.Red;
        ellipse.StrokeThickness = 2;
        ellipse.Stroke = Brushes.Black;
        paragraph.Inlines.Add(ellipse);

        //Add the figure to a paragraph.
        figure.Blocks.Add(paragraph);

        //Insert the figure into a new paragraph.
        flowDocument.Blocks.Add(new Paragraph(figure));

        //Add a final paragraph
        paragraph = new Paragraph();
        paragraph.Inlines.Add("This text is not intended to be read.");

        flowDocument.Blocks.Add(paragraph);

        return flowDocument;

    }
```

```
//Obtain a reference to a PrintQueue using a PrintDialog.
public PrintQueue GetPrintQueue()
{
    PrintDialog printDialog = new PrintDialog();

    bool? result = printDialog.ShowDialog();

    if (result.HasValue && result.Value)
    {
        return printDialog.PrintQueue;
    }

    return null;
}

//Prints a FlowDocument
public void PrintFlowDocument(PrintQueue printQueue)
{
    FlowDocument flowDocument = GetFlowDocument();

    DocumentPaginator documentPaginator =
        ((IDocumentPaginatorSource)flowDocument).DocumentPaginator;

    XpsDocumentWriter writer =
        PrintQueue.CreateXpsDocumentWriter(printQueue);

    writer.Write(documentPaginator);
}

//Prints a FixedDocument
public void PrintFixedDocument(PrintQueue printQueue)
{
    FixedDocument fixedDocument = GetFixedDocument();

    XpsDocumentWriter writer =
        PrintQueue.CreateXpsDocumentWriter(printQueue);

    writer.Write(fixedDocument);
}

//Event handler for the click event of the Print FixedDocument button.
private void btnPrintFixedDocument_Click(object sender, RoutedEventArgs e)
{
    PrintFixedDocument(GetPrintQueue());
}
```

```
        //Event handler for the click event of the Print FlowDocument button.
        private void btnPrintFlowDocument_Click(object sender, RoutedEventArgs e)
        {
            PrintFlowDocument(GetPrintQueue());
        }
    }
}
```

7-7. Asynchronously Print a Multipage FixedDocument

Problem

You need to print a multipage System.Windows.Documents.FlowDocument with each page being printed onto a separate page of paper. Because your multipage document could be quite large, you will want to perform the printing asynchronously, keeping the user informed of the progress and allowing them to cancel the print job if they want.

Solution

Use the System.Windows.Xps.XpsDocumentWriter.WriteAsync method, hooking into its various events to keep the user informed of the printing progress as well as to offer the chance to cancel the job.

Note You will need to add references to the System.Printing and ReachFramework assemblies in your project for this example.

How It Works

When printing a document using the Write method of an XpsDocumentWriter, the calling thread will wait until the Write method has completed. This is fine for small documents, but for larger documents, the Write method will take longer, preventing any further work on the UI thread.

To maintain a responsive UI, provide the user with feedback on the progress of the printing, and allow the printing to be cancelled, the printing needs to be performed asynchronously. Luckily, the XpsDocumentWriter easily allows for asynchronous printing with only a little extra code.

Obtaining a System.Windows.Printing.PrintQueue and XpsDocumentWriter for asynchronous printing is the same as when printing a Visual (see recipe 7-3). Once an XpsDocumentWriter has been created, instead of calling Write, WriteAsync is used. The extra code required is in adding handlers to the WritingProgressChanged and WritingCompleted events, which are raised by the XpsDocumentWriter once the writing begins. Code to cancel the printing is also required.

The `WritingProgressChanged` event is raised continuously by the `XpsDocumentWriter` as it writes each document part. A `System.Windows.Documents.Serialization.WritingProgressChangedEventArgs` object is passed to any methods handling the event. The event arguments detail the number of pages that have been written and a `WritingProgressChangeLevel` value indicating the scope of the event. The `WritingProgressChangeLevel` will be one of four possible values:

- `FixedDocumentSequenceWritingProgress`

- `FixedDocumentWritingProgress`

- `FixedPageWritingProgress`

- `None`

In this example, the value will be either `FixedDocumentWritingProgress` as pages are written or `FixedDocumentSequenceWritingProgress` as the final part of the document is written, indicating the printing is almost complete. Using the information in the event arguments, the user can be updated on the progress of the printing, for example, through a `System.Windows.Controls.ProgressBar` control.

The handler for the `WritingProgressCompleted` event is used to perform any cleaning up and determine whether the printing completed successfully.

Once the `WriteAsync` method has been called on the `XpsDocumentWriter`, the operation can be cancelled by calling the `CancelAsync` method on the same `XpsDocumentWriter`. This will stop the printing and fire off the `WritingProgressCompleted` event on the `XpsDocumentWriter`.

The `WritingCompleted` event will pass a `WritingCompletedEventArgs` object to the handler. The `WritingCompletedEventArgs` class derives from `System.ComponentModel.AsyncCompletedEventArgs` and provides information on whether the printing was cancelled or whether an error occurred. This information can then be relayed to the user if required.

■**Note** The objects being printed should not be released until printing has completed.

The Code

The following code demonstrates how to print a large `FixedDocument`, in an asynchronous manner, allowing the user to cancel the printing process. A large `FixedDocument` is generated and stored in a `DocumentViewer`. The Print button on the document viewer is overridden, executing the custom printing progress, starting with presenting the user with a `PrintDialog`. Once the `PrintDialog` is done with, a mask is displayed over the window, graying out the window and displaying a progress bar, which shows the current progress of the print job, and a button that allows the user to cancel the print job.

The following code defines the content of the application's `Window1.xaml` file:

```
<Window
  x:Class="Recipe_07_07.Window1"
  xmlns="http://schemas.microsoft.com/winfx/2006/xaml/presentation"
  xmlns:x="http://schemas.microsoft.com/winfx/2006/xaml"
```

```xml
      Title="Window1" Height="400" Width="600">
      <Grid>

        <DocumentViewer x:Name="dvDocumentViewer">
          <DocumentViewer.CommandBindings>
            <CommandBinding
              Command="ApplicationCommands.Print"
              Executed="DocumentViewer_PrintDocument" />
          </DocumentViewer.CommandBindings>
        </DocumentViewer>

        <Grid
          x:Name="spProgressMask"
          Background="#66000000"
          Visibility="Collapsed">
          <StackPanel
            VerticalAlignment="Center"
            HorizontalAlignment="Center">
            <TextBlock Text="Printing document..." />
            <ProgressBar
              x:Name="pbPrintProgress"
              Minimum="0"
              Maximum="100"
              Value="0"
              Width="100"
              Height="20"
            />
            <Button Content="Cancel" Click="btnCancelPrint_Click" />
          </StackPanel>
        </Grid>
      </Grid>
    </Window>
```

The following code defines the content of the Window1.xaml.cs code-behind file:

```csharp
using System;
using System.Printing;
using System.Windows;
using System.Windows.Controls;
using System.Windows.Documents;
using System.Windows.Documents.Serialization;
using System.Windows.Markup;
using System.Windows.Media;
using System.Windows.Shapes;
using System.Windows.Xps;
```

```csharp
namespace Recipe_07_07
{
    public partial class Window1 : Window
    {
        public Window1()
        {
            InitializeComponent();

            dvDocumentViewer.Document = CreateMultiPageFixedDocument();
        }

        //Creates a FixedDocument with lots of pages.
        public FixedDocument CreateMultiPageFixedDocument()
        {
            FixedDocument fixedDocument = new FixedDocument();
            fixedDocument.DocumentPaginator.PageSize = new Size(96 * 8.5, 96 * 11);

            //Create a large number of pages so we can see the progress
            //bar and cancel button in action.
            for (int i = 0; i < 1000; i++)
            {
                PageContent pageContent = new PageContent();
                fixedDocument.Pages.Add(pageContent);
                FixedPage fixedPage = new FixedPage();

                //Add a canvas with a TextBlock and a Rectangle as children.
                Canvas canvas = new Canvas();
                fixedPage.Children.Add(canvas);

                TextBlock textBlock = new TextBlock();

                textBlock.Text =
                    string.Format("Page {0} / {1}\n\nThis Is Page {0}.",
                                i + 1, 1000);

                textBlock.FontSize = 24;
                canvas.Children.Add(textBlock);

                Rectangle rect = new Rectangle();
                rect.Width = 200;
                rect.Height = 200;
                rect.Fill =
                    new SolidColorBrush(Color.FromArgb(200, 20, 50, 200));
                canvas.Children.Add(rect);

                ((IAddChild)pageContent).AddChild(fixedPage);
            }
```

```csharp
        return fixedDocument;
    }

    //Present the user with a PrintDialog and use it to
    //obtain a reference to a PrintQueue.
    public PrintQueue GetPrintQueue()
    {
        PrintDialog printDialog = new PrintDialog();

        bool? result = printDialog.ShowDialog();

        if (result.HasValue && result.Value)
        {
            return printDialog.PrintQueue;
        }

        return null;
    }

    //Keep a reference to the XPS document writer we use.
    private XpsDocumentWriter xpsDocumentWriter;

    public void PrintDocumentAsync(FixedDocument fixedDocument)
    {
        //Get a hold of a PrintQueue.
        PrintQueue printQueue = GetPrintQueue();

        //Create a document writer to print to.
        xpsDocumentWriter = PrintQueue.CreateXpsDocumentWriter(printQueue);

        //We want to know when the printing progress has changed so
        //we can update the UI.
        xpsDocumentWriter.WritingProgressChanged +=
            PrintAsync_WritingProgressChanged;

        //We also want to know when the print job has finished, allowing
        //us to check for any problems.
        xpsDocumentWriter.WritingCompleted += PrintAsync_Completed;

        StartLongPrintingOperation(fixedDocument.Pages.Count);

        //Print the FixedDocument asynchronously.
        xpsDocumentWriter.WriteAsync(fixedDocument);
    }

    private void PrintAsync_WritingProgressChanged(object sender,
        WritingProgressChangedEventArgs e)
```

```csharp
{
    //Another page of the document has been printed. Update the UI.
    pbPrintProgress.Value = e.Number;
}

private void PrintAsync_Completed(object sender,
    WritingCompletedEventArgs e)
{
    string message;
    MessageBoxImage messageBoxImage;

    //Check to see whether there was a problem with the printing.
    if (e.Error != null)
    {
        messageBoxImage = MessageBoxImage.Error;
        message =
            string.Format("An error occurred whilst printing.\n\n{0}",
                          e.Error.Message);
    }
    else if (e.Cancelled)
    {
        messageBoxImage = MessageBoxImage.Stop;
        message = "Printing was cancelled by the user.";
    }
    else
    {
        messageBoxImage = MessageBoxImage.Information;
        message = "Printing completed successfully.";
    }

    MessageBox.Show(message, "Recipe_07_07",
                    MessageBoxButton.OK, messageBoxImage);

    StopLongPrintingOperation();
}

private void StartLongPrintingOperation(int pages)
{
    pbPrintProgress.Value = 0;
    pbPrintProgress.Maximum = pages;

    spProgressMask.Visibility = Visibility.Visible;
}
```

```
        private void StopLongPrintingOperation()
        {
            spProgressMask.Visibility = Visibility.Collapsed;
        }

        private void DocumentViewer_PrintDocument(object sender, EventArgs e)
        {
            PrintDocumentAsync(CreateMultiPageFixedDocument());
        }

        private void btnCancelPrint_Click(object sender, RoutedEventArgs e)
        {
            //The user has clicked the Cancel button.
            //First ensure we have a valid XpsDocumentWriter.
            if (xpsDocumentWriter != null)
            {
                //Cancel the job.
                xpsDocumentWriter.CancelAsync();
            }
        }
    }
}
```

7-8. Programmatically Create and Save a Simple FixedDocument

Problem

You need to create a simple System.Windows.Documents.FixedDocument consisting of a few pages where each page will display some text. You also need to be able to save this document to disk using an XPS document.

Solution

Create a FixedDocument, and add as many System.Windows.Documents.FixedPage objects as required. The visual content of each page is built up by adding elements as children of the FixedPage. Once the FixedDocument is built, it is saved to disk using an XPS document.

How It Works

A FixedDocument consists of a collection of FixedPage objects. Each FixedPage can contain any number of controls including text, images, custom controls, and so on.

The FixedPage object is derived from FrameworkElement and as such has a child collection of type UIElementCollection.

The Code

The following XAML defines a System.Windows.Window that contains a System.Windows.Controls.
DocumentViewer and a System.Windows.Controls.Button. When the Window is loaded, a
FixedDocument is created and displayed in the DocumentViewer.

The Button is used to initiate the save progress; it displays a System.Windows.Forms.
SaveDialog to the user and allows them to specify where to save the XPS document, which
contains the FixedDocument.

```
<Window
  x:Class="Recipe_07_08.Window1"
  xmlns="http://schemas.microsoft.com/winfx/2006/xaml/presentation"
  xmlns:x="http://schemas.microsoft.com/winfx/2006/xaml"
  Title-"Window1"
  Height="600"
  Width="800"
  Loaded="Window_Loaded">
  <Grid>
    <Grid.RowDefinitions>
      <RowDefinition Height="*" />
      <RowDefinition Height="25" />
    </Grid.RowDefinitions>

    <DocumentViewer x:Name="dvDocumentViewer"  />

    <Button
      Grid.Row="1"
      Content="Save Document"
      Click="btnSaveDocument_Click"
    />
  </Grid>
</Window>
```

The following code defines the content of the Window1.xaml.cs file:

```
using System.IO;
using System.IO.Packaging;
using System.Windows;
using System.Windows.Controls;
using System.Windows.Documents;
using System.Windows.Markup;
using System.Windows.Xps;
using System.Windows.Xps.Packaging;
using Microsoft.Win32;
```

```
namespace Recipe_07_08
{
    /// <summary>
    /// Interaction logic for Window1.xaml
    /// </summary>
    public partial class Window1 : Window
    {
        public Window1()
        {
            InitializeComponent();
        }

        //Creates a FixedDocument and places it in the document viewer.
        private void Window_Loaded(object sender, RoutedEventArgs e)
        {
            dvDocumentViewer.Document = CreateMultiPageFixedDocument();
        }

        public FixedDocument CreateMultiPageFixedDocument()
        {
            FixedDocument fixedDocument = new FixedDocument();

            //Set the size of each page to be A4 (8.5" x 11").
            Size a4PageSize = new Size(8.5 * 96, 11 * 96);
            fixedDocument.DocumentPaginator.PageSize = a4PageSize;

            //Add 5 pages to the document.
            for (int i = 1; i < 6; i++)
            {
                PageContent pageContent = new PageContent();
                fixedDocument.Pages.Add(pageContent);

                FixedPage fixedPage = new FixedPage();
                //Create a TextBlock
                TextBlock textBlock = new TextBlock();
                textBlock.Margin = new Thickness(10, 10, 0, 0);
                textBlock.Text = string.Format("Page {0}", i);
                textBlock.FontSize = 24;
                //Add the TextBlock to the page.
                fixedPage.Children.Add(textBlock);
                //Add the page to the page's content.
                ((IAddChild)pageContent).AddChild(fixedPage);
            }

            return fixedDocument;
        }
```

```csharp
//Handles the click event of the save button defined in markup.
private void btnSaveDocument_Click(object sender, RoutedEventArgs e)
{
    //Show a save dialog and get a file path.
    string filePath = ShowSaveDialog();

    //If we didn't get a path, don't try to save.
    if (string.IsNullOrEmpty(filePath))
    {
        return;
    }

    //Save the document to disk to the given file path.
    SaveDocument(filePath, dvDocumentViewer.Document as FixedDocument);
}

//Present the user with a save dialog and return a path to a file.
private string ShowSaveDialog()
{
    SaveFileDialog saveFileDialog = new SaveFileDialog();
    saveFileDialog.Filter = "XPS Files | *.xps";
    saveFileDialog.OverwritePrompt = true;
    saveFileDialog.CheckFileExists = false;
    saveFileDialog.DefaultExt = ".xps";

    if (saveFileDialog.ShowDialog(this) == true)
    {
        return saveFileDialog.FileName;
    }

    return null;
}

//Save the document to disk to the given file path.
private void SaveDocument(string fileName, FixedDocument document)
{
    //Delete any existing file.
    File.Delete(fileName);

    //Create a new XpsDocument at the given location.
    XpsDocument xpsDocument =
        new XpsDocument(fileName, FileAccess.ReadWrite,
                        CompressionOption.NotCompressed);

    //Create a new XpsDocumentWriter for the XpsDocument object.
    XpsDocumentWriter xdw = XpsDocument.CreateXpsDocumentWriter(xpsDocument);
```

```
            //Write the document to the Xps file.
            xdw.Write(document);

            //Close down the saved document.
            xpsDocument.Close();
        }
    }
}
```

7-9. Use Figures and Floaters in a FlowDocument

Problem

You need to create a System.Windows.Documents.FlowDocument, which contains inline content such as images, tables, and so on.

Solution

Use the System.Windows.Documents.Floater and System.Windows.Documents.Figure objects to place rich content inline with your text.

How It Works

Floater and Figure objects allow content to be placed in a FlowDocument that is positioned independently of the document's content flow. Floater and Figure objects are for use only in FlowDocument objects and cannot be used in a System.Windows.Documents.FixedDocument.

There are a few differences between Figure and Floater that need to be considered when choosing which to use in a document. Generally, you will want to use a Figure when you require control over the dimensions and location of the Figure's content. If this level of control isn't required, a Floater will be the better choice.

A Floater cannot be positioned in a document; it will simply be placed wherever space can be made available, whereas a Figure can be placed relatively using anchors or absolutely using pixel offsets.

Figure and Floater also differ in the way they can be sized. A Figure's height and width can be sized relative to a page, column, or content or absolutely using pixel values. For relative sizing, expressions are used to indicate by how much the Figure should be sized and relative to what object; for example, use "0.8 page" to occupy 80 percent of the height or width of a page, "0.5 column" to occupy 50 percent of the height or width of a column, or "0.1 content" to occupy 10 percent of the height or width of the content in which the Figure is placed. For page and content relative sizing, 1.0 is the upper limit of the allowed scaling; for example, "2 page" will simply be treated as "1 page."

Sizing a Floater is limited to the width of the Floater, and this can be set using only an absolute pixel value; in other words, "0.25 column" is not a valid value for the width of a Floater. The width of a Floater is also restrained to the width of a column, with the width of a column being the default width for a Floater. If the specified width is greater than the width of a column, the size is capped at the width of a column.

The final major difference between a `Figure` and `Floater` is the way in which the two objects are paginated. A `Figure` will not paginate, and as such, any content that does not fit will simply be clipped. The content within a `Floater`, on the other hand, will be split across columns and pages.

The Code

The following XAML code defines a window with a `System.Windows.Controls.FlowDocumentReader`. Inside the `FlowDocumentReader` is a sample `FlowDocument` containing some paragraphs of text, a list, a `Figure`, and a `Floater`. Resizing the window will demonstrate the way in which the `Floater` and `Figure` behave in terms of flow layout.

```
<Window
  x:Class="Recipe_07_09.Window1"
  xmlns="http://schemas.microsoft.com/winfx/2006/xaml/presentation"
  xmlns:x="http://schemas.microsoft.com/winfx/2006/xaml"
  Title="Recipe_07_09
  Height="300"
  Width="300">
  <Grid>
    <FlowDocumentReader>
      <FlowDocument>
        <Paragraph>
          <Run>This is a simple run of text inside a paragraph.</Run>
          <Run>This is another simple run of text inside a paragraph.</Run>
          <Run>This is another simple run of text inside a paragraph.</Run>
          <Run>This is another simple run of text inside a paragraph.</Run>
        </Paragraph>
        <Paragraph>
          <Run>This is a simple run of text inside another paragraph.</Run>
          <Run>This is another simple run of text inside another paragraph.</Run>
          <Run>This is another simple run of text inside another paragraph.</Run>
          <Run>This is another simple run of text inside another paragraph.</Run>
        </Paragraph>
        <Paragraph>
          <Figure HorizontalAnchor="PageCenter" VerticalAnchor="PageCenter"
                  Background="WhiteSmoke" BorderThickness="2" BorderBrush="Black">
            <Paragraph>This is a simple paragraph inside a Figure.
              This is a simple paragraph inside a Figure.
              This is a simple paragraph inside a Figure.
              This is a simple paragraph inside a Figure.
              This is a simple paragraph inside a Figure.
            </Paragraph>
          </Figure>
        </Paragraph>
        <Paragraph>
          <Bold>This is a line of bold text inside another paragraph.</Bold>
          <Bold>This is another line of bold text inside another paragraph.</Bold>
```

```
            <Bold>This is another line of bold text inside another paragraph.</Bold>
            <Bold>This is another line of bold text inside another paragraph.</Bold>
          </Paragraph>
          <List>
            <ListItem><Paragraph>This is a list item.</Paragraph></ListItem>
            <ListItem><Paragraph>This is a list item.</Paragraph></ListItem>
            <ListItem><Paragraph>
                <Bold>This is a bold list item.</Bold>
            </Paragraph></ListItem>
          </List>
          <Paragraph>
            <Floater Background="Silver">
              <Paragraph>
                This is a simple paragraph inside a floater.
                This is a simple paragraph inside a floater.
                This is a simple paragraph inside a floater.
                This is a simple paragraph inside a floater.
                This is a simple paragraph inside a floater.
              </Paragraph>
            </Floater>
          </Paragraph>
        </FlowDocument>
      </FlowDocumentReader>
    </Grid>
</Window>
```

7-10. Programmatically Create and Save a FlowDocument

Problem

You need to create a simple `System.Windows.Documents.FlowDocument` in code and save it to disk as a `.xaml` file.

Solution

Open an existing XPS document for reading, and extract the document content from the file. The content is then displayed in a `System.Windows.Controls.RichTextBox` where it can be edited. Once editing is complete, the content is then saved to the XPS document.

How It Works

Loading a document into a document viewer is similar to that shown in recipe 7-6, which loads a `System.Windows.Documents.FixedDocument` from a `System.Windows.Xps.Packaging.XpsDocument`. The document is loaded and then placed into a `FlowDocumentPaginator`. This can then be provided as the content to a `RichTextBox` where the user can edit the content.

The Code

```xml
<Window
  x:Class="Recipe_07_10.Window1"
  xmlns="http://schemas.microsoft.com/winfx/2006/xaml/presentation"
  xmlns:x="http://schemas.microsoft.com/winfx/2006/xaml"
  Title="Window1"
  Height="300"
  Width="300"
  Loaded="Window_Loaded">
  <DockPanel>
    <Button
      DockPanel.Dock="Bottom"
      Height="25"
      Content="Save..."
      Click="btnSave_Click"
    />

    <FlowDocumentReader x:Name="fdrViewer" />
  </DockPanel>
</Window>
```

The following code defines the content of the code-behind file for the previous markup:

```csharp
using System;
using System.IO;
using System.Windows;
using System.Windows.Documents;
using System.Windows.Markup;
using System.Windows.Media;
using System.Windows.Shapes;
using System.Xml;
using Microsoft.Win32;

namespace Recipe_07_10
{
    /// <summary>
    /// Interaction logic for Window1.xaml
    /// </summary>
    public partial class Window1 : Window
    {
        public Window1()
        {
            InitializeComponent();
        }

        /// <summary>
        /// This method handles the click event on the only button
```

```csharp
/// in the application's main window. The user is presented
/// with a dialog in which a file path is chosen. A call
/// to the save method is then made.
/// </summary>
private void btnSave_Click(object sender, RoutedEventArgs e)
{
    string filePath = ShowSaveDialog();

    if (string.IsNullOrEmpty(filePath))
    {
        return;
    }

    SaveFile(filePath, fdrViewer.Document);
}

/// <summary>
/// Creates and displays a SaveFileDialog allowing the user to
/// select a location to save the document to.
/// </summary>
/// <returns>
/// When the save dialog is closed via the OK button, the
/// method returns the chosen file path; otherwise it returns
/// null.
/// </returns>
private string ShowSaveDialog()
{
    SaveFileDialog saveFileDialog = new SaveFileDialog();
    saveFileDialog.Filter = "XAML Files | *.xaml";
    saveFileDialog.OverwritePrompt = true;
    saveFileDialog.CheckFileExists = false;
    saveFileDialog.DefaultExt = ".xaml";

    if (saveFileDialog.ShowDialog(this) == true)
    {
        return saveFileDialog.FileName;
    }

    return null;
}

/// <summary>
/// Saves a FixedDocument to a .xaml file at the target location.
/// </summary>
/// <param name="fileName">
/// The target location for the document.
/// </param>
```

```csharp
/// <param name="documentSource">
/// An IDocumentPaginatorSource for the FixedDocument to be saved
/// to disk.
/// </param>
private void SaveFile(string fileName,
                      IDocumentPaginatorSource documentSource)
{
    XmlTextWriter xmlWriter = null;
    TextWriter writer = null;
    Stream file = null;

    try
    {
        file = File.Create(fileName);
        writer = new StreamWriter(file);

        xmlWriter = new XmlTextWriter(writer);

        // Set serialization mode
        XamlDesignerSerializationManager xamlManager =
            new XamlDesignerSerializationManager(xmlWriter);

        // Serialize
        XamlWriter.Save(documentSource.DocumentPaginator.Source,
                        xamlManager);

    }
    catch (Exception e)
    {
        string msg = string.Format("Error occurred during saving.{0}{0}{1}",
            Environment.NewLine,
            e.Message);

        MessageBox.Show(msg,
                        "Recipe_07_10",
                        MessageBoxButton.OK,
                        MessageBoxImage.Error);
    }
    finally
    {
        if (!ReferenceEquals(xmlWriter, null))
        {
            xmlWriter.Close();
        }
```

```csharp
            if (!ReferenceEquals(writer, null))
            {
                writer.Close();
            }

            if (!ReferenceEquals(file, null))
            {
                file.Close();
            }
        }
    }

    private void Window_Loaded(object sender, RoutedEventArgs e)
    {
        //Programmatically create a FlowDocument
        FlowDocument flowDocument = new FlowDocument();

        //Create a new paragraph to add to the document.
        Paragraph paragraph = new Paragraph();

        //Add some text to the paragraph.
        paragraph.Inlines.Add("This is a paragraph.");
        paragraph.Inlines.Add(" This is a paragraph.");
        paragraph.Inlines.Add(" This is a paragraph.");
        paragraph.Inlines.Add(" This is a paragraph.");
        paragraph.Inlines.Add(" This is a paragraph.");
        paragraph.Inlines.Add(" This is a paragraph.");
        paragraph.Inlines.Add(" This is a paragraph.");
        paragraph.Inlines.Add(" This is a paragraph.");

        //Add the paragraph to the document.
        flowDocument.Blocks.Add(paragraph);

        //Create a new figure and add an Ellipse to it.
        Figure figure = new Figure();
        paragraph = new Paragraph();
        Ellipse ellipse = new Ellipse();
        ellipse.Width = 50;
        ellipse.Height = 50;
        ellipse.Fill = Brushes.Red;
        ellipse.StrokeThickness = 2;
        ellipse.Stroke = Brushes.Black;
        paragraph.Inlines.Add(ellipse);

        //Add the figure to a paragraph.
        figure.Blocks.Add(paragraph);
```

```
//Insert the figure into a new paragraph.
flowDocument.Blocks.Add(new Paragraph(figure));

//Add a final paragraph
paragraph = new Paragraph();
paragraph.Inlines.Add("This is another paragraph.");
paragraph.Inlines.Add(" This is another paragraph.");
paragraph.Inlines.Add(" This is another paragraph.");
paragraph.Inlines.Add(" This is another paragraph.");
paragraph.Inlines.Add(" This is another paragraph.");
paragraph.Inlines.Add(" This is another paragraph.");
paragraph.Inlines.Add(" This is another paragraph.");
paragraph.Inlines.Add(" This is another paragraph.");

flowDocument.Blocks.Add(paragraph);

//Now set the content of the document reader to the
//new FlowDocument
fdrViewer.Document = flowDocument;
        }
    }
}
```

7-11. Asynchronously Save a FixedDocument to an XPS File

Problem

You need to write a System.Windows.Documents.FixedDocument to an XPS document file stored on disk. Because of the possibility of large files, the writing needs to be performed asynchronously so as to maintain a responsive UI.

Solution

XPS documents are actually System.Windows.Documents.FixedDocument objects and can be created from a range of object types. Create a System.Windows.Xps.XpsDocument in memory, pointing to a given location on disk. Then create a System.Windows.Xps.XpsDocumentWriter for the document, and write the content to be saved to the XpsDocument using the XpsDocumentWriter.WriteAsync method.

How It Works

Saving content to an XpsDocument on disk is similar to printing content (recipe 7-6). In this instance, we create a new XpsDocument in the required location on a physical storage device using the System.IO.FileAccess.ReadWrite mode. An XpsDocumentWriter is then created for the XpsDocument using the static method XpsDocument.CreateXpsDocumentWriter.

When the WriteAsync method gets called on the XpsDocumentWriter, it will now write to the same XPS file as the XpsDocument with which it was created. By hooking into the various events on the XpsDocumentWriter, the UI can be kept up-to-date, and it allows the user to cancel the saving if required.

The Code

> **Note** You will need to add a project reference to System.Printing and ReachFramework.

> **Caution** The following example generates an XPS document with 1,000 pages. On a dual-core machine with 2GB RAM, this allows a good period of time for interaction with the progress mask. You may want to reduce the number of pages that are created if you experience performance issues by adjusting the constant value passed to the CreateFixedPageDocument method from Window_Loaded.

```xml
<Window
  x:Class="Recipe_07_11.Window1"
  xmlns="http://schemas.microsoft.com/winfx/2006/xaml/presentation"
  xmlns:x="http://schemas.microsoft.com/winfx/2006/xaml"
  Title="Window1"
  Height="600"
  Width="800"
  Loaded="Window_Loaded">
  <Grid>
    <DockPanel>
      <Button
        DockPanel.Dock="Bottom"
        Click="btnSave_Click"
        Content="Save As..."
      />
      <DocumentViewer
        x:Name="dvDocumentViewer"
      />
    </DockPanel>

    <Grid
      x:Name="spProgressMask"
      Background="#66000000"
      Visibility="Collapsed">
      <StackPanel
        VerticalAlignment="Center"
        HorizontalAlignment="Center">
```

```
      <TextBlock Text="Saving document..." />
      <ProgressBar
        x:Name="pbSaveProgress"
        Minimum="0"
        Maximum="100"
        Value="0"
        Width="100"
        Height="20"
      />
      <Button
        Content="Cancel"
        Click="btnCancelSave_Click" />
    </StackPanel>
  </Grid>
 </Grid>
</Window>
```

The following code defines the content of the `Window1.xaml.cs` file:

```
using System.IO;
using System.Windows;
using System.Windows.Controls;
using System.Windows.Documents;
using System.Windows.Documents.Serialization;
using System.Windows.Markup;
using System.Windows.Xps;
using System.Windows.Xps.Packaging;
using Microsoft.Win32;

namespace Recipe_07_11
{
    /// <summary>
    /// Interaction logic for Window1.xaml
    /// </summary>
    public partial class Window1 : Window
    {
        private XpsDocumentWriter xdw = null;

        public Window1()
        {
            InitializeComponent();
        }

        private void btnSave_Click(object sender, RoutedEventArgs e)
        {
            //Present the user with a save dialog, getting the path
            //to a file where the document will be saved.
            SaveFileDialog saveFileDialog = new SaveFileDialog();
```

```
            saveFileDialog.Filter = ".xps|*.xps";
            saveFileDialog.OverwritePrompt = true;
            saveFileDialog.Title = "Save to Xps Document";

            //If the user cancelled the dialog, bail.
            if (saveFileDialog.ShowDialog(this) == false)
            {
                return;
            }

            //Save the document.
            SaveDocument(saveFileDialog.FileName,
                dvDocumentViewer.Document as FixedDocument);
        }

        private void SaveDocument(string fileName, FixedDocument document)
        {
            //Delete any existing file.
            File.Delete(fileName);

            //Create a new XpsDocument at the given location.
            XpsDocument xpsDocument =
                new XpsDocument(fileName, FileAccess.ReadWrite);

            //Create a new XpsDocumentWriter for the XpsDocument object.
            xdw = XpsDocument.CreateXpsDocumentWriter(xpsDocument);

            //We want to be notified of when the progress changes.
            xdw.WritingProgressChanged +=
                delegate(object sender, WritingProgressChangedEventArgs e)
                {   //Update the value of the progress bar.
                    pbSaveProgress.Value = e.Number;
                };

            //We want to be notified of when the operation is complete.
            xdw.WritingCompleted +=
                delegate(object sender, WritingCompletedEventArgs e)
                {
                    //We're finished with the XPS document, so close it.
                    //This step is important.
                    xpsDocument.Close();

                    string msg = "Saving complete.";

                    if (e.Error != null)
                    {
                        msg =
```

```
                        string.Format("An error occurred whilst " +
                                      "saving the document.\n\n{0}",
                                      e.Error.Message);
            }
            else if (e.Cancelled)
            {
                //Delete the incomplete file.
                File.Delete(fileName);

                msg =
                    string.Format("Saving cancelled by user.");
            }

            //Inform the user of the print operation's exit status.
            MessageBox.Show(msg,
                            "Recipe_07_11",
                            MessageBoxButton.OK,
                            MessageBoxImage.Information);

            spProgressMask.Visibility = Visibility.Collapsed;
        };

    //Show the long operation mask with the Cancel button and progress bar.
    spProgressMask.Visibility = Visibility.Visible;
    pbSaveProgress.Maximum = document.Pages.Count;
    pbSaveProgress.Value = 0;

    //Write the document to the XPS file asynchronously.
    xdw.WriteAsync(document);
}

private void btnCancelSave_Click(object sender, RoutedEventArgs e)
{
    //When the 'Cancel' button is clicked, we want to try and
    //stop the save process.
    if (xdw != null)
        xdw.CancelAsync();
}

private void Window_Loaded(object sender, RoutedEventArgs e)
{
    //Load the DocumentViewer with a simple FixedDocument.
    //A large number of pages are generated so that the progress
    //of the printing is slow enough to be observed.
    dvDocumentViewer.Document = CreateFixedPageDocument(1000);
}
```

```
private FixedDocument CreateFixedPageDocument(int numberOfPages)
{
    // Create a FixedDocument
    FixedDocument fixedDocument = new FixedDocument();
    fixedDocument.DocumentPaginator.PageSize = new Size(96 * 8.5, 96 * 11);

    for (int i = 0; i < numberOfPages; i++)
    {
        PageContent pageContent = new PageContent();
        fixedDocument.Pages.Add(pageContent);
        FixedPage fixedPage = new FixedPage();
        TextBlock textBlock = new TextBlock();
        textBlock.Text = string.Format("Page {0}", i);
        textBlock.FontSize = 24;
        fixedPage.Children.Add(textBlock);
        ((IAddChild)pageContent).AddChild(fixedPage);
    }

    return fixedDocument;
}
```

7-12. Display a Document

Problem

You need to display a System.Windows.Documents.FixedDocument or System.Windows.Documents.FlowDocument in your application.

Solution

Create a new instance of a System.Windows.Xps.Packaging.XpsDocument, passing in the path to the XPS file you want to load. A FixedDocumentSequence can then be retrieved from the XpsDocument and used to display the content of the file in a System.Windows.Controls.DocumentViewer in your application.

How It Works

Several controls are provided for viewing documents in WPF. The control you use for displaying a document will depend on the type of document being displayed and the functionality you want to offer the user. Each of the viewers provides built-in printing, text searching, and scaling. When displaying a FixedDocument, the choice is limited to a System.Windows.Controls.

DocumentViewer, whereas you have three options when it comes to displaying a FlowDocument. The possible controls are as follows:

- System.Windows.Controls.FlowDocumentPageViewer

- System.Windows.Controls.FlowDocumentReader

- System.Windows.Controls.FlowDocumentScrollViewer

The FlowDocumentReader is the most heavyweight of the three and allows the viewer to dynamically switch viewing modes. Three viewing modes are available; one displays the document a page at a time (single page), another displays two pages side by side (book reading format), and the last displays the document as a single, continuous page that the viewer scrolls through.

Should the requirements be such that the mode doesn't need to be dynamic, the FlowDocumentPageViewer can be used for displaying the document in terms of pages (single or book reading format), and the FlowDocumentScrollViewer can be used to display the document as a single scrollable page.

The Code

The following XAML defines a System.Windows.Window displaying a System.Windows.Controls. TabControl. The TabControl contains two System.Windows.Controls.TabItem objects, one of which contains a DocumentViewer for displaying a FixedDocument and the other contains a FlowDocumentReader for displaying a FlowDocument. Both TabItem elements also contain a Button, used for selecting a file to open and display in the appropriate viewer control.

```
<Window
  x:Class="Recipe_07_12.Window1"
  xmlns="http://schemas.microsoft.com/winfx/2006/xaml/presentation"
  xmlns:x="http://schemas.microsoft.com/winfx/2006/xaml"
  Title="Window1"
  Height="600"
  Width="800">
  <TabControl>
    <TabItem Header="Fixed Document">
      <DockPanel>
        <Button
          Height="24"
          Margin="5"
          DockPanel.Dock="Bottom"
          Content-"Open..."
          Click="btnOpenFixedDoc_Click"
        />
        <DocumentViewer x:Name="dvDocumentViewer" />
      </DockPanel>
    </TabItem>
    <TabItem Header="Flow Document">
      <DockPanel>
        <Button
```

```
            Height="24"
            Margin="5"
            DockPanel.Dock="Bottom"
            Content="Open..."
            Click="btnOpenFlowDoc_Click"
          />
          <FlowDocumentPageViewer x:Name="fdv"/>
        </DockPanel>
      </TabItem>
    </TabControl>
</Window>
```

The following code defines the content of the Window1.xaml.cs file:

```csharp
using System;
using System.IO;
using System.Windows;
using System.Windows.Documents;
using System.Windows.Markup;
using System.Windows.Xps.Packaging;
using System.Xml;
using Microsoft.Win32;

namespace Recipe_07_12
{
    /// <summary>
    /// Interaction logic for Window1.xaml
    /// </summary>
    public partial class Window1 : Window
    {
        public Window1()
        {
            InitializeComponent();
        }

        //Handles the click event of the 'Open...'
        //button for the fixed document viewer.
        private void btnOpenFixedDoc_Click(object sender,
            RoutedEventArgs e)
        {
            string filePath =
                GetFileName("XPS Document (*.xps)|*.xps");

            if (string.IsNullOrEmpty(filePath))
            {
                ShowFileOpenError(filePath);
                return;
            }
```

```csharp
    IDocumentPaginatorSource documentSource =
        OpenFixedDocument(filePath);

    if (documentSource == null)
    {
        ShowFileOpenError(filePath);
    }

    dvDocumentViewer.Document = documentSource;
}

//Handles the click event of the 'Open...'
//button for the flow document viewer.
private void btnOpenFlowDoc_Click(object sender,
    RoutedEventArgs e)
{
    string filePath =
        GetFileName("XAML Document (*.xaml)|*.xaml");

    if (string.IsNullOrEmpty(filePath))
    {
        ShowFileOpenError(filePath);
        return;
    }

    FlowDocument flowDocument = OpenFlowDocument(filePath);

    if (flowDocument == null)
    {
        ShowFileOpenError(filePath);
        return;
    }

    fdv.Document = flowDocument;
}

//Presents the user with an open file dialog and returns
//the path to any file they select to open.
private string GetFileName(string filter)
{
    //First get the file to be opened
    OpenFileDialog openFileDialog = new OpenFileDialog();
    openFileDialog.Filter = filter;
    openFileDialog.Multiselect = false;
    openFileDialog.CheckFileExists = true;
    openFileDialog.CheckPathExists = true;
```

```
        if (openFileDialog.ShowDialog() == true)
        {
            return openFileDialog.FileName;
        }

        return null;
    }

    private IDocumentPaginatorSource OpenFixedDocument(
        string fileName)
    {
        try
        {
            //Load the XpsDocument into memory.
            XpsDocument document =
                new XpsDocument(fileName, FileAccess.Read);

            if (document == null)
            {
                return null;
            }

            //Get an IDocumentPaginatorSource for the document.
            return document.GetFixedDocumentSequence();
        }
        catch (Exception)
        {
            return null;
        }
    }

    private FlowDocument OpenFlowDocument(string fileName)
    {
        Stream file = null;
        TextReader reader = null;
        XmlTextReader xmlReader = null;

        try
        {
            //Load the file into memory.
            file = File.OpenRead(fileName);
            reader = new StreamReader(file);
            //Create an XmlTextReader to use with
            //the XamlReader below.
            xmlReader = new XmlTextReader(reader);
```

```
            //Parse the XAML file and load the FlowDocument.
            return XamlReader.Load(xmlReader) as FlowDocument;
        }
        catch (Exception)
        {
            return null;
        }
        finally
        {
            if (file != null)
                file.Dispose();

            if (reader != null)
                reader.Dispose();

            if (xmlReader != null)
                xmlReader.Close();
        }
    }

    //Display a message if the file cannot be opened.
    private void ShowFileOpenError(string filePath)
    {
        string msg = string.Format("Unable to open " + filePath);
        MessageBox.Show(msg, "Recipe 7-12",
            MessageBoxButton.OK, MessageBoxImage.Error);
        return;
    }
    }
}
```

7-13. Annotate a Document with Sticky Notes

Problem

You are displaying a System.Windows.Documents.FixedDocument System.Windows.Documents. FlowDocument in your application, and you want to allow the user to annotate the document with sticky notes, just as you would with a hard-copy document.

Solution

Adding sticky notes to a document allows you to annotate sections of the document with text notes.

How It Works

Annotations are widely used on hard-copy documents and as such have been included in the document support in .NET 3.0. Sticky notes are a type of annotation that can be applied to content being displayed in any of the following controls:

- DocumentViewer

- FlowDocumentPageViewer

- FlowDocumentReader

- FlowDocumentScrollViewer

The Annotation APIs in the framework provide all the functionality to manage annotations but provide no entry point on the UI to do so. This requires a little extra work on your part. To make life easier, the System.Windows.Annotations.AnnotationService provides a collection of commands to manage the annotations in one of the previous controls. For the purpose of this recipe, the management of annotations will be handled in code.

A context menu item is added to the FlowDocumentViewer, which is where the handler will create the sticky note. This method retrieves the current username and then creates a new sticky note for the current text selection in the document viewer.

The newly created sticky note is placed into the AnnotationStore from where it can be retrieved later. (See recipe 7-15 for more information on AnnotationStore.)

The Code

The following XAML defines a Window containing a System.Windows.Controls.TabControl with two System.Windows.Controls.TabItem elements. The first TabItem contains a System.Windows.Controls.DocumentViewer, and the second contains a System.Windows.Controls.FixedDocumentReader.

When the Window is loaded, a simple FixedDocument and a simple FlowDocument are created and placed into the DocumentViewer and FlowDocumentReader, respectively. Adding sticky notes is as simple as selecting some text, right-clicking, and selecting the Add Comment menu item.

```xaml
<Window
  x:Class="Recipe_07_13.Window1"
  xmlns="http://schemas.microsoft.com/winfx/2006/xaml/presentation"
  xmlns:x="http://schemas.microsoft.com/winfx/2006/xaml"
  Title="Window1"
  Height="300"
  Width="300"
  Loaded="Window_Loaded">
  <TabControl>
    <TabItem Header="Fixed Document">
      <DocumentViewer x:Name="xdv">
        <DocumentViewer.ContextMenu>
          <ContextMenu>
            <MenuItem
              Header="Add Comment..."
```

```
                Click="Xdv_AddComment_Click" />
            </ContextMenu>
          </DocumentViewer.ContextMenu>
        </DocumentViewer>
      </TabItem>

      <TabItem Header="Flow Document">
        <FlowDocumentPageViewer x:Name="fdv">
          <FlowDocumentPageViewer.ContextMenu>
            <ContextMenu>
              <MenuItem
                Header="Add Comment..."
                Click="Fdv_AddComment_Click" />
            </ContextMenu>
          </FlowDocumentPageViewer.ContextMenu>
        </FlowDocumentPageViewer>
      </TabItem>
    </TabControl>
</Window>
```

The following code defines the content of the Window1.xaml.cs file:

```
using System;
using System.IO;
using System.Reflection;
using System.Windows;
using System.Windows.Annotations;
using System.Windows.Annotations.Storage;
using System.Windows.Documents;
using System.Windows.Media;
using System.Windows.Xps.Packaging;

namespace Recipe_07_13
{
    /// <summary>
    /// Interaction logic for Window1.xaml
    /// </summary>
    public partial class Window1 : Window
    {
        //FixedDoxument specifics
        AnnotationService fixedAnnotationService;
        AnnotationStore fixedAnntationStore;
        MemoryStream fixedAnnotationBuffer;

        //FlowDocument specifics
        AnnotationService flowAnnotationService;
        AnnotationStore flowAnntationStore;
        MemoryStream flowAnnotationBuffer;
```

```csharp
public Window1()
{
    InitializeComponent();
}

//When the Window is loaded, we want to get hold of some
//test document to try the sticky notes on, then
//start up the annotation services that make it possible.
private void Window_Loaded(object sender, RoutedEventArgs e)
{
    //Load in our sample FixedDocument
    LoadFixedDocument();
    //Create a new FlowDocument
    fdv.Document = CreateFlowDocument();

    //Start the annotation services
    StartFixedDocumentAnnotations();
    StartFlowDocumentAnnotations();
}

//Handles the user clicking the Add Comment context menu item
//on the document viewer in the FixedDocument tab.
private void Xdv_AddComment_Click(object sender, RoutedEventArgs e)
{
    //Get the current user's name and
    //use as the comment's author
    string userName = System.Environment.UserName;

    //The AnnotationHelper.CreateTextStickyNoteForSelection method
    //will throw an exception if no text is selected.
    try
    {
        AnnotationHelper.CreateTextStickyNoteForSelection(
            fixedAnnotationService, userName);
    }
    catch (InvalidOperationException)
    {
        MessageBox.Show("Please select some text to annotate.");
    }
}

//Handles the user clicking the Add Comment context menu item
//on the document viewer in the FlowDocument tab.
private void Fdv_AddComment_Click(object sender, RoutedEventArgs e)
{
    //Get the current user's name as the author
    string userName = System.Environment.UserName;
```

```csharp
        //The AnnotationHelper.CreateTextStickyNoteForSelection method
        //will throw an exception if no text is selected.
        try
        {
            AnnotationHelper.CreateTextStickyNoteForSelection(
                flowAnnotationService, userName);
        }
        catch (InvalidOperationException)
        {
            MessageBox.Show("Please select some text to annotate.");
        }
    }

    private void StartFixedDocumentAnnotations()
    {
        //Create a new annotation service for the fixed document viewer.
        fixedAnnotationService = new AnnotationService(xdv);

        //Open a stream for our annotation store.
        fixedAnnotationBuffer = new MemoryStream();

        //Create an AnnotationStore using the stream.
        fixedAnntationStore = new XmlStreamStore(fixedAnnotationBuffer);

        //Enable the AnnotationService against the new annotation store.
        fixedAnnotationService.Enable(fixedAnntationStore);
    }

    private void StartFlowDocumentAnnotations()
    {
        //Create a new annotation service for the fixed document viewer.
        flowAnnotationService = new AnnotationService(fdv);

        //Open a stream for our annotation store.
        flowAnnotationBuffer = new MemoryStream();

        //Create an AnnotationStore using the stream.
        flowAnntationStore = new XmlStreamStore(flowAnnotationBuffer);

        //Enable the AnnotationService against the new annotation store.
        flowAnnotationService.Enable(flowAnntationStore);
    }

    //Create a simple FlowDocument that can be used for testing out
    //sticky notes.
    private FlowDocument CreateFlowDocument()
```

```
{
    FlowDocument flowDocument = new FlowDocument();
    Paragraph paragraph = new Paragraph();
    paragraph.FontSize = 12;
    paragraph.Foreground = Brushes.Black;
    paragraph.FontWeight = FontWeights.Bold;
    paragraph.Inlines.Add(new Run("This is a FlowDocument."));

    flowDocument.Blocks.Add(paragraph);

    paragraph = new Paragraph();
    paragraph.FontWeight = FontWeights.Normal;
    paragraph.Inlines.Add(
        new Run("This is a paragraph in the FlowDocument."));

    flowDocument.Blocks.Add(paragraph);

    return flowDocument;
}

//An XPS document is loaded and displayed in the document viewer,
//ready for annotating.
private void LoadFixedDocument()
{
    string documentPath =
        Path.GetDirectoryName(Assembly.GetExecutingAssembly().Location)
        + "\\SampleDocument\\FixedDocument.xps";

    //Create a URI for the file path.
    Uri documentUri = new Uri(documentPath, UriKind.Absolute);

    XpsDocument xpsDocument = null;

    try
    {
        //Attempts to open the specified XPS document with
        //read and write permission.
        xpsDocument = new XpsDocument(documentPath, FileAccess.ReadWrite);
    }
    catch (Exception)
    {
        //You may want to handle any errors that occur during
        //the loading of the XPS document. For example, an
        //UnauthorizedAccessException will be thrown if the
        //file is marked as read-only.
    }
```

```
        //If the document is null, it's not a valid XPS document.
        if (xpsDocument == null)
        {
            //You may want to log an error here.
            return;
        }

        //Get the FixedDocumentSequence of the loaded document.
        FixedDocumentSequence fixedDocumentSequence
            = xpsDocument.GetFixedDocumentSequence();

        //If the document's FixedDocumentSequence is not found,
        //the document is corrupt.
        if (fixedDocumentSequence == null)
        {
            //Handle as required.
            return;
        }

        //Load the document's FixedDocumentSequence into
        //the DocumentViewer control.
        xdv.Document = fixedDocumentSequence;
    }
  }
}
```

7-14. Use Highlighting in a Document

Problem

You need to allow a user to highlight sections of a document.

Solution

Use the `System.Windows.Annotations.AnnotationHelper` to create highlighted sections of text in content displayed in a document viewer.

How It Works

Highlighting is another form of annotating a document and is performed in much the same way as creating sticky notes. The `AnnotationHelper` class provides a method for applying highlighting to a selection of text in a document being presented in a document viewer through the `CreateHighlightForSelection` method. This method takes the following parameters: a `System.Windows.Annotations.AnnotationService` object on which to create the highlight, a `System.String` giving the name of the author; and a `System.Windows.Media.Brush` that is used as the highlight color.

As you would imagine, removing highlighting from sections of text is just as simple. This time, you use the `ClearHighlightForSelection` method of the `AnnotationHelper`, passing in the `AnnotationService` on which the highlight is to be cleared. This method will clear only the highlighting applied to the selected text in the document viewer. This allows you to add or remove highlights on a character-by-character basis or to clear all the highlights in a selection of text where only some text is selected.

Calling either of these two methods when there is no text selected will cause a `System.InvalidOperationException` to be thrown.

The Code

The following XAML defines a window containing a `System.Windows.Controls.TabControl` with two `System.Windows.Controls.TabItem` elements. The first `TabItem` contains a `System.Windows.Controls.DocumentViewer`, and the second contains a `System.Windows.Controls.FixedDocumentReader`.

When the `Window` is loaded, a simple `FixedDocument` and a simple `FlowDocument` are created and placed into the `DocumentViewer` and the `FlowDocumentReader`, respectively. Adding sticky notes is as simple as selecting some text, right-clicking, and selecting the Add Highlight menu item. Removing highlights is performed in the same manner, although you select the Clear Highlight(s) menu item.

```
<Window
  x:Class="Recipe_07_14.Window1"
  xmlns="http://schemas.microsoft.com/winfx/2006/xaml/presentation"
  xmlns:x="http://schemas.microsoft.com/winfx/2006/xaml"
  Title="Window1"
  Height="800"
  Width="600"
  Loaded="Window_Loaded">
  <Grid>
    <Grid.RowDefinitions>
      <RowDefinition Height="*" />
      <RowDefinition Height="20" />
    </Grid.RowDefinitions>

    <TabControl>
      <TabItem Header="Fixed Document">
        <DocumentViewer x:Name="xdv">
          <DocumentViewer.ContextMenu>
            <ContextMenu>
              <MenuItem
                Header="Add Highlight"
                Click="DocumentViewer_AddHighlight"
                Tag="fixed" />
              <MenuItem
                Header="Clear Highlight(s)"
                Click="DocumentViewer_ClearHighlight"
                Tag="fixed" />
```

```
          </ContextMenu>
        </DocumentViewer.ContextMenu>
      </DocumentViewer>
    </TabItem>

    <TabItem Header="Flow Document">
      <FlowDocumentPageViewer x:Name="fdv">
        <FlowDocumentPageViewer.ContextMenu>
          <ContextMenu>
            <MenuItem
              Header="Add Highlight"
              Click="DocumentViewer_AddHighlight"
              Tag="flow" />
            <MenuItem
              Header="Clear Highlight(s)"
              Click="DocumentViewer_ClearHighlight"
              Tag="flow" />
          </ContextMenu>
        </FlowDocumentPageViewer.ContextMenu>
      </FlowDocumentPageViewer>
    </TabItem>
  </TabControl>
</Grid>
</Window>
```

The following code defines the content of the Window1.xaml.cs file:

```
using System;
using System.IO;
using System.Reflection;
using System.Windows;
using System.Windows.Annotations;
using System.Windows.Annotations.Storage;
using System.Windows.Controls;
using System.Windows.Documents;
using System.Windows.Media;
using System.Windows.Xps.Packaging;

namespace Recipe_07_14
{
    /// <summary>
    /// Interaction logic for Window1.xaml
    /// </summary>
    public partial class Window1 : Window
    {
        //FixedDoxument specifics
        AnnotationService fixedAnnotationService;
```

```
AnnotationStore fixedAnntationStore;
MemoryStream fixedAnnotationBuffer;

//FlowDocument specifics
AnnotationService flowAnnotationService;
AnnotationStore flowAnntationStore;
MemoryStream flowAnnotationBuffer;

XpsDocument xpsDocument;

public Window1()
{
    InitializeComponent();
    //Fire up the annotation services.
    StartFixedDocumentAnnotations();
    StartFlowDocumentAnnotations();
}

private void Window_Loaded(object sender, RoutedEventArgs e)
{
    //Populate the two document viewers.
    LoadFixedDocument();
    fdv.Document = CreateFlowDocument();
}

private void StartFixedDocumentAnnotations()
{
    //Create a new annotation service for the fixed document viewer.
    fixedAnnotationService = new AnnotationService(xdv);

    //Open a stream for our annotation store.
    fixedAnnotationBuffer = new MemoryStream();

    //Create an AnnotationStore using the stream.
    fixedAnntationStore = new XmlStreamStore(fixedAnnotationBuffer);

    //Enable the AnnotationService against the new annotation store.
    fixedAnnotationService.Enable(fixedAnntationStore);
}

private void StartFlowDocumentAnnotations()
{
    //Create a new annotation service for the fixed document viewer.
    flowAnnotationService = new AnnotationService(fdv);

    //Open a stream for our annotation store.
    flowAnnotationBuffer = new MemoryStream();
```

```csharp
    //Create an AnnotationStore using the stream.
    flowAnntationStore = new XmlStreamStore(flowAnnotationBuffer);

    //Enable the AnnotationService against the new annotation store.
    flowAnnotationService.Enable(flowAnntationStore);
}

//This method is called when the Add Highlight context menu is
//clicked by the user on either of the two document viewer controls.
private void DocumentViewer_AddHighlight(object sender,
    RoutedEventArgs e)
{
    //Work out which document viewer we are dealing with
    //and get the appropriate store.
    string tag = ((MenuItem)sender).Tag.ToString();

    AnnotationService annotationService =
        tag == "fixed"
        ? fixedAnnotationService
        : flowAnnotationService;

    //Get the current user's name as the author
    string userName = System.Environment.UserName;

    try
    {
        //Creates a yellow highlight
        AnnotationHelper.CreateHighlightForSelection(
            annotationService, userName, Brushes.Yellow);
    }
    catch (InvalidOperationException)
    {
        MessageBox.Show("Please select some text to highlight.");
    }
}

private void DocumentViewer_ClearHighlight(object sender, RoutedEventArgs e)
{
    //Work out which document viewer we are dealing with
    //and get the appropriate store.
    string tag = ((MenuItem)sender).Tag.ToString();

    AnnotationService annotationService =
        tag == "fixed"
        ? fixedAnnotationService
        : flowAnnotationService;
```

```csharp
        try
        {
            //Clear the selected text of any highlights.
            AnnotationHelper.ClearHighlightsForSelection(
                annotationService);
        }
        catch (InvalidOperationException)
        {
            MessageBox.Show("Please select some text to clear.");
        }
}

//Creates a simple FlowDocument containing text that can be
//highlighted.
private FlowDocument CreateFlowDocument()
{
    FlowDocument flowDocument = new FlowDocument();
    Paragraph paragraph = new Paragraph();
    paragraph.FontSize = 12;
    paragraph.Foreground = Brushes.Black;
    paragraph.FontWeight = FontWeights.Bold;
    paragraph.Inlines.Add(new Run("This is a FlowDocument."));

    flowDocument.Blocks.Add(paragraph);

    paragraph = new Paragraph();
    paragraph.FontWeight = FontWeights.Normal;
    paragraph.Inlines.Add(
        new Run("This is a paragraph in the FlowDocument."));

    flowDocument.Blocks.Add(paragraph);

    return flowDocument;
}

//An XPS document is loaded and displayed in the document viewer,
//ready for annotating.
private void LoadFixedDocument()
{
    string documentPath =
        Path.GetDirectoryName(Assembly.GetExecutingAssembly().Location)
        + "\\SampleDocument\\FixedDocument.xps";

    //Create a URI for the file path.
    Uri documentUri = new Uri(documentPath, UriKind.Absolute);

    xpsDocument = null;
```

```
        try
        {
            //Attempts to open the specified XPS document with
            //read and write permission.
            xpsDocument = new XpsDocument(documentPath,
                FileAccess.ReadWrite);
        }
        catch (Exception)
        {
            //You may want to handle any errors that occur during
            //the loading of the XPS document. For example an
            //UnauthorizedAccessException will be thrown if the
            //file is marked as read-only.
        }

        //If the document is null, it's not a valid XPS document.
        if (xpsDocument == null)
            return; //Handle as required.

        //Get the FixedDocumentSequence of the loaded document.
        FixedDocumentSequence fixedDocumentSequence
            = xpsDocument.GetFixedDocumentSequence();

        //If the document's FixedDocumentSequence is not found,
        //the document is corrupt.
        if (fixedDocumentSequence == null)
            return; //Handle as required.

        //Load the document's FixedDocumentSequence into
        //the DocumentViewer control.
        xdv.Document = fixedDocumentSequence;
    }
  }
}
```

7-15. Load and Save User-Defined Annotations

Problem

You need to display an XPS document-based System.Windows.Documents.FixedDocument in your application, including any annotations that may be in the document. Any new annotations made on the document also need to be persisted.

Solution

The annotation framework in WPF allows different methods for serializing annotations on a document. Using XML to store the annotations, you can add or load them from a System.Windows.Xps.Packaging.XpsDocument stored on disk.

How It Works

Annotations are stored and managed using a System.Windows.Annotations.Storage.AnnotationStore. The AnnotationStore class is an abstract class and implemented by System.Windows.Annotations.Storage.XmlStreamStore, an XML-based data store for annotation data. With an XmlStreamStore, it is possible to add annotations to an XpsDocument simply by adding a new System.IO.Packaging.PackagePart to the System.IO.Packaging.Package, containing the annotations.

For the purpose of this example, commands found in the System.Windows.Annotations namespace have been used to add and remove annotations from the document. This ensures that the provided code is more focused on the persistence of the annotations, rather than their creation/deletion.

Note You will need to add references to the System.Printing and ReachFramework assemblies in your project for this example.

Caution Each time this sample is built, the sample XPS document supplied with the source code is copied to the output directory, overwriting any existing one. This means that any saved annotations will be lost after each build. Should you want to use a different document, just print a document on your computer, and select Microsoft XPS Document Writer as your target printer.

The Code

```
<Window
  x:Class="Recipe_07_15.Window1"
  xmlns="http://schemas.microsoft.com/winfx/2006/xaml/presentation"
  xmlns:x="http://schemas.microsoft.com/winfx/2006/xaml"
  xmlns:a="clr-namespace:System.Windows.Annotations;assembly=PresentationFramework"
  Title="Window1"
  Height="600"
  Width="800"
  Closed="Window_Closed">
  <DockPanel>

    <Grid DockPanel.Dock="Bottom">
      <Grid.ColumnDefinitions>
```

```xml
      <ColumnDefinition Width="0.5*" />
      <ColumnDefinition Width="0.5*" />
    </Grid.ColumnDefinitions>

    <Button
      Content="Open XPS..."
      Click="btnOpenXps_Click"
    />

    <Button
      Content="Save Annotations"
      Click="btnSaveXps_Click"
      Grid.Column="1"
    />
  </Grid>

  <DocumentViewer x:Name="dvViewer">
    <DocumentViewer.ContextMenu>
      <ContextMenu>
        <MenuItem
          Header="Add Comment"
          Command="a:AnnotationService.CreateTextStickyNoteCommand"
        />

        <MenuItem
          Header="Add Highlight"
          Command="a:AnnotationService.CreateHighlightCommand"
        />

        <Separator />

        <MenuItem
          Command="a:AnnotationService.DeleteStickyNotesCommand"
          Header="Remove Notes"
        />

        <MenuItem
          Command="a:AnnotationService.ClearHighlightsCommand"
          Header="Remove Highlight"
        />
      </ContextMenu>
    </DocumentViewer.ContextMenu>
  </DocumentViewer>
 </DockPanel>
</Window>
```

The following code defines the content of the `Window1.xaml.cs` file:

```
using System;
using System.IO;
using System.IO.Packaging;
using System.Linq;
using System.Reflection;
using System.Windows;
using System.Windows.Annotations;
using System.Windows.Annotations.Storage;
using System.Windows.Documents;
using System.Windows.Xps.Packaging;
using Microsoft.Win32;

namespace Recipe_07_15
{
    /// <summary>
    /// Interaction logic for Window1.xaml
    /// </summary>
    public partial class Window1 : Window
    {
        private AnnotationService fixedAnnotationService;
        private AnnotationStore fixedAnntationStore;
        private Stream fixedAnnotationBuffer;
        private Uri documentUri;
        private Package xpsPackage;
        private XpsDocument xpsDocument;

        private bool hasOpenDocument;

        private const string fixedDocumentSequenceContentType =
            "application/vnd.ms-package.xps-fixeddocumentsequence+xml";

        private const string annotRelsType =
            "http://schemas.microsoft.com/xps/2005/06/annotations";

        private const string annotContentType =
            "application/vnd.ms-package.annotations+xml";

        public Window1()
        {
            InitializeComponent();

            hasOpenDocument = false;
        }

        //Handles the Click event raised by the
        //Open button, defined in markup.
```

```csharp
private void btnOpenXps_Click(object sender, RoutedEventArgs e)
{
    CloseFixedDocument();

    LoadFixedDocument();
}

//Handles the Click event raised by the
//Save button, defined in markup.
private void btnSaveXps_Click(object sender, RoutedEventArgs e)
{
    SaveAnnotations();
}

//Handles the Closed event, raised by the window
//defined  in markup, clearing up.
private void Window_Closed(object sender, EventArgs e)
{
    StopFixedDocumentAnnotations();
}

//Closes an open document and tidies up.
private void CloseFixedDocument()
{
    if (hasOpenDocument)
    {
        StopFixedDocumentAnnotations();

        PackageStore.RemovePackage(documentUri);

        xpsDocument.Close();
        xpsDocument = null;

        xpsPackage.Close();
        xpsPackage = null;
    }
}

//Presents the user with an OpenFileDialog, used to get a path
//to the XPS document they want to open. If this succeeds,
//the XPS document is loaded and displayed in the document viewer,
//ready for annotating.
private void LoadFixedDocument()
{
    //Get a path to the file to be opened.
    string fileName = GetDocumentPath();
    //If we didn't get a valid file path, we're done.
```

```csharp
//You might want to log an error here.
if (string.IsNullOrEmpty(fileName))
{
    return;
}

//Create a URI for the file path.
documentUri = new Uri(fileName, UriKind.Absolute);

try
{
    //Attempts to open the specified XPS document with
    //read and write permission.
    xpsDocument = new XpsDocument(fileName, FileAccess.ReadWrite);
}
catch (Exception)
{
    //You may want to handle any errors that occur during
    //the loading of the XPS document. For example, an
    //UnauthorizedAccessException will be thrown if the
    //file is marked as read-only.
}

//Get the document's Package from the PackageStore.
xpsPackage = PackageStore.GetPackage(documentUri);

//If either the package or document are null, the
//document is not valid.
if ((xpsPackage == null) || (xpsDocument == null))
{
    //You may want to log an error here.
    return;
}

//Get the FixedDocumentSequence of the loaded document.
FixedDocumentSequence fixedDocumentSequence
    = xpsDocument.GetFixedDocumentSequence();

//If the document's FixedDocumentSequence is not found,
//the document is corrupt.
if (fixedDocumentSequence == null)
{
    //Handle as required.
    return;
}
```

```
        //Load the document's FixedDocumentSequence into
        //the DocumentViewer control.
        dvViewer.Document = fixedDocumentSequence;

        //Enable user annotations on the document.
        StartFixedDocumentAnnotations();

        hasOpenDocument = true;
    }


    //Present the user with an OpenFileDialog, allowing
    //them to select a file to open. If a file is selected,
    //return the path to the file; otherwise, return an empty
    //string.
    private string GetDocumentPath()
    {
        OpenFileDialog openFileDialog = new OpenFileDialog();
        openFileDialog.Filter = "XPS Document | *.xps";
        openFileDialog.Multiselect = false;
        openFileDialog.CheckFileExists = true;
        openFileDialog.CheckPathExists = true;

        openFileDialog.InitialDirectory =
            Path.GetFullPath(Assembly.GetExecutingAssembly().Location);

        string result = string.Empty;

        if (openFileDialog.ShowDialog(this) == true)
        {
            result = openFileDialog.FileName;
        }

        return result;
    }


    //Saves the document's annotations by flushing their buffers.
    //The package is also flushed so that the changes are persisted
    //to disk.
    private void SaveAnnotations()
    {
        //Check that we have a valid fixed annotation service.
        if (fixedAnnotationService != null
            && fixedAnnotationService.IsEnabled)
        {
            fixedAnnotationService.Store.Flush();
            fixedAnnotationBuffer.Flush();
        }
```

```
            if (xpsPackage != null)
            {
                xpsPackage.Flush();
            }
        }

    private void StartFixedDocumentAnnotations()
    {
        //If there is no AnnotationService yet, create one.
        if (fixedAnnotationService == null)
        {
            fixedAnnotationService = new AnnotationService(dvViewer);
        }

        //If the AnnotationService is currently enabled, disable it
        //because you'll need to reenable it with a new store object.
        if (fixedAnnotationService.IsEnabled)
        {
            fixedAnnotationService.Disable();
        }

        //Open a stream to the file for storing annotations.
        fixedAnnotationBuffer =
            GetAnnotationPart(GetFixedDocumentSequenceUri()).GetStream();

        //Create a new AnnotationStore using the file stream.
        fixedAnntationStore = new XmlStreamStore(fixedAnnotationBuffer);

        //Enable the AnnotationService using the new store object.
        fixedAnnotationService.Enable(fixedAnntationStore);
    }

    //When closing the application, or just the document it is
    //important to close down the existing annotation service,
    //releasing any resources. Note that the annotation service
    //is stopped without saving changes.
    public void StopFixedDocumentAnnotations()
    {
        //If the AnnotationStore is active, flush and close it.
        if ((fixedAnnotationService != null)
            && fixedAnnotationService.IsEnabled)
        {
            fixedAnnotationService.Store.Dispose();
            fixedAnnotationBuffer.Close();
        }
```

```csharp
            //If the AnnotationService is active, shut it down.
            if (fixedAnnotationService != null)
            {
                if (fixedAnnotationService.IsEnabled)
                {
                    fixedAnnotationService.Disable();
                }

                fixedAnnotationService = null;
            }
        }


        //Searches the parts of a document, looking for the
        //FixedDocumentSequence part. If the part is found,
        //its URI is returned; otherwise, null is returned.
        private Uri GetFixedDocumentSequenceUri()
        {
            Uri result = null;
            PackagePart packagePart;

            //Get the FixedDocumentSequence part from the Package.
            packagePart = xpsPackage.GetParts().Single<PackagePart>(
                part =>
                    part.ContentType == fixedDocumentSequenceContentType);

            //If we found the part, note its URI.
            if (packagePart != null)
            {
                result = packagePart.Uri;
            }

            return result;
        }

        private PackagePart GetAnnotationPart(Uri uri)
        {
            Package package = PackageStore.GetPackage(documentUri);

            if (package == null)
            {
                return null;
            }

            // Get the FixedDocumentSequence part from the package.
            PackagePart fdsPart = package.GetPart(uri);
```

```csharp
// Search through all the document relationships to find the
// annotations relationship part (or null, of there is none).
PackageRelationship annotRel = null;

annotRel
    = fdsPart.GetRelationships().FirstOrDefault<PackageRelationship>(
        pr => pr.RelationshipType == annotRelsType);

PackagePart annotPart;

//If annotations relationship does not exist, create a new
//annotations part, if required, and a relationship for it.
if (annotRel == null)
{
    Uri annotationUri =
        PackUriHelper.CreatePartUri(new Uri("annotations.xml",
                                    UriKind.Relative));

    if (package.PartExists(annotationUri))
    {
        annotPart = package.GetPart(annotationUri);
    }
    else
    {
        //Create a new Annotations part in the document.
        annotPart = package.CreatePart(annotationUri, annotContentType);
    }

    //Create a new relationship that points to the Annotations part.
    fdsPart.CreateRelationship(annotPart.Uri,
                               TargetMode.Internal,
                               annotRelsType);
}
else
{
    //If an annotations relationship exists,
    //get the annotations part that it references.

    //Get the Annotations part specified by the relationship.
    annotPart = package.GetPart(annotRel.TargetUri);

    if (annotPart == null)
    {
        //The annotations part pointed to by the annotation
        //relationship URI is not present. Handle as required.
        return null;
    }
```

```
        }

        return annotPart;
      }
    }
}
```

7-16. Print a Document's Annotations

Problem

You need to print a document including all of its annotations, as displayed in a document viewer.

Solution

Use a System.Windows.Annotations.AnnotationDocumentPaginator to decorate a document with its associated annotations.

How It Works

Printing a document with its annotations is similar to printing a document on its own; just a few extra steps are required to include any annotations in the printout. The document's annotations, if present, are added to the document being printed by using an AnnotationDocumentPaginator. This class's constructor takes two arguments, a System.Windows. Documents.DocumentPaginator (that is, the document paginator for the document you are printing) and a System.Windows.Annotations.AnnotationStore (or an annotation storage stream). The AnnotationDocumentPaginator wraps the source DocumentPaginator and adds the annotations found in the AnnotationStore to the supplied document. This paginator is then used in the same way as writing a normal paginator to a print queue or disk. In this instance, you will pass the annotation paginator as a parameter to the Write method of a System.Windows. Xps.XpsDocumentWriter, created against a System.Printing.PrintQueue (see recipe 7-6).

When printing in this way, a copy of the document's paginator must be used in the AnnotationDocumentPaginator's constructor; otherwise, you will have all sorts of odd behavior happening. This is due to the document becoming corrupt during the printing process and can manifest itself in many ways.

Another gotcha happens when printing annotations asynchronously. If a reference to the annotation store object is used and the annotations in the UI are changed while the document is printing, those changes may well make their way onto the printed document. To combat this, there is a constructor on the AnnotationDocumentPaginator, which accepts a System.IO.Stream object for the annotation store. Use this and pass in a copy of your annotation store Stream object.

Finally, when a document is printed using an AnnotationDocumentPaginator, the annotations will be printed exactly as they appear on the document in the document viewer. Sticky notes that obscure any text will obscure the same text in the final document.

Note You will need to add references to the System.Printing and ReachFramework assemblies in your project for this example.

The Code

```xml
<Window
  x:Class="Recipe_07_16.Window1"
  xmlns="http://schemas.microsoft.com/winfx/2006/xaml/presentation"
  xmlns:x="http://schemas.microsoft.com/winfx/2006/xaml"
  Title="Window1"
  Height="300"
  Width="300">
  <DockPanel>
    <DocumentViewer x:Name="dvDocumentViewer">
      <DocumentViewer.CommandBindings>
        <CommandBinding
          Command="ApplicationCommands.Print"
          Executed="DocumentViewer_PrintDocument" />
      </DocumentViewer.CommandBindings>
      <DocumentViewer.ContextMenu>
        <ContextMenu>
          <MenuItem
            Header="Add Comment..."
            Click="DocumentViewer_AddComment" />
        </ContextMenu>
      </DocumentViewer.ContextMenu>
    </DocumentViewer>
  </DockPanel>
</Window>
```

The following code defines the content of Window1.xaml.cs:

```csharp
using System;
using System.IO;
using System.Printing;
using System.Reflection;
using System.Windows;
using System.Windows.Annotations;
using System.Windows.Annotations.Storage;
using System.Windows.Controls;
using System.Windows.Documents;
using System.Windows.Xps;
using System.Windows.Xps.Packaging;
```

```csharp
namespace Recipe_07_16
{
    /// <summary>
    /// Interaction logic for Window1.xaml
    /// </summary>
    public partial class Window1 : Window
    {
        //Fields to handle our Annotation specifics.
        private AnnotationService fixedAnnotationService;
        private AnnotationStore fixedAnntationStore;
        private Stream fixedAnnotationBuffer;

        private XpsDocument xpsDocument;
        private FixedDocumentSequence fixedDocumentSequence;

        public Window1()
        {
            InitializeComponent();
            //Load in our fixed document.
            LoadFixedDocument();
            //Fire up the annotation service...
            StartFixedDocumentAnnotations();
        }

        private void  DocumentViewer_AddComment(object sender, RoutedEventArgs e)
        {
            //Get the current user's name as the author
            string userName = System.Environment.UserName;

            //The AnnotationHelper.CreateTextStickyNoteForSelection method
            //will throw an exception if no text is selected.
            try
            {
                AnnotationHelper.CreateTextStickyNoteForSelection(
                    fixedAnnotationService, userName);
            }
            catch (InvalidOperationException)
            {
                MessageBox.Show("Please select some text to annotate.");
            }
        }


        //An XPS document is loaded and displayed in the document viewer,
        //ready for annotating.
        private void LoadFixedDocument()
```

```
    {
        string documentPath =
            Path.GetDirectoryName(Assembly.GetExecutingAssembly().Location)
            + "\\SampleDocument\\FixedDocument.xps";

        //Create a URI for the file path.
        Uri documentUri = new Uri(documentPath, UriKind.Absolute);

        xpsDocument = null;

        try
        {
            //Attempts to open the specified XPS document with
            //read and write permission.
            xpsDocument = new XpsDocument(documentPath,
                FileAccess.ReadWrite);
        }
        catch (Exception)
        {
            //You may want to handle any errors that occur during
            //the loading of the XPS document. For example an
            //UnauthorizedAccessException will be thrown if the
            //file is marked as read-only.
        }

        //If the document is null, it's not a valid XPS document.
        if (xpsDocument == null)
            return; //Handle as required.

        //Get the FixedDocumentSequence of the loaded document.
        fixedDocumentSequence
            = xpsDocument.GetFixedDocumentSequence();

        //If the document's FixedDocumentSequence is not found,
        //the document is corrupt.
        if (fixedDocumentSequence == null)
            return; //Handle as required.

        //Load the document's FixedDocumentSequence into
        //the DocumentViewer control.
        dvDocumentViewer.Document = fixedDocumentSequence;
    }

    private void StartFixedDocumentAnnotations()
    {
        //If there is no AnnotationService yet, create one.
        if (fixedAnnotationService == null)
```

```
        fixedAnnotationService
            = new AnnotationService(dvDocumentViewer);

    //If the AnnotationService is currently enabled, disable it
    //because you'll need to reenable it with a new store object.
    if (fixedAnnotationService.IsEnabled)
        fixedAnnotationService.Disable();

    //Open a memory stream for storing annotations.
    fixedAnnotationBuffer = new MemoryStream();

    //Create a new AnnotationStore using the above stream.
    fixedAnntationStore = new XmlStreamStore(fixcdAnnotationBuffer);

    //Enable the AnnotationService using the new store object.
    fixedAnnotationService.Enable(fixedAnntationStore);
}

//Present the user with a PrintDialog, allowing them to
//select and configure a printer.
public PrintQueue ShowPrintDialog()
{
    PrintDialog printDialog = new PrintDialog();

    if (printDialog.ShowDialog() == true)
        return printDialog.PrintQueue;

    return null;
}

//Handles the click of the print button in the document
//viewer, overriding the default behavior.
private void DocumentViewer_PrintDocument(object sender, RoutedEventArgs e)
{
    //Get a print queue
    PrintQueue printQueue = ShowPrintDialog();

    if (printQueue == null)
        return;

    try
    {
        //Create a new XPS writer using the chosen print queue.
        XpsDocumentWriter writer
            = PrintQueue.CreateXpsDocumentWriter(printQueue);
```

```
                    //We need to use a copy of the document's fixed document
                    //sequence when creating the AnnotationDocumentPaginator.
                    FixedDocumentSequence fds
                        = xpsDocument.GetFixedDocumentSequence();

                    //You now need to create a document paginator for any
                    //annotations in the document.
                    AnnotationDocumentPaginator adp =
                        new AnnotationDocumentPaginator(fds.DocumentPaginator,
                            fixedAnnotationService.Store);

                    //Write out the document, with annotations using the annotation
                    //document paginator.
                    writer.Write(adp);
                }
                catch (Exception ex)
                {
                    MessageBox.Show(ex.Message);
                }
            }

        }
    }
```

CHAPTER 8

Multithreading

Internally, WPF leverages multithreading by executing the rendering and composition of elements on a separate thread from the UI thread. However, from the point of view of developers, it is fundamentally a single-threaded apartment (STA) model of threading, like the Windows Forms architecture. Initially, the WPF development team wanted to remove the dependency on the STA model, in favor of a mechanism of thread rental, whereby UI objects could be accessed on any thread. However, this design introduced substantial complexity for single-threaded applications and made it more difficult to interoperate with existing services (such as the Win32 API, Clipboard, Internet Explorer, and so on).

The fact that WPF objects have STA threading means that they can be accessed only on the thread that created them. However, the .NET Framework provides great support for creating and using multiple threads, and the WPF team has exposed a number of useful classes and mechanisms to allow WPF developers to leverage multithreading within their applications.

The recipes in this chapter describe how to:

- Schedule operations for execution on the UI thread (recipes 8-1, 8-2, and 8-3)

- Check and ensure that code is running on the UI thread (recipes 8-4 and 8-5)

- Execute a method asynchronously using a background thread (recipes 8-6, 8-7, 8-8, and 8-9)

- Update the UI asynchronously on a thread-safe timer (recipe 8-10)

- Show a continuous animation during an asynchronous process (recipe 8-11)

- Show a progress bar while processing on a background thread (recipes 8-12, 8-13, and 8-14)

- Implement Application.DoEvents in WPF (recipe 8-15)

- Create a separate thread for each window in a multiwindow application (recipe 8-16)

8-1. Execute a Method Asynchronously Using the Dispatcher Queue

Problem

You need to execute a method asynchronously without blocking the UI thread.

Solution

Invoke the method on the `Dispatcher` property for a UI element, and specify a `System.Windows.Threading.DispatcherPriority` that is lower than the `Render` event (see Table 8-1).

How It Works

In WPF, most objects ultimately derive from `System.Windows.Threading.DispatcherObject`, and only the thread that created a `DispatcherObject` may access that object. For example, a background thread cannot update the contents of a `System.Windows.Controls.TextBox` that was created on the UI thread.

The `DispatcherObject` has a method called `BeginInvoke`, which takes a `System.Delegate` as one of its parameters. When `BeginInvoke` is called, the `Dispatcher` will schedule this delegate for execution in its event queue. When it is due execution, the `Dispatcher` will execute this delegate on the same thread on which its owner was created. The `BeginInvoke` method is asynchronous and returns to the caller immediately.

The second parameter expected by `BeginInvoke` is a `DispatcherPriority`, which controls when the delegate is due execution. It does this by informing the `Dispatcher` of the priority of this event, relative to the other pending operations in the event queue. Events will be executed only when there are no higher priority events in the queue. This is useful for specifying that a certain process should be executed, for example, in the background or when the application is idle, but should not block more important events such as those concerned with loading or rendering the element.

■**Note** Microsoft Word accomplishes spell checking using this mechanism. Spell checking is done in the background using the idle time of the UI thread.

Table 8-1 shows the values of the `DispatcherPriority` enum in ascending order of priority.

Because the `Dispatcher` executes the delegate in the same thread that was used to create the component, the code in the delegate can update and interact with the control. This is the simplest way possible of executing a method asynchronously, without exposing yourself to complex synchronization issues such as race conditions, deadlocks, live locks, and memory corruption. We will cover more advanced ways using the `System.ComponentModel.BackgroundWorker` later in this chapter.

Table 8-1. *Dispatcher Priorities, Lowest to Highest*

Name	Value
Invalid	−1
Inactive	0
SystemIdle	1
ApplicationIdle	2
ContextIdle	3
Background	4
Input	5
Loaded	6
Render	7
DataBind	8
Normal	9
Send	10

The Code

The following example demonstrates a simple application with a window containing a System. Windows.Controls.Button and a System.Windows.Controls.TextBlock. When the user clicks the Button, there is code in the code-behind that counts upward from 3, searching for prime numbers. When the program finds a prime number, it updates the TextBlock with the number. The user can click the Button again to stop the search.

The example schedules a prime number check on the window's Dispatcher property. It uses a DispatcherPriority of SystemIdle, which ensures that any pending UI events are processed in between each check.

The XAML for the window is as follows:

```
<Window x:Class="Recipe_08_01.Window1"
    xmlns="http://schemas.microsoft.com/winfx/2006/xaml/presentation"
    xmlns:x="http://schemas.microsoft.com/winfx/2006/xaml"
    Title="WPF Recipes 8_01" Width="220" Height="104" >
    <StackPanel Orientation="Vertical">
        <Button
            Click="StartStop_Click"
            Name="btnStartStop"
            Margin="5"
            Height="34">Start</Button>
        <StackPanel Orientation="Horizontal">
            <TextBlock Margin="5">Biggest Prime Found:</TextBlock>
            <TextBlock Name="txtBiggestPrime" Margin="5" />
        </StackPanel>
    </StackPanel>
</Window>
```

The code-behind for the window is as follows:

```
using System;
using System.Windows;
using System.Windows.Threading;
using Recipe_08_01;

namespace Recipe_08_01
{
    public partial class Window1 : Window
    {
        private bool continueCalculating = false;

        public Window1() : base()
        {
            InitializeComponent();
        }

        private void StartStop_Click(object sender, RoutedEventArgs e)
        {
            if(continueCalculating)
            {
                continueCalculating = false;
                btnStartStop.Content = "Start";
            }
            else
            {
                continueCalculating = true;
                btnStartStop.Content = "Stop";

                // Execute the CheckPrimeNumber method on
                // the current Dispatcher queue
                this.Dispatcher.BeginInvoke(
                    DispatcherPriority.Normal,
                    new Action<int>(CheckPrimeNumber), 3);
            }
        }

        public void CheckPrimeNumber(int current)
        {
            if(PrimeNumberHelper.IsPrime(current))
            {
                txtBiggestPrime.Text = current.ToString();
            }
```

```
        if(continueCalculating)
        {
            // Execute the CheckPrimeNumber method
            // again, using a lower DispatcherPriority
            this.Dispatcher.BeginInvoke(
                DispatcherPriority.SystemIdle,
                new Action<int>(CheckPrimeNumber), current + 2);
        }
    }
  }
}
```

The code in the `PrimeNumberHelper` class that searches for prime numbers is omitted for the sake of brevity, but the full code is available with the online examples for this chapter.

Figure 8-1 shows the resulting window. If you resize the window whilst the calculation is running, you can see that whilst the calculation slows down, the repainting of the window does not. This is because the paint messages are given higher priority by the dispatcher queue.

Figure 8-1. *Executing a method asynchronously using the* Dispatcher

8-2. Load the Data for a Window Asynchronously After It Has Rendered

Problem

You need to show a window or control that loads a lot of data and have it load the data after the control has finished loading and rendering correctly.

Solution

In the Loaded event of the window or control, execute the method to load the data by calling the BeginInvoke method of the System.Windows.Threading.DispatcherObject for the UI element, and specify a System.Windows.Threading.DispatcherPriority of Background.

How It Works

Suppose you have a window or control that displays some data and it takes a noticeable amount of time to generate and display this data. If you execute the method that loads this data in the window or control's constructor, then the entire UI element will not be displayed until after the method has completed. Furthermore, if you execute the method in the Loaded event, then whilst the control or window will be displayed immediately, it will not be rendered correctly until the data has finished being loaded.

When you use the BeginInvoke method of a window or control's Dispatcher property, it adds the delegate to the Dispatcher's event queue but gives you the opportunity to specify a lower priority for it. This ensures that the Dispatcher processes all loading and rendering events before executing the delegate that loads the data. This allows the control or window to be displayed and rendered immediately, whilst the data waits in the background to be loaded.

The Code

The following example displays a window containing a System.Windows.Controls.TextBlock and a System.Windows.Controls.ListBox. In the code-behind for the window, there is a method called LoadNumbers, which generates a list of 1 million numbers and sets them as the ItemsSource for the ListBox.

The XAML for the window is as follows:

```
<Window x:Class="Recipe_08_02.Window1"
    xmlns="http://schemas.microsoft.com/winfx/2006/xaml/presentation"
    xmlns:x="http://schemas.microsoft.com/winfx/2006/xaml"
    Title="WPF Recipes 8_02" Height="200" Width="300"
    Loaded="Window_Loaded">
    <Grid>
        <Grid.RowDefinitions>
            <RowDefinition Height="24"/>
            <RowDefinition />
        </Grid.RowDefinitions>

        <TextBlock Margin="4">
            One Million Numbers:
        </TextBlock>

        <ListBox x:Name="listBox"
                Grid.Row="1"
                />
    </Grid>
</Window>
```

In the code-behind, there are comments that show three possible ways of calling the LoadNumbers method. If you uncomment any one of the three options and comment out the other two, you can see the effect on the loading and rendering of the window. Option 3 is the one that is uncommented by default, and it is the only option that allows the window to be loaded and rendered correctly, before trying to generate and display the million numbers.

It works by calling the BeginInvoke method of the window's Dispatcher property and setting a DispatcherPriority of Background. The code-behind is as follows:

```
using System.Windows;
using System.Windows.Threading;
using System.Collections.Generic;
```

```
namespace Recipe_08_02
{
    public partial class Window1 : Window
    {
        public Window1()
        {
            InitializeComponent();

            // Option 1.
            // If LoadNumbers is called here, the window
            // doesn't show until the method has completed.
            //
            // LoadNumbers();
        }

        private void Window_Loaded(object sender, RoutedEventArgs e)
        {
            // Option 2.
            // If LoadNumbers is called here, the window
            // loads immediately, but it doesn't display
            // properly until the method has completed.
            //
            // LoadNumbers();

            // Option 3.
            // If LoadNumbers is invoked here on the
            // window's Dispatcher with a DispatcherPriority of
            // Background, the window will load and be displayed
            // properly immediately, and then the list of numbers
            // will be generated and displayed once the
            // method has completed.
            //
            this.Dispatcher.BeginInvoke(
                DispatcherPriority.Background,
                new LoadNumbersDelegate(LoadNumbers));
        }

        // Declare a delegate to wrap the LoadNumbers method
        private delegate void LoadNumbersDelegate();

        // Load one million numbers into a list and
        // set it as the ItemsSource for the ListBox
        private void LoadNumbers()
        {
            List<string> numberDescriptions = new List<string>();
```

```
            for(int i = 1; i <= 1000000; i++)
            {
                numberDescriptions.Add("Number " + i.ToString());
            }

            // Set the ItemsSource
            listBox.ItemsSource = numberDescriptions;
        }
    }
}
```

Figure 8-2 shows the resulting window.

Figure 8-2. *Loading the data for a control after it has rendered*

8-3. Load the Items in a ListBox Asynchronously

Problem

You need to show a System.Windows.Controls.ListBox, or any System.Windows.Controls. ItemsControl, and load its data one item at a time, allowing the window to receive other input, binding, and rendering events whilst the items are loading.

Solution

In the Loaded event of the window or control, execute the method to load the first item of data by calling the BeginInvoke method of the System.Windows.Threading.DispatcherObject for the UI element, and specify a System.Windows.Threading.DispatcherPriority of Background. When this method has finished generating the data and adding it to the list, add the same method to the Dispatcher's queue recursively, each time adding just one item and then queuing the call to add the next one with a DispatcherPriority of Background.

How It Works

Suppose you have a window or control that displays some data and it takes a noticeable amount of time to generate and display this data. If you have one method that loads all the data at one go, then none of the data will appear until the entire list has been loaded.

When you use the BeginInvoke method of a window or control's Dispatcher property, it adds the delegate to the Dispatcher's event queue but gives you the opportunity to specify a lower priority for it. By executing a method that loads just one item at a time, the window is given the chance to execute any other higher-priority events in between items. This allows the control or window to be displayed and rendered immediately and loads each item one at a time.

The Code

The following example displays a window containing a System.Windows.Controls.TextBlock and a System.Windows.Controls.ListBox. In the code-behind for the window, the ListBox is bound to a System.Collections.ObjectModel.ObservableCollection of strings. The ObservableCollection class represents a dynamic collection that provides notifications when items get added, when items get removed, or when the whole list is refreshed. There is a method called LoadNumber, which adds a number to this list, increments the number, and calls itself recursively 10,000 times. Each time LoadNumber is called, it is executed by a delegate that is added to the window's Dispatcher queue, using a priority of Background. This means any higher-priority events added to the queue while the list items are being generated, such as events concerned with input, loading, binding, or rendering, are executed first.

The XAML for the window is as follows:

```
<Window x:Class="Recipe_08_03.Window1"
    xmlns="http://schemas.microsoft.com/winfx/2006/xaml/presentation"
    xmlns:x="http://schemas.microsoft.com/winfx/2006/xaml"
    Title="WPF Recipes 8_03" Height="200" Width="300"
    Loaded="Window_Loaded">

    <Window.Resources>
        <DataTemplate
            x:Key="ListItemTemplate">
            <StackPanel
                Orientation="Horizontal">
                <Image
                    Margin="4"
                    Source="Apress.gif"
                    />
                <TextBlock
                    Margin="4"
                    Text="{Binding}"
                    VerticalAlignment="Center"
                    />
            </StackPanel>
        </DataTemplate>
    </Window.Resources>

    <Grid>
```

```xml
<Grid.RowDefinitions>
    <RowDefinition Height="24"/>
    <RowDefinition />
</Grid.RowDefinitions>

<TextBlock
    Margin="4">
    Loading 10,000 Numbers, one at a time:
</TextBlock>

<ListBox
    x:Name="listBox"
    Grid.Row="1"
    ItemTemplate=
      "{StaticResource ListItemTemplate}"
    />

    </Grid>
</Window>
```

The code-behind is as follows:

```csharp
using System.Collections.ObjectModel;
using System.Windows;
using System.Windows.Threading;

namespace Recipe_08_03
{
    public partial class Window1 : Window
    {
        // ObservableCollection of strings
        private ObservableCollection<string> numberDescriptions;

        public Window1()
        {
            InitializeComponent();
        }

        private void Window_Loaded(object sender, RoutedEventArgs e)
        {
            // Initialize an ObservableCollection of strings
            numberDescriptions =
                new ObservableCollection<string>();

            // Set it as the ItemsSource for the ListBox
            listBox.ItemsSource = numberDescriptions;
```

```
            // Execute a delegate to load
            // the first number on the UI thread, with
            // a priority of Background.
            //
            this.Dispatcher.BeginInvoke(
                DispatcherPriority.Background,
                new LoadNumberDelegate(LoadNumber), 1);
        }

        // Declare a delegate to wrap the LoadNumber method
        private delegate void LoadNumberDelegate(int number);

        private void LoadNumber(int number)
        {
            // Add the number to the observable collection
            // bound to the ListBox
            numberDescriptions.Add("Number " + number.ToString());

            if(number < 10000)
            {
                // Load the next number, by executing this method
                // recursively on the dispatcher queue, with
                // a priority of Background.
                //
                this.Dispatcher.BeginInvoke(
                    DispatcherPriority.Background,
                    new LoadNumberDelegate(LoadNumber), ++number);
            }
        }
    }
}
```

Figure 8-3 shows the resulting window.

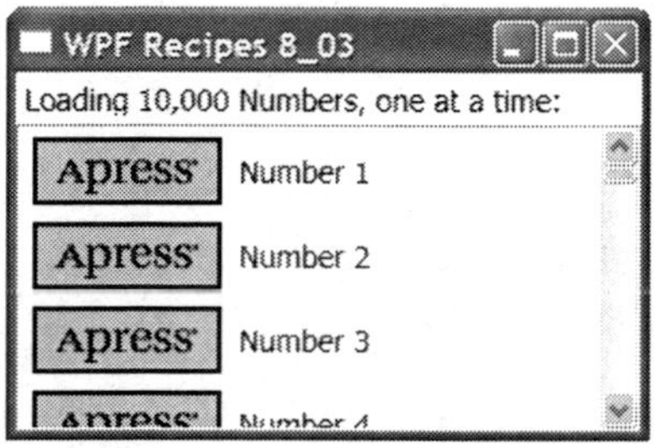

Figure 8-3. *Loading the data for a ListBox, one item at a time*

8-4. Check Whether You Are Running on the UI Thread

Problem

You need to determine whether the code being executed is running on the UI thread. This is necessary, for example, if the code needs to interact with a UI element. In such a case, if the code is not running on the UI thread, it will cause a System.InvalidOperationException, with the error message "The calling thread cannot access the object because a different thread owns it."

Solution

Use the Dispatcher property of any of your UI elements, and call the CheckAccess method.

How It Works

System.Windows.UIElement inherits from System.Windows.Threading.DispatcherObject, which exposes a System.Windows.Threading.Dispatcher property. The Dispatcher class has a method called CheckAccess that returns True if the calling thread is the current thread and False if not.

Tip This CheckAccess method is the WPF equivalent of the InvokeRequired property of the Control object in Windows Forms, which shares similar thread-affinity rules to WPF.

The Code

The following example displays a window containing two System.Windows.Controls.Button controls and a System.Windows.Controls.TextBox. In the code-behind for the window, there is a method called CheckAccess that calls the CheckAccess method of the TextBox's Dispatcher property. In the click event for the button on the left, this CheckAccess method is called on the UI thread. In the click event for the button on the right, the method is invoked asynchronously using the BeginInvoke method of a delegate. The result of the call to Dispatcher.CheckAccess is then displayed in the TextBox.

The XAML for the window is as follows:

```
<Window x:Class="Recipe_08_04.Window1"
    xmlns="http://schemas.microsoft.com/winfx/2006/xaml/presentation"
    xmlns:x="http://schemas.microsoft.com/winfx/2006/xaml"
    Title="WPF Recipes 8_04" Height="120" Width="364">
    <Grid>
        <Grid.ColumnDefinitions>
            <ColumnDefinition/>
            <ColumnDefinition/>
        </Grid.ColumnDefinitions>
```

```xml
    <Grid.RowDefinitions>
        <RowDefinition/>
        <RowDefinition Height="30"/>
    </Grid.RowDefinitions>

    <Button
        Grid.Column="0"
        Click="ButtonTrue_Click"
        Margin="4">
        UI Thread
    </Button>

    <Button
        Grid.Column="1"
        Click="ButtonFalse_Click"
        Margin="4">
        Non-UI Thread
    </Button>

    <TextBlock
        Grid.Row="1"
        Margin="4">
        Dispatcher.CheckAccess() =
    </TextBlock>

    <TextBlock
        x:Name="txtResult"
        Grid.Row="1"
        Grid.Column="1"
        Margin="4"
        />
    </Grid>
</Window>
```

The code for the window is as follows:

```csharp
using System.Windows;
using System.Windows.Threading;

namespace Recipe_08_04
{
    public partial class Window1 : Window
    {
        public Window1()
        {
            InitializeComponent();
        }
```

```csharp
private void ButtonTrue_Click(object sender, RoutedEventArgs e)
{
    // Call CheckAccess on the UI thread
    CheckAccess();
}

private void ButtonFalse_Click(object sender, RoutedEventArgs e)
{
    // Invoke a call to CheckAccess
    // on a different thread
    CheckAccessDelegate del =
        new CheckAccessDelegate(CheckAccess);
    del.BeginInvoke(null, null);
}

// Declare a delegate to wrap the CheckAccess method
private delegate void CheckAccessDelegate();

// Declare a delegate to wrap the SetResultText method
private delegate void SetResultTextDelegate(string result);

private void CheckAccess()
{
    // Check if the calling thread is in the UI thread
    if(txtResult.Dispatcher.CheckAccess())
    {
        SetResultText("True");
    }
    else
    {
        // The calling thread does not have access to the UI thread.
        // Execute the SetResult method on the Dispatcher of the UI thread.
        txtResult.Dispatcher.BeginInvoke(
            DispatcherPriority.Normal,
            new SetResultTextDelegate(SetResultText),
            "False");
    }
}

private void SetResultText(string result)
{
    // Display the result of the CheckAccess method
    txtResult.Text = result;
}
    }
}
```

Figure 8-4 shows the resulting window.

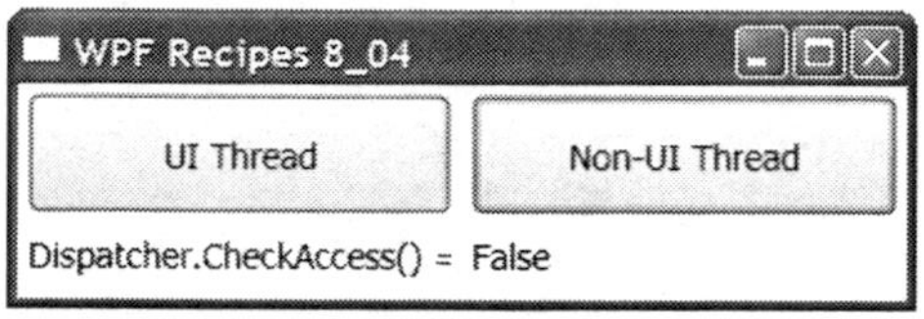

Figure 8-4. *Determining whether the calling thread has access to the UI thread*

8-5. Ensure That You Are Running on the UI Thread

Problem

You need to verify that the code being executed is running on the UI thread and throw an exception if not.

Solution

Use the Dispatcher property of any of your UI elements, and call the VerifyAccess method.

How It Works

System.Windows.UIElement inherits from System.Windows.Threading.DispatcherObject, which exposes a System.Windows.Threading.Dispatcher property. The Dispatcher class has a method called VerifyAccess that throws a System.InvalidOperationException if the calling thread is not the current thread.

The Code

The following example displays a window containing two System.Windows.Controls.Button controls. In the code-behind for the window, there is a method called VerifyAccess that calls the VerifyAccess method of the window's Dispatcher property. In the click event for the button on the left, this VerifyAccess method is called on the UI thread. In the click event for the button on the right, the method is invoked asynchronously using the BeginInvoke method of a delegate. This results in an InvalidOperationException with an error message stating that "The calling thread cannot access this object because a different thread owns it."

The XAML for the window is as follows:

```
<Window x:Class="Recipe_08_05.Window1"
    xmlns="http://schemas.microsoft.com/winfx/2006/xaml/presentation"
    xmlns:x="http://schemas.microsoft.com/winfx/2006/xaml"
    Title="WPF Recipes 8_05" Height="100" Width="300">
```

```xml
<Grid>
    <Grid.ColumnDefinitions>
        <ColumnDefinition/>
        <ColumnDefinition/>
    </Grid.ColumnDefinitions>

    <Button
        Grid.Column="0"
        Click="ButtonTrue_Click"
        Margin="4">
        UI Thread
    </Button>

    <Button
        Grid.Column="1"
        Click="ButtonFalse_Click"
        Margin="4">
        Non-UI Thread
    </Button>

</Grid>
</Window>
```

The code for the window is as follows:

```csharp
using System.Windows;

namespace Recipe_08_05
{
    public partial class Window1 : Window
    {
        public Window1()
        {
            InitializeComponent();
        }

        private void ButtonTrue_Click(object sender, RoutedEventArgs e)
        {
            // Call VerifyAccess on the UI thread
            VerifyAccess();
        }

        private void ButtonFalse_Click(object sender, RoutedEventArgs e)
        {
            // Invoke a call to VerifyAccess
            // on a different thread
```

```
        VerifyAccessDelegate del =
            new VerifyAccessDelegate(VerifyAccess);
        del.BeginInvoke(null, null);
    }

    // Declare a delegate to wrap the VerifyAccess method
    private delegate void VerifyAccessDelegate();

    private void VerifyAccess()
    {
        this.Dispatcher.VerifyAccess();
    }
}
}
```

Figure 8-5 shows the resulting window.

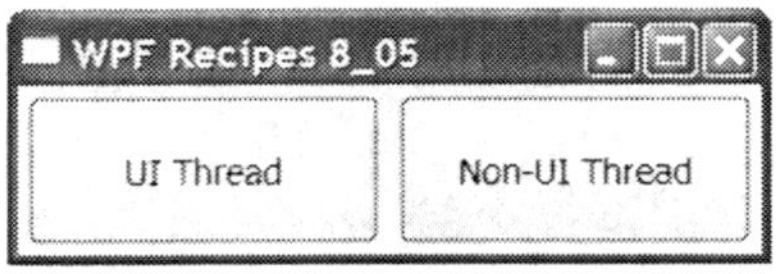

Figure 8-5. *Verifying that the calling threads has access to the UI thread*

8-6. Execute a Method Asynchronously Using a Background Worker Thread

Problem

You need to execute a method asynchronously on a background thread.

Solution

Create an instance of the System.ComponentModel.BackgroundWorker class, attach event handlers to its DoWork and RunWorkerCompleted events, and call the RunWorkerAysnc method to start the background thread.

How It Works

The BackgroundWorker component gives you the ability to execute time-consuming operations asynchronously. It automatically executes the operation on a different thread to the one that created it and then automatically returns control to the calling thread when it is completed.

The BackgroundWorker's DoWork event specifies the delegate to execute asynchronously. It is this delegate that is executed on a background thread when the RunWorkerAsync method is called. When it has completed the operation, it calls the RunWorkerCompleted event and executes the attached delegate on the same thread that was used to create it.

The DoWork method takes an argument of type System.ComponentModel.DoWorkEventArgs, which allows you to pass an argument to the method. The RunWorkerCompleted event is passed an instance of the System.ComponentModel.RunWorkerCompletedEventArgs class, which allows you to receive the result of the background process and any error that might have been thrown during processing.

If the BackgroundWorker object is created on the UI thread, for example, in the constructor method for a window or control, then you can access and update the UI in the RunWorkerCompleted event without having to check that you are on UI thread again. The BackgroundWorker object handles all the thread marshaling for you.

The Code

The following example creates a window with two System.Windows.Controls.TextBlock controls and a System.Windows.Controls.Button. The values in the TextBlock controls specify a range of numbers. In the constructor for the window, an instance of the BackgroundWorker class is created, and event handlers are attached to its DoWork and the RunWorkerCompleted events.

When the Button is clicked, the RunWorkerAsync method is called, which starts the BackgroundWorker and executes the DoWork event. In the code for this event, a PrimeNumberHelper class is used to search for the largest prime number within the range of numbers. When it finishes, the code for the RunWorkerCompleted event is executed, which updates a System.Windows.Controls.TextBlock on the window.

The XAML for the window is as follows:

```xml
<Window x:Class="Recipe_08_06.Window1"
    xmlns="http://schemas.microsoft.com/winfx/2006/xaml/presentation"
    xmlns:x="http://schemas.microsoft.com/winfx/2006/xaml"
    Title="WPF Recipes 8_06" Width="240" Height="140" >
    <StackPanel Orientation="Vertical">
        <StackPanel Orientation="Horizontal">
            <TextBlock Margin="5" VerticalAlignment="Center">From:</TextBlock>
            <TextBox Name="txtFrom" Margin="5" Width="64" Text="1" />
            <TextBlock Margin="5" VerticalAlignment="Center">To:</TextBlock>
            <TextBox Name="txtTo" Margin="5" Width="64" Text="1000000"/>
        </StackPanel>
        <Button
            Click="Start_Click"
            Name="btnStart"
            Margin="5"
            Height="34">Start</Button>
        <StackPanel Orientation="Horizontal">
            <TextBlock Margin="5">Biggest Prime Found:</TextBlock>
            <TextBlock Name="txtBiggestPrime" Margin="5" />
        </StackPanel>
    </StackPanel>
</Window>
```

The code-behind for the window is as follows:

```
using System;
using System.Windows;
using System.ComponentModel;
using Recipe_08_06;

namespace Recipe_08_06
{
    public partial class Window1 : Window
    {
        private BackgroundWorker worker;

        private long from;
        private long to;
        private long biggestPrime;

        public Window1()
            : base()
        {
            InitializeComponent();

            // Create a Background Worker
            worker = new BackgroundWorker();

            // Attach the event handlers
            worker.DoWork +=
                new DoWorkEventHandler(worker_DoWork);
            worker.RunWorkerCompleted +=
                new RunWorkerCompletedEventHandler(worker_RunWorkerCompleted);
        }

        private void Start_Click(object sender, RoutedEventArgs e)
        {
            try
            {
                if(!long.TryParse(txtFrom.Text, out from))
                    throw new ApplicationException("From is not a valid number");

                if(!long.TryParse(txtTo.Text, out to))
                    throw new ApplicationException("To is not a valid number");

                // Start the Background Worker
                worker.RunWorkerAsync();
```

```csharp
                btnStart.IsEnabled = false;
                txtBiggestPrime.Text = string.Empty;
            }
            catch(Exception ex)
            {
                MessageBox.Show(
                        ex.Message, "Error",
                        MessageBoxButton.OK, MessageBoxImage.Error);
            }
        }

        private void worker_RunWorkerCompleted(
            object sender, RunWorkerCompletedEventArgs e)
        {
            btnStart.IsEnabled = true;
            txtBiggestPrime.Text = biggestPrime.ToString();
        }

        private void worker_DoWork(
            object sender, DoWorkEventArgs e)
        {
            // Loop through the numbers, finding the biggest prime
            for(long current = from; current <= to; current++)
            {
                if(PrimeNumberHelper.IsPrime(current))
                {
                    biggestPrime = current;
                }
            }
        }
    }
}
```

Figure 8-6 shows the resulting window.

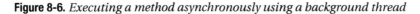

Figure 8-6. *Executing a method asynchronously using a background thread*

8-7. Track the Progress of a Background Worker Thread

Problem

You need to track the progress of a background worker thread. This is useful to keep the user informed during a long-running process.

Solution

Create an instance of the System.ComponentModel.BackgroundWorker class to process an operation on a background thread. Set its WorkerReportsProgress property to True, and attach an event handler to its ProgressChanged event. Call the ReportProgress method from the DoWork event handler.

How It Works

The BackgroundWorker component provides built-in support for tracking the progress of its operation. This is useful for displaying how much work has been completed on the UI. Three steps are involved. First, you need to set the BackgroundWorker's WorkerReportsProgress property to True. It is False by default. Second, you need to call its ReportProgress method during the operation, passing in the percentage of work that has been completed. Third, you need to attach an event handler to the ProgressChanged event, which is automatically raised each time the ReportProgress method is called.

The BackgroundWorker class executes the ProgressChanged event on the thread that created it, so if this is the UI thread, you can update the UI directly in this event handler.

The Code

The following example creates a window that instantiates a BackgroundWorker object in its constructor and sets its WorkerReportsProgress property to True. It displays a number of controls, including a System.Windows.Controls.Button. When this Button is clicked, the BackgroundWorker starts an operation to search for the largest prime number within a range of numbers.

After each prime number is found, the ReportProgess method is called, passing in an estimated percentage of completion. This executes the code in the worker_ProgressChanged method, which displays the percentage in a System.Windows.TextBlock on the window.

The XAML for the window is as follows:

```
<Window x:Class="Recipe_08_07.Window1"
    xmlns="http://schemas.microsoft.com/winfx/2006/xaml/presentation"
    xmlns:x="http://schemas.microsoft.com/winfx/2006/xaml"
  Title="WPF Recipes 8_07" Width="228" Height="168" >
    <StackPanel Orientation="Vertical">
```

```
        <StackPanel Orientation="Horizontal">
            <TextBlock Margin="5" VerticalAlignment="Center">From:</TextBlock>
            <TextBox Name="txtFrom" Margin="5" Width="60" Text="1" />
            <TextBlock Margin="5" VerticalAlignment="Center">To:</TextBlock>
            <TextBox Name="txtTo" Margin="5" Width="60" Text="10000"/>
        </StackPanel>
        <Button
            Click="StartStop_Click"
            Name="btnStartStop"
            Margin="5"
            Height="34">Start</Button>
        <StackPanel Orientation="Horizontal">
            <TextBlock Margin="5">Percent complete:</TextBlock>
            <TextBlock Name="txtPercent" Margin="5" />
        </StackPanel>
        <StackPanel Orientation="Horizontal">
            <TextBlock Margin="5">Biggest Prime Found:</TextBlock>
            <TextBlock Name="txtBiggestPrime" Margin="5" />
        </StackPanel>
    </StackPanel>
</Window>
```

The code-behind for the window is as follows:

```
using System;
using System.ComponentModel;
using System.Windows;
using Recipe_08_07;

namespace Recipe_08_07
{
    public partial class Window1 : Window
    {
        private BackgroundWorker worker;

        private long from;
        private long to;
        private long biggestPrime;

        public Window1()
            : base()
        {
            InitializeComponent();

            // Create a Background Worker
            worker = new BackgroundWorker();
            worker.WorkerReportsProgress = true;
```

```csharp
    // Attach the event handlers
    worker.DoWork +=
        new DoWorkEventHandler(worker_DoWork);
    worker.RunWorkerCompleted +=
        new RunWorkerCompletedEventHandler(worker_RunWorkerCompleted);
    worker.ProgressChanged += worker_ProgressChanged;
}

private void StartStop_Click(object sender, RoutedEventArgs e)
{
    try
    {
        if(!long.TryParse(txtFrom.Text, out from))
            throw new ApplicationException("From is not a valid number");

        if(!long.TryParse(txtTo.Text, out to))
            throw new ApplicationException("To is not a valid number");

        // Start the Background Worker
        worker.RunWorkerAsync();

        btnStartStop.IsEnabled = false;
        txtBiggestPrime.Text = string.Empty;
    }
    catch(Exception ex)
    {
        MessageBox.Show(
                ex.Message, "Error",
                MessageBoxButton.OK, MessageBoxImage.Error);
    }
}

private void worker_RunWorkerCompleted(
    object sender, RunWorkerCompletedEventArgs e)
{
    btnStartStop.IsEnabled = true;
    txtBiggestPrime.Text = biggestPrime.ToString();
}

private void worker_DoWork(
    object sender, DoWorkEventArgs e)
{
    // Loop through the numbers, finding the biggest prime
    for(long current = from; current <= to; current++)
    {
```

```
        if(PrimeNumberHelper.IsPrime(current))
        {
            biggestPrime = current;

            // Call report progress to fire the ProgressChanged event
            int percentComplete = Convert.ToInt32(
                                                ((double) current / to)
                                                    * 100d);

            worker.ReportProgress(percentComplete);

            System.Threading.Thread.Sleep(10);
        }
    }
}

private void worker_ProgressChanged(
    object sender, ProgressChangedEventArgs e)
{
    // Update the progress bar
    txtPercent.Text = e.ProgressPercentage.ToString() + "%";
}
    }
}
```

Figure 8-7 shows the resulting window.

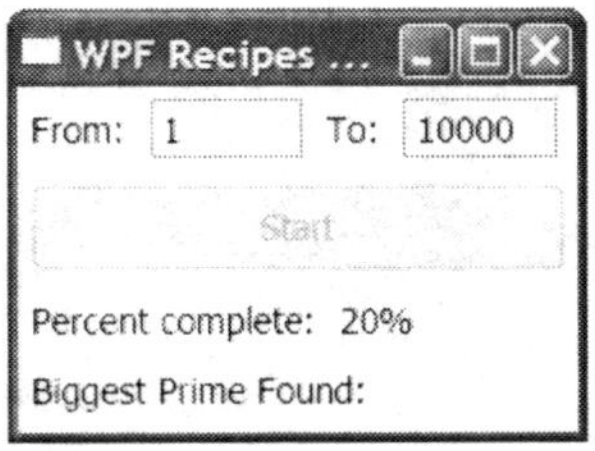

Figure 8-7. *Tracking the progress of a background worker thread*

8-8. Support the Cancellation of a Background Worker Thread

Problem

You need to allow a user to cancel an operation on a background worker thread.

Solution

Create an instance of the `System.ComponentModel.BackgroundWorker` class to process an operation on a background thread. Set its `WorkerSupportsCancellation` property to `True`, and call the `CancelAsync` method when the user wants to cancel the operation. In the `DoWork` event handler, check the `CancellationPending` property, and if this is `True`, use the `Cancel` property of `System.ComponentModel.DoWorkEventArgs` to notify the `RunWorkerCompleted` event handler that the operation was cancelled.

How It Works

A few steps are involved in allowing an operation on a background worker thread to be cancelled. First, set the `WorkerSupportsCancellation` property of the `BackgroundWorker` to `True`. It is `False` by default. Second, you need to call its `CancelAsync` method when the user has requested the cancellation, for example, by clicking a `System.Windows.Controls.Button` marked Cancel. This doesn't automatically cancel the operation; it just sets the `BackgroundWorker`'s `CancellationPending` property to `True`. So, the next thing you need to do is check the value of this property during the operation. When it is `True`, you must set the `Cancel` property of the `DoWorkEventArgs` parameter to `True` and exit the method. Finally, in the `RunWorkerCompleted` event handler, you can check the `Cancelled` property of the `System.ComponentModel.RunWorkerCompletedEventArgs` parameter. If it is `True`, you know that the operation was cancelled by the user.

The Code

The following example creates a window that instantiates a `BackgroundWorker` object in its constructor and sets its `WorkerSupportsCancellation` property to `True`. It displays a number of controls, including a `System.Windows.Controls.Button`. The first time this `Button` is clicked, it runs the `BackgroundWorker`, which starts an operation to search for the largest prime number within a range of numbers. It also sets the text on the `Button` to Cancel. When it is clicked again, it calls the `CancelAsync` method of the `BackgroundWorker`.

Each time the code in the `DoWork` method checks whether a number is prime, it also checks to see whether the `BackgroundWorker`'s `CancellationPending` property is `True`. If it is, it sets the `Cancel` property of the `DoWorkEventArgs` parameter to `True` and exits the method. In the `RunWorkerCompleted` method, it checks the `Cancelled` property of the `RunWorkerCompletedEventArgs` parameter and displays a `System.Windows.Messagebox` if it is `True`.

The XAML for the window is as follows:

```
<Window x:Class="Recipe_08_08.Window1"
    xmlns="http://schemas.microsoft.com/winfx/2006/xaml/presentation"
    xmlns:x="http://schemas.microsoft.com/winfx/2006/xaml"
    Title="WPF Recipes 8_08" Width="230" Height="148" >
    <StackPanel Orientation="Vertical">
        <StackPanel Orientation="Horizontal">
            <TextBlock Margin="5" VerticalAlignment="Center">From:</TextBlock>
            <TextBox Name="txtFrom" Margin="5" Width="64" Text="1" />
            <TextBlock Margin="5" VerticalAlignment="Center">To:</TextBlock>
            <TextBox Name="txtTo" Margin="5" Width="64" Text="1000000"/>
        </StackPanel>
```

```
        <Button
            Click="StartStop_Click"
            Name="btnStartStop"
            Margin="5"
            Height="34">Start</Button>
        <StackPanel Orientation="Horizontal">
            <TextBlock Margin="5">Biggest Prime Found:</TextBlock>
            <TextBlock Name="txtBiggestPrime" Margin="5" />
        </StackPanel>
    </StackPanel>
</Window>
```

The code-behind for the window is as follows:

```
using System;
using System.ComponentModel;
using System.Windows;
using Recipe_08_08;

namespace Recipe_08_08
{
    public partial class Window1 : Window
    {
        private BackgroundWorker worker;

        private long from;
        private long to;
        private long biggestPrime;

        public Window1()
            : base()
        {
            InitializeComponent();

            // Create a Background Worker
            worker = new BackgroundWorker();

            // Enable support for cancellation
            worker.WorkerSupportsCancellation = true;

            // Attach the event handlers
            worker.DoWork +=
                new DoWorkEventHandler(worker_DoWork);
            worker.RunWorkerCompleted +=
                new RunWorkerCompletedEventHandler(worker_RunWorkerCompleted);
        }
```

```csharp
private void StartStop_Click(object sender, RoutedEventArgs e)
{
    if(!worker.IsBusy)
    {
        try
        {
            if(!long.TryParse(txtFrom.Text, out from))
                throw new ApplicationException(
                        "From is not a valid number");

            if(!long.TryParse(txtTo.Text, out to))
                throw new ApplicationException("To is not a valid number");

            // Start the Background Worker
            worker.RunWorkerAsync();

            btnStartStop.Content = "Cancel";
            txtBiggestPrime.Text = string.Empty;
        }
        catch(Exception ex)
        {
            MessageBox.Show(
                    ex.Message, "Error",
                    MessageBoxButton.OK, MessageBoxImage.Error);
        }
    }
    else
    {
        // Cancel the Background Worker
        worker.CancelAsync();
    }
}

private void worker_RunWorkerCompleted(
    object sender, RunWorkerCompletedEventArgs e)
{
    if(e.Cancelled)
    {
        // The user cancelled the operation
        MessageBox.Show("Operation was cancelled");
    }

    btnStartStop.Content = "Start";
    txtBiggestPrime.Text = biggestPrime.ToString();
}
```

```
private void worker_DoWork(
    object sender, DoWorkEventArgs e)
{
    // Loop through the numbers, finding the biggest prime
    for(long current = from; current <= to; current++)
    {
        // Check if the BackgroundWorker
        // has been cancelled
        if(worker.CancellationPending)
        {
            // Set the Cancel property
            e.Cancel = true;
            return;
        }

        if(PrimeNumberHelper.IsPrime(current))
        {
            biggestPrime = current;
        }
    }
}
```

Figure 8-8 shows the resulting window.

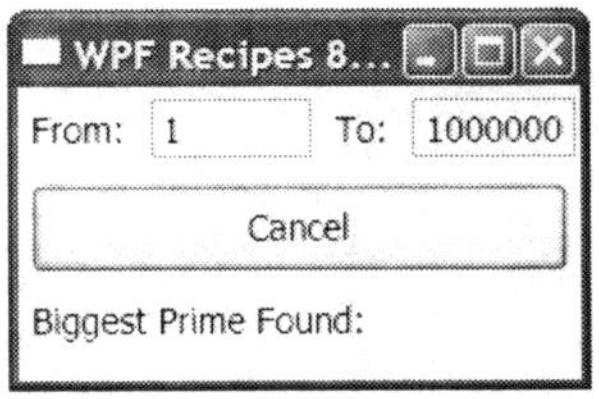

Figure 8-8. *Supporting the cancellation of a background worker thread*

8-9. Create a Background Worker Thread in XAML

Problem

You need to declare a System.ComponentModel.BackgroundWorker in XAML.

Solution

Reference the System.ComponentModel namespace in the XAML for your window, and define an instance of the BackgroundWorker in the Window.Resources collection.

How It Works

When the window is initialized, the instance of the BackgroundWorker will be instantiated. You can set its properties and attach its event handlers using attributes in the XAML.

The Code

The following example demonstrates a window that declares a BackgroundWorker in the Window. Resources collection. It imports the System.ComponentModel namespace by referencing it in the Window attributes. The BackgroundWorker is given a key, has its properties set, and has delegates attached to its events, all in the inline XAML.

The window also declares a System.Windows.Controls.ProgressBar and a System.Windows. Controls.Button. When the Button is clicked, the BackgroundWorker that was declared in the Resources is started asynchronously and reports its progress to the ProgressBar.

In the window's constructor, the FrameworkElement.FindResource method is called to retrieve a reference to the BackgroundWorker declared in the XAML. This reference is then used to start and cancel the BackgroundWorker when the Button is clicked.

The XAML for the window is as follows:

```
<Window x:Class="Recipe_08_09.Window1"
   xmlns="http://schemas.microsoft.com/winfx/2006/xaml/presentation"
   xmlns:x="http://schemas.microsoft.com/winfx/2006/xaml"
   xmlns:ComponentModel="clr-namespace:System.ComponentModel;assembly=System"
   Title="WPF Recipes 8_09" Height="100" Width="200">

   <Window.Resources>
      <ComponentModel:BackgroundWorker
         x:Key="backgroundWorker"
         WorkerReportsProgress="True"
         WorkerSupportsCancellation="True"
         DoWork="BackgroundWorker_DoWork"
         RunWorkerCompleted="BackgroundWorker_RunWorkerCompleted"
         ProgressChanged="BackgroundWorker_ProgressChanged"
         />
   </Window.Resources>

   <Grid>

      <Grid.RowDefinitions>
         <RowDefinition/>
         <RowDefinition/>
      </Grid.RowDefinitions>

      <ProgressBar
         Name="progressBar" Margin="4"/>
```

```
        <Button
            Name="button"
            Grid.Row="1"
            Click="button_Click"
            HorizontalAlignment="Center"
            Margin="4"
            Width="60">
            Start
        </Button>
    </Grid>
</Window>
```

The code-behind for the window is as follows:

```
using System.ComponentModel;
using System.Threading;
using System.Windows;
using System.Windows.Input;

namespace Recipe_08_09
{
    public partial class Window1 : Window
    {
        private readonly BackgroundWorker worker;

        public Window1()
        {
            InitializeComponent();

            // Retrieve a reference to the
            // BackgroundWorker declared in the XAML
            worker = this.FindResource("backgroundWorker")
                    as BackgroundWorker;
        }

        private void button_Click(object sender, RoutedEventArgs e)
        {
            if(!worker.IsBusy)
            {
                this.Cursor = Cursors.Wait;

                worker.RunWorkerAsync();
                button.Content = "Cancel";
            }
            else
            {
                worker.CancelAsync();
            }
        }
```

```
    private void BackgroundWorker_DoWork(
                    object sender,
                    System.ComponentModel.DoWorkEventArgs e)
    {
        for(int i = 1; i <= 100; i++)
        {
            if(worker.CancellationPending)
                break;

            Thread.Sleep(100);
            worker.ReportProgress(i);
        }
    }

    private void BackgroundWorker_RunWorkerCompleted(
                    object sender,
                    System.ComponentModel.RunWorkerCompletedEventArgs e)
    {
        this.Cursor = Cursors.Arrow;

        if(e.Error != null)
            MessageBox.Show(e.Error.Message);

        button.Content = "Start";
    }

    private void BackgroundWorker_ProgressChanged(
                    object sender,
                    System.ComponentModel.ProgressChangedEventArgs e)
    {
        progressBar.Value = e.ProgressPercentage;
    }
  }
}
```

8-10. Update the UI Asynchronously on a Timer

Problem

You need to execute a method that updates the UI on a timer.

Solution

Use a System.Windows.Threading.DispatcherTimer that utilizes the Dispatcher object of the thread that creates it and raises the Tick event on the Dispatcher queue at a specified time and at a specified priority.

How It Works

There are three timer classes in the .NET Framework Base Class Library (BCL): System.Threading.Timer, System.Timers.Timer, and System.Windows.Forms.Timer. Each of these timers is different, but essentially they all support specifying a time interval between ticks, as well as the code to run when this interval is reached. WPF introduces a new timer that is also designed specifically to utilize the threading model in WPF. It ensures that when the Tick event handler is raised, the delegate is added to the dispatcher queue of the thread that created it. So if the DispatcherTimer is created on the UI thread, the delegate added to the Tick event handler will automatically be executed on the UI thread.

The DispatcherTimer class has an overloaded constructor that allows you to specify a DispatcherPriority parameter. If this parameter is omitted, the default is Normal. It can be used to specify that the tick event should be fired in the background and not interfere with higher-priority events such as those to do with loading, binding, and rendering.

The Code

The following example creates a window with a System.Windows.Controls.Button and a System.Windows.Controls.TextBlock. When the Button is clicked, there is logic in the code-behind to initialize an instance of the DispatcherTimer class and to give it an interval of one second, and there is a Tick event handler that displays the current second in the TextBlock control. Because the DispatcherTimer is created on UI thread, there is no need for any special code in the Tick event handler to ensure it is being executed on the UI thread.

The XAML for the window is as follows:

```
<Window x:Class="Recipe_08_10.Window1"
    xmlns="http://schemas.microsoft.com/winfx/2006/xaml/presentation"
    xmlns:x="http://schemas.microsoft.com/winfx/2006/xaml"
    Title="WPF Recipes 8_10" Height="100" Width="300">
    <Grid>
        <Grid.ColumnDefinitions>
            <ColumnDefinition />
            <ColumnDefinition />
        </Grid.ColumnDefinitions>

        <Button
            x:Name="button"
            Click="Button_Click">Start Timer</Button>

        <TextBlock
            x:Name="txtStatus"
            Grid.Column="1"
            Margin="4"
            VerticalAlignment="Center"
            HorizontalAlignment="Center">
        </TextBlock>
    </Grid>
</Window>
```

The code-behind for the window is as follows:

```csharp
using System;
using System.Windows;
using System.Windows.Threading;

namespace Recipe_08_10
{
    public partial class Window1 : Window
    {
        private DispatcherTimer timer;

        public Window1()
        {
            InitializeComponent();
        }

        private void Button_Click(object sender, RoutedEventArgs e)
        {
            if(timer == null || !timer.IsEnabled)
            {
                timer = new DispatcherTimer();

                timer.Interval = TimeSpan.FromMilliseconds(1000);
                timer.Tick += new EventHandler(timer_Tick);

                timer.Start();
                button.Content = "Stop Timer";
            }
            else
            {
                timer.Stop();
                button.Content = "Start Timer";
            }
        }

        private void timer_Tick(object sender, EventArgs e)
        {
            txtStatus.Text = DateTime.Now.Second.ToString();
        }
    }
}
```

8-11. Show a Continuous Animation During an Asynchronous Process

Problem

You need to show a continuous animation whilst processing an operation on a background thread.

Solution

Create a System.Windows.Media.Animation.Storyboard to animate some visual elements, whilst processing an operation asynchronously using a System.ComponentModel.BackgroundWorker object. Set the RepeatBehavior property of the Storyboard to System.Windows.Threading. DispatcherTimer.Forever. Specify that the Storyboard should be interactively controllable by calling its Begin method with a value of True for the isControllable parameter. In the BackgroundWorker's RunWorkerCompleted event handler, call the Storyboard's Stop method.

How It Works

Setting the RepeatBehavior property of the Storyboard class to Forever ensures that the animation runs continuously until explicitly stopped. It can then be started when the asynchronous process is begun and stopped when it completes.

■**Caution** If the Begin method of the Storyboard is not called with the isControllable parameter explicitly set to True, then calling the Stop method programmatically will not terminate the animation.

The Code

The following example demonstrates a window that displays a System.Windows.Shapes.Ellipse and a System.Windows.Controls.Button. A Storyboard is declared in the Resources collection of the Window, which changes the color of the Ellipse from gray to green when run.

In the code-behind for Button's Click event, the Storyboard is started, and a BackgroundWorker object is run asynchronously. It simulates a background process by calling System.Threading. Thread.Sleep a number of times. In the code for the RunWorkerCompleted event, the Storyboard is stopped.

The XAML for the window is as follows:

```
<Window x:Class="Recipe_08_11.Window1"
    xmlns="http://schemas.microsoft.com/winfx/2006/xaml/presentation"
    xmlns:x="http://schemas.microsoft.com/winfx/2006/xaml"
    Title="WPF Recipes 8_11" Height="220" Width="180">
    <Window.Resources>
        <Storyboard  x:Key="PulseStoryboard" AutoReverse="True" >
```

```xml
                <ColorAnimationUsingKeyFrames BeginTime="00:00:00"
                        Storyboard.TargetName="ellipse"
                        Storyboard.TargetProperty=
                "(Shape.Fill).(GradientBrush.GradientStops)[0].(GradientStop.Color)">
                    <SplineColorKeyFrame KeyTime="00:00:00.5000000" Value="Lime"/>
                </ColorAnimationUsingKeyFrames>
                <ColorAnimationUsingKeyFrames BeginTime="00:00:00"
                        Storyboard.TargetName="ellipse"
                        Storyboard.TargetProperty=
                "(Shape.Fill).(GradientBrush.GradientStops)[1].(GradientStop.Color)">
                    <SplineColorKeyFrame KeyTime="00:00:00.5000000" Value="Green"/>
                </ColorAnimationUsingKeyFrames>
            </Storyboard>
        </Window.Resources>

        <Grid x:Name="LayoutRoot" >

            <Grid.RowDefinitions>
                <RowDefinition Height="*"/>
                <RowDefinition Height="60" />
            </Grid.RowDefinitions>

            <Ellipse
             Width="100"
             Height="100"
             Margin="10"
             Stroke="{x:Null}" x:Name="ellipse">
                <Ellipse.Fill>
                    <RadialGradientBrush GradientOrigin="0.25,0.25">
                        <GradientStop Offset="0" Color="#A8FFFFFF"/>
                        <GradientStop Offset="1" Color="#FF9C9F97"/>
                    </RadialGradientBrush>
                </Ellipse.Fill>
            </Ellipse>

            <Button Margin="10"
                    Content="Start"
                    Grid.Row="1"
                    x:Name="button"
                    Click="button_Click"/>
        </Grid>
    </Window>
```

The code-behind for the window is as follows:

```
using System.Windows;
using System.Threading;
using System.ComponentModel;
using System.Windows.Media.Animation;

namespace Recipe_08_11
{
    public partial class Window1 : Window
    {
        private Storyboard pulseStoryboard;
        private BackgroundWorker worker;

        public Window1()
        {
            InitializeComponent();

            pulseStoryboard
                = (Storyboard) this.Resources["PulseStoryboard"];

            // Set the animation to repeat indefinitely
            pulseStoryboard.RepeatBehavior = RepeatBehavior.Forever;

            // Create a Background Worker
            worker = new BackgroundWorker();

            worker.DoWork +=
                new DoWorkEventHandler(worker_DoWork);
            worker.RunWorkerCompleted +=
                new RunWorkerCompletedEventHandler(worker_RunWorkerCompleted);
        }

        private void button_Click(
            object sender, RoutedEventArgs e)
        {
            // Begin the animation
            pulseStoryboard.Begin(this, true);

            // Start the Background Worker
            worker.RunWorkerAsync();

            button.IsEnabled = false;
        }
```

```
    private void worker_RunWorkerCompleted(
        object sender, RunWorkerCompletedEventArgs e)
    {
        button.IsEnabled = true;

        // Stop the animation
        pulseStoryboard.Stop(this);
    }

    private void worker_DoWork(
        object sender, DoWorkEventArgs e)
    {
        for(int i = 1; i <= 50; i++)
        {
            Thread.Sleep(50);
        }
    }
  }
}
```

Figure 8-9 shows the resulting window.

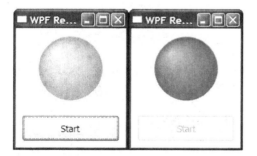

Figure 8-9. *Showing a continuous animation during an asynchronous process*

8-12. Show a ProgressBar While Processing on a Background Thread

Problem

You need to show a System.Windows.Controls.ProgressBar whilst processing an operation on a background thread.

Solution

Create a System.ComponentModel.BackgroundWorker object, set its WorkerReportsProgress property to True, and add an event handler to its ProgressChanged event. Call the ReportProgress method of the BackgroundWorker whilst processing the operation on the background thread, and in the code for this ProgressChanged event handler, update the Value property of a ProgressBar.

How It Works

The BackgroundWorker class has a Boolean property called WorkerReportsProgress, which indicates whether the BackgroundWorker can report progress updates. It is set to False by default. When this is set to True, calling the ReportProgress method will raise the ProgressChanged event.

The ReportProgress method takes an integer parameter specifying the percentage of progress completed by the BackgroundWorker. This parameter is passed to the ProgressChanged event handler via the ProgressPercentage property of the System.ComponentModel. ProgressChangedEventArgs class.

The ProgressBar control sets the default value for its Maximum property to 100, which lends itself perfectly and automatically to receive the ProgressPercentage as its Value property.

The Code

The following example demonstrates a window that declares a ProgressBar control and a Button. An instance of the BackgroundWorker class is created in the window's constructor, and its WorkerReportsProgress property is set to True. Event handlers are added to the ProgressBar's DoWork, RunWorkerCompleted, and ProgressChanged events.

In the code-behind for the button's Click event, the BackgroundWorker is started asynchronously. This executes the worker_DoWork method on a background thread, which loops through 1 to 100, simulating some processing using Thread.Sleep and calling the ReportProgress method of the BackgroundWorker.

Each time ReportProgress is called, the worker_ProgressChanged method is executed, which sets the Value property of the ProgressBar to the ProgressPercentage property of the ProgressChangedEventArgs.

The XAML for the window is as follows:

```
<Window x:Class="Recipe_08_12.Window1"
    xmlns="http://schemas.microsoft.com/winfx/2006/xaml/presentation"
    xmlns:x="http://schemas.microsoft.com/winfx/2006/xaml"
    Title="WPF Recipes 8_12" Height="100" Width="200">
    <Grid>

        <Grid.RowDefinitions>
            <RowDefinition/>
            <RowDefinition/>
        </Grid.RowDefinitions>

        <ProgressBar
            Name="progressBar" Margin="4"/>
```

```
        <Button
            Name="button"
            Grid.Row="1"
            Click="button_Click"
            HorizontalAlignment="Center"
            Margin="4"
            Width="60">
            Start
        </Button>
    </Grid>
</Window>
```

The code-behind for the window is as follows:

```
using System.ComponentModel;
using System.Threading;
using System.Windows;
using System.Windows.Input;

namespace Recipe_08_12
{
    public partial class Window1 : Window
    {
        private BackgroundWorker worker;

        public Window1()
        {
            InitializeComponent();

            // Create a Background Worker
            worker = new BackgroundWorker();

            // Enable progress reporting
            worker.WorkerReportsProgress = true;

            // Attach the event handlers
            worker.DoWork += new DoWorkEventHandler(worker_DoWork);
            worker.RunWorkerCompleted +=
                    new RunWorkerCompletedEventHandler(
                            worker_RunWorkerCompleted);
            worker.ProgressChanged += worker_ProgressChanged;
        }

        private void button_Click(object sender, RoutedEventArgs e)
        {
            // Start the Background Worker
            worker.RunWorkerAsync();
```

```
            this.Cursor = Cursors.Wait;
            button.IsEnabled = false;
        }

        private void worker_RunWorkerCompleted(
            object sender, RunWorkerCompletedEventArgs e)
        {
            this.Cursor = Cursors.Arrow;

            if(e.Error != null)
                MessageBox.Show(e.Error.Message);

            button.IsEnabled = true;
        }

        private void worker_DoWork(
            object sender, DoWorkEventArgs e)
        {
            for(int i = 1; i <= 100; i++)
            {
                // Simulate some processing by sleeping
                Thread.Sleep(100);

                // Call report progress to fire the ProgressChanged event
                worker.ReportProgress(i);
            }
        }

        private void worker_ProgressChanged(
            object sender, ProgressChangedEventArgs e)
        {
            // Update the progress bar
            progressBar.Value = e.ProgressPercentage;
        }
    }
}
```

Figure 8-10 shows the resulting window.

Figure 8-10. *Showing a progress bar while processing on a background thread*

8-13. Show a Cancellable ProgressBar While Processing on a Background Thread

Problem

You need to show a System.Windows.Controls.ProgressBar whilst processing an operation on a background thread and allow the user to cancel the operation during processing.

Solution

Create a System.ComponentModel.BackgroundWorker object, and set its WorkerSupportsCancellation property to True. Add a System.Windows.Controls.Button to your window, and call the CancelAsync method of the BackgroundWorker in its Click event handler.

How It Works

The BackgroundWorker class has a Boolean property called WorkerSupportsCancellation, which, when set to True, allows the CancelAsync method to interrupt the background operation. It is set to False by default.

In the RunWorkerCompleted event handler, you can use the Cancelled property of the RunWorkerCompletedEventArgs to check whether the BackgroundWorker was cancelled.

The Code

The following example demonstrates a window that declares a ProgressBar control and a Button. An instance of the BackgroundWorker class is created in the window's constructor, and its WorkerSupportsCancellation property is set to True.

When the Button is clicked, the code in the Click handler runs the BackgroundWorker asynchronously and changes the text of the Button from Start to Cancel. If it is clicked again, the IsBusy property of the BackgroundWorker returns True, and the code calls the CancelAsync method to cancel the operation.

In the RunWorkerCompleted event handler, a System.Windows.MessageBox is shown if the Cancelled property of the RunWorkerCompletedEventArgs parameter is True.

The XAML for the window is as follows:

```
<Window x:Class="Recipe_08_13.Window1"
    xmlns="http://schemas.microsoft.com/winfx/2006/xaml/presentation"
    xmlns:x="http://schemas.microsoft.com/winfx/2006/xaml"
    Title="WPF Recipes 8_13" Height="100" Width="200">
<Grid>

    <Grid.RowDefinitions>
        <RowDefinition/>
        <RowDefinition/>
    </Grid.RowDefinitions>
```

```
        <ProgressBar
            Name="progressBar" Margin="4"/>

        <Button
            Name="button"
            Grid.Row="1"
            Click="button_Click"
            HorizontalAlignment="Center"
            Margin="4"
            Width="60">
            Start
        </Button>
    </Grid>
</Window>
```

The code-behind for the window is as follows:

```
using System.ComponentModel;
using System.Threading;
using System.Windows;
using System.Windows.Input;

namespace Recipe_08_13
{
    public partial class Window1 : Window
    {
        private BackgroundWorker worker;

        public Window1()
        {
            InitializeComponent();

            // Create a Background Worker
            worker = new BackgroundWorker();
            worker.WorkerReportsProgress = true;

            // Enable support for cancellation
            worker.WorkerSupportsCancellation = true;

            // Attach the event handlers
            worker.DoWork +=
                new DoWorkEventHandler(worker_DoWork);
            worker.RunWorkerCompleted +=
                new RunWorkerCompletedEventHandler(worker_RunWorkerCompleted);
            worker.ProgressChanged +=
                worker_ProgressChanged;
        }
```

```
private void button_Click(
    object sender, RoutedEventArgs e)
{
    if(!worker.IsBusy)
    {
        this.Cursor = Cursors.Wait;

        // Start the Background Worker
        worker.RunWorkerAsync();
        button.Content = "Cancel";
    }
    else
    {
        // Cancel the Background Worker
        worker.CancelAsync();
    }
}

private void worker_RunWorkerCompleted(
    object sender, RunWorkerCompletedEventArgs e)
{
    this.Cursor = Cursors.Arrow;

    if(e.Cancelled)
    {
        // The user cancelled the operation
        MessageBox.Show("Operation was cancelled");
    }
    else if(e.Error != null)
    {
        MessageBox.Show(e.Error.Message);
    }

    button.Content = "Start";
}

private void worker_DoWork(
    object sender, DoWorkEventArgs e)
{
    for(int i = 1; i <= 100; i++)
    {
        // Check if the BackgroundWorker
        // has been cancelled
```

```
                if(worker.CancellationPending)
                {
                    // Set the Cancel property
                    e.Cancel = true;
                    return;
                }

                // Simulate some processing by sleeping
                Thread.Sleep(100);
                worker.ReportProgress(i);
            }
        }

        private void worker_ProgressChanged(
            object sender, ProgressChangedEventArgs e)
        {
            progressBar.Value = e.ProgressPercentage;
        }
    }
}
```

Figure 8-11 shows the resulting window.

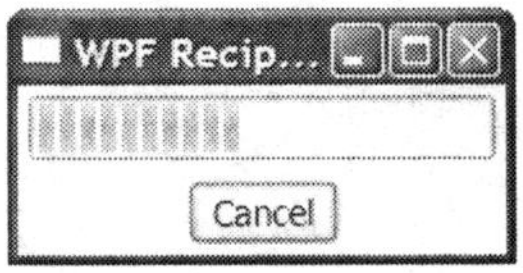

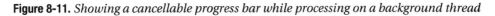

Figure 8-11. *Showing a cancellable progress bar while processing on a background thread*

8-14. Show a Continuous Progress Bar While Processing on a Background Thread

Problem

You need to show a continuous System.Windows.Controls.ProgressBar whilst processing an operation on a background thread, until the operation either completes or is cancelled by the user.

Solution

Create a System.ComponentModel.BackgroundWorker object, and add a ProgressBar to your window. Before calling the RunWorkerAsync method to start the BackgroundWorker, set the IsIndeterminate property of your ProgressBar to True. When the operation has completed, set the IsIndeterminate property to False again.

How It Works

The ProgressBar class has a Boolean property called IsIndeterminate. When this property is True, the ProgressBar animates a few bars moving across the ProgressBar in a continuous manner and ignores the Value property. It continues indefinitely until IsIndeterminate is set back to False again.

The Code

The following example demonstrates a window that declares a ProgressBar control and a Button. When the Button is clicked, a BackgroundWorker object is run that simulates a long-running operation by counting from 1 to 500 and calling the System.Threading.Thread.Sleep method in between each number. When the BackgroundWorker is run, the IsIndeterminate property of the ProgressBar is set to True, which starts its animation. When the RunWorkerCompleted event is raised, IsIndeterminate is set back to False, and the ProgressBar stops.

The XAML for the window is as follows:

```
<Window x:Class="Recipe_08_14.Window1"
    xmlns="http://schemas.microsoft.com/winfx/2006/xaml/presentation"
    xmlns:x="http://schemas.microsoft.com/winfx/2006/xaml"
    Title="WPF Recipes 8_14" Height="100" Width="200">
    <Grid>

        <Grid.RowDefinitions>
            <RowDefinition/>
            <RowDefinition/>
        </Grid.RowDefinitions>

        <ProgressBar
            Name="progressBar" Margin="4"/>

        <Button
            Name="button"
            Grid.Row="1"
            Click="button_Click"
            HorizontalAlignment="Center"
            Margin="4"
            Width="60">
            Start
        </Button>
    </Grid>
</Window>
```

The code-behind for the window is as follows:

```
using System.ComponentModel;
using System.Threading;
using System.Windows;
using System.Windows.Input;
```

```csharp
namespace Recipe_08_14
{
    public partial class Window1 : Window
    {
        private BackgroundWorker worker;

        public Window1()
        {
            InitializeComponent();

            // Create a Background Worker
            worker = new BackgroundWorker();

            // Enable support for cancellation
            worker.WorkerSupportsCancellation = true;

            worker.DoWork +=
                new DoWorkEventHandler(worker_DoWork);
            worker.RunWorkerCompleted +=
                new RunWorkerCompletedEventHandler(worker_RunWorkerCompleted);
        }

        private void button_Click(
            object sender, RoutedEventArgs e)
        {
            if (!worker.IsBusy)
            {
                this.Cursor = Cursors.Wait;

                // Set the ProgressBar's IsInderterminate
                // property to true to start the progress indicator
                progressBar.IsIndeterminate = true;
                button.Content = "Cancel";

                // Start the Background Worker
                worker.RunWorkerAsync();
            }
            else
            {
                worker.CancelAsync();
            }
        }

        private void worker_RunWorkerCompleted(
            object sender, RunWorkerCompletedEventArgs e)
        {
            this.Cursor = Cursors.Arrow;
```

```
            if (e.Error != null)
            {
                MessageBox.Show(e.Error.Message);
            }

            button.Content = "Start";

            // Reset the ProgressBar's IsInderterminate
            // property to false to stop the progress indicator
            progressBar.IsIndeterminate = false;
        }

        private void worker_DoWork(
            object sender, DoWorkEventArgs e)
        {
            for (int i = 1; i <= 500; i++)
            {
                if (worker.CancellationPending)
                    break;

                Thread.Sleep(50);
            }
        }
    }
}
```

Figure 8-12 shows the resulting window.

Figure 8-12. *Showing a continuous progress bar while processing on a background thread*

8-15. Implement Application.DoEvents in WPF

Problem

You need to implement the Application.DoEvents method in Windows Forms in order to force the UI thread to process rendering events during a long-running process.

Solution

Use the Invoke method of the current System.Windows.Threading.Dispatcher to queue a place-holder delegate with a System.Windows.Threading.DispatcherPriority of Background.

How It Works

Whereas the BeginInvoke method of Dispatcher is asynchronous, the Invoke method is synchronous. This means that the call to Invoke will not return until the event has been executed. If a dummy event is queued with a Background priority, then it will not be executed until all higher-priority operations have completed.

Caution Using Application.DoEvents is not always advisable, and it must be used with caution. For example, consider the case where a call to DoEvents is followed by code that accesses a window's Controls collection. It is possible that one of the events processed during the DoEvents may have been the user clicking the window's Close button. This would result in a call to the window's Dispose method, which in turn would clear the Controls collection. If the code following the call to DoEvents makes assumptions about the existence of controls in the window, this would cause an exception.

The Code

The following example displays a window containing two System.Windows.Controls.Button controls and a System.Windows.Controls.ListBox control. In the Click events for the buttons, a method called LoadNumbers is called that loads 10,000 numbers into the ListBox. When the button on the left is clicked, the window freezes whilst the numbers are loaded. It cannot receive any other events, and the numbers don't get displayed until all of them are added to the list.

However, when the button on the right is clicked, a method called DoEvents is called after each number is added to the ListBox. This ensures that the ListBox is updated between numbers and the window can still receive other input events.

In the code for DoEvents, an empty delegate is placed on the dispatcher queue using the Invoke method and given a DispatcherPriority of Background. This ensures the DoEvents method does not return until all the rendering events in the queue are processed.

The XAML for the window is as follows:

```
<Window x:Class="Recipe_08_15.Window1"
    xmlns="http://schemas.microsoft.com/winfx/2006/xaml/presentation"
    xmlns:x="http://schemas.microsoft.com/winfx/2006/xaml"
    Title="WPF Recipes 8_15" Height="200" Width="300">
    <Grid>

        <Grid.RowDefinitions>
            <RowDefinition Height="48"/>
            <RowDefinition/>
        </Grid.RowDefinitions>

        <StackPanel
            Orientation="Horizontal">
```

```xml
        <Button x:Name="btnWithout"
                Click="btnWithout_Click"
                Margin="4">
            Without DoEvents
        </Button>

        <Button x:Name="btnWith"
                Click="btnWith_Click"
                Margin="4">
            With DoEvents
        </Button>

    </StackPanel>

    <ListBox x:Name="listBox"
             Grid.Row="1" />
</Grid>
</Window>
```

The code for the window is as follows:

```csharp
using System.Windows;
using System.Windows.Threading;

namespace Recipe_08_15
{
    public partial class Window1 : Window
    {
        public Window1()
        {
            InitializeComponent();
        }

        private void btnWithout_Click(
            object sender, RoutedEventArgs e)
        {
            LoadNumbers(false);
        }

        private void btnWith_Click(
            object sender, RoutedEventArgs e)
        {
            LoadNumbers(true);
        }
```

```csharp
        private void LoadNumbers(bool callDoEvents)
        {
            listBox.Items.Clear();

            btnWithout.IsEnabled = false;
            btnWith.IsEnabled = false;

            // Load ten thousand numbers into a listbox
            for(int i = 1; i <= 10000; i++)
            {
                listBox.Items.Add("Number " + i.ToString());

                // Optionally call DoEvents
                if(callDoEvents)
                    DoEvents();
            }

            btnWithout.IsEnabled = true;
            btnWith.IsEnabled = true;
        }

        /// <summary>
        /// Process all messages in the current dispatcher queue
        /// </summary>
        public static void DoEvents()
        {
            // Add an empty delegate to the
            // current thread's Dispatcher, and
            // invoke it synchronously but using a
            // a Background priority.
            // It won't return until all higher-priority
            // events in the queue are processed.
            Dispatcher.CurrentDispatcher.Invoke(
                DispatcherPriority.Background,
                new EmptyDelegate(
                    delegate{}));
        }

        private delegate void EmptyDelegate();
    }
}
```

Figure 8-13 shows the resulting window.

Figure 8-13. *Loading a* ListBox *of numbers and calling* DoEvents *between each number*

8-16. Create a Separate Thread for Each Window in a Multiwindow Application

Problem

You have an application with multiple windows and need each window to have its own UI thread so that long-running operations in one window do not interfere with the rendering and operations in the other windows.

Solution

Instead of initializing and showing a new window from the UI thread of the main window, create a new System.Threading.Thread, and then create and show a new window from the starting point of this new thread.

How It Works

If you create and show child windows from the UI thread of the main window in an application with multiple windows, then each window shares the same thread and System.Windows.Threading.Dispatcher object. This is perfectly fine for many applications, but it means that each window shares the same event queue for all its UI events. This means that if one window initiates a long-running operation, none of the other windows can receive their events until it is finished.

When you create a new thread, WPF automatically creates a new Dispatcher object to manage it. So if you create each new window from a new thread, they will get their own Dispatcher object and events in the Dispatcher queue because one window will not affect the processing of events in the other windows.

To create a new thread, instantiate a new Thread object, and specify a System.Threading.ThreadStart delegate as its starting point. In this method, create and show a new window and then call Dispatcher.Run to start processing events on the thread's Dispatcher queue.

The Code

The following example demonstrates a window that functions as the main window of a multi-window application. There is a System.Windows.Controls.Button with the text New Window. When this is clicked, it launches a new window. If the Create Separate Threads System.Windows.Controls.CheckBox is checked, then it creates a new thread to spawn the new window. If it is not checked, then it creates it directly from the UI thread.

The new child windows contain a Button marked Start that, when clicked, executes a method that searches for prime numbers. To simulate a long-running blocking process, there is a CheckBox marked Sleep Between Numbers. If this is checked, the child window sleeps for 200 milliseconds between checking for each number.

To see the effects of creating each window on a separate thread, first create a few child windows with the Create Separate Threads CheckBox unchecked. If you then check the Sleep Between Numbers option on one of the child numbers, you will see that the simulated long-running process affects the processing on *all* the child windows. By slowing down the operation on one child window, it slows down the processing of events on all the other windows too.

However, by checking the Create Separate Threads CheckBox before creating new windows, you will see that even when we slow down the operation on one or more of the child windows, the other ones are not affected. They still execute the search for prime numbers and process their rendering and painting events, just as quickly as if they were the only window.

The XAML for the main window is as follows:

```xml
<Window x:Class="Recipe_08_16.MainWindow"
    xmlns="http://schemas.microsoft.com/winfx/2006/xaml/presentation"
    xmlns:x="http://schemas.microsoft.com/winfx/2006/xaml"
    Title="WPF Recipes 8_16"
    Height="108"
    Width="230" >
    <StackPanel Orientation="Vertical">

        <StackPanel Orientation="Horizontal">
            <Button Content="New Window"
                Click="btnNewWindow_Click"
                Margin="4"
                Height="40"
                Width="104"/>
            <Button Content="Close Windows"
                Click="btnCloseWindows_Click"
                Margin="4"
                Height="40"
                Width="104"/>
        </StackPanel>

        <CheckBox x:Name="chkCreateThread"
                Content="Create separate threads"
                Margin="4"/>
    </StackPanel>
</Window>
```

The code-behind for the main window is as follows:

```csharp
using System.Windows;
using System.Threading;
using System.Collections.Generic;

using Recipe_08_16;

namespace Recipe_08_16
{
    public partial class MainWindow : Window
    {
        private List<ChildWindow> windows = new List<ChildWindow>();
        private List<Thread> threads = new List<Thread>();

        public MainWindow()
        {
            InitializeComponent();
        }

        private void btnNewWindow_Click(object sender, RoutedEventArgs e)
        {
            if(chkCreateThread.IsChecked.Value)
            {
                // Create a new Thread
                // which will create a new window
                Thread newWindowThread =
                        new Thread(
                            new ThreadStart(
                                ThreadStartingPoint));
                newWindowThread.SetApartmentState(ApartmentState.STA);
                newWindowThread.IsBackground = true;
                newWindowThread.Start();

                threads.Add(newWindowThread);
            }
            else
            {
                // Create a new window
                ChildWindow window = new ChildWindow();
                window.Show();

                windows.Add(window);
            }
        }
```

```
        private void ThreadStartingPoint()
        {
            // Create a new window
            ChildWindow window = new ChildWindow();
            window.Show();

            // Start the new window's Dispatcher
            System.Windows.Threading.Dispatcher.Run();
        }

        private void btnCloseWindows_Click(object sender, RoutedEventArgs e)
        {
            foreach(ChildWindow window in windows)
            {
                window.Stop();
                window.Close();
            }
            windows.Clear();

            foreach(Thread thread in threads)
            {
                thread.Abort();
            }
            threads.Clear();
        }
    }
}
```

The XAML for the child window is as follows:

```
<Window x:Class="Recipe_08_16.ChildWindow"
    xmlns="http://schemas.microsoft.com/winfx/2006/xaml/presentation"
    xmlns:x="http://schemas.microsoft.com/winfx/2006/xaml"
    Title="Child Window" Width="228" Height="128" >
    <StackPanel Orientation="Vertical">
        <Button
            Click="StartStop_Click"
            Name="btnStartStop"
            Margin="4"
            Height="34">Start</Button>
        <CheckBox x:Name="chkSleep"
                Margin="4"
                Content="Sleep between numbers"/>
```

```
        <StackPanel Orientation="Horizontal">
            <TextBlock Margin="4">Biggest Prime Found:</TextBlock>
            <TextBlock Name="txtBiggestPrime" Margin="4" />
        </StackPanel>
    </StackPanel>
</Window>
```

The code-behind for the child window is as follows:

```
using System;
using System.Windows;
using System.Windows.Threading;

namespace Recipe_08_16
{
    public partial class ChildWindow : Window
    {
        private bool continueCalculating = false;

        private PrimeNumberHelper primeNumberHelper
            = new PrimeNumberHelper();

        public ChildWindow()
            : base()
        {
            InitializeComponent();
        }

        private void StartStop_Click(object sender, RoutedEventArgs e)
        {
            if(continueCalculating)
                Stop();
            else
                Start();
        }

        public void Start()
        {
            continueCalculating = true;
            btnStartStop.Content = "Stop";

            // Execute the CheckPrimeNumber method on
            // the current Dispatcher queue
            this.Dispatcher.BeginInvoke(
                DispatcherPriority.Normal,
                new Action<int>(CheckPrimeNumber), 3);
        }
```

```
        public void Stop()
        {
            continueCalculating = false;
            btnStartStop.Content = "Start";

            // Add an empty delegate to the
            // current thread's Dispatcher, and
            // invoke it synchronously but using a
            // a Background priority.
            // This ensures the Stop method won't return
            // until the CheckPrimeNumber method has completed.
            Dispatcher.CurrentDispatcher.Invoke(
                DispatcherPriority.Background,
                new EmptyDelegate(
                    delegate{}));
        }

        public void CheckPrimeNumber(int current)
        {
            if(primeNumberHelper.IsPrime(current))
            {
                txtBiggestPrime.Text = current.ToString();
            }

            if(continueCalculating)
            {
                // Execute the CheckPrimeNumber method
                // again, using a lower DispatcherPriority
                this.Dispatcher.BeginInvoke(
                    DispatcherPriority.SystemIdle,
                    new Action<int>(CheckPrimeNumber), current + 2);

                if(chkSleep.IsChecked.Value)
                    System.Threading.Thread.Sleep(200);
            }
        }

        private delegate void EmptyDelegate();
    }
}
```

Figure 8-14 shows the resulting windows. The child window with the Sleep Between Numbers option checked takes much longer to find the prime numbers. However, the other windows are not affected.

Figure 8-14. *Creating a separate thread for each window in an application with multiple windows*

CHAPTER 9

■ ■ ■

Working with 2D Graphics

WPF fundamentally changes the way Windows application developers will use graphics within their applications' user interfaces. WPF offers the application developer a vast range of powerful and flexible graphics capabilities that they can integrate tightly into the user interface of their applications. Developers no longer need to make a technical decision as to whether they should use graphics or forms and controls for the UI of their application. WPF makes it so easy to integrate and interact with both graphics and controls that developers will start to use graphics far more regularly than they did in the days of WinForms and GDI development. Unfortunately, knowing how to use these features is not enough to create truly beautiful and usable applications, but that is the topic of another book.

The recipes in this chapter describe how to:

- Draw straight lines and sequences of connected lines (recipes 9-1 and 9-2)

- Format lines and the outlines of shapes (recipe 9-3)

- Draw curved lines (recipe 9-4)

- Draw shapes (recipes 9-5 and 9-6)

- Create reusable shapes (recipe 9-7)

- Display tool tips on graphics (recipe 9-8)

- Display graphical content in a tool tip (recipe 9-9)

- Use the currently configured system colors in your graphics (recipe 9-10)

- Draw or fill a shape using a solid color (recipe 9-11)

- Fill a shape with a linear of radial color gradient (recipe 9-12)

- Fill a shape with an image (recipe 9-13)

- Fill a shape with a pattern or texture (recipe 9-14)

- Fill a shape with a view of active UI elements (recipe 9-15)

- Apply blur effects on UI elements (recipe 9-16)

- Apply glow effects on UI elements (recipe 9-17)

- Apply drop shadow effects on UI elements (recipe 9-18)

- Scale, skew, rotate, and position graphics elements using transforms (recipe 9-19)

9-1. Draw a Line

Problem

You need to draw a simple straight line.

Solution

Use the System.Windows.Shapes.Line class to represent the line. Use the X1 and Y1 properties of the Line class to specify the line's start point and the X2 and Y2 properties to specify its end point.

How It Works

The Line class allows you to easily draw a single straight line between two points in a two-dimensional plane. The X1 and Y1 properties of the Line class identify its start point, and the X2 and Y2 properties identify its end point. Both points are relative to the base position of the Line object in its container (see Chapter 2 for details of how to position UI elements in the various types of containers provided by WPF).

By default, the unit for the X1, Y1, X2, and Y2 values are assumed to be px (pixels) but can also be in (inches), cm (centimeters), or pt (points). You can also use negative values to refer to points above and to the left of the Line object's base position. This can cause the line to draw outside the boundaries of its container.

The Stroke property of the Line defines the brush used to draw the line. Usually, for a line you will want to use a solid color by specifying a name or numeric color value for the Stroke property (recipes 9-11 through 9-15 discuss brushes in more detail). The StrokeThickness sets the thickness of the line expressed as a number and an optional unit identifier. By default, the unit is assumed to be px (pixels) but can also be in (inches), cm (centimeters), or pt (points).

The Code

The following XAML demonstrates how to use Line elements in both a System.Windows.Controls.StackPanel and a System.Windows.Controls.Canvas (see Figure 9-1). The Canvas gives total flexibility over the positioning of the Line elements, whereas the StackPanel tries to stack the Line elements vertically. Using a negative value for the Y1 property of the third Line element in the StackPanel, the example demonstrates the possibility of drawing the Line outside its container.

```
<Window x:Class="Recipe_09_01.Window1"
    xmlns="http://schemas.microsoft.com/winfx/2006/xaml/presentation"
    xmlns:x="http://schemas.microsoft.com/winfx/2006/xaml"
    Title="WPF Recipes 9_01" Height="250" Width="500">
    <StackPanel Orientation="Horizontal">
        <StackPanel Margin="5">
```

```
            <TextBlock FontSize="14" Text="Lines in a StackPanel:"/>
            <Line X1="10" Y1="10" X2="230" Y2="40"
                    Stroke="Black" StrokeThickness="5"/>
            <Line X1="10" Y1="80" X2="230" Y2="20"
                    Stroke="Black" StrokeThickness="8"/>
            <Line X1="2.5cm" Y1="-1.25cm" X2="3.5cm" Y2="1.5cm"
                    Stroke="Black" StrokeThickness=".1cm"/>
        </StackPanel>
        <Canvas Margin="5">
            <TextBlock FontSize="14" Text="Lines in a Canvas:"/>
            <Line Canvas.Top="100" Canvas.Left="20"   X2="200" Y2="40"
                    Stroke="Black" StrokeThickness="5"/>
            <Line X1="50" Y1="200" X2="230" Y2="20"
                    Stroke="Black" StrokeThickness="8"/>
            <Line Canvas.Bottom="30" Canvas.Left="180"
                    X1="0" Y1="30" X2="-10" Y2="-130"
                    Stroke="Black" StrokeThickness="5"/>
        </Canvas>
    </StackPanel>
</Window>
```

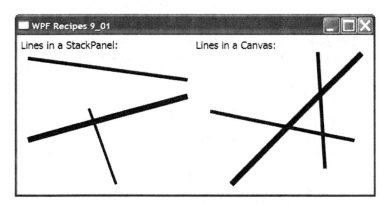

Figure 9-1. *Lines in a StackPanel and a Canvas*

9-2. Draw a Sequence of Connected Lines

Problem

You need to draw a sequence of connected lines.

Solution

Use the System.Windows.Shapes.PolyLine class. Use the Points property of the PolyLine
element to specify the sequence of points that you want connected to form the sequence of
connected lines.

How It Works

The PolyLine element makes it easy and efficient to create a sequence of connected lines. Instead of using a sequence of individual System.Windows.Shapes.Line elements (described in recipe 9-1), you use a single PolyLine element and simply specify the sequence of points you want connected to form the line sequence.

You can declare the points for the PolyLine statically by specifying a sequence of coordinate pairs in the Points property of the PolyLine element. Each of these coordinate pairs represents the X and Y offset of a point from the base position of the PolyLine within its container (see Chapter 2 for details of how to position UI elements in the various types of containers provided by WPF). For clarity, you should separate the X and Y coordinates of a pair with a comma and separate each coordinate pair with a space (for example, x1,y1 x2,y2 x3,y3, and so on).

To configure the points of a PolyLine programmatically, you need to add System.Windows.Point objects to the System.Windows.Media.PointsCollection collection contained in the Points property of the PolyLine object.

The Code

The following XAML demonstrates how to use PolyLine elements to draw a sequence of connected lines (see Figure 9-2). The first PolyLine is configured statically in XAML, while the second is configured in the code-behind.

```
<Window x:Class="Recipe_09_02.Window1"
    xmlns="http://schemas.microsoft.com/winfx/2006/xaml/presentation"
    xmlns:x="http://schemas.microsoft.com/winfx/2006/xaml"
    Title="WPF Recipes 9_02" Height="270" Width="300" Loaded="Window_Loaded">
    <Canvas>
        <TextBlock Canvas.Top="40" Canvas.Left="20"
                    FontSize="14" Text="Static Points Collection" />
        <Polyline Stroke="Black" StrokeThickness="3"
                    Points="10,10 270,10 270,100 10,100 10,25
                    255,25 255,85 230,40 205,85 180,40 155,85 35,85" />
        <TextBlock Canvas.Top="150" Canvas.Left="20"
                    FontSize="14" Text="Programmatic Points Collection" />
        <Polyline Name="plLine" Stroke="Black" StrokeThickness="3" />
    </Canvas>
</Window>
```

The following code-behind configures the Points used to generate the second PolyLine shown in Figure 9-2:

```
using System.Windows;

namespace Recipe_09_02
{
    /// <summary>
    /// Interaction logic for Window1.xaml
    /// </summary>
```

```csharp
public partial class Window1 : Window
{
    public Window1()
    {
        InitializeComponent();
    }

    private void Window_Loaded(object sender, RoutedEventArgs e)
    {
        // Populate the PointsCollection of the PolyLine.
        plLine.Points.Add(new Point(10, 140));
        plLine.Points.Add(new Point(270, 140));
        plLine.Points.Add(new Point(270, 220));
        plLine.Points.Add(new Point(255, 220));
        plLine.Points.Add(new Point(230, 175));
        plLine.Points.Add(new Point(205, 220));
        plLine.Points.Add(new Point(180, 175));
        plLine.Points.Add(new Point(155, 220));
        plLine.Points.Add(new Point(130, 175));
        plLine.Points.Add(new Point(10, 175));
        plLine.Points.Add(new Point(10, 220));
        plLine.Points.Add(new Point(125, 220));
    }
}
```

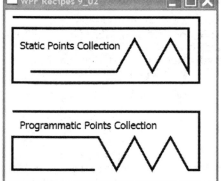

Figure 9-2. *PolyLine objects in a Canvas*

9-3. Format Lines

Problem

You need to format a line or the outline of a shape by defining its color and thickness; whether it is dashed or solid; the appearance of its ends; and the shape of joins in the line.

Solution

Use the Stroke and StrokeThickness properties to control the color and thickness of the line; the StrokeStartLineCap and StrokeEndLineCap properties to control the shape of the line's ends; the StrokeDashArray, StrokeDashCap, and StrokeDashOffset properties to make the line dashed; and the StrokeLineJoin property to control the appearance of line joins.

How It Works

The System.Windows.Shapes.Shape class provides a host of properties that allow you to control the format of the lines used to draw the Shape. Because the Shape class is the base class for all the basic 2D drawing objects, you have access to a common set of formatting options regardless of which subclass of Shape you are using. This includes the Ellipse, Line, Path, Polygon, Polyline, and Rectangle classes from the System.Windows.Shapes namespace. Table 9-1 summarizes the properties of the Shape class that you can use to format the lines used to draw these shapes.

Table 9-1. *Properties of the Shape Class Used to Format Lines*

Value	Description
Stroke	Defines the System.Windows.Media.Brush that is used to paint the line. There are many different types of brushes, but the easiest and most commonly used brush used when drawing lines is the System.Windows.Media.SolidColorBrush. You can use a SolidColorBrush in XAML simply by specifying a predefined color name or one of the many numeric representations of a color for the Stroke property value. Recipes 9-11 through 9-15 discuss brushes in more detail.
StrokeThickness	Sets the thickness of the line expressed as a number and an optional unit identifier. By default, the unit is assumed to be px (pixels) but can also be in (inches), cm (centimeters), or pt (points).
StrokeStartLineCap	The shape to apply to the start of the line; available values are Flat, Round, Square, and Triangle. This property has an effect only if the line is not part of a closed shape and actually has visible ends. All but the Flat option will extend the length of the line slightly. See the System.Windows.Media.PenLineCap enumeration for more information.
StrokeEndLineCap	Same as for StrokeStartLineCap, except it applies to the end of a line.
StrokeDashArray	A sequence of System.Double values that define the pattern of dashes and gaps for the line. The first value defines the length (in pixels) of the first line segment in the dash pattern, and the second value defines the length of the first gap. Further values continue to alternate between defining the length of the next line segment and the next gap until the line is completed. If there are not enough values provided in the StrokeDashArray sequence to complete the line, the values that are given are simply repeated. Using this flexible mechanism, you can provide a single value to create a uniform dash pattern on a line, or you can provide multiple values to create complex nonuniform patterns.
StrokeDashOffset	A System.Double value that defines the distance (in pixels) within the dash pattern (defined by StrokeDashArray) where the pattern should begin. This allows you to make the first dash a different length than would be achieved using StrokeDashArray alone.

Table 9-1. *Properties of the Shape Class Used to Format Lines*

Value	Description
StrokeDashCap	Same as for StrokeStartLineCap, except it applies to the start and end of dashed line sections.
StrokeLineJoin	The shape to apply to the joins or vertices in the line or shape; available values are Bevel, Miter, and Round. See the System.Windows.Media.PenLineJoin enumeration for more information.

The Code

The following XAML uses a set of the System.Windows.Shapes.PolyLine elements arranged in a grid (see Figure 9-3) to demonstrate how to use the Shape properties described in Table 9-1 to format lines:

```
<Window x:Class="Recipe_09_03.Window1"
    xmlns="http://schemas.microsoft.com/winfx/2006/xaml/presentation"
    xmlns:x="http://schemas.microsoft.com/winfx/2006/xaml"
    Title="WPF Recipes 9_03" Height="300" Width="400">
    <UniformGrid Columns="3" HorizontalAlignment="Center"
            VerticalAlignment="Center">
        <Polyline Margin="10" Stroke="Black" StrokeThickness="5"
            Points="0,0 100,0 100,100 0,100 0,20 80,20 80,80
                20,80, 20,40 60,40 60,60 40,60" />
        <Polyline Margin="10" Stroke="Navy" StrokeThickness="8"
                StrokeStartLineCap="Triangle" StrokeEndLineCap="Triangle"
            Points="0,0 100,0 100,100 0,100 0,20 80,20 80,80
                20,80, 20,40 60,40 60,60 40,60" />
        <Polyline Margin="10" Stroke="Red" StrokeThickness="5"
                StrokeDashArray="2" StrokeDashCap="Triangle"
            Points="0,0 100,0 100,100 0,100 0,20 80,20 80,80
                20,80, 20,40 60,40 60,60 40,60" />
        <Polyline Margin="10" Stroke="Black" StrokeThickness="5"
                StrokeDashArray="5 2 2 2" StrokeDashCap="Round"
            Points="0,0 100,0 100,100 0,100 0,20 80,20 80,80
                20,80, 20,40 60,40 60,60 40,60" />
        <Polyline Margin="10" Stroke="DarkCyan" StrokeThickness="8"
                StrokeLineJoin="Bevel"
            Points="0,0 100,0 100,100 0,100 0,20 80,20 80,80
                20,80, 20,40 60,40 60,60 40,60" />
        <Polyline Margin="10" Stroke="Black" StrokeThickness="8"
                StrokeEndLineCap="Round" StrokeStartLineCap="Round"
                StrokeLineJoin="Round" StrokeDashCap="Round"
                StrokeDashArray="10 2" StrokeDashOffset="10"
```

```
            Points="0,0 100,0 100,100 0,100 0,20 80,20 80,80
                    20,80, 20,40 60,40 60,60 40,60" />
    </UniformGrid>
</Window>
```

Figure 9-3. *Examples of formatted* PolyLine *objects*

9-4. Draw a Curved Line

Problem

You need to draw a curved line.

Solution

Represent the curved line using a System.Windows.Shapes.Path element. In the Data property of the Path object, define the shape of the curved line as a PathGeometry element containing one PathFigure element for each line you need to draw. Construct each line as a sequence of one or more ArcSegment, LineSegment, and BezierSegment elements within the PathFigure element (PathGeometry, PathFigure, ArcSegment, LineSegment, and BezierSegment are all classes from the System.Windows.Media namespace).

■**Tip** Defining complex curved lines manually can be time-consuming, error prone, and frustrating. For complex curved lines, you should consider using a visual design tool that generates XAML to draw the line and then use the output of the tool in your application.

How It Works

Drawing a curved line is not as simple in WPF as you would hope. Unlike lines, ellipses, and rectangles, there is no simple class that draws a curved line for you. However, at the expense of a little complexity, you get a great deal of flexibility and control, which is what you really want if you need to draw all but the simplest curved lines.

To draw a curved line, you must use a combination of elements. First, you need a Path element, which is the element (derived from System.Windows.Shapes.Shape) that defines the settings—such as color and thickness—used to actually draw the line (see recipe 9-3 for details on how you can control the formatting of a line). Path also implements events for handling mouse and keyboard interaction with the line.

The Data property of the Path element must contain the description—expressed using a PathGeometry element—of the line that the Path element should draw when rendered. The PathGeometry element can define multiple lines, so you must declare each line inside the PathGeometry element within its own PathFigure element. The StartPoint property of the PathFigure element defines the point where WPF will start to draw your line. The StartPoint property takes a pair of System.Double values representing the X and Y offsets from the root position of the Path element within its container.

Within the PathFigure element, you finally get to define what your line is going to look like using one or more ArcSegment, LineSegment, and BezierSegment elements. When rendered, each segment defines how your line continues from the point where the previous segment ended (or the StartPoint of the PathFigure if it is the first segment).

A LineSegment defines a straight line drawn from the end of the last segment to the point defined in its Point property. The Point property takes a pair of Double values representing the X and Y offsets from the root position of the Path element.

An ArcSegment defines an elliptical arc drawn between the end of the last segment and the point defined in its Point property. The Point property takes a pair of Double values representing the X and Y offsets from the root position of the Path element. Table 9-2 defines the properties of the ArcSegment class that let you configure the shape of the curved line it defines.

Table 9-2. *Properties of the ArcSegment Class*

Value	Description
IsLargeArc	Specifies whether the line drawn between the start and end of the ArcSegment is the small or the large section of the ellipse used to calculate the arc.
IsSmoothJoin	A Boolean that defines whether the join between the previous line and the ArcSegment should be treated as a corner. This determines how the StrokeLineJoin property (discussed in recipe 9-3) of the Path element affects the rendering of the join.
RotationAngle	A double that defines the amount in degrees by which the ellipse (from which the arc is taken) is rotated about the x-axis.
Size	A pair of Double values that specify the x- and y-radii of the ellipse used to calculate the arc.
SweepDirection	Defines the direction in which WPF draws the ArcSegment; available values are Clockwise and Counterclockwise.

A BezierSegment defines a Bezier curve drawn between the end of the last segment and the point defined in its Point3 property. The Point3 property takes a pair of Double values representing the X and Y offsets from the root position of the Path element. The Point1 and Point2 properties of the BezierSegment define the control points of the Bezier curve that exert a "pull" on the line causing it to create a curve. You can read more about Bezier curves at http://en.wikipedia.org/wiki/Bezier_curves.

Note WPF defines a mini-language that provides a concise syntax by which you can define complex geometries. Because it is terse and difficult to read, this language is primarily intended for tools that generate geometry definitions automatically but can also be used in manual definitions. A discussion of this mini-language is beyond the scope of this book. To find out more, read the MSDN article at http://msdn.microsoft.com/de-de/library/ms752293(VS.85).aspx.

The Code

The following XAML demonstrates how to use ArcSegment, LineSegment, and BezierSegment elements to draw curved lines on a System.Windows.Controls.Canvas (see Figure 9-4). The PathGeometry element contains two PathFigure elements resulting in two separate lines.

```xaml
<Window x:Class="Recipe_09_04.Window1"
    xmlns="http://schemas.microsoft.com/winfx/2006/xaml/presentation"
    xmlns:x="http://schemas.microsoft.com/winfx/2006/xaml"
    Title="WPF Recipes 9_04" Height="300" Width="290">
    <Canvas Margin="10">
        <Path Stroke="Black" StrokeThickness="5" StrokeLineJoin="Round"
              StrokeStartLineCap="Round" StrokeEndLineCap="Round">
            <Path.Data>
                <PathGeometry>
                    <PathFigure IsClosed="False" StartPoint="10,100">
                        <LineSegment Point="150,100" />
                        <ArcSegment Point="250,50" IsLargeArc="False"
                                    Size="100,80" SweepDirection="Clockwise"/>
                        <ArcSegment Point="50,150" IsLargeArc="False"
                                    Size="100,80" />
                        <BezierSegment Point1="200,300" Point2="200,-80"
                                       Point3="250,230"/>
                    </PathFigure>
                    <PathFigure IsClosed="False" StartPoint="10,150">
                        <LineSegment Point="30,230" />
                        <ArcSegment Point="110,230"
                                    IsLargeArc="False" Size="100,100" />
                        <ArcSegment Point="240,240"
                                    IsLargeArc="False" Size="100,100"
                                    SweepDirection="Clockwise"/>
                    </PathFigure>
```

```
            </PathGeometry>
          </Path.Data>
        </Path>
    </Canvas>
</Window>
```

Figure 9-4. *Examples of curved lines in a canvas*

9-5. Draw Simple Shapes

Problem

You need to draw simple shapes such as a circle, a rectangle, or another simple polygon.

Solution

Use the Ellipse, Rectangle, or Polygon classes from the System.Windows.Shapes namespace.

How It Works

The Ellipse, Rectangle, and Polygon classes all derive from the System.Windows.Shapes.Shape class and provide a quick and easy way to draw simple shapes.

To use an Ellipse or Rectangle element, you need only specify a Height property and a Width property to control the basic size of the shape. The values are assumed to be px (pixels) but can also be in (inches), cm (centimeters), or pt (points). For the Rectangle element, you can also specify values for the RadiusX and RadiusY properties, which set the radius of the ellipse used to round the corners of the rectangle.

The Polygon allows you to create shapes with as many sides as you require by constructing a shape from a sequence of connected lines. To do this, you specify the sequence of points you want connected by lines to form your shape. The Polygon automatically draws a final line segment from the final point back to the first point to ensure the shape is closed.

You can declare the points for the Polygon statically by specifying a sequence of coordinate pairs in the Points property of the Polygon element. Each of these coordinate pairs represents the X and Y offset of a point from the base position of the Polygon within its container (see Chapter 2 for details of how to position UI elements in the various types of containers provided by WPF). For clarity, you should separate the X and Y coordinates of a pair with a comma and separate each coordinate pair with a space (for example, x1,y1 x2,y2 x3,y3, and so on).

To configure the points of a Polygon programmatically, you need to add System.Windows. Point objects to the System.Windows.Media.PointsCollection collection contained in the Points property of the Polygon object.

The Code

The following XAML demonstrates how to use Ellipse, Rectangle, and Polygon elements to draw simple shapes in a System.Windows.Controls.UniformGrid (see Figure 9-5).

```
<Window x:Class="Recipe_09_05.Window1"
    xmlns="http://schemas.microsoft.com/winfx/2006/xaml/presentation"
    xmlns:x="http://schemas.microsoft.com/winfx/2006/xaml"
    Title="WPF Recipes 9_05" Height="350" Width="300">
    <UniformGrid Columns="3" HorizontalAlignment="Center"
                 VerticalAlignment="Center">
        <Rectangle Stroke="Black" StrokeThickness="3"
                   Height="60" Width="90" />
        <Rectangle Stroke="Black" StrokeThickness="3"
                   Height="100" Width="70"
                   RadiusX="10" RadiusY="10"/>
        <Rectangle Stroke="Black" StrokeThickness="3"
                   Height="70" Width="70"
                   RadiusX="5" RadiusY="30"/>
        <Ellipse Stroke="Black" StrokeThickness="3"
                 Height="100" Width="70"/>
        <Ellipse Stroke="Black" StrokeThickness="3"
                 Height="50" Width="90"/>
        <Ellipse Stroke="Black" StrokeThickness="3"
                 Height="70" Width="70"/>
        <Polygon Stroke="Black" StrokeThickness="3"
                 Margin="5"
                 Points="40,10 70,80 10,80"/>
        <Polygon Stroke="Black" StrokeThickness="3"
                 Margin="5"
                 Points="20,0 60,0 80,20 80,60 60,80
                 20,80 0,60 0,20"/>
        <Polygon Stroke="Black" StrokeThickness="3"
                 Margin="5"
                 Points="20,0 50,10 50,50 80,60 60,80 0,20"/>
    </UniformGrid>
</Window>
```

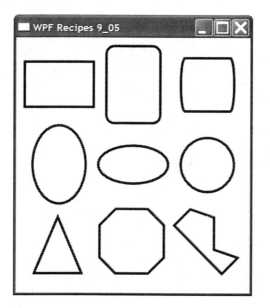

Figure 9-5. *Examples of simple shapes in a grid*

9-6. Draw Complex Shapes

Problem

You need to draw a complex shape.

Solution

Use a System.Windows.Shapes.Path element to represent the overall shape. In the Data property of the Path object, include a GeometryGroup element containing one or more EllipseGeometry, LineGeometry, PathGeometry, or RectangleGeometry elements that together describe your shape. GeometryGroup, EllipseGeometry, LineGeometry, PathGeometry, and RectangleGeometry are all classes from the System.Windows.Media namespace.

■**Tip** Defining complex shapes manually can be time-consuming, error prone, and frustrating. For complex shapes, you should consider using a visual design tool (such as Microsoft Expression Design) that generates XAML to draw the shape and then use the output of the tool in your application.

How It Works

Recipe 9-5 describes how to draw polygons with many sides using the System.Windows.Shapes. Polygon class. Although the Polygon class allows you to create somewhat complex shapes easily, it allows you to use only straight edges on those shapes. Polygon also includes significant overhead because of all the functionality inherited from the System.Windows.Shapes.Shape class.

For complex and lightweight shapes over which you have more control, you should use the classes derived from the System.Windows.Media.Geometry class, including PathGeometry, EllipseGeometry, LineGeometry, and RectangleGeometry. To make shapes that consist of multiple simpler shapes, you must encapsulate the collection of simpler shapes in a GeometryGroup element.

The EllipseGeometry, LineGeometry, and RectangleGeometry elements are lighter-weight equivalents of the Ellipse, Line, and Rectangle classes from the System.Windows.Shapes namespace intended for use when creating more complex shapes.

To draw an ellipse with the EllipseGeometry class, position the ellipse using the Center property, and specify the width and height of the ellipse using the RadiusX and RadiusY properties. To draw a line with the LineGeometry class, specify the starting point of the line using the StartPoint property and the end of the line using the EndPoint property. To draw a rectangle with the RectangleGeometry class, specify the position of the top-left corner of the rectangle as well as the width and height of the rectangle using the Rect property. You can also specify values for the RadiusX and RadiusY properties, which set the radius of the ellipse used to round the corners of the rectangle. All coordinates are relative to the root position of the Path element within its container.

Recipe 9-4 describes how to draw complex curved lines using the PathGeometry element. To use these techniques to draw a closed shape instead of a line, the System.Windows.Media.PathFigure element provides the IsClosed property, which, when set to the value True, ensures that WPF automatically draws a final line between your last point and the first point of the line, making it a closed shape.

The Code

The following XAML demonstrates how to create a complex shape using multiple simple shapes defined using EllipseGeometry, LineGeometry, PathGeometry, or RectangleGeometry elements contained in a GeometryGroup element (see Figure 9-6).

```
<Window x:Class="Recipe_09_06.Window1"
    xmlns="http://schemas.microsoft.com/winfx/2006/xaml/presentation"
    xmlns:x="http://schemas.microsoft.com/winfx/2006/xaml"
    Title="WPF Recipes 9_06" Height="200" Width="200">
    <Canvas Margin="10">
        <Path Canvas.Left="45" Stroke="Black" StrokeThickness="3" >
            <Path.Data>
                <GeometryGroup>
                    <!--Head and hat-->
                    <PathGeometry>
                        <PathFigure IsClosed="True" StartPoint="40,0">
                            <LineSegment Point="70,100" />
                            <ArcSegment Point="70,110" IsLargeArc="True"
                                    Size="10,10" SweepDirection="Clockwise"/>
                            <ArcSegment Point="10,110" Size="30,30"
                                    SweepDirection="Clockwise"/>
```

```
                  <ArcSegment Point="10,100" IsLargeArc="True"
                         Size="10,10" SweepDirection="Clockwise"/>
              </PathFigure>
          </PathGeometry>
          <!--Hat buttons-->
          <EllipseGeometry Center="40,40" RadiusX="2" RadiusY="2"/>
          <EllipseGeometry Center="40,50" RadiusX="2" RadiusY="2"/>
          <EllipseGeometry Center="40,60" RadiusX="2" RadiusY="2"/>
          <!--Eyes-->
          <EllipseGeometry Center="30,100" RadiusX="3" RadiusY="2"/>
          <EllipseGeometry Center="50,100" RadiusX="3" RadiusY="2"/>
          <!--Nose-->
          <EllipseGeometry Center="40,110" RadiusX="3" RadiusY="3"/>
          <!--Mouth-->
          <RectangleGeometry Rect="30,120 20,10"/>
      </GeometryGroup>
    </Path.Data>
  </Path>
 </Canvas>
</Window>
```

Figure 9-6. *Drawing a complex shape from multiple simple shapes*

9-7. Create Reusable Shapes

Problem

You need to create a shape that you can use many times without having to define it each time.

Solution

Define the geometry of the shape as a static resource, and give it a Key. You can then use binding syntax to reference the geometry from the Data property of a System.Windows.Shapes.Path element wherever you need it.

Note Chapter 1 discusses how to create and manage static resources in more detail.

How It Works

Geometries describing complex shapes can be long and complicated, so you will not want to repeat the geometry description in multiple places. Instead, you can define the geometry once as a static resource and refer to the resource wherever you would normally use that geometry.

You can declare instances of any of the classes that inherit from the System.Windows.Media. Geometry class in the resource dictionary of a suitable container. This includes the PathGeometry, EllipseGeometry, LineGeometry, RectangleGeometry, and GeometryGroup classes from the System. Windows.Media namespace. The only special action you need to take is to give the geometry resource a name by assigning a value to the x:Key property.

Once defined, refer to the geometry resource from the Data property of a Path element using the following syntax:

```
… Data="{StaticResource GeometryKey}" …
```

The Code

The following XAML demonstrates how to create a System.Windows.Media.GeometryGroup static resource with the key Clown, and its subsequent use to display a clown shape multiple times in a System.Windows.Controls.UniformGrid. Each clown displayed uses the same underlying geometry but different stroke settings to change the color and format of the lines (see Figure 9-7).

```xml
<Window x:Class="Recipe_09_07.Window1"
    xmlns="http://schemas.microsoft.com/winfx/2006/xaml/presentation"
    xmlns:x="http://schemas.microsoft.com/winfx/2006/xaml"
    Title="WPF Recipes 9_07" Height="350" Width="300">
    <Window.Resources>
        <GeometryGroup x:Key="Clown">
            <!--Head and hat-->
            <PathGeometry>
                <PathFigure IsClosed="True" StartPoint="40,0">
                    <LineSegment Point="70,100" />
                    <ArcSegment Point="70,110" IsLargeArc="True"
                                Size="10,10" SweepDirection="Clockwise"/>
                    <ArcSegment Point="10,110" Size="30,30"
                                SweepDirection="Clockwise"/>
                    <ArcSegment Point="10,100" IsLargeArc="True"
                                Size="10,10" SweepDirection="Clockwise"/>
                </PathFigure>
            </PathGeometry>
```

```xml
            <!--Hat buttons-->
            <EllipseGeometry Center="40,40" RadiusX="2" RadiusY="2"/>
            <EllipseGeometry Center="40,50" RadiusX="2" RadiusY="2"/>
            <EllipseGeometry Center="40,60" RadiusX="2" RadiusY="2"/>
            <!--Eyes-->
            <EllipseGeometry Center="30,100" RadiusX="3" RadiusY="2"/>
            <EllipseGeometry Center="50,100" RadiusX="3" RadiusY="2"/>
            <!--Nose-->
            <EllipseGeometry Center="40,110" RadiusX="3" RadiusY="3"/>
            <!--Mouth-->
            <RectangleGeometry Rect="30,120 20,10"/>
        </GeometryGroup>
    </Window.Resources>
    <UniformGrid Columns="2" Rows="2">
        <Path HorizontalAlignment="Center" Data="{StaticResource Clown}"
              Stroke="Black" StrokeThickness="1" Margin="5" Fill="BurlyWood"/>
        <Path HorizontalAlignment="Center" Data="{StaticResource Clown}"
              Stroke="Blue" StrokeThickness="5" Margin="5" />
        <Path HorizontalAlignment="Center" Data="{StaticResource Clown}"
              Stroke="Red" StrokeThickness="3"  StrokeDashArray="1 1"/>
        <Path HorizontalAlignment="Center" Data="{StaticResource Clown}"
              Stroke="Green" StrokeThickness="4" StrokeDashArray="2 1"/>
    </UniformGrid>
</Window>
```

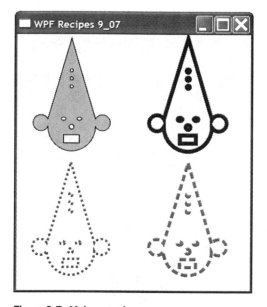

Figure 9-7. *Using static geometry resources to create reusable shapes*

9-8. Display a Tool Tip on a Shape

Problem

You need to display a tool tip when a user hovers over a System.Windows.Shapes.Shape with the mouse pointer.

Solution

Assign a System.Windows.Controls.ToolTip control to the ToolTip property of the Shape on which you want to display the tool tip.

How It Works

The Shape class extends System.Windows.FrameworkElement, meaning it inherits the ToolTip property, providing a simple mechanism through which to display a tool tip on any Shape.

The ToolTip property is of type System.Object, so you can assign it any object, and the property will attempt to render the object as a tool tip for display. For simple textual tool tips, you can specify the text to display as the value of the control's ToolTip attribute. When creating richer, more complex tool tips, you should use property element syntax to specify structured ToolTip content (see recipe 3-16 for an example).

On shapes, the ToolTip will not display if the user has positioned the mouse over a transparent area of the shape. So, for example, if a shape has lines but no fill, the ToolTip will be shown only when the user hovers over the lines.

Note Recipes 3-16, 3-17, and 3-18 provide more details about how to control the content, positioning, and visible duration of a ToolTip.

The Code

The following XAML demonstrates how to define a ToolTip for display when the user hovers the mouse pointer over various graphics elements derived from the Shape class (see Figure 9-8). The ToolTip is visible on the clown only when the mouse is actually on one of the lines because the clown has a transparent fill.

```
<Window x:Class="Recipe_09_08.Window1"
    xmlns="http://schemas.microsoft.com/winfx/2006/xaml/presentation"
    xmlns:x="http://schemas.microsoft.com/winfx/2006/xaml"
    Title="WPF Recipes 9_08" Height="200" Width="400">
    <Canvas>
```

```xml
        <Canvas.Resources>
            <Style TargetType="{x:Type ToolTip}">
                <Setter Property="FontSize" Value="20" />
            </Style>
            <GeometryGroup x:Key="Clown">
                <!--Head and hat-->
                <PathGeometry>
                    <PathFigure IsClosed="True" StartPoint="40,0">
                        <LineSegment Point="70,100" />
                        <ArcSegment Point="70,110" IsLargeArc="True"
                                    Size="10,10" SweepDirection="Clockwise"/>
                        <ArcSegment Point="10,110" Size="30,30"
                                    SweepDirection="Clockwise"/>
                        <ArcSegment Point="10,100" IsLargeArc="True"
                                    Size="10,10" SweepDirection="Clockwise"/>
                    </PathFigure>
                </PathGeometry>
                <!--Hat buttons-->
                <EllipseGeometry Center="40,40" RadiusX="2" RadiusY="2"/>
                <EllipseGeometry Center="40,50" RadiusX="2" RadiusY="2"/>
                <EllipseGeometry Center="40,60" RadiusX="2" RadiusY="2"/>
                <!--Eyes-->
                <EllipseGeometry Center="30,100" RadiusX="3" RadiusY="2"/>
                <EllipseGeometry Center="50,100" RadiusX="3" RadiusY="2"/>
                <!--Nose-->
                <EllipseGeometry Center="40,110" RadiusX="3" RadiusY="3"/>
                <!--Mouth-->
                <RectangleGeometry Rect="30,120 20,10"/>
            </GeometryGroup>
        </Canvas.Resources>
        <Rectangle Canvas.Top="10" Canvas.Left="20"
                   Stroke="Black" StrokeThickness="4" Fill="Blue"
                   Height="140"  Width="70" ToolTip="A rectangle."/>
        <Path Canvas.Top="10" Canvas.Left="130"
              Stroke="Black" StrokeThickness="4"
              Data="{StaticResource Clown}" ToolTip="A clown." />
        <Ellipse Canvas.Top="10" Canvas.Left="235"
                 Stroke="Black" StrokeThickness="1"
                 Height="135" Width="135" ToolTip="An author.">
            <Ellipse.Fill>
                <ImageBrush ImageSource="WeeMee.jpg" Stretch="Fill" />
            </Ellipse.Fill>
        </Ellipse>
    </Canvas>
</Window>
```

Figure 9-8. *Displaying tool tips on graphics elements*

9-9. Display Graphics Elements in a Tool Tip

Problem

You need to include graphics elements in the body of a System.Windows.Controls.ToolTip control.

Solution

Within the body of the ToolTip element, use a top-level layout panel such as a StackPanel, Grid, or Canvas to allow you to create structured content within it. Position the graphical content in the layout panel as described in Chapter 2. (StackPanel, Grid, and Canvas are all members of the System.Windows.Controls namespace.)

How It Works

WPF allows you to freely mix graphics and more traditional UI controls and content. This means you are free to include graphics within normal panels as well as pop-up windows and tool tips.

To use graphics in a ToolTip in XAML, you will need to define the ToolTip element using property element syntax within the body of the UI element you want to associate the ToolTip with. You should then define some form of top-level layout panel to allow you to position the graphics within the body of the ToolTip appropriately.

The Code

The following XAML demonstrates how to use graphics in a ToolTip applied to a System.Windows. Controls.Button control (see Figure 9-9).

```
<Window x:Class="Recipe_09_09.Window1"
    xmlns="http://schemas.microsoft.com/winfx/2006/xaml/presentation"
    xmlns:x="http://schemas.microsoft.com/winfx/2006/xaml"
    Title="WPF Recipes 9_09" Height="100" Width="300">
```

```xml
<Grid>
    <Grid.Resources>
        <!--A static linear gradient brush containing light spectrum-->
        <LinearGradientBrush x:Key="VisibleSpectrumBrush"
                             StartPoint="0,0" EndPoint="1,0">
            <GradientStop Color="Red" Offset="0.15" />
            <GradientStop Color="Orange" Offset="0.2" />
            <GradientStop Color="Yellow" Offset="0.35" />
            <GradientStop Color="Green" Offset="0.5" />
            <GradientStop Color="Blue" Offset="0.65" />
            <GradientStop Color="Indigo" Offset="0.75" />
            <GradientStop Color="Violet" Offset="0.9" />
        </LinearGradientBrush>
    </Grid.Resources>
    <!--A button with a ToolTip containing graphics elements-->
    <Button Content="A button with a graphical tooltip."
            MaxHeight="25" Margin="10">
        <Button.ToolTip>
            <StackPanel>
                <Rectangle Height="30" Width="280"
                           Fill="{StaticResource VisibleSpectrumBrush}" />
                <TextBlock HorizontalAlignment="Center"
                           Text="The visible light spectrum." />
            </StackPanel>
        </Button.ToolTip>
    </Button>
</Grid>
</Window>
```

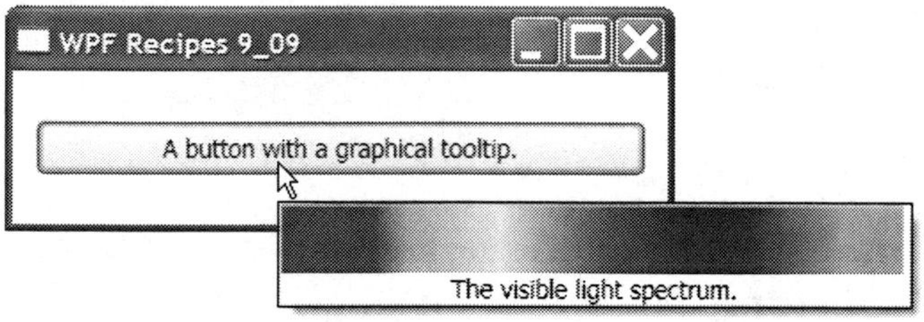

Figure 9-9. *A Button with a ToolTip containing graphics elements*

9-10. Use System Colors in Your Graphics

Problem

You need to use colors in your graphics that match those defined for use in the Microsoft Windows user interface.

Solution

Use the static properties of the System.Windows.SystemColors class to obtain a System.Windows. SolidBrush object representing one of the colors used by Microsoft Windows for a particular visual element.

How It Works

The SystemColors class implements about 30 static properties that allow you to obtain SolidBrush objects configured with the colors Windows uses to draw various visual elements used in the operating system UI. Some examples of these properties are WindowBrush, WindowFrameBrush, InfoBrush, and DesktopBrush.

To use these colors in code, you simply get the desired property value and assign the returned SolidBrush object to whatever needs to use it. To use these colors in XAML, you must use binding syntax to refer to the static properties of the SystemColors class as follows:

```
<Rectangle Fill="{x:Static SystemColors.ActiveBorderBrush}" />
```

The Code

The following XAML demonstrates how to use Windows system colors obtained through the properties of the SystemColors object to fill a set of rectangles (see Figure 9-10):

```
<Window x:Class="Recipe_09_10.Window1"
    xmlns="http://schemas.microsoft.com/winfx/2006/xaml/presentation"
    xmlns:x="http://schemas.microsoft.com/winfx/2006/xaml"
    Title="WPF Recipes 9_10" Height="300" Width="300">
<UniformGrid>
    <UniformGrid.Resources>
        <Style TargetType="{x:Type Rectangle}">
            <Setter Property="Height" Value="50" />
            <Setter Property="Width" Value="50" />
            <Setter Property="Margin" Value="5" />
        </Style>
    </UniformGrid.Resources>
    <Rectangle Fill="{x:Static SystemColors.ActiveBorderBrush}" />
    <Rectangle Fill="{x:Static SystemColors.ActiveCaptionBrush}" />
    <Rectangle Fill="{x:Static SystemColors.ScrollBarBrush}" />
    <Rectangle Fill="{x:Static SystemColors.AppWorkspaceBrush}" />
    <Rectangle Fill="{x:Static SystemColors.ControlBrush}" />
    <Rectangle Fill="{x:Static SystemColors.ControlDarkBrush}" />
    <Rectangle Fill="{x:Static SystemColors.ControlDarkDarkBrush}" />
    <Rectangle Fill="{x:Static SystemColors.ControlLightBrush}" />
    <Rectangle Fill="{x:Static SystemColors.HotTrackBrush}" />
    <Rectangle Fill="{x:Static SystemColors.ControlTextBrush}" />
    <Rectangle Fill="{x:Static SystemColors.DesktopBrush}" />
    <Rectangle Fill="{x:Static SystemColors.InfoBrush}" />
    <Rectangle Fill="{x:Static SystemColors.MenuBarBrush}" />
    <Rectangle Fill="{x:Static SystemColors.GrayTextBrush}" />
```

```
        <Rectangle Fill="{x:Static SystemColors.HighlightBrush}" />
        <Rectangle Fill="{x:Static SystemColors.WindowFrameBrush}" />
    </UniformGrid>
</Window>
```

Figure 9-10. *Using Windows system colors in graphics*

9-11. Draw or Fill a Shape Using a Solid Color

Problem

You need to draw or fill a shape using a solid color.

Solution

For shapes derived from System.Windows.Shapes.Shape, set the Stroke or Fill property to an instance of System.Windows.Media.SolidColorBrush configured with the color you want to use.

How It Works

The SolidColorBrush class represents a brush with a single solid color that you can use to draw or fill shapes. To draw a shape derived from Shape using a solid color, assign an instance of a SolidColorBrush to the Stroke property of the Shape. To fill a shape derived from Shape using a solid color, assign an instance of a SolidColorBrush to the Fill property of the Shape.

There are a variety of ways to obtain SolidColorBrush objects in both XAML and code, but you need to understand how WPF represents color to best understand how to create and use SolidColorBrush objects.

WPF represents color with the System.Windows.Media.Color structure, which uses four channels to define a color: alpha, red, green, and blue. Alpha defines the amount of transparency the color has, and the red, green, and blue channels define how much of that primary color is included in the aggregate color.

The Color structure supports two common standards for defining the values for these channels: RGB and scRGB. The RGB standard uses 8-bit values for each channel, and you use a number between 0 and 255 to specify the value. This gives you 32 bits of color information, which is usually sufficient when displaying graphics on a computer screen.

However, when you are creating images for printing or further digital processing, a wider range of colors is required. The scRGB standard uses 16-bit values for each channel, and you use a floating-point number between 0 and 1 to specify the value. This gives you 64 bits of color information.

To support both the RGB and scRGB standards, the Color structure provides two sets of properties to represent the alpha, red, green, and blue channels of a color. The properties that provide RGB support are named A, R, G, and B and take System.Byte values. The properties that provide scRGB support are named ScA, ScR, ScG, and ScB and take System.Single values. The two sets of properties are synchronized, so, for example, if you change the A property of a Color object, the ScA property changes to the equivalent value on its own scale.

To obtain a Color object in code, you can use the static properties of the System.Windows.Media.Colors class, which provide access to more than 140 predefined Color objects. To create a custom Color object, call the static FromArgb, FromAValues, FromRgb, FromScRgb, or FromValues methods of the Color structure.

Once you have a Color object, you can pass it as an argument to the SolidColorBrush constructor and obtain a SolidColorBrush instance that will draw or fill your shape with that color. You can also obtain a SolidColorBrush instance preconfigured with current system colors using the static properties of the System.Windows.SystemColors class, as described in recipe 9-10.

XAML provides flexible syntax support to allow you to specify the color of a SolidColorBrush within the Stroke or Fill property of a shape. You can use RGB syntax, scRGB syntax, or the names of the colors defined in the Colors class.

If you want to reuse a specific SolidColorBrush, you can declare it as a resource within the resources collection of a suitable container and assign it a key. Once defined, refer to the SolidColorBrush resource from the Fill or Stroke property of a Shape element using the following syntax:

```
... Fill="{StaticResource SolidColorBrushKey}" ...
```

Note Chapter 1 discusses how to create and manage static resources in more detail.

The Code

The following XAML uses a set of Rectangle, Ellipse, and Line objects (from the System.Windows.Shapes namespace) to demonstrate how to use SolidColorBrush objects to draw and fill shapes (see Figure 9-11). The XAML demonstrates how to use named colors, RGB syntax, and scRGB syntax, as well as how to create and use a static SolidColorBrush resource.

```xml
<Window x:Class="Recipe_09_11.Window1"
    xmlns="http://schemas.microsoft.com/winfx/2006/xaml/presentation"
    xmlns:x="http://schemas.microsoft.com/winfx/2006/xaml"
    Title="WPF Recipes 9_11" Height="300" Width="300">
    <Canvas Margin="5">
        <Canvas.Resources>
            <!--scRGB semi-transparent color-->
            <SolidColorBrush Color="sc# 0.8,0.3,0.9,0.25" x:Key="Brush1" />
        </Canvas.Resources>

        <!--SolidColorBrush resource-->
        <Rectangle Fill="{StaticResource Brush1}" Height="180" Width="80" />
        <!--Named color-->
        <Rectangle Canvas.Top="10" Canvas.Left="50"
            Fill="RoyalBlue" Height="70" Width="220" />
        <!--RGB semi-transparent color-->
        <Ellipse Canvas.Top="30" Canvas.Left="90"
            Fill="#72ff8805" Height="150" Width="100" />
        <!--RGB solid color-->
        <Ellipse Canvas.Top="150" Canvas.Left="70"
            Fill="#ff0000" Height="100" Width="200" />
        <!--scRGB semi-transparent color-->
        <Line X1="20" X2="260" Y1="200" Y2="50"
            Stroke="sc# 0.6,0.8,0.3,0.0" StrokeThickness="40"/>
        <!--scRGB solid color-->
        <Line X1="20" X2="270" Y1="240" Y2="240"
            Stroke="sc# 0.1,0.5,0.1" StrokeThickness="20"/>
    </Canvas>
</Window>
```

Figure 9-11. *Drawing and filling shapes with solid colors*

9-12. Fill a Shape with a Linear or Radial Color Gradient

Problem

You need to draw or fill a shape with a linear or radial color gradient (that is, a fill that transitions smoothly between two or more colors).

Solution

For shapes derived from System.Windows.Shapes.Shape, to use a linear gradient, set the Fill or Stroke property to an instance of System.Windows.Media.LinearGradientBrush. To use a radial gradient, set the Fill or Stroke property to an instance of System.Windows.Media.RadialGradientBrush.

How It Works

The LinearGradientBrush and RadialGradientBrush classes allow you to create a blended fill or stroke that transitions from one color to another. It is also possible to transition through a sequence of colors.

A LinearGradientBrush represents a sequence of linear color transitions that occur according to a set of gradient stops you define along a gradient axis. The gradient axis is an imaginary line that by default connects the top-left corner of the area being painted with its bottom-right corner. You define gradient stops using GradientStop elements inside the LinearGradientBrush element.

To position gradient stops along the gradient axis, you assign the System.Double value between 0 and 1 to the Offset property of a GradientStop. The Offset value represents the percentage distance along the gradient axis at which the gradient stop occurs. So, for example, 0 represents the start of the gradient axis, 0.5 represents halfway along, and 0.75 represents 75 percent along the gradient axis. You specify the color associated with a gradient stop using the Color property of the GradientStop element. Recipes 9-10 and 9-11 discuss how you can define colors in XAML.

You can change the position and orientation of the gradient axis using the StartPoint and EndPoint properties of the LinearGradientBrush. Each of the StartPoint and EndPoint properties takes a pair of Double values that allow you to position the point using a coordinate system relative to the area being painted. The point "0,0" represents the top left of the area, and the point "1,1" represents the bottom right. So, to change the gradient axis from its default diagonal orientation to a horizontal one, set StartPoint to the value "0,0.5" and EndPoint to the value "1,0.5"; to make the gradient axis vertical, set StartPoint to the value "0.5,0" and EndPoint to the value "0.5,1"

■**Note** By setting the MappingMode property of the LinearGradientBrush to the value Absolute, you change the coordinate system used by the StartPoint and EndPoint properties from being one relative to the area being filled to being one expressed as device-independent pixels. Refer to the MSDN documentation on the MappingMode property for details at http://msdn.microsoft.com/en-us/library/system.windows.media.gradientbrush.mappingmode.aspx.

Using the StartPoint and EndPoint properties of the LinearGradientBrush, you can assign negative numbers or numbers greater than 1 to create a gradient axis that starts or ends outside the area being filled. You can also define a gradient axis that starts or ends somewhere inside the body of the area being filled.

Where the gradient axis does not start and end on the boundary of the area being painted, WPF calculates the gradient as specified but does not paint anything that lies outside the area. Where the gradient does not completely fill the area, WPF by default fills the remaining area with the final color in the gradient. You can change this behavior using the SpreadMethod property of the LinearGradientBrush element. Table 9-3 lists the possible values of the SpreadMethod property.

Table 9-3. *Possible Values of the SpreadMethod Property*

Value	Description
Pad	The default value. The last color in the gradient fills all remaining area.
Reflect	The gradient is repeated in reverse order.
Repeat	The gradient is repeated in the original order.

The RadialGradientBrush is similar in behavior to the LinearGradientBrush except that it has an elliptical gradient axis that radiates out from a defined focal point. You still use GradientStop elements in the RadialGradientBrush to define the position and color of transitions, but you use the RadiusX and RadiusY properties to define the size of the elliptical area covered by the gradient and the Center property to position the ellipse within the area being painted. You then use the GradientOrigin property to specify the location from where the sequence of gradient stops and starts within the gradient ellipse. As with the LinearGradientBrush, all of these properties' values are relative to the area being painted.

Tip If you want to reuse LinearGradientBrush or RadialGradientBrush elements, you can declare them as a resource within the resources collection of a suitable container and assign them a key. Once defined, refer to the gradient resource from the Fill or Stroke property of the Shape element using the following syntax:

… Fill="{StaticResource GradientKey}" …

The Code

The following XAML uses a set of Rectangle, Ellipse, and Line objects (from the System.Windows. Shapes namespace) to demonstrate how to use LinearGradientBrush and RadialGradientBrush objects to draw and fill shapes (see Figure 9-12). The XAML also demonstrates how to create and use static LinearGradientBrush and RadialGradientBrush resources.

```xml
<Window x:Class="Recipe_09_12.Window1"
    xmlns="http://schemas.microsoft.com/winfx/2006/xaml/presentation"
    xmlns:x="http://schemas.microsoft.com/winfx/2006/xaml"
    Title="WPF Recipes 9_12" Height="300" Width="300">
    <Canvas Margin="5">
        <Canvas.Resources>
            <!--Vertical reflected LinearGradientBrush static resource-->
            <LinearGradientBrush x:Key="LGB1" SpreadMethod="Reflect"
                            StartPoint="0.5,-0.25" EndPoint="0.5,.5">
                <GradientStop Color="Aqua" Offset="0.5" />
                <GradientStop Color="Navy" Offset="1.0" />
            </LinearGradientBrush>
            <!--Centered RadialGradientBrush static resource-->
            <RadialGradientBrush Center="0.5,0.5" RadiusX=".8" RadiusY=".5"
                            GradientOrigin="0.5,0.5" x:Key="RGB1">
                <GradientStop Color="BlanchedAlmond" Offset="0" />
                <GradientStop Color="DarkGreen" Offset=".7" />
            </RadialGradientBrush>
        </Canvas.Resources>

        <!--Fill with LinearGradientBrush static resource-->
        <Rectangle Canvas.Top="5" Canvas.Left="5"
            Fill="{StaticResource LGB1}" Height="180" Width="80" />
        <!--Fill with RadialGradientBrush static resource-->
        <Rectangle Canvas.Top="10" Canvas.Left="50"
                Fill="{StaticResource RGB1}" Height="70" Width="230" />
        <!--Fill with offset RadialGradientBrush-->
        <Ellipse Canvas.Top="130" Canvas.Left="30" Height="100" Width="230">
            <Ellipse.Fill>
                <RadialGradientBrush RadiusX=".8" RadiusY="1"
                            Center="0.5,0.5" GradientOrigin="0.05,0.5">
                    <GradientStop Color="#ffffff" Offset="0.1" />
                    <GradientStop Color="#ff0000" Offset="0.5" />
                    <GradientStop Color="#880000" Offset="0.8" />
                </RadialGradientBrush>
            </Ellipse.Fill>
        </Ellipse>
        <!--Fill with diagonal LinearGradientBrush-->
        <Ellipse Canvas.Top="30" Canvas.Left="110" Height="150" Width="150">
            <Ellipse.Fill>
                <LinearGradientBrush StartPoint="1,1" EndPoint="0,0">
                    <GradientStop Color="#DDFFFFFF" Offset=".2" />
                    <GradientStop Color="#FF000000" Offset=".8" />
                </LinearGradientBrush>
            </Ellipse.Fill>
        </Ellipse>
```

```
    <!--Stroke with horizontal multi-color LinearGradientBrush-->
    <Line X1="20" X2="280" Y1="240" Y2="240" StrokeThickness="30">
        <Line.Stroke>
            <LinearGradientBrush StartPoint="0,0.5" EndPoint="1,0.5">
                <GradientStop Color="Red" Offset="0.15" />
                <GradientStop Color="Orange" Offset="0.2" />
                <GradientStop Color="Yellow" Offset="0.35" />
                <GradientStop Color="Green" Offset="0.5" />
                <GradientStop Color="Blue" Offset="0.65" />
                <GradientStop Color="Indigo" Offset="0.75" />
                <GradientStop Color="Violet" Offset="0.9" />
            </LinearGradientBrush>
        </Line.Stroke>
    </Line>
  </Canvas>
</Window>
```

Figure 9-12. *Filling and drawing shapes with linear and radial gradients*

9-13. Fill a Shape with an Image

Problem

You need to fill a shape derived from System.Windows.Shapes.Shape with an image.

Solution

Assign an instance of System.Windows.Media.ImageBrush to the Fill property of the Shape. Use the Stretch, AlignmentX, AlignmentY, and ViewBox properties of the ImageBrush element to control the way the image fills the shape.

How It Works

The abstract System.Windows.Media.TileBrush class contains the functionality required to use a graphical image to paint a specified area. Classes derived from TileBrush include ImageBrush, DrawingBrush, and VisualBrush (all from the System.Windows.Media namespace). Each TileBrush subclass allows you to specify a different source for the graphics used to fill the area: ImageBrush lets you use a graphics file, DrawingBrush lets you use a drawing object, and VisualBrush lets you use an existing screen element (see recipe 9-15).

To use an image to fill a shape, you simply assign an ImageBrush element to the Fill property of the Shape you want to fill. You specify the name of the source image file using the Source property of the ImageBrush. You can use a local file name or a URL. The image can be loaded from any of the following image formats:

- .bmp
- .gif
- .ico
- .jpg
- .png
- .wdp
- .tiff

The default ImageBrush behavior (inherited from TileBrush) is to stretch the source image to completely fill the shape. This does not maintain the aspect ratios of the source image and will result in a stretched and distorted image if the source image is not the same size as the shape. You can override this behavior using the Stretch property of the ImageBrush. Table 9-4 lists the possible values you can assign to the Stretch property and describes their effect.

Table 9-4. *Possible Values of the Stretch Property*

Value	Description
None	Don't scale the image at all. If the image is smaller than the area of the shape, the rest of the area is left empty (transparent fill). If the image is larger than the shape, the image is cropped.
Uniform	Scale the source image so that it all fits in the shape while still maintaining the original aspect ratio of the image. This will result in some parts of the shape being left transparent unless the source image and shape have the same aspect ratios.
UniformToFill	Scale the source image so that it fills the shape completely while still maintaining the original aspect ratio of the image. This will result in some parts of the source image being cropped unless the source image and shape have the same aspect ratios.
Fill	The default behavior. Scale the image to fit the shape exactly without maintaining the original aspect ratio of the source image.

When using None, Uniform, and UniformToFill values for the Stretch property, you will want to control the positioning of the image within the shape. ImageBrush will center the image by default, but you can change this with the AlignmentX and AlignmentY properties of the ImageBrush element. Valid values for the AlignmentX property are Left, Center, and Right. Valid values for the AlignmentY property are Top, Center, and Bottom.

You can also configure the ImageBrush to use only a rectangular subsection of the source image as the brush instead of the whole image. You do this with the Viewbox property of the ImageBrush element. Viewbox takes four comma-separated System.Double values that identify the coordinates of the upper-left and lower-right corners of the image subsection relative to the original image. The point "0,0" represents the top left of the original image, and the point "1,1" represents the bottom right. If you want to use absolute pixel values to specify the size of the Viewbox, set the ViewboxUnits property of the ImageBrush to the value Absolute.

The Code

The following XAML uses a set of Rectangle, Ellipse, Polygon, and Line objects (from the System. Windows.Shapes namespace) to demonstrate how to use ImageBrush objects to fill shapes with an image (see Figure 9-13). The XAML also demonstrates how to create and use a static ImageBrush resource.

```
<Window x:Class="Recipe_09_13.Window1"
    xmlns="http://schemas.microsoft.com/winfx/2006/xaml/presentation"
    xmlns:x="http://schemas.microsoft.com/winfx/2006/xaml"
    Title="WPF Recipes 9_13" Height="300" Width="300">
  <Canvas Margin="5">
    <!--Define a static ImageBrush resource-->
    <Canvas.Resources>
        <ImageBrush x:Key="IB1" ImageSource="WeeMee.jpg" />
    </Canvas.Resources>

    <!--Fill ellipse using static ImageBrush resource-->
    <Ellipse Height="160" Width="160"
            Canvas.Top="0" Canvas.Left="110"
            Stroke="Black" StrokeThickness="1"
            Fill="{StaticResource IB1}" />
    <!--Fill rectangle with UniformToFill ImageBrush-->
    <Rectangle Height="180" Width="50"
            Canvas.Top="5" Canvas.Left="5"
            Stroke="Black" StrokeThickness="1" >
        <Rectangle.Fill>
            <ImageBrush ImageSource="WeeMee.jpg" Stretch="UniformToFill"/>
        </Rectangle.Fill>
    </Rectangle>
    <!--Fill Polygon with Left aligned Uniform ImageBrush-->
    <Polygon Canvas.Top="110" Canvas.Left="45"
            Points="40,0 150,100 10,100"
            Stroke="Black" StrokeThickness="1">
```

```
        <Polygon.Fill>
            <ImageBrush ImageSource="WeeMee.jpg" Stretch="Uniform"
                        AlignmentX="Left" />
        </Polygon.Fill>
    </Polygon>
    <!--Draw a line using a part of the source image-->
    <Line X1="20" X2="280" Y1="240" Y2="240" StrokeThickness="30">
        <Line.Stroke>
            <ImageBrush ImageSource="WeeMee.jpg"
                        Viewbox="30,46,42,15" ViewboxUnits="Absolute" />
        </Line.Stroke>
    </Line>
    </Canvas>
</Window>
```

Figure 9-13. *Filling and drawing shapes with images*

9-14. Fill a Shape with a Pattern or Texture

Problem

You need to fill a shape with a repeating pattern or texture.

Solution

To fill shapes derived from System.Windows.Shapes.Shape, assign an instance of System.Windows.Media.ImageBrush to the Fill property of the Shape. Use the Stretch, TileMode, ViewBox, and ViewPort properties of the ImageBrush element to control the way WPF uses the image to fill the shape.

How It Works

Recipe 9-13 describes how to fill a shape with an image using an ImageBrush. To fill a shape with a pattern or texture, you typically load some abstract graphic or texture from a file and apply it repeatedly to cover the entire area of a given shape. You do this using the same techniques discussed in recipe 9-13 but use a number of additional ImageBrush properties (inherited from TileBrush) to completely fill the shape by drawing the image repeatedly instead of once.

The first step is to define the tile that the ImageBrush will use to fill the shape. The ImageBrush uses the concept of a viewport to represent the tile. By default, the viewport is a rectangle with the dimensions equal to those of the image that the ImageBrush would normally use to fill the shape. Normally the viewport would be completely filled with the source image, but you can define what proportion of the viewport is filled by the source image using the Viewport property of the ImageBrush.

The Viewport property takes four comma-separated System.Double values that identify the coordinates of the upper-left and lower-right corners of the rectangle within the viewport where you want the ImageBrush to insert the source image. So, for example, you can take the original image and configure it to cover only a fraction of the viewport. The point "0,0" represents the top-left corner of the viewport, and the point "1,1" represents the bottom-right corner.

With your base tile defined, you use the TileMode property of the ImageBrush to define how the ImageBrush fills the shape using the tile defined by the viewport. Table 9-5 lists the possible values you can assign of the TileMode property and describes their effect.

Table 9-5. *Possible Values of the TileMode Property*

Value	Description
None	The default value. The base tile is drawn but not repeated. You get a single image, and the rest of the shape is empty (transparent fill).
Tile	The base tile is used repeatedly to fill the shape. Each tile is placed next to the other using the same orientation.
FlipX	The base tile is used repeatedly to fill the shape except that the tiles in alternate columns are flipped horizontally.
FlipY	The base tile is used repeatedly to fill the shape except that the tiles in alternate rows are flipped vertically.
FlipXY	The base tile is used repeatedly to fill the shape except that the tiles in alternate columns are flipped horizontally and the tiles in alternate rows are flipped vertically.

The Code

The following XAML uses a set of Rectangle, Ellipse, and Line objects (from the System.Windows. Shapes namespace) to demonstrate how to use ImageBrush objects to fill shapes with repeating patterns loaded from image files (see Figure 9-14). The XAML also demonstrates how to create and use static ImageBrush resources for the purpose of tiling.

```xml
<Window x:Class="Recipe_09_14.Window1"
    xmlns="http://schemas.microsoft.com/winfx/2006/xaml/presentation"
    xmlns:x="http://schemas.microsoft.com/winfx/2006/xaml"
    Title="WPF Recipes 9_14" Height="300" Width="380">
    <StackPanel Orientation="Horizontal">
        <StackPanel Margin="10">
            <StackPanel.Resources>
                <!--Style for the tile swabs-->
                <Style TargetType="{x:Type Image}">
                    <Setter Property="Margin" Value="5"/>
                    <Setter Property="MaxHeight" Value="50"/>
                </Style>
            </StackPanel.Resources>
            <!--Display the basic tiles used in the example-->
            <TextBlock Text="Tiles:" />
            <Image Source="bubble_dropper.jpg" />
            <Image Source="mini_mountains.jpg" />
            <Image Source="fly_larvae.jpg" />
            <Image Source="fishy_rainbow.jpg" />
        </StackPanel>
        <Canvas Margin="5">
            <Canvas.Resources>
                <!--Define static ImageBrush resource with TileMode FlipXY-->
                <ImageBrush x:Key="IB1" ImageSource="bubble_dropper.jpg"
                        Stretch="UniformToFill" TileMode="FlipXY"
                        Viewport="0,0,0.2,0.2" />
                <!--Define static ImageBrush resource with TileMode FlipX-->
                <ImageBrush x:Key="IB2" ImageSource="mini_mountains.jpg"
                        Stretch="UniformToFill" TileMode="FlipX"
                        Viewport="0,0,0.5,0.2" />
            </Canvas.Resources>

            <!--Fill Rectangles with static ImageBrush resources-->
            <Rectangle Canvas.Top="5" Canvas.Left="5"
                    Height="180" Width="80"
                    Fill="{StaticResource IB1}" />
            <Rectangle Canvas.Top="10" Canvas.Left="50"
                    Height="70" Width="230"
                    Fill="{StaticResource IB2}" />
            <!--Fill Ellipse with custom ImageBrush - TileMode Tile-->
            <Ellipse Canvas.Top="130" Canvas.Left="30"
                    Height="100" Width="230">
```

```xml
                <Ellipse.Fill>
                    <ImageBrush ImageSource="fishy_rainbow.jpg"
                                Stretch="Fill" TileMode="Tile"
                                Viewport="0,0,0.25,0.5" />
                </Ellipse.Fill>
            </Ellipse>
            <!--Fill with custom ImageBrush - TileMode Tile-->
            <Ellipse Canvas.Top="30" Canvas.Left="110"
                    Height="150" Width="150">
                <Ellipse.Fill>
                    <ImageBrush ImageSource="fly_larvae.jpg" Opacity=".7"
                                Stretch="Uniform" TileMode="Tile"
                                Viewport="0,0,0.5,.5" />
                </Ellipse.Fill>
            </Ellipse>
            <!--Draw Stroke with tiled ImageBrush - TileMode Tile-->
            <Line X1="20" X2="280" Y1="240" Y2="240" StrokeThickness="30">
                <Line.Stroke>
                    <ImageBrush ImageSource="ApressLogo.gif"
                                Stretch="UniformToFill" TileMode="Tile"
                                Viewport="0,0,0.25,1" />
                </Line.Stroke>
            </Line>
        </Canvas>
    </StackPanel>
</Window>
```

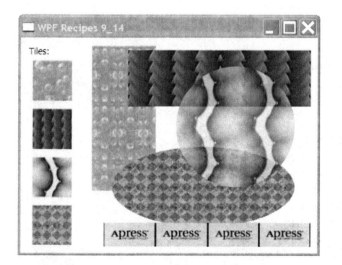

Figure 9-14. *Filling and drawing shapes with patterns*

9-15. Fill a Shape with a View of Active UI Elements

Problem

You need to fill a shape with an image of some active UI elements from another part of the UI.

Solution

Assign an instance of System.Windows.Media.VisualBrush to the Fill property of the Shape. Set the value of the Visual property of the VisualBrush to reference the UI element with which you want to fill the Shape.

How It Works

Just as System.Windows.Media.ImageBrush (discussed in recipes 9-13 and 9-14) allows you to fill a shape with an image or a texture, the VisualBrush allows you to fill a shape with a dynamic but noninteractive view of a UI element. Like ImageBrush, the VisualBrush class is derived from System.Windows.Media.TileBrush and so offers all the image scaling and tiling capabilities discussed in recipes 9-13 and 9-14. The only difference is that instead of configuring VisualBrush with a reference to an image, you set the Visual property of the VisualBrush to reference an active UI element. WPF will then use the current state of the specified UI element (and the configuration of the VisualBrush) to fill the Shape. As the referenced UI elements change, any shapes painted with the VisualBrush are dynamically updated. You set the value of the Visual property using element binding syntax of the following form:

```
… Visual="{Binding ElementName=someElementName }" …
```

The Code

The following XAML uses some Rectangle and Ellipse objects (from the System.Windows. Shapes namespace) to demonstrate how to use VisualBrush objects to fill shapes with views of active UI elements (see Figure 9-15). The XAML also demonstrates how to create and use static VisualBrush resources.

```xml
<Window x:Class="Recipe_09_15.Window1"
    xmlns="http://schemas.microsoft.com/winfx/2006/xaml/presentation"
    xmlns:x="http://schemas.microsoft.com/winfx/2006/xaml"
    Title="WPF Recipes 9_15" Height="250" Width="550">
    <StackPanel Orientation="Horizontal">
        <StackPanel Margin="5" MinWidth="180">
            <TextBlock FontSize="15" Text="Active Controls:"/>
            <StackPanel Name="spInnerLeftPanel" Margin="5">
                <ListBox>
                    <ListBoxItem Content="First List Item" IsSelected="True"/>
                    <ListBoxItem Content="Second List Item" />
                    <ListBoxItem Content="Third List Item" />
                </ListBox>
```

```xml
                        <Button Content="Button 1" Margin="5" MinWidth="80"/>
                        <Button Content="Button 2" Margin="5" MinWidth="80"/>
                        <GroupBox BorderBrush="Black" BorderThickness="2"
                                  Header="Check Boxes" Name="gbCheckBoxes">
                            <StackPanel>
                                <CheckBox Content="First CheckBox" Margin="2"
                                          IsChecked="True" />
                                <CheckBox Content="Second CheckBox" Margin="2" />
                                <CheckBox Content="Third CheckBox" Margin="2" />
                            </StackPanel>
                        </GroupBox>
                    </StackPanel>
                </StackPanel>
                <Canvas Margin="5">
                    <Canvas.Resources>
                        <VisualBrush x:Key="VB1"
                                     Visual="{Binding ElementName=spInnerLeftPanel}" />
                        <VisualBrush x:Key="VB2" Viewbox="0,0,0.5,0.2"
                                     Visual="{Binding ElementName=spInnerLeftPanel}"
                                     Stretch="UniformToFill" TileMode="FlipX" />
                    </Canvas.Resources>

                    <!--Fill Rectangles with static VisualBrush resources-->
                    <Rectangle Canvas.Top="5" Canvas.Left="5"
                               Stroke="Black" StrokeThickness="2"
                               Height="180" Width="80"
                               Fill="{StaticResource VB1}"
                               SnapsToDevicePixels="True" />
                    <Rectangle Canvas.Top="10" Canvas.Left="100"
                               Stroke="Black" StrokeThickness="2"
                               Height="70" Width="220"
                               Fill="{StaticResource VB2}"
                               SnapsToDevicePixels="True" />
                    <!--Fill Ellipse with custom VisualBrush-->
                    <Ellipse Canvas.Top="90" Canvas.Left="100"
                             Stroke="Black" StrokeThickness="2"
                             Height="110" Width="220"
                             SnapsToDevicePixels="True">
                        <Ellipse.Fill>
                            <VisualBrush
                                Visual="{Binding ElementName=spInnerLeftPanel}" />
                        </Ellipse.Fill>
                    </Ellipse>
                </Canvas>
            </StackPanel>
        </Window>
```

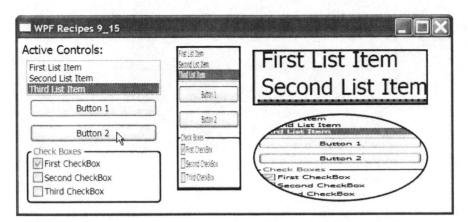

Figure 9-15. *Filling shapes with views of active UI elements*

9-16. Apply Blur Effects on UI Elements

Problem

You need to apply a blur effect to your UI elements.

Solution

Create a System.Windows.Media.Effects.BlurBitmapEffect element, and assign it to the BitmapEffect property of the element you want to blur. Use the Radius property of the BlurBitmapEffect element to control how blurred the target element appears.

How It Works

Assigning a BlurBitmapEffect element to the BitmapEffect property of an element causes that element to be blurred according to the configuration of the BlurBitmapEffect element. The BitmapEffect property is declared by the System.Windows.UIElement class, which means you can apply a blur effect to anything that inherits from UIElement, which includes all the standard control and graphics elements. Table 9-6 summarizes the properties of the BlurBitmapEffect class that allow you to control the specific blur effect applied to a target element.

Table 9-6. *Properties of the BlurBitmapEffect Class*

Property	Description
KernelType	Defines the type of blur kernel used to perform the blurring. The default value is Gaussian. The other possible value is Box. The Gaussian kernel produces a smoother blur effect but uses more processing power.
Radius	Defines the magnitude of blurring; larger numbers produce more blurring.

> **Note** Bitmap effects such as the `BlurBitmapEffect` element are rendered in software and do not take advantage of any graphics hardware acceleration you may have available. This means you should think carefully before using these effects. Small regions of blurring will not noticeably affect application performance, but blurring large areas may.

The Code

The following XAML demonstrates how to apply a blur effect to a variety of UI elements using the `BlurBitmapEffect` element. Figure 9-16 shows the output of the example and highlights the effect of assigning higher values to the `Radius` property of the `BlurBitmapEffect` element.

```xaml
<Window x:Class="Recipe_09_16.Window1"
    xmlns="http://schemas.microsoft.com/winfx/2006/xaml/presentation"
    xmlns:x="http://schemas.microsoft.com/winfx/2006/xaml"
    Title="WPF Recipes 9_16" Height="300" Width="300">
    <UniformGrid Columns="3" Rows="4">
        <UniformGrid.Resources>
            <GeometryGroup x:Key="Clown">
                <!--Head and hat-->
                <PathGeometry>
                    <PathFigure IsClosed="True" StartPoint="40,0">
                        <LineSegment Point="70,100" />
                        <ArcSegment Point="70,110" IsLargeArc="True"
                                    Size="10,10" SweepDirection="Clockwise"/>
                        <ArcSegment Point="10,110" Size="30,30"
                                    SweepDirection="Clockwise"/>
                        <ArcSegment Point="10,100" IsLargeArc="True"
                                    Size="10,10" SweepDirection="Clockwise"/>
                    </PathFigure>
                </PathGeometry>
                <!--Hat buttons-->
                <EllipseGeometry Center="40,40" RadiusX="2" RadiusY="2"/>
                <EllipseGeometry Center="40,50" RadiusX="2" RadiusY="2"/>
                <EllipseGeometry Center="40,60" RadiusX="2" RadiusY="2"/>
                <!--Eyes-->
                <EllipseGeometry Center="30,100" RadiusX="3" RadiusY="2"/>
                <EllipseGeometry Center="50,100" RadiusX="3" RadiusY="2"/>
                <!--Nose-->
                <EllipseGeometry Center="40,110" RadiusX="3" RadiusY="3"/>
                <!--Mouth-->
                <RectangleGeometry Rect="30,120 20,10"/>
            </GeometryGroup>
        </UniformGrid.Resources>
        <TextBlock Text="A TextBlock" FontSize="16"
                HorizontalAlignment="Center" VerticalAlignment="Center" />
```

```xml
<TextBlock Text="A TextBlock"  FontSize="16"
           HorizontalAlignment="Center" VerticalAlignment="Center">
    <TextBlock.BitmapEffect>
        <BlurBitmapEffect Radius="1" KernelType="Gaussian"/>
    </TextBlock.BitmapEffect>
</TextBlock>
<TextBlock Text="A TextBlock"  FontSize="16"
           HorizontalAlignment="Center" VerticalAlignment="Center">
    <TextBlock.BitmapEffect>
        <BlurBitmapEffect Radius="2" />
    </TextBlock.BitmapEffect>
</TextBlock>
<Button Content="A Button" FontSize="16" Margin="5" MaxHeight="30"/>
<Button Content="A Button" FontSize="16" Margin="5" MaxHeight="30">
    <Button.BitmapEffect>
        <BlurBitmapEffect Radius="1" />
    </Button.BitmapEffect>
</Button>
<Button Content="A Button" FontSize="16" Margin="5" MaxHeight="30">
    <Button.BitmapEffect>
        <BlurBitmapEffect Radius="2" />
    </Button.BitmapEffect>
</Button>
<Path HorizontalAlignment="Center" VerticalAlignment="Center"
      Data="{StaticResource Clown}" Stroke="Blue" StrokeThickness="4">
    <Path.LayoutTransform>
        <ScaleTransform ScaleX=".5" ScaleY=".45" />
    </Path.LayoutTransform>
</Path>
<Path HorizontalAlignment="Center" VerticalAlignment="Center"
      Data="{StaticResource Clown}" Stroke="Blue" StrokeThickness="4">
    <Path.LayoutTransform>
        <ScaleTransform ScaleX=".5" ScaleY=".45" />
    </Path.LayoutTransform>
    <Path.BitmapEffect>
        <BlurBitmapEffect Radius="1" />
    </Path.BitmapEffect>
</Path>
<Path HorizontalAlignment="Center" VerticalAlignment="Center"
      Data="{StaticResource Clown}" Stroke="Blue" StrokeThickness="4">
    <Path.LayoutTransform>
        <ScaleTransform ScaleX=".5" ScaleY=".45" />
    </Path.LayoutTransform>
    <Path.BitmapEffect>
        <BlurBitmapEffect Radius="2" />
    </Path.BitmapEffect>
</Path>
```

```
        <Ellipse Margin="5" Stroke="Black" StrokeThickness="1" >
            <Ellipse.Fill>
                <ImageBrush ImageSource="WeeMee.jpg" />
            </Ellipse.Fill>
        </Ellipse>
        <Ellipse Margin="5" Stroke="Black" StrokeThickness="1" >
            <Ellipse.BitmapEffect>
                <BlurBitmapEffect Radius="1" />
            </Ellipse.BitmapEffect>
            <Ellipse.Fill>
                <ImageBrush ImageSource="WeeMee.jpg" />
            </Ellipse.Fill>
        </Ellipse>
        <Ellipse Margin="5" Stroke="Black" StrokeThickness="1" >
            <Ellipse.BitmapEffect>
                <BlurBitmapEffect Radius="2" />
            </Ellipse.BitmapEffect>
            <Ellipse.Fill>
                <ImageBrush ImageSource="WeeMee.jpg" />
            </Ellipse.Fill>
        </Ellipse>
    </UniformGrid>
</Window>
```

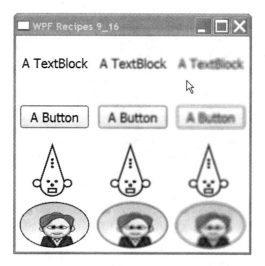

Figure 9-16. *Text, controls, shapes, and images blurred to varying degrees*

9-17. Apply a Glow Effect to Your UI Elements

Problem

You need to apply a glow effect to your UI elements.

Solution

Create a System.Windows.Media.Effects.OuterGlowBitmapEffect element, and assign it to the BitmapEffect property of the element you want to glow. Use the GlowColor property of the OuterGlowBitmapEffect element to define the color of the glow and the GlowSize property to define the size of the glowing halo around the target element.

How It Works

Assigning an OuterGlowBitmapEffect element to the BitmapEffect property of an element creates a glowing halo around the target element according to the configuration of the OuterGlowBitmapEffect element. The BitmapEffect property is declared by the System.Windows.UIElement class, which means you can apply a glow effect to anything that inherits from UIElement, which includes all the standard control and graphics elements. Table 9-7 summarizes the properties of the OuterGlowBitmapEffect class that allow you to control the nature of the glow applied to a target element.

Table 9-7. *Properties of the OuterGlowBitmapEffect Class*

Property	Description
GlowColor	The color of the glowing halo around the target element. See recipes 9-10 and 9-11 for a discussion of the options you have for defining colors in WPF.
GlowSize	The thickness of the glowing halo in device-independent pixels—the larger the number, the bigger the glow. Valid values are between 1 and 199, with the default value being 20.
Noise	Defines the level of noise (graininess) in the halo. Valid values are between 0 and 1. A value of 0 gives a smooth halo, while any other value introduces a proportional amount of graininess into the glow effect. The default value is 0.
Opacity	Defines the opacity of the glowing halo. Valid values are between 0 and 1. A value of 0 means the glow is completely transparent, while a value of 1 means the glow is completely opaque. Values between 0 and 1 introduce a proportional level of opacity. The default value is 1.

Note Bitmap effects such as the OuterGlowBitmapEffect element are rendered in software and do not take advantage of any graphics hardware acceleration you may have available. This means you should think carefully before using these effects. Small regions of glow will not noticeably affect application performance, but using glow on large areas may.

The Code

The following XAML demonstrates how to apply a glow effect to a variety of graphics elements using the OuterGlowBitmapEffect element. Figure 9-17 shows the output of the example and highlights the effect of assigning higher values to the GlowSize and Noise properties of the OuterGlowBitmapEffect element.

```xml
<Window x:Class="Recipe_09_17.Window1"
    xmlns="http://schemas.microsoft.com/winfx/2006/xaml/presentation"
    xmlns:x="http://schemas.microsoft.com/winfx/2006/xaml"
    Title="WPF Recipes 9_17" Height="230" Width="500">
    <Canvas Margin="10">
        <Canvas.Resources>
            <GeometryGroup x:Key="Clown" FillRule="Nonzero">
                <!--Head and hat-->
                <PathGeometry>
                    <PathFigure IsClosed="True" StartPoint="40,0">
                        <LineSegment Point="70,100" />
                        <ArcSegment Point="70,110" IsLargeArc="True"
                                    Size="10,10" SweepDirection="Clockwise"/>
                        <ArcSegment Point="10,110" Size="30,30"
                                    SweepDirection="Clockwise"/>
                        <ArcSegment Point="10,100" IsLargeArc="True"
                                    Size="10,10" SweepDirection="Clockwise"/>
                    </PathFigure>
                </PathGeometry>
                <!--Hat buttons-->
                <EllipseGeometry Center="40,40" RadiusX="2" RadiusY="2"/>
                <EllipseGeometry Center="40,50" RadiusX="2" RadiusY="2"/>
                <EllipseGeometry Center="40,60" RadiusX="2" RadiusY="2"/>
                <!--Eyes-->
                <EllipseGeometry Center="30,100" RadiusX="3" RadiusY="2"/>
                <EllipseGeometry Center="50,100" RadiusX="3" RadiusY="2"/>
                <!--Nose-->
                <EllipseGeometry Center="40,110" RadiusX="3" RadiusY="3"/>
                <!--Mouth-->
                <RectangleGeometry Rect="30,120 20,10"/>
            </GeometryGroup>
        </Canvas.Resources>

        <TextBlock Text="A TextBlock with Noise" FontSize="16">
            <TextBlock.BitmapEffect>
                <OuterGlowBitmapEffect Noise="0.5"
                                       GlowColor="Red" GlowSize="25" />
            </TextBlock.BitmapEffect>
        </TextBlock>
```

```xml
<Polyline Canvas.Left="0" Canvas.Top="40"
          Margin="10" Stroke="Black" StrokeThickness="5"
          Points="0,0 100,0 100,100 0,100 0,20 80,20 80,80
                  20,80, 20,40 60,40 60,60 40,60" >
    <Polyline.BitmapEffect>
        <OuterGlowBitmapEffect GlowColor="Blue" GlowSize="10" />
    </Polyline.BitmapEffect>
</Polyline>
<Path Canvas.Left="170" Canvas.Top="10" Data="{StaticResource Clown}"
      Stroke="Black" StrokeThickness="4" Fill="Wheat">
    <Path.BitmapEffect>
        <OuterGlowBitmapEffect GlowColor="Green" GlowSize="30" />
    </Path.BitmapEffect>
</Path>
<Ellipse Canvas.Right="20" Canvas.Top="5"
         Height="150" Width="150" Stroke="Black" StrokeThickness="1">
    <Ellipse.BitmapEffect>
        <OuterGlowBitmapEffect GlowColor="Black" GlowSize="80" />
    </Ellipse.BitmapEffect>
    <Ellipse.Fill>
        <ImageBrush ImageSource="WeeMee.jpg" />
    </Ellipse.Fill>
</Ellipse>
    </Canvas>
</Window>
```

Figure 9-17. *Text, shapes, and images glowing to varying degrees*

9-18. Apply a Drop Shadow Effect to Your UI Elements

Problem

You need to apply a drop shadow effect to your UI elements.

Solution

Create a System.Windows.Media.Effects.DropShadowBitmapEffect element, and assign it to the BitmapEffect property of the element you want to have a shadow. Use the Color property of the DropShadowBitmapEffect element to define the color of the shadow and the ShadowDepth property to define the size of the shadow on the target element.

How It Works

Assigning a DropShadowBitmapEffect element to the BitmapEffect property of an element creates a shadow on the target element according to the configuration of the DropShadowBitmapEffect element. The BitmapEffect property is declared by the System.Windows.UIElement class, which means you can apply a shadow effect to anything that inherits from UIElement, which includes all the standard control and graphics elements. Table 9-8 summarizes the properties of the DropShadowBitmapEffect class that allow you to control the nature of the shadow applied to a target element.

Table 9-8. *Properties of the DropShadowBitmapEffect Class*

Property	Description
Color	The color of the shadow on the target element. See recipes 9-10 and 9-11 for a discussion of the options you have for defining colors in WPF.
Direction	Defines the angle in degrees at which the shadow is cast from the target element. A value of 0 (or 360) means the shadow is cast to the right, a value of 90 means the shadow is cast directly upward, a value of 180 means the shadow is cast to the left, and so on. The default value is 315, causing the shadow to be cast to the lower right of the target element.
Noise	Defines the level of noise (graininess) in the shadow. Valid values are between 0 and 1. A value of 0 gives a smooth shadow, while any other value introduces a proportional amount of graininess into the shadow effect. The default value is 0.
Opacity	Defines the opacity of the shadow. Valid values are between 0 and 1. A value of 0 means the shadow is completely transparent, while a value of 1 means the shadow is completely opaque. Values between 0 and 1 introduce a proportional level of opacity. The default value is 1.
ShadowDepth	The distance in device-independent pixels between the target object and the shadow cast. Valid values are between 0 and 300, with the default value being 5.
Softness	Defines the softness of the shadow, that is, whether the shadow is sharp or diffuse. Valid values are between 0 and 1. A value of 0 means the shadow is sharply defined, while a value of 1 means the shadow is very diffuse. Values between 0 and 1 introduce a proportional level of softness. The default value is 0.5.

Note Bitmap effects such as the `DropShadowBitmapEffect` element are rendered in software and do not take advantage of any graphics hardware acceleration you may have available. This means you should think carefully before using these effects. Small regions of shadow will not noticeably affect application performance, but using shadow on large areas may.

The Code

The following XAML demonstrates how to apply a drop shadow effect to a variety of UI elements using the `DropShadowBitmapEffect` element. Figure 9-18 shows the output of the example and highlights the effect of assigning a variety of values to the `Direction`, `Noise`, `ShadowDepth`, and `Softness` properties of the `DropShadowBitmapEffect` element.

```xaml
<Window x:Class="Recipe_09_18.Window1"
    xmlns="http://schemas.microsoft.com/winfx/2006/xaml/presentation"
    xmlns:x="http://schemas.microsoft.com/winfx/2006/xaml"
    Title="WPF Recipes 9_18" Height="230" Width="500">
    <Canvas Margin="10">
        <Canvas.Resources>
            <GeometryGroup x:Key="Clown" FillRule="Nonzero">
                <!--Head and hat-->
                <PathGeometry>
                    <PathFigure IsClosed="True" StartPoint="40,0">
                        <LineSegment Point="70,100" />
                        <ArcSegment Point="70,110" IsLargeArc="True"
                                    Size="10,10" SweepDirection="Clockwise"/>
                        <ArcSegment Point="10,110" Size="30,30"
                                    SweepDirection="Clockwise"/>
                        <ArcSegment Point="10,100" IsLargeArc="True"
                                    Size="10,10" SweepDirection="Clockwise"/>
                    </PathFigure>
                </PathGeometry>
                <!--Hat buttons-->
                <EllipseGeometry Center="40,40" RadiusX="2" RadiusY="2"/>
                <EllipseGeometry Center="40,50" RadiusX="2" RadiusY="2"/>
                <EllipseGeometry Center="40,60" RadiusX="2" RadiusY="2"/>
                <!--Eyes-->
                <EllipseGeometry Center="30,100" RadiusX="3" RadiusY="2"/>
                <EllipseGeometry Center="50,100" RadiusX="3" RadiusY="2"/>
                <!--Nose-->
                <EllipseGeometry Center="40,110" RadiusX="3" RadiusY="3"/>
                <!--Mouth-->
                <RectangleGeometry Rect="30,120 20,10"/>
            </GeometryGroup>
        </Canvas.Resources>
```

```xml
    <Polyline Canvas.Left="10" Canvas.Top="30"
            Margin="10" Stroke="Black" StrokeThickness="5"
            Points="0,0 100,0 100,100 0,100 0,20 80,20 80,80
                    20,80, 20,40 60,40 60,60 40,60" >
        <Polyline.BitmapEffect>
            <DropShadowBitmapEffect Color="Blue" Direction="35"
                                    ShadowDepth="7" Softness=".3" />
        </Polyline.BitmapEffect>
    </Polyline>
    <Path Canvas.Left="170" Canvas.Top="10" Data="{StaticResource Clown}"
        Stroke="Black" StrokeThickness="4" Fill="Wheat">
        <Path.BitmapEffect>
            <DropShadowBitmapEffect Color="Green" Direction="30" Noise="1"
                                    ShadowDepth="20" Softness="3" />
        </Path.BitmapEffect>
    </Path>
    <Ellipse Canvas.Right="20" Canvas.Top="5"
        Height="150" Width="150" Stroke="Black" StrokeThickness="1">
        <Ellipse.BitmapEffect>
            <DropShadowBitmapEffect Color="Black" Direction="-50"
                                    ShadowDepth="40" Softness=".7" />
        </Ellipse.BitmapEffect>
        <Ellipse.Fill>
            <ImageBrush ImageSource="WeeMee.jpg" />
        </Ellipse.Fill>
    </Ellipse>
  </Canvas>
</Window>
```

Figure 9-18. *Shapes and images with drop shadows*

9-19. Scale, Skew, Rotate, or Position Graphics Elements

Problem

You need to scale, skew, rotate, or position graphics elements.

Solution

Assign a RotateTransform, SkewTransform, ScaleTransform, or TranslateTransform element to the LayoutTransform or RenderTransform property of the graphic element you want to manipulate. RotateTransform, SkewTransform, ScaleTransform, or TranslateTransform are members of the System.Windows.Media namespace.

How It Works

When working with graphics, it is incredibly useful and efficient to be able to take a graphic element and rotate it from its default orientation, change its size, skew it, or display it displaced from its default position using a transformation matrix. WPF provides this capability (see System.Windows.Media.MatrixTransform) but also exposes the same functionality through a set of easy-to-use transform classes: RotateTransform, SkewTransform, ScaleTransform, and TranslateTransform. There is also a class named TransformGroup, which allows you to group together more than one of the transform elements so that they are applied together.

Assigning one of the transform elements (or the TransformGroup element) to the LayoutTransform or RenderTransform property of an element applies the defined transformation to the target element. The LayoutTransform and RenderTransform properties are declared by the System.Windows.UIElement class, meaning you can apply transforms to anything that inherits from UIElement, which includes all the standard control and graphics elements.

The difference between the LayoutTransform and RenderTransform is the order in which WPF executes the transformation. WPF executes the LayoutTransform as part of the layout processing, so the rotated position of the control affects the layout of controls around it. The RenderTransform, on the other hand, is executed after layout is determined, which means the rotated control does not affect the positioning of other controls and can therefore end up appearing partially over or under other controls.

Table 9-9 summarizes the unique properties of each transform class that describe how they affect their target elements.

The UIElement class also declares a property named RenderTransformOrigin, which allows you to define a center point on an element that will be used by any RenderTransform elements applied to it. The benefit of using RenderTransformOrigin over CenterX and CenterY (described in Table 9-9) is that RenderTransformOrigin allows you to specify a relative distance instead of an absolute pixel value, as is the case with CenterX and CenterY. RenderTransformOrigin takes a pair of System.Double values between 0 and 1, with "0,0" representing the top left of the element and "1,1" representing the bottom right. The center of the object is represented by the point "0.5,0.5".

Table 9-9. *Properties of the Transform Classes*

Property	Description
RotateTransform	
Angle	The angle in degrees by which you rotate the target element. Positive values rotate clockwise, and negative values rotate anticlockwise. The rotation occurs around the point specified by the CenterX and CenterY properties.
CenterX	The x-coordinate (in device-independent pixels) of the point around which the transformation occurs.
CenterY	The y-coordinate (in device-independent pixels) of the point around which the transformation occurs.
ScaleTransform	
CenterX	See CenterX under RotateTransform.
CenterY	See CenterY under RotateTransform.
ScaleX	The proportion by which the target element is scaled in the x-axis.
ScaleY	The proportion by which the target element is scaled in the y-axis.
SkewTransform	
AngleX	The angle in degrees counterclockwise from the y-axis by which the target element is skewed.
AngleY	The angle in degrees counterclockwise from the x-axis by which the target element is skewed.
CenterX	See CenterX under RotateTransform.
CenterY	See CenterY under RotateTransform.
TranslateTransform	
X	The distance to translate (move) the target element along the x-axis.
Y	The distance to translate (move) the target element along the y-axis.

■**Note** You can get and manipulate the underlying matrix (as a System.Windows.Media.Matrix) used by each of the transform classes mentioned in this recipe via the Value property of the transform class.

The Code

The following XAML demonstrates how to use a variety of individual and grouped layout and render transforms to manipulate graphics elements (see Figure 9-19). Of particular interest are the series of clown heads that are fundamentally located at the same position in the canvas but translated, scaled, and rotated using a set of render transforms grouped together in a TransformGroup element.

```xml
<Window x:Class="Recipe_09_19.Window1"
    xmlns="http://schemas.microsoft.com/winfx/2006/xaml/presentation"
    xmlns:x="http://schemas.microsoft.com/winfx/2006/xaml"
    Title="WPF Recipes 9_19" Height="300" Width="450">
    <Canvas>
        <Canvas.Resources>
            <GeometryGroup x:Key="Clown" FillRule="Nonzero">
                <!--Head and hat-->
                <PathGeometry>
                    <PathFigure IsClosed="True" StartPoint="40,0">
                        <LineSegment Point="70,100" />
                        <ArcSegment Point="70,110" IsLargeArc="True"
                                    Size="10,10" SweepDirection="Clockwise"/>
                        <ArcSegment Point="10,110" Size="30,30"
                                    SweepDirection="Clockwise"/>
                        <ArcSegment Point="10,100" IsLargeArc="True"
                                    Size="10,10" SweepDirection="Clockwise"/>
                    </PathFigure>
                </PathGeometry>
                <!--Hat buttons-->
                <EllipseGeometry Center="40,40" RadiusX="2" RadiusY="2"/>
                <EllipseGeometry Center="40,50" RadiusX="2" RadiusY="2"/>
                <EllipseGeometry Center="40,60" RadiusX="2" RadiusY="2"/>
                <!--Eyes-->
                <EllipseGeometry Center="30,100" RadiusX="3" RadiusY="2"/>
                <EllipseGeometry Center="50,100" RadiusX="3" RadiusY="2"/>
                <!--Nose-->
                <EllipseGeometry Center="40,110" RadiusX="3" RadiusY="3"/>
                <!--Mouth-->
                <RectangleGeometry Rect="30,120 20,10"/>
            </GeometryGroup>
        </Canvas.Resources>
        <Polyline Canvas.Left="50" Canvas.Top="10"
                Stroke="Black" StrokeThickness="5"
                Points="0,0 100,0 100,100 0,100 0,20 80,20 80,80
                        20,80, 20,40 60,40 60,60 40,60">
            <Polyline.LayoutTransform>
                <ScaleTransform CenterX="50" CenterY="50"
                                ScaleX="0.2" ScaleY="0.7"/>
            </Polyline.LayoutTransform>
        </Polyline>
        <Polyline Canvas.Left="90" Canvas.Top="10"
                Stroke="Black" StrokeThickness="5"
                Points="0,0 100,0 100,100 0,100 0,20 80,20 80,80
                        20,80, 20,40 60,40 60,60 40,60" >
```

```
        <Polyline.LayoutTransform>
            <RotateTransform Angle="45" CenterX="50" CenterY="50"/>
        </Polyline.LayoutTransform>
    </Polyline>
    <Polyline Canvas.Left="225" Canvas.Top="10"
            Stroke="Black" StrokeThickness="5"
            Points="0,0 100,0 100,100 0,100 0,20 80,20 80,80
                    20,80, 20,40 60,40 60,60 40,60" >
        <Polyline.LayoutTransform>
            <SkewTransform CenterX="50" CenterY="50" AngleX="-45" />
        </Polyline.LayoutTransform>
    </Polyline>
    <Path Canvas.Left-"20" Canvas.Top="110"
        Data="{StaticResource Clown}"
        Stroke="Black" StrokeThickness="4">
    </Path>
    <Path Canvas.Left="20" Canvas.Top="110"
        Data="{StaticResource Clown}" RenderTransformOrigin="0.5,0.5"
        Stroke="Black" StrokeThickness="4">
        <Path.RenderTransform>
            <TransformGroup>
                <ScaleTransform ScaleX=".8" ScaleY=".8" />
                <RotateTransform Angle="50" CenterX="40" CenterY="40" />
                <TranslateTransform X="80" Y="20" />
            </TransformGroup>
        </Path.RenderTransform>
    </Path>
    <Path Canvas.Left="20" Canvas.Top="110"
        Data="{StaticResource Clown}" RenderTransformOrigin="0.5,0.65"
        Stroke="Black" StrokeThickness="4">
        <Path.RenderTransform>
            <TransformGroup>
                <ScaleTransform ScaleX=".6" ScaleY=".6" />
                <RotateTransform Angle="90" CenterX="40" CenterY="40" />
                <TranslateTransform X="120" Y="0" />
            </TransformGroup>
        </Path.RenderTransform>
    </Path>
    <Path Canvas.Left="20" Canvas.Top="110"
        Data="{StaticResource Clown}" RenderTransformOrigin="0.5,0.5"
        Stroke="Black" StrokeThickness="4">
        <Path.RenderTransform>
            <TransformGroup>
                <ScaleTransform ScaleX="0.4" ScaleY="0.4" />
                <RotateTransform Angle="130" CenterX="40" CenterY="40" />
                <TranslateTransform X="200" Y="10" />
            </TransformGroup>
```

```
            </Path.RenderTransform>
        </Path>
    </Canvas>
</Window>
```

Figure 9-19. *Skewing, rotating, translating, and scaling graphics using transforms*

CHAPTER 10

Working with 3D Graphics

3D graphics programming is often a daunting task and can get quite hairy with all those vectors, matrices, and quaternion math, not to mention hit testing and texture mapping. Luckily, WPF provides a rich set of classes to help simplify and speed up the use of 3D in your applications. On the downside, though, you may still need to get your hands dirty with polygons to define the 3D content you want to display, such as a 3D model.

This chapter will be of most value to those who have at least a basic understanding of 3D coordinate spaces and who are familiar with mathematical concepts such as *points* (a position in space given as an offset from the coordinate system's origin), *vectors* (a direction and a magnitude), and *matrices* (a table of values).

Although 3D can take your user interfaces to the next level, it should be used sparingly and only where it will add value to your application. Using too much may also slow your application down on some older machines.

It is important to note that the WPF 3D graphics engine does not work like a ray-tracer where light values are calculated on a per-pixel basis, because this is very costly. Instead, the light is calculated for each vertex of a triangle and then interpolated to color the remainder of the triangle's surface. This means that although the output will have a realistic look, it won't be able to achieve the same level of realism possible with a ray-tracer. Despite this, you are still able to quickly and easily build fully interactive, 3D content right in to your application.

The recipes in this chapter describe how to:

- Use 3D content in your application (recipe 10-1)

- Use cameras to view your 3D models (recipe 10-2)

- Render a 3D model (recipe 10-3)

- Add lighting to your 3D scenes (recipe 10-4)

- Deal with materials and textures of objects (recipes 10-5 and 10-6)

- Interact with 3D objects, responding to user input and more (recipe 10-7)

- Use existing 2D content in a 3D scene (recipe 10-8)

10-1. Use 3D in Your Application

Problem

You need to display some 3D content in your application, be it a simple control or a complex 3D model.

Solution

Use a `System.Windows.Controls.Viewport3D` control to display 3D content in your 2D application.

How It Works

The `Viewport3D` control is a 2D control that hosts 3D content, rendering (or projecting) the content on to its 2D surface, much like 3D objects around us are projected onto the 2D surface of a camera's viewfinder. Like the viewfinder on a standard camera displays whatever the camera is looking at, the content displayed in a `Viewport3D` control is directed by a `System.Windows.Media.Media3D.Camera` implementation (see recipe 10-2 for more information about the `Camera` class).

The content of a `Viewport3D` is set through its `Children` property, a `System.Windows.Media.Media3D.Visual3DCollection`. The `Visual3DCollection` is a collection of objects implementing the abstract `System.Windows.Media.Media3D.Visual3D` class, which currently includes `System.Windows.Media.Media3D.ModelVisual3D`, `System.Windows.Media.Media3D.Viewport2DVisual3D` (see recipe 10-8), and `System.Windows.UIElement` objects.

`Viewport3D` derives from `System.Windows.FrameworkElement` so provides support for user input and focus, as well as methods for performing hit tests within the control, a very useful feature indeed. If something a little lighter is needed, the `System.Windows.Media.Media3D.Viewport3DVisual` is available. This derives from `System.Windows.Visual`, as opposed to `Viewport3D`, which derives from `FrameworkElement`. When using a `Viewport3DVisual`, you still get support for hit testing, but you lose built-in user input handling. A `Viewport3DVisual` is good to use when displaying 3D content within a 2D control and when the view is likely to be printed.

The Code

The following XAML demonstrates how to use the `Viewport3D` element in a simple scenario of displaying a single polygon (see Figure 10-1):

```
<Window
  x:Class="Recipe_10_01.Window1"
  xmlns="http://schemas.microsoft.com/winfx/2006/xaml/presentation"
  xmlns:x="http://schemas.microsoft.com/winfx/2006/xaml"
  Title="Recipe_10_01" Height="400" Width="600">
  <Viewport3D>
    <Viewport3D.Camera>
      <PerspectiveCamera
```

```
            LookDirection="0,0,-1"
            Position="0,0,5" />
        </Viewport3D.Camera>
        <ModelVisual3D>
          <ModelVisual3D.Content>
            <AmbientLight Color="White" />
          </ModelVisual3D.Content>
        </ModelVisual3D>
        <ModelVisual3D>
          <ModelVisual3D.Content>
            <GeometryModel3D>
              <GeometryModel3D.Geometry>
                <MeshGeometry3D
                  Positions="-1,-1,0 1,-1,0 1,1,0"
                  TriangleIndices="0 1 2" />
              </GeometryModel3D.Geometry>
              <GeometryModel3D.Material>
                <DiffuseMaterial Brush="Firebrick" />
              </GeometryModel3D.Material>
            </GeometryModel3D>
          </ModelVisual3D.Content>
        </ModelVisual3D>
      </Viewport3D>
    </Window>
```

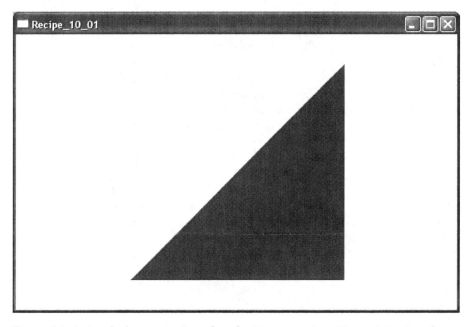

Figure 10-1. *A simple demonstration of rendering content in a* Viewport3D *control*

10-2. Use a 3D Camera

Problem

You need to be able to control and alter the characteristics of the view in a System.Windows.Controls.Viewport3D, as well as choose the type of projection method used to render your 3D scene.

Solution

Use an implementation of the System.Windows.Media.Media3D.Camera class, defining the location, view direction, field of view, and so on, for the camera.

How It Works

Cameras are an important part of 3D graphics and control how the scene appears to the viewer when it is projected on to the image plane of the camera. This is just like the camera on a movie set that defines what the user sees on the screen in the theater.

The area of 3D space that is visible to the camera is inferred from the camera's configuration such as its location, direction it is looking, orientation, field of view, focal length near plane distance, and far plane distance. This area of space is known as the *frustum*; see http://en.wikipedia.org/wiki/Viewing_frustum for more information about a view frustum.

The camera's other function is to create a *view matrix*, a matrix that defines how objects in the world should be transformed so that the scene appears as expected from the given view. This view matrix also contains a projection matrix, which defines how points should be transformed so that they appear according to the camera's projection type, either perspective or orthographic. WPF provides both support for both of these types of camera in the System.Windows.Media.Media3D.PerspectiveCamera and System.Windows.Media.Media3D.OrthographicProjection camera..

The choice of projection method will depend on how you want your 3D scene to appear. When using a perspective projection camera, parallel lines will converge giving the perception of depth, or *perspective*. This type of projection gives more realistic projections, with objects appearing as they do in real life. When using orthographic projection, lines that are parallel remain parallel and never converge. This type of projection is ideally suited to computer-aided design (CAD) packages, where measurements need to be accurate. Figure 10-2 shows the difference between a view rendered using a PerspectiveCamera and an OrthographicProjection camera.

There is a third type of camera, the MatrixCamera, that allows a great deal of control over the way the camera constructs its view matrix. It does also mean that you need to do a great deal of work to get the camera functioning properly. By specifying a view matrix for the camera, you can define how your objects appear. For example, you may want to create a camera that simulates a fish-eye lens.

The Code

The following XAML demonstrates how to use Camera objects and how they can affect the way in which rendered objects appear. Of the two Viewport3D controls defined in the code, the first uses an OrthographicCamera, and the second uses a PerspectiveCamera. Both Viewport3D controls contain three System.Windows.Media.Media3D.ModelVisual3D objects, each defining a square of a different orientation and color (see Figure 10-2).

```xml
<Window x:Class="Recipe_10_02.Window1"
    xmlns="http://schemas.microsoft.com/winfx/2006/xaml/presentation"
    xmlns:x="http://schemas.microsoft.com/winfx/2006/xaml"
    Title="Recipe_10_02" Height="300" Width="300">
  <Window.Resources>
    <!-- Front, left square -->
    <MeshGeometry3D
      x:Key="squareMeshFrontLeft"
      Positions="-1,0,1 1,0,1 1,1,1 -1,1,1"
      TriangleIndices="0 1 2 0 2 3" />
    <!-- Front, right square -->
    <MeshGeometry3D
      x:Key="squareMeshFrontRight"
      Positions="1,0,1 1,0,-1 1,1,-1 1,1,1"
      TriangleIndices="0 1 2 0 2 3" />
    <!-- Top square -->
    <MeshGeometry3D
      x:Key="squareMeshTop"
      Positions="-1,1,1 1,1,1 1,1,-1 -1,1,-1"
      TriangleIndices="0 1 2 0 2 3" />

    <DiffuseMaterial x:Key="diffuseFrontLeft" Brush="Firebrick" />
    <DiffuseMaterial x:Key="diffuseFrontRight" Brush="CornflowerBlue" />
    <DiffuseMaterial x:Key="diffuseTop" Brush="OrangeRed" />
  </Window.Resources>
  <Grid>
    <Grid.ColumnDefinitions>
      <ColumnDefinition Width="0.5*"/>
      <ColumnDefinition Width="0.5*"/>
    </Grid.ColumnDefinitions>

    <DockPanel>
      <TextBlock
        Text="Orthographic Projection"
        DockPanel.Dock="Bottom"
        HorizontalAlignment="Center" />
    <Viewport3D x:Name="OrthographicView">
      <Viewport3D.Camera>
        <OrthographicCamera
          Width="4"
          Position="10,10,10"
          LookDirection="-1,-1,-1"
          UpDirection="0,1,0" />
      </Viewport3D.Camera>
```

```xml
        <!--Front left side-->
        <ModelVisual3D>
          <ModelVisual3D.Content>
            <GeometryModel3D
            Geometry="{StaticResource squareMeshFrontLeft}"
            Material="{StaticResource diffuseFrontLeft}" />
          </ModelVisual3D.Content>
        </ModelVisual3D>
        <!-- Front right side -->
        <ModelVisual3D>
          <ModelVisual3D.Content>
            <GeometryModel3D
              Geometry="{StaticResource squareMeshFrontRight}"
              Material="{StaticResource diffuseFrontRight}" />
          </ModelVisual3D.Content>
        </ModelVisual3D>
        <!-- Top side -->
        <ModelVisual3D>
          <ModelVisual3D.Content>
            <GeometryModel3D
            Geometry="{StaticResource squareMeshTop}"
            Material="{StaticResource diffuseTop}" />
          </ModelVisual3D.Content>
        </ModelVisual3D>
        <ModelVisual3D>
          <ModelVisual3D.Content>
            <AmbientLight Color="White" />
          </ModelVisual3D.Content>
        </ModelVisual3D>
      </Viewport3D>
      </DockPanel>

    <DockPanel Grid.Column="1">
      <TextBlock
        Text="Perspective Projection"
        DockPanel.Dock="Bottom"
        HorizontalAlignment="Center" />
    <Viewport3D x:Name="PerpesctiveView" Grid.Column="1">
      <Viewport3D.Camera>
        <PerspectiveCamera Position="3,3,3" LookDirection="-1,-1,-1" />
      </Viewport3D.Camera>
      <!--Front left side-->
      <ModelVisual3D>
        <ModelVisual3D.Content>
        <GeometryModel3D
          Geometry="{StaticResource squareMeshFrontLeft}"
```

```
          Material="{StaticResource diffuseFrontLeft}" />
          </ModelVisual3D.Content>
      </ModelVisual3D>
      <!-- Front right side -->
      <ModelVisual3D>
        <ModelVisual3D.Content>
        <GeometryModel3D
          Geometry="{StaticResource squareMeshFrontRight}"
          Material="{StaticResource diffuseFrontRight}" />
          </ModelVisual3D.Content>
      </ModelVisual3D>
      <!-- Top side -->
      <ModelVisual3D>
        <ModelVisual3D.Content>
        <GeometryModel3D
          Geometry="{StaticResource squareMeshTop}"
          Material="{StaticResource diffuseTop}" />
          </ModelVisual3D.Content>
      </ModelVisual3D>

      <ModelVisual3D>
        <ModelVisual3D.Content>
          <AmbientLight Color="White" />
        </ModelVisual3D.Content>
      </ModelVisual3D>
    </Viewport3D>
    </DockPanel>
  </Grid>
</Window>
```

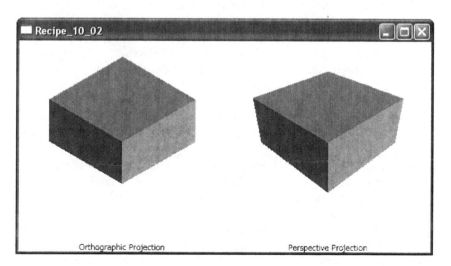

Figure 10-2. *Demonstrates the differences between orthographic and perspective projection*

10-3. Draw a 3D Model

Problem

You need to render a 3D model or shape within a `System.Windows.Controls.Viewport3D` control.

Solution

Use a `System.Windows.Media.Media3D.ModelVisual3D` or a `System.Windows.Media.Media3D.ModelUIElement3D` object, providing a `System.Windows.Media.Media3D.GeometryModel3D` object as its content. The `GeometryModel3D` will contain the data representing the model through its Geometry property, storing a `System.Windows.Media.Media3D.MeshGeometry3D`.

How It Works

In 3D graphics, shapes are generally broken down into triangles; a triangle is the simplest closed shape that can be rendered in three dimensions. It might come as a surprise to find that a line is not the simplest shape, but a line is a one-dimensional object, having only a length. In 3D, a line is a series of squares or cubes, each of which is made up of several triangles. There are myriad reasons as to why a triangle was selected to be the fundamental object in 3D graphics, but it's a discussion that is beyond the scope of this recipe. For more information, see http://en.wikipedia.org/wiki/Polygon_(computer_graphics).

Knowing this, it will come as no surprise to learn that the data for defining a mesh (remember, a collection of tessellated triangles) is based around triangles. The way in which the data for a mesh is defined may seem odd at first but will soon seem more logical as you become accustomed to the 3D world. The first stage in defining a mesh is to provide a `System.Windows.Media.Media3D.Point3DCollection` object for the mesh's Positions property, detailing the points for each vertex of each triangle in the mesh. In XAML, the values can be defined in a list, with or without separating commas. It is important to ensure the number of 3D points defined (X, Y, and Z coordinates) is a multiple of 3. The order in which the points are defined is not important, as long as each individual point is kept together.

The second stage is to define a `System.Windows.Media.Int32Collection` object for the mesh's TriangleIndicies property, detailing the order in which the points defined in the mesh's Positions property are to be used. Again, these values can be defined as a string of space-separated values when defined in XAML. The order of the values in this case is important and is used when determining the surface normal for the triangle. When the points of a triangle are specified in counterclockwise order, the triangle is rendered facing toward the camera, whereas triangles that are defined in clockwise order are rendered such that they are facing away from the camera.

The two preceding stages will give you a model that is ready for rendering. Once the model is given a material (see recipe 10-5), it will be visible in your 3D viewport. An additional stage of configuration is to define a list of vertex normals for the triangles you have defined. A vertex normal is given for each vertex (a point at the corner of the model where several triangles meet and is used when lighting a model. A vertex normal is defined as a normalized vector and is calculated as being the average of the surface normals of each triangle that shares a given vertex. The surface normal of a triangle is a vector that is perpendicular (at a right angle to) the face of the triangle.

If no value is defined for the Normals property of a MeshGeometry3D object, WPF will determine the values for you, based on the winding order of your triangles. Should you want to override the inferred values or specify your own vertex normals to achieve a desired effect or smooth out an artifact, you can provide a System.Windows.Media.Media3D.Vector3DCollection containing the vector that describes each vertex normal. The order that vertex normals are supplied should match the order in which the positions of each vertex are given, in the Positions property.

The Code

The following XAML demonstrates rendering some simple models within a Viewport3D control. Four triangles are created and displayed in the Viewport3D, with each triangle having the same color and a different rotation as the others.

```xml
<Window Background="Black"
  x:Class="Reipce_10_03.Window1"
  xmlns="http://schemas.microsoft.com/winfx/2006/xaml/presentation"
  xmlns:x="http://schemas.microsoft.com/winfx/2006/xaml"
  Title="Window1" Height="300" Width="300" Loaded="Window11_Loaded">
  <Window.Resources>
    <MeshGeometry3D
      x:Key="triangleMesh"
      Positions="-1,-1,0 1,-2,-1 1,1,0"
      TriangleIndices="0 1 2" />
  </Window.Resources>
  <Viewport3D x:Name="vp">
    <Viewport3D.Camera>
      <PerspectiveCamera
        LookDirection="0,0,-1"
        Position="0,0,5" />
    </Viewport3D.Camera>
    <ModelVisual3D>
      <ModelVisual3D.Content>
        <PointLight Position="0,-1,1" Color="White" />
      </ModelVisual3D.Content>
    </ModelVisual3D>
  </Viewport3D>
</Window>
```

The following code defines the content for the previous markup's code-behind file. The code defines a handler for the System.Windows.Window.Loaded event, which is added in the previous markup. When the method is invoked, it creates four triangles and rotates them before adding them to the Viewport3D. Figure 10-3 demonstrates the scene.

```csharp
using System.Windows;
using System.Windows.Media;
using System.Windows.Media.Media3D;
```

```csharp
namespace Reipce_10_03
{
    public partial class Window1 : Window
    {
        public Window1()
        {
            InitializeComponent();
        }

        private void Window11_Loaded(object sender, RoutedEventArgs e)
        {
            //Get a reference to the triangleMesh defined in markup
            MeshGeometry3D triangleMesh
                = (MeshGeometry3D)TryFindResource("triangleMesh");
            //Create four triangles
            for (int i = 0; i < 4; i++)
            {
                //Create a new model and geometry object
                ModelVisual3D modelVisual3D = new ModelVisual3D();
                GeometryModel3D geometryModel3D
                    = new GeometryModel3D();
                //Set the GeometryModel3D's Geometry to the triangleMesh
                geometryModel3D.Geometry = triangleMesh;
                //Give the model a material
                geometryModel3D.Material
                    = new DiffuseMaterial(Brushes.Firebrick);
                //Set the content of the ModelVisual3D
                modelVisual3D.Content = geometryModel3D;
                //We want to rotate each triangle so that they overlap
                //and intersect
                RotateTransform3D rotateTransform
                    = new RotateTransform3D();
                rotateTransform.Rotation
                    = new AxisAngleRotation3D(new Vector3D(0, 0, -1),
                                                    i * 90);
                //Apply the transformation
                modelVisual3D.Transform = rotateTransform;
                //Add the new model to the Viewport3D's children
                vp.Children.Add(modelVisual3D);
            }
        }
    }
}
```

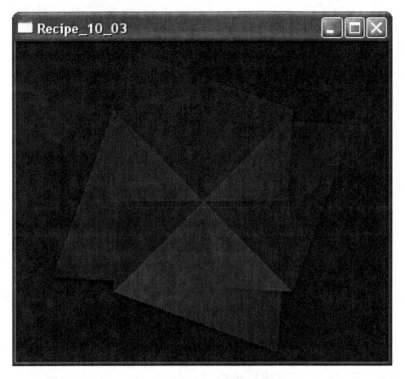

Figure 10-3. *Demonstration of a simple 3D scene containing four triangles that overlap and intersect. The single point light at the bottom of the scene provides illumination.*

10-4. Light a Scene

Problem

You need to be able to set the lighting within a scene, either using a natural ambient light or replicating other types of light sources.

Solution

Use an implementation of the abstract `System.Windows.Media.Media3D.Light` class to add point or directional lighting to your `System.Windows.Controls.Viewport3D`. WPF provides support for the following light source types:

- Ambient light (`System.Windows.Media.Media3D.AmbientLight`)

- Directional light (`System.Windows.Media.Media3D.DirectionalLight`)

- Point light (`System.Windows.Media.Media3D.PointLight`)

- Spotlight (`System.Windows.Media.Media3D.SpotLight`)

How It Works

The way a 3D scene is lit can have a huge impact on how realistic it appears to the user. All 3D scenes require some level of lighting; otherwise, you wouldn't be able to see anything. It would be in the dark. The actual type and number of lights required will depend on what you are trying to achieve. If you wanted to create a simple carousel control, you would not need anything more than some bright ambient lighting, whereas if you were creating a program for real-estate agents to provide virtual walk-throughs, lighting would be very important.

Each type of light has a `Color` dependency property, enabling you to set the color of your light source to any `System.Windows.Media.Color` value. It may be useful to note that because lights are actually models themselves, you are able to transform and animate them in the same way you would transform or animate other models.

Of the different types of lighting, ambient light is the simplest and can be thought of as daylight, a uniform level of light that is present in all parts of a scene. It doesn't cast any shadows but provides the most basic form of illumination for your 3D objects.

Directional lighting is a step on from ambient lighting and adds a direction, as a `System.Windows.Media.Media3D.Vector3D`, into the mix. Directional light travels in the given direction with uniform coverage.

The final two types of light, `PointLight` and `SpotLight`, derive from `System.Windows.Media.Media3D.PointLightBase`, which itself inherits from `Light`. A `PointLight` can be thought of as a positional light, a light source from a point in space. `PointLight` objects have a `Position` dependency property, of type `System.Windows.Media.Media3D.Point3D`, defining the location of the light in space, from which light of the specified color is emitted uniformly in all directions.

The `PointLight` and `SpotLight` objects also support attenuation factors, a value that indicates the distance at which the brightness (or luminosity) of the light begins to fade. This is handy if you want to model low-power light sources that don't have an infinite range such as candles or lightbulbs.

■**Note** You can also create a light source by giving a model a `System.Windows.Media.Media3D.EmissiveMaterial`. An emissive material is effectively a light source where you can specify the size and shape, and it is taken into account during any lighting calculations.

The Code

The following XAML uses a series of `Viewport3D` controls, each with a single polygon and different type of lighting, to demonstrate the effect that lighting has on your 3D scenes (see Figure 10-4).

```
<Window
  x:Class="Recipe_10_04.Window1"
  xmlns="http://schemas.microsoft.com/winfx/2006/xaml/presentation"
  xmlns:x="http://schemas.microsoft.com/winfx/2006/xaml"

  Title="Recipe_10_04" Height="300" Width="300" Loaded="Window1_Loaded">
  <Window.Resources>
```

```xml
  <MeshGeometry3D
    x:Key="triangleMesh"
    Positions="-1,-1,0 1,-1,-2 1,1,0"
    TriangleIndices="0 1 2" />
</Window.Resources>
<UniformGrid>
  <!-- Ambient light -->
  <Viewport3D x:Name="vp1">
    <Viewport3D.Camera>
      <PerspectiveCamera LookDirection="0,0,-1" Position="0,0,5" />
    </Viewport3D.Camera>
    <ModelVisual3D>
      <ModelVisual3D.Content>
        <AmbientLight Color="White" />
      </ModelVisual3D.Content>
    </ModelVisual3D>
  </Viewport3D>
  <!-- Point light -->
  <Viewport3D x:Name="vp2">
    <Viewport3D.Camera>
      <PerspectiveCamera LookDirection="0,0,-1" Position="0,0,5" />
    </Viewport3D.Camera>
    <ModelVisual3D>
      <ModelVisual3D.Content>
        <PointLight Position="0,-1,1" Color="White" />
      </ModelVisual3D.Content>
    </ModelVisual3D>
  </Viewport3D>
  <!-- Directional light -->
  <Viewport3D x:Name="vp3">
    <Viewport3D.Camera>
      <PerspectiveCamera LookDirection="0,0,-1" Position="0,0,5" />
    </Viewport3D.Camera>
    <ModelVisual3D>
      <ModelVisual3D.Content>
        <DirectionalLight Direction="-1,-1,-1" Color="White" />
      </ModelVisual3D.Content>
    </ModelVisual3D>
  </Viewport3D>
  <!-- Spotlight  >
  <Viewport3D x:Name="vp4">
    <Viewport3D.Camera>
      <PerspectiveCamera LookDirection="0,0,-1" Position="0,0,5" />
    </Viewport3D.Camera>
    <ModelVisual3D>
      <ModelVisual3D.Content>
        <SpotLight
```

```
                    Range="10"
                    Direction="0,0,-1"
                    OuterConeAngle="25"
                    InnerConeAngle="20"
                    Position="0,0,9"
                    LinearAttenuation="0.1"
                    Color="White" />
            </ModelVisual3D.Content>
        </ModelVisual3D>
    </Viewport3D>
  </UniformGrid>
</Window>
```

The following code defines the content of the Window1.xaml.cs file. This code contains the handler for the System.Windows.Window.Loaded event that was added in markup. The handler creates four triangles in each of the Viewport3D controls defined in markup. Although the same effect could have been achieved in markup, performing the triangle generation in code keeps the markup less cluttered, drawing focus to the lighting objects.

```csharp
using System.Windows;
using System.Windows.Controls;
using System.Windows.Media;
using System.Windows.Media.Media3D;

namespace Recipe_10_04
{
    public partial class Window1 : Window
    {
        public Window1()
        {
            InitializeComponent();
        }

        //Handler for the Window1.Loaded event
        private void Window1_Loaded(object sender, RoutedEventArgs e)
        {
            //Get a reference to the triangleMesh defined in markup
            MeshGeometry3D triangleMesh
                = (MeshGeometry3D)TryFindResource("triangleMesh");
            //Create our pattern of triangles for each Viewport3D
            CreateTriangles(vp1, 4, triangleMesh);
            CreateTriangles(vp2, 4, triangleMesh);
            CreateTriangles(vp3, 4, triangleMesh);
            CreateTriangles(vp4, 4, triangleMesh);
        }

        private void CreateTriangles(Viewport3D viewport3D,
            int triangleCount, MeshGeometry3D triangleMesh)
```

```
{
    //Create four triangles
    for (int i = 0; i < 4; i++)
    {
        //Create a new model and geometry object
        ModelVisual3D modelVisual3D = new ModelVisual3D();
        GeometryModel3D geometryModel3D
            = new GeometryModel3D();
        //Set the GeometryModel3D's Geometry to the triangleMesh
        geometryModel3D.Geometry = triangleMesh;
        //Give the model a material
        geometryModel3D.Material
            = new DiffuseMaterial(Brushes.Firebrick);
        //Set the content of the ModelVisual3D
        modelVisual3D.Content = geometryModel3D;
        //We want to rotate each triangle so that they overlap
        //and intersect
        RotateTransform3D rotateTransform
            = new RotateTransform3D();
        rotateTransform.Rotation
            = new AxisAngleRotation3D(new Vector3D(0, 0, -1),
                                        i * 90);
        //Apply the transformation
        modelVisual3D.Transform = rotateTransform;
        //Add the new model to the Viewport3D's children
        viewport3D.Children.Add(modelVisual3D);
    }
}
}
}
```

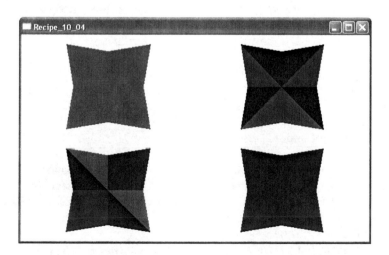

Figure 10-4. *Demonstrates the different types of lighting when used to light the same collection of models*

10-5. Specify a Material for a Model

Problem

You need to be able to specify the type and characteristics of the material applied to a System.Windows.Media.Media3D.GemoetryModel3D or System.Windows.Media.Media3D. Viewport2DVisual3D.

Solution

Use an implementation of the abstract class System.Windows.Media.Media3D.Material to specify the type of material to be used and characteristics such as color.

How It Works

The type of material used when creating a 3D object will affect the way light interacts with the object, as well as the final color of the object and any light that is reflected. WPF provides support for three categories of material: diffuse, specular, and emissive. Each material type has a Brush dependency property that is used to specify the color/visual used to paint the material.

The most basic and commonly used material is the diffuse material, implemented with the System.Windows.Media.Media3D.DiffuseMaterial class. A diffuse material is one that has a very uneven surface, causing reflected light rays that strike its surface to be scattered in all directions. This scattered light uniformly spreads out over a hemisphere around the point of incident and will appear the same, regardless of the camera's position. When lighting a diffuse material, gradients are often seen where the intensity of the reflected light drops off as you move out from the point of incident, giving some very pleasing and realistic effects. Diffuse materials are used when modeling a matte surface.

A specular material is quite different from a diffuse material and is used when modeling hard, glossy objects like some plastics or metals, because specular material will show highlights where light is reflected. The amount by which a highlight is spread over the surface of the material surrounding a point of incident is configured using the SpecularPower property of a System.Windows.Media.Media3D.SpecularMaterial. A lower value will result in a larger spread, and a higher value will give smaller, more concentrated highlights. Specular materials also differ from diffuse materials in the way their color contributes to the overall value. Generally, these values are averaged and combined, but for a specular material, the values are additive and will add to the value of light at that point. If there is a great deal of light being reflected, the value may exceed 100 percent, in which case the material will be colored white in this area. For this reason, a specular material is almost always defined within a System.Windows.Media. Media3D.MaterialGroup, over the top of some DiffuseMaterial, adding any highlights that may be present.

The third type of material is an emissive material. These materials are different again from the other two materials in that objects with an emissive material will emit light evenly across its surface. Despite this, an object with an emissive material is not classed as a light source, and its contribution to the final color of a light ray is calculated differently. Like SpecularMaterial objects, an EmissiveMaterial is almost always used in a MaterialGroup.

You may also notice that objects that have a Material property also have a BackMaterial property. During the rendering process of a 3D scene, any polygons that are facing away from the camera, that is, when the angle between the polygon's surface normal and the view direction is greater than 90 degrees, are removed because they are not visible. This process is known as *back-face culling*; in other words, polygons facing their backs toward the camera are culled.

This is not a problem when you have a closed, solid 3D shape, but it can be problematic when dealing with lamina objects, composed only of a single layer of polygons, such as a flag. In this instance, you may want to see the BackMaterial property to some material that will be displayed when the model is facing away from the camera. The back material could be as simple as a mirror image of the front material or something different altogether.

The Code

The following XAML demonstrates how to use the different types of materials outlined earlier. The example contains three Viewport3D controls, each with a single polygon, rendered with one of the material types listed earlier. This example illustrates how the material of a 3D object can affect the way it appears when rendered (see Figure 10-5).

```xaml
<Window x:Class="Recipe_10_05.Window1"
    xmlns="http://schemas.microsoft.com/winfx/2006/xaml/presentation"
    xmlns:x="http://schemas.microsoft.com/winfx/2006/xaml"
    Title="Recipe_10_05" Height="300" Width="800" Loaded="Window1_Loaded">
  <Window.Resources>
    <MeshGeometry3D
      x:Key="triangleMesh"
      Positions="-1,-1,0 1,-1,-2 1,1,0"
      TriangleIndices="0 1 2" />

    <DiffuseMaterial x:Key="diffuseMaterial" Brush="Firebrick" />

    <MaterialGroup x:Key="specularMaterial">
      <StaticResource ResourceKey="diffuseMaterial" />
      <SpecularMaterial
        Brush="White"
        SpecularPower="5" />
    </MaterialGroup>

    <MaterialGroup x:Key="emissiveMaterial">
      <StaticResource ResourceKey="diffuseMaterial" />
      <EmissiveMaterial Color="Yellow" />
    </MaterialGroup>

  </Window.Resources>
  <Grid>
    <Grid.ColumnDefinitions>
      <ColumnDefinition />
      <ColumnDefinition />
      <ColumnDefinition />
    </Grid.ColumnDefinitions>
```

```xml
<Grid.RowDefinitions>
  <RowDefinition />
  <RowDefinition Height="20" />
</Grid.RowDefinitions>

<!-- Diffuse Material -->
<Viewport3D x:Name="vp1">
  <Viewport3D.Camera>
    <PerspectiveCamera LookDirection="0,0,-1" Position="0,0,5" />
  </Viewport3D.Camera>
  <ModelVisual3D>
    <ModelVisual3D.Content>
      <PointLight Position="0,-1,2" Color="White" />
    </ModelVisual3D.Content>
  </ModelVisual3D>
</Viewport3D>
<!-- Specular Material -->
<Viewport3D x:Name="vp2" Grid.Column="1">
  <Viewport3D.Camera>
    <PerspectiveCamera LookDirection="0,0,-1" Position="0,0,5" />
  </Viewport3D.Camera>
  <ModelVisual3D>
    <ModelVisual3D.Content>
      <PointLight Position="0,-1,2" Color="White" />
    </ModelVisual3D.Content>
  </ModelVisual3D>
</Viewport3D>
<!-- Emissive Material -->
<Viewport3D x:Name="vp3" Grid.Column="2">
  <Viewport3D.Camera>
    <PerspectiveCamera LookDirection="0,0,-1" Position="0,0,5" />
  </Viewport3D.Camera>
  <ModelVisual3D>
    <ModelVisual3D.Content>
      <PointLight Position="0,-1,2" Color="White" />
    </ModelVisual3D.Content>
  </ModelVisual3D>
</Viewport3D>

<!-- Labels -->
<TextBlock
  Text="Diffuse Material"
  Grid.Row="1"
  HorizontalAlignment="Center" />
<TextBlock
  Text="Specular Material"
  Grid.Row="1"
```

```
      Grid.Column="1"
      HorizontalAlignment="Center" />
    <TextBlock
      Text="Emissive Material"
      Grid.Row="1"
      Grid.Column="2"
      HorizontalAlignment="Center" />
  </Grid>
</Window>
```

The following code defines the content of the Window1.xaml.cs file. This code contains the handler for the System.Windows.Window.Loaded event that was added in markup. The handler creates four triangles in each of the Viewport3D controls defined in markup. Although the same effect could have been achieved in markup, performing the triangle generation in code keeps the markup less cluttered, drawing focus to the lighting objects.

```
using System.Windows;
using System.Windows.Controls;
using System.Windows.Media.Media3D;

namespace Recipe_10_05
{
    /// <summary>
    /// Interaction logic for Window1.xaml
    /// </summary>
    public partial class Window1 : Window
    {
        public Window1()
        {
            InitializeComponent();
        }

        //Handler for the Window1.Loaded event
        private void Window1_Loaded(object sender, RoutedEventArgs e)
        {
            //Get a reference to the triangleMesh defined in markup
            MeshGeometry3D triangleMesh
                = (MeshGeometry3D)TryFindResource("triangleMesh");
            //Create our pattern of triangles for each Viewport3D
            CreateTriangles(vp1, 4, triangleMesh,
                (Material)TryFindResource("diffuseMaterial"));
            CreateTriangles(vp2, 4, triangleMesh,
                (Material)TryFindResource("specularMaterial"));
            CreateTriangles(vp3, 4, triangleMesh,
                (Material)TryFindResource("emissiveMaterial"));
        }
```

```
private void CreateTriangles(Viewport3D viewport3D,
    int triangleCount, MeshGeometry3D triangleMesh,
    Material material)
{
    //Create four triangles
    for (int i = 0; i < 4; i++)
    {
        //Create a new model and geometry object
        ModelVisual3D modelVisual3D = new ModelVisual3D();
        GeometryModel3D geometryModel3D
            = new GeometryModel3D();
        //Set the GeometryModel3D's Geometry to the triangleMesh
        geometryModel3D.Geometry = triangleMesh;
        //Give the model a material
        geometryModel3D.Material = material;
        //Set the content of the ModelVisual3D
        modelVisual3D.Content = geometryModel3D;
        //We want to rotate each triangle so that they overlap
        //and intersect
        RotateTransform3D rotateTransform
            = new RotateTransform3D();
        rotateTransform.Rotation
            = new AxisAngleRotation3D(new Vector3D(0, 0, -1),
                                        i * 90);
        //Apply the transformation
        modelVisual3D.Transform = rotateTransform;
        //Add the new model to the Viewport3D's children
        viewport3D.Children.Add(modelVisual3D);
    }
}
```

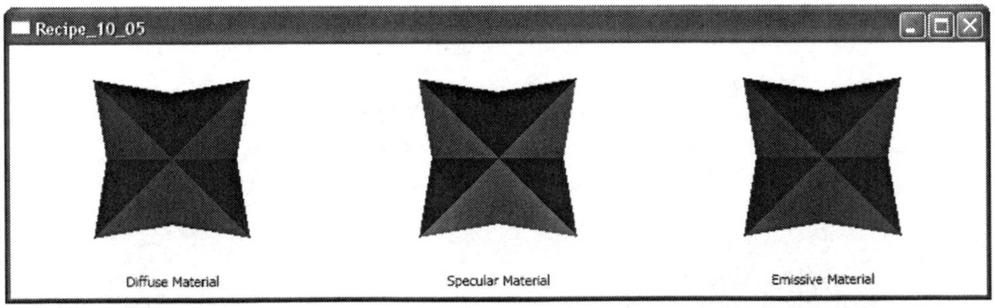

Figure 10-5. *Examples of the different types of materials and their effects on a model's lighting*

10-6. Apply Textures to a Model

Problem

You have a 3D model that you want to apply a texture to, giving it a rich and possibly realistic appearance.

Solution

When defining a 3D model, supply the TextureCoordinates property of a System.Windows. Media.Media3D.MeshGeometry3D with a System.Windows.Media.PointCollection detailing the texture coordinates when mapping a texture on to the object. Then supply the desired texture as a System.Windows.Media.Brush, that is, a System.Windows.Media.ImageBrush.

How It Works

Texture mapping is an age-old technique in computer graphics and is the process of applying some image or texture to a rendered object. This allows you to wrap your 3D objects in lush images, increasing the richness of the application and providing a realistic image to the viewer. Performing texture mapping is often a perilous task and involves you mapping values between coordinate systems, thereby transforming the points to fit the profile of the object they are being mapped to. Luckily, WPF does a huge amount of work for you, leaving little more than for you to specify the texture coordinates for each vertex in your model and what you want to use to paint the object.

When defining a MeshGeometry3D object, you have the option of supplying texture coordinates as a PointCollection. The idea is that for each vertex in the model, you specify the coordinate it maps to on the source texture. This is done by listing the 2D texture coordinates in the same order as the vertices were defined; for example, the first texture coordinate you specify in your PointCollection will be used when texture mapping the first triangle in the model.

The texture coordinates are specified as a value between 0 and 1, inclusive, where $x = 0$ maps to the left of the texture image and $x = 1$ maps to the right of the texture image. Similarly for y, 0 maps to the top of the source image, and 1 maps to the bottom. Think of them as a ratio, describing how far across or down the source image a point should map to.

So, now that you know how to specify your texture coordinates, you need to specify the texture! In true WPF style, this process is fairly painless and is carried out using a System. Windows.Media.Media3D.Material object. Because the Brush property of a Material object is a System.Windows.Media.Brush, objects such as a System.Windows.Media.ImageBrush and System. Windows.Media.VisualBrush can be used. To use an image file from disk as a texture, you would create a System.Windows.Media.Media3D.DiffuseMaterial and specify an ImageBrush as the value for its Brush property, setting the ImageSource property of the ImageBrush to the path of the image you want to display.

Should you use a transparent image or control as the brush for your model, you may want to place the texture in a System.Windows.Media.Media3D.MaterialGroup and place a soft-colored material underneath the texture.

The Code

The following XAML demonstrates how to use Ellipse, Rectangle, or Polygon elements to draw simple shapes in a System.Windows.Controls.UniformGrid (see Figure 10-6).

```xml
<Window
  x:Class="Recipe_10_06.Window1"
  xmlns="http://schemas.microsoft.com/winfx/2006/xaml/presentation"
  xmlns:x="http://schemas.microsoft.com/winfx/2006/xaml"
  Background="Thistle" Height="400" Width="400" Title="Recipe_10_06">
  <Window.Resources>
    <!-- Front, left square -->
    <MeshGeometry3D
      x:Key="squareMeshFrontLeft"
      Positions="-1,-1,1 1,-1,1 1,1,1 -1,1,1"
      TriangleIndices="0 1 2 0 2 3"
      TextureCoordinates="0,1 1,1 1,0 0,0" />
    <!-- Front, right square -->
    <MeshGeometry3D
      x:Key="squareMeshFrontRight"
      Positions="1,-1,1 1,-1,-1 1,1,-1 1,1,1"
      TriangleIndices="0 1 2 0 2 3"
      TextureCoordinates="0,1 1,1 1,0 0,0" />
    <!-- Top square -->
    <MeshGeometry3D
      x:Key="squareMeshTop"
      Positions="-1,1,1 1,1,1 1,1,-1 -1,1,-1"
      TriangleIndices="0 1 2 0 2 3"
      TextureCoordinates="0,1 1,1 1,0 0,0" />

    <DiffuseMaterial x:Key="textureFrontLeft">
      <DiffuseMaterial.Brush>
        <ImageBrush ImageSource="weesam.jpg" />
      </DiffuseMaterial.Brush>
    </DiffuseMaterial>

    <DiffuseMaterial x:Key="textureFrontRight">
      <DiffuseMaterial.Brush>
        <ImageBrush ImageSource="weejayne.jpg" />
      </DiffuseMaterial.Brush>
    </DiffuseMaterial>

    <MaterialGroup x:Key="textureTop">
      <DiffuseMaterial Brush="Olive" />
      <DiffuseMaterial>
        <DiffuseMaterial.Brush>
          <VisualBrush Stretch="Uniform">
            <VisualBrush.Visual>
```

```xml
            <Border
              Margin="50,0"
              BorderThickness="1"
              CornerRadius="5"
              BorderBrush="Firebrick">
              <Border.RenderTransform>
                <RotateTransform Angle="-45" />
              </Border.RenderTransform>
              <TextBlock Text="I am a VisualBrush!" />
            </Border>
          </VisualBrush.Visual>
        </VisualBrush>
      </DiffuseMaterial.Brush>
    </DiffuseMaterial>
  </MaterialGroup>
</Window.Resources>

<Viewport3D>
  <Viewport3D.Camera>
    <PerspectiveCamera Position="4,3.5,4" LookDirection="-1,-0.7,-1" />
  </Viewport3D.Camera>
  <!--Front left side-->
  <ModelVisual3D>
    <ModelVisual3D.Content>
    <GeometryModel3D
      Geometry="{StaticResource squareMeshFrontLeft}"
      Material="{StaticResource textureFrontLeft}" />
    </ModelVisual3D.Content>
  </ModelVisual3D>
  <!-- Front right side -->
  <ModelVisual3D>
    <ModelVisual3D.Content>
    <GeometryModel3D
      Geometry="{StaticResource squareMeshFrontRight}"
      Material="{StaticResource textureFrontRight}" />
    </ModelVisual3D.Content>
  </ModelVisual3D>
  <!-- Top side -->
  <ModelVisual3D>
    <ModelVisual3D.Content>
    <GeometryModel3D
      Geometry="{StaticResource squareMeshTop}"
      Material="{StaticResource textureTop}" />
    </ModelVisual3D.Content>
  </ModelVisual3D>

  <ModelVisual3D>
    <ModelVisual3D.Content>
```

```
            <AmbientLight Color="White" />
        </ModelVisual3D.Content>
      </ModelVisual3D>
    </Viewport3D>
</Window>
```

Figure 10-6. *Examples of texture mapping using both images loaded from disk as well as a visual brush*

10-7. Interact with 3D Objects

Problem

You need to detect when your 3D objects are clicked with the mouse or when the mouse is placed over the object. This includes clicking objects that overlap but at different distances from the camera.

Solution

Build your 3D models as System.Windows.Media.Media3D.ModelUIElement3D objects in a System.Windows.Controls.Viewport3D. The ModelUIElement3D object provides support for input, focus, and the associated events.

How It Works

The ModelUIElement3D object is very similar to the ModelVisual3D object, with both classes descending from System.Windows.Media.Media3D.Visual3D, although ModelUIElement provides the added richness that is user input and focus handling. This extra functionality isn't quite free, though, because it will add overhead to your 3D scene. If performance is key to your application, you may want to implement your own user input handling, implementing only the functionality you require.

Harnessing the extra functionality is as simple as adding event handlers to the required events and executing your custom code. This enables you to add things like tool tips or apply animations to your models, something not possible in XAML because ModelVisual3D objects and its descendents do not support triggers.

When handling user input in a scene with more than one model, the distance that an object is from the camera will be taken into consideration when determining which object was clicked. This means that if you have two objects that overlap each other but are positioned at different depths, the object closest to the camera, and only that object, will receive the event.

> **Note** If two or more objects overlap and the mouse click event is at a point where both objects are at the same depth, you will encounter z-fighting! This is where two pixels at the same depth may be selected at random in a nondeterministic fashion and will be particularly noticeable in animation.

The Code

The following XAML demonstrates how to use handling user input events on layered objects in a 3D scene. A single Viewport3D control contains three polygons as ModelUIElement3D objects, with handlers on each of the polygon's MouseDown events. Observe how it doesn't matter where on the foremost triangle you click; the polygon1_MouseDown method is invoked as polygon1 is closer to the camera than the other two polygons in the scene (see Figure 10-7).

```
<Window
  x:Class="Recipe_10_07.Window1"
  xmlns="http://schemas.microsoft.com/winfx/2006/xaml/presentation"
  xmlns:x="http://schemas.microsoft.com/winfx/2006/xaml"
  Title="Recipe_10_07" Height="300" Width="300">
  <Viewport3D>
    <Viewport3D.Camera>
      <PerspectiveCamera LookDirection="0,0,-1" Position="0,0,5" />
    </Viewport3D.Camera>
    <ModelVisual3D>
      <ModelVisual3D.Content>
        <AmbientLight Color="White" />
      </ModelVisual3D.Content>
    </ModelVisual3D>
    <!-- Polygon 1 -->
    <ModelUIElement3D MouseDown="polygon1_MouseDown">
      <GeometryModel3D>
        <GeometryModel3D.Geometry>
          <MeshGeometry3D
            Positions="-1,-1,1 1,-1,1 1,1,1"
```

```
                TriangleIndices="0 1 2" />
            </GeometryModel3D.Geometry>
            <GeometryModel3D.Material>
              <DiffuseMaterial Brush="Firebrick" />
            </GeometryModel3D.Material>
          </GeometryModel3D>
        </ModelUIElement3D>
        <!-- Polygon 2 -->
        <ModelUIElement3D MouseDown="polygon2_MouseDown">
          <GeometryModel3D>
            <GeometryModel3D.Geometry>
              <MeshGeometry3D
                Positions="1,-1,0 1,1,0 -1,1,0"
                TriangleIndices="0 1 2" />
            </GeometryModel3D.Geometry>
            <GeometryModel3D.Material>
              <DiffuseMaterial Brush="CornflowerBlue" />
            </GeometryModel3D.Material>
          </GeometryModel3D>
        </ModelUIElement3D>
        <!-- Polygon 3 -->
        <ModelUIElement3D MouseDown="polygon3_MouseDown">
          <GeometryModel3D>
            <GeometryModel3D.Geometry>
              <MeshGeometry3D
                Positions="1,0,0 1,1,0 0,1,0"
                TriangleIndices="0 1 2" />
            </GeometryModel3D.Geometry>
            <GeometryModel3D.Material>
              <DiffuseMaterial Brush="OrangeRed"/>
            </GeometryModel3D.Material>
          </GeometryModel3D>
        </ModelUIElement3D>
      </Viewport3D>
</Window>
```

The following code defines the content of the code-behind for the previous markup. The code defines the three event handlers that are added in the markup.

```
using System.Windows;
using System.Windows.Input;

namespace Recipe_10_07
{
    public partial class Window1 : Window
    {
        public Window1()
```

```
        {
            InitializeComponent();
        }

        private void polygon1_MouseDown(object sender,
            MouseButtonEventArgs e)
        {
            MessageBox.Show("polygon1_MouseDown", "Recipe_10_07");
        }

        private void polygon2_MouseDown(object sender,
            MouseButtonEventArgs e)
        {
            MessageBox.Show("polygon2_MouseDown", "Recipe_10_07");
        }

        private void polygon3_MouseDown(object sender,
            MouseButtonEventArgs e)
        {
            MessageBox.Show("polygon3_MouseDown", "Recipe_10_07");
        }
    }
}
```

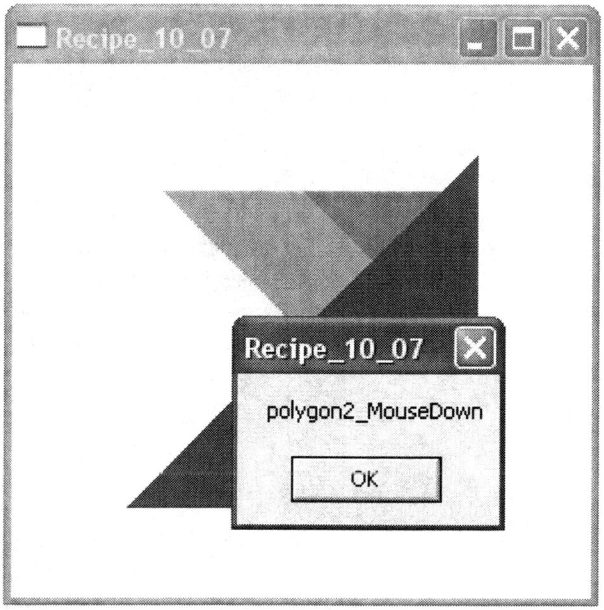

Figure 10-7. *Example of user input on objects that overlap but are at different depths with respect to the camera*

10-8. Use a 2D Control in a 3D Scene

Problem

You need to use some of the standard 2D controls such as System.Windows.Controls.Button or System.Windows.Controls.TextBox in a 3D scene, allowing the control to be fully interactive.

Solution

Use a System.Windows.Media.Media3D.Viewport2DVisual3D to host the required 2D control.

How It Works

The Viewport2DVisual3D control is used to host 2D content in a 3D content control, complementing the System.Windows.Media.Media3D.Viewport3DVisual control that hosts 3D content within a 2D visual. This is a very powerful feature that enables you to easily build a powerful and rich 3D user interface, retaining the use of 2D controls such as System.Windows.Controls.Button objects and System.Windows.Controls.TextBox objects.

When using 2D content in a 3D visual, WPF can carry out coordinate system transformations, mapping the position of any input events such as mouse clicks in to their 2D equivalents. This is great if you are displaying a custom control with multiple interactive regions or child controls because you are able to process user interaction in the same way you would normally in 2D.

> **Note** The System.Windows.Media.Media3D.Viewport2DVisual3D class was introduced in .NET 3.5.

The Code

The following XAML demonstrates how to use 2D content in a 3D model by rendering various standard controls on to the faces of three squares, which are joined together to form the visible half of a cube (see Figure 10-8). Notice how all the controls respond to user input such as hover states, click states, and so on. When the button is clicked, a message is displayed that shows the location at which the mouse was pressed, relative to the button's own coordinate system, implicitly projecting and transforming the 3D point into 2D.

```
<Window
  x:Class="Recipe_10_08.Window1"
  xmlns="http://schemas.microsoft.com/winfx/2006/xaml/presentation"
  xmlns:x="http://schemas.microsoft.com/winfx/2006/xaml"
  Title="Recipe_10_08" Height="300" Width="300">
  <Window.Resources>
    <!-- Front, left square -->
    <MeshGeometry3D
      x:Key="squareMeshFrontLeft"
      Positions="-1,-1,1 1,-1,1 1,1,1 -1,1,1"
```

```xml
      TriangleIndices="0 1 2 0 2 3"
      TextureCoordinates="0,1 1,1 1,0 0,0" />
  <!-- Front, right square -->
  <MeshGeometry3D
    x:Key="squareMeshFrontRight"
    Positions="1,-1,1 1,-1,-1 1,1,-1 1,1,1"
    TriangleIndices="0 1 2 0 2 3"
    TextureCoordinates="0,1 1,1 1,0 0,0" />
  <!-- Top square -->
  <MeshGeometry3D
    x:Key="squareMeshTop"
    Positions="-1,1,1 1,1,1 1,1,-1 -1,1,-1"
    TriangleIndices="0 1 2 0 2 3"
    TextureCoordinates="0,1 1,1 1,0 0,0" />


  <DiffuseMaterial
    x:Key="visualHostMaterial"
    Brush="White"
    Viewport2DVisual3D.IsVisualHostMaterial="True" />
</Window.Resources>
<Viewport3D>
  <Viewport3D.Camera>
    <PerspectiveCamera Position="4,2.5,4" LookDirection="-1,-0.7,-1" />
  </Viewport3D.Camera>
  <Viewport2DVisual3D
    Material="{StaticResource visualHostMaterial}"
    Geometry="{StaticResource squareMeshFrontLeft}">
    <StackPanel>
      <Slider />
      <Button Click="Button_ClickMe_Click" >
        <DockPanel>
          <Ellipse
            Width="20"
            Height="20"
            Stroke="Black"
            Fill="Purple"
            DockPanel.Dock="Right" />
          <TextBlock VerticalAlignment="Center" Text="Click me!" />
        </DockPanel>
      </Button>
    </StackPanel>
  </Viewport2DVisual3D>

  <Viewport2DVisual3D
    Material="{StaticResource visualHostMaterial}"
    Geometry="{StaticResource squareMeshFrontRight}">
    <TextBox
```

```xml
              Text="This is a TextBox!"
              AcceptsReturn="True"
              Width="200"
              Height="200" />
        </Viewport2DVisual3D>

        <Viewport2DVisual3D
          Material="{StaticResource visualHostMaterial}"
          Geometry="{StaticResource squareMeshTop}">
          <StackPanel>
            <RadioButton GroupName="rgTest" IsChecked="True" Content="RadioButton 1" />
            <RadioButton GroupName="rgTest" Content="RadioButton 2" />
            <RadioButton GroupName="rgTest" Content="RadioButton 3" />
            <CheckBox IsChecked="True" Content="CheckBox 1" />
            <CheckBox IsChecked="True" Content="CheckBox 2" />
            <CheckBox IsChecked="True" Content="CheckBox 3" />
            <ComboBox>
              <ComboBox.Items>
                <ComboBoxItem Content="Item 1" />
                <ComboBoxItem Content="Item 2" />
                <ComboBoxItem Content="Item 3" />
              </ComboBox.Items>
            </ComboBox>
          </StackPanel>
        </Viewport2DVisual3D>

        <ModelVisual3D>
          <ModelVisual3D.Content>
            <AmbientLight Color="White" />
          </ModelVisual3D.Content>
        </ModelVisual3D>
      </Viewport3D>
</Window>
```

The following code defines the content of the Window1.xaml.cs file:

```csharp
using System;
using System.Windows;
using System.Windows.Controls;
using System.Windows.Input;

namespace Recipe_10_08
{
    /// <summary>
    /// Interaction logic for Window1.xaml
    /// </summary>
    public partial class Window1 : Window
```

```
{
    public Window1()
    {
        InitializeComponent();
    }

    private void Button_ClickMe_Click(object sender,
        RoutedEventArgs e)
    {
        //Get the position of the mouse, relative to the
        //button that was clicked.
        Point? position = Mouse.GetPosition(sender as Button);
        //Build a message string to display to the user.
        string msg = string.Format("Wow, you just clicked a " +
            "2D button in 3D!{0}{0}You clicked the button at" +
            " x = {1}, y = {2}", Environment.NewLine,
            (int)position.Value.X, (int)position.Value.Y);

        MessageBox.Show(msg, "Recipe_10_08");
    }
}
}
```

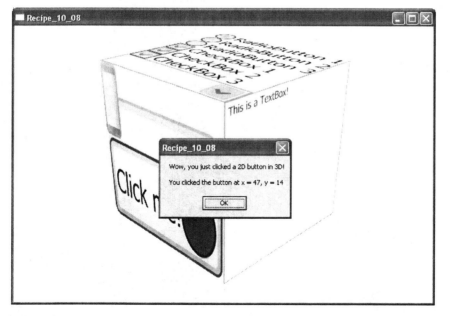

Figure 10-8. *Demonstrating the use of 2D content in a 3D model. Clicking the button also retrieves the point at which the button was clicked, relative to the button's model coordinate system.*

CHAPTER 11

■ ■ ■

Creating Animation

WPF is big on animation and includes a vast array of objects to help you get your application looking and feeling as slick as possible. A great deal of work is done for you, the developer, saving you time and headaches and greatly speeding up the whole process. This means that more and more applications will be able to include savvy animations with ease, increasing the user experience quality and also looking cool. With careful design and planning, animation can really bring an application to life; although use too much animation, and the performance of your application may suffer.

The recipes in this chapter describe how to:

- Animate the value of a property (recipe 11-1)

- Animate data-bound properties (recipe 11-2)

- Remove existing animations (recipe 11-3)

- Overlap two animations (recipe 11-4)

- Run several animations in parallel (recipe 11-5)

- Create an animation that uses keyframes (recipe 11-6)

- Interactively control the progress of an animation (recipe 11-7)

- Animate the shape of a path object (recipe 11-8)

- Loop and reverse animations (recipe 11-9)

- Limit the frame rate of animations (recipes 11-10 and 11-11)

- Animate an object along a path (recipe 11-12)

- Play back audio or video files (recipe 11-13)

- Synchronize animation playback with an audio or video file (recipe 11-14)

- Receive notification when an animation completes (recipe 11-15)

- Animate a property with indirect property targeting (recipe 11-16)

- Control animations using triggers (recipe 11-17)

- Animate text (recipe 11-18)

11-1. Animate the Property of a Control

Problem

You need to change the value of a property on a control with respect to time, be it the opacity of a button, the color of a rectangle, or the height of an expander.

Solution

Animate the value of the property using one or more System.Windows.Media.Animation. Timeline objects in a System.Windows.Media.Animation.Storyboard.

How It Works

Owing to the richness of WPF's animation framework, there are myriad options when it comes to animating something. In essence, you are able to animate just about any System.Windows. DependencyProperty of an object that derives from System.Windows.Media.Animation.Animatable. Couple that with the range of types for which Timeline objects already exist, and you find yourself in a position of endless possibilities.

To animate the property of a control, you will generally declare one or more AnimationTimeline objects that target the data type of the property being animated. These timelines are defined as children of a System.Windows.Media.Animation.Storyboard, with the root Storyboard being activated by a System.Windows.Media.Animation.BeginStoryboard when used in markup. It is also possible to nest Storyboard objects and ParallelTimeline objects as children. Each AnimationTimeline can target a different property of a different object, a different property of the same object, or the same property of the same object. The target object or target property can also be defined at the level of the parent ParallelTimeline or Storyboard.

For each data type that WPF supports, there exists an AnimationTimeline. Each timeline will be named *<Type>Animation*, possibly with several variants for special types of Timeline, where *<Type>* is the target data type of the Timeline. With the exception of a few AnimationTimeline objects, the animation's effect on a target property is defined by specifying values for one or more of the To, From, or By properties. If the From property of an AnimationTimeline is not specified, the value of the property at the point the timeline's clock is applied will be used. This is useful because it means you do not need to worry about storing a property's initial value and then restore it at a later date. If a value for the From property is specified, the property will be set with that value when the Timeline is applied. Again, the original value of the property will be restored when the timeline's clock is removed.

The abstract Timeline class, from which all AnimationTimeline, Storyboard, and ParallelTimeline objects derive, defines several properties that allow you to define the characteristics of an animation. Table 11-1 describes these properties of the Timeline class.

Table 11-1. *Commonly Used Properties of the* Timeline *Class*

Property	Description
AccelerationRatio	Used to specify a percentage of the timeline's duration that should be used to accelerate the speed of the animation from 0 to the animation's maximum rate. The value should be a System.Double ranging between 0 and 1, inclusive, and is 0 by default. The sum of a timeline's AccelerationRatio and DeceleratioRatio must not be greater than 1.
AutoReverse	A System.Boolean property that specifies whether the Timeline should play back to the beginning once the end has been reached. See recipe 11-9 for more details on this property.
BeginTime	A System.Nullable(TimeSpan) that specifies when a timeline should become active, relative to its parent's BeginTime. For a root Timeline, the offset is taken from the time that it becomes active. This value can be negative and will start the Timeline from the specified offset, giving the appearance that the Timeline has already been playing for the given time. The SpeedRatio of a Timeline has no effect on its BeginTime value, although it is affected by its parent SpeedRatio. If the property is set to null, the Timeline will never begin.
DecelerationRatio	Used to specify a percentage of the timeline's duration that should be used to reduce the speed of the animation from the maximum rate down to 0. The value should be a System.Double ranging between 0 and 1, inclusive, and is 0 by default. The sum of a timeline's AccelerationRatio and DeceleratioRatio must not be greater than 1.
Duration	A nullable System.Windows.Duration specifying the length of time the animation should take to play from beginning to end. For Storyboard and ParallelTimeline objects, this value will default to the longest duration of its children. For a basic AnimationTimeline object—for example, System.Windows.Media.Animation.DoubleAnimation—this value will default to one second, and a keyframe-based animation will have a value equal to the sum of System.Windows.Media.Animation.KeyTime values for each keyframe.
FillBehavior	A value of the System.Windows.Media.Animation.FillBehavior enumeration is used to define an animation's behavior once it has completed, but its parent is still active, or its parent is in its hold period. The FillBehavior.HoldEnd value is used when an animation should hold its final value for a property until its parent is no longer active or outside of its hold period. The FillBehavior.Stop value will cause the timeline to not hold its final value for a property once it completes, regardless of whether its parent is still active.
RepeatBehavior	A System.Windows.Media.Animation.RepeatBehavior value indicating whether and how an animation is repeated. See recipe 11-9 for more details on this property.
SpeedRatio	A property of type System.Double that is used as a multiplier to alter the playback speed of an animation. A speed ratio of 0.25 will slow the animation down such that it runs at a quarter of its normal speed. A value of 2 will double the speed of the animation, and a speed ratio of 1 means the animation will play back at normal speed. Note that this will affect the actual duration of an animation.

The Code

The following example demonstrates some of the functionality available with animations. Properties of various controls are animated using different values for the previous properties to indicate their effect.

```
<Window
  x:Class="Recipe_11_01.Window1"
  xmlns="http://schemas.microsoft.com/winfx/2006/xaml/presentation"
  xmlns:x="http://schemas.microsoft.com/winfx/2006/xaml"
  Title="Recipe_11_01"
  Height="300"
  Width="300">
  <Window.Resources>
    <Storyboard
      x:Key="ellipse1Storyboard"
      Storyboard.TargetName="ellipse1">
      <ParallelTimeline>
        <DoubleAnimation
          To="50"
          Duration="0:0:5"
          AccelerationRatio="0.25"
          DecelerationRatio="0.25"
          Storyboard.TargetProperty="Width"
          RepeatBehavior="5x" />
        <DoubleAnimation
          To="50"
          Duration="0:0:5"
          AccelerationRatio="0.5"
          DecelerationRatio="0.25"
          Storyboard.TargetProperty="Height"
          RepeatBehavior="5x"
          SpeedRatio="4" />
      </ParallelTimeline>
    </Storyboard>

    <Storyboard
      x:Key="rect1Storyboard"
      Storyboard.TargetName="rect1">
      <ParallelTimeline>
        <DoubleAnimation
          To="50"
          Duration="0:0:10"
          FillBehavior="Stop"
          Storyboard.TargetProperty="Width" />
        <DoubleAnimation
          To="50"
          Duration="0:0:5"
```

```xml
              FillBehavior="HoldEnd"
              AccelerationRatio="0.5"
              DecelerationRatio="0.25"
              Storyboard.TargetProperty="Height" />
        </ParallelTimeline>
      </Storyboard>
    </Window.Resources>
    <Window.Triggers>
      <EventTrigger
        RoutedEvent="Ellipse.Loaded"
        SourceName="ellipse1">
        <BeginStoryboard
          Storyboard="{DynamicResource ellipse1Storyboard}" />
      </EventTrigger>
      <EventTrigger
        RoutedEvent="Rectangle.Loaded"
        SourceName="rect1">
        <BeginStoryboard
          Storyboard="{StaticResource rect1Storyboard}" />
      </EventTrigger>
    </Window.Triggers>
    <Grid>
      <Grid.ColumnDefinitions>
        <ColumnDefinition Width="0.5*" />
        <ColumnDefinition Width="0.5*" />
      </Grid.ColumnDefinitions>

      <Ellipse
        x:Name="ellipse1"
        Margin="10"
        Width="100"
        Height="100"
        Fill="CornflowerBlue" />

      <Rectangle
        x:Name="rect1"
        Margin="10"
        Width="100"
        Height="100"
        Fill="Firebrick"
        Grid.Column="1" />
    </Grid>
</Window>
```

11-2. Animate a Property of a Control Set with a Data Binding

Problem

You need to animate the value of some property on a control, but that property is set using a data binding. When the value of the property changes, you need the animation to be updated to reflect the new value.

Solution

When the source value of a property changes, the animation needs to be restarted so that the new value can be used within the animation.

How It Works

Data binding is commonplace in WPF applications, and you may find that you are animating properties of a control that are data bound to some object or you are using data bindings to set values of your System.Windows.Media.Animation.Timeline objects. For example, you may be animating the Width property of a System.Windows.Shapes.Ellipse, where the Width is bound to the value of a System.Windows.Controls.Slider, or you have bound the AutoReverse property of a System.Windows.Media.Animation.DoubleAnimation to a System.Windows.Controls.CheckBox. You would expect that when the source value of a data binding changes that the animation would update, but sadly this is one thing that doesn't come for free.

When a Storyboard is activated, it and its child Timeline objects are copied and frozen. A System.Windows.Media.Animation.Clock object is then created for each Timeline object, including the root Storyboard that has a generated Clock used to control any child Clock objects. The Clock objects that are created for the storyboard's children are then used to carry out the animation on the target properties. This means any changes to the root Storyboard or its children will not have any effect on the Clock objects that have been created. To reflect any changes to a property's data-bound value or a change to a property of a Timeline object, the animation's Clock objects need to be re-created with these new values.

In reapplying a Storyboard, the current position of the existing Storyboard will be lost, starting the animation over. To combat this, you need to record the current position in time of the active Storyboard and use the Seek method on the new root Storyboard to advance the animation to where it was before the Storyboard was reapplied. This means the animation can continue with the new values but also means you will have to write some code.

The Code

The following XAML demonstrates how to use data bindings in animations. The Duration property of the Timeline objects are bound to a dependency property defined in the window's code-behind and is set using the System.Windows.Controls.Slider. The AutoReverse property of the Timeline objects is also bound but this time to a System.Windows.Controls.CheckBox.

```xml
<Window
  x:Class="Recipe_11_02.Window1"
  xmlns="http://schemas.microsoft.com/winfx/2006/xaml/presentation"
  xmlns:x="http://schemas.microsoft.com/winfx/2006/xaml"
  Title="Recipe_11_02"
  Height="350"
  Width="350">
  <Window.Triggers>
    <EventTrigger RoutedEvent="Window.Loaded">
      <BeginStoryboard Name="ellipseBeginStoryboard">
        <Storyboard x:Name="ellipseStoryboard">
          <ParallelTimeline x:Name="ellipseTimeline" RepeatBehavior="Forever">
            <DoublcAnimation
              Storyboard.TargetProperty="Width"
              Storyboard.TargetName="ellipse"
              AutoReverse="{Binding Path=AutoReverseAnimation}"
              Duration="{Binding Path=StoryboardDuration}"
              To="50"
              From="200" />
            <DoubleAnimation
              Storyboard.TargetProperty="Height"
              Storyboard.TargetName="ellipse"
              AutoReverse="{Binding Path=AutoReverseAnimation}"
              Duration="{Binding Path=StoryboardDuration}"
              To="50"
              From="200" />
          </ParallelTimeline>
        </Storyboard>
      </BeginStoryboard>
    </EventTrigger>
  </Window.Triggers>

  <DockPanel>
    <StackPanel Margin="5" DockPanel.Dock="Bottom">
      <TextBlock
        Text="Storyboard Duration (s):" Margin="0,5" />
      <Slider
        Width="250"
        Height="30"
        Minimum="0"
        Maximum="60"
        Value="5"
        ValueChanged="Slider_ValueChanged"
        Margin="0,5" />
      <CheckBox
        Content="AutoReverse"
        IsChecked="{Binding Path=AutoReverseAnimation, Mode=TwoWay}"
```

```
        Margin="0,5" />
    </StackPanel>

    <Ellipse
      x:Name="ellipse"
      Fill="{Binding Path=EllipseFillBrush}"
      Stroke="Black"
      StrokeThickness="1" />
  </DockPanel>
</Window>
```

The following code-behind contains the dependency properties that are used to supply the animations defined in the previous markup with their data-bound values. When the value of any of these properties changes, the animation is reapplied, reflecting the new values.

```
using System;
using System.Windows;
using System.Windows.Media;
using System.Windows.Media.Animation;

namespace Recipe_11_02
{
    public partial class Window1 : Window
    {
        public Window1()
        {
            InitializeComponent();

            Loaded += delegate(object sender, RoutedEventArgs e)
                    {
                        //Set the data context of the Window to itself.
                        //This will make binding to the dependency properties,
                        //defined below, a great deal easier.
                        DataContext = this;
                    };
        }

        // Gets or sets the AutoReverseAnimationProperty
        public bool AutoReverseAnimation
        {
            get { return (bool)GetValue(AutoReverseAnimationProperty); }
            set { SetValue(AutoReverseAnimationProperty, value); }
        }

        public static readonly DependencyProperty AutoReverseAnimationProperty =
            DependencyProperty.Register("AutoReverseAnimation", typeof(bool),
                typeof(Window1),
                    new UIPropertyMetadata(false, DependencyProperty_Changed));
```

```csharp
// Gets or sets the value of the StoryboardDuration property.
public Duration StoryboardDuration
{
    get { return (Duration)GetValue(StoryboardDurationProperty); }
    set { SetValue(StoryboardDurationProperty, value); }
}

public static readonly DependencyProperty StoryboardDurationProperty =
    DependencyProperty.Register("StoryboardDuration", typeof(Duration),
        typeof(Window1),
        new UIPropertyMetadata(new Duration(TimeSpan.FromSeconds(1)),
            DependencyProperty_Changed));

// Handles changes to the value of either the StoryboardDuration dependency
// property or the EllipseFillBrush dependency property and invokes the
// ReapplyStoryboard method, updating the animation to reflect the new
// values.
private static void DependencyProperty_Changed(DependencyObject sender,
    DependencyPropertyChangedEventArgs e)
{
    Window1 window1 = sender as Window1;

    if (window1 != null)
    {
        window1.ReapplyStoryboard();
    }
}

// Reapplies the 'ellipseStoryboard' object to the 'ellipse' object
// defined in the associated markup of the window.
private void ReapplyStoryboard()
{
    if (!this.IsInitialized)
    {
        return;
    }

    //Attempt to get the current time of the active storyboard.
    //If this is null, a TimeSpan of 0 is used to start the storyboard
    //from the beginning.
    TimeSpan? currentTime = ellipseStoryboard.GetCurrentTime(this)
                            ?? TimeSpan.FromSeconds(0);
    //Restart the storyboard.
    ellipseStoryboard.Begin(this, true);
    //Seek to the same position that the storyboard was before it was
    //restarted.
    ellipseStoryboard.Seek(this, currentTime.Value,
```

```
                TimeSeekOrigin.BeginTime);
    }

    private void Slider_ValueChanged(object sender,
                    RoutedPropertyChangedEventArgs<double> e)
    {
        StoryboardDuration = TimeSpan.FromSeconds(e.NewValue);
    }
  }
}
```

11-3. Remove Animations

Problem

You need to remove one or more animations that have been applied to a control, either to stop them running or to free up composited animations (see recipe 11-4).

Solution

Several options are available, depending on whether you are working in XAML or in code. The options are as follows:

- In code, call Remove on a System.Windows.Media.Animation.Storyboard, supplying a reference to the same object used in the call to Begin.

- In markup, use a System.Windows.Media.Animation.RemoveStoryboard object.

- In code, call the ApplyAnimationClock or BeginAnimation method on the object being animated, supplying the property being animated and a value of null. This will stop any animation clocks running against the property.

- In code, obtain a System.Windows.Media.Animation.ClockController from the Controller property of an animation clock, and call its Remove method. This will remove the clock in question.

How It Works

Based on where you need to remove the animation—in other words, from within code or markup—you'll use one of the previous options or maybe even a combination of them.

   The first option allows you to remove all the animation clocks defined within a Storyboard and is performed in code. You need to obtain a reference to the Storyboard you want to remove and simply call its Remove method. The method has two signatures, both taking a single parameter that points to either a System.Windows.FrameworkElement or a System.Windows. FrameworkContentElement. This must point to an object that was used in a call to a storyboard's Begin method or used in a System.Windows.Media.Animation.BeginStoryboard. This will have

the effect of removing all clocks that were created for the storyboard's child System.Windows.
Media.Animation.Timeline objects, regardless of any FillBehavior settings of System.Windows.
Media.Animation.FillBehavior.HoldEnd.

The Sytem.Winows.Media.Animation.ControllableStoryboard and System.Windows.Media.
Animation.RemoveStoryboard can be used to achieve the same effect as calling Remove on a
Storyboard within XAML markup. The RemoveStoryboard can be used to remove any clocks
applied by a Storyboard that was activated using a named System.Windows.Media.Animation.
BeginStoryboard, within the same name scope as the RemoveStoryboard. The RemoveStoryboard.
BeginStoryboardName property, of type System.String, is used to identify the BeginStoryboard
used to activate the Storyboard being removed.

Should you want to remove all clocks applied to a specific property of a control, you should
use either the ApplyAnimationClock method or the BeginAnimation method of the object to
which the property belongs. The two methods are available to any object that descends from
System.Windows.Media.Animation.Animatable, System.Windows.ContentElement, System.
Windows.Media.UIElement, or System.Windows.Media.Media3D.Visual3D. The ApplyAnimationClock
method takes two parameters: a System.Windows.DependencyProperty indicating the property
you want to remove any clocks from and a System.Windows.Media.Animation.AnimationClock
to apply to the property. Specifying a value of null here will remove any clocks applied to the
property of the owning object.

Using BeginAnimation is similar to using ApplyAnimationClock, and behind the
scenes, both methods end up in the same place when their second parameter is null. Like
the ApplyAnimationMethod, BeginAnimation takes two parameters, a DependencyProperty indicating the property on the owning object to be cleared of clocks and a System.Windows.Media.
Animation.AnimationTimeline from which all Timeline objects are derived. Again, a null value
is supplied for the second parameter, clearing all the clocks applied to the property.

To remove a specific clock from a specific property, you will need to use the fourth option
given earlier. This method is used in the code-behind and is a little trickier because it is used with
animations that have been created and applied to a property using an AnimationClock object in
code. A reference to an AnimationClock is usually obtained by calling the CreateClock method
of an AnimationTimeline object, which is no use for working with an already active clock. To
remove an instance of an AnimationClock, a reference to its ClockController is required. This is
easily obtained through the Controller property on an AnimationTimeline object. The Remove
method of the clock's controller doesn't require any parameters and will result in any instances
of that clock and its child clocks being removed from any properties they are animating.

The Code

The following example demonstrates the four different options for removing any animations
that are active on a property of some object. The following XAML defines four buttons, each of
which has an animation applied to its Width property. When each button is clicked, the animations running on it will be stopped using one of the previous four methods.

```
<Window
  x:Class="Recipe_11_03.Window1"
  xmlns="http://schemas.microsoft.com/winfx/2006/xaml/presentation"
  xmlns:x="http://schemas.microsoft.com/winfx/2006/xaml"
  Title="Recipe_11_03"
  Height="300"
```

```xml
    Width="300">
    <Window.Resources>
      <Storyboard x:Key="Storyboard1">
        <ParallelTimeline>
          <DoubleAnimation
            x:Name="Animation1"
            Storyboard.TargetProperty="Width"
            From="140"
            To="50"
            AutoReverse="True"
            RepeatBehavior="Forever" />
          <DoubleAnimation
            Storyboard.TargetProperty="Opacity"
            To="0.5"
            AutoReverse="True"
            RepeatBehavior="Forever" />
        </ParallelTimeline>
      </Storyboard>
    </Window.Resources>

    <UniformGrid>
      <Button Margin="5" Content="Method 1">
        <Button.Triggers>
          <EventTrigger RoutedEvent="Button.Loaded">
            <BeginStoryboard
              Storyboard="{DynamicResource Storyboard1}"
              x:Name="BeginStoryboard1" />
          </EventTrigger>
          <EventTrigger RoutedEvent="Button.Click">
            <RemoveStoryboard BeginStoryboardName="BeginStoryboard1" />
          </EventTrigger>
        </Button.Triggers>
      </Button>

      <Button
        Margin="5"
        Content="Method 2"
        Click="Button2_Click">
        <Button.Triggers>
          <EventTrigger
            RoutedEvent="Button.Loaded">
            <BeginStoryboard
              Storyboard="{DynamicResource Storyboard1}" />
          </EventTrigger>
        </Button.Triggers>
      </Button>
```

```
    <Button
      x:Name="button3"
      Margin="5"
      Content="Method 3"
      Click="Button3_Click"
      Loaded="Button3_Loaded" />

    <Button
      Margin="5"
      Content="Method 4"
      Click="Button4_Click"
      Loaded="Button4_Loaded" />
  </UniformGrid>
</Window>
```

The following code-behind declares the methods that handle the click events for three of the four System.Windows.Controls.Button objects, defined in the previous XAML:

```
using System;
using System.Windows;
using System.Windows.Controls;
using System.Windows.Media.Animation;

namespace Recipe_11_03
{
    public partial class Window1 : Window
    {
        public Window1()
        {
            InitializeComponent();
        }

        #region Method 2

        /// <summary>
        /// Handler for the Button.Click event on the 'Method 2' button.
        /// This method removes the animations affecting the button
        /// using the BeginAnimation() method, passing a null reference
        /// for the value of the System.Windows.Media.Animation.AnimationTimeline.
        /// </summary>
        private void Button2_Click(object sender, RoutedEventArgs e)
        {
            //Cast the sender to a button.
            Button button2 = sender as Button;
            //Remove any active animations against the Button's width property.
            button2.BeginAnimation(Button.WidthProperty, null);
            //Remove any active animations against the Button's height property.
            button2.BeginAnimation(Button.OpacityProperty, null);
        }
```

```
#endregion

#region Method 3

//Store a reference to the AnimationClock objects when they are created.
//This allows for the clocks to be accessed later when it comes to
//removing them.
private AnimationClock opacityClock;
private AnimationClock widthClock;

//Method that handles the Button.Loaded event on the 'Method 3' button.
//Animations are created and applied to 'button3', storing a reference to
//the clocks that are created.
private void Button3_Loaded(object sender, RoutedEventArgs e)
{
    DoubleAnimation opacityAnimation =
        new DoubleAnimation(1d, 0.5d, TimeSpan.FromSeconds(1),
                        FillBehavior.HoldEnd);
    opacityAnimation.RepeatBehavior = RepeatBehavior.Forever;
    opacityAnimation.AutoReverse = true;
    opacityClock = opacityAnimation.CreateClock();
    button3.ApplyAnimationClock(Button.OpacityProperty, opacityClock);

    DoubleAnimation widthAnimation =
        new DoubleAnimation(140d, 50d, TimeSpan.FromSeconds(1),
                        FillBehavior.HoldEnd);
    widthAnimation.RepeatBehavior = RepeatBehavior.Forever;
    widthAnimation.AutoReverse = true;
    widthClock = widthAnimation.CreateClock();
    button3.ApplyAnimationClock(Button.WidthProperty, widthClock);
}

//Handles the Button.Click event of 'button3'. This uses the third
//method of removing animations by removing each of the clocks.
private void Button3_Click(object sender, RoutedEventArgs e)
{
    opacityClock.Controller.Remove();
    widthClock.Controller.Remove();
}

#endregion

#region Method 4

//Store a local reference to the storyboard we want to
//interact with.
private Storyboard method4Storyboard;
```

```
private void Button4_Loaded(object sender, RoutedEventArgs e)
{
    method4Storyboard = TryFindResource("Storyboard1") as Storyboard;

    method4Storyboard.Begin(sender as FrameworkElement, true);
}

//Handles the Button.Click event of the 'Method 4' button.
private void Button4_Click(object sender, RoutedEventArgs e)
{
    //Make sure we got a valid reference.
    if (method4Storyboard != null)
    {
        //Remove the storyboard by calling its Remove method, passing the
        //control that it is currently running against.
        method4Storyboard.Remove(sender as FrameworkElement);
    }
}

#endregion
    }
}
```

11-4. Overlap Animations

Problem

You need to specify how a newly applied animation interacts with an existing animation, if present.

Solution

Specify a System.Windows.Media.Animation.HandoffBehavior value of HandoffBehavior.Compose to overlap animations applied to a property.

How It Works

When an animation is applied to a property of a System.Windows.FrameworkElement, it is possible to specify how any existing animations applied to the property should be handled. Two options are available to you. One stops and removes any existing animations before applying the new animation, and the second blends the two animations, merging the existing animation into the new one. Table 11-2 details these values.

Table 11-2. *The Values of HandoffBehavior*

Value	Description
Compose	The new animation will be partly merged into any existing ones, creating a smoother transition between the two.
SnapshotAndReplace	Any existing animation will be stopped at its current position, and the new one will begin. This creates a sharper transition between the two animations.

It is important to note that when animations are applied with a HandoffBehavior of HandoffBehavior.Compose, any existing animation will not free up the resources it is using until the owning object of the property the animation is applied to is freed. This can cause considerable performance overheads when compositing several large animations. The best way to ensure that your application doesn't suffer a performance hit is to manually free up any composited animations. You can easily achieve this by adding a handler to the Completed event of your System.Windows.Media.Animation.Timeline object (see recipe 11-15) and removing any animations from the property in question (see recipe 11-3).

The behavior is strange if To or From is specified. If either is specified, the animation will jump straight to the value of To.

The Code

```
<Window
  x:Class="Recipe_11_04.Window1"
  xmlns="http://schemas.microsoft.com/winfx/2006/xaml/presentation"
  xmlns:x="http://schemas.microsoft.com/winfx/2006/xaml"
  Title="Recipe_11_04"
  Height="300"
  Width="300">
  <Window.Resources>
    <Storyboard x:Key="LowOpacity">
      <DoubleAnimation Storyboard.TargetProperty="Opacity" />
    </Storyboard>

    <Storyboard x:Key="HighOpacity">
      <DoubleAnimation
        Storyboard.TargetProperty="Opacity"
        To="1"
        AutoReverse="True"
        RepeatBehavior="Forever" />
    </Storyboard>
  </Window.Resources>

  <Grid>
    <Grid.ColumnDefinitions>
```

```
        <ColumnDefinition Width="0.5*" />
        <ColumnDefinition Width="0.5*" />
      </Grid.ColumnDefinitions>

      <Grid.RowDefinitions>
        <RowDefinition Height="*" />
        <RowDefinition Height="35" />
      </Grid.RowDefinitions>

      <Border
        Background="Firebrick"
        Width="100"
        Height="100"
        x:Name="Rect1"
        Opacity="0.4">
        <Border.Triggers>
          <EventTrigger RoutedEvent="Mouse.MouseEnter">
            <BeginStoryboard Storyboard="{DynamicResource HighOpacity}" />
          </EventTrigger>
          <EventTrigger RoutedEvent="Mouse.MouseLeave">
            <BeginStoryboard Storyboard="{DynamicResource LowOpacity}" />
          </EventTrigger>
        </Border.Triggers>
      </Border>

      <Rectangle
        Fill="Firebrick"
        Width="100"
        Height="100"
        Grid.Column="1" />
    </Grid>
</Window>
```

11-5. Animate Several Properties in Parallel

Problem

You need to animate several properties of a control at the same time, that is, its height, width, and color.

Solution

Define your animations as normal but as children of a `System.Windows.Media.Animation.ParallelTimeline`.

How It Works

The `ParallelTimeline` is a special type of `System.Windows.Media.Animation.Timeline` that allows for one or more child `Timeline` objects to be defined as its children, with each child `Timeline` being run in parallel. Because `ParallelTimeline` is a `Timeline` object, it can be used like any other `Timeline` object. Unlike a `Storyboard` where animations are activated based on the order in which its child `Timeline` objects are declared, a `ParallelTimeline` will activate its children based on the value of their `BeginTime` properties. If any of the animations overlap, they will run in parallel.

The `Storyboard` class actually inherits from `ParallelTimeline` and simply gives each child a `BeginTime` based on where in the list of child objects a `Timeline` is declared and the cumulative `Duration` and `BeginTime` values of each preceding `Timeline`. The `Storyboard` class goes further to extend the `ParallelTimeline` class by adding a great deal of methods for controlling the processing of its child `Timeline` objects. Because `ParallelTimeline` is the ancestor of a `Storyboard`, `ParallelTimeline` objects are more suited to nesting because they are much slimmer objects.

Like other `Timeline` objects, the `ParallelTimeline` has a `BeginTime` property. This allows you to specify an offset from the start of the owning `Storyboard` to the activation of the `ParallelTimeline`. As a result, if a value for `BeginTime` is given by the `ParallelTimeline`, its children's `BeginTime` will work relative to this value, as opposed to being relative to the `Storyboard`.

It is important to note that a `Storyboard.Completed` event will not be raised on the owning `Storyboard` until the last child `Timeline` in the `ParallelTimeline` finishes. This is because a `ParallelTimeline` can contain `Timeline` objects with different `BeginTime` and `Duration` values, meaning they won't all necessarily finish at the same time.

The Code

The following example defines a `System.Windows.Window` that contains a single `System.Windows.Shapes.Rectangle`. When the mouse is placed over the rectangle, the `Rectangle.Height`, `Rectangle.Width`, and `Rectangle.Fill` properties are animated. The animation continues until the mouse is moved off the rectangle.

```
<Window
  x:Class="Recipe_11_05.Window1"
  xmlns="http://schemas.microsoft.com/winfx/2006/xaml/presentation"
  xmlns:x="http://schemas.microsoft.com/winfx/2006/xaml"
  Title="Recipe_11_05"
  Height="300"
  Width="300">
  <Grid>
    <Rectangle
      Height="100"
      Width="100"
      Fill="Firebrick"
      Stroke="Black"
      StrokeThickness="1">
      <Rectangle.Style>
```

```xml
            <Style TargetType="Rectangle">
              <Style.Triggers>
                <EventTrigger RoutedEvent="Rectangle.MouseEnter">
                  <BeginStoryboard>
                    <Storyboard>
                      <ParallelTimeline
                        RepeatBehavior="Forever"
                        AutoReverse="True">
                        <DoubleAnimation
                          Storyboard.TargetProperty="Width"
                          To="150" />
                        <DoubleAnimation
                          Storyboard.TargetProperty="Height"
                          To="150" />
                        <ColorAnimation
                          Storyboard.TargetProperty="Fill.Color"
                          To="Orange" />
                      </ParallelTimeline>
                    </Storyboard>
                  </BeginStoryboard>
                </EventTrigger>
                <EventTrigger
                  RoutedEvent="Rectangle.MouseLeave">
                  <BeginStoryboard>
                    <Storyboard>
                      <ParallelTimeline>
                        <DoubleAnimation
                          Storyboard.TargetProperty="Width"
                          To="100" />
                        <DoubleAnimation
                          Storyboard.TargetProperty="Height"
                          To="100" />
                        <ColorAnimation
                          Storyboard.TargetProperty="Fill.Color"
                          To="Firebrick" />
                      </ParallelTimeline>
                    </Storyboard>
                  </BeginStoryboard>
                </EventTrigger>
              </Style.Triggers>
            </Style>
          </Rectangle.Style>
        </Rectangle>
      </Grid>
</Window>
```

11-6. Create a Keyframe-Based Animation

Problem

You need to create an animation that uses keyframes to specify key points in the animation.

Solution

Use a keyframe-based animation such as System.Windows.Media.Animation.Double AnimationUsingKeyFrames. You can then use several System.Windows.Media.Animation. IKeyFrame objects to define the keyframes in your animation.

How It Works

The use of keyframes will be familiar to anyone who has ever touched on animation. For those who are new, keyframes basically allow you to specify key points in an animation where the object being animated needs to be at a required position or in a required state. The frames in between are then interpolated between these two keyframes, effectively filling in the blanks in the animation. This process of interpolating the in-between frames is often referred to as *tweening*.

When defining an animation using keyframes, you will need to specify one or more keyframes that define the animation's flow. These keyframes are defined as children of your keyframe animation. It is important to note that the target type of the keyframe must match that of the parent animation. For example, if you are using a System.Windows.Media. Animation.DoubleAnimationUsingKeyFrames, any keyframes must be derived from the abstract class System.Windows.Media.Animation.DoubleKeyFrame.

You will be pleased to hear that a good number of types have keyframe objects, from System.Int to System.String and System.Windows.Thickness to System.Windows.Media. Media3D.Quarternion. (For a more complete list of the types covered, please see http:// msdn.microsoft.com/en-us/library/ms742524.aspx.) All but a few of the types covered by animations have a choice of interpolation methods, allowing you to specify how the frames in between two keyframes are generated. Each interpolation method is defined as a prefix to the keyframe's class name and is listed in Table 11-3.

Table 11-3. *Interpolation Methods for Keyframe Animation*

Type	Description
Discrete	A discrete keyframe will not create any frames in between it and the following keyframe. Once the discrete keyframe's duration has elapsed, the animation will jump to the value specified in the following keyframe.
Linear	Linear keyframes will create a smooth transition between it and the following frame. The generated frames will animate the value steadily at a constant rate to its end point.
Spline	Spline keyframes allow you to vary the speed at which a property is animated using the shape of a Bezier curve. The curve is described by defining its control points in unit coordinate space. The gradient of the curve defines the speed or rate of change in the animation.

Although keyframes must match the type of the owning animation, it is possible to mix the different types of interpolation, offering variable speeds throughout.

The Code

The following XAML demonstrates how to use linear and double keyframes to animate the Height and Width properties of a System.Windows.Shapes.Ellipse control (see Figure 11-1). The animation is triggered when the System.Windows.Controls.Button is clicked.

```
<Window
  x:Class="Recipe_11_06.Window1"
  xmlns="http://schemas.microsoft.com/winfx/2006/xaml/presentation"
  xmlns:x="http://schemas.microsoft.com/winfx/2006/xaml"
  Title="Recipe_11_06"
  Height="300"
  Width="300">
  <Window.Resources>
    <Storyboard
      x:Key="ResizeEllipseStoryboard">
      <ParallelTimeline>
        <DoubleAnimationUsingKeyFrames
          Storyboard.TargetName="ellipse"
          Storyboard.TargetProperty="Height">
          <LinearDoubleKeyFrame Value="150" KeyTime="0:0:1" />
          <LinearDoubleKeyFrame Value="230" KeyTime="0:0:2" />
          <LinearDoubleKeyFrame Value="150" KeyTime="0:0:2.5" />
          <LinearDoubleKeyFrame Value="230" KeyTime="0:0:5" />
          <LinearDoubleKeyFrame Value="40" KeyTime="0:0:9" />
        </DoubleAnimationUsingKeyFrames>

        <DoubleAnimationUsingKeyFrames
          Storyboard.TargetName="ellipse"
          Storyboard.TargetProperty="Width">
          <DiscreteDoubleKeyFrame Value="150" KeyTime="0:0:1" />
          <DiscreteDoubleKeyFrame Value="230" KeyTime="0:0:2" />
          <DiscreteDoubleKeyFrame Value="150" KeyTime="0:0:2.5" />
          <DiscreteDoubleKeyFrame Value="230" KeyTime="0:0:5" />
          <DiscreteDoubleKeyFrame Value="40" KeyTime="0:0:9" />
        </DoubleAnimationUsingKeyFrames>
      </ParallelTimeline>
    </Storyboard>
  </Window.Resources>

  <Grid>

    <Grid.RowDefinitions>
      <RowDefinition />
      <RowDefinition Height="40" />
    </Grid.RowDefinitions>
```

```
<Ellipse
  Height="40"
  Width="40"
  x:Name="ellipse"
  HorizontalAlignment="Center"
  VerticalAlignment="Center">
  <Ellipse.Fill>
    <RadialGradientBrush
      GradientOrigin="0.75,0.25">
      <GradientStop Color="Yellow" Offset="0.0" />
      <GradientStop Color="Orange" Offset="0.5" />
      <GradientStop Color="Red" Offset="1.0" />
    </RadialGradientBrush>
  </Ellipse.Fill>
</Ellipse>

<Button
  Content="Start..."
  Margin="10"
  Grid.Row="1">
  <Button.Triggers>
    <EventTrigger RoutedEvent="Button.Click">
      <BeginStoryboard
        Storyboard="{DynamicResource ResizeEllipseStoryboard}" />
    </EventTrigger>
  </Button.Triggers>
</Button>

  </Grid>
</Window>
```

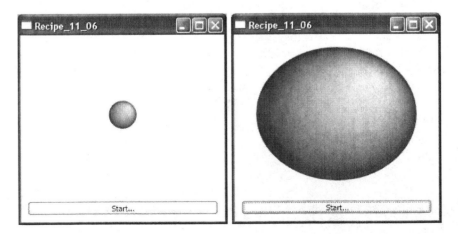

Figure 11-1. *An animated ellipse in its initial state (left) and after several seconds have passed (right)*

11-7. Control the Progress of an Animation

Problem

You need to be able to control the location of the playhead in an animation.

Solution

Use the Seek method on a System.Windows.Media.Animation.Storyboard to programmatically set the location of the playhead from the offset from the start of a Storyboard.

How It Works

The Seek method on a Storyboard object allows you to specify a duration relative to a specified origin to which the playhead should be positioned. This allows you to move the current position of the animation with great precision. The method takes three parameters—one being the object being animated, the second being a System.TimeSpan providing the offset to seek to, and the third a System.Windows.Media.Animation.TimeSeekOrigin value. The TimeSeekOrigin enumeration defines two values, details of which are given in Table 11-4.

Table 11-4. *The Values of a TimeSeekOrigin Enumeration*

Value	Description
BeginTime	The specified offset is relative to the start of the animation.
Duration	The specified offset is relative to end of the animation.

By looking at the total duration of the Storyboard, it is possible to drive the position of the animation using a control such as a System.Windows.Controls.Slider. Handling the Slider.ValueChanged event on a slider control, you can seek to a location in the animation based on the new location of the slider.

The Code

The following code demonstrates how to use a System.Windows.Controls.Slider to control the progress of an animation (see Figure 11-2). It is important to note that the animation is paused while the user is interacting with the Slider control so as to prevent the animation from progressing while the slider is being moved.

```
<Window
  x:Class="Recipe_11_07.Window1"
  xmlns="http://schemas.microsoft.com/winfx/2006/xaml/presentation"
  xmlns:x="http://schemas.microsoft.com/winfx/2006/xaml"
  Title="Recipe_11_07"
  Height="300"
  Width="600">
  <Grid>
```

```
<Rectangle
  x:Name="Rectangle"
  Height="100"
  Width="100"
  Fill="Firebrick">
  <Rectangle.RenderTransform>
    <MatrixTransform x:Name="RectangleMatrixTransform" />
  </Rectangle.RenderTransform>

  <Rectangle.Triggers>
    <EventTrigger RoutedEvent="Rectangle.Loaded">
      <BeginStoryboard x:Name="RectangleStoryboard">
        <Storyboard
          x:Name="Storyboard"
          CurrentTimeInvalidated="Storyboard_Changed">

          <MatrixAnimationUsingPath
            Storyboard.TargetName="RectangleMatrixTransform"
            Storyboard.TargetProperty="Matrix"
            Duration="0:0:10"
            RepeatBehavior="Forever">
            <MatrixAnimationUsingPath.PathGeometry>
              <PathGeometry Figures="M -100,0 300, 0" />
            </MatrixAnimationUsingPath.PathGeometry>
          </MatrixAnimationUsingPath>
        </Storyboard>
      </BeginStoryboard>
    </EventTrigger>
  </Rectangle.Triggers>
</Rectangle>

<Slider
  x:Name="Seeker"
  Minimum="0"
  Maximum="1"
  SmallChange="0.001"
  ValueChanged="Seeker_ValueChanged">
  <Slider.Triggers>
    <EventTrigger RoutedEvent="Slider.MouseLeftButtonDown">
      <StopStoryboard BeginStoryboardName="RectangleStoryboard" />
    </EventTrigger>
    <EventTrigger RoutedEvent="Slider.MouseLeftButtonUp">
      <ResumeStoryboard BeginStoryboardName="RectangleStoryboard" />
    </EventTrigger>
  </Slider.Triggers>
</Slider>
    </Grid>
</Window>
```

The following code-behind defines methods that update the value of the Slider, defined in the previous markup, and respond to the user moving the slider, seeking to a new point in the animation:

```
using System;
using System.Windows;
using System.Windows.Media.Animation;
using System.Windows.Input;

namespace Recipe_11_07
{
    /// <summary>
    /// Interaction logic for Window1.xaml
    /// </summary>
    public partial class Window1 : Window
    {
        public Window1()
        {
            InitializeComponent();
        }

        bool ignoreValueChanged = false;

        private void Storyboard_Changed(object sender, System.EventArgs e)
        {
            ClockGroup clockGroup = sender as ClockGroup;

            AnimationClock animationClock =
                clockGroup.Children[0] as AnimationClock;

            if (animationClock.CurrentProgress.HasValue)
            {
                ignoreValueChanged = true;
                Seeker.Value = animationClock.CurrentProgress.Value;
                ignoreValueChanged = false;
            }
        }

        private void Seeker_ValueChanged(object sender,
            RoutedPropertyChangedEventArgs<double> e)
        {
            if (ignoreValueChanged && Mouse.LeftButton != MouseButtonState.Pressed)
            {
                return;
            }

            Storyboard.Seek(Rectangle,
            TimeSpan.FromTicks((long)(Storyboard.Children[0].Duration.TimeSpan.Ticks
```

```
                         * Seeker.Value)),
                                TimeSeekOrigin.BeginTime);
            }
        }
    }
```

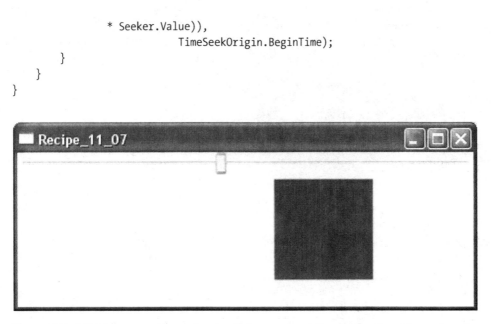

Figure 11-2. *A* Slider *control is used to track the progress of an animation. The animation moves the rectangle from one side of the window to the other.*

11-8. Animate the Shape of a Path

Problem

You need to animate the shape of a System.Windows.Shapes.Path.

Solution

Use a System.Windows.Media.PointAnimation object to animate the points of your path.

How It Works

A PointAnimation allows you to animate the value of a System.Windows.Point. By naming the sections of your path, you have complete access to the object, for example, a System.Windows.Media.LineSegment. By referring to the appropriate property, you are able to animate them, giving the appearance that the shape is changing. It is possible to target any point of a System.Windows.Media.PathSegment object, including the control points in a System.Windows.Media.BezierSegment.

The Code

The following XAML defines several different shapes within a path (see Figure 11-3). Each shape is animated using either a System.Windows.Media.Animation.DoubleAnimation or a PointAnimation.

```xml
<Window
  x:Class="Recipe_11_08.Window1"
  xmlns="http://schemas.microsoft.com/winfx/2006/xaml/presentation"
  xmlns:x="http://schemas.microsoft.com/winfx/2006/xaml"
  Title="Recipe_11_08"
  Height="300"
  Width="300">
  <Grid>
    <Path Stroke="Black" StrokeThickness="1">
      <Path.Data>
        <GeometryGroup>
          <LineGeometry
            x:Name="line1"
            StartPoint="20,20"
            EndPoint="264,20" />
          <LineGeometry
            x:Name="line2"
            StartPoint="38,40"
            EndPoint="248,40" />
          <LineGeometry
            x:Name="line3"
            StartPoint="140,60"
            EndPoint="140,150" />
          <LineGeometry
            x:Name="line4"
            StartPoint="160,60"
            EndPoint="160,150" />
          <EllipseGeometry
            x:Name="ellipse"
            Center="150,150"
            RadiusX="5"
            RadiusY="5" />
          <PathGeometry>
            <PathFigure>
              <BezierSegment
                x:Name="bezierSegment1"
                IsStroked="True"
                Point1="200,200"
                Point2="105,205"
                Point3="280,0" />
            </PathFigure>
          </PathGeometry>
          <PathGeometry>
            <PathFigure StartPoint="0,265">
              <BezierSegment
                x:Name="bezierSegment2"
                IsStroked="True"
```

```
                Point1="100,100"
                Point2="206,117"
                Point3="280,267" />
          </PathFigure>
        </PathGeometry>
      </GeometryGroup>
    </Path.Data>
    <Path.Triggers>
      <EventTrigger RoutedEvent="Path.Loaded">
        <BeginStoryboard>
          <Storyboard
            AutoReverse="True"
            RepeatBehavior="Forever">
            <PointAnimation
              To="40,20"
              Storyboard.TargetName="line1"
              Storyboard.TargetProperty="EndPoint" />
            <PointAnimation
              To="280,40"
              Storyboard.TargetName="line2"
              Storyboard.TargetProperty="StartPoint" />
            <PointAnimation
              To="20,60"
              Storyboard.TargetName="line3"
              Storyboard.TargetProperty="EndPoint" />
            <PointAnimation
              To="280,60"
              Storyboard.TargetName="line4"
              Storyboard.TargetProperty="EndPoint" />
            <ParallelTimeline
              Storyboard.TargetName="ellipse">
              <DoubleAnimation
                To="80"
                Storyboard.TargetProperty="RadiusX" />
              <DoubleAnimation
                To="80"
                Storyboard.TargetProperty="RadiusY" />
            </ParallelTimeline>
            <ParallelTimeline Storyboard.TargetName="bezierSegment1">
              <PointAnimation Storyboard.TargetProperty="Point1" To="300,0" />
              <PointAnimation Storyboard.TargetProperty="Point2" To="0,270" />
              <PointAnimation Storyboard.TargetProperty="Point3" To="300,263" />
            </ParallelTimeline>
            <ParallelTimeline Storyboard.TargetName="bezierSegment2">
              <PointAnimation Storyboard.TargetProperty="Point1" To="0,0" />
              <PointAnimation Storyboard.TargetProperty="Point2" To="260,300" />
              <PointAnimation Storyboard.TargetProperty="Point3" To="280,0" />
```

```
                </ParallelTimeline>
              </Storyboard>
            </BeginStoryboard>
          </EventTrigger>
        </Path.Triggers>
      </Path>
    </Grid>
  </Window>
```

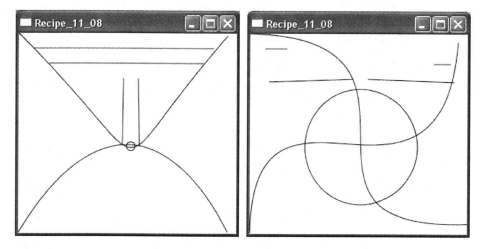

Figure 11-3. *The initial state of the shapes (left) and the final state of the shapes after being animated (right)*

11-9. Loop and Reverse an Animation

Problem

You need to run an animation indefinitely and reverse the animation each time it reaches the end.

Solution

Animation offers two properties, RepeatBehavior and AutoReverse, to control the looping and reversal of your animation.

How It Works

The two properties mentioned earlier allow you to perform tricky functionality very quickly and easily. As you might have guessed, the RepeatBehavior property of a System.Windows. Media.Animation.Timeline-based object allows you to control how many times an animation is repeated. You can specify this value in one of three ways, each of which is described in Table 11-5.

Table 11-5. *Specifying the Repeat Behavior of an Animation*

Mode	Description
Iteration Count	Specify the number of times that the animation should repeat, prefixed with the character x. The value is of type System.Double and must be greater than 0. It is important to note that when accessing the Count property of a RepeatBehavior structure in code, you should first check the value of the HasCount property to ensure the RepeatBehavior is driven by an iteration count. Should the HasCount property return False, accessing the Count property will throw a System.InvalidOperationException exception. To have an animation play through twice, set the value of RepeatBehavior to 2x. The value 2.5x would play the animation through twice.
Duration	A repeat duration can be specified as a whole number of days, a whole number of hours, a whole number of minutes, a number of seconds, or a whole number of fractional seconds.
Forever	The special Forever value is used to run the animation indefinitely. In this case, the Completed event will not be raised.

The System.Windows.Media.Animation.Storyboard.Completed event does not get raised until the last Timeline in the animation has completed. This means that if your animation has a repeat behavior of RepeatBehavior.Forever, the Storyboard.Completed event will never get raised.

The AutoReverse property of a Timeline is a great deal simpler and is of type System.Boolean. Setting the value to True will result in the animation playing from end to beginning, each time it reaches the end of the timeline. The default value of this property is False, resulting in the animation playing again from the beginning if any repeat behavior is defined. Automatically reversed animations count as a playback in terms of duration but not in terms of iterations. That is, if your animation has a repeat behavior of 2x and AutoReverse is True, the animation will play through from beginning to end and back again twice. If, however, the duration of the animation is one second and a RepeatBehavior of two seconds is specified, the animation will play from beginning to end and back again only once.

The Code

The following example demonstrates how to use the RepeatBehavior and AutoReverse properties. The code defines a System.Windows.Window that contains four System.Windows.Shapes.Ellipse controls. Each of the Ellipse objects has a different animation applied to it, demonstrating how to use the AutoReverse and RepeatBehavior properties.

```
<Window
  x:Class="Recipe_11_09.Window1"
  xmlns="http://schemas.microsoft.com/winfx/2006/xaml/presentation"
  xmlns:x="http://schemas.microsoft.com/winfx/2006/xaml"
  Title="Recipe_11_09"
  Height="600"
  Width="600">
  <UniformGrid>
    <Ellipse
```

```
      Height="200"
      Width="200"
      Fill="Firebrick">
      <Ellipse.Triggers>
        <EventTrigger
          RoutedEvent="Ellipse.Loaded">
          <BeginStoryboard>
            <Storyboard
              AutoReverse="True"
              RepeatBehavior="Forever">
              <ColorAnimation
                Storyboard.TargetProperty="Fill.Color"
                To="White" />
            </Storyboard>
          </BeginStoryboard>
        </EventTrigger>
      </Ellipse.Triggers>
    </Ellipse>

    <Ellipse
      Height="200"
      Width="200"
      Fill="Firebrick">
      <Ellipse.Triggers>
        <EventTrigger
          RoutedEvent="Ellipse.Loaded">
          <BeginStoryboard>
            <Storyboard
              Duration="0:0:1"
              RepeatBehavior="0:0:4">
              <ColorAnimation
                Storyboard.TargetProperty="Fill.Color"
                To="White" />
            </Storyboard>
          </BeginStoryboard>
        </EventTrigger>
      </Ellipse.Triggers>
    </Ellipse>

    <Ellipse
      Height="200"
      Width="200"
      Fill="Firebrick">
      <Ellipse.Triggers>
        <EventTrigger
          RoutedEvent="Ellipse.Loaded">
          <BeginStoryboard>
```

```xml
                    <Storyboard
                      RepeatBehavior="5x">
                      <ColorAnimation
                        Storyboard.TargetProperty="Fill.Color"
                        To="White" />
                    </Storyboard>
                  </BeginStoryboard>
                </EventTrigger>
              </Ellipse.Triggers>
            </Ellipse>

            <Ellipse
              Height="200"
              Width="200"
              Fill="Firebrick">
              <Ellipse.Triggers>
                <EventTrigger
                  RoutedEvent="Ellipse.Loaded">
                  <BeginStoryboard>
                    <Storyboard
                      AutoReverse="True"
                      RepeatBehavior="0:0:2">
                      <ColorAnimation
                        Storyboard.TargetProperty="Fill.Color"
                        To="White" />
                    </Storyboard>
                  </BeginStoryboard>
                </EventTrigger>
              </Ellipse.Triggers>
            </Ellipse>
          </UniformGrid>
        </Window>
```

11-10. Limit the Frame Rate of a Storyboard

Problem

You need to set the desired frame rate of a `System.Windows.Media.Animation.Storyboard` object for performance reasons or otherwise.

Solution

Use the `Timeline.DesiredFrameRate` attached property to specify a desired frame rate for a Storyboard.

How It Works

The Timeline.DesiredFrameRate attached property can be used to set a desired frame rate for a Storyboard and is applied to each of its child Timeline objects, if present. The property is a nullable System.Int32 value and must be greater than 0, where the specified value is measured in frames per second (fps). Setting the value to null will cause the desired frame rate to be set to the default value of 60 fps.

The desired frame rate of an animation should be thought of more as a frame rate limit that should not be exceeded. The animation framework will attempt to run the animation at the specified value, although this may not always be possible, depending on the performance and load of the host machine. For example, if the desired frame rate is set to 200 fps and the host machine is running several other animations, 200 fps may not be achievable, in which case the animation will run at the fastest possible frame rate, up to 200 fps.

You may want to limit the frame rate of a Storyboard to reduce the amount of processing required to run the animation as less work needs to be carried out each second. This is suited to slower animations that do not require a high frame rate. You may also want to set a high frame rate to allow animations with fast-moving objects to appear smoother and free from tearing.

The Code

The following example demonstrates how to use the Timeline.DesiredFrameRate attached property. Three System.Windows.Media.Animation.Storyboard objects are defined, each with a single System.Windows.Media.Animation.DoubleAnimation. Each child DoubleAnimation targets the Y property of a System.Windows.Media.TranslateTransform, applied to each of the three System.Windows.Shapes.Ellipse controls. Each Timeline runs at the same speed but has a different frame rate, highlighting the effects of altering the frame rate.

The Ellipse to the far left of the window will be animated with the smoothest movement and least tearing. The center Ellipse will be animated with a smooth movement but will be affected by tearing. The final Ellipse to the far right of the window will appear to jump from its start position to its final position because of its frame rate of 1 fps (see Figure 11-4).

```
<Window x:Class="Recipe_11_10.Window1"
    xmlns="http://schemas.microsoft.com/winfx/2006/xaml/presentation"
    xmlns:x="http://schemas.microsoft.com/winfx/2006/xaml"
    Title="Recipe_11_10" Height="300" Width="300">
  <Window.Triggers>
    <EventTrigger
      RoutedEvent="Window.Loaded">
      <BeginStoryboard>
        <Storyboard>
          <DoubleAnimation
            AutoReverse="True"
            RepeatBehavior="Forever"
            Storyboard.TargetName="tt1"
            Storyboard.TargetProperty="Y"
            Duration="0:0:1"
            To="-90" />
```

```xml
        </Storyboard>
      </BeginStoryboard>

      <BeginStoryboard>
        <Storyboard
          Timeline.DesiredFrameRate="1">
          <DoubleAnimation
            AutoReverse="True"
            RepeatBehavior="Forever"
            Storyboard.TargetName="tt2"
            Storyboard.TargetProperty="Y"
            To="-90"
            Duration="0:0:1" />
        </Storyboard>
      </BeginStoryboard>
    </EventTrigger>
  </Window.Triggers>
  <Grid>
    <Ellipse
      Width="75"
      Height="75"
      Fill="Firebrick"
      Stroke="Black"
      StrokeThickness="1">
      <Ellipse.RenderTransform>
        <TranslateTransform
          x:Name="tt1"
          X="-75"
          Y="90" />
      </Ellipse.RenderTransform>
    </Ellipse>

    <Ellipse
      Width="75"
      Height="75"
      Fill="Plum"
      Stroke="Black"
      StrokeThickness="1">
      <Ellipse.RenderTransform>
        <TranslateTransform
          x:Name="tt2"
          X="75"
          Y="90" />
      </Ellipse.RenderTransform>
    </Ellipse>
  </Grid>
</Window>
```

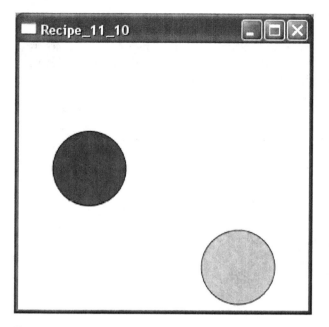

Figure 11-4. *The ellipse to the left of the window is smoothly animated between its start and end points, and the ellipse to the right jumps between the top and bottom of the screen.*

11-11. Limit the Frame Rate for All Animations in an Application

Problem

You need to set the desired frame rate for all animations within your application.

Solution

Override the default value for the System.Windows.Media.Animation.Timeline.DesiredFrameRate dependency property.

How It Works

The default value for the Timeline.DesiredFrameRate property is set to null, meaning that a value for the default desired frame rate will be calculated. Because this property is a standard dependency property, its property metadata can be overridden (see recipe 1-5 for more information on overriding the PropertyMetaData of a dependency property), allowing you to specify a new default value for any Timeline objects in your application.

To ensure that all the animations used in your application receive the new default value, it is best to perform the override at some point during the application's startup. This value can be changed later, giving a new default value to any animations created later in the application's life.

Because the override affects only the property's default value, animations can still be given other desired frame rate values by explicitly setting a value on the parent System.Windows.Media.Animation.Storyboard. This allows you to ensure that only certain animations are run at a higher or lower frame rate than the desired default value, which is useful if the majority of animations in your application are slow running in the background.

The Code

The following example demonstrates how to override the PropertyMetadata for the Timeline.DesiredFrameRateProperty dependency property. The following code details the content of the App.xaml.cs file. Here an event handler is registered against the System.Windows.Application.Startup event, which, when invoked, overrides the property metadata for the DesiredFrameRateProperty dependency property.

```
using System.Windows;
using System.Windows.Media.Animation;

namespace Recipe_11_11
{
    public partial class App : Application
    {
        public App()
        {
            Startup += delegate(object sender, StartupEventArgs e)
            {
                Timeline.DesiredFrameRateProperty.OverrideMetadata(typeof(Timeline),
                                            new PropertyMetadata(1));
            };
        }
    }
}
```

The following XAML declares two System.Windows.Shapes.Ellipse objects, both of which are animated, moving them in a vertical direction. The first animation, affecting the Ellipse to the left of the window, runs with the overridden default desired frame rate. The second animation that affects the Ellipse to the right of the window runs at an explicitly defined frame rate.

```
<Window x:Class="Recipe_11_11.Window1"
    xmlns="http://schemas.microsoft.com/winfx/2006/xaml/presentation"
    xmlns:x="http://schemas.microsoft.com/winfx/2006/xaml"
    Title="Recipe_11_11" Height="300" Width="300">
  <Window.Triggers>
    <EventTrigger
      RoutedEvent="Window.Loaded">
      <BeginStoryboard>
        <Storyboard>
          <DoubleAnimation
            AutoReverse="True"
            RepeatBehavior="Forever"
```

```xml
                    Storyboard.TargetName="tt1"
                    Storyboard.TargetProperty="Y"
                    Duration="0:0:1"
                    To="-90" />
            </Storyboard>
        </BeginStoryboard>

        <BeginStoryboard>
            <Storyboard
                Timeline.DesiredFrameRate="60">
                <DoubleAnimation
                    AutoReverse="True"
                    RepeatBehavior="Forever"
                    Storyboard.TargetName="tt2"
                    Storyboard.TargetProperty="Y"
                    To="-90"
                    Duration="0:0:1" />
            </Storyboard>
        </BeginStoryboard>
    </EventTrigger>
</Window.Triggers>
<Grid>
    <Ellipse
        Width="75"
        Height="75"
        Fill="Firebrick"
        Stroke="Black"
        StrokeThickness="1">
        <Ellipse.RenderTransform>
            <TranslateTransform
                x:Name="tt1"
                X="-75"
                Y="90" />
        </Ellipse.RenderTransform>
    </Ellipse>

    <Ellipse
        Width="75"
        Height="75"
        Fill="Plum"
        Stroke="Black"
        StrokeThickness="1">
        <Ellipse.RenderTransform>
            <TranslateTransform
                x:Name="tt2"
                X="75"
                Y="90" />
```

```
        </Ellipse.RenderTransform>
      </Ellipse>
    </Grid>
</Window>
```

11-12. Animate an Object Along a Path

Problem

You need to animate some control so that it moves along a path.

Solution

Use one of the three available path animation timeline objects.

How It Works

WPF kindly provides you with three ways of animating an object along a path. Each of these methods takes a System.Windows.Media.PathGeometry as its input, defining the shape of the path that the object will follow, and produces some kind of output, depending on the timeline's target type. All three timelines generate their output values by linearly interpolating between the values of the input path. Table 11-6 describes each of these three methods.

Table 11-6. *Path Animation Types*

Type	Description
DoubleAnimationUsingPath	Outputs a single System.Double value, generated from the input PathGeometry. Unlike the other two path-based timelines, the DoubleAnimationUsingPath also exposes a Source property that is a System.Windows.Media.Animation.PathAnimationSource. Table 11-7 describes the value of this enumeration.
PointAnimationUsingPath	Generates a series of System.Windows.Point objects, describing a position along the input PathGeometry, based on the current time of the animation. PointAnimationUsingPath is the only timeline of the three that does not provide any values for the angle of rotation to the tangent of the path at the current point.
MatrixAnimationUsingPath	Generates a series of System.Windows.Media.Matrix objects describing a translation matrix relating to a point in the input path. If the DoesRotateWithTrangent property of a MatrixAnimationUsingPath timeline is set to True, the output matrix is composed of a translation and rotation matrix, allowing both the position and orientation of the target to be animated with a single animation.

Table 11-7. *Values of the PathAnimationSource Enumeration*

Value	Description
X	Values output by the DoubleAnimationUsingPath correspond to the interpolated X component of the current position along the input path.
Y	Values output by the DoubleAnimationUsingPath correspond to the interpolated Y component of the current position along the input path.
Angle	Values output by the DoubleAnimationUsingPath correspond to the angle of rotation to the tangent of the line at the current point along the input path.

It should be clear that each of the path timelines has a specific use and offers different levels of functionality. The MatrixAnimationUsingPath provides the neatest method for animating both the position and the orientation of an object. The same effect is not possible at all using a PointAimationUsingPath and would require three DoubleAnimationUsingPath timelines, each with a different PathAnimationSource value for the Source property.

When using a value of PathAnimationSource.Angle for the Source property of a DoubleAnimationUsingPath timeline or setting the DoesRotateWithTangent property of a MatrixAnimationUsingPath timeline to True, you ensure that the object being animated is correctly rotated so that it follows the gradient of the path. If an arrow is translated using a path-driven animation, its orientation will remain the same throughout the timeline's duration. If, however, the arrow's orientation is animated to coincide with the path, the arrow will be rotated relative to its initial orientation, based on the gradient of the path. If you have a path defining a circle and the arrow initially points in to the center of the circle, the arrow will continue to point into the center of the circle as it moves around the circle's circumference.

Although the MatrixAnimationUsingPath has the most compact output, controls will rarely expose a Matrix property that you can directly animate. The target property of a MatrixAnimationUsingPath timeline will most commonly be the Matrix property of a System.Windows.Media.MatrixTransform, where the MatrixTransform is used in the render transform or layout transform of the control you want to animate. In a similar fashion, DoubleAnimationUsingPath can be used to animate the properties of a System.Windows.Media. TranslateTransform and System.Windows.Media.RotateTransform or any just about any System.Double property of the target control.

The Code

The following XAML demonstrates how to use a MatrixAnimationUsingPath, where a System.Windows.Controls.Border is translated and rotated, according to the shape of the path. The path is also drawn on the screen to better visualize the motion of the Border (see Figure 11-5).

```
<Window
  x:Class="Recipe_11_12.Window1"
  xmlns="http://schemas.microsoft.com/winfx/2006/xaml/presentation"
  xmlns:x="http://schemas.microsoft.com/winfx/2006/xaml"
  Title="Recipe_11_12"
  Height="300"
  Width="550">
```

```xml
<Window.Resources>
  <PathGeometry
    x:Key="AnimationPathGeometry"
    Figures="M 50,150 C 100,-200 500,400 450,100 400,-100 285,400 50,150" />

  <Storyboard x:Key="MatrixAnimationStoryboard">
    <MatrixAnimationUsingPath
      RepeatBehavior="Forever"
      Duration="0:0:5"
      AutoReverse="True"
      Storyboard.TargetName="BorderMatrixTransform"
      Storyboard.TargetProperty="Matrix"
      DoesRotateWithTangent="True"
      PathGeometry="{StaticResource AnimationPathGeometry}" />
  </Storyboard>
</Window.Resources>
<Grid>
  <Path
    Stroke="Black"
    StrokeThickness="1"
    Data="{StaticResource AnimationPathGeometry}" />

  <Border
    HorizontalAlignment="Left"
    VerticalAlignment="Top"
    Width="100"
    Height="50"
    CornerRadius="5"
    BorderBrush="Black"
    BorderThickness="1"
    RenderTransformOrigin="0,0">
    <Border.Background>
      <LinearGradientBrush
        StartPoint="0.5,0"
        EndPoint="0.5,1">
        <GradientStop
          Color="CadetBlue"
          Offset="0" />
        <GradientStop
          Color="CornflowerBlue"
          Offset="1" />
      </LinearGradientBrush>
    </Border.Background>
    <Border.RenderTransform>
      <MatrixTransform
        x:Name="BorderMatrixTransform" />
    </Border.RenderTransform>
```

```
        <Border.Triggers>
          <EventTrigger
            RoutedEvent="Border.Loaded">
            <BeginStoryboard
              Storyboard="{StaticResource MatrixAnimationStoryboard}" />
          </EventTrigger>
        </Border.Triggers>
        <TextBlock
          Text="^ This way up ^"
          HorizontalAlignment="Center"
          VerticalAlignment="Center" />
      </Border>
    </Grid>
</Window>
```

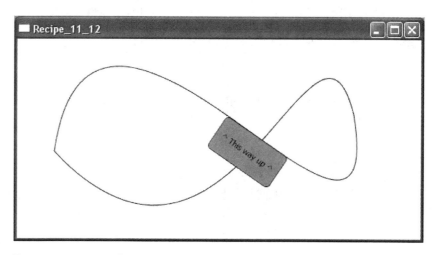

Figure 11-5. *A control midway through a path animation. Notice how the control is oriented such that it follows a tangent to the gradient of the curve.*

11-13. Play Back Audio or Video with a MediaTimeline

Problem

You need to play a media file, such as a WMV video file or WAV audio file, in your application.

Solution

Use a System.Windows.Media.MediaTimeline to provide the playback of animated media objects through a System.Windows.Controls.MediaElement control, such as audio and video files.

How It Works

The MediaElement control on its own can be used to display static content, but when driven by a MediaTimeline, it is able to provide the playback of media files. The MediaTimeline class inherits from System.Windows.Media.Animation.Timeline and as such can be configured using the properties listed in recipe 11-1. The MediaTimeline is given the location of a media file as its Source property and, when activated, will play the media file through the MediaElement it is targeting. Because the MediaTimeline is a Timeline object, it can be controlled by the several System.Windows.Media.Animation.ControllableStoryboardAction objects, allowing the media to be paused, resumed, stopped, skipped through, and so on. This allows you to create a rich media player very easily and all in XAML. For more information on using the MediaElement control, see http://msdn.microsoft.com/en-us/library/system.windows.controls.mediaelement.aspx.

By default, the Duration property of a MediaTimeline will be set to the duration of the media it is playing, also accessible through the MediaElement.NaturalDuration property, which returns a System.TimeSpan. Combine this with the MediaElement.Position property, also a TimeSpan, and you instantly have the ability to display the progress of a media file as it plays through, something that is commonplace in media playback.

The Code

The following XAML demonstrates how to use a MediaTimeline to drive the playback of a video file through a MediaElement (see Figure 11-6).

```xml
<Window
  x:Class="Recipe_11_13.Window1"
  xmlns="http://schemas.microsoft.com/winfx/2006/xaml/presentation"
  xmlns:x="http://schemas.microsoft.com/winfx/2006/xaml"
  Title="Recipe_11_13"
  Height="300"
  Width="300">
  <Viewbox>
    <MediaElement
      x:Name="mePlayer"
      Stretch="Fill">
      <MediaElement.Triggers>
        <EventTrigger
          RoutedEvent="MediaElement.Loaded">
          <BeginStoryboard>
            <Storyboard>
              <MediaTimeline
                Storyboard.TargetName="mePlayer"
                Source="clock.avi"
                RepeatBehavior="Forever" />
            </Storyboard>
          </BeginStoryboard>
        </EventTrigger>
      </MediaElement.Triggers>
```

```
        </MediaElement>
      </Viewbox>
</Window>
```

Figure 11-6. *A video file (with sound), eight seconds into its playback*

11-14. Synchronize Timeline Animations with a MediaTimeline

Problem

You need to ensure that any System.Windows.Media.Animation.Timeline animations remain synchronized with a System.Windows.Media.MediaTimeline defined in the same System.Windows.Media.Animation.Storyboard.

Solution

Set the SlipBehavior property of the parent System.Windows.Media.Animation.ParallelTimeline object to SlipBehavior.Slip.

How It Works

Often when playing back rich content such as audio or video, loading times or workload on the host machine can affect the smoothness of the media. If other Timeline animations are running alongside the media, they can get out of sync if the media's playback is disrupted. For example, if you have a Timeline animation that is the same length as a video file played using a MediaTimeline and the start of the MediaTimeline is delayed by a second because of loading or buffering, the

`Timeline` animation will have played for one second before the `MediaTimeline` starts to play the video. This will give the appearance that the `Timeline` has started early or finished too early.

The `ParallelTimeline.SlipBehavior` property defines how loss of synchronization between `MediaTimeline` and `Timeline` objects should be handled. The default value is `SlipBehavior.Grow` and displays the behavior described earlier. Any `Timeline` animations running alongside a `MediaTimeline` can start or finish at different times to the `MediaTimeline`. To combat this, the other value of the `SlipBehavior` enumeration, `SlipBehavior.Slip`, should be used.

When a `Timeline` slips, it effectively waits for any `MediaTimeline` objects to start/resume playback if hindered in any way. So if a `MediaTimeline` takes two seconds to load, any `Timeline` animations running in parallel to the `MediaTimeline` will not be activated until after two seconds, when the `MediaTimeline` is ready to continue. If during the playback of some media the `MediaTimeline` halts while the media is buffered, any `Timeline` animations running in parallel to the `MediaTimeline` will also halt and wait for the `MediaTimeline` to begin again.

The Code

The following XAML demonstrates how to use the `SlipBehavior.Slip` value. A video file is played back using a `MediaTimeline`, with two animations running alongside it. One of the animations is synchronized; the other is not. The red `System.Windows.Shapes.Ellipse` is not synchronized and uses the default `SlipBehavior.Grow` value, whereas the green `Ellipse` does slip. You should observe that the green `Ellipse` pauses briefly while the video is loaded, but the red `Ellipse` starts straightaway (see Figure 11-7).

```
<Window
  x:Class="Recipe_11_14.Window1"
  xmlns="http://schemas.microsoft.com/winfx/2006/xaml/presentation"
  xmlns:x="http://schemas.microsoft.com/winfx/2006/xaml"
  Title="Recipe_11_14"
  Height="320"
  Width="450">
  <Window.Resources>
    <PathGeometry
      x:Key="AnimationSyncPathGeometry"
      Figures="M 30,260 L 400,260" />

    <PathGeometry
      x:Key="AnimationNonSyncPathGeometry"
      Figures="M 30,230 L 400,230" />
  </Window.Resources>

  <Window.Triggers>
    <EventTrigger RoutedEvent="Window.Loaded">
      <BeginStoryboard>
        <Storyboard SlipBehavior="Slip">
          <MediaTimeline
            Storyboard.TargetName="mePlayer1"
            Source="clock.avi"
            RepeatBehavior="Forever" />
```

```xml
          <MatrixAnimationUsingPath
            RepeatBehavior="Forever"
            Duration="0:0:12"
            Storyboard.TargetName="SyncEllipseMatrixTransform"
            Storyboard.TargetProperty="Matrix"
            DoesRotateWithTangent="True"
            PathGeometry="{StaticResource AnimationSyncPathGeometry}" />
        </Storyboard>
      </BeginStoryboard>

      <BeginStoryboard>
        <Storyboard SlipBehavior="Grow">
          <MediaTimeline
            Storyboard.TargetName="mePlayer2"
            Source="clock.avi"
            RepeatBehavior="Forever" />

          <MatrixAnimationUsingPath
            RepeatBehavior="Forever"
            Duration="0:0:12"
            Storyboard.TargetName="NonSyncEllipseMatrixTransform"
            Storyboard.TargetProperty="Matrix"
            PathGeometry="{StaticResource AnimationNonSyncPathGeometry}" />
        </Storyboard>
      </BeginStoryboard>
    </EventTrigger>
</Window.Triggers>
<Grid>
  <Grid>
    <Grid.ColumnDefinitions>
      <ColumnDefinition Width="0.5*" />
      <ColumnDefinition Width="0.5*" />
    </Grid.ColumnDefinitions>

    <MediaElement
      Margin="10"
      Width="200"
      Height="200"
      x:Name="mePlayer1"
      Stretch="Fill"
      HorizontalAlignment="Center"
      VerticalAlignment="Top" />

    <MediaElement
      Margin="10"
      Width="200"
      Height="200"
      x:Name="mePlayer2"
```

```
        Stretch="Fill"
        HorizontalAlignment="Center"
        VerticalAlignment="Top"
        Grid.Column="1" />
    </Grid>

    <Path
      Stroke="Black"
      StrokeThickness="1"
      Data="{StaticResource AnimationSyncPathGeometry}"
      Grid.ColumnSpan="2" />

    <Path
      Stroke="Black"
      StrokeThickness="1"
      Data="{StaticResource AnimationNonSyncPathGeometry}"
      Grid.ColumnSpan="2" />

    <Ellipse
      Width="20"
      Height="20"
      Fill="ForestGreen"
      x:Name="syncElipse"
      HorizontalAlignment="Left"
      VerticalAlignment="Top">
      <Ellipse.RenderTransform>
        <MatrixTransform
          x:Name="SyncEllipseMatrixTransform" />
      </Ellipse.RenderTransform>
    </Ellipse>

    <Ellipse
      Width="20"
      Height="20"
      Fill="Firebrick"
      x:Name="nosyncElipse"
      HorizontalAlignment="Left"
      VerticalAlignment="Top">
      <Ellipse.RenderTransform>
        <MatrixTransform
          x:Name="NonSyncEllipseMatrixTransform" />
      </Ellipse.RenderTransform>
    </Ellipse>
  </Grid>

</Window>
```

Figure 11-7. *Two media files are being played back in separate storyboards. The green Ellipse is an animation that runs alongside the left video. It is slightly behind the red Ellipse because it slipped while the video was being loaded, whereas the red Ellipse started its animation immediately. The actual observed behavior will depend on the performance and workload of your machine.*

11-15. Receive Notification When an Animation Completes

Problem

You need to execute custom code when a System.Windows.Media.Animation.Storyboard completes, that is, all the child System.Windows.Media.Animation.Timeline objects have completed.

Solution

Register an event handler against the Timeline.Completed event, performing any custom tasks such as cleaning up composited Timeline objects (see recipe 11-3).

How It Works

The Timeline class defines a Completed System.EventHandler, which is raised when the Timeline finishes. Generally, this is when the timeline's Duration has elapsed. By adding an event handler to the event, the handler will be invoked when the Timeline completes. Because any Timeline object can notify listeners of its completion, the behavior may not be quite as expected.

When several `Timeline` objects are declared as children of a single `Storyboard` or `System.Windows.Media.Animation.ParallelTimeline`, no `Timeline.Completed` events will be raised until every `Timeline` in the parent `System.Windows.Media.Animation.TimelineGroup` have completed. So if you have a `Storyboard` with several `Timeline` children, each of which has a duration of one second and a single `Timeline` with a duration of ten seconds, the `Completed` event will not be raised on the `Storyboard` or its children until the final ten-second `Timeline` has completed. When the last animation has finished, the `Completed` events will be raised in a depth-first fashion, starting with the root `Timeline` object, in this case, the `Storyboard`.

It should be obvious that if a `Timeline` object is given a `System.Windows.Media.Animation.RepeatBehavior` of `Forever`, no completed events on any of the child objects of a `TimelineGroup`, or the `TimelineGroup` object itself, will be raised.

The Code

The following code example demonstrates the behavior of completion events. The markup file contains a few simple controls, each of which has an animation applied to it. Each animation supplies a `System.EventHandler` that displays a simple message when the animation finishes.

```
<Window
  x:Class="Recipe_11_15.Window1"
  xmlns="http://schemas.microsoft.com/winfx/2006/xaml/presentation"
  xmlns:x="http://schemas.microsoft.com/winfx/2006/xaml"
  Title="Recipe_11_15"
  Height="300"
  Width="300"
  Background="Black">
  <Window.Triggers>
    <EventTrigger
      RoutedEvent="Window.Loaded">
      <BeginStoryboard>
        <Storyboard
          Completed="Storyboard_Completed">
          <ParallelTimeline
            Completed="ParallelTimeline_Completed">
            <ColorAnimation
              Duration="0:0:1"
              Completed="Animation1_Completed"
              Storyboard.TargetProperty="Background.Color"
              To="White" />
            <ColorAnimation
              Duration="0:0:2"
              Completed="Animation2_Completed"
              Storyboard.TargetName="bd"
              Storyboard.TargetProperty="Background.(SolidColorBrush.Color)"
              To="Black" />
          </ParallelTimeline>
          <ColorAnimation
            Duration="0:0:3"
```

```
              Completed="Animation3_Completed"
              Storyboard.TargetName="rect"
              Storyboard.TargetProperty="(Shape.Fill).(SolidColorBrush.Color)"
              To="Firebrick" />
        </Storyboard>
      </BeginStoryboard>
    </EventTrigger>
  </Window.Triggers>

  <Border
    x:Name="bd"
    Margin="20"
    Background="HotPink">
    <Rectangle
      x:Name="rect"
      Width="100"
      Height="100"
      Fill="WhiteSmoke" />
  </Border>
</Window>
```

The following code details the content of the previous markup's code-behind file. The code defines several event handlers for various Completed events, defined in the markup.

```
using System;
using System.Windows;

namespace Recipe_11_15
{
    /// <summary>
    /// Interaction logic for Window1.xaml
    /// </summary>
    public partial class Window1 : Window
    {
        public Window1()
        {
            InitializeComponent();
        }

        private void Storyboard_Completed(object sender, EventArgs e)
        {
            MessageBox.Show("Storyboard complete.", "Recipe_11_15");
        }

        private void ParallelTimeline_Completed(object sender, EventArgs e)
        {
            MessageBox.Show("ParallelTimeline complete.", "Recipe_11_15");
        }
```

```csharp
        private void Animation1_Completed(object sender, EventArgs e)
        {
            MessageBox.Show("Animation 1 complete.", "Recipe_11_15");
        }

        private void Animation2_Completed(object sender, EventArgs e)
        {
            MessageBox.Show("Animation 2 complete.", "Recipe_11_15");
        }

        private void Animation3_Completed(object sender, EventArgs e)
        {
            MessageBox.Show("Animation 3 complete.", "Recipe_11_15");
        }
    }
}
```

11-16. Animate the Color of a Brush with Indirect Property Targeting

Problem

You need to animate some color property of a control. The target property may be of type System.Windows.Media.Color or be exposed as the abstract type System.Windows.Media.Brush.

Solution

Use a System.Windows.Media.Animation.ColorAnimation to animate the color of the target property. If the target property is a Brush type, you will need to use an indirect property path to access the brush's color property.

How It Works

The ColorAnimation is no different from its siblings, other than it targets a property of type Color. It allows you to animate a color to a given value from either a specified value or the current value of the property. Animating a color property of a control such as System.Windows. Shapes.Rectangle.Fill, which is of type Color, is a trivial exercise and like any other animation. Animating the color of a System.Windows.Media.SolidColorBrush, or the value of a System. Windows.Media.GradientStop in a System.Windows.Media.LinearGradientBrush, is also trivial because they all expose a Color dependency property.

Should you want to animate the color of a property that is exposed as a Brush, you do not have a Color property against which you can apply the animation. For example, if you attempted to use a ColorAnimation to animate a System.Windows.Controls.Border.Background property using Background.Color as the target property of the animation, you will see a System.InvalidOperationException thrown when the app is started. The exception will inform you that it cannot resolve the given property path. The trick here is to use a combination of indirect property targeting and partial path qualification, specifying that the property you are accessing belongs to a SolidColorBrush (if the background is actually set to a SolidColorBrush). If the background is null, an exception will be thrown; if the property is set to a different implementation of Brush, the animation will have no effect.

Indirect property targeting and partial path qualification are features of the System.Windows. PropertyPath object (for more information on the PropertyPath object, refer to http:// msdn.microsoft.com/en-us/library/ms742451.aspx). Indirect property targeting basically allows you to specify the value for a property of a property, as long as all subproperties used in the path are dependency properties. The properties must also be either primitive types (for example, System.Double, System.Int, and so on) or System.Windows.Freezable types. In the example of targeting the background of a Border control, the indirect property path would be Background.Color. This alone, though, is not enough; as stated earlier, attempting to use this path will result in an exception. This is where partial path qualification comes in.

Partial path qualification enables you to define a target property that doesn't have a specified target type; that is, it is defined in a style or template. For example, the value of a Border.Background property could be any of the available brush types, and it is not known until the property is set which type is being used. Paths that are intended to be used in this manner are indicated by wrapping them in parentheses. This can be an entire path or subsections of a path. In the example of targeting the background property of a Border control, you would need to use the path Background.(SolidColorBrush.Color) to target the background's color.

To take this a step further, if the properties used in the path are defined on some base object, you are able to use the name of the base class in the path. An example of this is when dealing with the System.Windows.Shapes.Rectangle.Fill property. The Fill dependency property is defined in the abstract class System.Windows.Shapes.Shape. So, should you have an animation that targets the Fill property of any given shapes, the property path can be defined as (Shape.Fill).(SolidColorBrush.Color). Pretty neat!

The Code

The following example demonstrates three different ways of targeting a property for animation. The examples use a combination of partial path qualification and indirect property targeting to access the target properties.

```xml
<Window
  x:Class="Recipe_11_16.Window1"
  xmlns="http://schemas.microsoft.com/winfx/2006/xaml/presentation"
  xmlns:x="http://schemas.microsoft.com/winfx/2006/xaml"
  Title="Recipe_11_16"
  Height="300"
  Width="300"
  Background="Black">
  <Window.Triggers>
    <EventTrigger
      RoutedEvent="Window.Loaded">
      <BeginStoryboard>
        <Storyboard
          AutoReverse="True"
          RepeatBehavior="Forever">
```

```
            <ColorAnimation
              Storyboard.TargetProperty="Background.Color"
              To="White" />
            <ColorAnimation
              Storyboard.TargetName="bd"
              Storyboard.TargetProperty="Background.(SolidColorBrush.Color)"
              To="Black" />
            <ColorAnimation
              Storyboard.TargetName="rect"
              Storyboard.TargetProperty="(Shape.Fill).(SolidColorBrush.Color)"
              To="Firebrick" />
          </Storyboard>
        </BeginStoryboard>
      </EventTrigger>
    </Window.Triggers>
    <Border
      x:Name="bd"
      Margin="20"
      Background="HotPink">
      <Rectangle
        x:Name="rect"
        Width="100"
        Height="100"
        Fill="WhiteSmoke" />
    </Border>
  </Window>
```

11-17. Control Animations Through Triggers

Problem

You need to pause/resume, stop, skip forward, or skip backward in an animation once it has begun.

Solution

Use a derived class of the abstract System.Windows.Media.Animation.ControllableStoryboardAction class to control a running animation through triggers.

How It Works

When working with animations in XAML, they are usually started through some trigger such as a control being loaded, the user running the mouse over a control, or the user clicking something in your app and invoking a System.Windows.BeginStoryboard. WPF allows you to further

CHAPTER 11 ▨ CREATING ANIMATION647

control animations in a similar fashion through the use of a set of classes that derive from ControllableStoryboardAction. Table 11-8 lists the actions that are available and how they affect an animation, all of which can be found in the System.Windows.Media.Animation namespace.

Table 11-8. *Implementations of ControllableStoryboardAction*

Type	Description
PauseStoryboard	Halts an animation at its current position, leaving animated properties in their current state. A subsequent call to a BeginStoryboard will result in the animation's clocks being replaced with new clocks and the animation restarting.
RemoveStoryboard	Removes a Storyboard, halting any child Timeline objects and freeing up any resources they may be using. See recipe 11-3 for more information on removing storyboards.
ResumeStoryboard	Resumes a paused animation, continuing the animation from the position at which it was paused. Applying this action to a storyboard that has not been paused will have no effect.
SeekStoryboard	Seeks, or moves, the target storyboard to an offset specified in the Offset property. It is important to note that seeking in a storyboard ignores a SpeedRatio value, treating the property as having a value of 1 and no SlipBehavior. For example, if a Storyboard has a Duration of two seconds and a SpeedRatio of two, an Offset of one second will seek to the midpoint of the animation. The Origin property is set to a value of the System.Windows.Media.Animation.TimeSeekOrigin enumeration, indicating whether the supplied offset is relative to the start or end of the target Storyboard.
SetStoryboardSpeedRatio	Allows you to alter the playback speed of an animation by setting the value of the SpeedRatio property to some System.Double value. A speed ratio of 0.25 will slow the animation down such that it runs at a quarter of its normal speed. A value of 2 will double the speed of the animation, and a speed ratio of 1 means the animation will play back at normal speed. Note that this will affect the actual duration of an animation.
SkipStoryboardToFill	Advances a Storyboard and all child Timeline objects to its fill period, if set (see recipe 11-1 for more information).
StopStoryboard	Stops and resets a Storyboard. When a Storyboard is stopped in this fashion, the Completed event does not get raised, although both the CurrentGlobalSpeedInvalidated and CurrentStateInvalidated events are raised.

Each of these actions is relevant only to animations that were started using a named BeginStoryboard object. The actions all have a BeginStoryboardName property, defined in ControllableStoryboardAction, which is used to specify the name of the BeginStoryboard that was used to start the target Storyboard. Applying any of the previous actions to a Storyboard that isn't active will have no effect.

The Code

The following example demonstrates how to use the storyboard actions that derive from
ControllableStoryboardAction. There are three shapes displayed in the window, each of which
is animated in a different way by a single Storyboard. Beneath the controls are several buttons,
each of which performs a different action on the storyboard when clicked.

```xml
<Window
  x:Class="Recipe_11_17.Window1"
  xmlns="http://schemas.microsoft.com/winfx/2006/xaml/presentation"
  xmlns:x="http://schemas.microsoft.com/winfx/2006/xaml"
  Title="Recipe_11_17"
  Height="350"
  Width="400">
  <Window.Resources>
    <Storyboard
      x:Key="Storyboard"
      RepeatBehavior="10x">
      <DoubleAnimation
        Storyboard.TargetName="rect1"
        Storyboard.TargetProperty="Width"
        To="250"
        FillBehavior="HoldEnd"
        AutoReverse="False" />
      <DoubleAnimation
        Storyboard.TargetName="rect2"
        Storyboard.TargetProperty="Width"
        To="250"
        AutoReverse="True" />
      <ColorAnimation
        Storyboard.TargetName="ellipse1"
        Storyboard.TargetProperty="Fill.(SolidColorBrush.Color)"
        To="Orange"
        AutoReverse="True" />
    </Storyboard>
  </Window.Resources>

  <Window.Triggers>
    <EventTrigger
      RoutedEvent="Button.Click"
      SourceName="btnBegin">
      <BeginStoryboard
        x:Name="beginStoryboard"
        Storyboard="{StaticResource Storyboard}" />
    </EventTrigger>

    <EventTrigger
      RoutedEvent="Button.Click"
```

```
    SourceName="btnPause">
    <PauseStoryboard
      BeginStoryboardName="beginStoryboard" />
  </EventTrigger>

  <EventTrigger
    RoutedEvent="Button.Click"
    SourceName="btnResume">
    <ResumeStoryboard
      BeginStoryboardName="beginStoryboard" />
  </EventTrigger>

  <FventTrigger
    RoutedEvent="Button.Click"
    SourceName="btnStop">
    <StopStoryboard
      BeginStoryboardName="beginStoryboard" />
  </EventTrigger>

  <EventTrigger
    RoutedEvent="Button.Click"
    SourceName="btnSeek">
    <SeekStoryboard
      BeginStoryboardName="beginStoryboard"
      Offset="0:0:5"
      Origin="BeginTime" />
  </EventTrigger>

  <EventTrigger
    RoutedEvent="Button.Click"
    SourceName="btnSkipToFill">
    <SkipStoryboardToFill
      BeginStoryboardName="beginStoryboard" />
  </EventTrigger>

  <EventTrigger
    RoutedEvent="Button.Click"
    SourceName="btnDoubleSpeed">
    <SetStoryboardSpeedRatio
      BeginStoryboardName="beginStoryboard"
      SpeedRatio="2" />
  </EventTrigger>

  <EventTrigger
    RoutedEvent="Button.Click"
    SourceName="btnHalfSpeed">
    <SetStoryboardSpeedRatio
```

```
            BeginStoryboardName="beginStoryboard"
            SpeedRatio="0.5" />
      </EventTrigger>

  </Window.Triggers>
  <Grid>
    <StackPanel>
      <Rectangle
        x:Name="rect1"
        Width="50"
        Height="100"
        Stroke="Black"
        Fill="CornflowerBlue"
        Margin="5" />

      <Ellipse
        x:Name="ellipse1"
        Width="50"
        Height="50"
        Stroke="Black"
        Fill="Firebrick"
        StrokeThickness="1"
        Margin="5" />

      <Rectangle
        x:Name="rect2"
        Width="50"
        Height="100"
        Stroke="Black"
        Fill="CornflowerBlue"
        Margin="5" />

      <StackPanel Orientation="Horizontal">
        <Button x:Name="btnBegin" Content="Begin" />
        <Button x:Name="btnPause" Content="Pause" />
        <Button x:Name="btnResume" Content="Resume" />
        <Button x:Name="btnStop" Content="Stop" />
        <Button x:Name="btnSeek" Content="Seek" />
        <Button x:Name="btnSkipToFill" Content="Skip To Fill" />
        <Button x:Name="btnDoubleSpeed" Content="Double Speed" />
        <Button x:Name="btnHalfSpeed" Content="Half Speed" />
      </StackPanel>
    </StackPanel>
  </Grid>
</Window>
```

11-18. Animate Text

Problem

You need to animate a string of characters.

Solution

Use a `System.Windows.Media.Animation.StringAnimationUsingKeyFrames` supplying the text to appear in each of the keyframes.

How It Works

The `StringAnimationUsingKeyFrames` timeline allows you to specify a series of `System.Windows.Media.Animation.StringKeyFrame` keyframes. Each keyframe defines the characters that appear at that point in time. The only built-in implementation of the abstract `StringKeyFrame` class is a `System.Windows.Media.Animation.DiscreteStringKeyFrame`, meaning you cannot create a smooth blend between two characters; they will simply appear.

This animation is useful for simulating characters being typed on a screen or an animated type banner (see Figure 11-8).

The Code

The following XAML demonstrates how to use an animation that uses `DiscreteStringKeyFrame` objects to animate the `Text` property of a `System.Windows.Controls.TextBlock` control.

```xml
<Window
  x:Class="Recipe_11_18.Window1"
  xmlns="http://schemas.microsoft.com/winfx/2006/xaml/presentation"
  xmlns:x="http://schemas.microsoft.com/winfx/2006/xaml"
  Title="Recipe_11_18"
  Height="130"
  Width="200">
  <Window.Resources>
    <Storyboard
      x:Key="StringAnimationStoryboard">
      <StringAnimationUsingKeyFrames
        AutoReverse="True"
        Storyboard.TargetName="MyTextBox"
        Storyboard.TargetProperty="Text">
        <DiscreteStringKeyFrame Value="" KeyTime="0:0:0" />
        <DiscreteStringKeyFrame Value="H" KeyTime="0:0:0.5" />
        <DiscreteStringKeyFrame Value="He" KeyTime="0:0:1" />
        <DiscreteStringKeyFrame Value="Hel" KeyTime="0:0:1.5" />
        <DiscreteStringKeyFrame Value="Hell" KeyTime="0:0:2" />
        <DiscreteStringKeyFrame Value="Hello" KeyTime="0:0:2.5" />
        <DiscreteStringKeyFrame Value="Hello T" KeyTime="0:0:3" />
        <DiscreteStringKeyFrame Value="Hello Th" KeyTime="0:0:3.5" />
```

```xml
          <DiscreteStringKeyFrame Value="Hello Tha" KeyTime="0:0:4" />
          <DiscreteStringKeyFrame Value="Hello Thar" KeyTime="0:0:4.5" />
          <DiscreteStringKeyFrame Value="Hello Thar!" KeyTime="0:0:5" />
          <DiscreteStringKeyFrame Value="Hello Thar!" KeyTime="0:0:5.5" />
        </StringAnimationUsingKeyFrames>
      </Storyboard>
    </Window.Resources>
    <DockPanel>
      <TextBlock
        x:Name="MyTextBox"
        DockPanel.Dock="Top"
        FontSize="30"
        Margin="5" HorizontalAlignment="Center" />
      <Button
        Content="Start Animation"
        Width="100"
        Height="20">
        <Button.Triggers>
          <EventTrigger
            RoutedEvent="Button.Click">
            <BeginStoryboard
              Storyboard="{DynamicResource StringAnimationStoryboard}" />
          </EventTrigger>
        </Button.Triggers>
      </Button>
    </DockPanel>
  </Window>
```

Figure 11-8. *The result of the text animation*

CHAPTER 12

Dealing with Multimedia and User Input

Being a technology for developing rich user interfaces, it makes sense that WPF should provide good support for integrating video and audio into your applications and for getting input from the user. This chapter takes a look at some of the video, audio, and user input capabilities provided by WPF.

As with so many things, WPF makes it relatively easy to add strong multimedia and user input support to your applications. The recipes in this chapter describe how to:

- Play standard Windows system sounds (recipe 12-1)

- Play sounds when users interact with controls (recipe 12-2)

- Play and control the playback characteristics of media files (recipes 12-3)

- Respond when the user clicks controls with the mouse (recipes 12-4 and 12-5)

- Respond when the user moves the mouse wheel (recipe 12-6)

- Handle drag and drop operations between controls (recipe 12-7)

- Handle keyboard events (recipe 12-8)

- Query the state of the keyboard (recipe 12-9)

- Suppress mouse and keyboard events (recipe 12-10)

12-1. Play System Sounds

Problem

You need to play one of the standard Windows system sounds.

Solution

Use the static properties of the System.Media.SystemSounds class to obtain a System.Media. SystemSound object representing the sound you want to play. Then call the Play method on the SystemSound object.

How It Works

The SystemSounds class provides a simple way of playing some of the most commonly used standard Windows system sounds. The SystemSounds class implements five static properties: Asterisk, Beep, Exclamation, Hand, and Question. Each of these properties returns a SystemSound object representing a particular sound. Once you have the appropriate SystemSound object, simply call its Play method to play the sound.

The sound played by each SystemSound object depends on the user's Windows configuration on the Sounds tab of the Sounds and Audio Devices control panel. If the user has no sound associated with the specific type of event, calling Play on the related SystemSound object will make no sound. You have no control over any aspect of the sound playback such as volume or duration.

The Code

The following XAML displays five buttons (see Figure 12-1). Each button is configured to play a different SystemSound using the SystemSounds class in the code-behind:

```xaml
<Window x:Class="Recipe_12_01.Window1"
    xmlns="http://schemas.microsoft.com/winfx/2006/xaml/presentation"
    xmlns:x="http://schemas.microsoft.com/winfx/2006/xaml"
    Title="WPF Recipes 12_01" Height="120" Width="300">
    <Canvas>
        <Canvas.Resources>
            <!-- Style all buttons the same -->
            <Style TargetType="{x:Type Button}">
                <Setter Property="Height" Value="25" />
                <Setter Property="MinWidth" Value="70" />
                <EventSetter Event="Click" Handler="Button_Click" />
            </Style>
        </Canvas.Resources>
        <Button Canvas.Top="15" Canvas.Left="30"
            Content="Asterisk" Name="btnAsterisk" />
        <Button Canvas.Top="15" Canvas.Left="110"
            Content="Beep" Name="btnBeep" />
        <Button Canvas.Top="15" Canvas.Left="190"
            Content="Exclamation" Name="btnExclamation" />
        <Button Canvas.Top="50" Canvas.Left="70"
            Content="Hand" Name="btnHand" />
        <Button Canvas.Top="50" Canvas.Left="150"
            Content="Question" Name="btnQuestion" />
    </Canvas>
</Window>
```

The following code-behind determines which button the user has clicked and plays the appropriate sound:

```
using System.Windows;
using System.Windows.Controls;

namespace Recipe_12_01
{
    /// <summary>
    /// Interaction logic for Window1.xaml
    /// </summary>
    public partial class Window1 : Window
    {
        public Window1()
        {
            InitializeComponent();
        }

        // Handles the click events for all system sound buttons.
        private void Button_Click(object sender, RoutedEventArgs e)
        {
            Button btn = sender as Button;

            if (btn != null)
            {
                // Simple switch on the name of the button.
                switch (btn.Content.ToString())
                {
                    case "Asterisk":
                        System.Media.SystemSounds.Asterisk.Play();
                        break;
                    case "Beep":
                        System.Media.SystemSounds.Beep.Play();
                        break;
                    case "Exclamation":
                        System.Media.SystemSounds.Exclamation.Play();
                        break;
                    case "Hand":
                        System.Media.SystemSounds.Hand.Play();
                        break;
                    case "Question":
                        System.Media.SystemSounds.Question.Play();
                        break;
```

```
                    default:
                        string msg = "Sound not implemented: " + btn.Content;
                        MessageBox.Show(msg);
                        break;
                }
            }
        }
    }
}
```

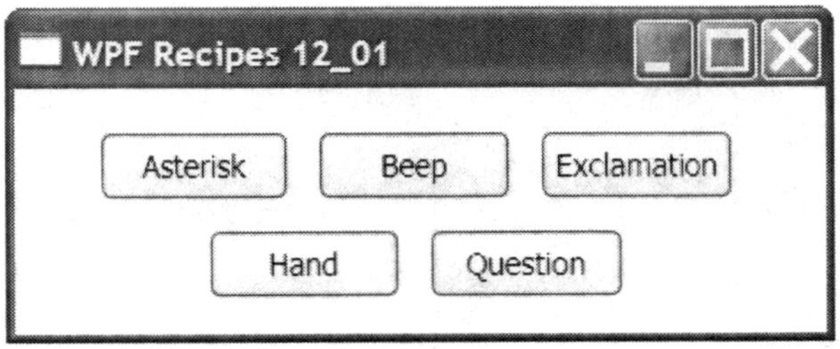

Figure 12-1. *A set of buttons playing system sounds*

12-2. Use Triggers to Play Audio When a User Interacts with a Control

Problem

You need to play a sound when the user interacts with a control, such as clicking a button or moving a slider.

Solution

Declare a System.Windows.Controls.MediaElement on your form. Configure an EventTrigger on the control, and use a StoryBoard containing a System.Windows.Media.MediaTimeline to play the desired audio through the MediaElement in response to the appropriate event.

How It Works

An EventTrigger hooks the event specified in its RoutedEvent property. When the event fires, the EventTrigger applies the animation specified in its Actions property. As the action, you can configure the animation to play a media file using a MediaTimeline.

You can define an EventTrigger directly on a control by declaring it in the Triggers collection of the control. In the RoutedEvent property of the EventTrigger, specify the name of the event you want to trigger the sound, for example, Button.Click. Within the Actions element of the Triggers collection, declare a BeginStoryboard element containing a Storyboard element. In the Storyboard element, you declare the MediaTimeline.

You specify the media file to play using the Source property of the MediaTimeline and the MediaElement that will actually do the playback in the Storyboard.TargetName property. When the user interacts with the control, the specified sound will play back asynchronously.

Note Chapter 6 provides more details on the use of triggers, and Chapter 11 provides extensive coverage of animation in WPF.

The Code

The following XAML demonstrates how to assign an EventTrigger to the Click event of a System.Windows.Controls.Button and the ValueChanged event of a System.Windows.Controls.Slider. Figure 12-2 shows the example running.

```
<Window x:Class="Recipe_12_02.Window1"
    xmlns="http://schemas.microsoft.com/winfx/2006/xaml/presentation"
    xmlns:x="http://schemas.microsoft.com/winfx/2006/xaml"
    Title="WPF Recipes 12_02" Height="100" Width="300">
    <StackPanel>
        <!-- MediaElement for sond playback. -->
        <MediaElement Name="meMediaElem" />
        <!-- The Button that goes Ding! -->
        <UniformGrid Height="70" Columns="2">
            <Button Content="Ding" MaxHeight="25" MaxWidth="70">
                <Button.Triggers>
                    <EventTrigger RoutedEvent="Button.Click">
                        <EventTrigger.Actions>
                            <BeginStoryboard>
                                <Storyboard>
                                    <MediaTimeline
                                        Source="ding.wav"
                                        Storyboard.TargetName="meMediaElem"/>
                                </Storyboard>
                            </BeginStoryboard>
                        </EventTrigger.Actions>
                    </EventTrigger>
                </Button.Triggers>
            </Button>
            <!-- The Slider that goes Ring! -->
            <Slider MaxHeight="25" MaxWidth="100" >
                <Slider.Triggers>
                    <EventTrigger RoutedEvent="Slider.ValueChanged">
                        <EventTrigger.Actions>
                            <BeginStoryboard>
                                <Storyboard>
                                    <MediaTimeline
```

```
                                    Source="ringin.wav"
                                    Storyboard.TargetName="meMediaElem" />
                            </Storyboard>
                        </BeginStoryboard>
                    </EventTrigger.Actions>
                </EventTrigger>
            </Slider.Triggers>
        </Slider>
      </UniformGrid>
    </StackPanel>
</Window>
```

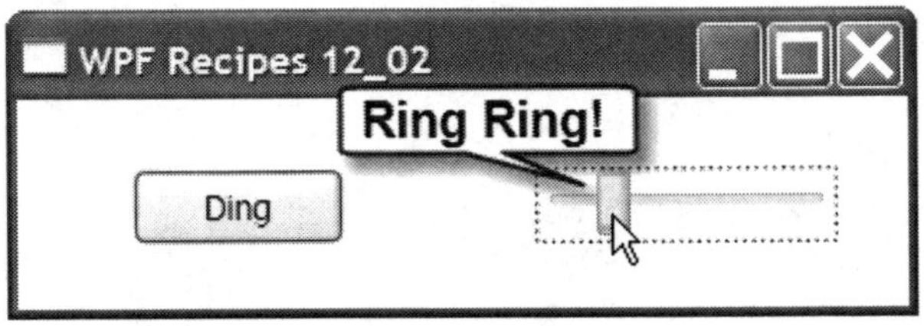

Figure 12-2. *Playing sound using triggers*

12-3. Play a Media File

Problem

You need to play a sound or music file and allow the user to control the progress of the play-back, volume, or balance.

Solution

Use a System.Windows.Controls.MediaElement to handle the playback of the media file. Use a System.Windows.Media.MediaTimeline to control the playback of the desired media through the MediaElement. Declare the set of controls that will enable the user to control the playback and associate triggers with these controls that start, stop, pause, and resume the animation controlling the MediaTimeline. For volume and balance, data bind controls to the Volume and Balance properties of the MediaElement.

How It Works

A MediaElement performs the playback of a media file, and you control that playback via animation using a MediaTimeline. To control the playback, you use a set of EventTrigger elements to start, stop, pause, and resume the animation Storyboard containing the MediaTimeline.

Either you can define the EventTrigger elements in the Triggers collection on the controls that control the playback or you can centralize their declaration by placing them on the container in which you place the controls. Within the Actions element of the Triggers collection, declare the Storyboard elements to control the MediaTimeline.

> ■**Note** Chapter 5 provides more details on using data binding, Chapter 6 discusses using triggers in more detail, and Chapter 11 provides extensive coverage of animation in WPF.

One complexity arises when you want a control, such as a System.Windows.Controls.Slider, to show the current position within the media file as well as allow the user to change the current play position. To update the display of the current play position, you must attach an event handler to the MediaTimeline.CurrentTimeInvalidated event, which updates the Slider position when it fires.

To move the play position in response to the Slider position changing, you attach an event handler to the Slider.ValueChanged property, which calls the Stoyboard.Seek method to change the current MediaTimeline play position. However, you must include logic in the event handlers to stop these events from triggering each other repeatedly as the user and MediaTimeline try to update the Slider position (and in turn the media play position) at the same time.

The Code

The following XAML demonstrates how to play an AVI file using a MediaElement and allow the user to start, stop, pause, and resume the playback. The user can also move quickly back and forth through the media file using a slider to position the current play position, as well as control the volume and balance of the audio (see Figure 12-3).

```xml
<Window x:Class="Recipe_12_03.Window1"
    xmlns="http://schemas.microsoft.com/winfx/2006/xaml/presentation"
    xmlns:x="http://schemas.microsoft.com/winfx/2006/xaml"
    Title="WPF Recipes 12_03" Height="450" Width="300">
    <StackPanel x:Name="Panel">
        <StackPanel.Resources>
            <!-- Style all buttons the same. -->
            <Style TargetType="{x:Type Button}">
                <Setter Property="Height" Value="25" />
                <Setter Property="MinWidth" Value="50" />
            </Style>
        </StackPanel.Resources>
        <StackPanel.Triggers>
            <!-- Triggers for handling playback of media file. -->
            <EventTrigger RoutedEvent="Button.Click" SourceName="btnPlay">
                <EventTrigger.Actions>
                    <BeginStoryboard Name="ClockStoryboard">
                        <Storyboard x:Name="Storyboard"  SlipBehavior="Slip"
                                CurrentTimeInvalidated="Storyboard_Changed">
                            <MediaTimeline BeginTime="0" Source="clock.avi"
                                Storyboard.TargetName="meMediaElement"
                                RepeatBehavior="Forever" />
                        </Storyboard>
                    </BeginStoryboard>
```

```xml
                    </EventTrigger.Actions>
                </EventTrigger>
                <EventTrigger RoutedEvent="Button.Click" SourceName="btnPause">
                    <EventTrigger.Actions>
                        <PauseStoryboard BeginStoryboardName="ClockStoryboard" />
                    </EventTrigger.Actions>
                </EventTrigger>
                <EventTrigger RoutedEvent="Button.Click" SourceName="btnResume">
                    <EventTrigger.Actions>
                        <ResumeStoryboard BeginStoryboardName="ClockStoryboard" />
                    </EventTrigger.Actions>
                </EventTrigger>
                <EventTrigger RoutedEvent="Button.Click" SourceName="btnStop">
                    <EventTrigger.Actions>
                        <StopStoryboard BeginStoryboardName="ClockStoryboard" />
                    </EventTrigger.Actions>
                </EventTrigger>
                <EventTrigger RoutedEvent="Slider.PreviewMouseLeftButtonDown"
                            SourceName="sldPosition" >
                    <PauseStoryboard BeginStoryboardName="ClockStoryboard" />
                </EventTrigger>
                <EventTrigger RoutedEvent="Slider.PreviewMouseLeftButtonUp"
                            SourceName="sldPosition" >
                    <ResumeStoryboard BeginStoryboardName="ClockStoryboard" />
                </EventTrigger>
            </StackPanel.Triggers>

            <!-- Media element to play the sound, music, or video file. -->
            <MediaElement Name="meMediaElement" HorizontalAlignment="Center"
                        Margin="5" MinHeight="300" Stretch="Fill"
                        MediaOpened="MediaOpened" />

            <!-- Button controls for play, pause, resume, and stop. -->
            <StackPanel HorizontalAlignment="Center" Orientation="Horizontal">
                <Button Content="_Play" Name="btnPlay" />
                <Button Content="P_ause" Name="btnPause" />
                <Button Content="_Resume" Name="btnResume" />
                <Button Content="_Stop" Name="btnStop" />
            </StackPanel>

            <!-- Slider shows the position within the media. -->
            <Slider HorizontalAlignment="Center" Margin="5"
                    Name="sldPosition" Width="250"
                    ValueChanged="sldPosition_ValueChanged">
            </Slider>

            <!-- Sliders to control volume and balance. -->
            <Grid>
```

```xml
        <Grid.ColumnDefinitions>
            <ColumnDefinition Width="1*"/>
            <ColumnDefinition Width="4*"/>
        </Grid.ColumnDefinitions>
        <Grid.RowDefinitions>
            <RowDefinition />
            <RowDefinition />
        </Grid.RowDefinitions>
        <TextBlock Grid.Column="0" Grid.Row="0" Text="Volume:"
                HorizontalAlignment="Right" VerticalAlignment="Center"/>
        <Slider Grid.Column="1" Grid.Row="0" Minimum="0" Maximum="1"
                TickFrequency="0.1" TickPlacement="TopLeft"
 Value="{Binding ElementName=meMediaElement, Path=Volume, Mode=TwoWay}" />
        <TextBlock Grid.Column="0" Grid.Row="1" Text="Balance:"
                HorizontalAlignment="Right" VerticalAlignment="Center"/>
        <Slider Grid.Column="1" Grid.Row="1" Minimum="-1" Maximum="1"
                TickFrequency="0.2" TickPlacement="TopLeft"
 Value="{Binding ElementName=meMediaElement, Path=Balance, Mode=TwoWay}" />
        </Grid>
    </StackPanel>
</Window>
```

The following code-behind shows the event handlers that allow the user to set the current play position using a slider and update the position of the slider to reflect the current play position:

```csharp
using System;
using System.Windows;
using System.Windows.Input;
using System.Windows.Media;
using System.Windows.Media.Animation;

namespace Recipe_12_03
{
    /// <summary>
    /// Interaction logic for Window1.xaml
    /// </summary>
    public partial class Window1 : Window
    {
        bool ignoreValueChanged = false;

        public Window1()
        {
            InitializeComponent();
        }
```

```csharp
// Handles the opening of the media file and sets the Maximum
// value of the position slider based on the natural duration
// of the media file.
private void MediaOpened(object sender, EventArgs e)
{
    sldPosition.Maximum =
        meMediaElement.NaturalDuration.TimeSpan.TotalMilliseconds;
}

// Updates the position slider when the media time changes.
private void Storyboard_Changed(object sender, EventArgs e)
{
    ClockGroup clockGroup = sender as ClockGroup;

    MediaClock mediaClock = clockGroup.Children[0] as MediaClock;

    if (mediaClock.CurrentProgress.HasValue)
    {
        ignoreValueChanged = true;
        sldPosition.Value = meMediaElement.Position.TotalMilliseconds;
        ignoreValueChanged = false;
    }
}

// Handles the movement of the slider and updates the position
// being played.
private void sldPosition_ValueChanged(object sender,
    RoutedPropertyChangedEventArgs<double> e)
{
    if (ignoreValueChanged)
    {
        return;
    }

    Storyboard.Seek(Panel,
        TimeSpan.FromMilliseconds(sldPosition.Value),
        TimeSeekOrigin.BeginTime);
}
}
}
```

Figure 12-3. *Controlling the playback of media files*

12-4. Respond When the User Clicks a UI Element with the Mouse

Problem

You need to take an action when the user clicks or double-clicks a UI element with the mouse.

Solution

Handle the MouseDown or MouseUp event inherited from System.Windows.UIElement, the MouseDoubleClick event inherited from System.Windows.Control, or the Click event inherited from System.Windows.Control.ButtonBase.

How It Works

Depending on the UI element you are working with and the kind of functionality you are trying to implement, you can handle mouse click events in a variety of ways. The MouseDown or MouseUp events are the most widely available because they are implemented by UIElement. The MouseDown event occurs as soon as the user clicks any mouse button while over a UIElement, but the MouseUp event occurs only when the user releases the button. The MouseDoubleClick event implemented by Control is raised when the user double-clicks a Control.

> **Note** The UIElement class also implements the MouseLeftButtonDown, MouseLeftButtonUp, MouseRightButtonDown, and MouseRightButtonUp, which as the names suggest allow you to be selective about which mouse button causes an event to be raised.

The ButtonBase class provides a special Click event support, which overrides the basic behavior of the MouseLeftButtonDown event implemented by UIElement.

The Code

The following XAML demonstrates how to hook various mouse click event handlers to a variety of control types including a Button, Label, and TextBlock (from the System.Windows.Controls namespace) as well as a System.Windows.Shapes.Rectangle:

```
<Window x:Class="Recipe_12_04.Window1"
    xmlns="http://schemas.microsoft.com/winfx/2006/xaml/presentation"
    xmlns:x="http://schemas.microsoft.com/winfx/2006/xaml"
    Title="WPF Recipes 12_04" Height="150" Width="300">
    <UniformGrid Columns="2" Rows="2">
        <Button Content="Click" Click="Button_Click"
                MaxHeight="25" MaxWidth="100" />
        <Label Background="LightBlue" Content="Double Click"
               HorizontalContentAlignment="Center"
               MaxHeight="25" MaxWidth="100"
               MouseDoubleClick="Label_MouseDoubleClick" />
        <TextBlock Background="Turquoise" Padding="25,7"
                   Text="Mouse Up" MouseUp="TextBlock_MouseUp"
                   HorizontalAlignment="Center" VerticalAlignment="Center"/>
        <Canvas>
            <Rectangle Canvas.Top="15" Canvas.Left="20"
                Height="25" Width="100" Fill="Aqua"
                MouseDown="Rectangle_MouseDown" />
            <TextBlock Canvas.Top="20" Canvas.Left="40" Text="Mouse Down"
                IsHitTestVisible="False"/>
        </Canvas>
    </UniformGrid>
</Window>
```

The following code-behind shows the simple event handler implementations for the various mouse click events:

```
using System;
using System.Windows;
using System.Windows.Input;

namespace Recipe_12_04
{
    /// <summary>
    /// Interaction logic for Window1.xaml
    /// </summary>
    public partial class Window1 : Window
    {
        public Window1()
        {
            InitializeComponent();
        }

        // Handles the Click event on the Button.
        private void Button_Click(object sender, RoutedEventArgs e)
        {
            MessageBox.Show("Mouse Click", "Button");
        }

        // Handles the MouseDoubleClick event on the Label.
        private void Label_MouseDoubleClick(object sender, MouseButtonEventArgs e)
        {
            MessageBox.Show("Mouse Double Click", "Label");
        }

        // Handles the MouseDown event on the Rectangle.
        private void Rectangle_MouseDown(object sender, MouseButtonEventArgs e)
        {
            MessageBox.Show("Mouse Down", "Rectangle");
        }

        // Handles the MouseUp event on the TextBlock.
        private void TextBlock_MouseUp(object sender, MouseButtonEventArgs e)
        {
            MessageBox.Show("Mouse Up", "TextBlock");
        }
    }
}
```

Figure 12-4 shows the resulting window.

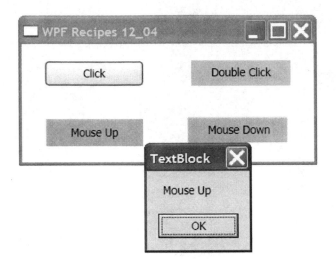

Figure 12-4. *Handling mouse click events*

12-5. Respond When the User Clicks a UI Element in a Container with the Mouse

Problem

You need to take an action when the user clicks one of a number of UI elements held in a container.

Solution

Handle the `System.Windows.UIElement.MouseUp`, `System.Windows.UIElement.MouseDown`, or `System.Windows.Control.ButtonBase.Click` event in the container of the controls.

How It Works

WPF automatically bubbles the `MouseDown`, `MouseUp`, and `Click` events up the containment hierarchy, making it a trivial exercise to handle these events at the container level instead of that of the individual controls. All you need to do is declare an event handler of the appropriate type at the container instead of the individual control. If the container does not support the event you want to handle—such as the `Click` event, which is implemented by `ButtonBase`—you use the attached event syntax `Buttonbase.Click` as the event name to ensure the correct event is handled.

If the control is nested within a number of containers, the bubbled events are automatically routed up through all container levels, so you can handle the event at one or more containers where appropriate.

The Code

The following XAML demonstrates how to handle control events at the container level. To demonstrate the bubbling of events through multiple containers, when the user clicks the Rectangle in the bottom-right corner (see Figure 12-5), the event is first handled by the Canvas and then by the UniformGrid, because both containers handle the MouseDown event.

```
<Window x:Class="Recipe_12_05.Window1"
    xmlns="http://schemas.microsoft.com/winfx/2006/xaml/presentation"
    xmlns:x="http://schemas.microsoft.com/winfx/2006/xaml"
    Title="WPF Recipes 12_05" Height="150" Width="300">
    <UniformGrid Columns="2" Rows="2" ButtonBase.Click="UniformGrid_Click"
                MouseDown="UniformGrid_MouseDown">
        <Button Content="Button" MaxHeight="25" MaxWidth="70" Name="Button"/>
        <Label Background="LightBlue" Content="Label" Name="Label"
                HorizontalContentAlignment="Center"
                MaxHeight="25" MaxWidth="100"/>
        <TextBlock Background="Turquoise" Padding="25,7" Text="TextBlock"
                HorizontalAlignment="Center" VerticalAlignment="Center"
                Name="TextBlock"/>
        <Canvas MouseDown="Canvas_MouseDown">
            <Rectangle Canvas.Top="15" Canvas.Left="20" Fill="Aqua"
                Height="25" Width="100" Name="Rectangle"/>
            <TextBlock Canvas.Top="20" Canvas.Left="45" Text="Rectangle"
                IsHitTestVisible="False"/>
        </Canvas>
    </UniformGrid>
</Window>
```

The following code-behind contains the event-handling code for the Canvas and UniformGrid controls:

```
using System.Windows;
using System.Windows.Input;

namespace Recipe_12_05
{
    /// <summary>
    /// Interaction logic for Window1.xaml
    /// </summary>
    public partial class Window1 : Window
    {
        public Window1()
        {
            InitializeComponent();
        }

        // Handles the MouseDown event on the Canvas.
        private void Canvas_MouseDown(object sender, MouseButtonEventArgs e)
```

```
        {
            FrameworkElement fe = e.OriginalSource as FrameworkElement;

            MessageBox.Show("Mouse Down on " + fe.Name, "Canvas");
        }

        // Handles the Click event on the UniformGrid.
        private void UniformGrid_Click(object sender, RoutedEventArgs e)
        {
            FrameworkElement fe = e.OriginalSource as FrameworkElement;

            MessageBox.Show("Mouse Click on " + fe.Name, "Uniform Grid");
        }

        // Handles the MouseDown event on the UniformGrid.
        private void UniformGrid_MouseDown(object sender, MouseButtonEventArgs e)
        {
            FrameworkElement fe = e.OriginalSource as FrameworkElement;

            MessageBox.Show("Mouse Down on " + fe.Name, "Uniform Grid");
        }
    }
}
```

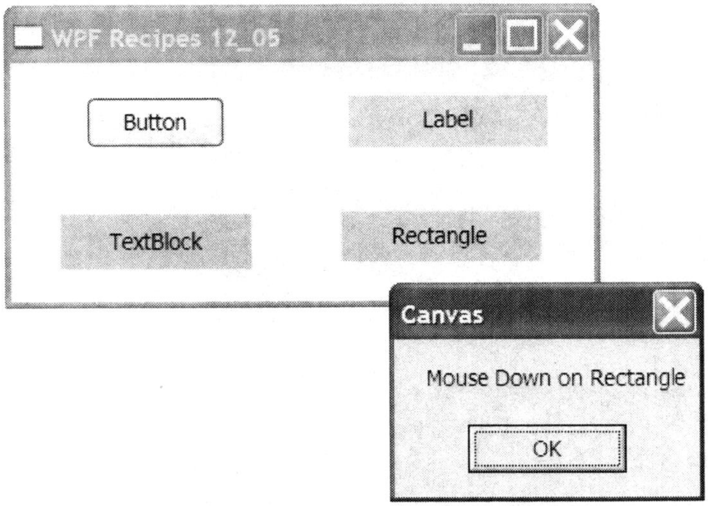

Figure 12-5. *Handling mouse click events at the control container*

12-6. Respond When the User Rotates the Mouse Wheel

Problem

You need to take an action when the user spins the mouse's scroll wheel.

Solution

On the control you want to respond to the mouse wheel, handle the MouseWheel event inherited from the System.Windows.UIElement class.

How It Works

When the mouse pointer is over an element and the user moves the mouse wheel, a MouseWheel event is raised on the element. To handle these events, simply attach an event handler to the MouseWheel event.

When WPF calls the event handler, it passes the handler a System.Windows.Input. MouseWheelEventArgs object that describes the mouse wheel event and the state of the mouse buttons. The Delta property of the MouseWheelEventArgs is positive if the mouse wheel is moved away from the user and negative if the mouse wheel is moved toward the user. The LeftButton and RightButton properties indicate whether the buttons are currently pressed or released using values of the System.Windows.Input.MouseButtonState enumeration.

The Code

The following XAML demonstrates how to attach mouse wheel event handlers to various UI elements. The application (shown in Figure 12-6) contains a Slider, a RichTextBox, and a Rectangle that each responds to the mouse wheel when the mouse pointer is over the element. The RichTextBox already has mouse wheel support built in to perform vertical scrolling of the content. The Slider uses a MouseWheel event handler to move the slider thumb left and right. The Rectangle uses a MouseWheel event handler to enlarge and decrease its Height and Width properties depending on whether the left mouse button is currently pressed.

```
<Window x:Class="Recipe_12_06.Window1"
    xmlns="http://schemas.microsoft.com/winfx/2006/xaml/presentation"
    xmlns:x="http://schemas.microsoft.com/winfx/2006/xaml"
    Title="WPF Recipes 12_06" Height="300" Width="300">
    <Canvas>
        <Slider Canvas.Top="10" Canvas.Left="20" Name="sldSlider"
                Minimum="0" Maximum="1000" Value="500"
                Width="250" MouseWheel="Slider_MouseWheel"/>
        <RichTextBox Canvas.Top="50" Canvas.Left="20"
            Width="250" Height="100"
            VerticalScrollBarVisibility="Visible">
            <FlowDocument>
                <Paragraph FontSize="12">
```

```
                        Lorem ipsum dolor sit amet, consectetuer adipiscing elit,
                        sed diam nonummy nibh euismod tincidunt ut laoreet dolore
                        magna aliquam erat volutpat.
                    </Paragraph>
                    <Paragraph FontSize="15">
                        Ut wisi enim ad minim veniam, quis nostrud exerci tation
                        ullamcorper suscipit lobortis nisl ut aliquip ex ea
                        commodo consequat. Duis autem vel eum iriure.
                    </Paragraph>
                    <Paragraph FontSize="18">A List</Paragraph>
                    <List>
                        <ListItem>
                            <Paragraph>
                                <Bold>Bold List Item</Bold>
                            </Paragraph>
                        </ListItem>
                        <ListItem>
                            <Paragraph>
                                <Italic>Italic List Item</Italic>
                            </Paragraph>
                        </ListItem>
                        <ListItem>
                            <Paragraph>
                                <Underline>Underlined List Item</Underline>
                            </Paragraph>
                        </ListItem>
                    </List>
                </FlowDocument>
            </RichTextBox>
            <Rectangle Canvas.Top="160" Canvas.Left="20" Name="shpRectangle"
                    Fill="LightBlue" Width="50" Height="50"
                    MouseWheel="Rectangle_MouseWheel">
            </Rectangle>
        </Canvas>
</Window>
```

The following code-behind shows the event handlers that handle the MouseWheel event for the Slider and Rectangle:

```
using System.Windows;
using System.Windows.Input;

namespace Recipe_12_06
{
    /// <summary>
    /// Interaction logic for Window1.xaml
    /// </summary>
    public partial class Window1 : Window
```

```
{
    public Window1()
    {
        InitializeComponent();
    }

    // Handles the MouseWheel event on the Slider.
    private void Slider_MouseWheel(object sender, MouseWheelEventArgs e)
    {
        // Increment or decrement the slider position depending on
        // whether the wheel was moved up or down.
        sldSlider.Value += (e.Delta > 0) ? 5 : -5;
    }

    // Handles the MouseWheel event on the Rectangle.
    private void Rectangle_MouseWheel(object sender,
        MouseWheelEventArgs e)
    {
        if (e.LeftButton == MouseButtonState.Pressed)
        {
            // If the left button is pressed, increment or
            // decrement the width.

            double newWidth =
                shpRectangle.Width += (e.Delta > 0) ? 5 : -5;

            if (newWidth < 10) newWidth = 10;
            if (newWidth > 200) newWidth = 200;

            shpRectangle.Width = newWidth;
        }
        else
        {
            // If the left button is not pressed, increment or
            // decrement the height.

            double newHeight =
                shpRectangle.Height += (e.Delta > 0) ? 5 : -5;

            if (newHeight < 10) newHeight = 10;
            if (newHeight > 200) newHeight = 200;

            shpRectangle.Height = newHeight;
        }
    }
}
}
```

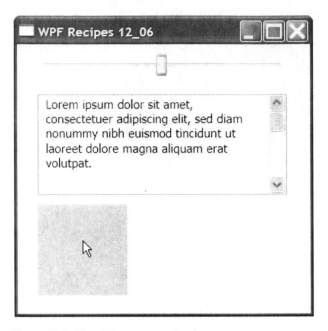

Figure 12-6. *Handling mouse wheel events*

12-7. Drag Items from a List and Drop Them on a Canvas

Problem

You need to allow the user to drag items from a System.Windows.Controls.ListBox to a System.Windows.Controls.Canvas.

Note Drag and drop is relatively simple to implement in WPF but contains a lot of variations depending on what you are trying to do and what content you are dragging. This example focuses on dragging content from a ListBox to a Canvas, but the principles are similar for other types of drag and drop operations and can be adapted easily.

Solution

On the ListBox or ListBoxItem, handle the PreviewMouseLeftButtonDown event to identify the start of a possible drag operation and identify the ListBoxItem being dragged. Handle the PreviewMouseMove event to determine whether the user is actually dragging the item, and if so, set up the drop operation using the static System.Windows.DragDrop class. On the Canvas (the target for the drop operation), handle the DragEnter and Drop events to support the dropping of dragged content.

How It Works

The static DragDrop class provides the functionality central to making it easy to execute drag and drop operations in WPF. First, however, you must determine that the user is actually trying to drag something.

There is no single best way to do this, but usually you will need a combination of handling MouseLeftButtonDown or PreviewMouseLeftButtonDown events to know when the user clicks something and MouseMove or PreviewMouseMove events to determine whether the user is moving the mouse while holding the left button down. Also, you should use the SystemParameters. MinimumHorizontalDragDistance and SystemParameters.MinimumVerticalDragDistance properties to make sure the user has dragged the item a sufficient distance to be considered a drag operation; otherwise, the user will often get false drag operations starting as they click items.

Once you are sure the user is trying to drag something, you configure the DragDrop object using the DoDragDrop method. You must pass the DoDragDrop method a reference to the source object being dragged, a System.Object containing the data that the drag operation is taking with it, and a value from the System.Windows.DragDropEffects enumeration representing the type of drag operation being performed. Commonly used values of the DragDropEffects enumeration are Copy, Move, and Link. The type of operation is often driven by special keys being held down at the time of clicking, for example, holding the Control key signals the user's intent to copy (see recipe 12-9 for information on how to query keyboard state).

On the target of the drop operation, implement event handlers for the DragEnter and Drop events. The DragEnter handler allows you to control the behavior seen by the user as the mouse pointer enters the target control. This usually indicates whether the control is a suitable target for the type of content the user is dragging. The Drop event signals that the user has released the left mouse button and indicates that the content contained in the DragDrop object should be retrieved (using the Data.GetData method of the DragEventArgs object passed to the Drop event handler) and inserted into the target control.

The Code

The following XAML demonstrates how to set up a ListBox with ListBoxItem objects that support drag and drop operations (see Figure 12-7):

```
<Window x:Class="Recipe_12_07.Window1"
    xmlns="http://schemas.microsoft.com/winfx/2006/xaml/presentation"
    xmlns:x="http://schemas.microsoft.com/winfx/2006/xaml"
    Title="WPF Recipes 12_07" Height="300" Width="300">
    <DockPanel LastChildFill="True" >
        <ListBox DockPanel.Dock="Left" Name="lstLabels">
            <ListBox.Resources>
                <Style TargetType="{x:Type ListBoxItem}">
                    <Setter Property="FontSize" Value="14" />
                    <Setter Property="Margin" Value="2" />
                    <EventSetter Event="PreviewMouseLeftButtonDown"
                        Handler="ListBoxItem_PreviewMouseLeftButtonDown"/>
                    <EventSetter Event="PreviewMouseMove"
                                Handler="ListBoxItem_PreviewMouseMove"/>
                </Style>
            </ListBox.Resources>
```

```
            </ListBox.Resources>
            <ListBoxItem IsSelected="True">Allen</ListBoxItem>
            <ListBoxItem>Andy</ListBoxItem>
            <ListBoxItem>Antoan</ListBoxItem>
            <ListBoxItem>Bruce</ListBoxItem>
            <ListBoxItem>Ian</ListBoxItem>
            <ListBoxItem>Matthew</ListBoxItem>
            <ListBoxItem>Sam</ListBoxItem>
            <ListBoxItem>Simon</ListBoxItem>
        </ListBox>
        <Canvas AllowDrop="True" Background="Transparent"
                DragEnter="cvsSurface_DragEnter" Drop="cvsSurface_Drop"
                Name="cvsSurface" >
        </Canvas>
    </DockPanel>
</Window>
```

The following code-behind contains the event handlers that allow the example to identify the ListBoxItem that the user is dragging, determine whether a mouse movement constitutes a drag operation, and allow the Canvas to receive the dragged ListBoxItem content.

```
using System;
using System.Windows;
using System.Windows.Controls;
using System.Windows.Input;

namespace Recipe_12_07
{
    /// <summary>
    /// Interaction logic for Window1.xaml
    /// </summary>
    public partial class Window1 : Window
    {
        private ListBoxItem draggedItem;
        private Point startDragPoint;

        public Window1()
        {
            InitializeComponent();
        }

        // Handles the DragEnter event for the Canvas. Changes the mouse
        // pointer to show the user that copy is an option if the drop
        // text content is over the Canvas.
        private void cvsSurface_DragEnter(object sender, DragEventArgs e)
        {
            if (e.Data.GetDataPresent(DataFormats.Text))
```

```
        {
            e.Effects = DragDropEffects.Copy;
        }
        else
        {
            e.Effects = DragDropEffects.None;
        }
    }

    // Handles the Drop event for the Canvas. Creates a new Label
    // and adds it to the Canvas at the location of the mouse pointer.
    private void cvsSurface_Drop(object sender, DragEventArgs e)
    {
        // Create a new Label.
        Label newLabel = new Label();
        newLabel.Content = e.Data.GetData(DataFormats.Text);
        newLabel.FontSize = 14;

        // Add the Label to the Canvas and position it.
        cvsSurface.Children.Add(newLabel);
        Canvas.SetLeft(newLabel, e.GetPosition(cvsSurface).X);
        Canvas.SetTop(newLabel, e.GetPosition(cvsSurface).Y);
    }

    // Handles the PreviewMouseLeftButtonDown event for all ListBoxItem
    // objects. Stores a reference to the item being dragged and the
    // point at which the drag started.
    private void ListBoxItem_PreviewMouseLeftButtonDown(object sender,
        MouseButtonEventArgs e)
    {
        draggedItem = sender as ListBoxItem;
        startDragPoint = e.GetPosition(null);
    }

    // Handles the PreviewMouseMove event for all ListBoxItem objects.
    // Determines whether the mouse has been moved far enough to be
    // considered a drag operation.
    private void ListBoxItem_PreviewMouseMove(object sender,
        MouseEventArgs e)
    {
        if (e.LeftButton == MouseButtonState.Pressed)
        {
            Point position = e.GetPosition(null);

            if (Math.Abs(position.X - startDragPoint.X) >
                    SystemParameters.MinimumHorizontalDragDistance ||
                Math.Abs(position.Y - startDragPoint.Y) >
                    SystemParameters.MinimumVerticalDragDistance)
```

```
            {
                // User is dragging, set up the DragDrop behavior.
                DragDrop.DoDragDrop(draggedItem, draggedItem.Content,
                    DragDropEffects.Copy);
            }
        }
    }
}
```

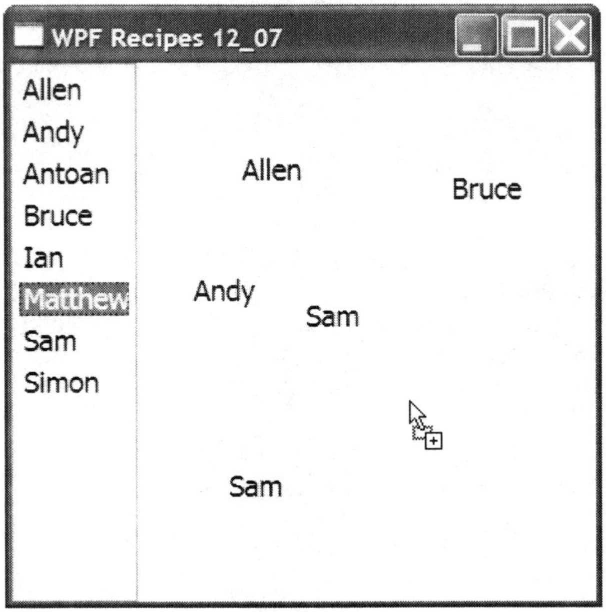

Figure 12-7. *Dragging items from a* ListBox *and dropping them on a* Canvas

12-8. Handle Keyboard Events

Problem

You need to take an action when the user presses keys on the keyboard.

Solution

To take an action when the user presses a key, handle the PreviewKeyDown or KeyDown event. To take an action when the user releases a key, handle the PreviewKeyUp or KeyUp event. To take an action as the target element receives the text input, handle the PreviewTextInput or TextInput event.

How It Works

When the user presses a key, WPF fires the following sequence of events:

1. PreviewKeyDown

2. KeyDown

3. PreviewTextInput

4. TextInput

5. PreviewKeyUp

6. KeyUp

The events that begin with Preview are *tunneling* events that go top down through the container hierarchy to the target control. The other events are *bubbling* events that go from the target control up through the container hierarchy. This sequence of events going both up and down the container hierarchy provides a great deal of flexibility as to when and where you want to handle keyboard events.

The KeyUp and KeyDown events (as well as their tunneling counterparts) fire every time the user presses a key, but the PreviewTextInput and TextInput events fire only when a control receives actual input, which may be the result of multiple keystrokes. For example, pressing the Shift key to enter a capital letter would result in a KeyDown event but no TextInput event. When the user subsequently pressed the desired letter, a second KeyDown event would fire, and finally the TextInput event would fire.

Note Some controls that do advanced text handling, such as the System.Windows.Controls.TextBox, suppress some of the keyboard events, meaning you may not always see the events when and where you would expect to handle them. If this is the case, you usually have to resort to using the Preview events.

The Code

The following XAML demonstrates how to handle keyboard events. The example handles all keyboard events raised on a TextBox control and logs them to another read-only TextBox. Figure 12-8 shows the example running after the user has pressed Shift+L and then lowercase letter *g*. You can see that the TextInput event is suppressed and so does not appear in the log.

```
<Window x:Class="Recipe_12_08.Window1"
    xmlns="http://schemas.microsoft.com/winfx/2006/xaml/presentation"
    xmlns:x="http://schemas.microsoft.com/winfx/2006/xaml"
    Title="WPF Recipes 12_08" Height="300" Width="300">
    <DockPanel LastChildFill="True">
        <TextBox DockPanel.Dock="Top" FontSize="14"
                Height="30" HorizontalAlignment="Stretch"
                PreviewKeyDown="TextBox_KeyEvent"
```

```
                    KeyDown="TextBox_KeyEvent"
                    PreviewKeyUp="TextBox_KeyEvent"
                    KeyUp="TextBox_KeyEvent"
                    TextInput="TextBox_TextEvent"
                    PreviewTextInput="TextBox_TextEvent"/>
        <TextBox Name="txtLog" HorizontalAlignment="Stretch"
                    IsReadOnly="True" VerticalScrollBarVisibility="Visible"/>
    </DockPanel>
</Window>
```

The following code-behind contains the keyboard event handlers that write details of the events to the log:

```
using System;
using System.Windows;
using System.Windows.Input;

namespace Recipe_12_08
{
    /// <summary>
    /// Interaction logic for Window1.xaml
    /// </summary>
    public partial class Window1 : Window
    {
        public Window1()
        {
            InitializeComponent();
        }

        // Handles all Key* events for the TextBox and logs them.
        private void TextBox_KeyEvent(object sender, KeyEventArgs e)
        {
            String msg = String.Format("{0} - {1}\n",
                e.RoutedEvent.Name, e.Key);

            txtLog.Text += msg;
            txtLog.ScrollToEnd();
        }

        // Handles all Text* events for the TextBox and logs them.
        private void TextBox_TextEvent(object sender,
            TextCompositionEventArgs e)
        {
            String msg = String.Format("{0} - {1}\n",
                e.RoutedEvent.Name, e.Text);
```

```
            txtLog.Text += msg;
            txtLog.ScrollToEnd();
        }
    }
}
```

Figure 12-8. *Capturing and logging keyboard events from a TextBox*

12-9. Query Keyboard State

Problem

You need to query the state of the keyboard to determine whether the user is pressing any special keys.

Solution

Use the IsKeyDown and IsKeyToggled methods of the static System.Windows.Input.Keyboard class.

How It Works

The static Keyboard class contains two methods that allow you to determine whether a particular key is currently pressed or whether keys that have a toggled state (for example, Caps Lock) are currently on or off.

To determine whether a key is currently pressed, call the IsKeyDown method, and pass a member of the System.Windows.Input.Keys enumeration that represents the key you want to test. The method returns True if the key is currently pressed. To test the state of toggled keys, call the IsKeyToggled method, again passing a member of the Keys enumeration to identify the key to test.

The Code

The following XAML defines a set of CheckBox controls representing various special buttons on the keyboard. When the Button is pressed, the program uses the Keyboard class to test the state of each button and update the IsSelected property of the appropriate CheckBox (see Figure 12-9).

```xml
<Window x:Class="Recipe_12_09.Window1"
    xmlns="http://schemas.microsoft.com/winfx/2006/xaml/presentation"
    xmlns:x="http://schemas.microsoft.com/winfx/2006/xaml"
    Title="WPF Recipes 12_09" Height="170" Width="200">
    <StackPanel HorizontalAlignment="Center">
        <UniformGrid Columns="2">
            <UniformGrid.Resources>
                <Style TargetType="{x:Type CheckBox}">
                    <Setter Property="IsHitTestVisible" Value="False" />
                    <Setter Property="Margin" Value="5" />
                </Style>
            </UniformGrid.Resources>
            <CheckBox Content="LeftShift" Name="chkLShift"/>
            <CheckBox Content="RightShift" Name="chkRShift"/>
            <CheckBox Content="LeftControl" Name="chkLControl"/>
            <CheckBox Content="RightControl" Name="chkRControl"/>
            <CheckBox Content="LeftAlt" Name="chkLAlt"/>
            <CheckBox Content="RightAlt" Name="chkRAlt"/>
            <CheckBox Content="CapsLock" Name="chkCaps"/>
            <CheckBox Content="NumLock" Name="chkNum"/>
        </UniformGrid>
        <Button Content="Check Keyboard" Margin="10" Click="Button_Click"/>
    </StackPanel>
</Window>
```

The following code-behind contains the Button.Click event that checks the keyboard and updates the CheckBox controls:

```csharp
using System.Windows;
using System.Windows.Input;

namespace Recipe_12_09
{
    /// <summary>
    /// Interaction logic for Window1.xaml
    /// </summary>
    public partial class Window1 : Window
```

```csharp
{
    public Window1()
    {
        InitializeComponent();
        CheckKeyboardState();
    }

    // Handles the Click event on the Button.
    private void Button_Click(object sender, RoutedEventArgs e)
    {
        CheckKeyboardState();
    }

    // Checks the state of the keyboard and updates the checkboxes.
    private void CheckKeyboardState()
    {
        // Control keys.
        chkLControl.IsChecked = Keyboard.IsKeyDown(Key.LeftCtrl);
        chkRControl.IsChecked = Keyboard.IsKeyDown(Key.RightCtrl);

        // Shift keys.
        chkLShift.IsChecked = Keyboard.IsKeyDown(Key.LeftShift);
        chkRShift.IsChecked = Keyboard.IsKeyDown(Key.RightShift);

        // Alt keys.
        chkLAlt.IsChecked = Keyboard.IsKeyDown(Key.LeftAlt);
        chkRAlt.IsChecked = Keyboard.IsKeyDown(Key.RightAlt);

        // Num Lock and Caps Lock.
        chkCaps.IsChecked = Keyboard.IsKeyToggled(Key.CapsLock);
        chkNum.IsChecked = Keyboard.IsKeyToggled(Key.NumLock);
    }
}
}
```

Figure 12-9. *Querying keyboard state*

12-10. Suppress Keyboard and Mouse Events

Problem

You need to suppress the events raised by the keyboard or mouse.

Solution

Handle the tunneling counterpart of the event you want to suppress. In the event handler, set the Handled property of the event argument object to the value True.

How It Works

Each of the main mouse and keyboard events like MouseDown, MouseUp, KeyDown, and KeyUp has tunneling event counterparts that start off at the top of the container hierarchy and travel down to the target control. These tunneling counterparts have the prefix Preview on their name. By handling these preview events, you can intercept an event before it happens at the target control and suppress it.

Every preview event handler takes two arguments: a System.Object that contains a reference to the event sender and an object that derives from System.Windows.RoutedEventArgs that contains data specific to the event being handled. RoutedEventArgs implements a Boolean property named Handled. By setting this property to the value True in your event handler, you stop the subsequent bubbling event from firing, effectively suppressing the event.

The Code

The following XAML demonstrates how to suppress the Button.Click event by handling the PreviewMouseDown event in the container of the Button:

```
<Window x:Class="Recipe_12_10.Window1"
    xmlns="http://schemas.microsoft.com/winfx/2006/xaml/presentation"
    xmlns:x="http://schemas.microsoft.com/winfx/2006/xaml"
    Title="WPF Recipes 12_10" Height="100" Width="200">
    <StackPanel Orientation="Horizontal">
        <StackPanel Orientation="Horizontal"
                    PreviewMouseDown="StackPanel_PreviewMouseDown">
            <Button Content="Blocked" Click="Button_Click"
                    Height="25" Margin="10" Width="70"/>
        </StackPanel>
        <Button Content="Not Blocked" Click="Button_Click"
                Height="25" Margin="10" Width="70"/>
    </StackPanel>
</Window>
```

The following code-behind shows how to suppress the Button.Click event by setting the Handled property to True in the PreviewMouseDown event handler:

```csharp
using System.Windows;
using System.Windows.Input;

namespace Recipe_12_10
{
    /// <summary>
    /// Interaction logic for Window1.xaml
    /// </summary>
    public partial class Window1 : Window
    {
        public Window1()
        {
            InitializeComponent();
        }

        private void Button_Click(object sender, RoutedEventArgs e)
        {
            MessageBox.Show("Button Clicked", "Button");
        }

        private void StackPanel_PreviewMouseDown(object sender,
            MouseButtonEventArgs e)
        {
            e.Handled = true;
        }
    }
}
```

CHAPTER 13

Migrating and Windows Forms Interoperability

Having learned how to create user interfaces in WPF, it would be fantastic to never have to worry about "old" technologies anymore. However, the reality is that most applications will not be completely rewritten just to take advantage of WPF. Many organizations with existing applications built using older UI technologies such as Windows Forms will opt to use WPF only for certain elements of their UI where it gives them specific advantages. Even if an organization does decide to adopt WPF totally, they aren't likely to stage any migration of existing applications.

In addition, given the amount of time and effort spent developing Windows Forms controls over the years, for some time you may find that there are many Windows Forms controls that you want to use that do not have a WPF equivalent.

These issues mean it is necessary to have WPF UI elements integrate with older UI technologies—and this situation will likely continue for many years. Fortunately, WPF provides very good integration with Windows Forms. The recipes in this chapter describe how to:

- Use WPF windows in Windows Forms applications (recipe 13-1)

- Use WPF controls in Windows Forms (recipe 13-2)

- Use Windows Forms forms in WPF applications (recipe 13-3)

- Use Windows Forms controls in WPF windows (recipe 13-4)

Note WPF also provides reasonable integration with older Win32 interfaces elements. We have chosen not to discuss Win32 integration here and instead focus only on Windows Forms. For a description on how to integrate WPF and Win32, see the article "WPF and Win32 Interoperation Overview" on MSDN at http://msdn.microsoft.com/en-us/library/ms742522.aspx.

13-1. Use WPF Windows in a Windows Forms Application

Problem

You need to display a WPF window in a Windows Forms application.

Solution

Create an instance of the System.Windows.Window you want to display in your Windows Forms code. Call Window.ShowDialog to display the window modal, or call Window.Show to display the window modeless.

How It Works

The only difficult thing about displaying a WPF window in a Windows Forms application is actually integrating the WPF source code into your project correctly if you are using Visual Studio. There is no option to add a WPF Window when you select Add New Item in Solution Explorer.

By far the easiest way around this is to import an existing WPF Window using the Add Existing option in Solution Explorer. This will set everything up appropriately (adding the necessary assembly references), and you can then edit the WPF Window as you would when creating a WPF application.

Once you have a WPF window declared, you can reference and instantiate the class the same as you would do any other class. Calling Window.ShowDialog will display the window modally, meaning that the user can interact with only that Window and must close it before they can interact again with the rest of the application. Calling Window.Show will display the window modeless, allowing the user to interact with the new Window as well as the rest of the application.

The Code

The following example (shown running in Figure 13-1) displays a Windows form with two buttons. The left button opens and closes a modeless WPF Window, and the right button opens a modal Window. When the example creates the modeless window, it subscribes an event handler to the Window.Closing event so that the application can update the button state should the user choose to close the Window directly instead of using the button. The following code is the code-behind for the main Windows form:

```
using System;
using System.Windows.Forms;
using System.ComponentModel;

namespace Recipe_13_01
{
```

```
public partial class Form1 : Form
{
    private Window1 modelessWindow;
    private CancelEventHandler modelessWindowCloseHandler;

    public Form1()
    {
        InitializeComponent();
        modelessWindowCloseHandler = new CancelEventHandler(Window_Closing);
    }

    // Handles the button click event to open and close the modeless
    // WPF Window.
    private void OpenModeless_Click(object sender, EventArgs e)
    {
        if (modelessWindow == null)
        {
            modelessWindow = new Window1();

            // Add an event handler to get notification when the window
            // is closing.
            modelessWindow.Closing += modelessWindowCloseHandler;

            // Change the button text.
            btnOpenModeless.Text = "Close Modeless Window";

            // Show the Windows Form.
            modelessWindow.Show();
        }
        else
        {
            modelessWindow.Close();
        }
    }

    // Handles the button click event to open the modal WPF Window.
    private void OpenModal_Click(object sender, EventArgs e)
    {
        // Create and display the modal window.
        Window1 window = new Window1();
        window.ShowDialog();
    }

    // Handles the WPF Window's Closing event for the modeless window.
    private void Window_Closing(object sender, CancelEventArgs e)
    {
        // Remove the event handler reference.
```

```
                modelessWindow.Closing -= modelessWindowCloseHandler;
                modelessWindow = null;

                // Change the button text.
                btnOpenModeless.Text = "Open Modeless Window";
            }
        }
    }
```

The following XAML provides the declaration of the WPF Window that is opened from the Windows Forms application:

```
<Window x:Class="Recipe_13_01.Window1"
    xmlns="http://schemas.microsoft.com/winfx/2006/xaml/presentation"
    xmlns:x="http://schemas.microsoft.com/winfx/2006/xaml"
    Title="WPF Recipes 13_01" Height="200" Width="300">
    <StackPanel Margin="20">
        <TextBlock FontSize="20" Text="A WPF Window" TextAlignment="Center"/>
        <Button Click="btnClose_Click" Content="Close" Margin="50"
                MaxWidth="50" Name="btnClose" />
    </StackPanel>
</Window>
```

The following is a small amount of code-behind used by the WPF Window to allow users to close the Window by clicking the Close button:

```
using System.Windows;
using System.Windows.Forms;

namespace Recipe_13_01
{
    /// <summary>
    /// Interaction logic for Window1.xaml
    /// </summary>
    public partial class Window1 : Window
    {
        public Window1()
        {
            InitializeComponent();
        }

        private void btnClose_Click(object sender, RoutedEventArgs e)
        {
            this.Close();
        }
    }
}
```

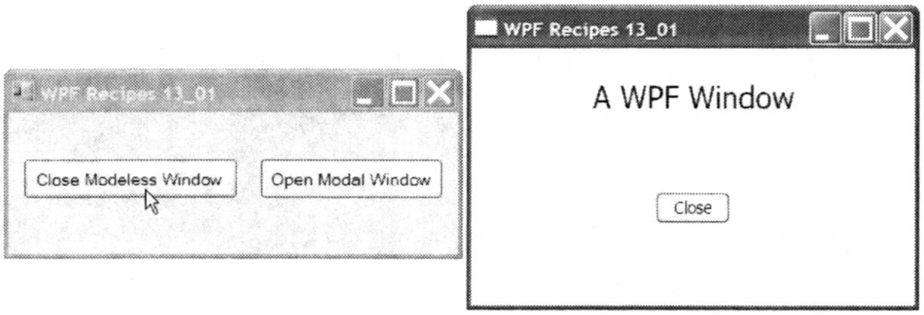

Figure 13-1. *Displaying a WPF Window from a Windows Forms application*

13-2. Use WPF Controls in Windows Forms

Problem

You need to display WPF UI elements alongside Windows Forms controls in a Windows form.

Solution

Use a System.Windows.Forms.Integration.ElementHost control on your Windows form, and host the WPF control inside it.

How It Works

The ElementHost control is a Windows Forms control that allows you to host WPF controls in Windows Forms. The ElementHost control makes integrating WPF controls into your Windows Forms application relatively simple and even provides some limited visual design-time support.

The ElementHost can contain a single WPF element that inherits from System.Windows.UIElement. This element can be one of the layout containers discussed in Chapter 2, which allows you to create rich structured WPF content within the ElementHost control. Often, the WPF element you place in the ElementHost control will be a WPF user control (see Chapter 4) but can also be any common WPF control.

To use the ElementHost control in Visual Studio's graphical design environment, open the Toolbox, and browse to the WPF Interoperability category. Drag the ElementHost control, and drop it on the Windows form as you would with any other control. Using the ElementHost Tasks window, you can then select any WPF user control currently in your project to place in the ElementHost control (see Figure 13-2).

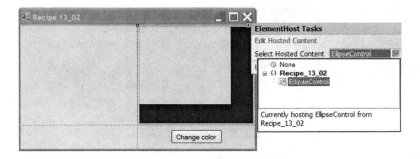

Figure 13-2. *Using* ElementHost *in Visual Studio*

If you do not want to use a user control, then you will need to populate the ElementHost control programmatically by assigning the desired WPF element to the Child property of the ElementHost control.

The Code

The following example demonstrates how to integrate WPF controls into a Windows Forms application. The example (shown in Figure 13-3) uses a simple WPF user control consisting of a System.Windows.Shapes.Ellipse that can change between red and blue color gradients. This EllipseControl is assigned to one ElementHost using the Visual Studio form builder. Another ElementHost is populated programmatically with a System.Windows.Controls.TextBox. A standard Windows Forms button triggers the EllipseControl to change color and then writes a log entry to the TextBox. Here is the XAML for the WPF user control:

```
<UserControl x:Class="Recipe_13_02.EllipseControl"
    xmlns="http://schemas.microsoft.com/winfx/2006/xaml/presentation"
    xmlns:x="http://schemas.microsoft.com/winfx/2006/xaml"
    Height="300" Width="300">
<Grid x:Name="Grid1">
    <Grid.Resources>
        <RadialGradientBrush x:Key="RedBrush" RadiusX=".8" RadiusY="1"
                             Center="0.5,0.5" GradientOrigin="0.05,0.5">
            <GradientStop Color="#ffffff" Offset="0.1" />
            <GradientStop Color="#ff0000" Offset="0.5" />
            <GradientStop Color="#880000" Offset="0.8" />
        </RadialGradientBrush>
        <RadialGradientBrush x:Key="BlueBrush" RadiusX=".8" RadiusY="1"
                             Center="0.5,0.5" GradientOrigin="0.05,0.5">
            <GradientStop Color="#ffffff" Offset="0.1" />
            <GradientStop Color="#0000ff" Offset="0.5" />
            <GradientStop Color="#000088" Offset="0.8" />
        </RadialGradientBrush>
    </Grid.Resources>
```

```
    <Ellipse Margin="5" Name="Ellipse1" ToolTip="A WPF Ellipse."
            Fill="{StaticResource RedBrush}">
    </Ellipse>
  </Grid>
</UserControl>
```

Here is the code-behind for the EllipseControl, which is used to control and query its current color gradient:

```csharp
using System.Windows.Controls;
using System.Windows.Media;

namespace Recipe_13_02
{
    /// <summary>
    /// Interaction logic for EllipseControl.xaml
    /// </summary>
    public partial class EllipseControl : UserControl
    {
        public EllipseControl()
        {
            InitializeComponent();
        }

        // Gets the name of the current color.
        public string Color
        {
            get
            {
                if (Ellipse1.Fill == (Brush)Grid1.Resources["RedBrush"])
                {
                    return "Red";
                }
                else
                {
                    return "Blue";
                }
            }
        }

        // Switch the fill to the red gradient.
        public void ChangeColor()
        {
            // Check the current fill of the ellipse.
            if (Ellipse1.Fill == (Brush)Grid1.Resources["RedBrush"])
            {
                // Ellipse is red, change to blue.
                Ellipse1.Fill = (Brush)Grid1.Resources["BlueBrush"];
            }
```

```
            else
            {
                // Ellipse is blue, change to red.
                Ellipse1.Fill = (Brush)Grid1.Resources["RedBrush"];
            }
        }
    }
}
```

The following is the code-behind for the main Windows Forms form—Form1. The Form1 constructor demonstrates the programmatic creation and configuration of an ElementHost control to display a standard WPF TextBox control. The button1_Click method is invoked when the user clicks the button, and it changes the color of the ellipse and appends a message to the content of the TextBox. The rest of the application code generated by Visual Studio is not shown here but is provided in the sample code.

```
using System;
using System.Windows;
using System.Windows.Forms;
using WPFControls=System.Windows.Controls;
using System.Windows.Forms.Integration;

namespace Recipe_13_02
{
    public partial class Form1 : Form
    {
        WPFControls.TextBox textBox;

        public Form1()
        {
            InitializeComponent();

            // Create a new WPF TextBox control.
            textBox = new WPFControls.TextBox();
            textBox.Text = "A WPF TextBox\n\r\n\r";
            textBox.TextAlignment = TextAlignment.Center;
            textBox.VerticalAlignment = VerticalAlignment.Center;
            textBox.VerticalScrollBarVisibility =
                WPFControls.ScrollBarVisibility.Auto;
            textBox.IsReadOnly = true;

            // Create a new ElementHost to host the WPF TextBox.
            ElementHost elementHost2 = new ElementHost();
            elementHost2.Name = "elementHost2";
            elementHost2.Dock = DockStyle.Fill;
            elementHost2.Child = textBox;
            elementHost2.Size = new System.Drawing.Size(156, 253);
            elementHost2.RightToLeft = RightToLeft.No;
```

```
            // Place the new ElementHost in the bottom left table cell.
            tableLayoutPanel1.Controls.Add(elementHost2, 1, 0);
        }

        private void button1_Click(object sender, EventArgs e)
        {
            // Change the ellipse color.
            ellipseControl1.ChangeColor();

            // Get the current ellipse color and append to TextBox.
            textBox.Text +=
                String.Format("Ellipse color changed to {0}\n\r",
                ellipseControl1.Color);

            textBox.ScrollToEnd();
        }
    }
}
```

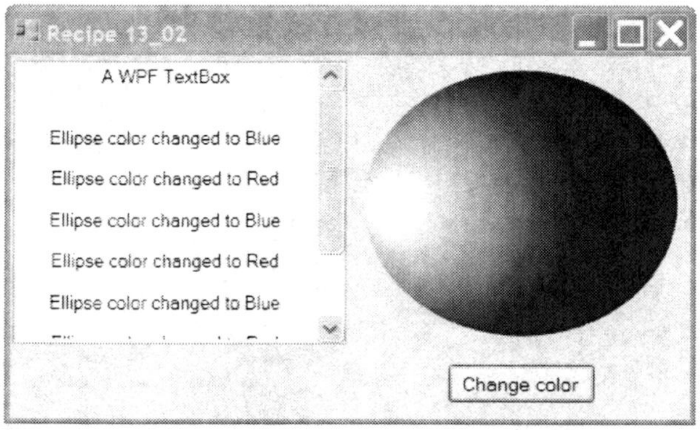

Figure 13-3. *Using WPF controls in a Windows Forms form*

13-3. Use Windows Forms in a WPF Application

Problem

You need to display a Windows form in a WPF application.

Solution

Create an instance of the System.Windows.Forms.Form you want to display in your WPF code. Call Form.ShowDialog to display the form modal or Form.Show to display the form modeless.

How It Works

It is straightforward to add a Windows form to your WPF application because Visual Studio allows you to select the Windows Forms template from the Add New Item option. You can then use Visual Studio's form builder to create the form visually.

Once you have a Form declared, you can reference and instantiate the class the same as you would do any other class. Calling Form.ShowDialog will display the Form modally, meaning the user can interact only with that Form and must close it before they can interact again with the rest of the application. Calling Form.Show will display the Form modeless, allowing the user to interact with the new Window as well as the rest of the application.

The Code

The following example (shown running in Figure 13-4) displays a WPF Window with two buttons. The left button opens and closes a modeless Form, and the right button opens a modal Form. When the example creates the modeless Form, it subscribes an event handler to the Form.FormClosing event so that the application can update the button state should the user choose to close the Form directly instead of using the button. The following is the XAML defining the application's main window:

```
<Window x:Class="Recipe_13_03.Window1"
    xmlns="http://schemas.microsoft.com/winfx/2006/xaml/presentation"
    xmlns:x="http://schemas.microsoft.com/winfx/2006/xaml"
    Title="WPF Recipes 13_03" Height="100" Width="300">
    <UniformGrid Columns="2">
        <Button HorizontalAlignment="Center" MaxHeight="25"
                Name="btnOpenModeless" Content="Open Modeless Form"
                Click="OpenModeless_Click" />
        <Button HorizontalAlignment="Center" MaxHeight="25"
                Name="btnOpenModal" Content="Open Modal Form"
                Click="OpenModal_Click" />
    </UniformGrid>
</Window>
```

The following is the code-behind for the main WPF window, which shows how the Form is manipulated by the WPF application:

```
using System.Windows;
using System.Windows.Forms;

namespace Recipe_13_03
{
    /// <summary>
    /// Interaction logic for Window1.xaml
    /// </summary>
    public partial class Window1 : Window
    {
        private Form1 modelessForm;
        private FormClosingEventHandler modelessFormCloseHandler;
```

```csharp
public Window1()
{
    InitializeComponent();
    modelessFormCloseHandler =
        new FormClosingEventHandler(ModelessFormClosing);
}

// Handles the Windows Form Closing event for the modeless form.
private void ModelessFormClosing(object sender, FormClosingEventArgs e)
{
    // Remove the event handler reference.
    modelessForm.FormClosing -= modelessFormCloseHandler;
    modelessForm = null;

    // Change the button text.
    btnOpenModeless.Content = "Open Modeless Form";
}

// Handles the button click event to open the modal Windows Form.
private void OpenModal_Click(object sender, RoutedEventArgs e)
{
    // Create and display the modal form.
    Form1 form = new Form1();
    form.ShowDialog();
}

// Handles the button click event to open and close the modeless
// Windows Form.
private void OpenModeless_Click(object sender, RoutedEventArgs e)
{
    if (modelessForm == null)
    {
        modelessForm = new Form1();

        // Add an event handler to get notification when the form
        // is closing.
        modelessForm.FormClosing += modelessFormCloseHandler;

        // Change the button text.
        btnOpenModeless.Content = "Close Modeless Form";

        // Show the Windows Form.
        modelessForm.Show();
    }
```

```
        else
        {
            modelessForm.Close();
        }
    }
}
}
```

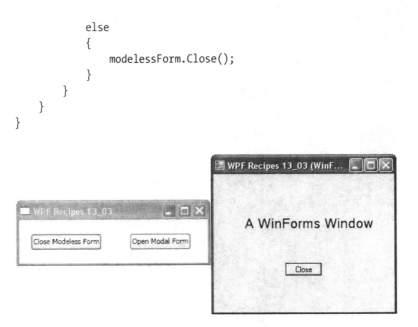

Figure 13-4. *Displaying a Windows Forms form from a WPF application*

13-4. Use Windows Forms Controls in a WPF Window

Problem

You need to display Windows Forms controls alongside WPF controls in a WPF window.

Solution

Use a `System.Windows.Forms.Integration.WindowsFormsHost` control on your WPF window, and host the Windows Forms control inside it.

Note WPF makes no specific provision for hosting ActiveX controls. To host an ActiveX control, you need to use it as you would in Windows Forms and then host the Windows Forms wrapper in WPF as described in this recipe. For further details, see the article on MSDN at `http://msdn.microsoft.com/en-us/library/ms742735.aspx`.

How It Works

The `WindowsFormsHost` control is a WPF control that allows you to host Windows Forms controls. The `WindowsFormsHost` control makes integrating Windows Forms controls into your WPF application simple.

The WindowsFormsHost can contain a single Windows Forms control that inherits from
System.Windows.Forms.Control.

The Code

The following code demonstrates how easy it is to use the WindowsFormsHost control to include
Windows Forms controls alongside WPF controls in your WPF applications.

The example (shown in Figure 13-5) uses a Windows Forms Button and a DataGridView to
demonstrate the ease of integration. Clicking the Button raises an event that causes the WPF
System.Windows.Shapes.Ellipse to change between a red and a blue gradient fill. The data in
the DataGridView is provided by binding its DataSource property to a CountryCollection
containing a set of Country objects defined directly in XAML as a static resource.

```xml
<Window x:Class="Recipe_13 04.Window1"
    xmlns="http://schemas.microsoft.com/winfx/2006/xaml/presentation"
    xmlns:x="http://schemas.microsoft.com/winfx/2006/xaml"
    xmlns:wf="clr-namespace:System.Windows.Forms;assembly=System.Windows.Forms"
    xmlns:rec="clr-namespace:Recipe_13_04"
    Title="WPF Recipes 13_04" Height="300" Width="500">
    <UniformGrid Columns="2" Rows="2" x:Name="Grid1">
        <UniformGrid.Resources>
            <RadialGradientBrush x:Key="RedBrush" RadiusX=".8" RadiusY="1"
                                 Center="0.5,0.5" GradientOrigin="0.05,0.5">
                <GradientStop Color="#ffffff" Offset="0.1" />
                <GradientStop Color="#ff0000" Offset="0.5" />
                <GradientStop Color="#880000" Offset="0.8" />
            </RadialGradientBrush>
            <RadialGradientBrush x:Key="BlueBrush" RadiusX=".8" RadiusY="1"
                                 Center="0.5,0.5" GradientOrigin="0.05,0.5">
                <GradientStop Color="#ffffff" Offset="0.1" />
                <GradientStop Color="#0000ff" Offset="0.5" />
                <GradientStop Color="#000088" Offset="0.8" />
            </RadialGradientBrush>
            <rec:CountryCollection x:Key="Countries">
                <rec:Country ID="1" Name="Australia" Capital="Sydney" />
                <rec:Country ID="2" Name="United Kingdom" Capital="London" />
                <rec:Country ID="3" Name="India" Capital="New Delhi" />
                <rec:Country ID="4" Name="Russia" Capital="Moscow" />
                <rec:Country ID="5" Name="Japan" Capital="Tokyo" />
            </rec:CountryCollection>
        </UniformGrid.Resources>
        <!-- A Winforms Button control-->
        <WindowsFormsHost >
            <wf:Button x:Name="btnWinFormButton" Text="Make Blue"
                       MaximumSize="100,25" BackColor="LightGray"
                       Click="btnWinFormButton_Click"/>
```

```
            </WindowsFormsHost>
            <!-- A WPF Ellipse-->
            <Ellipse Margin="5" Name="Ellipse1" ToolTip="A WPF Ellipse."
                    Fill="{StaticResource RedBrush}">
            </Ellipse>
            <!-- A WPF RichTextBox control-->
            <RichTextBox DockPanel.Dock="Bottom" ToolTip="A WPF Ellipse."
                    VerticalScrollBarVisibility="Visible">
                <FlowDocument>
                    <Paragraph FontSize="15">
                        A WPF Rich text Box.
                    </Paragraph>
                    <Paragraph FontSize="12">
                        Ut wisi enim ad minim veniam, quis nostrud exerci tation
                        ullamcorper suscipit lobortis nisl ut aliquip ex ea
                        commodo consequat. Duis autem vel eum iriure.
                    </Paragraph>
                </FlowDocument>
            </RichTextBox>
            <!-- A Winforms DataGridView control-->
            <WindowsFormsHost HorizontalAlignment="Center">
                <wf:DataGridView x:Name="dataGrid"
                            DataSource="{StaticResource Countries}"/>
            </WindowsFormsHost>
        </UniformGrid>
</Window>
```

The following is the code-behind that handles the click event raised when the user clicks the Windows Forms Button:

```
using System;
using System.Windows;
using System.Windows.Media;

namespace Recipe_13_04
{
    /// <summary>
    /// Interaction logic for Window1.xaml
    /// </summary>
    public partial class Window1 : Window
    {
        public Window1()
        {
            InitializeComponent();
        }
```

```
        // Handles the click of the Winforms button. Changes the fill
        // of the ellipse and changes the button text.
        private void btnWinFormButton_Click(object sender, EventArgs e)
        {
            // Check the current fill of the ellipse.
            if (Ellipse1.Fill == (Brush)Grid1.Resources["RedBrush"])
            {
                // Ellipse is red, change to blue.
                Ellipse1.Fill = (Brush)Grid1.Resources["BlueBrush"];

                // Change the Text on the Winforms button.
                btnWinFormButton.Text = "Make Red";
            }
            else
            {
                // Ellipse is blue, change to red.
                Ellipse1.Fill = (Brush)Grid1.Resources["RedBrush"];

                // Change the Text on the Winforms button.
                btnWinFormButton.Text = "Make Blue";
            }
        }
    }
}
```

Here is the code that defines the Country and CountryCollection classes used as data in the DataGridView:

```
using System;
using System.Collections.Generic;

namespace Recipe_13_04
{
    public class CountryCollection : List<Country> { }

    public class Country
    {
        public int ID { get; set; }
        public string Name { get; set; }
        public string Capital { get; set; }
    }
}
```

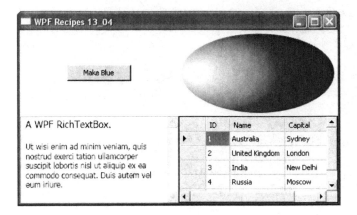

Figure 13-5. *Using Windows Forms controls in a WPF Window*

Index

Special Characters

{ } (braces), 100

/ character, 36

Numerics

2D controls, 590–593

2D graphics

lines

drawing, 512

drawing curved, 518–520

drawing sequences of connected, 513–514

formatting, 515–517

overview, 511–512

positioning, 558–561

rotating, 558–561

scaling, 558–561

shapes

drawing complex, 523–524

drawing simple, 521–522

drawing using solid colors, 533–534

filling using solid colors, 533–534

filling with active UI elements, 546–547

filling with images, 539–542

filling with linear color gradients, 536–539

filling with patterns, 542–545

filling with radial color gradients, 536–539

filling with textures, 542–545

reusable, 525–526

skewing, 558–561

Tool Tips

displaying graphics elements in, 530–531

displaying on shapes, 528–529

UI elements

applying blur effects to, 548–551

applying drop shadow effect to, 554–557

applying glow effects to, 552–554

using system colors in, 531–532

3D graphics

applying textures to, 583–585

drawing, 570–572

interacting with, 586–589

lighting scenes, 573–577

overview, 563

specifying material for, 578–582

using 2D controls in scenes, 590–593

using camera, 566–569

using in applications, 564–565

A

A property, 534

AccelerationRatio property, 597

Accepted property, 308

AcceptsReturn property, 105

AcceptsTab property, 105, 112

Actions element, 656, 658

Actions property, 656

ActualWidth property, 357

AddPersonCommand class, 251, 254, 256–257

AddValueChanged method, 19

aero.normalcolor.xaml file, 366

AffectsArrange property, 9

AffectsMeasure property, 9

AffectsParentArrange property, 9

AffectsParentMeasure property, 9

AffectsRender property, 9

AlignmentX property, 539, 541

AlignmentY property, 539, 541

AllowTransparency property, 82

AlternatingRowStyleSelector class, 345

Angle property, 559

Angle value, 633

AngleX property, 559

AngleY property, 559

animation
    of color of brush with indirect property
        targeting, 644–645
    controlling progress of, 617–619
    controlling through triggers, 646–650
    keyframe-based, 614–616
    limiting frame rate
        application, 629–630
        of storyboard, 626–627
    looping and reversing, 623–624
    MediaTimeline
        playing back audio or video with,
            635–636
        synchronizing Timeline animations
            with, 637–640
    notification of completion, 641–644
    object along path, 632–635
    overlapping, 609–611
    overview, 595
    parallel properties, 611–613
    property of control
        overview, 596–599
        set with data binding, 600–603
    removing, 604–609
    shape of path, 620–622

showing continuous during asynchronous
    process, 486–489

text, 651–652

AnimationTimeline object, 596–597, 605

AnimationTimeline property, 596

AnnotationDocumentPaginator class, 447, 452

AnnotationHelper class, 428–429, 431–432,
    435–436, 449

annotations
    loading and saving, 437–446
    printing, 447–452

AnnotationService class, 427, 429, 432–435,
    439–440, 444–445, 449–451

AnnotationStore class, 438

App_DispatcherUnhandledException
    property, 5

App.cs file, 42, 44

Appearance tab, 369

AppendText method, 105, 112

application: / / / authority, 36

Application class, 321–322, 338, 361, 499–503

application commands, supporting in user
    controls, 181–185

Application object, 2, 42, 46

application resource strings, binding to,
    321–323

application settings, binding to, 317–321

ApplicationCommands class, 111

ApplicationCommands command, 181

ApplicationDefinition object, 2, 4, 43

Application.DispatcherUnhandledException
    event, 4

Application.Properties property, 38

ApplicationPropertiesHelper object, 40

application-wide resources, 34–35

ApplyAnimationClock method, 604, 605, 608

applying textures to 3D models, 583–585

App.xaml file, 1–2, 4, 34, 37, 42, 368

App.xaml.cs file, 321–322

ArcSegment element, 518–520

AssemblyInfo.cs file, 366, 368

Asterisk property, 654

attached properties, 24–27, 54–55

audio

    playing using triggers, 656–657

    system sounds, 653–656

Auto value, 71

AutoReverse property, 597, 600, 623–624

■B

B property, 534

back-face culling, 579

Background property, 85, 165, 335, 337, 345, 349, 353, 458, 460

BackgroundWorker class, 469–471, 473–474, 477–478, 480–483, 486, 488–491, 493–498

BackgroundWorker threads

    creating in XAML, 480–483

    executing methods asynchronously using, 469–472

    showing ProgressBar while processing on

        cancellable, 493–496

        continuous, 496–499

        overview, 489–492

    supporting cancellation of, 476–480

    tracking progress of, 473–476

BackMaterial property, 578–579

Base Class Library (BCL), 484

BaseControlStyle property, 331

BasedOn attribute, 331

BCL (Base Class Library), 484

Beep property, 654–655

Begin method, 604

BeginAnimation method, 604–605

BeginChange method, 372

BeginInvoke method, 454, 457–458, 460–461, 464, 467, 500

BeginStoryboard element, 656

BeginStoryboardName property, 647

BeginTime property, 597, 612, 617

BezierSegment element, 518–520

binding. *See* data binding

Binding class, 230, 242

Binding declaration, 284

Binding property, 275

binding source, 229

Binding statement, 230, 233–234, 284

BindsDirectlyToSource property, 247, 260

BindsTwoWayByDefault property, 9

BitmapEffect property, 333, 548, 552, 555

BlurBitmapEffect element, 548–549

Body Text parameter, 79

Boolean property, 268, 275, 490, 682

Border control, 85

Border.Background property, 645

BorderBrush property, 85, 349

borders, 85–86

BorderThickness value, 85

Bottom value, 82, 140

bound data. *See also* data binding

braces ({ }), 100

Brush dependency property, 578

btnMessageHeaderButtonImage_Click event handler, 80

btnOpen_Click event handler, 116

btnSave_Click event handler, 116

bubbling events, 677

Build Action object, 2

Button 4 property, 60

Button 5 property, 60

Button class, 165, 193

Button click event, 157

Button controls, 122, 126, 165, 189, 196, 328, 331, 344

Button elements, 366

Button parameter, 79

Button property, 100

Button template, 357

button1_Click method, 692

ButtonBase class, 664

Buttonbase.Click event, 666

Button.Click event, 6, 147, 680, 682–683

buttons

    generating repeated click events, 124–125

    handling clicks, 122–124

    keyboard shortcuts to, 129–130

    setting default, 126–127

By property, 596

■ C

CAD (computer-aided design) packages, 566

Camera object, 566

cameras, 3D, 566–569

CancelAsync method, 399, 477, 493

CancellationPending property, 477

Cancelled property, 493

CanExecute event handler, 181–182, 182

CanExecute method, 250–251, 257, 259

CanExecute property, 182

CanExecuteChanged event, 251, 257–258

CanExecuteRoutedEventArgs class, 182

Canvas controls

    dragging elements inside, 225–227

    scrollable, 217–220

    zoomable, 221–225

Canvas method, 217

Canvas panel, 67

Canvas.Bottom value, 67

Canvas.Top value, 67

Canvas.ZIndex property, 68

Caption parameter, 79

CaretIndex property, 105

CaretPosition property, 112, 372

Center property, 82, 140, 537

CenterX property, 162, 558–559

CenterY property, 162, 558–559

centimeters (cm), 512

check boxes, 145–148

CheckAccess method, 464–466

CheckBox control, 146, 680

CheckBox.IsThreeState property, 146

Checked event, 142, 146

Child class, 31

Children collection, 221

Children property, 59, 564

Classic.xaml file, 366

Clear method, 105

ClearAllProperties method, 375

ClearHighlightForSelection method, 432

ClearValue method, 13

Click event, 122, 125, 134, 195–196, 206, 250–251, 664, 666

Click event handler, 89, 127, 130, 135, 340

Clock objects, 600

Closed event, 46

Closing event, 46

CLR objects, binding to, 235–241

cm (centimeters), 512

CoerceValueCallback value, 10, 16, 20

CollationCapability property, 386

CollectionChanged event, 296

collections

    applying custom grouping to, 313–316

    applying custom sorting logic to, 304–307

    filtering data in, 307–311

    grouping data in, 311–313

    with master-detail pattern, 295–302

    sorting data in, 302–304

CollectionView property, 296–297, 303

CollectionViewSource class, 297, 303–309, 311–312, 314–315

CollectionViewSource_EuropeFilter property, 308

color, brush, animating with indirect property targeting, 644–645

Color dependency property, 574

Color object, 534

Color property, 536, 555

Color Scheme drop-down box, 369

ColumnDefinition element, 65

columns, automatic wrapping of, 61–62

combo boxes, 159–162

ComboBox element, 160

ComboBoxItem element, 160

ComboBoxItem.Selected event, 160

ComboBox.SelectionChanged event,
    159–160

ComboBox.Text property, 160

Command property, 250–251

CommandBinding method, 181

CommandParameter property, 251, 253

commands, binding to, 250–259

Compare method, 304

Completed event, 642

Completed System.EventHandler object, 641

complex shapes, 523–524

ComponentCommands command, 181

Compose value, 610

computer-aided design (CAD) packages, 566

Conditions collection, 336

containers, responding when user clicks UI
    elements in, 666–668

Content property, 129, 154, 168–171

ContentControl class, 194

ContentControl property, 297, 300

ContentProperty attribute, 169

ContentTemplateSelector class, 278

context menus, displaying, 134–137

ContextMenu property, 134

Continent property, 309, 311, 315

continuous animation, 486–489

Control class, 97, 194, 464

Control. prefix, 328

control templates
    creating, 349–350
    customizing with properties, 353–354
    finding elements generated by, 356–358
    putting into styles, 351–353
    specifying named parts of, 354–356

ControllableStoryboardAction property,
    647–648

Controller property, 604

ControlNameAutomationPeer class, 202

controls
    button clicking
        generating repeated click events,
            124–125
        handling, 122–124
    changing appearance when mouse moves
        over, 333–334
    check boxes, 145–148
    combo boxes, 159–162
    displaying
        context menus, 134–137
        control content in braces, 100
        password entry boxes, 119–120
        rotated controls, 162–164
        simple text, 101–102
        static images, 103–104
    keyboard shortcuts
        to buttons, 129–130
        to text boxes, 128
    lists
        dynamically adding items to, 156–159
        viewing and selecting from, 153–155
    radio buttons, 142–145
    real-time spell checking, 120–121
    RichTextBox content, 115–118
    setting default buttons, 126–127
    Tool Tips
        displaying on controls, 137–138
        displaying on disabled controls, 139
        duration and position of, 140–142
    trees, 149–152
    user input
        rich text, 111–115
        simple text, 104–110
        sliders, 131–134

ControlTemplate class, 194–195

ControlTemplate property, 193, 349, 351,
    353, 355, 357

Convert method, 247–249, 260, 268–269, 271–273, 315

ConvertBack method, 269, 272, 274, 316

Converter property, 268–269, 314

converting bound data, 268–274

Copy method, 105, 112

CornerRadius property, 85

Counter property, 14

Country class, 311, 699

CountryCollection class, 699

CreateHighlightForSelection method, 431

CreateVisualCollator method, 383

Current property, 174

CurrentItem property, 297

curved lines, 518–520

custom business objects, 229

custom commands, 185–191

custom controls

    custom-drawn elements, 207–212

    dragging elements inside Canvas controls, 225–227

    lookless, 193–198

    numeric textbox controls, 212–216

    overview, 165–166

    scrollable Canvas controls, 217–220

    specifying parts required by, 198–202

    UI automation, supporting, 202–206

    zoomable Canvas controls, 221–225

custom-drawn elements, 207–212

CustomSort property, 304–305

Cut method, 105, 112

■D

data binding

    to application resource strings, 321–323

    to application settings, 317–321

    changing appearance of bound data, 274–277

    to CLR objects, 235–241

collections

    applying custom grouping to, 313–316

    applying custom sorting logic to, 304–307

    filtering data in, 307–311

    grouping data in, 311–313

    with master-detail pattern, 295–302

    sorting data in, 302–304

to commands, 250–259

converting bound data, 268–274

displaying bound data, 264–268

to existing object instances, 242–244

to IDataErrorInfo, 288–295

to methods, 247–250

overview, 229–230

properties of elements to self, 234–235

to properties of UI elements, 230–231

property of control set with, 600–603

selecting DataTemplate based on properties of data object, 278–282

specifying default value for, 262–264

specifying validation rules for, 283–288

two-way, 231–234

to values of enumeration, 260–262

to XML data, 244–246

data island, 245

data object, 229

Data property, 518–519, 523, 525–526

data templates, 264–268

data triggers, 274–277

DataContext property, 28, 236, 238, 242–244, 253–254, 289, 291, 297, 300

DataContextProperty property, 17

Data.cs file, 265

Data.GetData method, 673

DataGridView object, 697–699

DataItem class, 269, 275

DataSource property, 697

DataTemplate property, 264–268, 270, 274–283, 296–299, 311–314

DataTemplateSelector class, 278–279, 281

DataTrigger property, 274–276

debugging data bindings

    using attached properties, 54–55

    using IValueConverter, 51–54

DecelerationRatio property, 597

Decorator class, 194

Default Result parameter, 79

Default value, 232–233, 279, 306, 315, 317–318, 320

default value, specifying for binding, 262–264

DefaultStyleKeyProperty property, 194, 338

DefaultStyleKeyproperty.OverrideMetadata class, 195

defaultTaskTemplate property, 279, 282

DefaultValue value, 16

Delay property, 124

dependency properties

    adding PropertyChangedValueCallback, 19–20

    adding validation to, 20–23

    creating with property value inheritance, 28–31

    overriding metadata, 15–18

    overview, 7–12

    read-only, 13–15

DependencyObject object, 8

DependencyProperties property, 171

DependencyProperty field, 171

DependencyProperty property, 8, 10, 13, 16, 24, 213, 347, 602–603, 605

DependencyPropertyDescriptor property, 19

DependencyPropertyKey class, 13

DependencyPropertyKey.Dependency Property property, 13

Description property, 236, 239, 241, 297

design mode behavior, setting, 191–193

DesiredFrameRateProperty dependency property, 630

DesktopBrush property, 532

DiffuseMaterial class, 565, 567, 572, 577–579, 583–585, 588, 591

Direction property, 555–556

Disabled value, 71

Discrete keyframe, 614

DiscreteStringKeyFrame object, 651–652

Dispatcher class, 464, 467, 483, 503

Dispatcher method, 454

Dispatcher property, 454–455, 458, 461, 464, 467

Dispatcher queue, 454–457, 503

Dispatcher.CheckAccess class, 464

DispatcherObject class, 454

DispatcherPriority class, 454–455, 460, 484

DispatcherTimer class, 484

DispatcherUnhandledException event, 4, 6

displaying

    bound data, 264–268

    context menus, 134–137

    control content in braces, 100

    graphics elements in Tool Tips, 530–531

    password entry boxes, 119–120

    rotated controls, 162–164

    simple text, 101–102

    static images, 103–104

    Tool Tips

        on controls, 137–138

        on disabled controls, 139

        on shapes, 528–529

DisplayMemberPath property, 296

DistanceConverter class, 247, 249, 260

docking UI elements to edge of forms, 63–64

DockPanel property, 63, 93

DockPanel.Dock property, 63–64

Document property, 112, 115

DocumentPaginator object, 390, 394–395, 397, 401, 406, 413, 420, 447, 452

documents
 annotations
  loading and saving user-defined, 437–446
  printing, 447–452
  sticky note, 425–431
 displaying, 420–425
 FixedDocument
  asynchronously printing multipage, 398–404
  asynchronously saving to XPS file, 415–420
  programmatically creating and saving simple, 404–408
 FlowDocument
  programmatically creating and saving, 410–415
  using figures and floaters in, 408–410
 highlighting, 431–437
 simple, printing, 393–398
DocumentViewer object, 399–400, 404–405, 416, 419, 421, 426–427, 431–433, 435, 437, 439, 443, 448–451
DoDragDrop method, 673
DoesRotateWithTangent property, 633
DoEvents method, 453, 499–503
DoubleAnimationUsingPath method, 632
DoubleAnimationUsingPath object, 633
DoubleToWidthProperty property, 269
DoWork event, 469
DoWork event handler, 473
DoWorkEventArgs parameter, 477
DragCanvasControl control, 225, 227
DragDrop object, 673
DragDropEffects enumeration, 673
DragEnter event, 672–674
DragEventArgs object, 673
dragging
 elements inside Canvas controls, 225–227
 items from lists and dropping them on Canvas, 672–676

drawing
 3D models, 570–572
 lines
  curved, 518–520
  overview, 512
  sequences of connected, 513–514
 shapes
  complex, 523–524
  simple, 521–522
  using solid colors, 533–534
DrawingBrush class, 540
DrawingContext method, 207
DrawingContext object, 207
Drop event, 672–673
DropShadowBitmapEffect element, 555–556
Duration mode, 624
Duration property, 597, 636
Duration value, 612
DynamicResource markup extension, 361

E

EditingCommands class, 111
EditingCommands command, 181
ElementHost control, 689–690, 692
ElementName attribute, 230–231, 234, 242, 253, 271, 277, 286, 319–320
ElementName property, 195
Ellipse class, 516, 521, 534, 537, 541, 546
Ellipse element, 584
EllipseGeometry class, 523–524
EllipseGeometry element, 523
EmissiveMaterial object, 578–579
EndBatchWrite object, 383, 385
EndChange method, 372
EndPoint property, 536–537
ErrorContent class, 284–285, 289
ErrorContent property, 284
ErrorContent value, 284
EventManager class, 176
events, adding to user controls, 176–180

EventSetter element, 150

EventTrigger property, 656–660

exception handling, 4–7

Exclamation property, 654–655

Execute method, 250–251, 258–259

Executed event handler, 181–182

executing methods asynchronously

    using BackgroundWorker threads, 469–472

    using Dispatcher queue, 454–457

ExpandDirection property, 75

Expander control, 75

Expander element, 75

Expander.Header element, 75

expanders, 75–76

Explicit value, 233

ExternalAssembly value, 366

■F

FallbackValue property, 262

Figure object, 408

FileInputControl class, 169, 196, 199

FileInputControl control, 167, 169, 171, 182, 185, 201

FileInputControl method, 206

FileInputControlAutomationPeer class, 203

FileName property, 169, 171

Fill property, 269, 533–534, 539–540, 546

Fill value, 540

FillBehavior property, 597

filling shapes

    with active UI elements, 546–547

    with images, 539–542

    with linear color gradients, 536–539

    with patterns, 542–545

    with radial color gradients, 536–539

    with textures, 542–545

    using solid colors, 533–534

Filter property, 307–308, 314

FilterEventArgs class, 308–309

FilterEventHandler class, 308, 314

filtering data in collections, 307–311

FindName method, 356

FindResource method, 278–279, 282, 341

FixedDocument class

    asynchronously printing multipage, 398–404

    asynchronously saving to XPS file, 415–420

    simple, programmatically creating and saving, 404–408

FixedDocumentSequenceWritingProgress object, 399

FixedDocumentWritingProgress object, 399

FixedPage object, 404

FlipX value, 543

FlipXY value, 543

FlipY value, 543

Floater object, 408

FlowDirection property, 61

FlowDocument class

    programmatically creating and saving, 410–415

    using figures and floaters in, 408–410

FlowDocument element, 111

FlowDocument property, 112

FlowDocumentPageViewer object, 421–422, 426–427, 433

FlowDocumentPaginator object, 410

FlowDocumentReader object, 409–411, 421, 426, 432

FlowDocumentViewer object, 426

FontFamily property, 102, 331

FontSize property, 102, 331, 347

FontStyle property, 102, 331

FontWeight property, 102, 165, 344, 347

Foreground property, 366

Forever mode, 624

formatting lines, 515–517

Form.FormClosing event, 694

forms
    docking UI elements to edge of, 63–64
    sizing UI elements in, 94–96
    tab order in, 97
Form.ShowDialog object, 693–694
FrameworkElement class, 194, 338, 404, 564
FrameworkElement method, 341, 481
FrameworkElement property, 242–243, 279
FrameworkElementAutomationPeer class, 202
FrameworkElement-derived control, 137
FrameworkElements method, 217, 221
FrameworkPropertyMetadata object, 16, 28
FrameworkPropertyMetadataOptions enumeration, 9
FrameworkPropertyMetadataOptions.Inherits property, 28–29
From property, 596
FromArgb method, 534
FromAValues method, 534
FromRgb method, 534
FromScRgb method, 534
FromValues method, 534
frustum, 566

▪G

G property, 534
GemoetryModel3D class, 570
Generic ResourceDictionary class, 197
Generic.xaml resource dictionary, 194–195, 366
Geometry property, 570
GeometryGroup class, 523
GeometryGroup element, 523
GetDefaultView class, 304, 306
GetDefaultView method, 304
GetIsInDesignMode method, 191
GetPositionAtOffset method, 372
GetPrintCapabilities method, 386
GetTemplateChild class, 196, 199
GetTemplateChild method, 199

GetValue method, 13
GlowColor property, 552
GlowSize property, 552–553
GradientOrigin property, 537
GradientStop element, 536–537
graphics elements, using system colors in, 531–532
grid layout, 65–66
Grid panel, 73
Grid.Column property, 65
Grid.ColumnDefinitions element, 65
Grid.ColumnSpan property, 73
Grid.Row property, 65
Grid.RowDefinitions element, 65
Grid.RowSpan property, 73
GridSplitter control, 73
GridSplitter property, 73
group boxes, 77–78
GroupBox.Header element, 77
GroupDescriptions collection property, 311, 313
grouping data
    in collections, 311–313
    to collections, 313–316
groupingHeaderTemplate method, 311–313
GroupName property, 142

▪H

Hand property, 654–655
Handled property, 213, 682–683
HandoffBehavior.Compose object, 609–610
Header property, 75, 77, 88, 134
HeaderTemplate class, 311, 313–314
HeaderTemplateSelector property, 278
Heading attribute, 69
Height property, 58, 65, 94, 103, 269, 521, 654, 657, 659, 664, 667, 669–671, 673, 677, 680, 682
Hidden property, 217
Hidden value, 71
High property, 55

highlighting in documents, 431–437

highPriorityTaskTemplate property, 279–280, 282

horizontal stacks, 59–60

HorizontalAlignment property, 59–60, 73, 95

HorizontalOffset property, 82, 141

HorizontalScrollBarVisibility class, 217

HorizontalScrollBarVisibility property, 71, 112

■I

ICommand command, 186

ICommand object, 250–251, 257–258

IComparer class, 304

Icon parameter, 79

IDataErrorInfo class, 288–295

IDocumentPaginatorSource object, 394, 397, 413, 423–424

IEnumerable class, 295–297

Image class, 103

ImageBrush class, 540–541

ImageBrush element, 539

ImageBrush property, 543, 583–584

images

    displaying, 103–104

    filling shapes with, 539–542

ImageSource property, 583

in (inches), 512

IncreaseTotal command, 189

IncreaseTotal property, 186

Indeterminate event, 146

indirect property targeting, 644–645

InfoBrush property, 532

Inherits property, 9

INotifyCollectionChanged class, 296–297

INotifyPropertyChanged interface, 235–236, 239, 241, 254, 256, 292–293, 296–297

InsertTextIntoRun method, 372

interacting with 3D graphics, 586–589

Interval property, 124

InvalidateVisual method, 207

InvalidOperationException class, 467

Invoke method, 202, 500

InvokeRequired property, 464

IsChecked property, 52, 146

IsClosed property, 524

isControllable parameter, 486

IsDefault property, 126

IsEnabled property, 250–251

IsExpanded property, 52, 75

IsInDesignMode property, 191

IsIndeterminate property, 496–499

IsKeyDown method, 679–681

IsKeyToggled method, 679–681

IsLargeArc property, 519

IsMainMenu property, 87

IsMouseOver property, 333

IsMouseOverProperty property, 333

IsOpen property, 81

IsOutOfStock property, 275

IsPositive class, 275–276

IsReadOnly property, 105, 112

IsSelected property, 69, 142, 160, 347, 680

IsSelectedProperty property, 347

IsSmoothJoin property, 519

IsSnapToTickEnabled property, 131–132

IsSynchronizedWithCurrentItem property, 297

IsValid property, 283–284

ItemContainerStyleSelector property, 345

ItemsControl class, 271, 277, 295–296, 303–305, 308, 312–315

ItemsSource method, 458

ItemsSource property, 245, 265, 295–297

ItemTemplate property, 265, 278, 296–297

ItemTemplateSelector property, 278–279

Iteration Count mode, 624

IValueConverter class, 51–54, 268–269, 271–272, 313–315

IValueConverter interface, 269

IValueConverter.Convert method, 314

J

Journal property, 9

K

KernelType property, 548

Key property, 326, 328

Keyboard class, 679–680

keyboard events
  handling, 676–678
  suppressing, 682–683

keyboard shortcuts
  to buttons, 129–130
  to text boxes, 128

keyboard state, querying, 679–681

KeyDown event, 676–678, 682

keyframe-based animation, 614–616

KeyUp event, 676–678, 682

L

Label control, 128

LargeChange property, 131

LargerChange value, 132

LastChildFill property, 64

layout management
  autosizing main windows, 58
  borders, 85–86
  expanders, 75–76
  menus, 87–89
  message boxes, 78–80
  multitabbed interfaces, 69–70
  pop-up windows, 81–84
  resizable split panels, 73–74
  scrollable interfaces, 70–72
  status bars, 93–94
  toolbars, 90–92
  UI elements
    automatically wrapping rows or
      columns, 61–62
    docking to edge of form, 63–64
    grid layout, 65–66
    group boxes, 77–78

  horizontal or vertical stacking, 59–60
  positioning to exact coordinates, 67–68
  size control in form, 94–96
  tab order in form, 97

LayoutTransform property, 162–163,
  221–222, 558

Left value, 82, 140

LeftButton property, 669, 671, 675

Light object, 574

lighting scenes with 3D graphics, 573–577

Line class, 512, 516

Line elements, 512

Line object, 534, 537, 541

linear color gradients, filling shapes with,
  536–539

Linear keyframe, 614

LinearGradientBrush class, 536–537

LinearGradientBrush element, 537

LineCount property, 105

LineGeometry class, 523–524

LineGeometry element, 523

lines
  drawing, 512
  drawing curved, 518–520
  drawing sequences of connected, 513–514
  formatting, 515–517

LineSegment element, 518–520

list items
  changing appearance of alternate,
    345–347
  changing appearance of when selected,
    347–348

ListBox control, 458

ListBox element, 153, 460–463

ListBox property, 672–674, 676

ListBoxItem class, 347

ListBoxItem control, 157

ListBoxItem element, 153

ListBoxItem property, 153, 672–675

ListBoxItem.Selected event, 154

ListBox.SelectionChanged event, 154

ListCollectionView object, 305

lists

  dynamically adding items to, 156–159

  viewing and selecting from, 153–155

Loaded event, 341, 457, 460

loading

  items in ListBoxes asynchronously, 460–463

  window data asynchronously, 457–460

LoadNumber method, 461

LoadNumbers method, 458–459, 500–502

lookless custom controls, 193–198

looping animation, 623–624

LostFocus value, 233

Low property, 55

Luna.Homestead.xaml resource dictionary, 366–367

luna.metallic.xaml file, 366

luna.normalcolor.xaml file, 366

M

Main method, 2, 42

main windows, autosizing, 58

MappingMode property, 536

Margin property, 95, 331

master-detail pattern, collections with, 295–302

Material property, 578

MaterialGroup object, 578–579, 584–585

matrices, 563

MatrixAnimationUsingPath method, 632

MatrixAnimationUsingPath object, 618, 632–634, 639

MatrixCamera class, 566

MaxHeight property, 95

Maximum property, 131, 355, 490

Maximum value, 132

MaxLength property, 105

MaxWidth property, 95

Measure method, 217, 221

MeasureOverride method, 217, 221

media files, playing, 658–662

MediaCommands command, 181

MediaElement class, 636

MediaElement property, 656–660

MediaElement.NaturalDuration property, 636

MediaElement.Position property, 636

MediaTimeline

  playing back audio or video with, 635–636

  synchronizing Timeline animations with, 637–640

MediaTimeline class, 636

MediaTimeline property, 658

MediaTimeline.CurrentTimeInvalidated event, 659

Medium property, 55

Menu class, 87

MenuItem elements, 87

MenuItem object, 87–88, 134

menus, 87–89

MeshGeometry3D object, 571, 583

message boxes, 78–80

MessageBox class, 78

metadata, overriding, 15–18

MethodName property, 247–248, 260–261

MethodParameters collection, 247, 260

methods, binding to, 247–250

Microsoft.VisualBasic.ApplicationServices. StartupNextInstanceEventArgs property, 42

Microsoft.VisualBasic.ApplicationServices. WindowsFormsApplicationBase property, 42

Microsoft.Win32.OpenFileDialog file, 169, 182

MinHeight property, 95

Minimum property, 131, 355

Minimum value, 132

MinWidth property, 95

Mode property, 231–233, 284, 317

ModelUIElement object, 586

ModelUIElement3D object, 586–587

ModelVisual3D object, 586–587

mouse

  responding when user clicks UI elements in containers with, 666–668

  responding when user clicks UI elements with, 663–665

  responding when user rotates wheel, 669–671

mouse events, suppressing, 682–683

Mouse value, 82, 140

MouseDoubleClick event, 663–665

MouseDown event, 587, 663–668, 682

MouseLeftButtonDown event, 664, 673

MouseLeftButtonUp event, 664

MouseRightButtonDown event, 664

MouseRightButtonUp event, 664

MouseUp event, 663–666, 682

MouseWheel event, 669–671

MouseWheelEventArgs property, 669, 671

MSBuild property, 2

multimedia

  dragging items from lists and dropping them on Canvas, 672–676

  handling keyboard events, 676–678

  overview, 653

  playing media files, 658–662

  playing system sounds, 653–656

  querying keyboard state, 679–681

  responding when user clicks UI elements, 663–665

  responding when user clicks UI elements in containers, 666–668

  responding when user rotates mouse wheel, 669–671

  suppressing keyboard and mouse events, 682–683

  using triggers to play audio, 656–657

multiple windows, 46–51

multitabbed UIs, 69–70

multithreading

  BackgroundWorker threads

    creating in XAML, 480–483

    executing methods asynchronously using, 469–472

    supporting cancellation of, 476–480

    tracking progress of, 473–476

  creating separate threads for each window in multiwindow application, 503–509

  executing methods asynchronously using Dispatcher queue, 454–457

  implement Application.DoEvents in WPF, 499–503

  loading items in ListBoxes asynchronously, 460–463

  loading window data asynchronously after rendering, 457–460

  overview, 453

  ProgressBar, showing while processing

    cancellable, 493–496

    continuous, 496–499

    overview, 489–492

  showing continuous animation during asynchronous process, 486–489

  UI threads

    determining whether code is running on, 464–467

    verifying code is running on, 467–469

  updating UI asynchronously on timer, 483–485

MultiTrigger property, 336

multiwindow applications, 503–509

My Style key, 326

MyExternalAssembly assembly, 37

MyUserControl control, 191

■N

named styles, 325–327

NavigationCommands command, 181

Noise property, 552–553, 555–556

None property, 9, 55

None value, 366, 540, 543

Normals property, 571

NotDataBindable property, 9

notification of completion, 641–644

NotImplementedException event, 6

Number property, 213, 215

numeric textbox controls, 212–216

NumericTextBoxControl control, 215

■O

object instances, binding to existing, 242–244

ObjectDataProvider class, 247–248, 260–261

ObjectType property, 247–248, 260–261

ObservableCollection class, 461

ObservableCollection<T> class, 296–297

Offset property, 536

OnApplyTemplate method, 195–196, 199

OnClosing method, 317, 320

OnCreateAutomationPeer method, 202–203

OneTime value, 232

one-way binding, 231–232

OneWay value, 232–233, 235

OneWayToSource value, 232

OnNumberChanged method, 213

OnPreviewMouseLeftButtonDown method, 225

OnPreviewMouseLeftButtonUp method, 225

OnPreviewMouseMove method, 225

OnPreviewTextInput method, 213

OnPropertyChanged method, 236, 239–241, 254–257, 292–293

OnRender implementation, 160

OnRender method, 207

OnStartup method, 42, 321–322

OnStartupNextInstance method, 42

OnTextChanged method, 213

Opacity property, 552, 555

OpenFileDialog command, 182, 185

operating systems (OS), 365–369

Options parameter, 79

Orientation property, 59, 61

OriginalSource property, 122

OrthographicProjection class, 566

OS (operating systems), 365–369

OuterGlowBitmapEffect class, 552

OuterGlowBitmapEffect element, 552

OverrideMetadata method, 13, 15–16, 194

OverridesInheritenceBehaviour property, 9

■P

pack://authority/path path, 36

Pad value, 537

PageNumberControl control, 171, 173, 186, 189

Panel class, 194

parallel properties, 611–613

ParallelTimeline class, 596, 612

ParallelTimeline property, 596, 612

ParallelTimeline.SlipBehavior property, 638

Parent class, 30

PART_Browse element, 196

PART_ElementName element, 195, 199

PART_Indicator element, 195, 355

PART_Indicator method, 355

PART_Track element, 195, 355

PART_Xxx method, 355

password entry boxes, displaying, 119–120

Password property, 119

PasswordBox control, 119

PasswordBox property, 119

PasswordChar property, 119

Paste method, 105, 112

Path attribute, 230, 242, 247, 251, 260, 275, 317

Path class, 516, 518, 523

Path element, 519, 526

Path statement, 247, 260

PathAnimationSource value, 633

PathAnimationSource.Angle object, 633

PathFigure element, 518–519

PathGeometry class, 523–524

PathGeometry element, 518–520, 523

patterns, filling shapes with, 542–545

PauseStoryboard type, 647

Percent property, 269–270

PercentageRule class, 284, 286–287

PercentToFillConverter class, 269–270, 272

PercentToHeightConverter class, 269–271

Person class, 236, 239, 243, 251, 254, 265, 289, 292, 297, 301

PersonCollection class, 297, 300–301

perspective, 566

PerspectiveCamera class, 566

PieChartControl control, 207

pixels (px), 512

Placement property, 81

PlacementMode enumeration, 81, 140

PlacementMode option, 140

PlacementMode property, 81

PlacementMode value, 140

PlacementRectangle property, 82, 141

PlacementTarget property, 81–82, 141

Play method, 654

playing

    audio using triggers, 656–657

    media files, 658–662

    system sounds, 653–656

Point property, 519

Point3 property, 520

PointAimationUsingPath object, 633

PointAnimation value, 620

PointAnimationUsingPath method, 632

PointCollection object, 583

PointLight object, 574

points (pt), 512, 563

Points property, 513–514, 522

Polygon class, 516, 521, 523, 541

Polygon element, 584

polygon1_MouseDown method, 587

Polyline class, 516

PolyLine element, 513–514

PolyLine object, 514

pop-up windows, 81–84

PopupAnimation property, 82

Popup.HorizontalOffset property, 81

Popup.IsOpen property, 81

Popup.Placement property, 81

Popup.VerticalOffset property, 81

positioning graphics elements, 558–561

Positions property, 570–571

PresentationTraceLevel class, 54

PresentationTraceSource class, 54–55

Preview event, 677

PreviewKeyDown event, 676–677

PreviewKeyUp event, 676–678

PreviewMouseDown event, 682–683

PreviewMouseLeftButtonDown event, 672–673, 675

PreviewMouseMove event, 672, 675

PreviewTextInput event, 676–678

PrimeNumberHelper class, 457

PrintCapabilities document, 386

PrintCapabilities object, 386

PrintDialog object, 379–381, 384–385, 390, 394, 397, 399, 402, 451

printing

    configuring printing options using PrintTicket, 386–393

    multipage FixedDocument asynchronously, 398–404

    simple documents, 393–398

    WPF visuals

        collection of, 382–386

        overview, 379–382

PrintQueue object, 379–383, 385–386, 389–390, 393–394, 397, 402, 451

PrintServer object, 379

PrintTicket class, 386–393

Priority property, 279

ProbabilityToOpacityConverter property, 269

ProgressBar class, showing while processing
cancellable, 493–496
continuous, 496–499
overview, 489–492

ProgressBar element, 338

ProgressBar property, 366

ProgressChanged event, 473, 476, 489–490, 492

ProgressChanged event handler, 490

ProgressChangedEventArgs class, 476, 483, 490, 492, 496

ProgressPercentage class, 476, 483, 490, 492, 496

properties
adding to user controls, 171–175
sharing throughout application, 37–41

properties of control, animating, 596–603

Properties property, 38, 317

Properties.Resources class, 321

Properties.Settings.Default class, 317

Property property, 10

property value inheritance, 28–31

PropertyChanged value, 232–236, 238, 241, 248, 253, 256–258, 284, 286, 290–291, 293, 298, 319–320

PropertyChangedCallback value, 16, 20

PropertyChangedCallbacks method, 21

PropertyChangedEventArgs class, 236

PropertyChangedValueCallback value, 19–20

PropertyGroupDescription class, 311–313, 315

PropertyMetadata property, 630

PropertyNameChanged event, 236

PropertyThatDoesNotInherit property, 29

PropertyThatInherits property, 29

pt (points), 512, 563

public static readonly DependencyProperty property, 13

px (pixels), 512

Q

querying keyboard state, 679–681

Question property, 654

R

R property, 534

radial color gradients, filling shapes with, 536–539

RadialGradientBrush class, 536–537

radio buttons, 142–145

RadioButton property, 100

RadioButton.Checked event, 142–143

Radius property, 548–549

RadiusX property, 537

RadiusY property, 537

RaiseEvent method, 176

ReachFramework assembly, 380, 383, 387, 394, 398, 416, 438, 448

read-only dependency properties, 13–15

Rectangle class, 516, 521, 534, 537, 541, 546

Rectangle element, 355, 584

RectangleGeometry class, 523–524

RectangleGeometry element, 523

Reflect value, 537

Register method, 8, 13

RegisterReadOnly method, 13

RegisterReadOnly property, 13

Relative value, 82, 140

RelativeSource property, 234–235, 242, 285, 289–290

RelativeSource.Self property, 234, 285, 289

Remove method, 604

RemoveStoryboard type, 647

RemoveStoryboard.BeginStoryboardName property, 605

RemoveValueChanged method, 19

Render event, 454

RenderTransform elements, 558

RenderTransform property, 162–163, 558

RenderTransformOrigin property, 163, 558

Repeat value, 537

RepeatBehavior property, 486, 597, 623–624

RepeatBehavior.Forever event, 624

RepeatButton control, 124

ReportProgress class, 473, 476, 483, 489–490, 492, 496

ReportProgress method, 473, 490

resizable split panels, 73–74

resource dictionaries, 32–33

ResourceDictionarty.MergedDictionaries property, 32

ResourceDictionary class, 36–37, 37, 197, 201

ResourceDictionary markup extension, 361

ResourceDictionary property, 32, 34, 36

ResourceDictionary.MergedDictionaries property, 32

ResourceFile.xaml file, 36–37

ResourceKey property, 321

resources, application-wide, 34–35

Resources class, 321–322

Resources collection, 341, 344

Resources property, 328

ResumeStoryboard type, 647

reusable shapes, 525–526

reversing animation, 623–624

rich text, user input in form of, 111–115

RichTextBox class, 372–374, 372–376, 410

RichTextBox control
    loading content of, 115–118
    real time spell checking, 120–121
    saving content of, 115–118

RichTextBox element, 669–670

RichTextBox property, 111–112

RichTextBox.Document property, 111, 115–116

Right value, 82, 140

RightButton property, 669

rotated controls, displaying, 162–164

RotateTransform element, 558

RotateTransform property, 162

rotating graphics elements, 558–561

RotationAngle property, 519

RoutedCommand command, 185–186

RoutedEvent method, 176

RoutedEvent property, 656

RoutedEventArgs class, 655, 665, 668, 681–683

RoutedEventArgs.OriginalSource property, 123

RoutedUICommand command, 186

RowDefinition element, 65–66

rows, automatic wrapping of, 61–62

Royale.NormalColor.xaml file, 366

Run method, 42

RunWorkerAsync method, 469–470, 496

RunWorkerCompleted event, 469–470, 477, 486, 493, 497

RunWorkerCompleted method, 477

RunWorkerCompletedEventArgs class, 470, 472, 475, 477, 479, 483, 489, 492–493, 495, 498

RunWorkerCompletedEventArgs parameter, 477, 493

■S

ScA property, 534

ScaleTransform element, 558

ScaleTransform method, 221, 223

ScaleX property, 222, 559

ScaleY property, 222, 559

scaling graphics elements, 558–561

ScB property, 534

ScG property, 534

ScR property, 534

scrollable Canvas controls, 217–220

scrollable UIs, 70–72

ScrollableCanvasControl control, 218–219

ScrollViewer class, 217

ScrollViewer element, 71

ScrollViewer method, 217, 221

ScrollViewer property, 222

SearchChanged control, 177

SearchChanged event, 176

SearchChanged RoutedEvent control, 178

SearchControl control, 176, 180

Seek method, 600

SeekStoryboard type, 647

Select method, 105

SelectAll method, 106, 112

Selected event, 149, 153, 159–160

Selected event handler, 150

SelectedItem property, 149–150, 153, 160

SelectedItemChanged property, 150

SelectedItems property, 153

SelectedText property, 105

selecting

    from check boxes, 145–148

    from combo boxes, 159–162

    from lists, 153–155

    from radio buttons, 142–145

    from trees, 149–152

Selection property, 112

SelectionChanged event, 153, 160

SelectStyle method, 345

SelectTemplate method, 278–279, 281

SetOccupationCommand class, 251, 254, 256, 258

SetStoryboardSpeedRatio type, 647

Setter object, 275

Setter property, 328

Setters collection, 326

Setters property, 275

Settings property, 317

Settings.Default.Save method, 317

SetValue method, 13

ShadowDepth property, 555–556

Shape class, 516–517, 528

Shape property, 533

shapes

    displaying Tool Tips on, 528–529

    drawing

        complex, 523–524

        simple, 521–522

        using solid colors, 533–534

    filling

        with active UI elements, 546–547

        with images, 539–542

        with linear color gradients, 536–539

        with patterns, 542–545

        with radial color gradients, 536–539

        with textures, 542–545

        using solid colors, 533–534

    reusable, 525–526

Show method, 78

ShowOnDisabled property, 139

single instance application, 42–45

SingleInstanceManager property, 43

single-threaded apartment (STA) model, 453

Size property, 519

SizeToContent property, 58

sizing main windows, 58

skewing graphics elements, 558–561

SkewTransform element, 558

skins, dynamically changing, 361–365

SkinsComboBox System.Windows.Controls.ComboBox control, 361

SkipStoryboardToFill type, 647

Slices property, 207

Slider control, 131, 221, 223, 230–234, 284, 286

sliders, 131–134

Slider.ValueChanged event, 617

Slider.ValueChanged property, 659

SlipBehavior.Grow value, 638

SmallChange property, 131

SnapshotAndReplace value, 610

Softness property, 555–556

solid colors, drawing and filling shapes using, 533–534

SolidBrush class, 530

SolidColorBrush class, 533–534

SolidColorBrush property, 33

SortableCountries class, 305–306

SortCountries class, 305

SortDescription property, 303, 305

SortDescriptions collection, 303

sorting data

    in collections, 302–304

    to collections, 304–307

Source property, 36, 233, 242–243, 245–246, 248–249, 261, 267, 271, 277, 280–281, 285, 290, 303–304, 308, 312–315, 317–318, 540

<Source Type or Name>To<Target Type>Converter convention, 269

SourceAssembly value, 366

specifying material for 3D models, 578–582

SpecularMaterial object, 578–579

SpecularPower property, 578

SpeedRatio property, 597

spell checking

    RichTextBox, 120–121

    TextBox, 120–121

SpellCheck control, 121

SpellCheck.IsEnabled property, 121

Spline keyframe, 614

split panels, resizable, 73–74

SpotLight object, 574

SpreadMethod property, 537

STA (single-threaded apartment) model, 453

StackPanel property, 59–60

standard WPF applications, 1–3

StartPoint property, 519, 536–537

static XamlReader class, 115

StaticResource markup extension, 321

status bars, 93–94

StatusBar element, 93

StaysOpen property, 82

sticky notes, 425–431

Stop method, 486

StopStoryboard type, 647

storyboard, limiting frame rate of, 626–627

Storyboard class, 486, 596, 600, 617

Storyboard element, 656

Storyboard property, 596

Storyboard.Completed event, 624

Storyboard.TargetName property, 657

Stoyboard.Seek method, 659

Stretch property, 539–540, 542

StringAnimationUsingKeyFrames timeline, 651

StringKeyFrame class, 651

Stroke property, 512, 516, 533–534

StrokeDashArray property, 516

StrokeDashCap property, 516–517

StrokeDashOffset property, 516

StrokeEndLineCap property, 516

StrokeLineJoin property, 516–517

StrokeStartLineCap property, 516

StrokeThickness property, 512, 516

Style object, 165

Style property, 326, 331, 343

styles

    controls, changing appearance of when mouse moves over, 333–334

    ignoring implicit, 343–344

    inheriting from common base, 331–333

    list items

        changing appearance of alternate, 345–347

        changing appearance of when selected, 347–348

    named, 325–327

    overriding properties of, 330–331

    overview, 325

    programmatically extracting, 338–340

    putting control templates into, 351–353

    setting programmatically, 341–343

    that adapt to current OS theme, 365–369

ToolTip, 358–360

triggers

   applying multiple to same element, 335–336

   evaluating multiple properties for same, 336–337

   typed, 327–329

StyleSelector class, 345

SubPropertiesDoNotAffectRender property, 9

suppressing keyboard and mouse events, 682–683

SweepDirection property, 519

Syntax highlighting, 375–379

system colors, 531–532

system sounds, playing, 653–656

System.AppDomain property, 46

System.ArgumentException exception, 21

System.Collections.Generic.List<T> interface, 295

System.Collections.ICollection interface, 295

System.Collections.IComparer interface, 304

System.Collections.IDictionary property, 38

System.Collections.IEnumerable interface, 295

System.Collections.IList interface, 295, 304

System.Collections.ObjectModel.Collection <ResourceDictionary> property, 32

System.Collections.ObjectModel.Collection <T> interface, 295

System.Collections.ObjectModel.Observable Collection class, 461

System.Collections.ObjectModel.Observable Collection<T> class, 296, 305

System.Collections.Specialized.INotify CollectionChanged control, 295–296

System.Collections.Specialized.Notify CollectionChangedEventArgs class, 296

SystemColors class, 366, 532

SystemColors property, 366

System.ComponentModel namespace, 480–481

System.ComponentModel. RunWorkerCompletedEventArgs parameter, 477

System.ComponentModel.AsyncCompleted EventArgs object, 399

System.ComponentModel.BackgroundWorker class, 454, 469, 473, 477, 480, 486, 489, 493, 496

System.ComponentModel.BackgroundWorker event, 6

System.ComponentModel.Dependency PropertyDescriptor property, 19

System.ComponentModel.Dependency PropertyDescriptor.FromProperty static method, 19

System.ComponentModel.DesignerProperties property, 191

System.ComponentModel.DesignerProperties. GetIsInDesignMode method, 191

System.ComponentModel.DoWorkEventArgs class, 470, 477, 483

System.ComponentModel.IDataErrorInfo interface, 288

System.ComponentModel.INotifyProperty Changed control, 233, 235, 296

System.ComponentModel.ProgressChanged EventArgs class, 490

System.ComponentModel.PropertyChanged EventArgs class, 236

System.ComponentModel.RunWorkerComp letedEventArgs class, 470

System.ComponentModel.SortDescription control, 302–303

System.Data.DataSet object, 242

System.Delegate class, 454

System.Diagnostics.PresentationTraceLevel value, 54

System.Diagnostics.PresentationTraceSources. TraceLevel property, 54

System.Double value, 558

System.EventHandler event, 642

SystemFonts property, 366

SystemIdle property, 455

System.Int object, 614

System.Int32 value, 140

System.InvalidOperationException class, 432, 464, 467

System.InvalidOperationException property, 624, 644

System.IO.FileAccess.ReadWrite mode, 415

System.IO.FileStream object, 115

System.IO.Packaging.Package object, 438

System.IO.Packaging.PackagePart object, 438

System.IO.Stream class, 338, 447

System.Media.SystemSounds class, 654

System.NotImplementedException event, 6

System.NotImplementedException instance, 269

System.Object argument, 673, 682

SystemParameters property, 366

SystemParameters.MinimumHorizontal DragDistance property, 673, 675

SystemParameters.MinimumVertical DragDistance property, 673, 675

System.Printing assembly, 379–384, 387, 389, 394–395, 398, 400, 416, 438, 448

System.Printing.Collation method, 386

System.Printing.PrintCapabilities method, 386

System.Printing.PrintQueue method, 379, 382, 386, 447

System.Printing.PrintServer object, 379

System.Printing.PrintTicket object, 379, 386, 394

System.Reflection namespace, 321, 338

System.Security.SecureString property, 119

SystemSounds class, 654

System.String object, 614

System.String property, 119

System.Threading.Thread class, 476, 503, 508

System.Threading.Thread.Sleep class, 486

System.Threading.Thread.Sleep method, 497

System.Threading.ThreadStart class, 503

System.Threading.Timer class, 484

System.Thread.Mutex objects, 42

System.Timers.Timer class, 484

System.TimeSpan object, 617

System.Type parameter, 199

System.Type property, 328

SystemWidows.Window property, 34

System.Windows namespace, 245

System.Windows.Annotations namespace, 438

System.Windows.Annotations.Annotation DocumentPaginator object, 447

System.Windows.Annotations.Annotation Helper object, 431

System.Windows.Annotations.Annotation Service object, 426, 431

System.Windows.Annotations.AnnotationStore object, 447

System.Windows.Annotations.Storage. AnnotationStore object, 438

System.Windows.Annotations.Storage. XmlStreamStore object, 438

System.Windows.Application class, 2, 38, 321

System.Windows.Application property, 42

System.Windows.Application.Current. Windows property, 46

System.Windows.Application.Dispatcher UnhandledException event, 4

System.Windows.Application.LoadComponent class, 361

System.Windows.Application.Startup event, 630

System.Windows.Automation.Peers. FrameworkElementAutomationPeer class, 202

System.Windows.Automation.Provider. IInvokeProvider class, 202

System.Windows.BeginStoryboard object, 646

System.Windows.Button control, 331, 338, 366

System.Windows.Button element, 357

System.Windows.Button property, 330

System.Windows.CheckBox control, 331

System.Windows.Condition class, 336

System.Windows.ContentElement object, 605

System.Windows.Control class, 663

System.Windows.Control control, 344

System.Windows.Control property, 331

System.Windows.Control.ButtonBase class, 663

System.Windows.Control.ButtonBase.Click event, 666

System.Windows.Controls property, 99

System.Windows.Controls.BooleanTo VisibilityConverter class, 268

System.Windows.Controls.Border control, 165, 265, 353, 357

System.Windows.Controls.Border object, 633

System.Windows.Controls.Border property, 85, 349

System.Windows.Controls.Border.Background property, 644

System.Windows.Controls.Button background property, 33

System.Windows.Controls.Button class, 69, 328, 373, 384, 405, 455, 464, 467, 470, 473, 477, 481, 484, 486, 493, 504, 607, 615, 657

System.Windows.Controls.Button control, 5, 122, 124, 126, 129, 165, 176, 186, 219, 250, 297, 305, 464, 467, 500, 530, 590

System.Windows.Controls.Button property, 17, 60, 64, 66, 68, 75, 79, 91, 96–97, 157, 326, 333

System.Windows.Controls.Canvas class, 221, 225, 512, 520, 672

System.Windows.Controls.Canvas control, 217, 221, 225

System.Windows.Controls.Canvas property, 67

System.Windows.Controls.Canvas.Top, System.Windows.Controls. DockPanel.Dock property, 24

System.Windows.Controls.CheckBox class, 504, 600

System.Windows.Controls.CheckBox property, 52, 146

System.Windows.Controls.ComboBox control, 159, 236, 247, 251, 260, 331

System.Windows.Controls.ContentControl class, 278, 295

System.Windows.Controls.ContentControl control, 166, 169, 359

System.Windows.Controls.ContentPresenter class, 278

System.Windows.Controls.Control control, 333, 349, 353

System.Windows.Controls.Control elements, 355

System.Windows.Controls.Control property, 32, 34

System.Windows.Controls.Control.Foreground property, 268

System.Windows.Controls.ControlTemplate class, 275, 338, 349, 351, 355–356

System.Windows.Controls.ControlTemplate control, 165, 353, 359

System.Windows.Controls.ControlTemplate property, 355

System.Windows.Controls.ControlTemplate resource, 353

System.Windows.Controls.DataError ValidationRule class, 288

System.Windows.Controls.DataTemplate Selector class, 278

System.Windows.Controls.DockPanel property, 63, 82, 90

System.Windows.Controls.DocumentViewer object, 405, 420–421, 426, 432

System.Windows.Controls.Expander property, 52, 75

System.Windows.Controls.FixedDocument
Reader object, 426, 432

System.Windows.Controls.FlowDocument
Reader object, 409, 421

System.Windows.Controls.Grid control, 265

System.Windows.Controls.Grid property, 35,
52, 65, 73, 77

System.Windows.Controls.Grid.Row
property, 24

System.Windows.Controls.GridSplitter
property, 73

System.Windows.Controls.GridView control,
278

System.Windows.Controls.GroupBox
property, 77

System.Windows.Controls.GroupStyle
control, 311

System.Windows.Controls.HeaderedContent
Control class, 278

System.Windows.Controls.HeaderedItems
Control class, 278

System.Windows.Controls.Image control,
165, 265

System.Windows.Controls.Image method,
341

System.Windows.Controls.Image property,
349

System.Windows.Controls.ItemCollection
collection, 156

System.Windows.Controls.ItemsControl
class, 460

System.Windows.Controls.ItemsControl
control, 269, 275, 295, 303, 305, 311,
314

System.Windows.Controls.ItemsControl
property, 159

System.Windows.Controls.Label control,
128, 353

System.Windows.Controls.ListBox class, 347,
458, 460–461, 672

System.Windows.Controls.ListBox control,
245, 265, 278–279, 295–296, 500

System.Windows.Controls.ListBox method,
345

System.Windows.Controls.ListBox property,
153, 156, 159

System.Windows.Controls.ListBoxItem
object, 156, 347

System.Windows.Controls.ListView control,
295–296

System.Windows.Controls.MediaElement
class, 656, 658

System.Windows.Controls.MediaElement
control, 635

System.Windows.Controls.Menu property,
87

System.Windows.Controls.MenuItem
property, 87, 134

System.Windows.Controls.PasswordBox
control, 119

System.Windows.Controls.Primitives.Button
Base class, 250

System.Windows.Controls.Primitives.
PlacementMode enumeration, 81, 140

System.Windows.Controls.Primitives.Popup
property, 81

System.Windows.Controls.Primitives.Repeat
Button control, 124

System.Windows.Controls.Primitives.Status
Bar property, 93

System.Windows.Controls.ProgressBar class,
195, 355, 481, 489, 493, 496

System.Windows.Controls.ProgressBar
control, 338, 366

System.Windows.Controls.RadioButton
property, 91, 142

System.Windows.Controls.RichTextBox
control, 105, 111

System.Windows.Controls.RichTextBox
object, 372, 375, 410

System.Windows.Controls.RichTextBox
property, 91, 93, 115, 120

System.Windows.Controls.ScrollBarVisibility.
Visible class, 217

System.Windows.Controls.ScrollViewer
class, 217, 221

System.Windows.Controls.ScrollViewer
property, 71

System.Windows.Controls.Separator property, 88

System.Windows.Controls.Slider class, 657, 659

System.Windows.Controls.Slider control, 131, 221, 230–231, 233–234, 284, 617

System.Windows.Controls.Slider object, 600

System.Windows.Controls.SpellCheck class, 121

System.Windows.Controls.StackPanel class, 69, 331, 512

System.Windows.Controls.StackPanel property, 59, 64, 75, 96, 142

System.Windows.Controls.StyleSelector class, 345

System.Windows.Controls.TabControl control, 278

System.Windows.Controls.TabControl method, 426, 432

System.Windows.Controls.TabControl object, 69, 421

System.Windows.Controls.TabItem object, 421, 426, 432

System.Windows.Controls.TextBlock class, 455, 458, 461, 470, 484

System.Windows.Controls.TextBlock control, 215, 230, 232–233, 236, 247, 260, 265, 284, 322, 331, 470, 651

System.Windows.Controls.TextBlock property, 13, 29, 35, 40

System.Windows.Controls.TextBox class, 335, 337, 359, 454, 464

System.Windows.Controls.TextBox control, 21, 104, 111, 119, 176, 212, 231, 236, 243, 247, 251, 260, 263, 288, 297, 331, 335, 337, 590

System.Windows.Controls.TextBox file, 169, 182

System.Windows.Controls.TextBox method, 341

System.Windows.Controls.TextBox object, 373, 690

System.Windows.Controls.TextBox property, 17, 43, 88, 120, 126, 128, 157

System.Windows.Controls.ToggleButton class, 349

System.Windows.Controls.ToggleButton control, 351

System.Windows.Controls.ToolBar property, 90, 93

System.Windows.Controls.ToolBarTray property, 90

System.Windows.Controls.ToolTip control, 137, 358, 528, 530

System.Windows.Controls.ToolTip property, 81, 140

System.Windows.Controls.ToolTipService class, 139–140

System.Windows.Controls.TreeView control, 295–296

System.Windows.Controls.TreeView property, 149

System.Windows.Controls.TreeViewItem property, 149

System.Windows.Controls.UniformGrid class, 522, 584

System.Windows.Controls.UniformGrid property, 86

System.Windows.Controls.UserControl control, 166, 168, 171, 176, 181, 185, 191

System.Windows.Controls.UserControl property, 10, 26

System.Windows.Controls.ValidationResult class, 283

System.Windows.Controls.ValidationRule class, 283

System.Windows.Controls.Viewbox property, 13

System.Windows.Controls.Viewport3D control, 564, 566, 570, 573, 586

System.Windows.Controls.WrapPanel property, 61

System.Windows.ControlTemplate class, 194

System.Windows.Data.Binding control, 230–231, 234–235, 242, 268–269, 283, 288, 317

INDEX

System.Windows.Data.Binding markup
extension, 230–231, 234

System.Windows.Data.BindingBase control,
262

System.Windows.Data.Binding.BindingMode
control, 297

System.Windows.Data.BindingExpression
class, 232

System.Windows.Data.BindingMode
control, 231–232, 235

System.Windows.Data.BindingMode
enumeration, 232

System.Windows.Data.BindingMode.Two
Way attribute, 231, 317

System.Windows.Data.CollectionView class,
296, 303–304

System.Windows.Data.CollectionViewSource
class, 296, 304

System.Windows.Data.CollectionViewSource
control, 296, 302, 307, 311, 313

System.Windows.Data.Error exception, 245

System.Windows.Data.FilterEventArgs class,
308

System.Windows.Data.FilterEventHandler
class, 307

System.Windows.Data.IMultiValueConverter
class, 269

System.Windows.Data.IValueConverter
interface, 268, 313

System.Windows.Data.IValueConverter
property, 51

System.Windows.Data.ListCollectionView
class, 304

System.Windows.Data.MultiBinding class,
269

System.Windows.Data.ObjectDataProvider
class, 247

System.Windows.Data.PropertyGroup
Description class, 311

System.Windows.Data.RelativeSource
control, 234

System.Windows.Data.RelativeSource
property, 195

System.Windows.DataTemplate class, 264,
269, 274–275, 278, 311

System.Windows.DataTrigger class, 274

System.Windows.Data.UpdateSourceTrigger
enumeration, 232

System.Windows.Data.UpdateSourceTrigger.
PropertyChanged control, 297

System.Windows.Data.ValueConversion
Attribute class, 269

System.Windows.Data.XmlDataProvider
control, 245

System.Windows.DependencyObject object,
7, 20

System.Windows.DependencyObject
property, 13

System.Windows.DependencyObject.
SetValue property, 20

System.Windows.DependencyProperty
class, 212

System.Windows.DependencyProperty field,
171

System.Windows.DependencyProperty
property, 8, 14–15, 24, 230, 233, 236,
596, 605

System.Windows.DependencyPropertyKey
property, 13–14

System.Windows.DependencyProperty.
RegisterReadOnly property, 13

System.Windows.Dialogs.PrintDialog object,
379, 384, 394

System.Windows.Document.Run object, 372

System.Windows.Documents.Document
Paginator object, 447

System.Windows.Documents.Figure object,
408

System.Windows.Documents.FixedDocument
object, 393, 404, 408, 410, 415, 420,
437

System.Windows.Documents.FixedDocument
System.Windows.Documents.Flow
Document object, 425

System.Windows.Documents.FixedPage
object, 383, 404

System.Windows.Documents.Floater object, 408

System.Windows.Documents.FlowDocument object, 115, 393, 398, 408, 410, 420

System.Windows.Documents.FlowDocument property, 111

System.Windows.Documents.Serialization. WritingProgressChangedEventArgs object, 399

System.Windows.Documents.TextElement class, 375

System.Windows.Documents.TextPointer object, 372, 375

System.Windows.Documents.TextPointer Context enum, 375

System.Windows.Documents.TextRange object, 372, 375

System.Windows.Documents.TextSelection object, 111, 372

System.Windows.Documents.XpsDocument Writer object, 379

System.Windows.DragDrop class, 672

System.Windows.DragDropEffects enumeration, 673

System.Windows.EventHandler parameter, 19

System.Windows.FontWeight property, 326, 330, 333

System.Windows.Forms.Control object, 697

System.Windows.Forms.Form object, 693

System.Windows.Forms.Integration. ElementHost control, 689

System.Windows.Forms.Integration. WindowsFormsHost control, 696

System.Windows.Forms.SaveDialog object, 405

System.Windows.Forms.Timer class, 484

System.Windows.FrameworkContentElement class, 328, 604

System.Windows.FrameworkElement class, 137, 207, 278, 326, 328, 359, 528, 564, 604, 609

System.Windows.FrameworkElement control, 242, 284

System.Windows.FrameworkElement property, 28

System.Windows.FrameworkElement. DataContextProperty property, 16

System.Windows.FrameworkElement.Find Resource method, 341

System.Windows.FrameworkElement.Width property, 268

System.Windows.FrameworkProperty Metadata object, 9, 16

System.Windows.FrameworkProperty MetadataOptions enumeration, 9

System.Windows.FrameworkTemplate class, 356

System.Windows.Input namespace, 111, 181, 186

System.Windows.Input.ApplicationCommands class, 181

System.Windows.Input.CanExecuteRouted EventArgs class, 182

System.Windows.Input.CommandBinding class, 181, 185

System.Windows.Input.CommandManager class, 181, 185

System.Windows.Input.ICommand control, 250

System.Windows.Input.InputGesture class, 185

System.Windows.Input.InputGestureCollection class, 182

System.Windows.Input.Keyboard class, 679

System.Windows.Input.Keys enumeration, 680

System.Windows.Input.MouseButtonState enumeration, 669

System.Windows.Input.MouseWheelEventArgs object, 669

System.Windows.Input.RoutedCommand property, 185

System.Windows.Input.TextComposition EventArgs class, 213

System.Windows.LogicalDirection object, 372

System.Windows.Markup namespace, 115

System.Windows.Markup.ContentProperty Attribute attribute, 168

System.Windows.Markup.NullExtension markup extension, 343

System.Windows.Markup.XamlWriter. Save method, 338

System.Windows.Media namespace, 526

System.Windows.Media.Animation namespace, 647

System.Windows.Media.Animation. Animatable object, 596, 605

System.Windows.Media.Animation. AnimationClock object, 605

System.Windows.Media.Animation. AnimationTimeline object, 605, 607

System.Windows.Media.Animation. BeginStoryboard object, 596, 604–605

System.Windows.Media.Animation. Clock object, 600

System.Windows.Media.Animation. ClockController object, 604

System.Windows.Media.Animation. ColorAnimation property, 644

System.Windows.Media.Animation. ControllableStoryboardAction class, 636, 646

System.Windows.Media.Animation.Discrete StringKeyFrame keyframe, 651

System.Windows.Media.Animation.Double Animation object, 597, 600, 620, 627

System.Windows.Media.Animation.Double AnimationUsingKeyFrames object, 614

System.Windows.Media.Animation.Double KeyFrame class, 614

System.Windows.Media.Animation. FillBehavior.HoldEnd object, 605

System.Windows.Media.Animation.Handoff Behavior object, 609

System.Windows.Media.Animation. IKeyFrame object, 614

System.Windows.Media.Animation.Parallel Timeline object, 611, 637, 642

System.Windows.Media.Animation.Remove Storyboard object, 604–605

System.Windows.Media.Animation.Repeat Behavior object, 597, 642

System.Windows.Media.Animation. Storyboard class, 486, 596, 604, 617, 626–627, 630, 637, 641

System.Windows.Media.Animation. Storyboard property, 596

System.Windows.Media.Animation. Storyboard.Completed event, 624

System.Windows.Media.Animation. StringAnimationUsingKeyFrames property, 651

System.Windows.Media.Animation. StringKeyFrame keyframes, 651

System.Windows.Media.Animation. Timeline object, 596, 600, 605, 610, 612, 623, 636–637, 641

System.Windows.Media.Animation. Timeline.DesiredFrameRate dependency property, 629

System.Windows.Media.Animation. TimelineGroup object, 642

System.Windows.Media.Animation. TimeSeekOrigin value, 617

System.Windows.Media.BezierSegment object, 620

System.Windows.Media.Brush class, 583

System.Windows.Media.Brush method, 431

System.Windows.Media.Brush property, 644

System.Windows.Media.Brush value, 269

System.Windows.Media.Brush.Background property, 326

System.Windows.Media.Brush.BorderBrush property, 326

System.Windows.Media.Color property, 644

System.Windows.Media.Color structure, 533

System.Windows.Media.Color value, 574

System.Windows.Media.Colors class, 534

System.Windows.Media.DrawingContext class, 207

System.Windows.Media.Effects.BlurBitmap Effect element, 548

System.Windows.Media.Effects. DropShadowBitmapEffect element, 555

System.Windows.Media.Effects. OuterGlowBitmapEffect element, 552

System.Windows.Media.Geometry class, 524, 526

System.Windows.Media.GeometryGroup static resource, 526

System.Windows.Media.GradientStop property, 644

System.Windows.Media.ImageBrush class, 539, 542, 546, 583

System.Windows.Media.Int32Collection object, 570

System.Windows.Media.LinearGradientBrush class, 536

System.Windows.Media.LinearGradientBrush property, 644

System.Windows.Media.LineSegment object, 620

System.Windows.Media.MatrixTransform object, 633

System.Windows.Media.Media3D.Camera class, 566

System.Windows.Media.Media3D.Camera control, 564

System.Windows.Media.Media3D. DiffuseMaterial class, 578

System.Windows.Media.Media3D.Emissive Material class, 574

System.Windows.Media.Media3D.Gemoetry Model3D class, 570, 578

System.Windows.Media.Media3D.Light class, 573

System.Windows.Media.Media3D.Material class, 578, 583

System.Windows.Media.Media3D. MaterialGroup class, 578, 583

System.Windows.Media.Media3D. MeshGeometry3D class, 570, 583

System.Windows.Media.Media3D. ModelUIElement3D class, 570, 586

System.Windows.Media.Media3D. ModelVisual3D class, 564, 567, 570

System.Windows.Media.Media3D. OrthographicCamera class, 566

System.Windows.Media.Media3D. PerspectiveCamera class, 566

System.Windows.Media.Media3D. Point3D class, 574

System.Windows.Media.Media3D. Point3DCollection object, 570

System.Windows.Media.Media3D. PointLightBase class, 574

System.Windows.Media.Media3D. Quarternion object, 614

System.Windows.Media.Media3D. SpecularMaterial class, 578

System.Windows.Media.Media3D. Vector3D class, 574

System.Windows.Media.Media3D. Vector3DCollection class, 571

System.Windows.Media.Media3D.Viewport 2DVisual3D class, 564, 578, 590

System.Windows.Media.Media3D.Viewport 3DVisual control, 564, 590

System.Windows.Media.Media3D.Visual3D class, 564, 586, 605

System.Windows.Media.Media3D.Visual3D Collection class, 564

System.Windows.Media.MediaTimeline class, 656, 658

System.Windows.Media.MediaTimeline object, 635, 637

System.Windows.Media.PathFigure element, 524

System.Windows.Media.PathGeometry object, 632

System.Windows.Media.PathSegment object, 620

System.Windows.Media.PointAnimation object, 620

System.Windows.Media.PointCollection class, 583

System.Windows.Media.PointsCollection class, 514, 522

System.Windows.Media.RotateTransform object, 633

System.Windows.Media.ScaleTransform property, 221

System.Windows.Media.SolidColorBrush class, 533

System.Windows.Media.SolidColorBrush property, 33–34, 644

System.Windows.Media.TileBrush class, 540, 546

System.Windows.Media.Transform.Layout Transform property, 221

System.Windows.Media.TranslateTransform object, 627, 633

System.Windows.Media.UIElement object, 605

System.Windows.Media.Visual objects, 382

System.Windows.Media.VisualBrush class, 546, 583

System.Windows.MessageBox class, 78, 477

System.Windows.MessageBox property, 43, 123

System.Windows.MessageBoxResult enumeration, 78

System.Windows.MultiTrigger control, 336

System.Windows.Point class, 514, 522, 620

System.Windows.Printing.PrintQueue method, 393, 398

System.Windows.Printing.PrintQueue object, 393

System.Windows.PropertyMetadata object, 8

System.Windows.PropertyMetadata.Coerce ValueCallback value, 16

System.Windows.PropertyMetadata.Property ChangedCallback value, 16

System.Windows.PropertyPath object, 645

System.Windows.ResourceDictionary class, 34, 326

System.Windows.ResourceDictionary control, 245, 265, 311, 321, 361

System.Windows.ResourceDictionary property, 32, 36

System.Windows.ResourceReferenceKeyNot FoundException method, 341

System.Windows.RoutedEvent event, 176

System.Windows.RoutedEventArgs class, 122, 682

System.Windows.Setter objects, 275, 326

System.Windows.Setter property, 351

System.Windows.Shapes namespace, 516

System.Windows.Shapes.Ellipse object, 600, 615, 624, 627, 630, 638, 690, 697

System.Windows.Shapes.Line class, 512

System.Windows.Shapes.Line elements, 514

System.Windows.Shapes.Path class, 351

System.Windows.Shapes.Path control, 620

System.Windows.Shapes.Path element, 518, 523, 525

System.Windows.Shapes.Polygon class, 523

System.Windows.Shapes.PolyLine class, 513, 517

System.Windows.Shapes.Rectangle class, 664

System.Windows.Shapes.Rectangle control, 269, 275

System.Windows.Shapes.Rectangle elements, 355

System.Windows.Shapes.Rectangle object, 612

System.Windows.Shapes.Rectangle.Fill property, 644–645

System.Windows.Shapes.Shape class, 516, 521, 524, 528, 533, 536, 539, 542, 645

System.Windows.SolidBrush object, 532

System.Windows.StaticResourceExtension class, 321, 326

System.Windows.Style class, 194, 275, 284, 288–289, 338, 351

System.Windows.Style control, 341, 343, 345

System.Windows.Style property, 330–331, 355, 358

System.Windows.Style resource, 326, 328, 333, 335–336, 347

System.Windows.Styles property, 349

System.Windows.SystemColors class, 365, 532, 534

System.Windows.SystemFonts class, 365

System.Windows.SystemParameters class, 365

System.Windows.SystemParameters. KeyboardDelay property, 124

System.Windows.SystemParameters. KeyboardSpeed property, 124

System.Windows.TemplateBindingExtension markup extension, 353

System.Windows.TemplatePart attribute, 195

System.Windows.TemplatePartAttribute attribute, 199

System.Windows.TemplatePartAttribute class, 355

System.Windows.TextBlock class, 473

System.Windows.Thickness object, 614

System.Windows.Threading.Dispatcher class, 464, 467, 499, 503, 506

System.Windows.Threading.Dispatcher property, 464, 467

System.Windows.Threading.DispatcherObject class, 454, 457, 460, 464, 467

System.Windows.Threading.DispatcherPriority class, 454, 457, 460, 499

System.Windows.Threading.DispatcherTimer class, 483, 486

System.Windows.Threading.DispatcherTimer property, 14

System.Windows.Threading.Dispatcher UnhandledExceptionEventArgs object, 4

System.Windows.Threading.Dispatcher UnhandledExceptionEventHandler event, 4

System.Windows.Trigger class, 347, 349, 351

System.Windows.Trigger property, 333

System.Windows.Triggers collection, 335

System.Windows.UIElement class, 176, 207, 464, 467, 548, 552, 555, 558, 564, 689

System.Windows.UIElement element, 663, 669

System.Windows.UIElement property, 24, 153, 156, 160, 333

System.Windows.UIElement.MouseDown event, 666

System.Windows.UIElement.MouseUp event, 666

System.Windows.ValidateValueCallback property, 10

System.Windows.Visibility value, 268

System.Windows.Visual control, 564

System.Windows.Window element, 58

System.Windows.Window method, 405, 421

System.Windows.Window object, 612, 686

System.Windows.Window property, 13–14, 17, 24, 33, 35, 52

System.Windows.WindowCollection property, 46

System.Windows.Window.Loaded event, 571, 576, 581

System.Windows.Window.RenderTransform property, 10

System.Windows.Xps.Packaging.XpsDocument object, 410, 420, 438

System.Windows.Xps.VisualsToXpsDocument object, 382–383

System.Windows.Xps.XpsDocument object, 415

System.Windows.Xps.XpsDocumentWriter object, 379, 383, 393, 415, 447

System.Windows.Xps.XpsDocumentWriter. WriteAsync method, 398

Sytem.Windows.Controls.Image control, 103

Sytem.Winows.Media.Animation. ControllableStoryboard object, 605

T

TabControl element, 69

TabIndex property, 97

TabItem element, 69

TabItem.Header element, 69

tabs, order of, 97

TabStripPlacement property, 69

Target property, 128

TargetName property, 275–276

TargetType property, 328, 331, 351, 355

TaskItemDataTemplateSelector class, 279, 281

Template property, 349, 351, 353, 355, 357

TemplateBinding markup extension, 353

TemplatePart attribute, 196, 199

TemplatePartAttribute property, 199, 355

templates, control

    creating, 349–350

    customizing by properties, 353–354

    finding elements generated by, 356–358

    putting into style, 351–353

    specifying named parts of, 354–356

text

    animation of, 651–652

    applying Syntax highlighting in text control, 375–379

    displaying, 101–102

    overview, 371

    programmatically inserting into RichTextBox, 372–374

    user input in form of, 104–110

text boxes, 128

Text property, 13, 21, 105, 191, 213, 230–233, 243, 251, 284, 286, 372

TextAlignment property, 102, 105

TextBlock control, 101, 230, 484

TextBlock property, 100

TextBox control, 105, 121, 157, 213, 231, 232

TextBox object, 120–121, 231–234, 236–237, 243–244, 248–249, 252, 263–264, 284–286, 289–291, 295, 298–299

TextBox property, 100, 337

TextBox.Text property, 22

TextChanged event, 106, 112

TextCompositionEventArgs class, 213

TextDecoration property, 102

TextInput event, 676–677

TextPointer object, 372

TextPointerContext class, 375, 378

TextSelection object, 111

TextureCoordinates property, 583

textures

    applying to 3D models, 583–585

    filling shapes with, 542–545

TextWrapping property, 102, 105

ThemeDictionaryExtension class, 368

ThemeDictionaryExtension control, 366

ThemeInfoAttribute attribute, 366, 368

themes, 365–369

Themes subfolder, 194, 197, 366, 367

themes\<ThemeName>.<ThemeColor>.xaml file, 366

threading, 453

three-dimensional graphics. *See* 3D graphics

Tick event, 483

Tick event handler, 484

TickFrequency property, 131

TickFrequency value, 132

TickPlacement property, 131

Ticks property, 132

Tile value, 543

TileBrush subclass, 540

TileMode property, 542–543

Timeline animations, synchronizing, 637–640

Timeline class, 596, 600

Timeline.Completed event, 641

Timeline.DesiredFrameRate property, 626–627, 629

Timeline.DesircdFrameRateProperty dependency property, 630

TimeSeekOrigin enumeration, 617

To property, 596

ToggleButton control, 349

ToggleButton method, 193

Tool Tips
    displaying graphics elements in, 530–531
    displaying on controls, 137–138
    displaying on disabled controls, 139
    displaying on shapes, 528–529
    duration and position of, 140–142

ToolBar element, 90

ToolBar object, 91

ToolBar.Rank property, 91

toolbars, 90–92

ToolBarTray property, 91

ToolTip class, 358

ToolTip element, 530

ToolTip property, 137, 138, 234, 284, 289, 528

ToolTip styles, 358–360

ToolTipService class, 139–141

ToolTipService property, 139

ToolTipService.HorizontalOffset property, 140–141

ToolTipService.Placement property, 140–141

ToolTipService.PlacementTarget property, 140

ToolTipService.ShowDuration property, 140

ToolTipService.ShowOnDisabled property, 139

ToolTipService.VerticalOffset property, 140–141

ToString method, 264–265, 296

ToString output, 154

Total property, 174

TransformGroup element, 559

TranslateTransform element, 558

trees, 149–152

TreeView control, 149

TreeView element, 149

TreeViewItem element, 149

TreeViewItem property, 150

TreeViewItem.Selected event, 150

TreeView.SelectionChanged event, 149

TriangleIndicies property, 570

Trigger objects, 335, 349

triggers
    apply multiple to same element, 335–336
    controlling animation through, 646–650
    evaluating multiple properties for same, 336–337

Triggers collection, 656

try…catch block, 6

tunneling events, 677

two-dimensional controls, 590–593

two-dimensional graphics. *See* 2D graphics

two-way binding, 231–234, 232

TwoWay value, 232–235, 237–238, 284, 286, 290–291, 297–299, 318–319

typed styles, 327–329

U

UI (user interface)
    supporting automation in custom controls, 202–206
    updating asynchronously on timer, 483–485

UI elements
    applying blur effects to, 548–551
    applying drop shadow effect to, 554–557
    applying glow effects to, 552–554
    automatically wrapping rows or columns, 61–62
    binding properties of to self, 234
    binding to properties of, 230–231
    data binding, 235
    docking to edge of form, 63–64

filling shapes with active, 546–547

grid layout, 65–66

grouping, 77–78

horizontal or vertical stacking, 59–60

positioning to exact coordinates, 67–68

responding when user clicks, 663–668

sizing in forms, 94–96

tab order, 97

UI threads

determining whether code is running on, 464–467

verifying code is running on, 467–469

UIElement class, 207, 548, 558

UIElementCollection type, 404

Unchecked event, 146

Undo method, 106, 112

Uniform value, 540

UniformGrid event, 657–658, 664, 667–668, 680

UniformToFill value, 540

UpdateSource property, 232

UpdateSourceTrigger attribute, 231–233, 284, 297

updating UI asynchronously on timer, 483–485

user controls

application commands, supporting, 181–185

Content property of, 168–171

creating, 166–168

custom commands, adding to, 185–191

design mode behavior, setting, 191–193

events, adding to, 176–180

overview, 165–166

properties, adding to, 171–175

user input

multimedia and

dragging items from lists and dropping on Canvas, 672–676

handling keyboard events, 676–678

overview, 653

playing media files, 658–662

playing system sounds, 653–656

querying keyboard state, 679–681

responding when user clicks UI elements, 663–665

responding when user clicks UI elements in containers, 666–668

responding when user rotates mouse wheel, 669–671

suppressing keyboard and mouse events, 682–683

using triggers to play audio, 656–657

rich text, 111–115

simple text, 104–110

sliders, 131–134

user interface (UI). *See also* UI elements; UI threads

supporting automation in custom controls, 202–206

updating asynchronously on timer, 483–485

UserControl control, 166, 169

UserControl property, 10

user-defined annotations, 437–446

UserValue dependency property, 21

■V

Validate method, 283, 287

ValidatesOnDataErrors property, 288

ValidatesOnErrors property, 288–289

ValidateValueCallback value, 16

validation

adding to dependency properties, 20–23

specifying rules for binding, 283–288

Validation.ErrorTemplate class, 283–285, 288–289

Validation.ErrorTemplate property, 284

Validation.HasError property, 284–285, 289

ValidationResult class, 283–284, 287

ValidationRule class, 283–284, 286–287

ValidationRules collection, 283–284, 288

ValidationRules property, 283–284

ValidationValueCallback handler, 20

ValidationValueCallback value, 20

value converters, 268–274

Value property, 131–132, 134, 221, 223, 230–234, 275, 284, 286, 355, 490

ValueChanged event, 131–132, 657

values of enumeration, binding to, 260–262

vectors, 563

Velocity property, 10

VelocityProperty property, 10

VerifyAccess method, 467

vertical stacks, 59–60

VerticalAlignment property, 60, 95

VerticalOffset property, 82, 141

VerticalScrollBarVisibility property, 71, 112, 217

view matrix, 566

ViewBox property, 539, 541–542

viewing

    check boxes, 145–148

    combo boxes, 159–162

    lists, 153–155

    radio buttons, 142–145

    trees, 149–152

ViewPort property, 542–543

Viewport2DVisual3D control, 590

Viewport3D control, 564–569, 571–572, 574–577, 579–582, 585–588, 591–592

Viewport3D element, 564

Viewport3DVisual class, 564

Visible value, 71

Visual object, 380

Visual property, 546

VisualBrush class, 540, 546

VisualsToXpsDocument object, 382–385

VisualsToXpsWriterDocument object, 383

W

Width property, 58, 65, 94, 103, 521, 600, 605, 654, 657, 659–661, 664, 667, 669–671, 673, 677, 680, 682

WidthAndHeight property, 58

Window attributes, 481

window data, loading asynchronously, 457–460

Window object, 58

Window parameter, 79

Window1.Rotation property, 24, 27

Window1.xaml file, 2–3, 35, 399

Window1.xaml.cs file, 2–3, 37, 389, 400, 405, 417, 422, 427, 433, 440, 448, 576, 581, 592

WindowBrush property, 532

Window.Closing event, 686

WindowFrameBrush property, 532

Window.Resources collection, 480–481

windows, sizing main, 58

Windows Forms

    overview, 685

    using controls in WPF Window, 696–699

    using WPF controls in, 689–693

    using WPF Windows in, 686–688

    in WPF application, 693–695

Windows property, 46

WindowsBase assembly, 54

WindowsFormsApplicationBase class, 42

WindowsFormsHost control, 696–697

Window.Show object, 686

Window.ShowDialog object, 686

worker_DoWork method, 490

worker_ProgressChanged method, 473, 490

WorkerReportsProgress property, 473–474, 481, 489–491, 494

WorkerSupportsCancellation property, 477–478, 481, 493–494, 498

WPF application
  application-wide resources, 34–35
  attached properties, 24–27
  debugging bindings
    using attached properties, 54–55
    using IValueConverter, 51–54
  dependency properties
    adding PropertyChangedValueCallback,
      19–20
    adding validation to, 20–23
    creating with property value
      inheritance, 28–31
    overriding metadata, 15–18
    overview, 7–12
    read-only, 13–15
  exception handling, 4–7
  implementing Application.DoEvents in,
    499–503
  managing multiple windows, 46–51
  properties, sharing throughout, 37–41
  resource dictionaries, 32–33, 36–37
  single instance application, 42–45
  standard, 1–3
  in Windows Forms, 693–695
WPF controls, 689–693
WPF visuals, printing, 379–386
WPF Window
  using in Windows Forms, 686–688
  using Windows Forms controls in,
    696–699
WrapPanel property, 61
wrapping, automatic, 61–62
Write method, 398
WritingCompleted event, 398–399
WritingCompletedEventArgs object, 399
WritingProgressChanged event, 398–399,
  402, 418
WritingProgressCompleted event, 399

X

X property, 336, 559
X value, 633
X1 property, 512
XAML, creating BackgroundWorker threads
  in, 480–483
XamlReader class, 115–116
XamlWriter class, 115
x:Key property, 526
XML data, binding to, 244–246
XML Paper Specification (XPS) technology,
  371
XmlDataProvider property, 245–246
xml:lang attribute, 121
XmlStreamStore class, 429, 434–435, 438,
  444, 451
x:Null markup extension, 344
XPath property, 245
XPS (XML Paper Specification) technology,
  371
XPS file, asynchronously saving
  FixedDocument to, 415–420
XpsDocument object, 407, 415–416, 418, 420,
  424, 430, 434, 437–438, 440, 442,
  449–450
XpsDocumentWriter method, 379, 381–383,
  385, 390, 393–394, 397–399, 402, 404,
  407, 415–418, 451

Y

Y property, 336, 559
Y value, 633
Y1 property, 512

Z

zoomable Canvas controls, 221–225
Zune.NormalColor.xaml file, 366

CPSIA information can be obtained at www.ICGtesting.com
Printed in the USA
LVOW110200071112

306200LV00008B/2/P